From the Inside Out

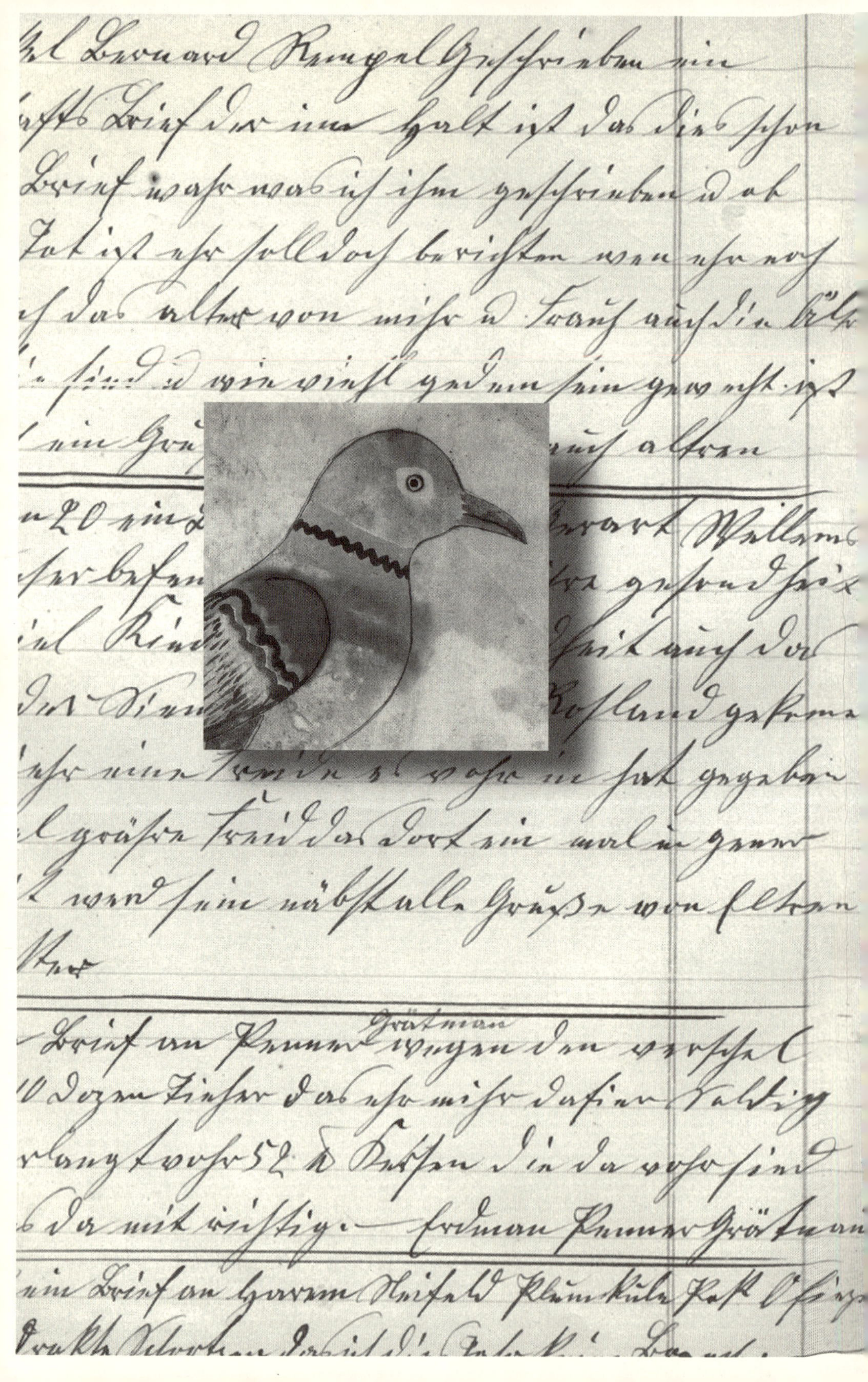

Contents

Preface ix

Introduction 1

I: Migrating Men

1. Cornelius W. Loewen,
   Gruenfeld, Manitoba, 1867–1877   21
2. Ezra R. Burkholder,
   Floradale, Ontario, 1876   29

II: Immigrant Women

3. Margaretha Jansen,
   Berlin, Ontario, 1874   41
4. Maria Stoesz Klassen,
   Ebenfeld, Manitoba, 1887   70

III: Old Men and Young Boys

5. Moses Weber,
   Lexington, Ontario, 1865   77
6. Heinrich Kornelsen,
   Lichtenau, Manitoba, 1875   86
7. Abraham F. Reimer,
   Blumenort, Manitoba, 1879   89
8. Moses S. Bowman,
   Mannheim, Ontario, 1890   114

IV: Merchant Fathers

9. Elias Eby,
   Bridgeport, Ontario, 1874   123
10. Klaas R. Reimer,
    Steinbach, Manitoba, 1885–1896   134

V: Married Men and their Work

- 11 Ephraim Cressman,
  Breslau, Ontario, 1890 — 149
- 12 Heinrich Friesen,
  Hochfeld, Manitoba, 1896–1898 — 164

VI: Bishops and Evangelists

- 13 Levi Jung,
  Center Valley, Pennsylvania, 1863 — 197
- 14 Peter R. Dueck,
  Steinbach, Manitoba, 1910–1913 — 210

VII: Farm Women

- 15 Margaretha Plett Kroeker,
  Steinbach, Manitoba, 1892 — 237
- 16 Laura Shantz,
  New Hamburg, Ontario, 1918 — 245
- 17 Maria Reimer Unger,
  Blumenhof, Manitoba, 1919 — 261
- 18 Judith Klassen Neufeld,
  Ebenfeld, Manitoba, 1922 — 294

VIII: Diverging Paths

- 19 Marie Schroeder,
  Morden, Manitoba, 1926 — 309
- 20 Cornelius T. Friesen,
  Osterwick, Manitoba, 1927 — 316
- 21 Ishmael Martin,
  St. Jacobs, Ontario, 1929 — 325

Notes — 335
Bibliography — 339
Selected Index — 345

For Mary Ann

Preface

This book contains selections of diaries from 21 Mennonites who were either Canadians or people visiting Canada. Most of these diaries were written by participants, or their descendants, of the first two waves of Mennonite immigration to Canada, the first from Pennsylvania to Upper Canada (Ontario) between 1786 and 1814, the second from New Russia (Ukraine) to Manitoba between 1874 and 1879.

Ten years ago, as I was writing my doctoral dissertation on one sub-group of these migrants – the Dutch-Russian Kleine Gemeinde Mennonites – I was astonished at the high number of existing personal diaries. These accounts provided the rich details of the everyday lives of these people. The following year, as a post-doctoral fellowship enabled me to undertake a study of the Swiss-South-German Mennonites of Waterloo County, Ontario, I was similarly surprised at the high number of diaries in that community. Then, over the years, I became aware of numerous diaries of Chortitzer and Sommerfelder Mennonites of Manitoba, usually identified by local historians Irene Enns Kroeker and John Dyck. Gerald Friesen, University of Manitoba, suggested one day that I might write an "instant book" by reproducing selections from these diaries.

A decade later the "instant book" is in your hands. I had many moments of doubt, as questions arose about the worthiness of these diaries. After all, most were written by ordinary men and women engaged in everyday farm life. But, once it became apparent that this very ordinariness was also the strength of this collection, it was easy for me to pursue the publication of a book. Then came the challenge of deciding which selections and which diaries to reproduce. At least 40 diaries, spanning the years between 1863 and 1943, were readily available for publication. But I had to make difficult decisions to reduce the number of diaries. Because the strength of the diaries was not in exhibiting the achievements of individuals but in representing a specific world, that is, everyday life from a particular perspective, I chose those diaries that reflected the widest possible range of experience within the Mennonite community. Thus, in the selection process I considered age, gender, class, church, region, livelihood, and marital status. It was my wish that both the young and the old, the women and the men, the married and the single, the church leaders and the community derelicts, farmers and merchants, the Manitobans and the Ontarians, the pietists and the communitarians, the settlers and the visitors, could be represented.

To further reduce the size of the manuscript, I have selected only a part of each diary, some of which spanned more than 20 years. Most often I selected a one-year span, a long enough time to portray the effects of seasonal change. And, because the focus within the diaries was not on the great events of the diarists themselves but on the rhythm of life, I have reproduced the selections in their entirety, including repetitious detail. To edit out sections of the diary would be to recast the world of the diarist.

In the end, then, only about half of the original selection is included here. The diaries that were included in the first draft of this manuscript but that are not reproduced here include those written by the following Manitoba diarists: David Stoesz (1872-1875); Abraham M. Friesen (1892); Aganetha Kornelsen (1901-1909); Gerhard Kornelsen (1891-1893); Jacob Schellenberg (1892); Jacob L. Dueck (1891); Justina Unger Dueck (1917); and Maria Plett Reimer (1929). And they include diaries written by the following Ontario diarists: David Bergey (1900); Isadore Snyder (1890); Clarence Wismer (1925); Susanna Cassel Shantz (1918); and Susanna Betzner Cressman (1939). Besides these, at least another dozen were at one point considered for inclusion.

Several principles guided the reproduction of these diaries. I wanted to reproduce the diaries as they were written. For the diaries originally written in English, this was rather simple; the material was transcribed as it was, including all the spelling and grammatical errors, inconsistencies and factual errors, and obscure abbreviations. Community volunteers and research assistants did this work. Occasionally I added editorial notes within square brackets to identify correct spelling and to clarify meaning. Where there was a clear error of fact, as in a date or a name, we offered the correction in square brackets rather than use the designation "sic." For the diaries written in German and translated into English, this principle was more difficult to follow; here, errors in spelling or punctuation were lost in the translation. In all the diaries, the first words in sentences were capitalized and essential punctuation was added. I also changed the format of the diaries; some were written in columns, some were double-spaced; some had indented first lines, others had indented second lines. I adopted a uniform indentation.

Several principles were considered in the translations, too. A literal translation of the temperatures in German would have read "degrees warm" or "degrees frozen"; I have usually simply rendered temperatures with the symbols for minus and plus. Where the German diaries used an occasional English word, the word was left in its original spelling; where the English diaries had occasional German phrases, those words were left intact, too. Some words in German were difficult to translate and thus they were usually left in German. They include: *Faspa,* or *Vesper,* a light afternoon meal served between lunch and supper; *Aeltester,* the head of the church, a bishop or elder; *Ohm,* technically meaning uncle, in Low German often refers to an honourable person, usually a minister; *Jenseits,* "the other side" of the Red River, either the West Reserve (in the vicinity of Altona and Winkler) or the Scratching River Reserve (in the vicinity of Rosenort); *Prüfung,* the annual April school examination that brought parents and community leaders to witness the end-of-year achievements of their children. The word *Bruderschaft,* the periodic church business meeting of all male members, has been translated as Brotherhood. The umlaut is used in proper names as the author used it; in my introductions to the diaries, the umlaut has usually been replaced with an *e,* as is common today where German words have been Anglicized; for example, I've used "Toews" in the introduction but "Töws" in the diary text.

I have also left terms of measurement intact; for example, I have made no attempt to change the temperatures, usually given in Fahrenheit (where water freezes at +32 and boils at +212) in Ontario and in Réaumur (where water freezes at 0 and boils at +80) in Manitoba. I have made no changes for variations in calendar usage, even though first-generation Manitobans often used the Gregorian calendar (10 days later than the Julian calendar) which was used in Russia until 1918. And I have made no changes to measurements of distance, usually noted as a *Werst* in Russia, approximately one kilometre, and *mile* in Canada. A question mark in square brackets – [?] – indicates that I am not certain of the intended meaning. An ellipsis (. . .) shows where words were illegible in the original. Only at one point in the manuscript has a name been changed, and this is where the name Jane Doe has been inserted to protect the privacy of her descendants.

This book would not have been published without the invaluable assistance of many friends and colleagues. I would like to express special thanks to Delbert Plett in Manitoba and Reg Good in Ontario, not only for identifying and overseeing the translation or transcription of several of the diaries included here, but also for their unending moral support of this project. As the editors of *Preservings* (Hanover Steinbach Historical Society newsletter) and *Mennogespräch* (Ontario Mennonite Historical Society newsletter), respectively, they allowed me to share my interpretations in short articles with local communities. Professors Gerry Friesen, James Urry, Doreen Klassen, Tom Nesmith, Angela Davis, Bill Brooks, Debra Lindsay, and Donald Akenson read the introduction in an earlier manifestation. Professors Jack Bumsted and Marlene Epp read the entire manuscript and offered helpful comments. Professor Dirk Hoerder invited me to give the introduction as a paper at a Social Science History Association conference in Chicago in 1992. A Multiculturalism Secretariat Junior Fellowship provided by the Secretary of State enabled the initial research trips to Waterloo County. A Social Sciences and Humanities Research Council of Canada grant allowed for the final selection, translation, and editing to be completed.

Special thanks are extended to the many people who participated in translating and editing these diaries and the diaries that I have set aside for another publication. They include: Ben Hoeppner, Irene Enns Kroeker, Peter U. Dueck, Margaret Toews, Priscilla Reimer, Sarah Reimer, Lorna Bergey, Dave K. Schellenberg, Henry Fast, Mary Enns, Richard Taylor, George H. Enns, Betty Loewen, and Ken Klassen. Student assistants Jennifer Rogalsky and Charlene Turner helped input the diaries. Dave Schellenberg prepared and wrote background notes to help interpret the diaries. David Carr, Director, Carol Dahlstrom, Managing Editor, and Allison Campbell, Promotion Coordinator, of the University of Manitoba Press, provided valuable expertise once the manuscript was in production.

My family is a source of personal strength in all my endeavours: my children, Rebecca, Meg, and Sasha, and my wife, Mary Ann, are all "remarkable human beings who communicate their natures abundantly."[1]

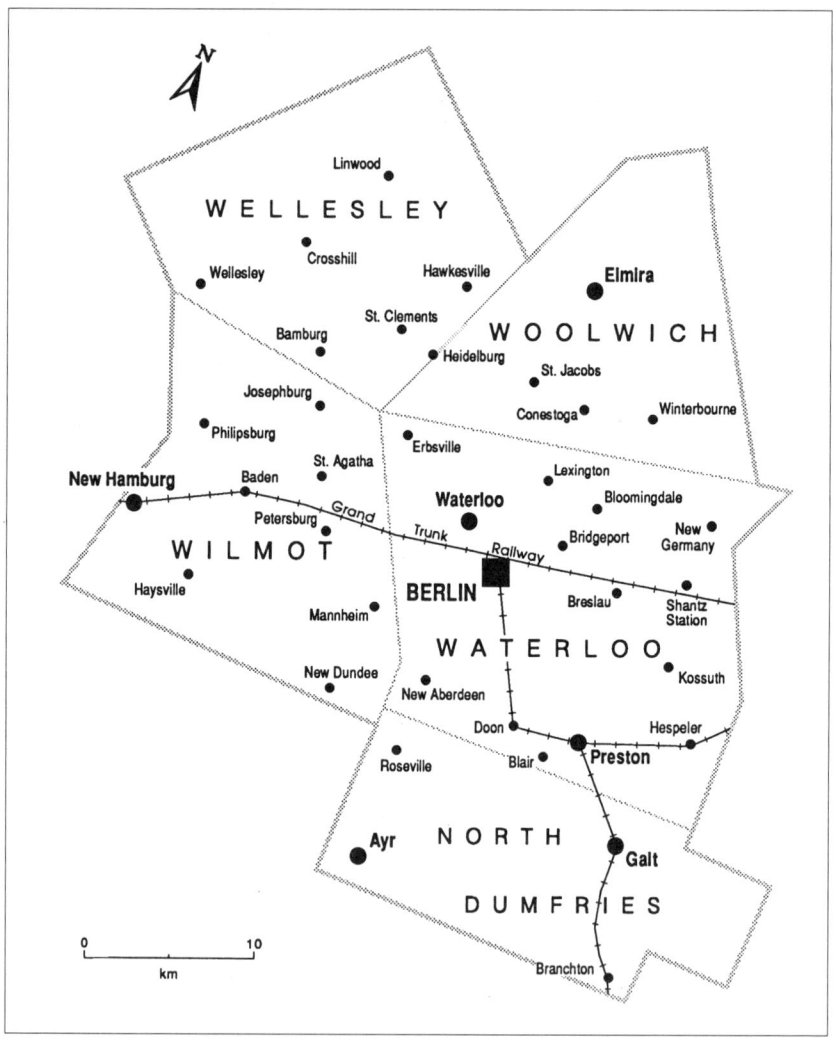

Waterloo County, 1890s.

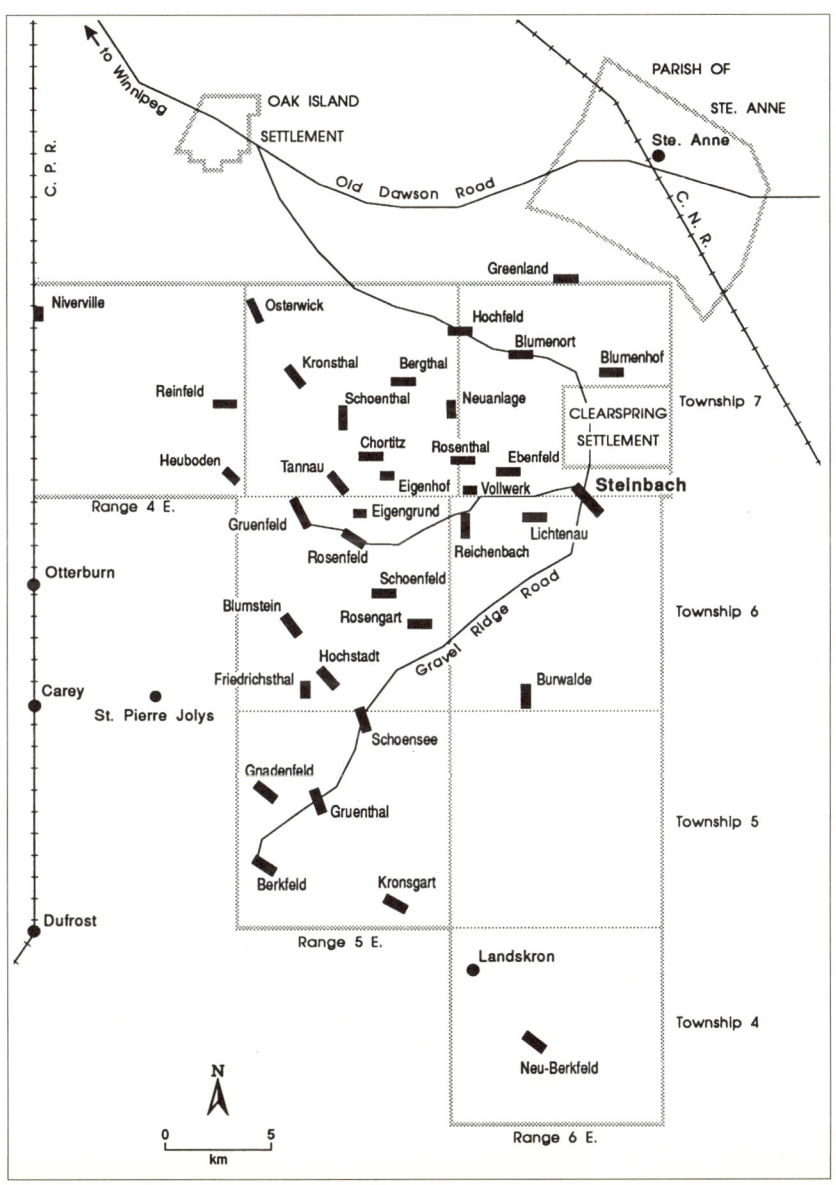

Rural Municipality of Hanover, 1895.

A Waterloo County farmstead, typical of many Old Order Mennonite properties. Note the pioneer stone cottage, which was erected in the 1830s, the two-storey house made from native fieldstones, which was erected in the 1850s, and the one-storey "Doddy House," which was built for the grandparents in the 1880s. (Courtesy Lorna Bergey)

Isaac S. and Elizabeth (Schneider) Cressman family. Diarist Ephraim Cressman is standing in the back row, second from left. (Courtesy Reg Good)

Moses Bowman's daughter Louisa and her husband, David Bergey, in 1928. David kept what is perhaps the most detailed farm diary in Waterloo County. (Courtesy Lorna Bergey)

The Kleine Gemeinde church building in Steinbach, Manitoba, built in 1911. This was Peter Dueck's home church. (From *Preservings*, June 1997, 75.)

The 1892 flour mill of Klaas Reimer and partners in Steinbach, Manitoba, 1892. (From *Preservings*, December 1996, 43.)

Laura Shantz and her parents and siblings. Back row: Laura, Lincoln, Marion. Front row: Noah S. Shantz, Walter, Stauffer, and Susannah (Cassel) Shantz. (Courtesy Lorna Bergey)

Heinrich and Agatha (Hiebert) Friesen. (Courtesy Irene Enns Kroeker)

The SS *International* arrived in Winnipeg on 31 July 1874 with the first contingent of Mennonite settlers in western Canada. The ship had steamed down the Red River from Fargo, North Dakota. Cornelius W. Loewen was one of the passengers. (Courtesy Peter S. Koop)

Introduction

"The great mass of diary writing is poor stuff, interesting only to the antiquarian or social historian," wrote Robert Fothergill in his 1974 history of English diaries.[1] His study, thus, disregarded this "poor stuff" and focussed on those diaries that exhibited "marvellous richness and vitality" and were kept by "remarkable human beings [who] communicat[ed] their natures abundantly."[2] The "poor stuff" of the diary world, however, is also often outside the purview of social histories. In their attempts to recreate the social dynamic within communities, social historians have relied on less personal sources, such as demographic data, ethnic newspapers, and the reports of parochial schools, mutual aid societies, and other community organizations. One reason for the absence of personal writings is simple: as Tamara Hareven has observed, "very few ordinary men and women left behind diaries and correspondence."[3] The "linguistic turn" may represent another reason: writings that expose sentiment and offer frank evaluation are, no doubt, the most promising pages for textual analysis. Certainly, the most recent works that examine the writings of everyday life focus on autobiographies, letters, memoirs, fiction, poetry, and community histories.[4] The daily diary has been left relatively unexamined.

This book contains examples of what Fothergill knows as the "poor stuff" of diary-keeping and what Hareven sees as a rarity. They are the personal writings that were abundant in one North American rural minority group: the Mennonites. The diaries contain few expressed emotions and little personal analysis. They are different from the immigrant diaries most often reproduced. Most bear little similarity to the Mennonite diaries published by other university presses. James Nyce's 1982 edition, *The Gordon C. Eby Diaries: Chronicle of a Mennonite Farmer, 1911-1913*, and Harvey Dyck's 1991 translation, *A Mennonite in Russia: The Diaries of Jacob D. Epp, 1851-1880*, for example, are the accounts of "extraordinary" Mennonites who analyze personal relationships, comment on new technologies, evaluate social boundaries, and exhibit "intensely personal" faith experiences."[5] Most of the diaries in this selection record daily acts, not emotion and analysis; they reflect the contours of social units – household, congregation, and community – not the inner thoughts of the individual.

Why then study these diaries? For the very reason that the daily diary written by the ordinary person about everyday life turns the often hidden contours of household and community "inside out," allowing the student to see a dynamic to which census, newspaper, and parish records can only hint. These diaries reveal the nature of social relationships in rural society. They suggest the fundamental importance of the agrarian household in the community. They mirror the preoccupation of household members with work routines, food procurement, crop selection, marketing procedures, weather patterns, and seasonal change. The diaries also outline the social boundaries of the rural community, defined by kinship ties, village and district politics, and congregational life. Specifically, they include references to daily comings and goings of kin; they record the illnesses, funerals, weddings, and childbirths of neighbours; they document the worship services, revival meetings, and disciplinary actions of the congregation.

By contrasting and comparing a number of diaries, one can identify different kinds of social patterns within apparently homogeneous communities. Region, for example, was an especially important variable. Most of the diaries examined in this study include those of two Mennonite communities in Canada: the Swiss-American Mennonite community in Waterloo County, Ontario, founded between 1800 and 1812; and the Dutch-Russian Mennonite East Reserve (known later as the Rural Municipality of Hanover) in Manitoba, established between 1874 and 1879. The Manitoba and Ontario diaries show the differences among various groups of Mennonites. The Ontario diaries, for example, were located in the Mennonite archives and the homes of the diarists' descendants in Waterloo County, as well as in Pennsylvania, Indiana, and Kansas, where other Swiss-Mennonite communities were established. The Manitoba diaries were located in Manitoba Mennonite archives, but also in Nebraska and Kansas where other Russian Mennonites lived, and in Mexico, Belize, and Paraguay, where descendants later migrated.[6] Moreover, all but one of the Ontario diaries were written in English, reflecting the decline of the German Palatine dialect, Pennsylvania Dutch, and the length of time since the early 1700s, when the first Swiss Mennonites arrived in North America. The Manitoba diaries, on the other hand, were recorded by immigrants from Europe, and thus all but one of these diaries in this collection were kept in the German language and written in the Gothic script.

The diaries also exhibit differences in the demographic, physiological, and economic makeup of the two communities. The East Reserve was an almost homogeneous Mennonite community that comprised an eight-township land bloc that had been set aside in 1873 for the exclusive settlement by Mennonites from Russia.[7] Here, some 2,000 Mennonites from the conservative "Bergthaler" and "Kleine Gemeinde" congregations made permanent homes while 6,000 other Mennonites settled in the West Reserve, 100 kilometres to the west. Although the exclusivity of the East Reserve was lifted in 1891, and Ukrainian and German Lutheran settlers began entering the reserve, Hanover Municipality remained a predominantly Mennonite enclave. By 1901, the 2,373 Mennonites of Hanover still represented fully 79 percent of the municipality's 3,003 inhabitants.[8] Waterloo County, on the other hand, had a polyglot population. In 1803, when Pennsylvania Mennonites acquired a 60,000-acre tract of land in the heart of present-day Waterloo County, they secured the base for an almost homogeneously Mennonite settlement. In the 1820s, when the Mennonite population reached 1,500, settlements were extended westward into present-day Wilmot County. But during this time, immigration from Germany and England changed the area's ethnic composition, and by 1838, when Waterloo County was officially established by statute, Mennonites no longer comprised a majority.[9] In 1901, the 5,509 Mennonites of Waterloo County represented only 10.5 percent of the county's 52,594 inhabitants.[10] Adding to the difficulty of establishing a separate, agrarian Mennonite community in Waterloo County was its urban nature. Indeed, in 1901, when not a single Hanover resident lived in a town of more than 1,000 residents, almost 40 percent of Waterloo County residents lived in such towns. In 1901, Hanover's largest town was Steinbach, with 349 residents (97 percent of which were Mennonite); in Waterloo County, the largest urban centre was Berlin, with 9,700 residents (of which only 4.2 percent were Mennonite).[11]

Finally, Waterloo County was also more industrialized than Hanover. As early as 1856, Waterloo had been linked to Toronto by the Grand Trunk Railroad, and, in the years after 1880, steep Canadian tariffs and an aggressive board of trade transformed Berlin into an industrial city. It became known for its furniture, clothing articles, leather goods, rubber products, and sugar.[12] By 1910, this industrial march was crowned with a link to the Niagara Falls hydroelectricity plant. Hanover, on the other hand, produced primarily agricultural foodstuffs. They included wheat, oats, cheese, cream, eggs, vegetables, and meat, mostly for consumption in Winnipeg, a full day's travel away. Timber and firewood were the only other commodities of export.[13] Although a railway skirted both the east and west sides of Hanover by 1898, no railway was built through the heart of the municipality, and it was not until 1908 that a long-distance telephone connection was made to the outside. Clearly, just as Hanover was representative of a pre-industrial, agrarian society, Waterloo County was an example of a rural community that was quickly becoming industrialized and urbanized. Such regional differences revealed themselves in the two sets of Mennonite diaries reproduced here.

There were other significant variables to consider in determining the nature of the diaries. Class mattered. While the majority of known Mennonite diaries were kept by middle-aged land-owning farm householders, others were kept by well-to-do merchants, church leaders, landless farmers, and servants. Then, too, diaries were kept by girls and women, as well as by boys and men. Clearly, religion, ethnicity, and class drew women and men to share common concerns and perceptions, but gender affected what was said and left unsaid. Generation lines cut yet another line through the genre of diary writing. Unwed youth, middle-aged parents, and grandparents revealed outlooks specific to their particular place in the life cycle. By contrasting diaries specific to a particular region, class, gender, or generation, one can perceive in the profiles of the Mennonite diary a certain depth and clarity.

A second, and less obvious, reason for examining the daily records of common folk is that it offers a window on the writer's mindset and world view.

These daily records capture the perspective of the writers as they looked "from the inside out" – out, to make sense of successive layers of social relations; out, beyond the household, to the kinship network, the local community, and to the wider society of marketplace, government, and "English" society. Even though there may be little personal reflection in the daily "household" diaries, they nevertheless suggest the subjective viewpoint of the writers. They hint at what Adrian Wilson refers to as "document genesis" and the illumination of what the diarist was attempting to achieve in the very act of writing.[14] They answer questions such as: For whom and for what occasions did the diarist intend the writings? Why did the diarist choose to record some events but exclude others? Why are some members of the household and community given more attention than others? Why did the diarist take precious moments out of a busy daily schedule to write at all? Why was it not enough to leave noteworthy events to the rich oral tradition within agrarian society? To what extent was the diary kept to ensure a common social memory and construct a sense of community in the mind of the writer? What was the purpose of this enterprise? What is the significance of diary-keeping as a social practice? Answers to these questions can do much more than identify "the biases of the document."[15] They can identify the historical process that created the diary.

Theories of literacy and speculations of its effects on the perceptions of historical actors offer some answers to these questions. Jack Goody suggests that the very act of writing is at "once more reflective [than speech] and at the same time permits [one] to ... work out the meaning of things, to explicate more formally."[16] Walter Ong adds that the act of writing brings shape and control to the writer's world. He argues that "time is seemingly tamed if we treat it spatially, ... mak[ing] it appear as divided into separate units next to each other."[17] This may appear especially true to the diarist because "'backward scanning' makes it possible in writing to eliminate inconsistencies," providing a sense of order that may in fact be less orderly and more elusive than the writer would wish.[18] The views of Goody and Ong recently have been challenged by scholars such as Matthew Innes, who warn about having "'orality' and 'literacy' reified into categories in their own right, as types of society or mentality."[19] Nevertheless, the ideas of Goody and Ong seem to have stood the test of time and made their way through the historiography. Scholars of immigrant literature, for example, seem to agree that writers "invent" identities by representing daily life in certain ways. They may do it by borrowing the linguistic styles and literary vehicles of the host society, in this way legitimizing and securing the immigrant presence in the new society. But then, too, immigrant or minority writers sometimes contest the understandings of the host society. Werner Sollors has argued that, where host-society writers may catalogue instances of assimilation, immigrant writers may cast the ethnic community or ethnic culture as a "'natural' and timeless category," a process that leads to the assertion of ethnic identity, or ethnicization.[20]

It is within these categories of understanding that we can assert that diary-writing was important for Mennonites, especially as they sought to replicate their closed ethno-religious communities in a Canadian society that was becoming increasingly urbanized and industrialized. Both the Ontarians and Manitobans practised an oral culture, steeped in a German dialect, Pennsylvania Dutch (or Palatine German) for the former, and Low German (or West Prussian Platt) for the latter. The dialects effectively guarded social boundaries and facilitated a community-based household economy. Yet both communities also wrote about these social relationships in a recognized literary language, either High German or English. And, by writing diaries, Mennonites created what they considered the "essentials of all time," and they did this by mapping, defining, and articulating crucial social relationships. Thus when Mennonite diarists recorded the social outline of household, kin group, community, and wider society, they were mentally designing, even celebrating, an envisioned community. It was a community separated from the wider society, firmly rooted in an agrarian economy and anchored to the sectarian congregation. Mennonites, it would seem, joined other traditionalist societies, who according to Harvey Graff made "use of literacy for conservative ends."[21] The daily journal of the rural Mennonite householder secured social boundaries and social networks by simply making record of them. It was a subjective enterprise without personal reflection, admissions of alienation, boasts of triumph, or solipsistic preoccupation.

A final reason for paying attention to the writing of rural people with only an elementary education is that those writings attest to the manner in which a rudimentary literacy develops within rural society. Linking the history of the Mennonites and literacy provides at least one set of conditions that gave rise to a general ability to read and write in rural society.

Important for literacy among Mennonites was their status as a religious minority. Like other groups outside recognized state churches, Mennonites used literacy to defend themselves against persecuting state authorities and to create a common set of understandings within the minority group.[22] Indeed, the diaries illuminate a mechanism that allowed Mennonites to develop into an ethnic group. Widespread literacy among Mennonites had developed soon after their genesis during the sixteenth century. Mennonite historian Arnold Snyder has observed that "communication by handwritten epistle, confessions, accounts of martyrdom and exhortation was common among the early Anabaptists, whose leaders at least were generally literate in the vernacular."[23] Literature became even more important than before, as moderate Anabaptists, who had rejected the authority of state churches and seditiously preached "rebaptism," began to argue that they were not part of the mystical or the fanatically militant branches of Anabaptism. Thus, literacy was used by Anabaptist leaders to aid the movement to coalesce into a stable, even conservative, sectarian community. The very denotation of "Mennonite" rose after the Dutch-Anabaptist leader Menno Simons became the most prolific of the Anabaptist writers. In later centuries, his devotional writings and apologias were linked with a voluminous 1,660-page martyrology, the *Martyrs' Mirror*, and several catechisms and hymnals to create a literary corps that served to energize and direct a highly self-conscious, migrating people.²⁴ These books were carried by Mennonites from one country to another, and in time they became the very symbols of group identity. A sign of the importance that Mennonites placed on literacy was not seen in their ownership of the books but in their practice of reading them. Indeed, reading the lyrics of martyr hymns in worship and reading catechisms in preparation for baptism were mandatory exercises for all Mennonites. Arguably, not only baptism, but also the recitation of the catechism, a piece of writing, became a rite of passage into full adult membership in the community. Its direct consequence was a rudimentary, but universal, literacy within the Mennonite community.²⁵

This level of literacy also reflects the history of Mennonites as "free peasants." This status meant that they negotiated with local sympathetic lords to make deals that secured special privileges and land rights. This was a crucial feature of their successive migrations – of Dutch Mennonites to Polish Prussia, New Russia (present-day Ukraine), and Manitoba, and of Swiss Mennonites to southern Germany, Pennsylvania, and Ontario. And arguably, this status may have spurred the transformation of Mennonites from readers to writers.²⁶ As free peasants, Mennonites also engaged in an early market economy, the very act noted by François Furet and Jacques Ozouf to have contributed to a rudimentary literacy among French farmers. To participate in a national-based economy required the act of reading in order to transcend the bounds of the local community that orality imposed. Numeracy, that is, a preoccupation with quantifying daily life (or, calculating rationally the extent of yield, profit, and advantage), was another exercise that a market economy encouraged.²⁷ And, as "free peasants," Mennonites were also often required by the state to keep records.²⁸ The Dutch Mennonites who migrated to the Russian Empire at the close of the eighteenth century, for example, encountered a bureaucratic state that was intent on compelling foreign agricultural colonists to "become integrated into the rapidly developing rural economy of southern Russia" and to demonstrate that integration through the submission of annual village and district records. For Swiss Mennonites who migrated westward from the German Palatinate to Pennsylvania at the same time, the demands of a market economy required negotiations with colony officials, close attention to the particulars of "partible" inheritance and knowledge of the economic opportunities in different parts of the colony.²⁹ Each of these activities also encouraged a rudimentary literacy.

Literacy may also have risen as a result of migration itself. Not only did migration force negotiation with government, encourage the reading of land-sales agent reports, compel the writing of letters across distances, but it also took Mennonites outside the confines of local communities into wider worlds. At least one historian has argued, "It is much easier when travelling to perceive one's life as a progression by stages than when fixed in one place, in one occupation."³⁰ Diaries sometimes commenced at migration, when the farmer was introduced to a new terrain and new climate; seemingly the passage from one space to another was linked to an increased awareness of the passage of time. By the nineteenth century, when both Dutch and Swiss Mennonites arrived in Canada after successive migrations, diary-writing was widespread.³¹

The writers exhibited in this book were not "remarkable human beings." They were ordinary rural folk – young women and grandmothers, teenaged boys and old men, husbands and wives, farmers and merchants, rural preachers and landless householders. They wrote to record their everyday lives, quotidian drudgery to some, miracles of life and community for others. In the process, they provided glimpses of their lives, their mindsets and their history as a people.

The method by which the rural Mennonite householder sought to affect the immediate world, then, was to simply record life's social profile. For most Mennonites, the notion of household, community, and social boundary was so pervasive that little else was recorded – these were rural household journals.

There were, however, two kinds of diary-writing that skirted these issues: one was the travelogue; the other was the highly individualistic, private diary of Mennonites who lived in more urbanized worlds. Both the travelogue and the private diary reflect the life world of a Mennonite who stood aside from the everyday life in the rural community. Fothergill's suggestion that diaries can be seen on a scale that measures the intensity of individualism – that is, degrees of "evolution towards literary self-consciousness" – may be useful in understanding these two diverging types of Mennonite diary.[32] It may be argued that the travelogue and the private diary stand on either side of the rural household journal on this scale. Clearly, the private diaries of Mennonite town-folk and pietists reveal the greatest degree of "literary self-consciousness," while the travelogues of Mennonite farm migrants show such consciousness as only emerging. The travelogue demonstrates that migration can change one's sense of time and space; the private diary indicates a growing individualism when sectarian community and rural household lose their hold on one's life.

The diaries from section I, "Migrating Men," are travelogues that illustrate how journeying from familiar environs could stimulate a literary awareness. One of the diaries incorporates a sub-diary into a sketchy daily log book, the other seems to commence at the point of departure. One of the diaries was written by a farmer, the other by a university student.

One such diary was written by Manitoba farmer Cornelius Loewen, who migrated from the Borosenko Mennonite Colony, New Russia, in 1874 to settle in Gruenfeld, Manitoba, popularly known as the first Mennonite village in western Canada. Until the point of migration, Loewen's diary contains only sporadic accounts of his household's market transactions. Then, on 1 June 1874, the diary abruptly takes on a new style, suggesting that it may have been written by someone else and copied into Loewen's notebook. The first words – "here is the trip from Russia to America written up" – head a detailed daily description of the transoceanic voyage. The succession of cities – Odessa, Berlin, Hamburg, "Lieverpol," "Halifaks," "Qaebek," Toronto, Winnipeg – ties the new and old worlds together. The careful documentation of the method of travel – by wagon, riverboat, train, ferry, ocean liner, lake-size steamboats, and ox cart – and the hours spent at train stations and seaports complete the map.

References to the icebergs and whales off the coast of Newfoundland, to "walk[ing] on dry earth" at Halifax, to meeting "Canadian Mennonite brothers [in Toronto, who] gifted us with meat, lard, butter and dried apples" were the signposts of a new land. Loewen's immediate world was awry; the diary, however, provided a sense of control and order.[33]

A similar pattern characterizes the migration account of an Ontario youth of Mennonite heritage who travelled to the United States in 1876. In this year, 19-year-old Ezra Burkholder moved to Kansas to join his family, who had migrated earlier. Despite the fact that Burkholder was a University of Toronto student when he wrote his diary, his record is similar to the travelogue within Loewen's. Burkholder pays special attention to the details of the trip. In fact, his diary seems to begin on the day he left home: "July 7th, 1876, started from Floradale in company of Jesse Snyder in a big wagon."[34] After boarding the train in Berlin and being whisked out of Waterloo County, he soon began describing the unfamiliar – the landscape and farmland, strangers on the train, and the passage of time. His entry for 10 July, the third day of travel, was typical: "It commenced to rain at 12:45.... Got a glass of pop at Chatham, .5 cents. West of Chatham, prairie to the right and brush to a certain space to the left. I was informed by a gentleman that there is a space west of Chatham all marsh." Here was a young man, it seems, who sensed, as never before, the passage of time and space. Clearly, travel for both Loewen and Burkholder resulted in an unprecedented mapping of time and space outside familiar boundaries.

At the other end of the continuum of Mennonite diary-writing are the most personal of the diaries. These provide accounts of introspection and religious conscience and often of social analysis. Sometimes the personal reflections are almost solipsistic, nearly absolute self-absorption.

The first diary from section II, "Immigrant Women," illustrates this approach. It is the diary of Margaretha Jansen, the 24-year-old daughter of Russian Mennonite immigrant leader Cornelius Jansen and his wife, Helena Friesen, who temporarily lived in Waterloo County between August 1873 and June 1874. Margaretha Jansen was a woman in a strange land, responsible for her ailing mother and younger siblings during her father's and brother's lengthy land-scouting trips in the United States. If these events provided her with a strong self-awareness, her subjective religiosity rooted in the urban Mennonite church of Berdyansk on the Sea of Azov heightened that awareness.[35] Her diary frequently described doubt, fear, and religious calling. Her moods shifted from great gaiety when she "laughed so much" to times when she thought about the future and had "not been so afraid ... for a long time." She feared for her travelling father, her former servants in Russia, and her relatives in Prussia. And she was ecstatic, especially when she could hear revivalist Daniel Brenneman and realize "a strong love for Jesus." Through all this she had an expressed literary consciousness, wondering, for example, whether deriding an acquaintance, Heinrich, as tedious, and a visitor, Mr. Albert, as "avaric[ious]," in her diary was right, that is, "think[ing] this way about a person and then to writ[e] it also." Here was a diarist with a full "literary self-conscious."

The personal nature of Margaretha's diary is made especially apparent when it is contrasted to the other diary in section II. The diary of Maria Klassen of Manitoba reflects the outlook of a woman in very different circumstances from those of Jansen in Waterloo.[36] Klassen's diary, for example, recorded little emotional contemplation. Within it is a letter from a brother in Russia who denounced her for having joined the migration and boasted of his own liberation from the Mennonite community. But the diary itself was a household account, with careful detailing of the daily activities of all family members, the comings and goings of neighbours and kin, and the events in the community, especially within the Bergthaler congregation. Especially important for Klassen was the economic strength of the household. Interwoven in the description of work and weather were the numerical aggregates, that is, numbers that marked the economic strength of the farm; labour costs, harvest yields, and market prices were recorded with precision. Maria Klassen, for example, noted that, on her husband's 4 October trip to Winnipeg, he "went ... at 5 in the morning with 14 bags of wheat." And she noted that upon his return he had received "54 cents" a bushel for the wheat. She noted that on 18 October the Klassen household sold to Gerhard Unger a half share in an old stove, but she added that he paid for it with two sheep, which should be compared to the $10 that "Penner" received for his half. When, on 21 November the Klassens slaughtered a cow with neighbour "Hiebert and J. Rempel and Mrs. Peters," she noted that the animal "was nice and fat," measured by the fact that from it they "got two pounds tallow." Thus, although both women were immigrants who lived in Mennonite communities, Klassen was a group immigrant, a member of an immigrant unit that included transplanted household, kin and congregation. Life in a new land was marked by relatively little upheaval. Household activities and social ties differed little from those in Bergthal Colony in New Russia.

The same degree of difference in perception apparent in the diaries of Margaretha Jansen and Maria Klassen can be seen in the diaries in section VI, "Bishops and Evangelists." Intense introspection pervades the first diary in this section. The 1863 journal of Pennsylvania evangelist Levi Jung during a whirlwind preaching tour of the Niagara and Waterloo Mennonite settlements was no ordinary travelogue. Rather, it was a highly self-conscious exposé of how Jung, against his father's wishes, "resign[ed his] heart to Christ" and travelled north to engage in a seemingly endless cycle of emotionally charged public meetings and private visits. He preached with "assist[ance] from on high" in one part of the day and met with young "souls, deeply distressed about their ... salvation" in another; he experienced "spiritual darkness" in one hour but had a sense of having his "soul ... refreshed" the next.[37] The whole episode was a spiritual journey where Jung constantly analyzed his own relationships with other people and his personal encounters with God.

Juxtaposing Jung's diary to that of *Aeltester* (Bishop) Peter Dueck of Steinbach, Manitoba, illuminates a sharp difference in the way that spiritual leaders perceived their missions. Like Jung's diary, the journal of Dueck served as a running social commentary by a religious leader. Peter Dueck, however, recorded no personal spiritual reflection. Rather, he reported on the *Bruderschaft*, the Brotherhood, or church business meetings. His records continue from 1901, when he was elected *Aeltester*, to 1919, when he died. Throughout these years he commented on the "sins" in the community, naming those caught in theft, assault, adultery, and drunkenness. He held his sharpest criticism for those who "assimilate to the ways of the world," that is, those who purchased "ostentatious" cars, welcomed an ever-encroaching government with its public schools and military campaigns, and embraced "evil businesses that grow larger every day." The diary records a growing concern with rowdy youth who dressed in stylish clothes, participated in "worldly" wedding celebrations, and drove the "costly" cars. Particular concern was directed to those parents who seemed powerless to stop these activities and even seemed linked to them by their own support for a public school in Steinbach and a growing openness to a consumer culture. Peter Dueck's diary describes a congregation's attempt to contest the fracturing of an Old World community in the face of growing consumerism and individualism.

Dueck's diary is similar to the notes in section IV, "Merchant Fathers." These well-to-do community members were unusually candid in offering their opinions on the merits and moral nature of their fellows. It was a practice made possible, one might speculate, by their position in the Mennonite community. David Blackburn documents the manner in which shopkeepers stood between classes in Germany, and Clifford Geertz documents the way in which entrepreneurs in Indonesian villages "stand outside the immediate purview of village social structure ... insulated by ... rank from the localized bonds of village society."[38]

Such social distance was apparent in the diaries of both Manitoba merchant Klaas R. Reimer and Ontario miller Elias Eby. Both men offered evaluations of their fellows with unequivocal paternalism. Eby was the second son of Bishop Benjamin Eby, the founder of Berlin, Ontario; like his father, Elias became a noted miller and merchant. His diary reflects this elitist position, as he readily lauds some and denounces others. The Russian Mennonite immigrants who passed through Waterloo County in 1874 en route to Manitoba are noted as an "innocent, peaceful and modest people"; young Susanna Brubacher, who died in March 1876, is described as "this once blossoming virgin"; "old Jonathan Bauman," who died a month later, as "an obliging citizen, a good neighbour and an active reformer." But a neighbour who died in June 1876 is described as "a squanderer, wasting his own and the children's money," and another who died in July 1876 as a "clever doctor, but [one who] lost the confidence of many of his friends through heavy drinking."[39]

In Manitoba, the well-to-do Steinbach merchant Klaas Reimer, the grandson of *Aeltester* Klaas Reimer, founder of the Mennonite Kleine Gemeinde, kept a similar record. Although the medium shifted from memoir to autobiography to diary and then to descriptions of his correspondence, Klaas seemed always ready to assess the behaviour of his acquaintances. The notes of his correspondence reproduced in this book describe his religiousness and his deep bonds to family and community; they also offer frank appraisals of the behaviour of his clientele, kin, and congregational leadership. In February 1890, Reimer noted that, in a letter to the recently remarried Isaac Harms of Nebraska, he asked him how he found "such a marriage in his old age, in his 80th year [to] a wife of 38"; in his own notes, Reimer commented freely that "it is often not good when this happens." Reimer was also quick to denounce his foes. In 1895, when ministers from the conservative Kleine Gemeinde Mennonite church wrote to oppose the size of his "business deals," suggesting a motivation of "greed," Reimer noted that he had written back to complain that the leaders "[kept] on forgetting how much unrighteousness occurs because of poverty" and added frankly, "That does not seem right to me."[40] Reimer and Eby, unlike most farm householders, were able to disengage themselves from the immediacy of community affairs and to analyze their social intercourse.

Most Mennonite diaries contain neither personal reflection nor social commentary. They are household journals, offering records of those patterns of life that were the most important to the domestic unit: weather, seasonal changes, community networks, work routine, and, most important, household relationships.

These are the concerns found in the most common of Mennonite diaries, those kept by married male farm householders. The diaries chosen for section V, "Married Men and their Work," are those of Heinrich Friesen, a farmer of medium wealth from Hochfeld, Manitoba, and Ephraim Cressman, a young farmer from Breslau, Ontario. The Friesen and Cressman diaries differed in several significant ways.[41] Their families were at different points in their life cycles, their farms were located in different physical environments, and they operated in markedly different economic and cultural environments. Ontario's Cressman, for example, lived in a relatively temperate physical environment, within a highly commercialized milieu and in a township that was highly integrated into provincial and regional politics. Manitoba's Heinrich Friesen lived in a setting sharply divided by the seasons, shaped by a simple agrarian economy, and a community that was almost homogeneously Mennonite. Cressman, 35 in 1890, had a small and young family (he had three small children, one an infant); Friesen, 56 in 1898, had seven children and one foster child, aged 12 to 28, two of whom were married. Despite these differences, Cressman and Friesen recorded similar concerns. The locus of both diaries, after all, was the household, its economic concern and its internal and external social relationships.

The work described in Cressman's diary records the tasks required by a farmer in an Ontario milieu. Its array of markets, advanced technology, mixed economy, proximity to urban centres and moderate climate shaped Cressman's strategies. Each day during January, Cressman worked with the farm's swine and cattle, but he also travelled frequently to nearby Breslau to purchase "bran and shorts" or to Berlin to sell "wood, logs and stakes." By early April, Cressman began working the land, "spreading manure," and "gangploughing" the seedbed. He then seeded the wide variety of crops that Ontario's moderate climate sustained and diversified economy demanded: clover, wheat, barley, oats, peas, sugar beets, carrots, and turnips. No sooner were these crops planted than Cressman focussed his energies on his livestock, selling the first cattle and swine, and shearing the sheep and washing wool. By July, Cressman cut the first hay and "cradled" the winter wheat. After the crops had dried in the fields, they were hauled to Cressman's huge bank-barn for storage until the early winter "thrashing." In the meantime, Cressman reploughed the fields and by September began seeding winter wheat and rye. In autumn, too, Cresman began the "pulling" of the apples, the harvest of the feed roots (the turnips and the carrots) and once again marketed swine in Berlin. December reintroduced the routine of winter; the endless days of hauling wood to Berlin, broken only by the hog-butchering bee and the repayment of a loan at Waterloo's Molson Bank. Each day brought a task toward building the economic strength of the household within a highly commercialized setting. It was a routine so unyielding that not to work the field or not to market a product was an unusual day, duly noted with the words "tinkering around."

The routine of work on the Heinrich Friesen farm in Manitoba was similar to the routine at Cressman's, differing only in its adaptation to a simpler economy and a more extreme continental climate, with more arid conditions and a shorter growing season. January and February marked the time on the Friesen farm when the adult males hauled hay, not from bank-barns as in humid Ontario, but from the fields, where Manitoba's dry climate allowed storage of hay. But usually even more time was devoted to hauling wood – firewood and lumber – from the forests to the east of the East Reserve. In March, the last of the previous year's crop was marketed, in large part to make use of the last of the winter sleigh trails. In April, once the water was low at the dam near Bergthal and the boys had drained water from the ploughed fields, the next season could begin. The lambs were branded and the seed wheat was cleaned, and a short time later the sheep were let out onto the pasture and the seeding of wheat, peas, oats, and rye was started. After the garden, too, was seeded, the Friesens turned their attention to fencing and renovations. By July, it was time to pull the mustard and thistles from the grain field. August saw the entire Friesen family cut the hay on the newly purchased Métis lands and stook the wheat sheaves on the cultivated village land. September brought out the ploughs and even offered a forage into the nearby bush for wild fruit. October was the month of the harvest; the jointly owned threshing machine moved in succession in 1898 – to the Falks', the Hieberts', then to the Friesens', and after that to the farmyards bearing the names of Wiebe, Kehler, Gerbrand, Schultz, Krause. November was the month at the Friesens' and at other village households for successive days of hog butchering. By December, it was time to haul more of the wheat to the elevator in Niverville or Ste. Anne.

These records clearly indicate the range of opportunities and restrictions that shaped the world of the average male householder. Of the various restrictions, weather was the most immutable to human agency. The whole of life was shaped by temperatures, wind velocities, precipitation, and degrees of sunniness. Daily weather entries were not simply records maintained by idle minds; they were a crucial feature of all household diaries because they were critical aspects of life. A second signal of opportunity and restriction was the economic strength of the household. Like the diary of Maria Klassen, those of Cressman and Friesen, were records of the attempt to manipulate and secure the fruits of nature. By recording yields of produce and market prices, these diarists sought to objectify life in the household.

The diary enabled its authors to secure a measure of control over their lives by recording the events of the household and noting its social links with the wider community. In substance it was a fundamental cultural expression deeply rooted in Mennonite society. The diary demonstrated the remarkable degree to which this farm community was actually a culture of literacy. And a measure of this was the fact that diary-keeping crossed any lines of generation that may have existed. The married male's diary may have been the most common daily record, but married and unmarried men, male and female, elderly and young diarists alike, focussed on the everyday life of household work routine, kinship ties, and church congregation. Where they differed in descriptions of these community features, the diaries provided a unique glimpse of Mennonite society from the perspective of a specific age.

The diaries in section III, "Old Men and Young Boys," reveal just how early Mennonite youths began acquiring a sense of time and space. The possibility of shaping everyday life is apparent from the diaries of two boys, Ontario's Moses Weber, who was 17 in 1865, and Manitoba's Heinrich Kornelsen, who was 15 in 1875.[42] These diaries offer glimpses into the lives of rural youths of strikingly different settings. Weber was a third-generation Canadian in 1865; he lived in a highly commercialized milieu, attended high school, and wrote in English (only his spelling, such as rendering sugar trough as "shugar trauf," and his syntax, apparent in "Jacob went behind Berlin working," signalled his German background). Kornelsen was an immigrant who wrote in German, lived in a closed, agrarian community and recorded his fascination with the physical features of his new home. True, there are differences in the Weber and Kornelsen diaries, but there are also important parallels. Each describes a world that, while separate from the world of adults, is nevertheless similarly defined – by the household economy bound by nature and the local economy, and by the social ties of kin and Mennonite community.

Moses Weber's diary does not readily reveal his youth. The daily diary entries began, as all other household records did, with a description of weather; "a midlen clear day" or "a rough day" were typical entries. He described his daily work: "We did begin to plough" or "we did begin hauling dung." He identified closely with the household, noting, for example, that his father received "$1.04 for springwheet and $1.09 for faul wheet" in Waterloo or that "father [drove] to David Martins and did get five young pigs." When Moses recorded visits, it included all comings to and goings from the Weber household; his entry for 22 January was not only that he and his sister Susan "went to the meeting at Gressman's, and to John Webers' for dinner" but also that his father, who was a Mennonite preacher, and mother "went to the meeting at Martins." And his was clearly a mind in tune with the Mennonite community, noting the deaths and funerals of community members and the occurrence of special church meetings when "strange preachers" from either Pennsylvania or Ohio came calling. In 1865, the only entry that broke the routine of recording household and community life was the one for 14 April marked by six asterisks and noting that "President of the U.S. . . . was killed by another person."[43]

The diary of young Heinrich Kornelsen represents a somewhat different point of view. Heinrich was a young immigrant and a member of a stem family, with a father, step-mother, and half-siblings. His life, thus, was more independent than Moses's. Because the 1870s marked the beginning of the settlement period in Manitoba, Heinrich lived on a frontier and was clearly engrossed by his new physical environment. Besides listing weather patterns, he made special note of wildlife: on 28 December he "caught a rabbit . . . and found a wolf." But as a teenager he was also expected to work as a servant in neighbouring households, in his case in the households of his sisters or uncles. And he knew his rights under the unusual Mennonite inheritance system that stipulated an equal division of all land between boys and girls; thus, in the sections of the diary for 1876 and 1877, he recorded the visits of the *Waisenmann*, the estates administrator who came to calculate the exact size of his mother's estate, that is, exactly half of the household's net worth, and Heinrich listed the amount of the inheritance owing him at the age of majority. Still, his was not an isolated world; like the adult diarists, he carefully recorded the social ties that defined his wider world. He noted not only his visitors, but also the visitors of his father and step-mother, and the location of the Mennonite worship service for any given Sunday.[44]

A similar pattern of record-keeping pervaded the diaries of the community's elderly. Manitoba's Abraham Reimer, who turned 71 in 1879, lived the life of a poor elderly grandfather who witnessed[45] the dynamic households of his sons and daughters who were among the wealthiest merchants, millers and farmers in the district. Having been a ward of the church mutual aid society in the past and relying for much of the household income on his wife's work as a seamstress, he earned the dubious nickname "Foula Raema," that is, "Lazy Reimer." One reason for the designation is clear; he got little work done because he spent so much time observing others at work. And this habit was at least partly because of his age. This is the record not only of a poor man, but also of an old man. His concern was not with the nuclear family, but with the extended family, which included the households of his seven married children. In fact, few days passed when Reimer did not leave his cottage, visit one of his married children, and comment on their household activities. In a single week in April 1879, for example, Abraham Reimer recorded that son-in-law Abram Penner was building a barn at Peter Friesen's, that the "Abraham Reimers and Peter Reimers walked" the seven muddy kilometres to Steinbach to attend church, that both son-in-law Peter Toews and son Abram began plowing, that son Klaas sold him thread and coffee from his store, and that both daughter-in-law Maria Reimer and daughter Margaretha, or "Die Abram Pennersche" as he calls her, offered him six eggs for hatching. During the same week, Reimer visited – sometimes staying for a meal or for a night – each of his six children, two in his own village, Blumenort, and four in Steinbach, seven kilometres distant. During the course of the year, Reimer also detailed the household economies of his married children, recording the acres planted to various crops, their yields and the prices they earned in Winnipeg.

Ontario's Moses Bowman was more well-to-do than Reimer, and as a gifted preacher he held an important office in the church.[46] His life was an endless routine of church meetings, funerals and baptisms, speaking engagements, and consultations with other ministers. Despite his public profile, the greater part of his world was shaped by his 11 sons and daughters, 10 of whom were married by 1890. Like all Mennonite ministers, Bowman spent most of his time "at home"; and at age 71 his overriding concern was with the last details of generational succession. He had already distributed his 200 acres of land to his children and sold the family farm to one of his sons, Aaron. But he still needed to make some adjustments to ensure equality within the complex partible inheritance system; one day in May he mailed son Samuel in Michigan $800 and two days later collected $700 from another son, Moses Jr. His social life involved frequent visits to the households of both his sons and his daughters and his social space incorporated the farms of his sons. His diary revealed a mental mapping that designated a layer of kin identity over the Waterloo community; thus on 13 February 1890 when Bowman drove to Berlin, it was via the "middle Street throu [son] Aaron's Road, [and] came back through [son] Noah's Road." But the importance of his children's households in his life was most visible in his own work routine. It frequently involved working for one of his sons, especially Aaron, on whose farmyard he lived. He helped Aaron "tap . . . sugar trees" in March and "lay . . . his barn floor" in July; he stayed home to "help Aaron thrash" in August and "dig . . . Aaron's potatoes" in October. Bowman's diary reveals the viewpoint of a community church leader but also of an elderly agrarian householder.[47]

Like young Moses Weber and Heinrich Kornelsen, the elderly Abraham Reimer and Moses Bowman were not at the centre of a farm household, yet both the young and the old saw it as their role to comment on the households to which they were linked directly or indirectly.

The diaries in section II, those by Margaretha Jansen and Maria Klassen, indicated that the tradition of diary-keeping among Mennonites crossed not only lines of region, class, and generation, but of gender, too. The diaries in section VII, "Farm Women," reveal a common perspective among women farm householders. At various points in their life cycles, women, like men, kept journals that dispassionately documented the daily work routine within the household, as well as the social network in which the household was set. Seemingly, as long as the farm economy was rooted in a household mode of production, women diarists were preoccupied not with self but with family – both the household and kinship social networks. Studies of women diarists have sometimes demonstrated the usefulness of diaries in asserting the separate identity of women in a male-dominated world. Judy Simons has argued that, "dogged by conventions of femininity," literary women through the centuries were "able through their diaries to break with those conventions."[48] Margaret Conrad's study of rural Canadian east-coast women – women with "few literary pretensions" – makes a different argument: the diaries of women in her study reflected "the real power of women in rural families"; they revealed a "remarkable ... sharing of jobs" with men and a set of social concerns "often shared by the men in their lives."[49] Mennonite women lived less idyllically, but their diaries, too, reflected the social setting of the rural community and farm household that drew women and men to a common pursuit, and often to similar life perspectives.

To a degree the diaries of Mennonite farm women reflect marriage status, region, proximity to a town, and class. Four different women represent four worlds: Margaretha Plett Kroeker, who was 49 in 1892, came from a prosperous farm located within the boundaries of the bustling town of Steinbach, Manitoba; Laura Shantz, who was 34 in 1918, was a single woman who lived with her parents, the owners of a well-established Waterloo, Ontario, farm; Maria Reimer Unger, who was 43 in 1919, came from a similarly successful farm in the rural district of Blumenhof, Manitoba; Judith Klassen Neufeld, who was 53 in 1922, represented a Manitoba household that was forced to leave the farm during a year of depression.[50] Despite the marked difference in their worlds, these four women perceived society in similar ways. For each of these women the household was the primary social unit, and kinship and congregation marked its social tentacles.

Remarkably, Kroeker's 1892 diary sheds little light on the commercial and social dynamic of Steinbach. And only indirect evidence reveals the Kroekers' social standing in town. The diary, for example, reveals that although in 1892 the Kroekers had no children living at home, they relied on help from servants (including a Ukrainian and a German Lutheran) and were in a position to care for a foster daughter and an older handicapped woman. Clearly indicating the spaciousness of their house is the regular note that the Kroekers regularly hosted the worship service of the town's largest church; and inevitably this was a time too when at least some of Margaretha's brothers and sisters, the Pletts of Blumenort and Blumenhof, and other church friends from neighbouring villages would stay for lunch and perhaps for *Faspa*. But there is no evidence of ostentatious living and no reflection on the relative wealth of any of the Kroeker neighbours.

Like the diaries of men, the works by women farm householders usually omitted personal reflection. Even during times of obvious emotional pain or moments of ecstasy, there is a stoic tone in the female diaries. When Judith

Klassen Neufeld noted that she and her husband were forced to leave a rented farm that they had hoped to purchase, and only after considerable search rented a house that required cleaning, she offered no utterance of despair or fatigue or disappointment, just the short quip that on 22 June, a day on which it was "very hot," "we moved from our farm."[51] Her tone did not change, even in times of shock, joy or impatience. A tragedy in June was recorded as a matter of fact: "Peter K. Friesen was killed in Steinbach while cutting down a tree. A piece of iron struck his head." A moment of obvious joy in January received the same short shrift: after the opening note on this day, she wrote, "Papa and Johan went to the river to get wood," followed the simple phrase, "in the p.m. the children were blessed with a infant son." On 30 October, Judith recorded a moment of youthful indiscretion on the part of her unmarried son, Jacob, who slept "until noon, as he attended the wedding last evening [and] came home at 6 a.m.," but she recorded no judgement.

Like the diaries of the men, too, women's diaries carefully documented the economy of the household and the social events in the community. In 1918, Ontario's Laura Shantz, for example, recorded a range of work outside the house. Shantz secured her household's economic strength by working both the farmyard and garden. Records such as "Buzzard cow, calf" or the "Mooly heifer, calved," indicate her central role in the dairy barn. References to "set three hens in the corncrib" or "sow has eight pigs in sheep pen" place her in other corners of the farmyard. Notes such as "Eph's butchered five pigs, one for Mother Shantz" or "took up potatoes in truck patch" also link her to food procurement. But she also identified with the entire household economy, including the parts dominated by men. Thus, she documented when "men worked on land," the day that "Walter . . . took load of pigs out to Baden," and the time that "Pa fetched [the] new Ford." And these household records extended easily into community and kin records. In October she noted how neighbour "Rosenbergers filled silo," and in other months she wrote about land transactions, auction sales, barn fires and barn-raising bees within the community. She mentioned special church services, Bible conferences, baptism instruction meetings, singing hour, and successive protracted revival meetings, led by Ed Hess at the Geiger Church, David Garber in Blenheim, and C.F. Derstine in Kitchener. True, there are references to the invading outside world: the notes of "the death of Pte. Elgin Eby in Action overseas, 71 Battalion, machine gun section" or even of "young Howling [who] stole cigars . . . at Kavelmans store" were signs of a Mennonite community tied to a wider world. Still, Laura Shantz's diary was a record of the social ties and boundaries that allowed a Mennonite community to survive a time of rapid urbanization.

If the tone and subject of women's diaries are the same as those of the men, it is still true that men and women exhibited different perspectives on the household, based on gender. Unlike men, women seem to have viewed the farm from within the house. Laura Shantz's diary mentioned children, health, the comings and goings of other women, and the domestic duties of cleaning and baking. In the women's diaries there are fewer references to weather and season. When Shantz noted weather patterns, they were the views of someone on the inside of the house: the blizzard in January 1918 was so harsh that "Joe Shantz ... couldn't get home," the February cold snap so extreme that it froze the "water pipes ... from tank to house," the "ice storm" of March so severe that "tellphone wires broke." Like the men, she made reference to life-cycle events – deaths of children and of elderly neighbours – and to such tragedies as murder, suicide, and accidental death. Unlike the diaries of most men, however, Laura Shantz's more frequently referred to birth, marriage, and especially to health. Typical were entries such as the February notes, "Elvin Shantz has mumps and Moses B. congestion of the lungs" and that "Mary Tohman had operation for appendicitis was burst [and] Wesley Battler [ha]s scarlet fever." She showed even greater concern for the health of immediate family members with records such as "Walter had sore ear" and "Dr Gillespie put me to bed," and with weight statistics for each of the women in the house: on 17 March it was "Grandma ... 118, Ma 154, Nurse 161, Laura 144."

There are many similarities between the Ontario and Manitoba women's diaries. Middle-aged mother Maria Unger, who lived in Manitoba, lived in a more closed, less commercialized society and in a harsher physical environment than her Ontario counterpart. Still, the Shantz diary and the Unger diary show a common preoccupation with daily work in a farm household and a social network marked by kin and congregation. Maria Unger's diary also depicted a woman's world with references to female social networks, childbirths and quilting bees, and to interactions between mothers and daughters. Her diary, too, was written from the perspective of inside the farmhouse; there were few details of weather but many mentions of such domestic work as "whitewashing the kitchen," "mangling the wash," "baking bread," "spinning, knitting, and sewing," and caring for the small children. Yet, like Laura Shantz's diary, Maria Unger's was a farm household journal. The daily work activities of each member of the family, female and male, was described. Maria Unger's entry for 17 March 1919 was typical: "Papa and Johann drove to Giroux for wood and I wove. The girls patched and dyed wool." And, like that of Laura Shantz, Maria Unger's world included the farmyard, where calves were born, brooding hens were set on eggs, and gardens were harvested. The only difference in the work pattern of Shantz and Unger was that, in the context of Manitoba's short growing season, Unger and her teenaged daughters spent more time in the fields, especially piling wheat sheaves into stooks to dry in Manitoba's hot, arid July.

The final selection of diaries, section VIII, "Diverging Paths," reveals how security on the farm, without regard to gender or region, ultimately shaped one's perspective. These diaries reveal that advancements of urbanization and technology in the host society did not homogenize society, that conservative ways could continue in a changing and heterogeneous world in Ontario and that upheaval could visit a well-established farm in southern Manitoba.

Marie Schroeder, 19 in 1926, lived on a farm, but as a step-daughter of the male household head she faced an uncertain future.[51] Schroeder's parents, who had migrated from the East Reserve to the West as children, migrated again shortly after Marie's birth, when her youthful father suffered a serious accident. Her parents were forced to leave their rented farm and move to church property in the town of Lowe Farm, where they lived until her father died. Later, when her mother remarried, this time to a well-to-do farmer, the family moved to his farm, north of the town of Morden. But Marie was a step-child in a blended family of 18 children, and she faced the promise of only a small inheritance. The Schroeder diary reflects that of a woman who had cast her eyes beyond the homestead. Although she had much work to do on the farm, she had taken the opportunity of studying beyond the mandatory seventh grade, and thus when she milked the cows she thought poetically, and when she wrote her diary she did it in English and with frankness and introspection. Her descriptions are among the most literary in this collection. She recorded moments of heartfelt joy, even giddiness, and of self-doubt. She offered her resistance to joining the church, her fascination with young men browned by the Mexican sun, her joy at capitalizing on the one-cent sale in Morden, and her antipathy to the "Plum Coulee girls." But most telling is her "secret hope that [she might] write things that have a real worth someday; things that are worth printing, and things that other folks would love to read and pay for." Marie Schroeder was a farm woman but, finding little prospect of farming, she looked past the farm, into her own soul and out beyond the homestead. Specific mixes of gender, class, and generation produced specific worlds of Mennonite diarists.

The 1927 diary of 67-year-old Cornelius T. Friesen reveals a life in turmoil. Friesen had been a local community leader, head of the local estates and credit organization called the *Waisenamt*.[52] Now, in the late 1920s, the Chortitzer Mennonite community of Manitoba's East Reserve was splitting. Many of its members were prepared to contest Manitoba's 1916 School Attendance Act, which compelled Mennonite children to attend publicly inspected, English-language schools. These Chortitzer Mennonites sought to maintain their German-language parochial schools by leaving Canada and re-establishing themselves in distant Paraguay's Chaco region. An emotional intensity and social dislocation reveal themselves in Friesen's account as members took their farewell, often with a sense of permanent separation. And those Chortitzers who remained in Canada redoubled efforts to revitalize the old foundation of the church: they met to establish moral guidelines for the community, they welcomed ministers from other regions to strengthen a community weakened by emigration, and they made way for new *Waisenmänner* to fill in for Friesen, who had retired, and for others who had joined the emigration.

The 1929 diary of 35-year-old Ontario farmer Ishmael Martin provides some information on the introduction of new crops and the shift from selling cream and butter to whole milk. Yet this is no new world. Martin's life continued to revolve around the triad of household, kin group, and church congregation.⁵³ His traditionalist life seems to be safeguarded by his farm and his Old Order Mennonite roots; there are no references in his diary to any life-transforming technology, whether car or tractor, telephone or electricity. More important in bringing a change to the tradition of Mennonite diary-keeping than the simple passage of time from one century to another was the social setting of the diarist. Martin may have written his diary during the 1920s, but he reflected a less individualistic and introspective mindset than those diarists of the nineteenth century who lived in more heterogeneous settings. The diaries of Margaretha Jansen and Levi Jung reflect a growing individualism associated with a more subjective religiosity; the diaries of miller Elias Eby and merchant Klaas Reimer suggest their writers' ability to distance themselves from the immediate community and reflect on its nature. The diaries of Ontario and Manitoba farm women and men, however, reveal a different perspective. They reflect a preoccupation with the household's economy and an inveterate dependence on a local social network. The deeply rooted nature of this kind of diary is reflected in the fact that old men and teenaged boys, married and unmarried women, and farmers of the 1890s and the 1920s kept diaries of a similar nature.

This "poor stuff" of Mennonite diary-writing provides few direct glimpses into Mennonite consciousness and few analyses of the development of Mennonite community. Except for occasional references to community tragedies, church upheavals, or weather aberrations, these diaries contain little sensation. But this very absence offers an invaluable glance into the everyday worlds of rural Mennonites in Canada. More important than even the content, however, is the medium of diary-writing itself. To know what they chose to record is also to know something of their culture, that is, the symbols and systems of meaning constructed by ordinary people in their everyday lives to make sense of life, and particularly to make sense of changes and inconsistencies of life.⁵⁴ Here was an attempt to order one's life in the face of the immutability of physical forces, the uncertainty of the market economy, the vulnerability of the social boundaries, and the ambiguous circle of friend and foe within the community. Here was an attempt by members of a cultural minority to survive in a rapidly changing wider society. The diaries themselves reflect their authors' determination that, within their households, kinship networks, and church congregations, Mennonites might continue to fashion a sense of order in their worlds.

Migrating Men

I

1   Cornelius W. Loewen (1827 to 1893)

Gruenfeld, Manitoba

Diary selection: 1867 to 1877

Age: 39 in 1867

Cornelius Loewen was born in Lindenau, Molotschna Colony, New Russia, in 1827. His parents were Isaak Loewen and Margaretha Wiens, who had migrated to Russia from Polish Prussia as children in 1804. Isaak Loewen became a noted silkworm farmer and a well-known deacon in the Mennonite Kleine Gemeinde. At age 26, in 1853, Cornelius married 20-year-old Helena Bartel. Cornelius and Helena had only two children who survived: Cornelius Jr., born in 1863, and Isaak, born in 1865. In 1867, the Loewens sold their Molotschna farm for 3,400 rubles and migrated to the new sub-colony of Borosenko, 150 kilometres to the west, across the Dnieper River; here they settled in the village of Gruenfeld. Within 10 years, in 1874, the Loewens joined the great migration of Dutch Russian Mennonites to North America. The Loewens chose to settle in Manitoba's Mennonite East Reserve in the village of Gruenfeld, known as the first Mennonite village in western Canada. In 1876, a few months after a difficult childbirth, Helena died. Shortly thereafter, Cornelius married Katherina Rempel Barkman of Steinbach, a widow who had outlived three husbands; her third husband, Reverend Jacob M. Barkman, had drowned in the Red River in Winnipeg on 3 June 1875. After his marriage to Katherina, Cornelius moved to Katherina's farm in Steinbach where he farmed and worked in the lumber business. His son Cornelius B. Loewen later opened a lumberyard, a tradition that grandson Cornelius T. Loewen continued.

Cornelius's diary was sketchy, kept only to record the most important events of life and the barest details of the household economy. Sometimes, as in the 1874 "crib" death of his baby son Jakob or the 1875 freezing of Heinrich Wiebe in a village 20 kilometres away, he recorded tragic events. Yet, for Cornelius's purpose of managing his life, it was less important for him to record Helena's death in October than it was to document the process of probating her estate, a prerequisite for his remarriage. Only a rough annual chronological order shaped the diary; matters were recorded haphazardly, sometimes a month after they occurred.

Situated within this sketchy diary is a dense daily account of the transatlantic migration in the summer of 1874. The detail of this sub-diary attests to the significance that Loewen ascribed to this migration. The sub-diary, however, was probably not Loewen's but borrowed from one of several that circulated in the East Reserve's villages. Often these travel accounts were copied and recopied and appeared later in the papers of various families. Not only is the description of the migration in a different hand, but also the style is different, and details overlap with details in the journal kept in his own handwriting. The author of this sub-diary is not known; it was possibly his wife. A similarly detailed diary of the identical trip, but penned by farmer Jakob Koop of Neuanlage, was reproduced in Delbert Plett, *Storm and Triumph: The Mennonite Kleine Gemeinde, 1850-1875* (Steinbach, MB: 1986): 330-332. Among the many new scenes and people recorded was the Dutch Russian Mennonite group's arrival in Toronto, where it was met by a delegation of Waterloo, Ontario, Mennonites, which included Elias Eby (see diary 9).

Most of the people noted in this diary are Cornelius's brothers: David, Heinrich, Abram, and Johann. The diary also includes his brothers-in-law, Johann Warkentin, a dairy farmer, and Cornelius Plett, the village mayor of Kleefeld (Molotschna) and then of Blumenhoff (Borosenko). And it includes the numerous encounters with members of his church congregation, the Kleine Gemeinde. Other Mennonites in this diary bearing names such as Block, Braun, and Funk are fellow Mennonite colonists, but some were probably members of the main Mennonite church. Non-Mennonites are also noted in the diary; they include Jewish peddlers, "a soldier," and Loewen's farm labourers – Mischie or Mischa, Jedoch, Zwirith, Paraska, and Mawre. Finally, there is reference to "Cornelius" or "my husband," indicating that Helena took her turn at recording the events of the Loewen household.

The diary was preserved by Gerhard Giesbrecht, Steinbach, Manitoba. A photocopy of the original diary, spanning the years between 1863 and 1892 and written in German Gothic handwriting, is located at the Mennonite Village Museum in Steinbach. The diary was translated by Royden Loewen. For more information on Cornelius Loewen and for another translation of the travelogue, see Melvin J. Loewen, *The Descendants of Cornelius W. Loewen and Helena Bartel* (Goshen, IN: 1994).

1867

3 Feb. Paid principal [on the loan], 4 rubles.

4 Feb. Paid principal [on the loan] for Anna, 3 rubles.

17 Feb. Owing at Jakob Schmidt for the sleeping bench, 1 ruble, 22 1/2 kopecks. They have taken 10 pounds *Hirsegritze* [?] 25 kopecks and also a glass of *Haarlämer Topfen* [?] 30 kopecks, for the plough wood at Schmidt, 7 rubles.

28 Feb. I sold the farm [on Molotschna Colony] to Cornelius Funk from Sparrau, for 3,400 rubles and obtained 1,500 rubles silver; 1,000 rubles [to be] given in May and 900 rubles are owed from May to October.

5 March I gave Johann Warkentin 1,500 rubles to take along for the land purchase [on Borosenko Colony].

7 May I gave the man everything, including interest.

7 May I borrowed from Johann Löwen, Muntau, 275 rubles at 6%.

21 May I took along 600 silver rubles and gave them to [my brother] Abraham Löwen.

24 May Purchased merchandise in Nicopol for 4 rubles, 13 kopecks.

26 Sept. Borrowed oats from Johann Barkmans'.

21 Nov. Hired the maid for one year for 30 silver rubles. 2 April: she went home.

Nov. I purchased from Johann Warkentin, Blumenhoff, rye for seeding, 3 Mirks [?].

1868

19 Jan. I owe Abraham Löwen: for ... string I owe him 21 kopecks; for [string for cap ?], 6 kopecks.

31 Jan. One bottle Waar [?] I owe 8 kopecks.

7 Feb. half a quart of wine, 28 kopecks; half...@ 14 kopecks, 21 kopecks; 5 *Mäze* [?] cotton, 78 kopecks; one pail, 60 kopecks; 8 rolls cotton, 3 rubles, 20 kopecks; for fish he owes, 74 kopecks; I received small money, 1 ruble, 70 kopecks; received payment, 5.37; he...me, 1 ruble, 20 kopecks; Abraham Löwen, sugar . . . for 90 kopecks; we have cheese, 3 3/4 pounds, 57 kopecks; I received payment, 1 ruble; they took 3 rolls cotton, 60 kopecks; they took *Töst* [?] and *Kaukes*[?], 20 kopecks; paid Susanna, one basket, 45 kopecks.

22 April Hired Marianna [a young girl] for one year for 2 rubles and our clothes.

26 May Hired Mawre for 25 rubles till the first of October.

Harvest David Löwen purchased wheat – 5 *chetvert* [one chetvert = 26.35 litres or 5.7 bushels], 10 rubles, 50 kopecks, overall for 52 rubles, 50 kopecks.

1869

4 April We and the Regehrs drove to Molotschna [Colony, 100 kilometres to the east] and returned home safely on the 16th. Kornelius Pletts and Johan Löwens wish to leave for the Crimea on the 15th. They arrived at our place on the 26th. The Crimeans [of the Kleine Gemeinde congregation] arrived here on May 1: Jakob Wiebes, Peter Bärg, Aron Schellenbergs and the Fasts. These are [here] concerning the unification [within the fractious Kleine Gemeinde], which with God's help occurred.

On the 12th Wiebe and Bärg drove on to the Molotschna. The others, the Schellenbergs and the Fasts, departed here on the 8th for home.

On the 10th at 1 o'clock at night Mrs. Abram Löwen gave birth to a son and with that she died. On the 11th she was buried.

[no date] Jakob Wiebe's [Crimean chapter of the Kleine Gemeinde], after this year's harvest, seceded or departed from us with the others and allowed themselves to be baptized another time [thus establishing the Krimmer Mennonite Brethren].

5 Oct. I gave money along with David Löwen; 18 rubles.

21 Oct. Hired a maid, named Paraska [possibly a Ukrainian], for one year for 35 rubles.

31 Dec. Borrowed merchandise at Sowarow, 40 rubles 20 kopecks.

1870

9 Jan. Purchased paper and . . . for the school, 65 kopecks.

13 Jan. Johann Töws is indebted for 2 1/2 . . . , 1 ruble, 40 kopecks. Peter Löwen, Hochfeld, owes me for sheep, 12 rubles, 40 kopecks; when all is sold then he will pay me.

15 Jan. I lent the soldier 10 rubles and he gave me the horse from now until seeding time is ended.

27 Jan. Peter's register; he is to receive 60 rubles.

26 Feb. Gave the maid, Paraska, wine for 1 ruble.

4 April Borrowed merchandise from Johann Husof [likely a Jewish peddler], 11 rubles, 26 kopecks.

10 Sept. We elected Peter Töws as Ältester [Bishop or Elder] with 65 votes and Schellenberg received 8 votes and Goossen 2 votes. On October 26 he was ordained by our preachers.

1871

27 Jan. I hired Zwirith for one whole year for 43 rubles.

9 May We hired Anna till New Years for 20 rubles.

12 May We hired Marianna for one year for 8 rubles.

19 Aug. I brought Soworow merchandise, 7 [rubles], 59 [kopecks].

28 Aug. I brought Sefan Husow some merchandise [for] 21 [rubles], 76 [kopecks].

After the harvest [I] had 6 *chetvert* wheat milled [to last] till springtime.

30 Aug. Sold wheat [one pud is 16 kilograms]: 70.21 pud @ 82 [kopecks]; 57.00 pud @ 83; . . . 58.46 pud @ 91; 11 Sept. . . . 65.77 pud @ 93; 14 Sept. . . . 46.79 pud @ 93.5; . . . 26.25 pud @ 90; 1 Oct. . . . 38.50 pud @ 90.0/92.5 . . . ; 3 Nov., . . . 34.54 pud @ 84.

8 Oct. I sold Johann Warkentin, Blumenhoff, sheep: 12 head @ 2 rubles 35 kopecks, for a total of 28 rubles, 20 kopecks.

1872

7 Jan. We hired Mischa; receivable pay per year – 30 rubles.

15 Jan. Sold 1.75 *Kageln* [piece of land?] to him [Isaak Löwen]. Received 15.00; he owes principal of 11.25; thus, he owes total principal of 22.50.

6 March We hired Jedoch; receivable pay per year – 33 rubles.

April Sold wheat 40.80 pud @ .92 1/2.

In October I gave money for the interest along [to Molotschna Colony?] with Heinrich Reimer and he has also paid.

28 Oct. Borrowed 50 silver rubles from Franz Kröker, Steinbach. In November I borrowed another 50 rubles from him. All paid up.

1 Nov. We settled the account [with] Johann Warkentin, Hochfeld; I still owe him 140.35, written out as, "one hundred and forty rubles and thirty five kopecks."

28 Nov. I borrowed 50 silver rubles till April from Johann Löwen, Blumenhoff.

11 Dec. I rented land from Isaak Löwen, Rosenfeld – 7 1/2 *desiatini* [1.09 hectares, for] 4.50.

1873

15 Feb. Cornelius Töws [the Kleine Gemeinde land delegate] departed for America [with 11 other Mennonite and Hutterite leaders]. On the 15th of April he began his return and on the 5th of August he arrived.

11 March I again hired Jedoch; she will receive a salary of 43 rubles.

4 April Sold bulls: 2.73.

9 April Hired Mischie again; if it [works out] well then 40 rubles, when it [works out] badly then only 35 rubles.

In June Marianne was hired till Martin [the feast of St. Martin, 1 November] for 7 rubles.

4 June Breschke [Bröski] worked at our place; in May I sold him a cow for 37 rubles.

21 June Our Father [Deacon Isaak Löwen] died and this brought his life to 85 years, 11 months, 11 days. On the 23rd of June he was buried.

During the harvest I settled an account with Heinrich Wohlgemuth.

14 September borrowed money, 1.75.

In September Gerhard Wiebe bought a cow for 25 rubles.

16 October Paid principal and interest [on the Johann Löwen loan].

1874

[no date] Our purchased land cost 1,316.90; per *desiatina*, 52.67 3/5.

1874 Drove to the *Wolost* [county offices] with regard to our move to America; settled the accounts with Jakob Regehr – provided a complete "financial road account." Drove once again with Johann Töws with regard to the [emigration] passes.

16 Jan. Purchased for the village administration: schnapps, 6 . . . ; 3 pounds sugar, .60 . . . ; 1 quart beer, .22 . . . ; 1/2 quart brandy, .30 . . . . [Total] 7.12.

31 Jan. Johann Töws, Grünfeld, has borrowed 300 silver rubles until we have paid for our land.

Feb. We had the auction sale.

9 April He [Johann Töws] has paid everything.

19 Feb. We brought Elisabeth Wiens here.

1874 Here is the trip from Russia to America written up.

The 1st of June, according to Russian time, on Saturday, we drove from our old home and came to Nikopol, there loaded our baggage onto the ship, stayed the night and left Sunday by ship to Cherson, spent the night there and drove Monday till Odessa. There, Tuesday late in the evening, we boarded the train and left. On Wednesday evening we arrived in Schmeriuka. There we changed trains. We left and came Thursday forenoon to Wolotschick, where the passes were examined and tickets purchased to Podwolotschick [where we crossed] over the border; here the baggage was weighed and then we departed at dusk.

On the other day, Friday, we came to the large town, near Switzerland. There we were quartered and rested well that very night. Saturday, soon after dawn, or after breakfast, we took the tickets and departed for Breslau. From there we departed late in the evening for Berlin, where we arrived on Sunday near noon. We waited there in the train station or Wartesaal, and departed late evening for Hamburg, where we arrived Monday morning; we obtained quarters at Majer. There we also obtained food, for breakfast coffee, sugar and *Zwieback* [buns]; for lunch potatoes . . . with soup and fresh meat. We waited there till Friday and departed there in the evening by ship over the North Sea to Hull, where we arrived Sunday, the 16th, at 2 o'clock afternoon. But we were required to spend the night on the ship. Monday, at noon, we walked to the train station and travelled till Lieverpool, where we arrived at 6 o'clock in the evening; we went to the quarters and were provided with supper and rested well.

Now we had arrived at the great ocean. Tuesday, the 18th, in the morning [we] boarded the great ship and after *Vesper* we set sail and at first, for about four days, we had a lot of wind. On the next day [after setting sail] we came to Irrland [Ireland]; there [we] stopped for a little while. Then we travelled till . . . Thursday, the 21st of June at 8 o'clock in the morning. Then we came to Neu Fuenland [Newfoundland], to a city Sankjons [Saint Johns] and stopped there for three hours. There we loaded more people and merchandise. In that region we saw many icebergs and huge whales. Sunday, the 30th, at 8 o'clock in the morning, we came to Halifaks [Halifax], which is also a city on an island. There too people embarked and many pieces of merchandise were loaded and much coal taken on. There we finally walked on dry earth; but this was not yet the end to the ocean.

Monday, the 1st of July, at 6 o'clock in the evening, we departed from Halifax and on Friday, the 5th of July (according to American time, the 17th), as the sun was setting we arrived safely in Qäbek [Quebec]. There we waited in the train station till the sun went down. Then we boarded the train and departed at once and Saturday morning at breakfast time we arrived in Montreal; once we finished breakfast, we travelled once again by train and on Sunday at 9 o'clock in the morning arrived in Toronto. There the Canadian Mennonite brothers welcomed us and gifted us with meat, lard, butter and dried apples. They also arranged things with the authorities that we did not have to travel on the difficult Dawsonraute [Dawson Road]. We waited in Toronto till Tuesday at 2:30 in the afternoon [and] then we departed by train. At 9 o'clock we came to the Superior Sea and walked at once onto the ship. At 11:30 at night we departed from there and sailed for four days and four nights on the sea and on Saturday the 25th of July, according to their time, we arrived at 10 o'clock in the evening at Dulut. On Sunday we observed the day of rest. Monday at 2 o'clock in the afternoon we boarded the train again and departed and on Tuesday we arrived as the sun was setting in Mohrheit [Moorhead].

Now we were on the *Rothen Fluss* [Red River]. At 2 o'clock we walked onto the ship and also soon departed, and on Friday, the 31st of July, evening, we arrived in Winnipeg. We stayed on board the ship overnight. On Saturday we purchased foodstuffs and things. Several remained in Winnipeg and settled on the other side of the river. We travelled by ship back to a point adjacent to our land and arrived Sunday, the 2nd of August, at day break. Now the further transportation [supported] by the government came to an end. Two wagons had been brought along from Winnipeg. Then, too, Métis drivers were hired and we had ourselves driven to the Immigration Houses which were seven miles from the river. We spent 19 days in these houses. Thus we arrived safely in Winnipeg on the 31st of July.

2 Aug. According to our [Manitoba] time, we arrived on the shore of the Red River and moved to the immigration houses [10 kilometres in land].

16 Aug. This morning at 12:30 in the morning our son Jakob was born.

21 Aug. Today we arrived at our dwelling place [in the village of Grünfeld].

28 Aug. This morning we found Jakob dead in the cradle and today after *Vesper* we buried him and his age had come to 12 days.

25 Aug. [in Manitoba] Gave Breschke money to buy an ox and to register the land [take out a homestead] and more – 98 dollars and 4 cents.

6 Sept. Johann Töws's account: he has borrowed one hundred ten dollars; the last he paid on 9.

15 Sept. Today the Steinbachers and Annafelders arrived at the Red River.

24 Sept. Mrs. Johann Warkentin died and was buried on the 25th.

9 Oct. We moved into our house.

18 Oct. Today we had Johann Esau . . . [and] Abraham Kornelsen as guests.

25 Oct. Jakob Friesen's account: he has borrowed for the purchase of oxen – 88 dollars and 80 cents.

17 Nov. Today my husband had a misfortune in Winnipeg and arrived home on the 28th of November by foot.

1875

7 Jan. I got from Regehr the money he had loaned from Franz Kröker, namely 100 dollars, which I am to repay in springtime.

7 Jan. 1875 Concerning the estate which is administered by Cornelius Löwen, Grünfeld, and Jakob Barkman, Steinbach, [these] are the "orphan" children of Abram Löwen:

Name of the Inheritors	Dol.	Cents	Age		
Son, Abram	663	33 1/3	18	They are	The settle-
Daughter, Margaretha	With the		15	to remain	ment is so
Daughter, Helena	father in		12	at home	far as one
Daughter, Anna	the farm.		11	with father.	sees peaceful.

22 Feb. A letter to Peter Fast, Rosenfeld.

8 April It began to thaw and in the evening began to rain and during the night also rained heavily. Also the sleigh travel came to an end.

3 June Ohm Jakob Barkman and Jakob Friesen drowned in the *Rothen Fluss* [Red River].

20 Aug. And again on the 21st it froze.

9 Sept. And on the 10th it froze for the second time.

27 Sept. We moved into our new house.

1 Oct. I borrowed from David Löwen, Hochstadt, 200 dollars at 5 percent.

25 Oct. We had a thunderstorm.

Nov. In November I borrowed money from Johann Dück – thirty dollars, numerically written, 30 dollars.

1876

6 April Received from Johann Löwen, Rosenhoff, $500.

1 March From Johann Dück, Grünfeld, I borrowed $50 till New Year without interest, if I need it longer, then I shall pay interest.

2 March The house of Johann Esau, an unmarried man, burned down and he moved at once to our place. He has exchanged his land [with the land of another villager] and now is our neighbour.

7 March We drove to Rosenhof and Rosenort to visit.

15 March We returned home safe and healthy.

16 March At 10 p.m. [Delegate] Cornelius Töws's [house/barn] burned down.

May I borrowed another 20 dollars from Johann Dück.

15 July Cornelius got a cow from D. Friesen.

1 Aug. We brought our little Johann to Töwses' [for wet nursing], [the agreement is that it] will be 20 weeks till New Year and must give him till New Years $25.

13 Dec. In the evening a sudden snowstorm struck and many people suffered misfortunes. Heinrich Wiebe, Blumenort, was unable to find the way home and froze to death. We always have things to ponder: that we might be faithful to the end and not assume too many things; that, or what we must do when such weather strikes.

1877

8 Jan. I had a settlement of the estate and was married for the second time, with Widow [Elisabeth] Barkman of Steinbach, on the 2nd of April, the second Easter holiday, we had ourselves served with the marriage ceremony.

2   Ezra R. Burkholder (1856 to 1923)

Floradale, Ontario

Diary selection: 7 July to 7 August 1876

Age: 19

Ezra Reis Burkholder was born in Waterloo County, Canada West, on 14 November 1856. He was the son of Samuel and Eva (Reis) Burkholder. Eva's birthplace is not known; Samuel was born in Lancaster County, Pennsylvania, and came to Canada as a small child. Ezra was the fourth child in a family of six boys, which included: Joseph, Benjamin, John, Samuel, and Abraham. The Burkholders seem to have been a family in transition, rooted in a Mennonite society but associating easily with Waterloo's Evangelical Church and with Methodism in both Canada and the United States.

In September 1873, Ezra's parents and most of his brothers moved from Waterloo County, Ontario, to Marion County, Kansas. Ezra remained in Ontario to complete his education at the University of Toronto. In 1876, he travelled to Kansas to see his parents' place but returned to Canada for four more years of training, this time for the Methodist Ministry, which included two years as a probationary itinerant minister. In October 1883, suffering from ill health, Ezra left the ministry in Canada and joined his family in Kansas permanently, where he established a lumberyard, E.R. Burkholder Lumber Company, in Hillsboro. Later he acquired other yards in McPherson and Marion counties. In June 1885, Ezra married Vinnie Ream Tubbs, and together they had three children. He also involved himself in all aspects of community affairs, serving one term as county representative for Marion in the state legislature. He died in 1923, leaving a thriving business to two of his sons.

Ezra Burkholder was 19 years old in 1876 when he left his home in Floradale, Ontario, and boarded the train for Kansas. The diary seems to have begun the day he left Ontario, and it served as a travelogue, recording in incredible detail the people he met en route and the new lands he saw. His point of departure was clearly a familiar society: on the day he left, he visited Berlin in the company of friend Jacob Kaufman, later the founder of Berlin Rubber Company. He then saw Joel Good, a Mennonite land surveyor in Waterloo, who had Ezra driven to Enoch Erb's, Good's son-in-law farmer, in Woolwich Township. And, even as he left town, he noted the death of E. Wendel Bowman, a local miller and member of the revivalistic New Mennonites. But en route, Burkholder was similarly secure in a non-Mennonite environment, recording numerous encounters with non-Mennonites during his train ride. Once he arrived in Kansas, he made little reference to the large Dutch-Russian Mennonite contingent, referring to them vaguely as "Russians" and noting only a few of their kind: Reverend Jacob Wiebe, the Krimmer Mennonite Brethren of Gnadenau; Ewert and his company of "rich Russians"; the amicable and English-speaking "Funk brothers"; and a "slouchy Russian" servant girl.

His main associations were with fellow Pennsylvania-descendant Mennonites, and these included the members of his family. His very first stop in Marion County was at the home of his grandfather, Samuel Burkholder, who had arrived in Kansas in 1873. Over the next few weeks he integrated quickly with his nuclear family. He worked with his father and treated his mother to a bouquet of flowers. He undertook scouting, hunting, and haying outings with his brothers, Joseph, John, Benjamin, and Abraham. And he moved among other Swiss Mennonites: H.B. Burkholder, perhaps a relative; Reuben J. Heatwole, the Virginian who was Marion County's first Mennonite; "Misses Kraft" who accompanied Ezra in a walk through head-high weeds; John Funk of Elkhart, Indiana, the editor of the Mennonite newspaper the *Herald of Truth* and a promoter of immigration to Kansas; a Reverend Wenger, who preached in the local schoolhouse; and David Good, a neighbour. Throughout his first month in Kansas, however, he associated easily with a non-Mennonite world, visiting a Methodist church, reading United States history, and befriending men named Perry, Holloway, and Hugh.

The diary was kept in a notebook purchased from "R.J. Wright Storekeeper in Fort Gratiot." As were most diaries of Ontario Mennonites at this time, it was written in English. A copy of the original and a typescript of the diary are located at the Mennonite Archives of Ontario in Waterloo. It was transcribed by Ethel May Burkholder Dvorak in 1976 and later by Reg Good. For the family history of Ezra Burkholder, see Ezra Eby, *A Biographical History of Early Settlers and Their Descendants in Waterloo Township* 1895 (Waterloo, ON: 1971).

Friday, July 7th 1876 Started from Floradale in company of Jessie Snyder in a big wagon. Had $1.75 American silver and $1.15 Canadian currency. Received from J.S. Bowman Elmira $50 Canadian currency. Bought from ... [in]

Elmira $45 American currency for $38.50 Canadian currency. Bought from Benjamin Bowman, Waterloo [a] microscope $1 [no] a magnifying glass. Sent portraits of Livingstone to Schuyler, Smith and Co. London. Had dinner with A. Erb. Went to Teacher's Association in afternoon. Very warm. Lemonade 10 cents. Passed through "Button Works" and "Felt Shoe Works," in company of Joseph Bingeman and Jacob Kaufmann. Many men engaged. Expenses over $300 a day; mostly women at work. Had tea at Amos Wilfong's in Berlin with Kaufmann. Went to Waterloo – saw Blackwood and Joel Goods. Went to Joel Good's and on way met Samuel Wegenest who sent best respects to parents and brothers. Went to Joel Goods. Frank took us over to Enoch Erb. Stopped there all night. Excursion from Toledo on 12th July. Rain in the morning – oppressively warm during day and evening. Had $46.75 American currency and $11.80 Canadian currency. Was quite well.

Saturday, July 8th Were taken to Waterloo by Enoch Erb. Had conversations with H. Thomas. Rode with J. Ruppel to Berlin. Spent 5 cents for Lemonade, 10 cents [for] ice-cream. Was to Association – accounts of which will be found on notes taken elsewhere. Dinner at Weaver's Hotel 25 cents; lemonade powder 13 cents; pass book 10 cents. Wendel Bowman died at Blair.

Dr. Whiting died at Berlin. Went to Bridgeport and to Anna Erbs and in evening for tea to Uncle Dans on Sunday afternoon. All around here send best respects. Very warm and oppressive Sundays and Saturdays. Had Saturday evening spent 73 cents. Bought for $4.04 Canadian currency $5.05 American currency. Have $7.03 Canadian currency and $51.80 American currency. Went to bed at 9 – slept from 9.30 to 12.30.

10th Was taken by U. Dan to station [train] arrived 2:20; was informed no cars going till 10:25 – slept an hour in station house – went to Berlin – spent 20 cents. Rode with Mr. Jackson to Preston. Bought ticket for Detroit, $5. Grain ripe [in region] below Galt. Land hilly and stony. Remarkably hot. Passed through Galt, Harrisburg, Woodstock, Ingersoll, and then to London. West of Woodstock land most beautiful, but buildings not so good as at home – noticed Thames River. Ingersoll a nice place – also Woodstock. Took dinner at depot in London, 30 cents.... A most beautiful stretch of land west of London – also some marshes. Met with a school-teacher from Wellington, who left at Glencoe. It commenced to rain at 12:45 – had some heavy showers. Got a glass of pop at Chatham, 5 cents. West of Chatham, prairie to the right and brush at a certain space to the left. I was informed by a gentleman that there is a space of 11 miles length west of Chatham all marsh. This is mostly not under cultivation, but that which is, is on account of the great rainfall mostly covered with water. Land west of the marsh very level but bushland lie in connection [?]. Crops look good – a great deal of nice corn here – wheat (fall) ripe but none cut. Lake St. Clair is now in view. Buildings very inferior along here. Came to Detroit at 6 o'clock. Paid bus, 25 cents American money, to take me to C.E. Kelsey on 93 Gerwold Street. Found Kelsey an extremely amiable man. Bought ticket to go to Hutchison and return for $42 American currency. Met with a man from Sandwich named C.A. Grantshur, a fisher by trade. Invited me to call on him. Scenery fair – many apple, etc. trees – land in many places so low and level – apparently it rained very heavy here. Came to Toledo at 8:40. Spent 30 cents for eating materials. Met with a man named R.O. Dickson from 33 Adelaide Street E., Toronto, Traveller's Insurance Company. He lived 5 years in Kansas (from 1869 to 1874). He was in Davis County East of Dickinson County. Got to be School Superintendent there. He liked the country very much – got married there and then two years ago his wife dying and his friends all living in Canada he came back to the city of Toronto – not however before having purchased 320 acres of land in Davis County. He praises very highly the school system of Kansas but says people cannot as yet fill it out and bring it in operation[,] i.e. in country districts. He says it is extremely healthy, and the atmosphere is salubrious – although it lies in a latitude farther south, yet owing to an almost steady breeze it is not so hot as at times in Ontario. He intends to go out again and remain. Junction City was his home. They were not visited by grasshoppers any years while he was out, but 1874, when they made remarkable havoc. Left Toledo 12 o'clock Chicago time.

In counting money find I have $1.21 Canadian money and $9.15 American currency. Lost 50 cents or made some mistake.

11th, 1876 After sleeping very unsoundly till daylight we had passed through Ohio. In Indiana things look most magnificent – there is along the railroad very nice land – wheat was cut and on shocks, some had been drawn away – oats look very good, and 1 piece I observed was nearly ripe. Along the railroad the crops have a most favourable aspect. The farm buildings are not equal to those of Waterloo Co. In the towns and cities etc., buildings present a most magnificent sight. The notable places we passed through were Fort Wayne, Wabash, Peru, Logansport and Lafayette Junction; 25 cents. At Peru, Dickson left me. Saw some beautiful Murino sheep. We next came into Illinois. Crops look good, fall wheat all cut but two pieces in one of which a header was standing and in another a reel rake was used. Oats looked just about ripe but I saw none cut. Saw but little barley – no spring wheat; but by far the most land is planted with corn which seems to be far above the average. I saw some corn which I judged 7 feet high. The land through most parts in Illinois is beautiful – some is rather low and flat – especially that lying close to the Illinois River – this river cover[s] a surface of about 3 miles in width. As much as we could see of Springfield it had some admirable buildings. I sent from a small place called Bluff a post card to H.B. Bowman. I was very much agitated by the conductor of the train who tried to make out that my ticket was only valid from Toledo to Quincy – but he telegraphed to Detroit and made all right in the evening. It was most oppressively warm all today – it did not rain where I was but it apparently rained in places before we came there. We passed along the Mississippi but found it not a clear pure water – it is very high at present – on the east of it we came to the city of Quincy.

Was around the city after supper for which I paid 50 cents. Bought 3 apples for 5 cents, glass lemonade 10 cents, newspaper 3 cents. Was out to [the] park which is large and very admirable; 6 cents. In [the] public square is a fountain the water of which shoots up about 15 foots. But being by mechanical force brought from the Mississippi it is dirty. There are great quarries at the southern end of the city. Saw a block 12 feet long and 3 feet square. They have a peculiar mode of loading them with one horse. Business was dull – roads not paved – side-walks made of brick – most beautiful and ornamental trees decorate the city – saw some of the most beautiful residences I ever saw in my life. The city is infected with a very unpleasant stench. Spent today $1; [thus] $9.15 – $1 [leaves] $8.15.

12th We left Quincy at 10 p.m. for Atchison and came to the latter place 9:40 a.m. On the way we stopped at Cameron Junction for breakfast. Bought newspaper, 10 cents, and apples 5 cents. I did not see much of Missouri until 7 this morning and then there was a fog. There is some nice land here. Some is hilly, and along the Missouri River there is a regular marsh several miles long and varies from 1 mile to several miles in breadth. Wheat crop looks to have been heavier in Missouri than in Indiana and Illinois. Saw some herds of cattle and pigs, and many mules at work – these are about as large as a good-sized horse – vary however, but they look nicer than ours in Canada.

There seems to have [been] some mistake in my ticket, but Mills, the conductor between Quincy and Cameron Junction corrected it. The fruit trees all along are larger than those in Canada, except those which are young. Their tops are spread out much wider, but the same disease which infects the trees of Canada is also prevalent along the line out here. The ornamental trees of Canada are just as nice as those here but they have more trees, of what are rare specimens in Canada. The Locust trees are quite abundant, and large. There are flowers along the railroad track which kinds we have in our gardens. Hedges look nice but there are not many planted. Corn looks also nice. In Missouri I saw a couple of patches which looked exceedingly fine. Men were cultivating or scuffling it, some with two horses or donkeys and others with one. There are many threshing machines bound for the west seen at the railroad stations. The Missouri River is not so wide as the Mississippi and runs slower. The water looks very dirty. They have a large bridge at Atchison. I did not observe very closely from Atchison to Topeka. A cool mist near Carbondale.

At Burlingame is a corn crib at the side of which the cars run and a sheller stands at the side of a car so that the shelled corn runs right in. The land is most beautiful. It is what the other people have stated. It would be a discredit to rate any land as there is not much difference between it yet there are occasional strips which are not as good as others. Wheat is all cut and much taken on stacks. Corn is ahead of all that I have seen along the road. Some oats is cut, some ready to cut, and some green yet. Spent for pie 15 cents; lemonade, 10 cents; cup, 10 cents. Came to Florence at 6:45. Expect to go to Marion Centre [Kansas] tomorrow morning, and from thence home to Samuel Burkholder. Spent 50 cents; had $8.15, [leaving] $7.65.

13th Beef sold chiefly in hot weather. Pork and beef rate the same. Beef sells from 8 to 12 [cents a pound]. A good substantial wagon double box, with brakes, whipple-trees, and neck yoke attached $80. Spring seats to each. I.e. on 60 days or so time. At cash rate $77. Open buggy good style $140, cash $135. There is however a difference in prices, buggies can be had at a higher and a cheaper price. Spring wagon $140. Half inch wagon line is dealt with at Leavenworth Penitentiary and Mitchell, Wisconsin. The party informed me that they had already shipped wagons and they will have sale for more. Sugar 10 lbs. for $1. Lumber: shingles for $4.25 per M; flooring for $37 per M; siding for $25 per M. Dimension number from $25 to $50 [as written, could be $30.00]; i.e. 2 x 4, 2 x 6, 2 x 8. Surface lumber $27 per M.; marsh harvester with . . . Den Binder for wire $300. I saw this work about 2 miles west of Florence; cuts 5 feet broad – man said cuts from 10 to 15 acres per day. Marsh harvester Elvart and Maslin Harvesters $205.

Weeds. . . . Rag Weed – Kansas Parsley – Devil's Shoe Laces. Came to Marion Centre this morning at 10 o'clock. Cost me $1 for fare, $1 for bed and breakfast and 53 cents for post cards and thermometer. I met with a young man named M. Jacobs and came to Mr. Jacob's place at 11. Stayed over dinner and came home at near two. Took them quite by surprise. The country is very beautiful, especially around where my father lives. $7.65 - $2.53 = $5.12.

Very warm yesterday and today. Yesterday at one time was 99° above zero. This morning at 7, 79°. At noon 96°. A cool breeze however temporizes the country. When the sun [remains] behind a cloud it is very cool, but the sun has a powerful sway.

14th, 76 Got up at 6 – 79°. Felt not well; thermometer at noon 82° and in evening 78°. We had a very heavy shower of rain, no wind connected, but very heavy thunder, it lasted through most of the night from noon but did not rain continually. Joseph, Benjamin, and I drove out to section 6, found it cut by ravines. A creek passes through. Saw at one place a solid foundation of rocks, which will be most indispensable to build – a creek passes through the N.W. corner. We saw many prairie chickens and antelopes – about 2 dozen of the latter. They could easily be shot, and Abram shot one lately. The land out there is all one scene of beauty. It is settled to within a close distance. There was church here at the school-house tonight. Two Evangelical Methodist preachers preached – intend to have service here regularly. Were here overnight.

15th Thermometer at 78°, 90°, 76°. This was a pleasant day, warm at noon, and we had a slight shower in the forenoon – on previous night lightning struck into a man's house about a mile and a half from here – did no harm. Was out bathing in cottonwood creek – this creek flows very fast, but it was not deep, the water flows rapid and over rocks in most parts. I saw a marsh harvester work – bound on it twice around a piece of oats – it is easier binding on there than on the ground.

16th, Sunday Thermometer [at] 6:30 a.m., 76°, 90°, 83°. The weather was very pleasant – there was a beautiful day today, with a continuous breeze. Was to church here at school house in forenoon and to J. Krafts in the afternoon – find people quite amiable – Brondrick preached.

17th Thermometer, 72°, 94°, 78°. I find this morning that days here are longer than in Canada. A Russian brought a girl here to work, she was slouchy and the man asked $3 a week, I then went to [the town of] Canada and got a girl for $1.25 a week. Russians are continually pouring in, but they all get work as they come in. The town is quite long and contains houses variously built. I met with H.B. Burkholder and had tea at Heatwole's.

18th, Tuesday Thermometer, 74°, 96°, 78°. I was to Peabody with Heatwole. Enjoyed myself much – got acquainted with John Funk, and found him an agreeable and pleasant chap. Had roast ears, and cabbage at hotel – got dinner from Heatwole – had a dish of ice cream with John Funk, and a glass of lemonade, 20 cents, bought lemons, 15 cents. Peabody has a beautiful school-house and library – saw 12 carloads of Texas cattle going through to Kansas City. This town is 5 years old. We saw many improved farms on the road and this shows the beauty to which a Kansas home can be changed in a short time. Hedges three years old turn cattle if properly attended to, if not however they are not so nice. All people that I met with grumble about the excessive heat, but I thought it was quite pleasant, there being a steady breeze from the southeast. We passed one place where there was school – had a look at the schoolhouse – found everything neat and clean – desks and furniture of the highest class – scholars are not required to bring books. All will be furnished with all necessary books by the section. Evry school has a Webster dictionary. We met with herds of cattle. I remained over night at Heatwole's place. Spent 15 cents.

19th, Wednesday Thermometer, 72°, 94°, 81°. Came home this morning – went with John to blacksmith shop and had a bath in the Cottonwood River. Got acquainted with Perrys. This is the fifteenth year they live in the state and they pronounce it healthy – they have not met any cases of fever and ague. They have beautiful cottonwood groves and hedges.

20th, Thursday Thermometer, 73°, 94°, and 78°. I worked a little this day. Joseph was to Peabody with two neighbours and bought a machine for $555, i.e. a complete threshing machine.

21st, Friday Thermometer, 69°, 94°, 80°. I helped to stack oats today. We stacked 20 loads of oats. They had 20 acres of oats and expect 40 bush. or upwards to the acre. It was very pleasant to work today. Two teams were used to haul together etc. I am teaching the boys to sing tonight. Pleasant. I helped to stack oats today, it was a pretty hard but not at all unpleasant job. Father was pitching in the field, Benjamin and Joseph hauled together and John and I stacked.

22nd, Saturday Thermometer, 70°, 95°, 80°. Warm. John and I went to Marion Centre to the mill. We found the mill about 1 ... miles out of town. Two men named Funk own the mill, it has three run of stone, is three and a half stories high – when grist is brought it is handed over a platform - flour is handed out at the next story, a road passing by there also – chop is bagged in the first story and carried up a pair of steps about 7 feet high – in the basement the gearing is placed which consists of two powerful waterwheels and other connected machinery, etc.

The mill is built against a cliff at the side of the Cottonwood River across which a dam is made of stone – these are laid in tiers and form a flight of steps on the lower side – The water in the dam is 18 feet deep at the mill but not so deep farther up. John and I took the boat which is there and rowed up the stream about half a mile – on each side of the stream are black walnut, cottonwood and other varieties of trees, wild grapes and plums grow in great profusion. We took a bath in the stream – water was quite warm but not clear. Turtles are here to be seen in large numbers. We found the Funk Bro's. most pleasant and amiable gentlemen, had dinner with them, and although they had to look after their mill yet we enjoyed ourselves tolerably – (John was well acquainted with them) – they speak the English language so as to be readily understood although they had only about 2 ... years practice in the mill. The mill cost them $12,000 and at present they can hardly make their interest out of their mill and meet their instalments, but they said that this is a hard time for them in the year. For amusement the boys tried their powers in jumping – two Russians tried it also, but unfortunately for the one standing behind the other who swung stones for weights – when one of his stones hit him in the ribs he gave venture to the most foul-mouthed oaths one could hear and it nearly terminated in a fight. Got acquainted with Mr. Holloway and others. Bought 1 lb. cheese, 20 cents, [and] map of Kansas, 60 cents, equals 80 cents. Land west of the creek a little rocky but not used for farming.

23, Sunday Thermometer, 79°, 84°, 73°. It commenced to rain at noon and rained 2 hrs. Commenced to rain in the evening – had a terrible thunderstorm during night and also heavy rain and wind. Kraft's girls, Mrs. Brumbow, and Kleinsby were here.

24th Thermometer, 61°, 68°, 64°. The rain has not yet abated. It rained till evening then stopped. Weather was quite cool – Abram and I were out to shoot prairie-chicken but it was too wet – we saw but three and one Jack-Rabbit.

25th Thermometer, 59°, 78°, 68°. A person could be quite comfortable with a coat on. John and I went out to plough on his land but it was too wet, in places however where land has been sown in[,] people ploughed. Spent the day (so-so). The creek, i.e. the Cottonwood was very high.

26th Thermometer, 68°, 82°, 79°. Very pleasant. Ate fresh tomatoes for the first time this year. Corn grows most splendidly and the promises for a heavy crop are now fair. It is about 9 feet high and there are some stalks amongst it, 12 and 13 feet, high. Played checker and read history of United States.

27th Thermometer, 79°, 94°, 80°. Weather warm. John and I rode with Querings boys on the north side of Cottonwood. Saw some land which is in my estimation inferior to that around here – it is rather wet bottomland. Evert [Ewert] and some rich Russians live in this vicinity and a great deal of land under cultivation; it is reported that six times the amount of grain will be sown this fall in this country. People are all busy ploughing to put in their fall grain – the time they start for this is about the 1st of September but many sow a great deal later. Thrashing is also commencing – but wheat does not turn out as well as last year. Jacob and Valentine Jacobs and father bought a thrashing machine –

complete for $555. The machine is superior to any machine I have seen in many respects – it is called the Massilon. They thrash by the bushel and to avoid cheating there is a patent market by which no trickery can be accomplished. Joseph was to Peabody today and bought coal at $5.50 per ton, and some lumber for side boards on a manure wagon, but he could get none which were not planed on one side.

28th, Friday Thermometer, 72°, 94°, 82°. Do not feel very well – am troubled with a [diarrhoea].

29th 74°, 94°, 79° – Warm. Went with David Good and mother to Marion Centre – Mother bought me two shirts, etc., for a present. Spent the day in Marion Centre, had quite a good time, got acquainted with Mr Hogh and others. Baby powder for sore lip, 10 cents, cigar, 5 cents, dinner, 50 cents, . . . 65. Walked home in evening – had tea with Mr. Jacobs.

30th, Sunday Thermometer, 74°, 86°, 75°. Pleasant, quite a number of young men spent this afternoon at our place, gaming, etc., was the go. No girls around here. It rained a little last night. Rains come from the north and northeast. Intended to go to Crane ranch but did not get off.

31st, Monday Thermometer, 73°, 90°, 74°. Pleasant. Rained some and thundered heavily last night. Went to Marion Centre with David Good, etc. Rode back with Rev. Mr. Wenger to Mr. Jacobs . . . found him an agreeable man – rode with him to Gnadenau – saw Rev. Jacob Wiebe – had supper there. Wenger preached in schoolhouse this evening. He preaches again on 20th August and then there will be regular service.

1st August Thermometer, 72°, 88°, 76°. Pleasant. Thrashed today one stack of wheat 185 bushels – Commenced this morning and finished at 3 o'clock. Wheat is plump but the crop is not so heavy as last year.

Aug. 2nd Thermometer, 70°, 88°, 70°. Pleasant. Helped father to work in granary shovelling wheat. Read U.S. history.

Aug. 3rd, Thursday Thermometer, 69° 92°, 70°. Warm. Was down to see them thrash at Raissan's – wheat is very nice but does not give so much per acres. Got a bouquet of flowers for mother – one especially beautiful kind called Cock's Comb. Went over to Mr. Kraft's this afternoon. Mr Kraft was off to Florence, with 60 bushels of old wheat, but there is no demand for wheat farther than what is used on the border and eastern part of Kansas – His wheat was third class – got 60 cents; 1st class, 90 cents.

August 4th, Friday Thermometer, 72°, 89°, 70°. Warm. Kraft had corn last year over 14 feet high – the first crop being 7 feet from the ground – corn looks most beautiful here but it is not quite so high as it was last year – I ate "roasting hears" at Mr. Krafts – one was however enough – the cobbs are larger than those in Canada. I went home in the evening and had a bath in the Cottonwood which was nice and clear. Went to Mr. Jacobs for supper and got a Texas pony to go to Cranes Ranch on Durham Park. Was at Mr. Heatwoles and made arrangements to correspond occasionally. Went down and saw Henry Burkholder, thence home.

August 5th, Saturday Thermometer, 69°, 78°, 74°. Pleasant. Rain and thunder from the north in the evening. Henry Burkholder and I went up to Crane's Ranch. Came there before noon – had dinner which we took along – then saw the cattle – they have two bulls – the nicest in the park from Canada – one weighs 2,800 pounds. He weighed 3,000 but he got sickly here on account of change of atmosphere and they at one time thought they would lose him but he [recuperated]. The other is a nice red one weighing 2,400. They have 200 animals thoro'bred, and 1,300 Texas cattle. It is a perfect sight of beauty to see so many cattle in each of which it is a difficult matter to detect a misshape. Crane had three of his sons here who take a great interest in the stock. They have one man – Reid who has charge of everything and others working under him. Corn cribs that hold 20,000 bushels. A great number of mules and horses.

August 6th, Sunday Thermometer, 70°, 88°, 82°. Pleasant. Spent day at home – cut hair in the forenoon – Henry Burkholder and John T. here – had a bath in the Cottonwood in the evening – The Cottonwood is very clean now and flows very fast. Ben and Abram and I were down. The dew is very heavy here and the grass was quite wet before it was dark.

August 7th, Monday Thermometer, 68°, 92°, 78°. This day is beautiful. Mother is getting things ready for me to take along on the road tomorrow. Joseph presented me with a revolver. Got samples of wheat and corn. Some corn 13 feet high – So far it was very promising and unless something unexpected turns up it will yield richly. About the soil in Kansas – as far as I saw it was one mass of fructification producing something in all places. I saw a tract of very level land – so level that I could not like to have it, but it was only a small tract, and then there is some on ridges covered with gravel, but in all such places there are beds of soil prevalent. There are three kinds of land – bottom lands – bald bottom and uplands. The soil of the first is chiefly adapted for corn, oats, and hay, consequently very good for cattle; the second is adapted beside what was named to raising grain; and the other is most excellent land to produce wheat, etc., and pasturage. In a moderately moist year I think the uplands are best, but if the much spoken of drought should once present itself the bottom lands would be best. I have made a great deal of inquiry about hot winds and drought but they who have lived here for from 5 to 12 years know nothing farther than it was pretty dry in 1874, which passes by the appellation "grass-hopper year," and they experienced also hot winds at that time, but in that year wheat and oats had yielded favourably before the grass-hoppers came. As far as health is concerned the doctors can give a fair idea – there are three doctors in Marion Centre, 2 in Lincolnville 12 miles from the Centre, 1 in Florence also 12 miles, and 3 in Peabody 14 miles from M. Centre. Two of the doctors in Marion Centre do no more than make a living and the third does a tolerably fair trade – they charge beside their medicine, $ 1 per mile. Fever and ague is not very prevalent – people that live on bottom lands have had it but not many. I asked every man I got acquainted with nearby what he knew about fever and ague and 3 had it. One man however named Black got it from eating to excess of watermelons and he said he continued eating till he got freed from it again. I saw no consumptive persons while I was here, I saw no one have a cold. Heard of fever while here, and find my parents and brothers all very healthy. In some parts where fever and ague prevails it is attributed to the diet – people who live on corn bread bacon and melons are sometimes subjected to fever and ague, and other diseases. A person who is around creeks and water pools in the evening is also more liable to become sick as there is a certain ant, of Halbario cast from the water and weeds, [?] which grow to a height of from 5 to 15 feet. Along the waters edges being constantly fed by the rising of the water with the amount of rain falling. Misses Kraft and I passed along a road near the creek and the weeds between the tracks of the wheels were all so high and thick that we could not see each other. It is owing chiefly to negligence that these weeds are not cut – if cut they die off. There is one weed called – sciaenoid which they say is very healthy and feeds on the malaria which is excreted from plants and water. Money is very scarce here – they charge 12% interest, in the bank and 12% commission to handle it. This is very hard on a man that has to borrow, but a great deal of money [is thus] rented in the bank. Farmers get in the bank 12%, but they have to leave the money in for a certain length of time. It pays far better to put money on interest, than to invest in land. Yet land is worth from about $7 to $18 an acre. It depends much upon the improvements made. Trees grow finely and a little work will suffice to plant trees around a place as thousands of them grow along the creek.

The family of Cornelius and Helena (Friesen) Jansen at their home in Berdyansk on the Sea of Azov before their 1873 migration to Canada. Back row: Peter, Tante Annie, Cornelius Jr., Helena and Cornelius Jansen, Margaretha, the diarist. Front row: Anna, John, and Helena. (From Gustav E. Reimer and G.R. Gaeddert, *Exiled by the Czar: Cornelius Jansen and the Great Mennonite Migration* [Newton, KS: 1956], 103.)

Ezra Burkholder as a businessman in the 1890s in Hillsboro, Kansas. (Courtesy Ethel May Burkholder Dvorak)

Maria Stoesz Klassen's daughter Maria, with her husband, Abraham Kehler of Blumgart. (Courtesy Irene Enns Kroeker)

The family of Jacob Y. and Sarah (Shuh) Shantz with the Schantz children at their farm in Berlin, Ontario. The children were born to Jacob's first two wives, Barbara Biehn and Nancy Brubacher. This is the farm where Margaretha Jansen wrote her diary. (From Gustav E. Reimer and G.R. Gaeddert, *Exiled by the Czar: Cornelius Jansen and the Great Mennonite Migration, 1874* [Newton, KS: 1956].)

Immigrant Women

II

3 Margaretha Jansen (1849 to 1875)
Berlin, Ontario
Diary selection: January to July 1874
Age: 24

Margaretha Jansen was born in 1849 in West Prussia, the eldest child of Cornelius (1823-1894) and Helena Von Riesen (1822-1897) Jansen. In 1850, shortly after Margaretha's birth, the Jansen family migrated to the Sea of Azov port of Berdyansk in New Russia, in part to be close to Helena's extended family in Molotschna Colony. In Berdyansk, the Jansens established themselves as a well-to-do grain-merchant family, and Cornelius served as Prussian consul for a nine-year term. In 1873, the Jansens, together with Helena's sister, Anna, migrated again, this time to North America, after Cornelius was expelled by the Russian government for promoting the emigration of Mennonites. The Jansens made Berlin, Ontario, their initial base in the New World as Cornelius and his son Peter explored different parts of the United States in search of a site that could sustain a compact Mennonite community. The Jansens' choice was Jefferson County, Nebraska, where they settled in June 1874.

For almost a year, however, they were residents of Berlin, Ontario, living near the town in a cottage on the yard of the prominent Swiss-Ontario-Mennonite businessman and immigration agent Jacob Y. Shantz and his third wife, Sarah Shuh. The Shantz and Jansen children were all about the same age and spent much time together. In 1874, the Jansens had six unmarried children: Margaretha, 24; Peter, 22; John (Heine), 20; Anna, 18; Helena, 15, and Cornelius, 11. The Shantzes still had eight children at home: Moses, 21; Jacob, 19; Susannah, 18; Dilman, 17; twins Mary and John, 15; Ida, seven, and Eunice, four. There was also a young woman named Magdalena, likely a maid, in the household. Other people named in the diary include friends who wrote from

Berdyansk (Russia) and Danzig (West Prussia), and Ontario Mennonites whom Margaretha met in church or in the community. A person who appears prominently in the diary was Reverend Daniel Brenneman, a well-known Mennonite revivalist from Indiana and the subject of Margaretha's great admiration. Another of the diary's important subjects was Margaretha's brother Peter Jansen, later a state senator in Nebraska, but here in this diary the frequent subject of his sister's consternation. Another notable person was "Old Mr. Eby," who died on 23 May; he was Isaac Eby, 69, the son of Bishop Benjamin Eby, the founder of Berlin, Ontario.

Our selection of the diary begins on 1 January 1874, when the Jansens had lived in Ontario for four and a half months; it ends on 4 July 1874, six months later, soon after they arrived in Nebraska. Here they established a farm in Jefferson County, near the site of the future railway town founded by and named after Peter Jansen. On 19 January 1875, half a year after the move to Nebraska, Margaretha died after a brief illness, described as "inflammatory rheumatism." Her last entry was 5 January 1875, when she wrote: "This evening I made brother Peter very angry with some words, so that he coldly said good night and angrily looked at me, so that I always have to think of it now. Still, it is my fault! Shall I heal him from his conceit by doing this, or point out to him what he has done wrong? No! No! Oh, that I could be quiet and pray!" Margaretha was an intensely caring and reflective person to the very end.

The diary was translated by Anna Linscheid and transcribed by Reg Good. A copy of the original in Gothic handwritten German is located at the Mennonite Library and Archives, North Newton, Kansas, Cornelius Jansen Collection. For a biography of Cornelius Jansen, Margaretha's father, see Gustav E. Reimer and G.R. Gaeddert, *Exiled by the Czar* (Newton, KS: 1956); for a biography of Jacob Y. Shantz, the Jansens' host in Berlin, see Samuel J. Steiner, *Vicarious Pioneer: The Life of Jacob Y. Shantz* (Winnipeg: 1988).

Thursday, January 1, 1874 We have started this new year in America and how dark the future lies before us. Today, however, we were much more cheerful than I had expected us to be. We (Anna, Hans and I) haven't been home almost the whole day. Why? Yesterday evening guests came to the Shantz family, namely, two nephews of the old Mr. Dettweiler and with them they went to Shantz's for dinner and we had to go along. It was a nice ride. Anna, Hans, Jakob, Moses, Magdalene, Hanny Dettweiler and I were in the big sleigh, while Susanne went with Aron D. alone in the small one. When we arrived there, only Hanne and Levi Shantz were at home. We all felt sorry that the others, even the parents, were absent. I do not know whether we had an especially good time, but we had much laughter, because Aron and Levi acted so funny. They dressed in their father's old jacket and wore his old cap, etc. When Moses burst out with laughter so that tears ran out of his eyes, he always said: "But Moses, do not cry so badly!" I do not know whether it was quite right that we laughed so much. I often had to think of Anna and Heinrich. Who knows what they would have thought of it. But I think they would have been gay too. Who knows where we will be together with our friends the next time? In the evening we visited Susanne's uncle, but he and sister Dettweiler had gone directly home from Shantz's.

Sunday, January 4 Today it was very stormy and wet. Yesterday evening, however, we had a strange experience. We wanted to go to choir practice, and Jakob thought we could still use the sleigh for it, although the snow had melted during the day. We crossed the bridge and passed the wood, because we thought there would possibly be more snow there. When we had passed a second bridge, the sleigh stopped on the bare soil. It was too hard a strain for the horses to go on, so we all decided to get out of the sleigh, to which Jakob agreed, since he always tries to keep the horses from becoming over tired. There, in the midst of the forest, we got out. The two little boys, Johan and Heine, were sent back home with the sleigh. We were fortunate that there was moonshine, for that made the way rather romantic.

Since we had to go quite a distance, I think we walked for two hours. Everyone was very gay, and on the way back Moses also was with us. He said that we would probably not forget this day very easily. Today I taught the Sunday school class for the first time. Ifraim's [Ephraim's] wedding is today, but neither parents nor brothers nor sisters are present, since the wedding is in Waterloo and immediately after that they leave for a trip. I don't like this kind of wedding at all.

Monday, January 5 Today Christmas is being celebrated in Russia. We thought much of last year and especially of our people, and I think that they in turn thought much of us also. This night I dreamt very clearly of Gerika and the little Aproska, and I was afraid for them. We also experienced great joy today, because we finally received letters from our dear ones in Danzig and Welinke.– How fast the weather changes. Yesterday rain and storm and today wonderful, clear sunshine and frost.

Tuesday, January 6 We received letters from J. Sudermann, which made us very happy. Moses went back to Hamilton today. In the evening we wrote a bit to Anna and Heinrich. Aunt Anna and I washed, and Mother made dinner. The weather is very bad, stormy and very, very cold, so that everything freezes immediately.

Wednesday, January 7 The weather is milder now and so Papa and I walked to town this afternoon. We were looking for some material for an everyday dress for me, but all was in vain. We were also in a school for older boys, which Peter and Hans will probably attend.

Friday, January 9 Peter and Hans made a sofa for us like the one Grandaunt has. I hope that it will be comfortable, so that dear Papa can rest on it, for now we have only the hard wooden benches and chairs. Oh, that Papa would stay healthy and would not worry so much about other people. Oh, and the dear brother . . .

Sunday, January 11 Today was a beautiful winter day, the kind we seldom have. The morning was especially beautiful. Mrs. Shantz and the little girl went with us to her brother-in-law, who is sick. They wanted to take Mother and

Papa along, but Papa preferred to stay home. Since there was no meeting today, Papa came over to read the Scripture to us. The two Oberholzer girls were there for dinner. In the afternoon we went to Sunday school. Only small Milly Meuer was in my class. She is a lovely little girl. After Sunday school, Marianne Schneider and her brother came for a visit. For supper Peter, Hans and I were at the Shantz family and later Peter read a very pleasant story, which Papa had given to him for that purpose. Hans and Heine were noisy and misbehaved.

Monday, January 12 At Shantz's home one bull and two pigs were butchered today. Hans and I helped. It worked quite well, and this time I did not have a headache. When Hans and Jakob turned the sausage meat through the machine, we girls all had to help a little. Sister Anna also had to come, because Jakob says that it would be good for our health, especially for Anna's and Susanne's. They had also hired two butchers and another lady, so that we finished the work rather early. Now I want to sew for a while on *Tante's* [Auntie's] shoes.

Tuesday, January 13 Today Susanne and her two cousins went to Port Alkin [on Lake Huron] by train. They have relatives there on her mother's side. They will probably stay there for eight days. In the afternoon Mr. and Mrs. Shantz, Tante and Papa went to town, where Papa secretly bought a rocking chair. Later, when it was already dark, Hans went to get it and put it into the stable where we keep the wood. That same evening I made a wreath, using branches from a pine tree. Today we also received letters from Welinske. They write more often than anybody else, though they usually do it during the night. They told us how they had decorated their Christmas tree, which reminded us of the many years we had also been privileged to do this. I must confess that I often forget completely that we have already celebrated Christmas this year.

Wednesday, January 14 Tante's birthday is today. I think she was very happy about the chair and our little handicraft work. Oh, that the Lord would grant us this day also in the following years and keep our Aunt and our parents in good health. Mother did not feel well today at all, while Papa seemed better. I hope we soon receive letters from Weisshof.

Thursday, January 15 In the morning I had school with Heine and Eida for a while. Actually I did it because Papa seemed to want it. But after we had started, I did better and better. If only I would have more love and patience with them; and if they would only learn something! In the afternoon and for supper our parents and Shantzes were at Bill Meners', as were Mary and Helen. Rather late in the evening Ifraim and his young wife paid us a visit. They plan to go to Preston very early tomorrow morning and from there they will take the train to Niagara Falls.

Friday, January 16 When Mary came to get me for milking this morning, she told me a nice joke. Jakob had put on Ifraim's beautiful overcoat instead of his old one, and when Ifraim wanted to dress quickly, he realized what had happened. Dillman followed him and when he had reached him Jakob at first did not want to change, for he had already sneezed into the sleeve. But after all this they arrived in Preston on time.

I helped the Shantzes with their baking, because Susanne was not home. They baked thirty-three mincepies, whereas I only baked nine for our family.

Saturday, January 17 Today we received letters from the dear Uncle and Aunt Sudermann from Berdjansk and also from the children. From Weishof came also birthday congratulations for Tante, but there was nothing from Anna and Heinrich. I am quite glad about this, because now we can still look forward to theirs and when letters come from them, we will enjoy them so much more. Tante has been in Berlin with Mrs. Shantz.

In the evening we had quite a lot of fun at choir practice. Johann had met the old Mr. Shantz in the afternoon, and he had suggested that his children would pick us up again. After we had waited for them for rather a long time, we decided to walk ahead. Peter went with us, though actually only to please us. We had walked for a long distance and had almost arrived when the Shantz children reached us. Johann, who had not wanted to walk, was with them and he now laughed at us. Mrs. Shantz had visitors and therefore they were late. The roads were so slippery that five or six times I almost fell.

Sunday, January 18 In the morning we had a meeting. We children went there with Papa. Mother is too sick, so Tante and Helene stayed at home. In the afternoon Sunday school was held, and again only the little Milly Meuer was in my class. She is a very darling little girl. In the evening we had evening-hour at home. After that Peter read the letter from Uncle Sudermann.

Monday, January 19 We received letters from Anna and Heinrich. Aunt Sudermann also wrote to Helene. This makes us realize that our friends think very little about America. If the Lord grants it, Anna and Heinrich will come next summer. Sometimes, rather, often I think that it will finally not work out, but then everything takes its course according to the Lord's will! If we just would put our troubles into his hands, instead of keeping our minds busy with them! Our dear Mother is not well at all. Oh, that the dear Lord would keep her for us, and also our dear Papa here in the foreign country! It snows much.

Tuesday, January 20 Again Mother did not feel well. Papa was in the big school because of Helene, for she is expected there tomorrow. It froze very much.

Wednesday, January 21 We received a letter from Pötcher, thanking us for *Blach* [?]. He also wrote some extra lines for Tante, wherein he expressed once again his thankfulness for the slippers which Tante had knitted at one time for Baerbchen. In the morning Helene went to school with Papa and stayed there. But she seems to feel rather strange among so many unknown persons. The thaw is strong.

Thursday, January 22 This morning Papa and uncle Shantz left by train, in order to visit some other congregations in the Toronto area. They hope to be back on Monday. Immediately after they had gone, Tante and I started to wash. We were busy with that until suppertime. Tante fell down the stairs of the wash house and hurt herself rather badly.

Friday, January 23 When I was busy with pie-baking this afternoon and wanted to get it done quickly, Heine came (just at the time when Peter and Hans were ready to go to school) and said that a guest from Elkhart [Indiana] had arrived. His name is Mr. Brenneman. Peter learned to know him very well during his travel, and he went over to see him and soon came back saying: "Dearest children, you are baking here and my friend Brenneman wants to come here soon to learn to know you." In that first moment I was angry and wished Peter and Mr. Brenneman far away, because I had to take away all the pies I had already made, carry everything down to the basement and clean up in a hurry. About one hour later, when Peter and the guest had arrived, everything was in order and my anger too had disappeared. I must confess that we got to like the new friend very much. Before he left us he sang with us (he sings beautifully) and he prayed so heartily! Mrs. Shantz and the girls had all been with us, and we felt sorry that Helene was in school.

Saturday, January 24 We did not attend choir practice today. Only Peter, Jakob and Dillman went. At first they did not want to take us along because it was stormy, but when they were ready to go they began to plead so much that we go along with them that finally Susanne simply pushed them out the door and locked it. We still hoped Mr. Shantz would offer us a ride, but it was in vain. So we went to our place and consoled ourselves by playing games. We were still playing when the boys came back. They told us that almost no one had been there, and so Mr. Dettweiler had played the piano and his wife had sung very nicely. Peter said it had been so homey and beautiful to see and to hear this couple with their two small children that he would have gone much farther for the experience. I am glad that Peter is not so strange and rigid any more. We shall probably long for Canada.

Sunday, January 25 This Sunday there was no meeting. Anna, Susanna, Magdalene and her sister went to Berlin to the Methodist Church, where they then stayed. Helen and Mary had gone to the Richart family, and Mother, Tante, Peter, Hans and I stayed home. In the morning we read. I also wanted to write to Anna Sudermann, but I did not get much done. In the afternoon we young people went to Sunday school. Peter also taught a class today. After a concluding prayer, Peter and Jakob went to get the big sleigh, and we went all together to Bridgeport to the Dettweilers' home. There were a number of other guests, too, G. Dettweiler and Krafts. After supper we went to church, because we wanted to hear our friend Brenneman. He preached in English, and the church was crowded with many different people, but all of them seemed to listen very attentively. Reverend Wismer gave a short speech in German. Later when we were leaving the Dettweilers' and were all rather gay, Mr. Dettweiler reminded us in a very friendly way that on the way home we should not forget what we had heard that night. It might easily happen when a group of young people are together.

Monday, January 26 This evening our friend Brenneman again held the evening service at Hendrikers'. Just when we were leaving for it, Papa and Peter came. We went, but Papa stayed home with Mother and Heine. The place was very crowded. Tante got a ride with Mrs. Shantz, while we walked. It was a lovely evening, not cold at all, and the moonshine was lovely!

Friday, January 30 Today cousin Heinrich had his birthday. Oh, that the dear Lord would guide him also this coming year and give him strength to love Him all the more, and also help him to overcome his fear of other people. We also pray that the dear Lord help him if this year is hard and difficult for him because of his separation from his friends and loved ones. May also He bring Heinrich and our dear Anna to us, if it is His will!

I went uptown with Papa. We bought green cloth for curtains, and then Papa drove back while Heine and I walked.

Saturday, January 31 Today a great change took place, and our small living room is hard to recognize. At the windows and at the wall in front of mother's bed long green curtains are hanging, and the stove is moved to the other side. Thus, the room appears much bigger. Today we did not have choir practice. I wrote to Grete.

Sunday, February 1 In the morning Mr. Brenneman preached. The meetinghouse was crowded. He spoke about the town of Nineveh – how Thomas had preached and how they repented. Very urgently and powerfully he admonished everybody not to simply live our life away until it be too late.

The evening hour was in the home of the Shantz family. From our family everyone was there except Papa, Mother and Heine, and from their family all but little Erika and Magdalene's sister were present. I do not want to forget the singing hour, but I cannot write anything about it. For dinner Mr. Brenneman was with the Shantz family, and after dinner he came to visit us. It was a nice half hour which we shall remember for a long time. I think he likes Helen very much, and he spoke with her and prayed fervently.

Monday, February 2 This afternoon we had a lesson here. Mr. Brenneman spoke about the questions the apostles asked Jesus Christ: Are there only a few who will be saved? And Jesus answered: "Take care that you enter the narrow gate." It was very beautiful. Oh, I wished that Anna and Heinrich could have heard and seen Mr. Brenneman when he speaks thus freely and unafraid. And every time, though he has spoken so often, it seems as if it were the first time, so heartily and enthusiastically does he speak. He urges everyone to give his heart to Jesus now this very day: "So that you only can pray very strongly that the Lord might help you to love Him seriously."

In the evening he preached in Freeport in a free church [United Brethren], which is three miles from here. Because there were guests with Shantzes, Jakob drove us, that is, Magdalene, Heine and me and two girls who wanted to go and also Mr. Brenneman. I think we shall not forget this evening within the following months, at least I never want to forget it. He spoke so fervently and still so friendly, telling us how he had confessed his belief twenty-two years ago, and thereafter had soon begun to preach. How much his wife and his eight children think of him and pray for him. And that his wife willingly lets him go to serve the Lord. He has never repented being the dear Lord's servant, for he is happy and content in doing this. Oh! I wish I could write much more about all he said. We almost always spoke English together, because he prefers to speak English rather than German, though he speaks the latter much more correctly and better than the people here do. He is, after all, an educated man and also dressed very differently from the others. In the church of Freeport he preached in English about Zacchaeus and how he quickly climbed down from the mulberry tree when Jesus called him. When he stood there and again urgently asked us to come to Jesus now and spoke more and more powerfully so that he had to wipe the sweat from his face from time to time, I had to think, Oh! that we would have such a strong love for Jesus! Oh, that He would help us because we are so weak! But He can and he certainly will help us!

Saturday, February 7 We drove to Dettweilers' in Dumfries [Township]. We had planned to do this a long time before, but we never got around to really going there. We enjoyed the ride very much. There were six of us, Jakob, Susanne, Peter, Hans, Anna and I. We arrived there before the night fell and stayed with the old Mr. and Mrs. Dettweiler. Anna and I were very cold that night and when I awoke I dressed in almost all of my clothes. Susanne, who slept with Hanny, also was cold. But I almost forgot to tell about the evening. We sang very much. Besides us there was a school friend of Peter, a Mr. Clemens, who has a good voice. We stayed up late after the evening's blessing was said. The old Mr. Dettweiler is a nice man and dear to me. He spoke much with Peter and had him tell about Russia. He told us his part about uncle Sudermann and recited something from the latter's sermon, making it seem as if we heard the dear uncle himself. The next morning was an indescribably beautiful winter's day. We young people drove to a married daughter of the old Dettweilers' and stayed there for dinner. In the evening we visited other relatives and from there we went back home.

We regretted that we could not join in on the evening service, but Jakob did not want to go there. He said that his horses had to work the next day again and so he couldn't possibly ride till twelve at night. This was the first time I really longed for a horse and wagon. Peter also wanted to go there, because Brenneman was going to leave the next day. Aaron and Hanny drove to the evening service, because they *had* to. So Peter tore a piece of paper out of his notebook and wrote a few lines to Brenneman and gave the note to them. On the way home we sang very much, especially Clemens.

Monday, February [9] Peter and Mr. Shantz went travelling this morning. Anna, Mary, Magdalene and her sister drove to the Dettweiler place to Bridgeport to help Harriet with the quilting. In the afternoon I sat with Susanne in the kitchen, and I darned my stockings while she was sewing. Later we milked together. Once Jakob came and asked whether we were all alone and whether we would not have liked also to go to Bridgeport. Susanne told him that Magdalene had said she would drive. Jakob thought that was altogether wrong, and that Susanne had the right to drive, too. If she (Susanne) would not want to drive, only then Magdalene could do it. I was wondering about him in my mind, and finally he asked us whether we would not want to drive with him to the evening service, but we were to decide quickly. Susanne said yes, and we had to get our work done in a hurry. After supper we left. It was rather far, but all went well. Jakob already had said in the yard that I could drive if I would want to, because he knows that I, as well as Susanne, love to drive. Susanne drove back home. He was very nice today, which proves that he felt sorry about not driving us to the evening hour yesterday. He had mentioned this to Peter when he said goodbye to him. Very few people attended today's evening service. Not even a minister was present. Still it was very nice and one was reminded of Jesus saying: "Where there are two or three gathered in my name, I am among them." Jakob also rose and spoke a few words. He had never done that before, since we arrived here. On the way back we spoke about yesterday, and he said that he feels much better now, etc. We also spoke about the *Herzbüchlein* [heart booklet] with the silken heart of the people and what it contains. The distance seemed so short! When we arrived at home and were thanking him for taking us along, he thanked us in return for coming along with him.

Tuesday, February 10 Susanne, Einike, Heine and I drove to Ifraim's. At noon we stayed with the young woman for Ifraim was not home until night. In the evening we went to the old Krenzers'. We took Eidy with us, although she absolutely did not want to and cried bitterly. It was very cold.

Wednesday, February 11 Today we washed. It was a clear day, but rather cold and in the evening and during the night it rained.

Thursday, February 12 Today was my birthday. The day was beautiful and bright. How much I thought about last year's birthday, especially in the morning when I was alone! Dear Papa gave me two pretty shells, really, they are very pretty. Anna had made a wreath out of pine-tree branches decorated with self-made flowers. She also gave me two linen aprons. The dear Tante gave me some beautiful cloth for a dress. We were quite alone (Peter was not with us either) and we had also promised not to tell the Shantz family anything about it. In the afternoon Anna and I went there with some work, and while we were knitting there Papa dropped in for a little while. He was so glad to see us sitting there so peacefully that he remarked absentmindedly, "Now you should really sing a birthday song for Margarete." Then everybody shouted: "Is it really your birthday today?" Now it was out! We all had to laugh very much. I was only afraid that Mrs. Shantz would come with that dress again, but she didn't. In the evening, however, she brought some of her home-made flannel for a winter skirt, and I accepted it thankfully. I think it would have offended her if I would have refused it.

One, or better several, great pleasures were mine when Hans, coming from school, brought letters. And he brought so many! From Danzig, from Weslink, from Russia, from . . . , etc. Papa received one letter that he never would have expected, namely, from Hermann Pfoth from Berdjansk. They also want to come here in the spring. In the evening I read all the letters one after the other, for the Shantz family had come to hear them.

Friday, February 13 During the day the weather was cold. In the evening we – Jakob, Susanne, Anna and I – went to the evening service. It was very cold and stormy, although there was no snow. Jakob walked almost all the way there and back, while I drove. My hands almost froze, because I had forgotten to put on gloves, but I did not mention it until we arrived at home.

Saturday, February 14 In the morning we hurried with the cleaning, and in the afternoon we attended the funeral of a small child in our church. After that we went to teacher Dettweiler's. That is quite a long way to go, and in order to shorten the distance we walked along the railroad tracks. At first it was fun walking there, but all of a sudden the pleasure came to an end. In front of us there was a river with no bridge crossing it, only the railroad tracks. We did not want to go back, so finally we found a beam underneath the tracks. It was broad enough so that we could cross the river on it. Anna and Susanne happily were on the other side already when my turn came. I took all of my courage and had already arrived at the middle of the beam when I looked down into the water and felt so sick that I thought I would not be able to move one more step, for I thought I would surely fall down. But once again I mustered up all my courage and – thanks to the Lord – reached the other side. I certainly do not want to do that again! In the evening the others came to the choir practice. But I almost forgot to mention that after we had been there for a while, his sister and cousin came also and we were happy all together. Aaron played the harmonica. When we drove home from choir practice that evening, somebody drove behind us very silently without bells. I was wondering about that, but the others were quiet. Now I know what it was. Susanne had a visitor. It seems so strange to me. A person, whom she did not know, comes that late in the evening when all the others had already gone to bed! But that is a custom over here!

Sunday, February 15 When Mary called me for milking today, she at once told me that Mrs. Sengmüller had died that very night. I was frightened when I heard it, for yesterday she was still up and around; in the morning she had baked. Then in the evening Magdalene had been there and had milked the cows for her, because she felt weak. But nobody had thought that she would die. During the night she had spoken to her husband, asking him to rearrange the cushions for her. But then she wanted him to lie down and to sleep again. When he awoke the next morning, he found her dead in her bed. The poor man was awfully shocked. He came and knocked at the window of Mrs. Shantz and said that his wife was dead. Jakob immediately drove to Berlin to get a woman to help, and Magdalene also went there immediately. At noontime we children all went there and from there to Sunday school.

Monday, February 16 The weather was gloomy today. In the evening after supper we went to Shantzes' to help them cut apples. Tomorrow Magdalene will help them to bake pies for the funeral. While cutting and peeling the apples, the boys made a lot of noise. Later we brought Susanna and Anna there, because they will watch half of the night and at 12 o'clock Hans and Jakob will take over.

Tuesday, February 17 In the morning after the children had gone to school, Heine and I went to town because yesterday the shoemaker, who has this beautiful, big Newfoundland dog, said to Papa that the dog had pups. He had only two and if Papa would want one for three dollars, we could come and choose one. Thus, Heine and I went there and chose the biggest one today. We also received letters from Uncle and Tante and also one from David Isaak.

Wednesday, February 18 Today the funeral of Mary Rik took place. Often I had to think that she should become blessed. There were very many people in the funeral procession, and even the Ezra Schneider family was here. Lisinda asked us to come to her place on Sunday; when she also spoke about it with Jakob, he promised her that if nothing else intervened, he would come. Brenneman will probably have the evening service.

Friday, February 20 In the evening Hans and I went to the Young Men's Association. A minister from Hamilton was there, who spoke about the Harz Mountains, or better: his travel in these mountains. Mother wanted me to go with Hans. The others, that is Susanne, Anna, Helen, and Jakob, went to the evening service at the old Schneider couple's home. Up to Berlin we all walked together and then parted. How I regretted my not being there when I heard that Brenneman had been there and had spoken to them!

Saturday, February 21 Yesterday the weather was like spring, and today we again have so much snow that we could use the sleigh for going to choir practice. Mr. Shantz, his sister and the Stütters, whom they have as guests, came to pick us up. This time the sleigh carried its heaviest load, for besides all of us who usually go, Magdalene's sister and her brother also came along. On the way there we were fourteen persons and on the way back fifteen, all in one sleigh. (We sat rather piled up.) There will probably be only two more choir practices, which we all regret very much.

Sunday, February 22 In the morning it seemed as if we might not go to church, for Jakob said it would be far too late, because we had all slept a little too long. Susanne, however, pleaded with him so long that we finally started to go. Of course, we were too late to attend the meeting there, so we immediately drove to Ezra's, where nobody was at home and everything was locked. Susanne found a way to slip in through the wooden house, and we all sat comfortably around the stove and read until they came back from church. In the evening the service was held, but Brenneman was not there.

Monday, February 23 It is stormy today, and the wind blows forcefully through all the cracks in the house. In the morning I taught school for Heine and Idi as usual. Idi was rather disobedient during the reading period, but maybe I was too impatient. Oh, that I would have more patience and be more gentle! In the afternoon Susanne came and the three of us – Susanne, Anna and I – sat together upstairs. Later I went milking with Mary. We saw a small squirrel running along beside the fence. Hans and Dillman also came. Hans wants to study all evening. Now Susanne, Jakob and Anna have gone to Hundrikers' for the evening service, but I had to stay home because of my cold. Heine is sitting next to me, making a wagon for himself. He said that when he has grown up, he too will rise up during the evening service and speak. When I told him he could do so now, although he is still small, he answered, "Oh no! If only the people would not turn around and look at me!" I said to him that one should not be ashamed of confessing the Lord.

Tuesday, February 24 In the morning I wrote to Grossenel. In the evening we all, except Mother, Mrs. Shantz and Heine, went to Berlin to the Young Men's Association, where Mr. Brenneman gave a talk about war and peace. He spoke clearly and beautifully to the many listeners. We all pitied the dear Mr. Brenneman, for he looked so overworked and tired. I think he must be very sick already, which would be no surprise for he has preached every day for five weeks and often several times a day. Oh! he is such a nice man and sacrifices himself wholly to show the people the way which leads to Christ. That it might not be in vain! Or better: that it might be a blessing for us!

We received some letters from Anna and Heinrich and from Welinke again. They write so very friendly. I think according to what Anna writes, that Heinrich must be having a hard time now. If he would just put all his confidence in the Lord! Brenneman first read the fifth chapter of Matthew and then spoke most of the time about the words "Blessed are the peace lovers."

Wednesday, February 25 In the morning I held school with the children, and in the afternoon Anna and I visited the Shantzes. I knitted gloves and Susanne cut several patches for a quilt. I gave Dillman and Johann the little pigeons that I had knitted for them. They enjoyed them very much, especially Johann. He is a very candid boy. Now he and Heine are sitting with me at the table and playing, and I am writing to Weishof. I have to answer so many letters to Prussia and Russia that just the thought of it makes me afraid.

Thursday, February 26 It is very cold and getting up in the morning was rather hard for me. But when I was downstairs and had kindled a fire in the stove, all went well. Then I woke Anna and while she made breakfast, I went milking. Now I shall go upstairs to wake the dears. I wish Peter would come home today! In vain we waited for Pete and Uncle Shantz. In the afternoon and in the evening I ironed. I did so near the stove in our living room, and when I heard the boys outside talking very loudly, I opened the window a little bit and stuck my head through the opening and heard a bit of their conversation. Jakob, Dillman and Robin helped Hans with the wood sawing. Tomorrow I shall help them drive away the sawdust. Now I heard their eager conversation (during which they forgot to saw for a while), about the moon which really shines very beautifully. Robin said: "They say that men are dwelling on the moon, but what happens when the moon turns smaller?" Dillman gave him a very good answer: "You know, in that case they come closer and closer together." I almost had to laugh aloud about this conversation. They also talked about many more things. Johannes told them about the planetarium in Berlin, but his reports often were rather mixed up, because when he saw it, which was a long time ago, his interest in it was very little. I shut my window quietly.

Saturday, February 28 Rather late in the afternoon Mr. Brenneman and some other men came back to Shantzes' because Brenneman hoped that Uncle Shantz and Peter would be back already, and he also wanted to drive to the evening service. But it almost seemed as if Jakob would not drive, because the distance was too far. Finally he decided to go, and Susanne and Helene were allowed to go along. They had a very good time, which I can well imagine. My only regret was that Anna and Mary could not come. Oh, we would like so much to go with Brenneman. In the evening we had guests. Two gentlemen whom Papa had learned to know on his trip with Uncle Shantz to the Twenty [Mile Creek community, on the Niagara Peninsula]. One of them we like especially. About 12 o'clock, just when I wanted to go upstairs, Uncle Shantz and Pete arrived. The others, Mr. Brenneman and the children arrived at about 3:00; at least, that is when I heard them.

Brenneman is quite worn out now after all the preaching he has done, and he will return to his home tomorrow.

Sunday, March 1 In the morning we had a meeting, but Brenneman only spoke a few words. After church he came to say good-bye to us. Who knows whether we shall ever see him again? I hope that his visit here has not been in vain!!

Monday, March 2 In the afternoon Mother and the Shantzes drove to Marianne's. My throat has been awfully sore today, and so after I had taught school for the children, I lay down on my bed and slept from 10:00 a.m. till 5:00 p.m. When I awoke I was still very tired, but I did feel much better.

Wednesday, March 4 Yesterday and today were troublesome days and even though I shall not write much about them, I shall never forget them. I wish the Lord would have mercy upon us and restore the peace and love among members of our family in this strange country. How much we lack that love and peace! If brother Peter just would think a little less of himself and would be more humble – how many things would change! We were looking forward so eagerly to his return, and I longed so much for him, but now he seems to estimate himself even more highly and with that he always provokes Papa's discontentment.

Thursday, March 5 It was a lovely spring day, so wonderful that one hardly could stand to be inside. Anna, Heine and I walked to Berlin, for we had to buy some things, but mainly we went because we wanted to see our young dog. It has grown very much, but its gray colour is not very nice. We also sent letters to Danzig and Weslinke.

Friday, March 6 Today the weather has changed completely for it is like November weather. Really, one could think that winter just began. In the morning we baked twelve pies and in the morning, as well as in the evening, I milked with Mary. The lady from the States who has been visiting in Canada for the last three months is at Shantzes', and I am wondering about her.

Saturday, March 7 This evening, for the first time, we had a visitor – namely, Mr. and Mrs. Jack Dettweiler with their little daughter. They all – Mr. and Mrs.

Shantz also – stayed for tea and in the evening Peter read several nice stories to us from the *Landbote*.

Sunday, March 8 The weather is still bad. Yesterday Helen and Mary drove to Breslau to visit Ezra Schneiders. In the morning all of us were home. The Shantz family had guests for dinner, namely Bill Neuwes; Mother and Papa also went there. Susanne, Anna, and I were at home, and we read in the new *Traktaetchen* [tracts], which Papa had received. In the afternoon we went to Sunday school. It was very bad for walking, so Mother, Tante, Mrs. Shantz, Magdalene, and her sister stayed at home. Only a small group of people gathered and later Papa distributed some of the tracts. Schneiders drove home immediately after Sunday school. In the evening Susanne, Magdalene and her sister visited us, and we had tea together. After that we sang several songs, for which Jakob dear joined us. Later Uncle Shantz asked him to get the wagon ready, for somebody had arrived. We all were glad when, after a while, Jakob with Aron Dettweiler entered, for now we had one more singer. You can notice that Aron has changed, though he does not act as gaily.

Monday, March 9 The weather still is bad. Mary and Helene returned in the morning and in the afternoon we went to Shantzes' with our work.

Tuesday, March 10 I do not know what I should write today, for my heart is so heavy (just as stormy as it is outside, so it is in my soul). Oh, I have so many sorrows today about Brother Peter. But in the past time I have often found help, and the dear Lord, who has helped us thus far, will help us further, even though everything seems so dull and dark to us. We have such a dear Lord who cannot and will not forsake us. "In hope he believed against hope, that he should become the father of many nations; as he had been told, 'So shall your descendants be'" (Romans 4:18). This beautiful saying I remembered for my consolation.

Friday, March [13] The day was cold and stormy. Mother and Papa did not feel well at all, because of all their worrying and their griefs. During the afternoon while Peter was at home, we received a letter from Johannes Penner from Mariendorf, which Peter read to us with seemingly some emotions. Anna and I at once gained so much hope, but just when Peter was leaving to go to Georg Dettweiler's, Mr. Shantz stepped in and asked in a very friendly manner whether we wouldn't want to come to the evening service, and then addressing Peter directly he mentioned that only he and Susanne were going and that Peter should come also. I myself had no rest at all, and for Helene it is too far away, and thus only Anna joined them. Formerly I liked to go to the evening service, but I must confess that lately I do not have the desire to go there and do not find pleasure in it. I almost think that it is immoral, but I cannot help myself!!

Oh, Lord, please help that the beloved parents will become healthy again and also take their sorrows from them!

Friday, March [20] For a number of days I have not written into this diary, but I shall never forget this time even if I did not write it down. It is a time of much sorrow, grief and sadness. Mother's hair is becoming more and more gray, and all this because of our dear brother Peter, who wants to go his own way; in his blind infatuation he almost believes that they are the ways and the will of the Lord! Oh, I wish the dear Lord would help him, would open his eyes before it is too late. We cannot be joyful and happy any more, because all the time we have to think of Peter's plans, which I did not suspect at all. Sometimes I am ashamed of myself when I think that the others and I could have prevented it if we had not been such good friends with the Shantzes. But could we think of that! No, never had such a thought entered into my mind, and still I can scarcely believe it now, though it is true. Lord, have mercy upon him!

Today is Peter's birthday, but how does he start the new year? In the afternoon Papa, Helene and I took a walk in the forest where we never had been before, because we do not like to go there all alone. Neither Peter nor Johannes likes to walk with us. It was a wonderful walk and we shall remember it for a long time. We found a lovely fresh-green bush and cut a few branches off for a wreath for Anna.

Yesterday when Tante and I went to town, we brought letters back from the friends in Danzig and Weslinke. Hans and Heine went to get the little dog, because the owner did not want to keep it any longer. It cries now quite a bit. We want to call it Larry. From Papa Peter received a new coat, while Anna knitted socks for him, and I made a scarf.

Sunday, March 22 In the morning Peter and I went to the English Methodist Church where we have gone once before. I like to hear the sermons there, and they also sing very beautifully. To walk with Peter was no fun at all, for he hardly spoke a word and what should I say? There are so many things we could have talked about, both from past experiences and the future, but now? When I speak to him about *that* I always become too involved and therefore I would rather keep silent. I do not know whether that is right. In the afternoon we went to Sunday school, and there we sang in the German service, just like old times. We were just among ourselves, namely, Papa, the dear mother, Tante and us six children. We sang many of those old dear songs, and I think even Peter enjoyed it. But I think he forces himself to kill his feelings for everything nice and beautiful in the family and only sees faults and weaknesses. I hope the Lord ensures that he does not repent when it is already too late. We were interrupted by Susanne's coming. Peter and Johannes went to the English Church in Berlin.

Monday, March 23 Today was Anna's birthday, but I do not think she enjoyed it very much. In the evening we had the evening benediction, before which Tante had made Peter very angry by some uncontrolled words. Later when Tante and Peter went upstairs, he spoke rather viciously to her about that and Tante then started to preach to him a long sermon, which he had not expected at all, at least not from Tante. Thus, they got involved in a heated word exchange, which is not good for Peter and which hurts Mother and Papa. Papa and Mother are both rather exhausted as a result of their difficult times, and I hope the dear Lord will protect them!

Thursday, March 26 Today our dear Papa and Peter left on their travels again. (I had written the above line in the evening, but I was so tired that I could not write, which is also proved by my handwriting). Yes, our dear Papa and brother Peter have left again. That the dear Lord might be with them and lead them on their way. Papa did not feel well at all. If Peter would just be nice and polite towards Papa! They are going to Washington, because Papa was recommended to go there by a minister. From there they want to go – if it is the will of the Lord – to the western states in order to find a new homestead for us. Oh, that the Lord would grant us help so that we find a home soon and then we will be very thankful! But whether all of us? Oh, I wish we all could be happy together once more and in love without aliens among us!

Saturday, March 28 Very early this morning Tante and I went to the market in Berlin. This was the first time I had been in the market hall. We received letters from our dear Papa and brother Peter. Pastor Andres from the Methodist Church was buried today. We have known him very well; he was only 38 years old and he leaves a widow with seven small children. It is very sad to think of it.

Sunday, March 29 In the morning we had the service here, followed by the afternoon Sunday school. In the evening Anna, Magdalene, Dillman, Hans, Johannes and I went to the Methodist Church to hear the burial sermon for Pastor Andres. It was very sad to see how the poor widow had to be carried out by the brother of the deceased because she was almost fainting.

Wednesday, April 1 Hans and Tante went to town in the morning. Hans saw a little package lying at the road side. Quickly he ran to it and lifted it. Then he discovered that it was filled with sand. Tante laughed heartily because he had fallen for an April's-fool's joke. I almost did the same. Namely, in the evening I went over to Magdalene and asked her whether she could give me a package of yeast, because Tante still wanted to use it, the same evening. Seeing Hans there, I asked him to bring it over to us and Dillman said immediately, "I shall do it." It didn't matter to me who brought it, and so I didn't think about it any more. Later Dillman came; he put the package on the drawer close to the door and said: "Here is the yeast." I thanked him and said that Hans could very well have brought it. Then the thought came to my mind that maybe Dillman had brought something different than what he said he had brought, and I looked at it in the light. When I took the piece of yeast, he quickly asked whether I really thought the dough would be all right. That made me suspicious and once again I went to the light, and when I stirred it up, I put out a long piece of paper. Hans laughed, but I said that I would never have believed such a thing of Dillman!

Later Dillman came and asked whether we would like to play outside with them. I really did not want to, but because the others went, I joined them. We played *Habt Ihr Angst vor dem schwarzen Mann* (Are you afraid of the black man?). The moon shone brightly and the northern lights could also be seen in the sky. But it was rather cold, and so I soon went back inside. When the others came in Hans asked whether I would not want to make the dough for the pies, for he would help me with it. Although I would rather have sewed on my dress, I did not but went to stir the dough.

Thursday, April 2 We received a letter from Papa from Philadelphia. Thank the Lord that our dear Papa is healthy. Oh, I wish the Lord would grant His help for the future also and that He would give Peter the strength to be of good help for Papa! In the morning we baked pies, then I taught school. In the afternoon Heine – or better Cornelius – and I went to the post office with a letter for Papa. It was snowing quite a bit, but the snow did not lie on the ground for a long time. I bought some nice booklets for my pupils in the Sunday school and for sister Anna and in addition to these, a package with Bible illustrations.

Moses is home again. When we came home he was already at our place and had not even gone to see his mother, neither his Papa first, although the latter was not at home. One would like to be friendly towards him, but one cannot be quite as friendly as formerly and that is a pity. But what should one do? If I think of Peter, all my friendliness vanishes although I know that Moses is not to be blamed at all for it.

Friday, April 3 Today was Holy Friday. In the morning we had a meeting (this almost seems to be a wonder) and there were quite a number of people in church. In the afternoon an unknown pastor was at Shantzes', and they called us to come over because he wanted to sing and to pray with all of us before leaving. He also spoke rather friendly, especially to the young people, but there could be no comparison with Mr. Brenneman's speeches. When the latter spoke, it always touched and moved the heart! The pastor was a brother-in-law of Mrs. Shantz, and the children of Mr. Shantz (especially Jakob and Susanne) do not seem to love her and her relatives particularly. Jakob looked so moody, almost angry and did not join the singing at all. Later when the man was gone, Mr. Shantz said that we should sing now together. Ifraim and his young wife were there and also two girls from Bingemann's (cousins of Susanne). In the evening we had the evening service at D. Schneider's place. Mr. Shantz and Moses walked, while Susanne, Magdalene, Anna, Jakob, and I drove. Jakob was very gentle. He asked me whether we would like to go to their uncle's with them tomorrow. I am sorry that I did not give a decisive negation. I only said that we would probably not do it.

Saturday, April 4 Today it is terribly cold, as though we are in the midst of winter and everything wears a cover of snow. Although Anna and I rose early enough, our breakfast was rather late again. (I think it was about 7:30 a.m.), because the others sleep too long when Papa is absent. I think they don't miss anything, and Mother especially needs a lot of sleep. When we were just sitting at breakfast, Mr. Shantz came down unexpectedly, sat down and said: "The children Moses, Jakob, Susanne, and also Mary are going to their relatives in the afternoon and at least three of us should join them, because they would be taking the big carriage." This was quite a surprise, as we were not expecting Mr. Shantz himself to invite us because he usually does not care about the younger people at all. He asks so humbly for advice about the trip and what he should take along; whether woollen or cotton shirts or linen ones, because laundering them might be too expensive, etc. Therefore, it was difficult for Mother to say no decisively, which I really hoped she would do. But the dear mother said it would be better for us to stay home, because we had caught colds on our trips to Dumfries [Township], to Dettweiler's, etc. Mr. Shantz then replied that it would not be cold now and if anyone had a cold, the best way to cure it would be to drive in the fresh air. I still thought it would be better if we would not join them, and that our dear Papa would not have agreed to let us go, and I said I would rather stay home. That seemed to startle him, and then he asked whether Anna and Johannes would not like to go. Anna was in the other room, and she also stated that she did not want to go. Therefore Mrs. Shantz left with the impression that our refusal was wholly my fault, which makes me feel rather little and uncomfortable (bad).

Heine and I then walked to the market to buy eggs, and when we came back we heard, to our great surprise, that only Susanne and Jakob were going on that ride, because Moses had not even wished to do it, and Mary also wanted to stay home with Helene. Thus, only those two left, which is quite good after all. I think Moses needs to get out to some other place, for I am wondering about him staying home so quietly yesterday.

As I am writing this (actually I wanted to dress), I hear that letters arrived, and I could not resist the temptation to run downstairs. There were several letters. One came from Uncle Paul, another from Danzig, and one was from Aronchen Klassen, who caused so much enjoyment in Berdjansk, because of his peculiar character. I enjoyed the letter from cousin Anna very much. She is always the same dear Anna, and she writes exactly what she thinks. But I could not enjoy Heinrich's letter, particularly, especially the one addressed to Helen and me. He writes mostly about the weather and the wind. It seems as though he writes only for the sake of writing, and I do not like such letters at all. Then, I am always tempted to say: "Don't torture yourself so much, don't do it at all." But maybe I am disillusioned. If I write my thoughts like these into my diary, I always remember afterwards that I want Anna and maybe also Heinrich to read all of this.

Easter, April 5 In the morning Tante, Hans, Anna, Helen, Heine, Moses, and Magdalene found all of us in the Baptist Church in Berlin. We had heard that they would baptize some people there today, and this in the river, although almost all the water was frozen. But we were mistaken this time, and I regretted not attending an English church instead of this one. In the evening Moses, Magdalene and Mary visited us. We read several letters to them, which was quite nice. But I still wish that it would have been more serious, because, although I plan on it every day, I forget it so often.

It is a winter day with snow and freezing temperature, so much so that you think it is Christmas, not Easter.

I am so glad that we stayed home. In the evening when Mary and I went milking, I took eight eggs with me (six red ones and two yellow ones) and those we put into the *Futterkasten* [food box] after having made two nests in it, one for Johannes and one for Dillman. We often think of last year! And how one longs for those times again! In the afternoon we had Sunday school, and I gave my children each a booklet.

April 6 There is no church anywhere today. In the morning we had visitors, namely Mr. Albert and his son. I do not like Albert particularly, in fact he repulses me. I think one reason for it is his being such an avarice; he looks so sly and he did not even wash his hands before coming here, and also all his children are very neglected. But maybe it is not right to think this way about a person, and then to write it also! When Mary and I went milking this morning early, Dillman cried rather gaily: "Now I want to tell you a story. When I opened the food box I saw eight rats sitting there." We were terrified and really believed that the rats had been at the eggs. But then he continued: "When I looked at them more closely, I saw that there were six red ones and one yellow." I think they enjoyed them. In the afternoon I hid some [eggs] for Hans, Heine and Helene in the living room. They had a lot of fun looking for and finding all of them. Some I had hidden in the wood box, some others in the pockets of overcoats and one in the oven. Outside it is storming, and some sleighs have already passed by.

Thursday, April 9 We received two letters from dear Papa and even Peter had written some both times (and quite nicely too). He wrote that they would soon go to the West, and they hope to find a home for us there. Oh, that he might really wish this from the bottom of his heart!

About the granting of the request [for a Mennonite block settlement] in Congress, Papa cannot write anything definite, but there seems to be little hope for it. But Papa has found a loyal friend and supporter in a Quaker while on his search. By the end of the week the matter will be decided by Congress, and dear Papa thinks it his duty to work for it during this time, even to stay there. But then they will pursue their travels. Oh, that the dear Lord may grant that all the pain Papa endures and all the effort he puts into it might not be in vain!

Saturday, April 11 There is snow and it is stormy, as though it were midwinter. Yesterday was a lovely spring day. Anna, Heine and I went to Berlin and mailed some letters. On the way back we walked through the small wood. It was still rather muddy, but we sat down on a small hill where it was dry and read the *Landbote,* which we had received at the post office. Maybe it was not quite reasonable to sit on the humid soil, but everything was so romantic around about us and not cold at all. Today it is altogether different, for even when I got up in the morning everything was white. If the sun shone, then the snow would disappear in a few hours. The Red-Indians have a saying: "Seven times it will snow and the snow will melt seven times before it will be spring." And it seems to me that they are right.

Sunday, April 12 We had a service this morning, and although we had holy communion, no one from our family participated. I myself did not feel the wish to partake of it. Oh, it is altogether different from the way it was at home! In the afternoon we had Sunday school as usual. Anna had a toothache and, therefore, I instructed her class.

Monday, April 13 In the morning Tante and I had walked to town, because of the lovely weather. We bought cloth for Anna, Tante and me for everyday summer dresses. Hans went to the doctor for a shot. I, too, would like to get one, but Mother says that six miles from here a woman died because of a smallpox vaccination and six other people are sick with it. In the evening Moses came with a letter written in German script, which he cannot read so well and which was also written very badly. Mary and Susanne also came to visit us.

Tuesday, April 14 We are waiting longingly for letters from dear Papa. Mother cut the pattern for my dress, and this afternoon I began to sew. In the evening the Shantz girls came over and I had to teach Magdalene how to knit. We received letters from Gorien and Abraham Quiring.

Wednesday, April 15 Tante and I did the washing after I had taught school. We left the white wash in the water because the wind was blowing so strongly.

Thursday, April 16 Finally, we received, thanks to the Lord, a letter from dear Papa and from Peter, but the dear Papa does not seem to be very hopeful. Peter writes that Papa has to walk so much and, therefore, has aches in his back. We are very concerned about our dear Papa. Oh, that Peter might be a good help to him and not make it more difficult for Papa with his insistent will, his haughtiness and his thoughts.

Friday, April 17 Today we baked and because Tante and Anna went to town with Shantzes, I had quite a lot to do by myself. When they returned, the pies were finally in the oven and Tante's dough was kneaded. In the afternoon I ironed. This was very boring today, because I always had to wait until new heat was in the iron again and thus I did not finish all of it. Our dear mother does not feel well at all, and we are often very worried about her. Oh, that the dear Saviour would render health to Mother once again!

Saturday, April 18 The day was very beautiful and, therefore, we resolved to take a walk into the woods. Actually, I would have preferred to stay at home, but it would not have been appropriate to say no, since we had talked about it for such a long time. If we had not gone today, then they would have waited until Peter's return, which we did not want to see happen. We walked and met Dillman tapping trees for maple sugar, which was very interesting to see. He has a cottage right in the middle of the woods and there he boils the sap, regardless of bad weather, in two long pans, the largest being about eight feet long, and four feet wide. Dillman wanted to walk with us to a pond that was quite a distance away, but because he had not quite finished his work yet, we walked a while in the woods by ourselves, searching for flowers, but not finding any, only evergreen and moss. When we wanted to walk back, we did not know which way to go. We called Johannes's name very loudly and when he answered us, we soon found out that we had been on the wrong way. When we then finally did arrive at the sugar hut, Dillman's work was done and he was just pouring his syrup into a small keg. He gave us all as much to drink as we wanted. Then we started on our excursion to the pond. This way was much more exciting for us, because the forest was still completely wild! Sometimes long, fallen, half-rotten trees lay across a little rivulet and Hans and Dillman had to help us cross them; or they had to part all the branches of the cedar trees, so that we could walk through them. Often it was so shadowy that we could not see the sky and the sun at all. Finally we arrived at the small pond. It reminded us very much of the pond in Olivon where we had seen the gold fish. But the shore around is all moor, and if one walks on it the ground moves. When the boys stamped hard on it, even the trees moved. I was very afraid of sinking, because I had to think of the song "Three boys in the woods." They also told us that once a cow had drowned in it and was never seen again. Johannes put a long stick into the soft soil and it disappeared. I was glad when we returned. The walk back was fun; we got our feet quite wet, but we did not mind it. We all enjoyed this hike, but I wish we could enjoy it even more, not as we do now, only half as much as we actually could.

Sunday, April 19 In the morning we went to the Lutheran Church because of the confirmation exercises. I would have preferred to go to the Methodist Church, but it did not seem to work out this time. I shall not go there again very soon. While we sat there and heard the austere sermon of the minister, I realized so clearly how wrong it was to sit there and listen, how he persuaded those who were confirmed that the Lutheran belief is the only right one and that if they would cease to believe in it, they would also lose their belief in God, etc. I felt very "hot" and uneasy to hear this, and if Helene and Heine had sat close to me, I certainly would have risen and walked out with them. However, a little later, when the minister began to distribute the holy communion and several persons rose and left the building, I thought it would be done like we do it, namely, that all who wish to walk out could do so. Helene also thought so and had said to Susanne: "Now, walk out with me." We all left. There were others who also wanted to leave, but when we got to the middle of the church, the minister shouted as loud as he could: "But, please, shut the doors so that the people cannot leave. What a disturbance of the holy communion is this!" I held Heine's hands and pushed as much as I could, in order to get out of the church before his command would be executed. Happily, I succeeded in getting out, because nobody hurried to shut the doors. The man who was in charge of it only said half aloud to us: "Leave quickly now." At that moment the minister repeated his command with much more emphasis and another man jumped up and we were just out of doors when they were locked. Now we saw that Magdalene was not with us, and we were all sorry. We still had to laugh, because now she would probably have to sit inside for one more hour and she had actually only come with us to please Susanne. We thought she might be angry with us, but when she came to Sunday school in the afternoon (for dinner she had stayed in Berlin), she laughed very much and told us that when she had been close to the door it had been shut right in front of her nose. The pastor had been very angry and had scorned very much while distributing the holy communion. She also told us that behind her two girls had sat and one had asked the other: "Do you also go to the communion?" to which the other one had answered: "Oh – I don't know, I look so uncombed." Then the other said: "Oh, you look quite nice, I wish I would look like you do." And finally both took off their decorated hats and participated. Really – a fine preparation! Above the pulpit there was a picture with Luther's memorial and around it was written on the wall in golden letters: "God's word and Luther's teaching I shall never forsake." Heine and I modified this a little bit and we said: "God's word is my teaching, and in Luther I shall never believe."

No, really, if you think about it, how Luther and his followers have gained their free spirit by war and bloodshed, have persecuted our poor, loyal forefathers because the latter remained steadfast in their belief and were tortured and murdered because they did not defend themselves, I can scarcely love them as much as I actually should.

Monday, April 20 Yesterday evening D. Schneider came to visit at Shantzes', and he paid us a visit also. Schneider is a very nice, sincere man. He prayed so heartily also for Papa and Peter and also for Mother. Our dear mother is very sick and yesterday she stayed in bed the whole day, as well as this forenoon. Oh, that the Lord might help us and mercifully render back Mother's health! Oh, it is so hard! We don't want to write it to our dear Papa, because he would worry too much. We also do not know at all where they are at this time and for how long a time they will stay away. Perhaps a number of weeks yet. We are waiting for letters very much. We received letters from Weslinke today. The beloved ones write so heartily, but they wondered why we had waited such a long time before writing them and what the reasons might be. That was because we had always depended on Peter to remind us to write – but now? I hope next time they won't have to wait for such a long time for letters from us.

Tuesday, April 21 Our dear mother was quite ill today. Actually she was emotionally distressed rather than ill. This is caused by the recent times. As long as Papa and Peter were here, Mother restrained herself, but now, since a few days ago, Mother almost always thinks of Peter and Papa. I think she is afraid, especially during the night, and thinks so much about Peter's affair that often she cannot sleep at all. This then makes her so weak and troubled that the most insignificant happening excites her. Oh, I almost despaired today! Mother looks so miserable and weak, and we do not want to write Papa about it, and also Mother would not permit it, and thus we look for a different way for help. This is to complain to our beloved Saviour and to ask Him that He might mercifully help us! Oh, if Peter would not be so misguided, then we could speak of God's Will.

In the evening after supper we had a school meeting at Shantzes'. Almost all teachers were assembled, and Anna, Susanne and I also had to come. Susanne resigned, which she regrets already. To fill her place, they made a very unwise choice in my opinion, because if Susanne did not know much about teaching, Kathy Richera is even less able to teach. She is only in the Testament class. Mr.

Baumann, who is president, wanted me to take her class and my few children together, but I did not want to because I thought they would elect Kathy Oberholzer, and Susanne had mentioned to me that she [Kathy] would like to do it. Now I feel sorry, but I hope that we shall not be here for a long time any more. Moses was elected to teach the class in which Heine is. It is strange that at this type of a meeting everything is written in English, although everyone is German.

We received a letter from Papa today, but Peter did not write at all. They are still in Philadelphia, and we had hoped all the time that they would already have left there. I hope they will leave soon for Colorado. But how long will it take until they have found a new home for us?

Wednesday, April 22 The day was lovely. Mother was outside with Heine, and we thank the Lord that she feels so much better. In the evening Magdalene and Susanne were here. Mary is helping at Ezra's for some time. I would have preferred it if we could have been along, for it is not good for Mother if there is much talking, etc.

Thursday, April 23 In the morning it snowed a lot, so that everything looked white and one could think it was winter. When the sun began to shine, the snow melted very fast and the day became beautiful. I always milk alone in the morning now and with Magdalene in the evening. But since there is so little milk, I would prefer it if we would buy the milk at some other place, and I also mentioned this to her, but she said . . .

We received letters from Papa and Peter, still from Philadelphia. But by now I hope they are already on their way in search of a home. Peter writes that we should pack so that we can leave quickly. Oh, it sounds consoling to me that he writes in this way. The dear Papa and also Peter did not feel very well. May the Lord protect our dear Papa!

Friday, April 24 Today we baked. We ran out of apples, but we were happy to get three more bushels from the Shantzes. Maybe they will last for us till Papa comes to take us away from here. It is lovely spring weather, only a little bit chilly.

Saturday, April 25 The whole day the weather was cloudy, cold and windy. While the others slept, I quickly cleaned the small hall, after I had milked at Shantzes'. I never make a fire now before I come back from there. This way Anna can sleep quite a bit longer, which she really needs during these days. In the morning Heine and I went to the market by ourselves, which was strenuous for me. In the afternoon I sewed my dress. In the evening it snowed. Mr. and Mrs. Shantz and later also Susanne came to visit us.

Sunday, April 26 When I arose and looked out of the window, everything looked white, and a beautiful winter landscape was to be seen. The roofs and the trees were all thickly covered with snow. When I had finished milking, I had to actually dig a way into our yard. Who knows where our dear Papa and Peter are now? Our dear mother often is very worried, and because of this her condition does not improve at all. In the afternoon we had our service, to which everyone except Mother went. Outside it is very dirty, because as soon as the sun came out the snow melted. Since the three sisters and brothers of Mr. Shantz were at Shantzes' for dinner, the girls also visited us. We then went there to sing. In the evening the service was held at Senn. Shantz's. Anna and I went there, as did Susanne, Jakob and Mrs. Shantz. I would have preferred to stay home, but – on the other hand – I did not want Anna to go alone. I was very tired and cold. There was very little talking; it is so different since Brenneman has gone. I wanted to write to dear Grete today, but I could not do it.

Monday, April 27 Right after breakfast, Mother began to pack and that proved to be too much for her. Now our dear mother is sick again. Oh, what shall become of us if the Lord does not send His mercy upon us! For a long time we have been without news from Papa and Peter. I think the fear about Papa makes Mother so sick. But I also think that the effort of the packing was too much for her, because now she has awful intestinal pains.

Thursday, April 30 Today is Heine's birthday. He is now already eleven years old, and we still think of him as being so small. Anna and I baked before breakfast. I had prepared the yeast already yesterday evening, and we also made a wreath for Heine. Mother gave him cloth for summer clothes. He was especially thankful for a paint box, which Tante gave to him.

The day before yesterday we received letters from Anna and Heinrich. Both of them also had written to Heine, and we had expected these letters. Helene was promoted to the next class in school.

Friday, May 1 This morning we had a lot of baking to do. In the afternoon Anna and Susanne went to Schneiders', and when Helene came home from school, we followed them. We had planned to go there for a long time. The way through the woods is quite far, but a very nice, romantic walk. We also met the old Mr. Wismer there. In the evening the service was held, and we were convinced that Mr. Shantz or somebody else would come, but we were wrong. Nobody came, and so we had to walk along, which was not too pleasant a prospect for us girls to do alone, and I had to think that our dear Papa certainly would have sent somebody to take us home. Just as we came close to the woods, we saw something jumping behind a trunk, which frightened us, because we thought it was a hare or a wild cat, but it was our Hans and the river. Hans said that he had been there for quite a while, waiting for us so that we would not have to walk alone. I was very glad that Hans had come and from there on we enjoyed walking through the moonlit woods.

Saturday, May 2 Right after breakfast Tante and I went to town to do the shopping; I am still not quite used to it, because in Berdjansk we never did it. Our dear mother has packed a lot today. Now Mr. and Mrs. Shantz are visiting her. I think Mother would like to see them leave, because there is still so much to be packed.

Helene went to Mrs. Young in the afternoon, because she had been invited to go there. The little girl who lives there had asked her because Mrs. Young wished it. Hans went there immediately after the tea to get her, but he is not yet back. Oh, that he might also bring a letter from our dear Papa with him!! I think we have a full moon today. I can see it through my window up here, rising big and clear.

Sunday, May 3 This was the first quite warm day of spring. In the morning we girls and also Susanne attended the service at the Methodist church, where a new minister was preaching. In the afternoon I had new students. In the evening everybody except Moses gathered here to look at the illustrated Bible. I am astonished how little these grown children know about the Biblical stories.

Monday, May 4 A cold, dull day! We received letters from our dear Papa and Peter, and also from the Quirings, who told us, to our great surprise, that Annchen Dueck (or Classen) is married to O. Gunter.

Tuesday, May 5 Today we received the news of the death of Aunt Zimmerman. (Heinrich only wrote to Papa.) We also got a letter from Uncle Sudermann. According to that letter, the Gunters and even Dirkses are beginning to think very differently about the States.

Wednesday, May 6 We received a letter from our dear Papa from Colorado. He is longing to see us again. Oh, I wish that the dear Lord would help us out of all this, that they may find a home for us where we can live peacefully with our parents for many more years! Often I can hardly wait for Papa's and Peter's return, but when I want to be happy the thought of it on the other hand makes me afraid, for I do not know how things will turn out – only the Lord knows!

May 14 I have not written for quite some time, which I regret now, but almost every day passed like the others. The day before yesterday Hans became rather sick. We were afraid that it was the measles, but yesterday after he had stayed in bed quietly for the whole day, he was much better and also today until about to the evening. He caught a cold today, and now he is sick again. First he was cold and now his head feels hot and aches very badly. Yesterday afternoon Susanne came and invited the girls, as well as Jakob and Moses, to go with her for a whole day's ride. I resigned immediately (did I do right?), for I think this would have been Papa's wish. I regret only that Anna therefore did not want to go either, but actually I did not mind it. Now I have fallen out of Jakob and Susanne's graces, I suppose, especially when Jakob walked by the window and said: "I hope you will think it over and join us tomorrow." (When he says things like this it is always a great surprise.) I answered him that this time it would not work out this way.

Yesterday evening a huge pile of bushes were burnt in the garden, and I was reminded of Jeschka, who always hacked all the weeds and bushes.

Today Susanne and Jakob drove away very neatly in the buggy with Mr. and Mrs. Shantz, Tante and Helene! Of course Mr. Shantz dropped in already before breakfast to ask whether anybody would want to come along to the meeting. I said that we would not want to go, and then he asked whether or not Tante wanted to go, and when I asked her she decided yes. (Probably just to please us so that at least somebody would ride with them.) Helene and Mary joined them also. Anna, Magdalene and I went to the Methodist Church in the morning. On the way back, I stopped by the post office where I picked up letters from

Papa and Peter from Iowa. Thank the Lord that He has protected our father so far! They are now searching for a new home for us. Peter writes that they had visited Mennonites over there, where it had been so dirty that Peter did not eat anything the whole day. Oh, my heart is so full of sorrows today when I think about the future, and I haven't been so afraid for the future for a long time. I know that this is not right, for don't I have many reasons to be thankful? In the evening Mother, Heine, Idy and I visited with Hopses for a little while, where the three small brothers are quite sick because of their shots! How badly I have written!

Friday, May 15 Yesterday after I had written, I went upstairs to Hans who was very sick again. The dear boy was freezing and has had very bad headaches. Also it tortured him very much to vomit. After I sat by his side for some time, he asked me to read something to him, and after I had read a Psalm, he wanted to hear the Bible verse where it says: "He bore our debts and suffered our pains." I was very glad that he had uttered this wish. Oh, that the Lord might guide him even through his illness!

Sunday, May [17] Anna, Helen and Susanne and I went to the English Methodist Church, where we heard a nice sermon and some lovely singing. I like to attend this church very much. When we arrived there, it started raining and it rained all the time. We were very worried about how we could come home but, to our surprise and relief, we saw Cornelius at the door waiting for us with umbrellas. After Sunday school, the girls went to Mady Oberholzer's and stayed there for supper.

Monday, May [18] In the afternoon Tante and I walked to Mayers', which we had planned to do for a long time. After school Helene and Mary also came. I liked it much better than I had expected. The little Milly is a lovely little girl. I asked her whether she would not want to learn verses for Sunday school. She said, "Yes, but they are all so difficult and nobody ever reads them to me." Then I read to her the first five verses from John until she could say them from memory. I also walked across meadows and fields with the children, and we were all very happy. We played ball, searched for small shells at the creek, etc.

Tuesday, May [19] Today we have written birthday letters to our dear Grete. We also received letters this morning, one from our dear Papa; one from Uncle Buhler from Berdjansk, and also one from Tante and Uncle from Prussia. I am curious to know why Anna and Heinrich have not written for such a long time. Maybe they have so much to do because Uncle and Aunt Zimmermann are going to Russia one of these days.

Wednesday, May [20] Helene did not go to school today because yesterday and today she had awful pains in her arm, and I do not feel well either. Because of this Tante and Anna did not let me wash, which did not please me at all. Since they had only a little wash, they were finished by noon. Tante brought Marianne, Heine and the two little girls to school earlier, which they had planned to do a long time ago. Anna laid the lingerie on the lawn to bleach, starched the few coloured pieces, and then also was done with her work.

In the evening we stayed here with Susanne, Mary, Magdalene and Moses and sang and had a good time. I like it if they come here, but I do not like to go to their home often. Hans has a fever.

Thursday, May [21] Now I just finished writing in this my diary because it was in great disorder. The morning is lovely, but rather cold, because it had rained during the night. Everything outside in nature is so beautiful and fresh. Now I will prepare breakfast and let Anna sleep a little longer, because she is still tired from yesterday. Maybe I will have time in the evening to write that Papa and Peter have already come home . . . Yes, our beloved ones arrived here this evening when we just sat down for tea. Thank the Lord! Oh, how glad and thankful we should be. They have found a new homestead in a small town in Iowa. A short time before our dear ones arrived, Anna, Heine, Idy and I went for a walk in the small wood to look for some violets, because the children wanted to so badly, but in the meantime the old Johannes Schneiders and Mr. Brenneman had come and Brenneman wanted to say goodbye to all of us. He had waited for us some time, but it was in vain. When we came, they had just left, which I regretted very much.

Friday, May 22 In the afternoon Tante went to town with Marianne, during which time I washed the lingerie of Papa and Peter's clothes and also laid them on the lawn to bleach. It was not so very much, but still I was busy the whole afternoon. Anna also came to help a little.

Saturday, May 23 In the morning Mother and Papa attended the burial of the old Mr. Eby in church. Mr. and Mrs. Shantz and Susanne also went there. Then Magdalene came over and asked me whether I would not like to bake some lemon cakes with her. I was very pleased with that; I took the necessary things and went to Magdalene's place. I baked, with her help, some quite nice cakes. Later in our new home I hope I shall be able to make them alone. In the evening Magdalene left to visit her parents, but she does not want to come back until we leave.

Sunday, May 24 In the morning we had a meeting, and the Shantzes had many guests for dinner. In the afternoon several Baptists were baptized at the riverside, for which a large crowd had gathered. I regretted that I could not watch it, but we did not want to leave the Sunday school classes to themselves these last times, and so Susanne, Anna and I went to Sunday school. I still hoped to get there on time, but it was too late, for on our way back we met all the people coming from there.

Friday, May [29] In the afternoon the sheep were washed down the river [?], and Anna and I as well as Susanne and Mary watched them for a while. I do not know why, but I almost do not like Susanne any more. It is too obvious that she is trying to win Peter by all her personality, and is not that bad, very bad? Especially since we have told her at the beginning of our stay here that we hoped our dear friends would soon follow us, and that one was especially dear to Peter!

Saturday, May [30] In the morning Jakob, Johannes and Peter brought all our big trunks to Preston. In the evening, after they had returned, and had eaten supper, Peter asked me whether I would like to go up to town. It was quite a nice walk for we talked about a number of things. Unfortunately, something is now between us, and that makes me so sorry. Oh, where are the times when we so much liked to be alone and to talk and when Peter loved to speak to me about a beautiful future. While walking we sang some short songs. But once Peter started "It is decided . . . " etc., then I was altogether quiet, but when he was finished I sang the following self-made song: "Friend, I am happy to leave this place. Soon I will find another place out there. All will be new and charming where I will settle. Even if on earth there is no true loyalty."

When we came back it was almost dark, and yet Susanne stood on our porch, although Anna was not there. Oh, I do not know how she finds it possible always to show herself with her smile and friendly manner. Till now I always thought she was nice, but what I see now is more that I can say.

Sunday, May [31] In the morning I asked Peter to go with his three sisters to the Methodist Church for the last time, and he did it. Oh, I was so glad of it, because the Mennonite Church did not have a service this Sunday. When we left and passed by the garden, Susanne was there . . . and when we came back, she already stood in the doorway (we could see her from quite a distance). In the afternoon we taught Sunday school once again. Mr. Hugh told the children that some of their teachers would leave them soon and that they should pray for them. It was quite hard for me, and the children also were moved. (I think they still liked me a little.) The little Milly gave me her picture and now would like to get mine. After Sunday school the old Mr. and Mrs. Oberholzer visited us, and also stayed for tea. Our dear mother has been in bed the whole day. She felt sick last night already. Right after supper Peter went to the Young Men's Association and stayed there very late. In the meantime, Anna, Helen and I were at Shantzes', because they really had wanted us to come. We sang the old songs together. I was so happy that Peter was not with us.

I think the dear Lord will finally lead everything to its best without all our many worries if we just ask Him and trust Him!

Monday, June 1 Today our dear ones, Tante, Peter, Anna and Larry, [the dog] left. Who knows when we others will be ready to go. Jakob drove them to Preston. I was rather afraid of the parting moment, but again, without any significant reason, everything went by quickly. Heine wanted, by all means, that Larry should kiss the river, but he did not do it. At noon Hans brought a letter from Heinrich and Anna.

Saturday, June 6 In the morning I cleaned a little with Helene's help. Yesterday evening Papa and Helene drove to Mr. Young to say farewell. He was very moved for Papa says he had kissed Helene. Later when she could not hear it, he had said to Papa: "She is a lovely girl." This afternoon Jakob, Susanne, Mary, Papa and Helene drove to the love feast of the Tunker [church]. Now it is quite late, and we are waiting anxiously for them. I would like to go to bed now, but still I do not want to leave Mother alone. In the afternoon I visited Magdalene. We spoke about many things. Is it good? Later I helped her with milking.

Sunday, June 7 In the morning we had a service, and this will probably be the last one we will attend. In the afternoon we heard that somebody from the Amish people would preach in the House for the Poor, and Papa went. I, too, would like to have gone, but I thought of it only after Papa had already left. Finally we managed that Magdalene [?] and I walked there, which we do not regret. We arrived a little too late and stayed on the stairs or sat in a window, but we could hear the preacher very well. We also could see the children playing in the yard and also the peacock who reminded me so much of Berdjansk. He seemed to be quite tame. I had put some English tracts in my pocket, and when the poor passed us on the stairway, I handed them out, one for each, and they were very glad, because when they saw that I gave one to everybody, they already stretched out their hands for it.

Tuesday, June 9 We have so much to do that often I do not know what to do first. Often I wish Tante would be here. Who knows when we shall finally travel?! We wanted to leave tomorrow, but it will probably not work out. I would like to write to our dear Grete, but I do not think I can manage today. Yesterday I did not feel well at all, so that Papa thought I also would get the fever and therefore I had to swallow Hans's bitter medicine, which tasted awful. In the evening the old couple (Moses Schneider) visited us. They are such loveable people, as are the old Mr. Schrag and his wife.

Wednesday, June 10 We have just had evening devotions with Shantzes, at which our dear Papa prayed so heartily. It was a very busy day. Papa had painful headaches. That the dear Saviour, with His mercy, would help again! And help Mom stay healthy also. Magdalene had finished Hans's new coat, which was very kind of her. Papa gave the whip to Jakob, who enjoyed it more than I had expected. Susanne gave Heine her picture, which she probably had meant for somebody else!! That the dear, loyal Lord who has led us so mercifully this far may lead us furthermore is our prayer.

Saturday, July 4 For the past three weeks, we have been in our new preliminary home and during that time I have not written into this diary, which now I regret. I like it here. The people are all friendly. I think there is quite a difference between our strong feeling in Canada and our feeling here. We will be very careful in making our new friends and relations here, for we should have learned a good lesson in Canada. During the past weeks (or better, during the past time) we have been very busy and our dear Papa is suffering greatly. Oh, that the dear Lord would render him good health! Now we often think about Anna and Heinrich. That the dear Lord might protect them on their journey! Two weeks ago Friday we got our cow and calf. The cow is quite good, but the calf needs so much milk.

4   Maria Stoesz Klassen (1823 to 1893)

Ebenfeld, Manitoba

Diary selection: 25 September to 31 December 1887

Age: 63

Maria Stoesz was born on 10 November 1823 in Chortitza Colony, New Russia, and was raised in the Bergthal Colony in the village of Schoenthal. She was the sister of the well-known *Aeltester* David Stoesz and she was married to Johann Klassen. In July 1874, Maria and Johann immigrated to Manitoba, settling in the village of Ebenfeld, East Reserve. Maria and Johann had 16 children, 15 of whom lived to adulthood. A family history notes that they included: Jacob, who married Susanna Neufeld, whose family lived in Ebenfeld, Manitoba; Anna, who married Jakob Krahn; Helena, who married Peter Falk; Peter; Katherina, who died in 1869 at 20; Martin, who married Sara Harder; Barbara, who married David Friesen; Maria, who married Abraham Kehler from Blumengard; Johann; Margaretha, who married Peter Penner from Pastwa; Aganetha, who married Peter Wiebe, resident in Langham, Saskatchewan; Susanna, who married Peter Hiebert from Hochfeld, Manitoba; Sara, who married the Klassens' neighbour, Heinrich Neufeld; Elisabeth, who married Peter Funk from Bergthal; Judith, who married Peter Neufeld, Heinrich's brother.

In this diary, Maria referred to Sara, Elisabeth (also known as Lisa), and to Judith (also known as Ida); only these three daughters were still unmarried and at home in 1887. They thus worked with their father in the fields or accompanied him to the market. Daughter Judith was also a diarist (see diary 18). Throughout her diary, Maria Stoesz Klassen referred to her sons-in-law by their surnames (e.g., "Penner," or "Kehler," or "Neufeld") and to the families of her daughters by their married names (e.g., "Hieberts," "our Mrs. Krahn," "our children Falks and Wiebes," "our Kehlers," "our Friesens," "our children Penners"). "Neufeld" in 1887 referred to the household of daughter Susanna, for although daughter Sara eventually also became a Mrs. Neufeld, she was not yet married. The families of the sons were known by their first names – Jakob, Martin, and Johann. The Klassens were popularly known within their district as "the family that had the 12 girls." In 1893, Maria and Johann retired, selling their farm and moving to the village of Bergthal, about six kilometres to the northwest. Maria died that same year.

Beyond her family, Maria's world extended to neighbours within Ebenfeld village, especially neighbour Peter Peters. The diary also reveals an intimate knowledge of other Bergthal Colony descendant villages – Schoenthal, Reichenbach, Bergthal, and Blumengart, all lying between three and 10 kilometres from the Stoesz farm. The village of Steinbach, only five kilometres from Ebenfeld, was the growing trade centre that the Klassens visited for market reasons, most often by husband Johann alone. Other villages, such as Pastwa, lying some 15 kilometres to the west, and the villages of the West Reserve, about 100 kilometres to the west, were visited during 1887 only at times of crisis. At least some of the Klassen children lived in the West Reserve during 1887, and eventually children Jacob, Helena, Martin, Barbara, and Margaretha moved there. With the exception of Aganetha, who eventually settled in Langham, Saskatchewan, all the children stayed in Manitoba.

Maria was 63 and 64 in 1887 when she wrote the enclosed excerpt from her diary. Unfortunately, it is the only section that has been preserved. The complete diary is reported to have been lengthy, the last entry making mention of the Klassens' plans for retirement. A letter written to Maria and Johann, from her brother Peter Stoesz, was found among family papers, and it reveals something of her earlier life. It is evident that Peter disagreed with his sister's decision to move to Canada. Peter was not content to live among Mennonites and thus left his village of Schoenthal, Bergthal Colony, to experience the life of a non-Mennonite city. He obtained work in the civil service, married, and did not immigrate to Manitoba with the rest of the family in 1874. Of the Stoesz family, Peter alone remained in Russia. The letter is included here because it was part of Maria's personal papers and sheds light on her world. The diary was translated by Maria Enns, Steinbach, Manitoba. For more information on Maria Stoesz, see Linda Buhler, "Ebenfeld," *Historical Sketches of the East Reserve, 1874-1910*, edited by John Dyck (Steinbach, MB: 1994), 104-124.

Peter's Letter to Maria   *Köppenthal, 27th September, 1863.*

My dear sister and brother-in-law:

Right now I happen to have a few hours of leisure, and have been thinking about my past, which was sometimes quite colourful, as you have regularly reminded me from time to time, that is, when you could get hold of me. Whether this is for the better or worse, I am not sure.

You were right at times, sister, but not always. Granted, not every life is exemplary, and I have never tried to say that mine has been. Life there [in Bergthal Colony] was too routine and unbearable. You don't know how difficult it was for me, being a pawn, sheepishly following the flock. Although there were those, that seemed to have the right ... Well, maybe I had better not say. You know, yourself, how Babylonian it was at your place, and maybe still is.

I am quite fortunate here, for I am free and I serve voluntarily. The people here are content and morally good. However, there are also those that are nailheads, or Napoleons, as your husband would call them, but the morally good constitute the majority. But enough of politics.

I would really like to know how it's going at your place, if you are well, and if you had a good harvest. You have a very difficult life, dear sister; I think of all your children [12 in number at this time] that you need to support. But the Creator provides for all of His creations and He will also help your children through this world.

Have a happy life, greet your children, relatives and Abraham Hiebert from Schönthal.

Tell David to write to me soon, and anyone else that is able to. Tell as many to write as can.

Your loving brother,
Peter Stösz

1887

September The children were home. Father went with Ida to Schönfeld with 4 dozen eggs. They bought shoes and gas and 3 kerchiefs. At P. Peters' everything has been threshed from *Faspa* [afternoon tea] to evening.

Sunday the 25th Morning the weather fine, afternoon we got visitors, our Kehlers and Mrs. Peters.

Monday the 26th Weather gloomy, Johan Unger from Rosengart got his arm squashed at the threshing machine. They took him to Winnipeg to have it amputated.

The 27th Father went with 10 bags of barley to the mill.

Wed. the 28th At 10 a.m. Father, Lisa, Ida and Penner were called to Reichenbach to help thresh. Again on the 29th. It was very hot both days. At 10, Klippensteins from West Reserve came for a visit. They had dinner and went to Ungers.

Friday the 30th They came back and stayed till Saturday evening.

October, Sunday the 2nd Oct. We went to church, Klippensteins were there too. In the afternoon we went to Neufelds'.

Tuesday the 4th Father went to Winnipeg at 5 in the morning with 14 bags of wheat. It was cold; there was frost in the windows. At 5 in the evening [likely the next day] they came back from Wpg. For the wheat they received 54 cents. They brought 3 pair shoes.

The 6th in the afternoon We went to Bergthal to Klassens for a farewell. Tomorrow Klippensteins are leaving.

The 7th in the afternoon We went to Steinbach with 20 lbs. butter. We bought several things.

Sat. the 8th Cold and gloomy.

Sunday the 9th In the morning, weather fair. In the afternoon, Neufelds came to visit. In the evening Father went to Winnipeg with wheat, to Blumengart for the night. Lisa went along. They came back on the 11th in the evening, received 57 cents for the wheat and $1.55 for the bag of onions.

The 12th Father went to Steinbach. He brought me cucumbers at 15 cents. It is snowing.

It is also snowing on the 13th.

On the 14th In the morning the windows are frost covered; 5° frost. In the afternoon we made sauerkraut.

Sunday the 16th St. Quake day, foggy and cold, in the afternoon we went to Hochfeld.

Monday the 17th Father and Penner want to fix the roof, but the 18th Hieberts came. They got some sand out of the bush.

On the 19th In the afternoon we went to Reichenbach to visit.

The 20th It is cold. After *Faspa*, Father and Ida went to the Mill with 5 bags of barley. It is cold, there is frost on the windows.

Saturday the 22nd We went to Steinbach and bought some things, 11.5 yards of tricot at 30 cents. We met Cornelius Stöszes. When we went home they came to our place and were our guests. They went home by moonlight. In the evening we got more visitors; Falks' two daughters came visiting.

Sunday, the 23rd It is cold and snowing.

Monday Father took the wood for the trough to Reichenbach.

The 25th Father went to Schönthal with a paper. It was -15 in the morning.

26th 16° frost.

27th 10° frost. It is cold. Today we tore the old stove down and finished the new one, up to the upper part.

The 28th By noon the stove was finished. At 5:00 Heinrich Neufeld said we must go to his place. His dear mother has died. He went to Pastwa to Penners'. We went there and found her lying in her bed, dead. She had been sick for two hours.

Sunday, the 30th Fine weather. In the afternoon Father went to Peters' to invite them to our hog slaughtering. While he was gone, Hieberts came to visit and told us that on the West Reserve Mrs. P. Kehler, Mrs. Jacob Wiebe, and a man by the name of Stobbe had died.

Tuesday the 1st of November 1887 On the first, Mrs. Neufeld was taken to her resting place at the cemetery. Mrs. H. Berg and I put the last dress attire on her. Tomorrow, if it is the will of God, we want to slaughter hogs. I am sick.

Thursday the 3rd We are slaughtering pigs. Peter Peters and Cornelius Peters and J. Rempel are helping us, they were well. Thank God. One [of the pig carcasses] was hung up ready to be sold.

The 4th We went to Blumengart. In the evening we were well and lay down to sleep. At midnight Father said he was not well and soon he became shivery with great frost and pain in the back and legs. On the 6th he was delirious and it lasted till Sunday noon. Penner went to all the children to let them know. They came over before noon. Kehler took the slaughtered pig and 10 bags of wheat. He wanted to take them away [to Winnipeg] on Monday.

On the 7th Father again had the pain in his legs and back and he is sicker again. He got sicker every day till Tuesday the 11th in the morning when he was a bit better. At noon our Friesens came and Klassens came Saturday night on the 12th. Our children were all here on Sunday the 13th except Falks and Martin and Wiebes. Father is a little better. Klassen went back home on Monday the 14th.

On the 16th In the afternoon Friesens left. Soon Wiebes, Martin and our Mrs. Krahn were here.

Thursday the 17th They all left for their homes. Thank God that Father is getting better. Yesterday in the morning at 9 it snowed. There was wind but it soon turned into a storm so that the windows were soon covered with snow and dirt so that we could not look out.

The 18th In the morning mild, but it soon got colder and it snowed in the afternoon. Gerhard Unger came to pick up the stove. We are getting two sheep for our half-share in the stove, and Penner gets $10.00. It is 6:00 and still snowing.

Today, Saturday the 19th 16° frost, but not windy.

Sunday, the 20th Windy and cloudy, 14°. In the afternoon, Hieberts and Mrs. Peters came to visit.

Monday, the 21st Hiebert and J. Rempel and Mrs. Peters came and slaughtered our cow. The cow was nice and fat. We got two pounds of tallow.

The 24th In the afternoon Kehlers came to visit. In the morning, 17° frost.

The 25th Penner went to the mill and brought flour, and he also took five bags for the hogs. In the evening Falk came here and stayed for the night.

The 26th 20° frost.

Sunday, the 27th 28° frost, but otherwise nice. The windows were almost thawed by noon. In the evening Neufelds' children came over to visit.

Monday, the 28th 24° frost and we got a visitor, W. Rempel, from Rheinland. He ate dinner and went to Steinbach.

The 29th Falk came and got ready to go to Winnipeg.

The 30th At 6 they left; their cargo was meat. We gave along a hind quarter from the cow, and 12 dressed hens. In the evening Pr. V. came visiting, and Ungers Gerhard brought the sheep.

December 1887, the 1st 4° frost. It is raining mixed with snow.

The 2nd In the evening Falk came back from Wpg. The meat was 119 lbs. and we received 4.5 cents [per pound], the hens, 33 lbs. at 10 cents. Falk brought 5.5 yds. material at 75 cents a yd. and a plate for 50 cents.

Sunday the 4th Stormy and in the afternoon mild. Rev. Peters came over. In the evening our children Penners and Sara and Ida went to Neufelds', and Neufeld was our guest.

On the 7th In the morning Mrs. Peters came over. Around noon, Kehler came to visit and brought Hieberts with him. It was very nice.

Thursday the 8th A minister election shall be held – may God be with them and lead everything to the best.

Sunday the 11th A clear morning but cold 24° – in the afternoon we received a letter from Friesens and Wiebes.

Monday the 12th We went to Steinbach with 45 lbs. tallow at 6 cents a lb. and 6.5 lbs. butter at 14 cents. We bought *Kaba* [?] for 1 dollar, 3.5 K, and fruit.

The 14th In the morning Penner went to Otterburne with wheat. At noon, our children the Krahns came visiting. Krahn went to Steinbach, and Ida went along.

The 16th In the morning, mild and 5° frost. Penner again went with wheat to Otterburne. In the afternoon, Father went to Wiebes' with a funeral invitation. J. Stösz's daughter, Anna, is to be laid to rest, Sunday, the 18th of December. She was sick for 5 weeks and 5 days, reaching the age of 18 years and 8 months.

Saturday, the 17th In the morning we went to Mrs. Peters and in the afternoon we came back. It was very mild. 4° warm.

Sunday, the 18th In the morning we went to the funeral. It was colder, and had snowed during the night. The driving path was bad. We came home at 6:00 in the evening.

Monday, the 19th In the morning 26° cold. The other days it was not so cold.

On Saturday, the 24th Kehler was here.

The 25th The first holiday in the morning, 17° cold. In the afternoon, Father and Ida went to Neufelds and Penner went to Wielers. A storm seemed to be coming.

The 26th The second holiday in the morning, 25° and storming.

The 27th Penners and Lisa and Sara went to Ungers. In the evening Lisa got sick and she is still sick, today, the 28th. In the morning, 30° cold and clear.

The 29th 33° cold.

The 30th We went to Steinbach with one pail butter at 14 cents. It was 23 pounds. It was stormy. In the evening the wind got stronger, and it kept on blowing all night.

The 31st Last day of the year, very stormy. 14° cold. Grain for the year 1887: Wheat, 366 bushels; Oats, 677 bushels; Barley, 86 bushels. We threshed on the 17th of September.

Margaretha Jansen (From Betty A. Miller and Oscar R. Miller, *The Cornelius Jansen Family History, 1822-1973* [Berlin, OH: 1974], 29.)

Heinrich Kornelsen and family, about 1913. Back row, from left to right, children: Lizzie, Margaret, Gerhard, Katherine, and Annie. Front row: Heinrich, Susie, and Elisabeth. (Courtesy Dave K. Schellenberg)

Old Men and Young Boys

III

5   Moses Weber (1847 to 1937)
Lexington, Ontario
Diary selection: 1 January to 30 June 1865
Age: 17

Moses Weber was born in Woolwich Township, Waterloo County, Canada West, in 1847. He was the son of preacher Samuel (Sem) Weber (1821-1885) and Anna Martin (born in 1824), both of whose parents came from Pennsylvania. Moses Weber grew up on what contemporaries called a "large farm," a farm that his father, Samuel, had acquired near Lexington upon his marriage. Moses's father was also a highly respected community person, a farmer, a cooper, and the preacher responsible for three Mennonite meeting places – Conestoga, Martins, and Schneiders. A family history identifies Moses's father as "an eloquent speaker, a man of great influence and a good worker among his coreligionists."

Moses, a teenager when he wrote this section of the diary, seemed particularly attuned to his parents' social world. This included the following kin: his uncles Henry Shantz (married to Anna's sister Veronica) and Benjamin L. Eby (married to Anna's sister Barbara); uncles John, Levi, Joseph, Daniel, and Tilman Martin (Anna's brothers from various parts of the county); uncle Joseph L. Weber (the husband of Samuel's only sibling, Anna); and his parents' cousins, Reverend Peter Martin and Noah S. Bowman, and Sam's second cousin Martin Good of Michigan. The networks observed by Moses also include church ties, often linked to places beyond Woolwich Township. A parade of "strange" church clerics visit from outside Waterloo County; for example, Bishop George Weber and a Reverend Nisely of the Lancaster Conference, Pennsylvania, visit in May. On other occasions the church leaders who visit the Weber household hail from Waterloo County itself: Henry Shantz of North Dumfries Township, for example, was a bishop in the Waterloo District; Abraham Martin of Woolwich Township was a noted and highly traditionalist bishop; Old Abraham Weber was a retired preacher from Freeport. There are overnight trips by Moses's parents, seemingly to visit the homes of church members: in February, for example, Moses reports that his parents took an overnight trip that included visits to the families of Absalom Schneiders, Jacob Bretz, Abraham Clemens, and Joseph Hagey, each of whom lived between Bridgeport and Hespeler [present-day Cambridge].

Most important for Moses, however, are the "young people" associated with these households; although they come to visit frequently, Moses does not identify them by their first names. They are noted only as the "young folks of Absalom Snyder" or "Peter Martin's young folks." The young person Moses spends most of his time with is his older sister, Susan, 21; she was single during 1865, marrying David Horst, a Woolwich Township neighbour, in January 1866. A sign of his closeness to his sister was that in 1870 Moses married David's sister, Barbara. While his older sister dominates this record, Moses makes little mention of his six younger siblings, ages 12 to two: Henry (b. 1853), Anna (b. 1855), Veronica (b. 1857), Samuel Jr. (b. 1859), Leah (b. 1862), and baby Levi (b. 1863). Another person of the Weber household who figures prominently is 27-year-old Jacob Martin (1838-1905), referred to on 13 February; he was the family's hired man, or apprentice, who learned the cooperage trade from Samuel Weber.

The diary is not only a detailed account of social networks and work routine, but it is also a record of linguistic assimilation. The diary was written in English, but it is clear from the German phonetics that Pennsylvania Dutch was still spoken at home. Moses's spelling has been left intact and without "sic" qualifiers. They include such words as "glover seet" (clover seed), "shugar bush" (sugar bush), "potatoe pach" (potato patch), "Conostoga" (Conestoga), "preecher" (preacher), "wer" (were), "jours" (chores), "peese" (peas), "sider" (cider). His abbreviations for the days of the week, given as "mo", "tu," "we," and so on, have been left intact.

A copy of the original diary was located at the Mennonite Archives of Ontario in Waterloo, Ontario. The diary was transcribed by Reg Good. For the family history of Moses Weber, see Ezra Eby, *A Biographical History of Early Settlers and Their Descendants in Waterloo Township* 1895 (Waterloo, ON: Eldon D. Weber, 1971), 368ff.

New Year, January the 1, 1865

su the 1 New Year. Sunday the first. A midlen [middling] clever [clear] day. We went to the meeting at Elmira. Father went to Peter Martins for dinner. Susan and I went to Samuel Reist and to Aaron Ziegler on visit.

mo the 2 A midlen fine day. Father and mother sent to the Funeral of the child of Tilman Martin, his age was 1 month 4 days.

tu the 3 A fine day. Father went up on the other place. I hauled wood.

we the 4 A cold day. Father and Mother went to David Gressman's [Cressman] on visit and are going to visit out in Wilmot a few days.

th the 5 A fine day. I hauled wood.

fr the 6 A fine day. We hauled wood. Father and Mother came home again from Wilmot.

sa the 7 A fine day. We thrashed a little oats. Peter Martins and Jacob his brother and sister wer here on visit.

su the 8 A fine day. We sent to the meeting at Schneiders [Meeting House]. Old John Martins wer her[e] on visit. Menno Guth [26] and Isaac Martin [20] were here on visit.

mo the 9 A fine day. We butchered t[h]ree hogs. Peter Reists wer here on visit.

tu the 10 A snowy day. They hauled wood. I did begin to go to School [17 at this time].

we the 11 A cold day. Father went to the school meeting and they put in Jacob Martin for Trustee. Father and mother went to Benjamin Martin.

th the 12 A cold day. They hauled wood. Rudy Detweilers wer here on visit.

fr the 13 A midlen clear day. They hauled wood. Joseph M. Webers wer here on visit, and brought two men along, from Pennsylvania.

sa the 14 A stormy day. Father went with them up to John Groffs and to Joseph L Weber's for dinner and they came here again and mother went along and they sent down to Joseph Schneiders on visit.

su the 15 A snowy day. They went to the meeting at Conestoga, Father & mother went to John Brubaker and to David Brubakers on visit.

mo the 16 A cold day. They worked at home. Joseph Kropp's wer here on visit.

tu the 17 A cold day. They hauled wood.

we the 18 A midlen fine day. They hauled wood.

th the 19 A fine day. They hauled wood.

fr the 20 A fine day. They hauled wood. Christian Schneiders were on visit.

sa the 21 A rough day. We hauled wood. Father and Mother went to Daniel Webers on visit.

su the 22 A snowy and rainy day. Father and mother went to the meeting at Martins. Susan and I went to the meeting at Gressmans [Cressmans, later the Breslau Mennonite Church], and to John Weber's for dinner and to Rudy Detwiler's for supper.

mo the 23 A snowy day. We hauled wood. Abraham Webers wer here on visit.

tu the 24 A stormy day. They hauled wood.

we the 25 A cold and stormy day. They worked at home.

th the 26 A stormy day. They worked at home.

fr the 27 A cold and stormy. They hauled rails.

sa the 28 A rough day. Father went down to Christian Eby's meeting house [later, First Mennonite Church, Kitchener]. Susan and I went out in Wilmot to David Gressman's and out there to visit . . .

su the 29 A fine day. They wer at home.

mo the 30 A fine day. Father went up to Wolwich [Woolwich].

tu the 31 A fine day. They hauled rails. John Burkerd came here.

February, the first A fine day. They hauled rails.

th the 2 A fine day. Father and mother went to J.L. Weber's on visit. They hauled rails.

fr the 3 A fine day. They hauled rails.

sa the 4 A warm day. We thrashed faul [fall] wheet.

su the 5 A stormy day. We went to the meeting at Schneiders. Isaac Bowman's and Joseph Shantz's wer here on visit.

mo the 6 A midlen fine [day]. They hauled rails.

tu the 7th Feb. 1865 A fine day. Father went to Bridgeport. Jonas Wengers wer here on visit. Jacob Martin went to the funeral of Isaac Burkerd, a child of Joseph Burkerd; his age was 5 years 3 months and there was another funeral in Elmira, the child of Joseph Gingrich.

we the 8 A snowy day. Father and Mother went to Peter Weber's to Elias Weber's and to William Ebys and to Peter Reist's on visit.

th the 9 A fine day. They cleaned up in the barn.

fr the 10 A stormy day. They hauled rails. Christian Schneider and David Martin wer here to settle some in the [e]state.

sa the 11 A midlen fine day. We did get done hauling rails. Father and Mother went to Waterloo on business. Susan and I went to Abraham Martin's on visit. [My sister] Magdalena is sick.

su the 12 A fine day. We went to meeting at Conestoga. Father and Mother went to J.W. Brubackers for dinner and to Abraham Brubaker's for supper and to Levi Bowman's over night from there to P[eter] Martins.

mo the 13 A midlen fine day. Jacob hauled wood home in the shed. The thermamater [thermometer] was this morning down on twenty below zero.

tu the 14 A cold day. Father went in the pine bush.

we the 15 A midlen fine day. Jacob hauled wood. Father and Mother went to Absalom Schneiders, on visit, and to Jacob Bretz's over night, and to Abraham Clemens and to Joseph Hegis. I went with John Martin to Hespeler's [Mill]; we had a load of ... wh[eat]. Andrew Groff's wer here on visit.

th the 16 A fine day. Father and Mother came home again.

fr the 17 A fine day. Father hauled wood.

sa the 18 A snowy day. We hauled wood.

su the 19 A fine day. We went to the meeting at Martins. Susan and I went to Absalom Martins' for dinner and to John Martins over supper.

mo [the 19] A fine day. Father hauled wood. Jacob worked in the shop, preparing wood for buckets. Amos Martins and Old Ester Martin wer here on visit.

February tu the 21 1865 A fine day. They hauled wood. Eli Martins wer here on visit.

we the 22 A fine day. They worked at home. Father went to Daniel Wismers' to visit old Peter Erb.

th the 23 A fine day. Jacob hauled wood. Father and Mother and some of the children went over to Grandmother on visit.

fr the 24 A fine day. They did get done hauling wood to Waterloo. Old Peter Erb died this forenoon at ten o'clock. We had spelling School.

sa the 25 A midlen clever day. We made a couple saw logs out of bath trees. Father went to Joseph S. Martin to get some oats, for sowing.

su the 26 A rainy day. We went to the Funeral of old Peter Erb he brought his age to 78 years, 1 m[onth], 10 days. Peter Martin's young folks [Levi, Catherine, and Gideon] wer here on visit.

mo the 27 A midlen clever day. They hauled some sawlogs. Martin Bowmans and the old Widow of J. Bowman wer here on visit.

March fr the 17, 1865 A fine day. They worked at hom[e].

sa the 18 A fine day. We thrashed the glover-seet from the straw, with the horses. J. W. Brubaker was here.

su the 19 A fine day. We went to the Meeting at Martins. Father and Mother went to Solomon Martins and Christian Schneiders on visit. Jacob and I went to David Martins on visit.

mo the [20] A midlen fine day. We took out a load of buckets in the shugar bush and began to hang them up and set up some traufs [troughs].

tu the 21 A rainy day. We worked in the shugarbush.

we the 22 A snowy & rainy day. We did begin to boil sap. Abraham W. Martin and Martin Good from Michigan wer here on visit.

th the 23 A fine day. I boiled sap. Jacob made buckets. Father went with Martin Good to Daniel Webers'.

fr the 24 An unpleasant day. I boiled sap. They thrashed the glover seet.

sa the 25 A snowy day. We worked at home. Father went to Conostoga.

March the 26th A fine day. Father and Mother went to the Meeting at C. Eby's and to Samuel Brubakers' for their dinner.

mo the 27 A fine day. Father went to Bridgeport. We worked in the shugarbush.

tu the 28 A fine day. We worked in the shugar-bush.

we the 29 A midlen clear day. We boiled sap.

th the 30 A fine day. We worked in the shugar-bush.

fr the 31 A fine day. We worked in the shugar-bush. Father went to Bridgeport.

April the 1, 1865 A stormy day. We worked in the shugar-bush.

su the 2 A fine day. We went to the Meeting at Schneiders, Joseph L Webers and Jacob Martin wer here on visit.

mo the 3 A fine day. We did begin to plough sod.

tu the 4 A midlen fine day. Father went to Waterloo. We did plough, and boiled some sap.

we the 5 A fine day. We did plough. Father and Mother went to Waterloo, and to Andrew Groffs on visit.

April this day, the 6th A fine day. We did plough sod.

fr the 7th A rough day. We did plough. Father went to C. Eby's Meetinghouse [possibly for a semi-annual church conference].

sa the 8 A midlen fine day. I did plough. Father went up on the other place.

su the 9 A fine day. Father and Mother went to the Meeting at Conostoga, and to B. Eby's and Daniel Martins on visit.

mo the 10 A midlen fine day. We did plough.

tu the 11 A midlen fine day. We did plough. Father went to Waterloo.

we the 12 A stormy day. We did get done ploughing sod, and made some fence.

th the 13 A fine day. We fixed up fence.

fr the 14 A warm day. We went to the meeting at Martins.

sa the 15 A midlen fine day. We sowed the first spring . . .

su the 16 A fine day. We went to the Meeting at Martins. Eastern [Easter]. Father and Mother went to Daniel Martin's there was meeting in the afternoon.

April, Monday the 17th A fine day. Joseph S. Martins wer here on visit.

tu the 18 A midlen fine day. Father went to Waterloo and Berlin on business.

we the 19 A midlen clever day. We sowed some spring-wheat.

th the 20 A rainy day. We done some jours. The chimney-sweeper cleaned our chimneys. Abraham Lincoln was buried. President of U.S. he was killed by an other person (or shooted) on Friday evening, 14th of April.

fr the 21 A rainy day. We fetched home three steers from the other place; that we took up in fall.

sa the 22 A stormy day. Father and Mother went to Waterloo on business. Levi Martins wer here on visit.

su the 23 A rough day. Father and Mother went to the Meeting at Elmira ant [and] to Isaac Wengers' for dinner, and to Vental [Wendel] Bowmans' for supper.

April mo 24th 1865 A fine day. We hauled dung to the apple-trees.

tu the 25 A fine day. Jacob worked in Lexington with the team. I hauled stones from the grass-fields.

we the 26 A clever day. I rolled the grass-field. We sowed some gyps [lime].

th the 27 A fine day. We sowed some glover seet; and fixed up fence.

fr the 28 A rainy day. We sowed the first oats for this spring.

sa the 29 A rainy day. Father went to David Martins' and did get five young pigs. We fixed up fence.

su the 30 A fine day. We went to the meeting at Schneiders. Isaac Moyers wer here on visit.

May the 1, 1865 A snowy day. Father and Mother went to the Funeral of the wife of Samuel Bowman. She braught [brought] her age to 53 y[ears], 7 m[onths], 24 d[ays].

tu the 2 A fine day. We fixed up fence.

May Wednesday, the 3th A fine day. We shovelled dung on the potatoe pach. Father went off on business.

th the 4 A fine day. We sowed the peese [peas], and some oats.

fr the 5 A warm day. We draged, and plainted . . . potatoes.

sa the 6 A rainy day. We worked at home. We sold a . . . to Jesh Snyder.

su the 7 A . . . day. We went to the meeting at Conostoga . . . Peter Martins' for dinner.

mo the 8 We plainted potatoes.

tu the 9 A . . . day. We did get done planting potatoes.

we the 10 A . . . day. We sowed some oats.

th the 11 A . . . day. We sowed some oats. Jacob Martin [St. Jacob's] and Mary Frei [Crosshill] did get married.

fr the 12 A . . . day. I did plough. Jacob plought in . . . Father went to Waterloo on business.

sa the 13 A . . . day. I fetched the new buggy in Conostoga.

su the 14 A rainy day. We went to the meeting at Martins, and to Daniel Martins' for dinner. Daniel Webers wer here on visit.

mo the 15 A warm day. We did plough. Father and Mother went to David Schneiders' on visit.

tu the 16 A warm day. We did plough.

we the 17 A midlen fine day. We went to the funeral of the wife of old Abraham Weber. She brought her age to 80 years 26 days.

th the 18 A fine day. Father took two loads of sp[ring] wheat to Waterloo and did get $1.04 for springwheet and $1.09 for faul wheet.

fr the 19 A midlen clever day. We hauled some wheat to Waterloo.

sa the 20 A fine day. We washed the sheep. I did plough. John Brubakers wer here on visit.

su the 21 A rainy day. Father and Mother went to Elmira to meeting and to P Martins' for dinner. Jacob & I went to C Ebys and there wer two strange preechers from Pennsylvania named George Weber and Nisly.

mo the 22 A rainy day. They went to the meeting at Martins', Nisly and G. Weber wer there. Father took G Weber home.

tu the 23 A fine day. We sheared the sheep. Father and George Weber went over in Marcham [Markham Township, north of Toronto].

we the 24 A midlen fine day. We did plough.

th the 25 A fine day. We drove two cows to Waterloo; we sold them for $20 a head. Mother and Henry went to the meeting [Ascension Day] at Martins [Meeting House], and to Grandmother for dinner.

fr the 26 A fine day. I did drag. Jacob did plough.

sa the 27 A fine day. We worked on the folow fields.

su the 28 A fine day. We went to the meeting at Schneiders. Daniel Schneiders wer here on visit.

mo the 29 A warm day. We did get done ploughing with the folow field for the first time.

tu the 30 A fine day. We did drag.

we the 31 A fine day. I did plough. Jacob worked on the road.

June the 1 1865 A warm day. We worked on the road. Father & Mother went to the Meeting at Gressmans and there was George Weber, and they went to John, and Benjamin Weber's on visit.

fr the 2 A warm day. We worked on the road. Father went to Bridgeport.

sa the 3 A warm day. We did get done working on the road. Father went to Conostoga and did fetch me bran.

su the 4 A warm day. We went to the Meeting at Conostoga, and to Benjamin Eby's and to Michael Brubaker's, on visit.

mo the 5 A fine day, Father and Mother went to Elias Snyder's and to Joseph M. Weeks' on visit [Whit Monday].

tu the 6 A warm day. We did drag.

we the 7 A warm day. We did drag. Father went out in the pine-bush and to Waterloo on business.

June, Thursday the 8, 1865 A warm day. We did drag. Father went to Bridgeport.

fr the 9 A fine day. We did begin hauling dung.

sa the 10 A fine day. We had some rain last night. We hauled dung. Daniel Martins wer here on visit

su the 11 A fine day. We went to the meeting at Martins'.

mo the 12 A fine day. We hauled dung.

tu the 13 A fine day. We did get done hauling dung. Henry Shantzes wer here on visit.

we the 14 A fine day. We went to the meeting at Schneiders, and there wer two strange Preachers from Ohio from the name Peter Besieger and Jacob Smith and they wer both here on visit.

th 15 A fine day. They went to the meeting at Martins'. I sowed the turnips.

fr the 16 A warm day. We did plough.

sa the 17 A warm day. We did plough.

June su the 18 A warm day. We went to the Meeting at C Eby's, and to Abraham Webers' on visit.

mo the 19 A fine day. We did plough. Father and mother went to Noah Bowman's and Joseph S. Martin's on visit . . .

tu the 20 A fine day. We did plough. David Snyders wer here on visit.

we the 21 A fine day. I did plough. Father and Mother went to the funeral of old Jacob Snyder. He brought his age to 74 y[ears] 4 m[onths].

th the 22 A fine day. We worked on the sider press. Jacob went behind Berlin working on the road.

fr the 23 A fine day. We worked on the sider press. Jacob went behind Berlin working on the road.

sa the 24 A fine day. We fixed up fence. Father went to Waterloo on business.

su the 25 A fine day. We went to the Meeting at Schneiders. Ventil [Wendel] Bowmans, Michail Brubakers, Abraham Martins and Levi Martins wer here on visit.

June, mo, the 26 A fine day. We did plough.

tu the 27 A fine day. We did plough.

we the 28 A rainy day. We did plough.

th the 29 A rainy day. We did plough.

fr the 30 A fine day. We did plough.

6   Heinrich Kornelsen (1860 to 1931)

Lichtenau, Manitoba
Diary selection: 16 November to 31 December 1875
Age: 15

Heinrich Kornelsen was born in 1860 in Lichtenau, Molotschna Colony, New Russia; he was the youngest surviving child of Gerhard Kornelsen, a respected Kleine Gemeinde schoolteacher, and Maria Enns. In 1871, when Heinrich was 11, his mother died, and his father married widow Cornelia Warkentin Harms. In 1875, the Kornelsens joined the migration to Manitoba. Here they settled, with several of their married children, in the village of Lichtenau, just southwest of Steinbach. In Manitoba, Gerhard taught in the Steinbach school, while Cornelia farmed a small acreage.

Reproduced here are the first weeks of the diary that began in November 1875, just months after Heinrich's family arrived in Manitoba. The diary is clearly the work of an energetic youth, written in large, often almost illegible letters. His references to rabbits, muskrats, and wolves are matched by his sketches of horse-drawn sleighs, hunters, and a variety of animals including foxes, gophers, squirrels, rabbits, geese, woodpeckers, and bison. Then, too, from time to time Heinrich breaks into a code, combining numbers and letters to record some event, an arrangement that also appears in the diary of his older brother-in-law, schoolteacher Abram R. Friesen.

Heinrich's diary reflected the social relationships of a youth from a blended family. Jakob, 18, is a step-brother; there was also a step-sister, Sara, 16, but she is not mentioned in the diary, indicating perhaps that she was working as a servant. Heinrich did refer to the families of his older siblings. He kept in close contact with his older sister, Aganetha, and her husband, schoolteacher Abram R. Friesen of Blumenhof, some seven kilometres to the north. His most frequent social encounters were with the families of his older sisters who lived in Lichtenau: Jakob and Maria Enns, who later moved to Nebraska; Gerhard and Anna Giesbrecht. He also kept in touch with his brother Gerhard and his wife, Elisabeth Giesbrecht. Young Heinrich also travelled frequently to nearby Steinbach for supplies.

The diary hints at the fact that, as local legend has it, Heinrich was large and very strong. The sketchy diary does not, however, reflect the detailed and insightful columns he later wrote for the newspapers, the *Nordwesten,* the *Mennonitische Rundschau,* and the *Steinbach Post.* In 1886, Heinrich married Cornelia Niessen, and after Cornelia died in childbirth in 1887 he married Elisabeth Broeski. The Kornelsens farmed south of Steinbach and raised a family of eight children. By 1916, the Kornelsens had moved to Steinbach where Heinrich had a small store and worked as "a teamster, hauling freight to Winnipeg." He died at 71 in 1931.

The original diary, written in Gothic script, was preserved by G.G. Kornelsen, Heinrich's nephew, and was rediscovered by G.G. Kornelsen's grandson, Dave Schellenberg, Steinbach, Manitoba, in 1989. It was translated by Dave Schellenberg.

November H.K. 187[5]

16 12° frost, quite calm.

17 14° frost, blowing snow, Stöber S.O., 4-h-7-h- 3-9-g-2-m-2-s-2-8.

18 12° frost, quite cold, wind p.m., began constructing a sleigh, set rabbit traps.

19 15° frost, cloudy and quite calm, we washed, I helped mend, Father was in Rosenfeld. In the evening -20. During the day some snow flurries.

20 22° frost and I caught a rabbit. It was quite clear and it was bitterly cold.

21 30° frost, quite windy, I caught a rabbit. Church service was in Blumenort [10 kilometres to the north].

22 18° frost, cloudy; I trapped two rabbits and brought ... to Blumenort; I was also in Blumenhof.

23 26° frost, clear, set some [musk]rat snares. [The siblings] A[bram] F[riesens] and G[erhard] G[iesbrechts] were here in the evening ...

24 22° frost.

25 18° frost.

26 27° frost.

27 18° frost.

28 29° frost.

29 32° frost.

30 20° frost.

December H.K. 1875

1 20° frost.

2 7° frost.

3 15° frost, I helped at Giesbrechts'.

4 4° frost, caught some rabbits.

5 2° frost, by evening +2. I have already caught 13 rabbits. I had a fur cap made for me.

6 17° frost.

7 17° frost, cloudy and windy, caught a rabbit.

8 28° frost, caught a rabbit in the steel trap, I and r-4-b went to Steinbach and found a wolf.

9 14° frost; snowed in the evening. Giesbrechts and Friesens were at Ennses'.

10 24°, I caught a live rabbit. It snowed in the evening.

11 15° frost. I, [step-brother] Jakob and Araham Friesen, Steinbach, went to [inheritance] settlement. In the evening blowing snow and blustery.

12 Temperature, quite cold and windy. Ennses were at our place.

13 19° frost; the boys ... left for *Jenn Seit* [The Other Side of the River, i.e. Rosenort].

14 9° frost, A[bram] F[riesen], J[acob Enns], G[erhard] G[iesbrecht] were here. Have already caught 21 rabbits.

15 16° frost. Our people were in Blumenort, also the Ennses. Caught a rabbit. After noon, cloudy and snow.

16 25° frost, much wind and very cold, blustery; cleaned the oven.

17 26° frost, cloudy.

18 27° frost, quite cloudy.

19 15° frost, cloudy and windy. *Vaterche* [Daddy] was in Blumenort for church service.

20 15° frost. Our people were in Steinbach, brought in the rabbits.

21 14° frost; the brothers came home, quite cloudy.

22 3° frost. Gerhard was in Blumenort. I have caught 25 rabbits.

23 26° frost. Gerhard went to Blumenhof. "Glass" Friesen's [house or building] burnt down. In the evening Johann Friesen and Enns were at our place.

24 9° frost. Ennses went to Blumenhof. Christmas Eve. 28 rabbits [in] 1875.

25 26° frost. Giesbrechts were here. Ennses also ...

26 27° frost. Church [in] Steinbach.

27 25° frost. I was in Blumenhof. Clear, Schellenbergs were at our place.

28 20° frost. *Vaterche* was in Steinbach in the evening, clear.

29 30° during the day. I was in Steinbach. Cloudy. In the evening at Ennses'. I caught a rabbit.

30 13° frost. Father and Ennses went to Grünfeld.

31 21° frost, clear, last day of the year. This is the end of the old year.

7 Abraham F. Reimer (1808 to 1892)

Blumenort, Manitoba
Diary selection: 11 April to 30 September 1879
Age: 71

Abraham Reimer was born in Petershagen, Molotschna Colony, New Russia, in 1808. Although he was the son of Reverend Klaas Reimer, founder of the Mennonite Kleine Gemeinde, and Helena Friesen, Abraham did not become a villager of status. As family histories note, and as this diary indicates, Elisabeth Rempel, whom he married in the late 1830s, was responsible for generating much of the household's income, and Abraham himself had the dubious distinction of being an observer. In the mid-1860s, Abraham and Elisabeth relocated to Borosenko Colony with their married children and in 1874 came to Manitoba, where they settled in the East Reserve village of Blumenort. Here Abraham continued to be viewed as a slackard by fellow villagers. A 1958 family history notes that he "prospered neither spiritually or materially the way his father had.... On the whole he is said to have had a real interest in many areas in which others were uninformed. As is the case with so many so-called men of knowledge, he too did not always end up on a 'green twig.'" Fortunately for the student of history, Abraham Reimer wrote down his observations, leaving one of the most detailed and intricate records of daily life in the Mennonite communities during the 1870s, both in Russia and in Manitoba. There are observations of work, food, health, harvest yield, construction, church issues, and weather – four times a day by a Réaumur thermometer. Above all, however, the diary is an elaborate social record of village, kin, and congregation.

The site of his observations was Abraham and Elisabeth's Blumenort village retirement house, located on the yard of their son Deacon Abraham R. Reimer. Here the elderly Abraham recorded the details of his work in his garden and of his wife's work at the sewing machine, as she served neighbours as a seamstress and fur coat refitter. Here, too, Abraham recorded his daily interactions with the households of his married children, most of whom fared considerably better than he did. Within Blumenort were the households of three of his married children: the farmer/blacksmith Abraham, 38, and his wife, Maria Reimer, and their six children, aged 12 and under; the minister/farmer Peter, 34, his wife, Maria Plett, and two children under four years; and Margaretha, 27, her husband, Abraham Penner, and their six children, all under nine years. Abraham's observations also included the activities of his married children who lived in Steinbach, a six-kilometre walk to the south that he took regularly. Here he visited the households of another four sets of married children: well-to-do merchant son Klaas, 42 (see diary 10), his second wife, Helena Warkentin, and their 11 children, aged 21 to infancy; daughter Elisabeth, 36, her teamster husband, Peter Toews, and their seven children, aged 18 to infancy; son Johann, 31 (later a village mayor), his wife, Anna Warkentin, and their seven children, aged 9 to infancy; 29-year-old daughter Katherina and her husband, Abraham S. Friesen, a prominent miller, and their four children, aged 10 to infancy. By the end of 1879, Abraham was a grandfather to 50 children, two of whom were born in March 1879.

Abraham's life was also interwoven in the affairs of most of the fellow Blumenort villagers. He commented regularly on the farm activities of neighbours – Peter Friesen, Peter Wiebe, Peter Toews – and especially on their trips to Winnipeg. He also recorded visits and church activities in villages such as Gruenfeld (later, Kleefeld) and in Rosenort, or *Jenseit*, on the other side of the Red River. A Franco-Manitoban community that he visited was *Ponteschien*, Abraham's rendering of Point des Chesne (later, Ste. Anne des Chesne). Then, too, he referred to members of other Mennonite groups including the majority Bergthaler Mennonite group, and to non-Mennonite neighbours, the Scottish Ontario settlers, whom he simply calls the "English." Finally, Abraham's world extended to Nebraska, where the extended families of his recently deceased brother Klaas and that of his sister Margaretha lived.

Reflecting the evolving spelling of Mennonite surnames during these years, Abraham renders Dück as Dick, Koop as Kop, Thiessen as Tiessen, and Wohlgemuth as Wohlgemut. In the original diary, too, most first names are abbreviated: Helena as Hel.; Johann as Joh.; Abraham as Ab. or Abr.; Cornelius as Cornel.; Klaas as Kla.; Peter as Pet.; Elisabeth as El.

Reproduced here is the first section of the first extant diary book relating to Abraham's experiences in Canada. The diaries that have been located include those that span 1870 to 1874 and 1879 to 1889. The diary was written in a tiny and difficult-to-read Gothic handwriting, in an 11-by-8 1/2-inch book with no margins. It was preserved by the Reimer family and eventually passed into the hands of Abraham's great-grandson, Ernie Goossen, a Steinbach lawyer. Goossen's partner, Delbert Plett, identified the diary as belonging to Abraham Reimer. The diary was initially translated by Ben Hoeppner of Winnipeg. The original diary is deposited in the Evangelical Mennonite Conference Archives in Steinbach, Manitoba. For more information on Abraham Reimer, see: John C. Reimer, et al., *Familienregister der Nachkommen von Klaas und Helena Reimer mit Biographien der ersten drei Generationen* (Winnipeg, MB: 1958); Royden Loewen, *Blumenort: A Mennonite Community in Transition, 1874-1983* (Blumenort, MB: 183.)

April 1879

11 Fri. +4, day +14, *Vesper* +16, evening +10. It was quite calm, clear. The church service was at the old Töwses'. Abraham Löwen from Grünfeld preached and Peter Töwses from Steinbach came over yesterday in the morning and for the night he was at Abraham Reimers'. Abraham Friesens from Steinbach attended Johan Friesens' auction sale in the afternoon. They stayed overnight. *Vesper* they had at our place.

12 Sat. +6, day +10, lunch +8, *Vesper* +10, night +5 1/2. It rained very much during the night. Today Mrs. Abraham Reimer dug out parsnip and served it for lunch. Also this week, the English have seeded about 10 acres of wheat and ploughed. Also some of the Bergthalers have seeded wheat. Also, here, they nearly finished putting up the school roof. And today I was at Abraham Penners'.

13 Sun. +2, day +6, *Vesper* +6, evening +5. It was quite calm and very cloudy. The church service was in Grünfeld and in the morning we were at Abraham Reimers'. Peter Friesen came down there too with his young child and he was there also for lunch. In the afternoon he was also at our place with Margaret. And Mrs. Abraham Penner, was mostly sick this week, with an aching throat. Her Klaas is often somewhat sick also.

14 Mon. +2, and it had frozen a little, day +7, at *Vesper* +10, at night +3. East wind. Some clouds. The church service was in Steinbach. Abraham Löwen of Grünfeld preached. Abraham Reimers and Peter Reimers also walked there and Johan Kops also drove to Steinbach, but they did not drive 1/2 mile and they had to turn around for they nearly got stuck in the mud. And today we also walked to Abraham Penners' and [stayed] for *Vesper*. And I walked to visit the school a little.

15 Tues. +2, day +8, *Vesper* +6, evening +4. Northeast wind, some clouds. I walked to the young Cornelius Friesens' and there bought a writing book for 20 cents and also a fountain pen. And I was also at Abraham Friesens' and I was also at Peter Friesens' and had a look at the new barn. I was also at Abraham Penners' and meanwhile he was at Friesens'... And yesterday we had parsnip for lunch.

16 Wed. -2, day 0, *Vesper* +14, evening +6. It was quite calm and clear. The old Pletts were at our place for *Vesper*. And today at about 2 o'clock Wohlgemut and I walked to Steinbach and were at Abraham Töws' for *Vesper* and I also spent the night there. And here Peter Töws and 2 others plowed in the garden and in Steinbach they are all working in the garden. And from here, yesterday, Abraham Friesens drove to Winnipeg with Johan Friesens.

17 Thur. -1, day +13, *Vesper* +18, evening +7. South wind, some clouds. Sawed a little wood and then at 11 o'clock I walked to Peter Töwses' and I was there for lunch. And at 2:30 I walked to Johan Reimers' and at 7 p.m. I walked to Klaas Reimers' and stayed there overnight. Johan Wiebe, Steinbach, began to sow wheat and harrow [it in]. And here 4 or 5 have begun to plough; David Tiessen came along home yesterday.

18 Fri. -1/2, day +10, *Vesper* +14, evening +4. West wind, very cloudy, at places it rained a little. And I walked early in morning from Steinbach and came back around 11:30. At 5 early this morning I walked to [see] David Tiessens as they had arrived from *Jenseit*. The old Peter Barkmans from Steinbach came home this week Tuesday from the river, from Rosenort.

19 Sat. -1, day +8, *Vesper* +16, evening +6. Calm and cloudy. In the afternoon yesterday I was at Abraham Penners'. Yesterday I bought at Klaas Reimers' 2 pounds [white?] and 1 pound [blue thread?] and coffee for 25 cents a pound, in all 1 dollar. And I borrowed the little book. And this afternoon Johan Friesen from here and Abraham Friesen from Steinbach, came home via our place.

20 Sun. +4, day +16, *Vesper* +9, evening +10. Quite still, clear. Also, already on Easter Monday, Mrs. Abraham Reimer gave us 6 eggs and Mrs. Abraham Penner also wanted to give us 6 eggs. Today Johan Reimers were here with Johan Wiebe, Steinbach, for *Vesper* and Klaas Reimers' Abraham was here. And the young Peter Töwses from here were also at our place for *Vesper* and Johan Kops were also at our place and Abraham Penners were here for *Vesper*. Abraham Reimer ploughed . . .

21 Mon. +5, day +18, *Vesper* +21, evening +12. It was quite calm and cloudy. And the day before yesterday after *Vesper* I was in Blumenhof at Abraham Friesens' and I brought them a new peak cap. And at about 6 I left and got home at 9 o'clock and there was very much mud and water as there has been much snow this winter: from 7 inches to a foot deep snow; on the road from 1 to 1 and 1/2 feet, also to 2 feet; on the slopes 3 feet; by the fences till about 3 feet; in the forest up to 8 feet.

22 Tues. +6, day +10, *Vesper* +10, evening +8. Northeast breeze and in the morning it rained off and on at places. Here they were ploughing last Friday and Saturday. Also last week, about Thursday, they all hauled straw onto the street. And last week, too, about Wednesday, the big cattle were driven onto the pasture. And in Steinbach, too. As of last week the snow has almost disappeared and in 5 days the snow will be gone in the fields. Two weeks ago already the ice at the top of the wells was gone.

23 Wed. +6, day +8, *Vesper* +13 1/2, evening +10. Some lightning, very cloudy. Yesterday I was at Abraham Penners', and yesterday morning my wife was at Abraham Penners' and yesterday evening my wife was at Heinrich Reimers'. She gradually improves in health and strength. I was yesterday at Peter Reimers'. The young Mrs. Johan Dick from Grünfeld last week suffered much pain for 3 days and 3 nights until she had given birth with the assistance of Dr. Schwartz.

24 Thur. +7, day +11, *Vesper* +15, evening +8. Was quite calm with some clouds in the evening and rain during the night and much wind. I bought from Klaas Friesen, Steinbach, 14 lbs. of meat from a large calf and borrowed meat. Yesterday at Klaas Reimers' a young cow calved, she had a female. And I was at Abraham Penners', and yesterday [I was] at Peter Reimers'.

25 Fri. +6, day +10, *Vesper* +11, night +8. East wind, very cloudy, rainy. Yesterday I was at Schoolteacher Cornelius Friesen's place and bought from him a glass of ink. And I was also at Abraham Friesens' and also at Abraham Penners' and she was a little better again. But it varies; one day she is so sick that mostly she has to lie down, and then from 1 to 2 days she is better, although very weak. And I sawed lumber all day Tuesday.

26 Sat. +4, day +6, *Vesper* +6, evening +1 1/2. North wind, rained somewhat, and it snowed so that no one was ploughing. And I have in 3 days torn apart an old coat and an old fur coat. And my wife remade an old coat this week for Heinrich Reimer and also made 13 caps. And in the evening the young Peter Töws came here. And at 9 p.m. my wife had to go to Peter Reimers' as their Abraham was sick and died at 2:30.

27 Sun. +1/2, day +4, *Vesper* +8, evening +1 1/2. During the night it stormed and the wind was a north wind. The church service was at the old Peter Penners' where *Ältester* Peter Töws preached and for 1 1/2 hours there was Brotherhood [meeting] concerning Johan Friesen's carrying about which no one is to be allowed in the church and Peter Töws, Steinbach, was also there. Abraham Friesens were at Abraham Penners' for lunch and for *Vesper* they got a cat from Peter Reimers'. And we were at Abraham Penners' after *Vesper*.

28 Mon. +8, day +6, *Vesper* +7, evening +2 1/2. Rain and calm, yet with dark clouds. In the morning a little ploughing was done. Today Abraham Penner drove to Heuboden to [procure] a maid but he could [not] have her as they have moved to Pembina and so he got Peter Töws' Katrina for 2 weeks. And this afternoon the old Peter Töws from here drove to Winnipeg, but they came back, having travelled as far as Mrs. Heinrich Wiebe's place. And Klaas Reimer left today for Winnipeg.

29 Tues. +1, day +6, *Vesper* +12, evening +6. North wind and cloudy. Also they came back this afternoon. Funeral at Peter Reimers' as their son Abraham was buried, having reached an age of 2 weeks and 2 days. And they had invited 15 families, but only 9 families came. From Steinbach only Peter Töws and his Peter came by foot. They were here for lunch. And Aron Penner from Blumenhof and Peter Penners' boys returned from Winnipeg after *Vesper*. And Abraham Penner sold a pair of oxen in Winnipeg for $125.

30 Wed. +4, day +14, *Vesper* +16, evening +10. Quite still and calm. Last week, Saturday, Abraham Penners' castrated 2 weanlings, both of them and 1 boar ... On Sunday evening we were at Peter Töwses' to visit and yesterday I was at Abraham Penners'. Yesterday morning at 6, Peter Töws drove to Winnipeg with eggs and chickens. And yesterday I was at Abraham Penners' in the morning ...

May 1879

1 Thur. +5, day +15, *Vesper* +18, evening +10. Quite calm and clear. They all began to plough in the high places, but the low places are too wet. I rolled up 1 spool of wool and also white thread. And mine [my wife] made peak caps and tore up an old coat of Peter Dick. And I was at Abraham Penners'; they have not yet sown any grain ... This week I made 2 small flower [boxes?] for Mrs. Abraham Penner and Mrs. Abraham Friesen.

2 Fri. +4, day +20, *Vesper* +22, evening +14. Was somewhat cloudy, quite calm. I began to walk to Steinbach at 9 a.m. and arrived at about 11:30 at Abraham Friesens'. There Abraham Friesen was seeding for Klaas Reimer . . . and he began yesterday afternoon with the fence . . . and for *Vesper* I was at Abraham Friesens' and for night I walked to Klaas Reimers'. . .

3 Sat. +6, day +10, *Vesper* +10, evening +4. Was overcast during the night and in the morning and afternoon it became rainy, north wind. I was at Johan Reimers' for lunch and at Peter Töwses' for *Vesper* and for night. And for [supper] I was at Abraham Friesens' and brought them 2 [cotton bed coverings?] and paper. I left at about 3 p.m. and came home at about 6. My wife was at Abraham Penners' and I walked there too.

4 Sun. +2, day +14, *Vesper* +16, evening +2. It had rained during the night; there was a great north wind and during the day it was very dark and rained steadily. There was church service in Grünfeld, although no one from [our] village was there and for lunch I was at Abraham Friesens'; left there at 3 for home . . . And there was a strong wind, and [so] I got home at 6 o'clock, walked to Abraham Penners' [and found] my wife there too.

5 Mon. +1, it had rained somewhat, day +5, *Vesper* +7, evening 5. North wind, and dark and cloudy. Two weeks ago Peter Töws, Steinbach, butchered a pig which yielded 2 1/2 pails lard. Peter Töwses, Steinbach, have as yet not seeded anything. Several have already planted small vegetables in the gardens, also beans and cucumbers. For 3 days already Franz Krökers have planted in the garden.

6 Tues. 0 with hoarfrost, day +10, *Vesper* +12, evening +5. Quite calm, cloudy. I tore up the big fur coat of Peter Dick, Grünfeld, and in the afternoon we ploughed the garden and I dug in the garden. Here, already yesterday Mrs. Abraham Reimer planted all her flowers in the garden and [so too have] others in the village. And in Steinbach, Mrs. Abraham Friesen has planted a good part of her flowers and our others in Steinbach have all planted their flowers.

7 Wed. -1, a hard frost during night, day +10, *Vesper* +15, evening +8. I planted turnips in the garden. And today I was at Abraham Reimers' and they brought for us [from Point des Chesne] about 100 and about 15 pounds of wheat flour which cost 2 1/2 cents a pound. This Johan Friesen brought [to our place]. And today at Abraham Reimers' a sow gave birth and had a litter of 6. Mrs. Abraham Penner has been sick half of the time.

8 Thur. +5, day +12 1/2, *Vesper* +9, evening +8. Cloudy, rain. Also during the night the little mare had a colt and on Sunday Peter Reimers drove alone to Johan Pletts' in Blumenhof. The old Johan Warkentin, Blumenhof, was here (which has not happened now for half a year) and he brought a plough share [to Abraham Reimer for sharpening].

9 Fri. +2, day +16, *Vesper* +20, evening +12. Was quite calm and some clouds. I prepared our garden; also Mrs. Peter Reimer walked to Blumenhof in the afternoon and I dug in the garden. My wife made the big fur coat for Mrs. Peter Dick in Grünfeld. On the last of April the young Peter Penner [recently arrived from Kansas] had his farmstead written over in Winnipeg.

10 Sat. +12, day +16, *Vesper* +20, evening +11 1/2. Was sunny, quite calm. I dug in the garden and made 3 ridges . . . this week in 3 1/2 days. During the night it rained with lightning and thunder and heavy wind. And after lunch today I was at Johan Kops and returned the [band?]; they have finished planting their potatoes 3 days ago and transplanted all their [house-begun flowers?].

11 Sun. +12, day +20, *Vesper* +22, evening +19. Quite calm, somewhat overcast. The church service was in Steinbach, Heinrich Reimer preached . . . Peter Reimers, both, went and we went too, and were for *Vesper* at Abraham Penners'. Also [after one of their cows] calved and had a bull, the cow did not have any milk for 8 weeks . . .

12 Mon. +14, day +17, *Vesper* +17, evening +9. There was north wind and [it was] cloudy. In this week I planted 3 long [rows, or is it turnips, in the garden?], and in the previous week on Saturday I planted about 5 kinds of lettuce, onions, parsnip and cabbage and today I dug further in the garden. And mine [my wife] washed till noon: [hand-wash?], linen and clothes. Also Abraham Reimers' [cows] and most of the villagers' [cows] were let onto the pasture.

13 Tues. +6, day 14, *Vesper* +15 1/2, evening +8. Was clear and quite calm. At 7 a.m. my wife was taken to Johan Reimers', Steinbach, by Abraham Friesen with Johan Reimers' horses and at 2:30 a baby daughter appeared. She was named Helena. From before noon until 8 p.m. she was critically sick, so that it seemed she would die.

14 Wed. +2, day +16, *Vesper* +9, evening 10. Was clear and quite calm, clouds. Then my wife came home at 2 p.m.; Peter Töws from Steinbach brought her [home]. Things with Mrs. Johan Reimer's condition have stabilized. Yesterday I had breakfast and lunch at Abraham Reimers' and for *Vesper* at Peter Reimers'. My wife was at Friesens' for the night.

15 Thur. +8, day +22, *Vesper* +22 1/2, evening +12. There was south wind, clear. Yesterday after lunch I was at Abraham Penners' and also at Abraham Reimers' for breakfast. Lunch I had at Peter Reimers'. Also today Peter Reimer finished the ploughing and seeding. Abraham Reimer already planted potatoes at the end of April.

16 Fri. +12, day +22, *Vesper* +26, evening +10. Was cloudy and quite calm. I worked in the garden. My wife was in the morning, yesterday, at Abraham Penners'. Abraham Reimer finished his ploughing today. He seeded 30 acres of wheat, 7 acres of barley and 14 acres of oats.

17 Sat. +10, day +10, *Vesper* +15, evening +10. Was clear and quite calm. Johan Kop finished ploughing today. This week they have all seeded their beans. Yesterday and today I received 2 baskets full of parsnips from Abraham Penner, and I dug out 2 baskets full from our own garden.

18 Sun. +10, day +16, *Vesper* +19, evening +10. And it rained steadily and was quite calm. The church service was in Grünfeld. The work with the young people was begun. Peter Reimers went to Blumenhof. Peter Reimers and Abraham Penners were here for a while this morning. They wanted to come here in the afternoon, but they went to the young Peter Penners'.

19 Mon. +8, day +8, *Vesper* +12, evening +8. Rain. So I did not do any digging, nor was there any ploughing done. At Abraham Penners' they slaughtered a hog. It yielded 2 inches of fat and a pailful of lard. Abraham Reimers and the old Peter Penners helped. But from our place no one was there.

20 Tues. +16, day +16, *Vesper* +19, evening +10. Was very cloudy, quite calm. I did some digging. In the afternoon I was at Abraham Penners' and in the afternoon Abraham Penner went to Steinbach, as did Peter Reimer. These went to Johan Reimers. At 2:30 Johan Reimers from Steinbach came here to get my wife, as she is still in bed. Abraham Penners went home at 8 o'clock ...

21 Wed. +10, day +16, *Vesper* +20, evening +12. Was cloudy, calm. Rain in the south ... The young Jacob Töwses from the other side of Grünfeld came. Peter Töwses and Peter Dicks from Grünfeld were here after *Vesper* and he wanted to pick up his fur and his coats and his pants. My wife has [had trouble with our] cow as she did not want to stand for milking. Abraham Reimer repaired the bridge in Grünfeld this week.

22 Thur. Ascension Day: +12, day +18, *Vesper* +20, evening +15. There was south wind, cloudy and raining. At the old Penners' the church service took place. *Ältester* Töws from Grünfeld spoke. Afterwards Brotherhood with regard to the young people. There were 10 sons and 3 daughters and also about Johan Friesen and the young Peter Penner, that they went against the advice of the preachers and the church in writing over their farmsteads in Winnipeg.

23 Fri. +14, day +20, *Vesper* +16, evening +14. During the night it has rained with lightning and there was also thunder and produced a south wind. Yesterday morning Klaas Reimer and Peter Töws and their Lisbet from Steinbach and in the afternoon Abraham Dicks from Grünfeld and old Kornelsens from Eigengrund and Cornelius Töws from Grünfeld and Johan Ens from Grünfeld and Heinrich Brandt from Steinbach were here.

24 Sat. +12, day 20, *Vesper* +18, evening +12. Today it rained in the morning and afternoon it was nice and clear. Wind north. Yesterday and today I dug 2 plots behind the smith shop. Today I finished the digging for the year. I unrolled 2 balls of yarn. I was at Abraham Penners'. Yesterday after lunch Abraham Töwses slaughtered a hog and it [yielded] 5 pails of lard.

25 Sun. +10, day +16, *Vesper* +16, about 16, evening +10. Was cloudy, quite calm. The church service was in Grünfeld. Heinrich Reimer left already yesterday after lunch. The meat from Abraham Friesen's pig (the first that is butchered) was in total 370 pounds heavy. He sold 100 pounds of lard for $15.00 and 2 cents; and shingles for 6 dollars, at 10 cents a pound. And I walked at 1:30 p.m. to Steinbach and was for *Vesper* at Johan Reimers'.

26 Mon. +8, day +18, *Vesper* +19, evening +9. Quite calm. So, I was at Abraham Friesens' overnight and at Peter Töwses' for lunch and for *Vesper* at Klaas Reimers' and learned that since Thursday Mrs. Johan Reimer has been improving. Every day she gets up a little but is not sitting in bed. I and Cornelius Friesen left at 6:30 from Steinbach and got home at 9. Johan Kornelsen was here in the evening.

27 Tues. +10 degree, day +17 1/2, *Vesper* +20, evening +12. Quite calm, although very cloudy. At 7 a.m. yesterday Johan Friesens moved to Nebraska. They left Winnipeg, but first they went to *Jenseit* from Winnipeg and wanted to stay there for a time and then go to Nebraska. Last Thursday Johan Friesen apparently was here for the last time. Yesterday afternoon Abraham Reimer went to Tannenau.

28 Wed. +12, day +24, *Vesper* +23, evening +16. Quite calm although very cloudy. Had hard thunderstorm with rain for a better part of the night, so that the ditches were filled with water. And [from] the day before yesterday, since Monday 3 days, the cow, Katrina, has been lying down because of sore legs. Monday Peter Reimer had smith work done for over $10.00. Yesterday I was at Peter Reimers'. He has finished the ploughing and the seeding. And yesterday Abraham had 2000 board feet of lumber cut in Steinbach. Abraham Friesen has in 2 days nearly finished his house.

29 Thur. +15, day +19, *Vesper* +21, evening +13. Rain and lightning during the night all over the place, and there was also thunder. And all the driving was in water. Abraham Reimers' Abraham and Peter Töws built a fence around the garden. Peter Reimers went to Tannenau, also Abraham Penner was in Tannenau. And Cornelius Penner, the old Penner and I split firewood yesterday and on Tuesday, as it was lying in water.

30 Fri. +10, day +10, *Vesper* +6, evening +4. Before noon very cloudy, in the afternoon it rained often and there was a cool north wind. Abraham Reimer's Abraham castrated our pigs, both of them, and placed the pigs in the small pen. Also Mrs. Abraham Penner was here today, by foot, and she was here for lunch and for *Vesper*. Peter Töws finished his ploughing and seeding today.

31 Sat. +4, day +8, *Vesper* +12, evening +4. Quite calm. I was today at Abraham Penners' and I was also at Peter Reimers' and in the evening I was also at Abraham Penners'. There I bought 6 *Borgen Wier Halpins* [?] and my wife was at Abraham Penners since Sunday. And the day before yesterday, on Thursday, I made the first batch of butter from our cow and there was 10 pounds of butter from 10 days. And yesterday, at about *Vesper* time, water rose in the creek ...

June 1879

1 Sun, Pentecost +1 with hoarfrost, quite clear, south breeze; day +18, *Vesper* +20, evening +10. Church service in Steinbach; Heinrich Reimer preached. Brotherhood with regard to the young people: 9 sons and 3 daughters and I and my wife went along with Abraham Reimers on horses and we left at 7:30 and were at Klaas Reimers' for lunch and at Johan Reimers for *Vesper* and left at 6 for home. Mrs. Johan Reimer is already quite healthy.

2 Mon. 7, day +19, *Vesper* +23, evening +15. It was cloudy, southeast wind. There was church service in Grünfeld. Yesterday at the Brotherhood [meeting] there was a great discussion about [remaining separate?]. Klaas Reimers were at Peter Reimers' for lunch and for *Vesper* at Peter Töwses' and after *Vesper* both were at our place. Last week, on Tuesday, the other sow at Abraham Reimers gave birth and 8 piglets were born, 7 lived. And last week, Saturday, we bought 1 weanling from Abraham Reimer.

3 Tues. +14, day 24, *Vesper* +26 1/2, evening +16. Quite calm; cloudy, and then it was rainy. The piglets, 3 weeks and 3 days old, cost $1.00 a piece. Also today we cleared out an entire room and washed the floor and then the entire room was whitewashed with lime, as well as in the windows. Mrs. Abraham Reimer helped till about *Vesper*, and Mrs. Peter Reimer and my wife helped and nearly got sick. I went after *Vesper* to Abraham Penners'.

4 Wed. +10, day +12, *Vesper* +15 1/2, evening +10 1/2. Cloudy and quite calm. Abraham Reimer got today 3 loads of *dieben*[?] from Steinbach in about 3 1/2 hours. Yesterday Johan Reimer, Steinbach, was here for lunch and then went to pick up his maid from Blumenhof. In the afternoon today my wife walked over to Abraham Penners', and I was at Peter Reimers' for *Vesper*, who cut 2 pigs for me and after lunch they walked to Blumenhof.

5 Thur. +8, day +12, *Vesper* +14, evening +7. There was a north wind, cloudy. And at Abraham's a sow littered; it had 8 piglets; 1 was dead. Also Cornelius Penner left here by foot Monday with Tiessen's David to the other side to see his parents. David has hired himself out at the old David Klassens'. Peter Reimer began yesterday to paper our living room.

6 Fri. It was about 2:30 and it began to rain; day +16, *Vesper* +20, evening 12. Cloudy, south wind. Yesterday Abraham Reimer built a bake oven on our yard and repaired for me an old hand block. Today I was sawing firewood. After lunch I helped Abraham Penner mangle with Lisbet and Maria Töws near Johan Kops'. Today Abraham Reimer built a fence from the house to the street.

7 Sat. +20, day +20, *Vesper* +24, evening +7 1/2. Quite calm, cloudy. Today Abraham Reimer finished completely the fence from the house door as far as the street. Mine [wife] was sick this week, so that she hardly could be up. I made an outhouse at the Peter Töws boundary. Peter Töwses came here from Steinbach at about 5:30 and for the night they walked to Abraham Reimers' and on Sunday Katrina went home.

8 Sun. +16, day +22, *Vesper* +27, evening +18. Was cloudy in the evening, overcast, but became rainy and quite calm. The church service was at the old Penners' and *Ältester* Töws preached the articles. Klaas Reimers were at Abraham Reimers' for lunch and Peter Töwses were at Peter Reimers' and Abraham Friesens at Peter Reimers'. For *Vesper* Abraham Friesens and Peter Töwses were at Abraham Penners.

9 Mon. +15, day +21, *Vesper* +25, evening +15. Quite calm, rainy with lightning. Last week it was thundering. Our cow ran with the bull. Yesterday the old Heinrich Reimers and Johan Dicks from Grünfeld were at Abraham Reimers' for *Vesper*. They also went to Blumenhof and after *Vesper* Peter Töwses and Abraham Friesens drove here. After lunch the old Reimers and Johan Dicks left for home.

10 Tues. +16, day +16, *Vesper* +20, evening +14. North wind and heavy rain, so that the ditches filled with water. In the afternoon yesterday at 2 p.m. Abraham

Reimer and Johan Dick and Peter Töws and Heinrich Reimer, all with oats, barley, potatoes, eggs and roosters left for Winnipeg, but they had not gone half way when they became stuck in water and they returned home today this morning at 10:30, completely rained wet, having mostly walked.

11 Wed. +14, day +19, *Vesper* +22, evening +16. Quite calm, cloudy. Abraham Reimer went to Tannenau to Penner, where he bought one piece of cotton batting which cost 12 cents and one piece cotton calico which cost 7 cents a yard and 5 kinds of nails, all about 115 pounds and came home about at 9 o'clock. And our things, planted about 5 weeks ago in early May, have all surfaced and so in May, 14 days ago, our potatoes have surfaced. Also since Pentecost the beans have surfaced.

12 Thur. +16, day, *Vesper*, evening +25 and evening +18. Quite calm, very cloudy, rain in several places. Peter Reimer shingled the backside of his dwelling house. In the afternoon I began making a small cradle for Peter Töwses in Steinbach. Abraham Reimer planted on the 3rd of June some potatoes in the garden near the creek. Abraham Penner has done carpentry work 4 days – Monday to Thursday – in Steinbach for Klaas Reimer.

13 Fri. +18, day +20, *Vesper* +16 1/2, evening +16. Cloudy in the morning; rain in the afternoon and almost through the night. In the morning I worked on the cradle. Peter Reimer brought in the morning the work bench into the old barn. Abraham Reimer came home in the morning. I and my wife were at Abraham Penners' Monday for lunch.

14 Sat. +14, day +14, *Vesper* +up to 16, evening +14. Quite calm and rainy from early morning until lunch, at times hard, so that water came up at many places to the knees and till the belly ... The people dug almost all day on the land throughout the village, so much so that they got completely wet.

15 Sun. +14, day +20, *Vesper* +22, evening +16. Quite calm, rain at places. The church service in Grünfeld, but no one came because of the high water. Yesterday the water in the creek rose unto the bridge and to the fence in the garden. Cornelius, the son of Cornelius Töwses from Grünfeld, was here, and for *Vesper* Heinrich Reimers were visiting. They had walked. Abraham Penners were here for *Vesper*, also on foot. It was very muddy.

16 Mon. 15, day +21, *Vesper* +25, evening +15. South wind with clouds. After *Vesper* I was at Abraham Penners'. Peter Töws from Steinbach was there for *Vesper*. He had walked in deep water. He went to Abraham Penners' for supper. For night he was at our place. And in the village many are digging and repairing the bridge, as they were damaged and had floated away.

17 Tues. +16, day +24, *Vesper* +24, evening +16. South wind with clouds, during the night lightning. Peter Töws was here for breakfast and walked home at about 9:30. And this week Abraham Penner could not lift. I sawed firewood in the afternoon. The old Cornelius Pletts from Blumenhof at Johan Kops' and for the night at our place. Yesterday Peter Reimer finished covering [shingling] his house. The old Pletts on the way home got stuck with the horses in the swamp at Cornelius Friesens' and they had to travel with oxen.

18 Wed. +15, day +20, *Vesper* +23, evening +17. South wind, during the day very cloudy, and before *Vesper* it rained. June 12 I made 4 1/2 pounds of butter. Peter Reimer made me a churn June 13. It cost $1.30. Yesterday, Cornelius Töws from Grünfeld brought Mrs. David Tiessen from the other side [of the river] to Grünfeld, as she is nearly well. My wife was in the afternoon at Abraham Penners'. I was splitting firewood.

19 Thur. +17, day +21, *Vesper* +23, evening +17. South wind and a great thunderstorm. Also yesterday, Sawatzky from Bergthal was here and got 3 piglets from Abraham Penners' and 3 from Peter Reimers'. He paid $1 a piece. Abraham Reimer began sawing for his house. Peter, son of Klaas Reimers from Steinbach, was here for lunch and got some clothes. On June 16 my wife [reseeded?] and this week beans.

20 Fri. +16, day +20, *Vesper* +20, evening +14. Cloudy and rain. Abraham Peter Reimer began this morning to cover his house. The young Peter Töws worked all day at Peter Reimers' until the evening. I was at Abraham Penners' in the morning. He has spent 2 days this week [gathering?] and tomorrow he is ploughing at the English people and I worked on the small cradle in the barn and Peter Reimers' maid has spent 3 weeks plastering on the barn and the house . . .

21 Sat. +11, day +17, *Vesper* +18, evening +8. North wind, cloudy with rain at various places. So then I made a half . . . Abraham Reimer completed his house completely by *Vesper* time. And Cornelius Töws, Grünfeld [here] . . . [they] left at 6 o'clock in the evening, and because of water and mud . . . they drove for 5 hours. And Mrs. David Tiessen has become completely well . . .

22 Sun. +19, day . . . , *Vesper* +26 1/2, evening +19. Quite calm and with some rain; cloudy in the morning, in the afternoon quite clear . . . Abraham Reimer and Heinrich Reimer, Steinbach, came home at . . . o'clock . . . *Altester* Töws presented the articles and in the afternoon Mrs. Peter Reimer walked to Blumenhof . . . Also Mrs. Abraham Penner came in the afternoon and she was also at Peter Töws'.

23 Mon. +17 . . . , day +13, *Vesper* +21, evening +15. It began to rain at 7 and rained very hard for half an hour so that the foot paths were filled with water. And it was so stormy with a north [wind] that it seemed that the houses would collapse. At Abraham Penners' the windows rattled so much in the room that 2 window panes broke. Also, since the 15th of June completely ripe strawberries have been eaten, and I have eaten strawberries since the 16th of June. And in the morning I made butter and there were about 4 pounds of butter from 4 days.

24 Tues. +14, day +16, *Vesper* +16, evening +12. Quite calm. Heavy rain during the night. Much lightning. I was splitting firewood. Today I was at Abraham Penners'. The young Mrs. Peter Töws has been lying sick in bed for 5 days and the old Mrs. Töws has been sick 3 days. I was at Peter Töwses'. The old Mrs. Töws could sit up again. Yesterday my wife was there also.

25 Wed. +11, day +16, *Vesper* +20, evening +14. North wind, cloudy and rain. I split firewood. My wife was at Abraham Penners' in the morning. I worked on the cradle. At the end of village much work was done on the road about water, [especially] at the end of the village by the young Peter Penners' place where 4 loads of straw were taken from the farmyards and placed on the street; and here at the old Cornelius Friesens' 2 loads of straw and 1 load of straw on the street.

26 Thur. +13, day +15, *Vesper* +17, evening +12. There was a north wind, cloudy, with a little rain. In the afternoon I worked on the small cradle and repaired the gate by the smithy. On the road, or the street, at Peter Penners', 70 or 100 loads of straw were dumped and at the old Cornelius Friesens' 50 loads of straw, or 70 loads of straw, were hauled and driven into the mud.

27 Fri. +12, day +19, *Vesper* +20, evening +14. Quite calm, cloudy. The last ice in the bottom of the well melted Monday 8 a.m. On Monday Peter Reimer had gone to *Ponteschien*, but he had not gone even a half a mile and he turned around, he was completely wet. But he left again in an hour and he came home at 7 in the evening. I put the small cradle together at Peter Reimers'.

28 Sat. 10, day +20, *Vesper* +22, evening +14. Quite calm, cloudy, otherwise clear. In the morning I split firewood. In the afternoon at Abraham Reimers' I worked on his [old saddle?]. On Monday P. Töws made a ditch across the street and a bridge and closed the ditch. Today they made the ditch along the whole village. Peter Töws and Johan Kop dug in the fence on the street.

29 Sun. +14, day +24, *Vesper* +26, evening +20. South wind. The church service was in Grünfeld and there was also Brotherhood. There were not many because of the rain. On Pentecost in June, a son was born at Juhnkes'. Last week Monday a big piece of the bridge in front of Mrs. Tiessen's was broken off, so that people could not pass over it.

30 Mon. +10, day +23, *Vesper* +25, evening +19. South wind, rainy. Very heavy thundering. A young women from Bergthal Colony was struck dead [from lightning]. The old Cornelius Plett from Blumenhof came here in the morning at 7:30 and got my wife to the young Cornelius Pletts'. My wife was there the entire day. She stayed there for the night and a son arrived during the night.

July 1879

1 Tues. +17, day +16, *Vesper* +19, evening +16. South wind, rain. The old Cornelius Plett brought my wife home at 6:30 and with her it had been a serious condition and during the night it had been serious. For an hour she [the mother] had been very sick. My wife slept little during the night and today during the day [she was] tired and irksome. Yesterday afternoon I was at Abraham Penners' and in Steinbach at Peter Töws' they completed the house.

2 Wed. +14, day +22, *Vesper* +24, evening +16. Quite calm, cloudy. The young Mrs. Töws was here last week Saturday. Yesterday Aron Penner brought Mrs. Abraham Penner to Blumenhof for the night. Abraham Penner is doing carpentry there. Today Mrs. Penner walked down here and had *Vesper* here and after *Vesper* Abraham Penner and the old Peter Töws went to Steinbach for the night and were at Heinrich Reimers' and bought 5 loads of straw . . .

3 Thur. +15, day +21, *Vesper* +23, evening +15. Quite calm, very cloudy, rainy. Also on Tuesday afternoon Heinrich Reimer's maid walked away from the employer Heinrich Reimer ... and Peter Reimer made this week the window frames in both rooms. In the afternoon I worked on the small cradle. Today Abraham Penner helped Peter Töws with the shutters for the house.

4 Fri. +16, day +20, *Vesper* +22, evening +14. Quite calm, cloudy, rain towards evening. In the morning I was at Abraham Penners' and at *Vesper* I worked again on the small cradle. In the afternoon I split firewood. In the morning I was at Peter Friesens' and at the young Cornelius Friesens'. Abraham Penner made new undergirdings in the barn at the old Peter Penners'.

5 Sat. +16, day +22, *Vesper* +26, evening +22. Quite calm, rain during the night, clouds in the morning. I split firewood. In the afternoon until *Vesper* I finished the cradle for Peter Töwses' in Steinbach. Abraham Penner was sick for 2 weeks. This week he had difficulty walking. He developed a growth on his side, so that he could hardly sit.

6 Sun. +16 1/2, day +25 1/2, *Vesper* +24 and in that region. The church service was at the old Peter Penners'. No one from Grünfeld was there and from Steinbach was only Johan Reimer. He was there on horseback, and his horse had to walk because of the rain during the night. Our bridge was nearly under water and almost to the railings of the fence by the creek and at the most it would come up to the [chest?].

7 Mon. +17, day +18, *Vesper* +21, evening +15. There was a westerly wind and quite sunny. Johan Reimer at Abraham Penners' for lunch. We had no visitors and only Abraham, son of Klaas Reimers, was here. Heinrich Reimer preached yesterday. Today we braced our beans and yesterday afternoon there was water. I made the latch on the smith shop door and there was much to be hammered.

8 Tues. +14, day +14, *Vesper* +26, evening +16. Wind is west, quite sunny. On Sunday evening it was +22. For lunch I was at Peter Reimers'. He patched the chimney, and the small room and the kitchen he made into one room, and changed the wall in the rear part of the house. The young Peter Töws was very sick on Sunday.

9 Wed. +16, day +24, *Vesper* +26, evening +20. Clear and calm. I sawed firewood. After *Vesper* I was at Abraham Penners'. Yesterday Abraham Reimer began to lay the *Beinsaumen*[?] because *erauste hinoch lingen*[?]. And Mrs. Abraham Penner and Mrs. David Tiessen were very sick in the morning, so that it seemed they might die. Abraham Penner engaged in carpentry and completed Mrs. Heinrich Wiebe's barn.

10 Thur. +17, day +26, *Vesper* +28, evening +21. There were clouds; calm; rain at places. I cut beans in the afternoon. Picked some 100 pieces in Abraham Reimer's bush. Heinrich Reimer and Abraham Reimer have finished the undergirding. Our potatoes have been blooming for 8 days and have potatoes as big as chicken eggs.

11 Wed. +15, day +25, *Vesper* +28, evening +24. Clouds, calm. I winnowed the beans. I was at Abraham Penners', where 14 men began to build a new bridge on the other end of the village. [The health situation with] Joh. Friesen and with Abraham Reimer was greatly improved and he could already walk about.

12 Sat. +19, day +28, *Vesper* +29, evening +22. Clouds; calm; rain during the night; there was also thunder and there was severe lightning. I finished peeling out the beans and I also made butter; there were approximately 3 1/2 pounds. And in the evening I was at Peter Töwses' and the young Mrs. Peter Töws has improved a good deal, even though she was still in bed. The young Töwses' cow calved today, a female.

13 Sun. +16, day +24, *Vesper* +25, evening +20. Was quite calm; clear. The church service was in Rosenfeld. There were only Heinrich Reimer, Johan Wiebe and Johan Kop who drove there [from Blumenort]. Yesterday after *Vesper* I helped the elder Abraham Penner's Lisbet mangle at Johan Kops'. Yesterday much work was done on the bridge beyond Johan Friesens'. Ana, the daughter of Peter Töwses, Steinbach, came to Abraham Penners' and stayed overnight.

14 Mon. +17, day +21, *Vesper* +23, evening +11. Clouds; quite calm. In the morning yesterday we were at Abraham Reimers'. Lisbet and Ana, daughters of Peter Töwses, came down there also. For lunch, however, both were at our place and for *Vesper* both walked back to Steinbach. There Lisbet went into domestic service and received $1.25 and she has already been there for 6 weeks.

15 Tues. +14, day +20, *Vesper* +20 1/2, evening +14. It was cloudy with some westerly wind. At about 9 a.m. yesterday I walked to Steinbach [a distance of 7 kilometres] and brought Peter Töwses their little cradle. I got there at 12 p.m. and stayed there for lunch and *Vesper*. After *Vesper* I went to Johan Reimers' and for night I was at Abraham Friesens', who had been to the store at Tannenau and had come back at 10:30. In the morning I was in the new mill which he had built the previous week.

16 Wed. +16, day +18, *Vesper* +20, evening +14. It was quite clear and a bit of a westerly breeze. Two weeks ago, June 28, Peter Töwses, Steinbach, erected their house (45 x 25 x 8 1/2 up to the ceiling). Yesterday I was along and went to Klaas Reimers' for lunch and *Vesper*. At 5:30 I left Steinbach and arrived home at 8 p.m, but both times I had to walk along the fence across the creek and had to walk there.

17 Thur. +12, day +19, *Vesper* +23, evening +17. Cloudy; quite calm. Yesterday I was at Abraham Penners' for *Vesper*. Since Monday Abraham Reimer has worked hard in the smith shop, also on Monday he began to make a pair of reaper canvasses. Today I was at Peter Reimers' where I helped him erect the chimney.

The bridge was completed on Tuesday and today they began to mow the hayfields [*Dampel*].

18 Fri. +16, day +21, *Vesper* +24, evening +20. Wind south. Cloudy. In Blumenhof people began to build their long bridge. Also Abraham Reimer gave half a load of lumber for it, and others too, so that there were a total of 4 loads that came [from Blumenort]. Some from here helped with the carpentry. Today I was at Abraham Penners'. And at least for 14 days they *kosten*[?] at several places *Stonful lieren* [several places?].

19 Sat. +20, day +25, *Vesper* +26, evening +20. Wind south, overcast, stormy, rain in the morning. Yesterday I split firewood for 1/2 day. Kops cooked pods last week. Heinrich Reimer did the same thing yesterday, and half a day until noon today. Reimers picked ripe berries. Also Peter Bargs from Grünfeld came to our place after *Vesper*.

20 Sun. +18, day +20, *Vesper* +22, evening +16. Cloudy; quite calm. The church service was in Steinbach and we were there too; I went along with Reimers and my wife went with Abraham Reimers. And Peter Bargs were at Abraham Reimers' overnight. In the church service the young people sat on the first bench and they were instructed. Brotherhood meeting followed; it concerned the old Peter Töwses. Yesterday all the ministers were here at Peter Reimers'.

21 Mon. +13, day +18, *Vesper* +21, evening +15. It was cloudy, quite calm. In the afternoon I was at Abraham Penners' and also for *Vesper* and yesterday we and Abraham Reimers [were there] for lunch and *Vesper*. Today Klaas Reimers were here at Peter Töwses' for *Vesper* and were there also after *Vesper*, visiting. The young Mrs. Töws is steadily getting a little better. Although she could just barely sit up and lay in bed. Yet now she is quite well. And Heinrich Reimer has completed Abraham Reimer's [reaper?].

22 Tues. +14, day +18, *Vesper* +19, evening +16. Quite calm, cloudy. I was a little sickly and I had a little fever and other ailments. Then also Cornelius Töwses came from Grünfeld for lunch and stayed after lunch till *Vesper*, about 3 hours. *Vesper* they had at Heinrich Reimers' and for night they stayed in Blumenhof. In the afternoon my wife walked to Abraham Penners' and David Tiessens'. Also last week, Friday and Saturday, Peter Friesen from here began cutting and binding ripe barley. Also last week there were those in Grünfeld who worked with oats.

23 Wed. +14, day +24, *Vesper* +24, evening +14. It was very cloudy, calm. I was a little better. My feet and one leg got sore and swollen, so that I had to limp. Mrs. Abraham Penner walked down here in the morning and she was also at Peter Töwses'. Yesterday at Abraham Reimers' I unwound 2 balls of cotton thread and today I unwound another 2 balls of cotton thread. Also today Abraham and Heinrich Reimer began to work here on their bridge. Yesterday the herdsman, [Hildebrand?], was here.

24 Thur. +15, day +14, *Vesper* +19, evening +15. Clouds, some south wind. I was completely well again. I unwound some cotton thread for Abraham Reimer. Also Abraham Hiebert was here in the afternoon. My wife made a pair of pants for him and a jacket for him. The Reimers were working on their bridge. Cornelius Töwses from Grünfeld came today from Blumenhof. They had been there two nights and one day. For lunch they were at Töwses'.

25 Fri. +12, day +20, *Vesper* +20, evening +16. Windy and rain until *Vesper*. The two Reimers worked on their bridge. I was well, but my foot and leg were swollen. Sunday, July 20, two Bergthaler drowned – two [of three] Dörksen brothers: [one] married [was drowned]; one was able to save himself; [the other one who drowned was] about 13 years old. [This occurred in the] Rat River and 2 oxen also lost.

26 Sat. +13, day +20, *Vesper* +22, evening +16. It was cloudy, west wind. Also today they finished the bridge, so that they could drive across. Three big wagon loads of planks, including the freight wagon, were laid underneath. Also yesterday the drowned Derksens were found 9 miles behind [from] Winnipeg and were buried there although in Bergthal was the funeral.

27 Sun. +14, day +20, *Vesper* +20, evening +16. It was quite calm. The church service was in Grünfeld and there Peter Barg had the main sermon. Brotherhood concerning the young people [baptismal candidates] and Johan Hiebert, Grünfeld, was excommunicated because of his speaking about married couples and other things like it. Johan Reimers from Steinbach, with Mrs. Abraham Friesen came here at 1 p.m. and stayed for *Vesper*.

28 Mon. +11, day, *Vesper*, evening. It was clear, calm, also yesterday afternoon for 1/2 an hour we had a heavy rain, so that Johan Reimer got wet on the street, and there a west wind. Johan Reimers and Mrs. Abraham Friesen were at our place for *Vesper*. After *Vesper* Johan Reimer went to Abraham Penners'. We and Mrs. Abraham Friesen also went there, but Abraham Penner was in Grünfeld; they went home at 6 o'clock. Abraham Penner came home at 7 o'clock.

29 Tues. +10, day +22, *Vesper* +26, evening +14. It was clear, quite calm and after *Vesper* it rained for 1/2 an hour. Last week, Friday afternoon and Saturday until *Vesper*, Abraham Reimer and Peter Reimer repaired the grass mower and the grain machine and also cut Peter Reimers' 3 acres of ripe barley and yesterday Abraham Reimers' home field of 7 acres of barley. And in the afternoon I was at Abraham Penners' and on the ridge he repaired one frame.

30 Wed. +14, day +26, *Vesper* +27 1/2, evening +21 1/2. It was clear, quite calm. And this morning from 3 to 6, the young Mrs. Peter Töws was very sick, so that she could not speak and seemed that she would die. Also my dear wife, and Margaret, came in the morning. P. Töws went yesterday to Winnipeg and Aron Penner from Blumenhof and the young Peter Penner bought a number of things.

31 Thur. +15, day +18, *Vesper* +21, evening +15. It was very cloudy and it rained steadily and was quite calm. Also yesterday Heinrich Reimer cut himself in the leg with the [scythe?]. I was yesterday and today at Peter Töwses' and today I was at Peter Penners'. Also Peter Töws from Steinbach with his Ana had driven here the day before yesterday and Ana drove with Gerbrandt, each with a wagon of wheat to Point des Chesne for milling. Peter Töws was here for *Vesper* and walked home.

August 1879

1 Fri. +14, day +25 1/2, *Vesper* +16, evening +14. Very mild in the morning, somewhat cloudy and quite calm. But then at about 1 p.m. it was already raining heavily in the west and at 2:30 it began raining here very heavily with hail, pieces as big as walnuts, and also strong wind. It seemed as if many buildings could topple over. And it all came from the west, although as it struck us the wind came from the northwest. It lasted about an hour. We could hardly see the [neighbouring] house. And also many windows were broken at the others'.

2 Sat. +12, day +18, *Vesper* +20. It was quite clear, some west wind. Also the old Peter Töwses and Aron Penner from Blumenhof came and here, yesterday, the young Peter Penners came home at 7 p.m. And Aron Penner brought Abraham Penners' cow back and he wanted to charge $28.00, but could have only $24.00. Already last week, Thursday, Abraham Friesen from Steinbach burned his eye while pouring zinc into a [mould?].

3 Sun. +12, day +20, *Vesper* +24, evening +16. In the morning some clouds; quite calm; rain for half an hour and fair in the afternoon. The church service was in Rosenfeld; 11 baptismal candidates were baptized: 8 sons and 3 daughters. From Steinbach, Abraham, the son of Klaas Reimers and a daughter from Steinbach; and from here Lisbet, daughter of Mrs. David Tiessen, and the young Peter Penners' daughter, the eldest. Yesterday I took from the Young Peter Penners' coffee for 1 dollar and sugar for 2 dollars.

4 Mon. +11, day +21, *Vesper* +23, evening +15. Calm; at places rain. Yesterday morning Abraham Reimer, Abraham and Klaas, went with the spring buggy and horses to the church service in Rosenfeld. Peter Reimer walked down there. Abraham Reimers came home yesterday at 3 o'clock. For *Vesper* the old Margreta was at our place and the old Mrs. Cornelius Friesen was here in the afternoon for an hour.

5 Tues. +14, day +26, *Vesper* +12. Clear and calm; very cloudy; rain in Steinbach; lightning. Peter Töwses from Steinbach came and had supper at Abraham Penners'. I also was there. Today for breakfast they were at our place. At 8:30 I and Peter went to Steinbach. I had lunch and *Vesper* at Peter Töwses'.

6 Wed. +11, day +16, *Vesper* +16 1/2, evening +10. Very cloudy; wind west. I was at Johan Reimers' for the night and at Klaas Reimers' for lunch. Yesterday evening the old [Mrs.] Peter Barkman took very sick, suddenly as she came with a pail of milk from the fence to the house door. They had to carry her to the bed as she had had such a *Schlagflusz*[?] that she could not move the right side; she had fever.

7 Thur. +7, day +18, *Vesper* +21, evening +11. It was very cloudy; quite calm. I was overnight at Abraham's. In the morning yesterday *Sud* [half-year?] calf was *kreuzirt* [killed?] at Abraham Friesens'. In the morning I went to the old

Peter Barkmans'. Her condition had hardly changed. By *Vesper* she was a little improved, but could not speak nor eat.

8 Fri. +10, day +20, *Vesper* +24, evening +12. It was quite calm; cloudy in the afternoon. Yesterday I was at Klaas Reimers' for lunch and at 2 p.m. I went from Johan Reimers' and got home at 4:30. After *Vesper* I was at Peter Töwses'. There conditions were not too bad. In the morning yesterday the young Mrs. Peter Töws was very sick with great stomach pains.

9 Sat. +12, day +24, *Vesper* +26 1/2, evening +19 1/2. Quite calm. Fourteen days ago our cat brought into this world 6 kittens. Also Abraham Reimer hauled 30 wagons of oats home and he has also a *Grosz Welt Grad* [?] from an Englishman, which can give hay [?]. For 3 days they have done some cutting and hauled home his barley.

10 Sun. 20, day +24, *Vesper* +26 1/2, evening +20. Quite calm; some clouds. The church service was here for the first time in the new, although old, building. Peter Barg from Grünfeld had the main sermon. Brotherhood following; [we were] exhorted to be ready for communion church service. Klaas Reimers were here a little at Abraham Reimers' for lunch.

11 Mon. +20, day +25, *Vesper* +17, evening +13. Wind west; very cloudy. Johan Reimer from Steinbach was here a little. Peter Töwses from Steinbach were at Abraham Penners' for lunch and *Vesper*. Abraham Friesen from Steinbach were at Peter Reimers' for lunch and *Vesper*. Mrs. Peter Töws and Mrs. Abraham Friesen were here.

12 Tues. +14, day +16, *Vesper* +17 1/2, evening +14. Calm; very cloudy; calm. Klaas Reimer from Steinbach has gone with 2 wagons to Winnipeg, as did also Johan Reimer and Peter Töws and Aron with a wagon alone with many fresh potatoes and eggs, which sold for 12 to 15 a dozen. The potatoes from 50 to 70 a bushel.

13 Wed. +16, day +20, *Vesper* +21 1/2, evening +16. Was somewhat cloudy, quite calm. Also, already the day before yesterday Peter Reimer threshed his 3 acres of wheat at his farmstead. And Peter Reimer, his wife and the herdsman Hiebert were tying [sheaves]. I was there in the afternoon. Yesterday and today we are somewhat sick. Today Abraham Reimer began threshing his wheat.

14 Thur. +15, day +19, *Vesper* +21, evening +13. It was very cloudy; calm. On Monday and the day before yesterday Abraham Reimer measured out the hay. They went 52 times – all told about 43 loads of hay. The day before, Peter Reimer had received a big swelling on his hip, so that he can hardly work and almost not walk and barely sit.

15 Fri. +10, day +19, *Vesper* +22. Many clouds in the morning; in the afternoon nearly clear; quite calm. The day before yesterday Abraham Reimer developed a swelling on the same place as it had been before so that he has difficulty standing and sitting. And this week, Monday, Klaas Reimer and Johan Reimer and Mrs. Abraham Friesen came in the afternoon from Steinbach by wagon. They had *Vesper* at Peter Reimers'.

16 Sat. +10, day +20, *Vesper* +24, evening +16. It was quite calm and somewhat cloudy. At about 1:30 o'clock I walked to Steinbach and got there about 3 o'clock for *Vesper* at Abraham Friesens'. After *Vesper* they began cutting shingles, although he started on Monday. This week he cut over 4000 shingles. I was there overnight and in the evening I filled water into the steam engine.

17 Sun. +10, day +22, *Vesper* +26, evening +18. Quite calm, some clouds, a little rain for half an hour. In the evening lightning. The church service was in Steinbach. Abraham Löwen of Grünfeld had the sermon and there was Brotherhood meeting until 3:30. It dealt with Klaas Friesen from Steinbach; he withheld 2 bushels of wheat from Wiebe of the forest and had not taken them to Winnipeg. [It also dealt] with Klaas Friesen that he had preformed statutory labour only for half a day but took pay for a whole day and other things and he was excommunicated. For lunch I was at Klaas Reimers' in Steinbach.

18 Mon. +15, day +18, *Vesper* +21, evening +15 ... Calm; rain with lightning during the night. In the morning it still was raining off and on. Abraham Friesen from Steinbach started out for Winnipeg yesterday after *Vesper*. In the afternoon Klaas Reimer and Johan Reimer and Mrs. Abraham Friesen, Steinbach, all on one wagon drove to Peter Reimers'. Here they had *Vesper*, although Mrs. Abraham Friesen had *Vesper* at Abraham's; but they were also at Peter Reimers' for *Vesper*. And Mrs. Abraham Penner came to Peter Reimers'.

19 Tues. +14, day +19 1/2, *Vesper* +22, evening +19. There was south wind, very cloudy. In the afternoon I was at Abraham Penners'; they were cutting grain. In the village all the people were busily cutting wheat. And last week, about Thursday, I sharpened Abraham Reimer's wide scythe. My wife was at Abraham Penners' and Peter Reimer's swelling on his side improved in the afternoon, but also *ein am*[?] and also he lay as he could not *Glassen unrecht*[?]

20 Wed. +8, day +20, *Vesper* +22, evening +14. Some clouds, quite calm. In the morning I was at Peter Töwses'. The young Mrs. Peter Töws is a little better each day, as she can get across the yard and to the barn. The old Peter Töws got a load of [bricks?]. Abraham Friesen had not yet arrived home. I had already last week, Thursday, borrowed the big *Martyrs-Mirror* from Heinrich Reimer.

21 Thur. +11, day +21, *Vesper* +24, evening +17. Very cloudy; rain in the evening in many places; quite calm. I was splitting firewood yesterday. Yesterday also I found evermore what I had lost last Friday in the woods. And we had green beans yesterday. I sharpened today Abraham Reimer's *Schpan* [?] scythe and made a wheel for the children's wagon. And today I was somewhat sick.

22 Fri. +12, day +20, *Vesper* +22 1/2, evening +14. Cloudy, quite calm. I was cutting firewood. The day before yesterday my wife gave me a haircut. Abraham Reimer's ulcer on his side is nearly better. He ate daily one *Murkat*[?] for 4 to 5 days. Peter Reimer took one per day for 8 days. He also begins to improve. Yesterday he was quite a bit better.

23 Sat. +12, day +16, *Vesper* +20, evening +14. South wind; rain at 2 o'clock; hard lightning in the afternoon. Last week, Thursday, I helped Peter Reimer to carry the workbench from the barn to the dining room. Friday and Saturday he built for the old Cornelius Pletts a small buggy with several seats. For 10 days Peter Reimer could not work in the field.

24 Sun. +14, day +16 1/2, *Vesper* +16, evening +14. It was quite calm; it rained here in the morning. The church service was in Grünfeld and there was also Brotherhood Meeting. A decision was made to observe Communion in Steinbach within 3 weeks. Also the change in Nebraska was discussed, that they have been dismissed from the church. Abraham Reimers went at 7 in morning to Grünfeld and returned at 7 in the evening.

25 Mon. +15, day +18, *Vesper* +15, evening +13. It was quite calm, somewhat cloudy and yesterday afternoon, from 2 to 3:30, it rained with lightning, here and in Grünfeld. It was general. Abraham Penners came here for lunch and for *Vesper* they went to Peter Töwses'. In the evening they walked home in the mud.

26 Tues. +12, day +20, *Vesper* +20 1/2, evening +12. Clear, quite calm. Also yesterday, at about 8 a.m. [someone] came here to fetch my wife as she [the neighbour's wife] was very ill. My wife came home at about 10 o'clock and my wife was also somewhat sick, so much so that she could hardly walk. Mrs. Abraham Reimer was improved today, so that she was up most of the time. I was there in morning. She was very weak. The young Mrs. Töws was here yesterday from lunch time till evening.

27 Wed. +10, day +19, *Vesper* +22, evening +14. Quite calm, a little cloudy. In the afternoon I went to Krusen[?] in Hochstadt and got 5 yards red cotton. I left at 5 o'clock and arrived home at 6 o'clock in the evening. In the evening I was at Abraham Penners'. My wife was there also. Mrs. Abraham Penner sent [marketed?] the day before yesterday, a 3-year old rooster.

28 Thur. +15, day +21, *Vesper* +23, evening +18. Quite calm, cloudy. I picked a pail full of ripe white beans. There have been ripe beans for 8 days already. The young Mrs. Peter Töws was here in the morning. In the afternoon I was at Abraham Penners', as it was a little better yesterday [with her] and in the afternoon today. For 20 days she has been up merely half the time.

29 Fri. +18, day +24, *Vesper* +29, evening +10. Calm in the morning and in the afternoon a little south wind; very cloudy after *Vesper*. In the morning I was at Abraham Penners' and there by the [end?] house I made a shelter for the brooding hen and the chicks and with her [Mrs. Abraham Penner] it was a little better. The young Mrs. Töws was sick again, so that she was mainly in bed. The old Mrs. Peter Töws was completely sick. Klaas Reimer, Steinbach, went the day before yesterday to Winnipeg.

30 Sat. +14, day +22, *Vesper* +23 1/2, evening +16. It was quite calm, cloudy and rain at places. The young Peter Töws lay all day. The old Mrs. Peter Töws was very sick. In the afternoon I picked the large bowl full of ripe white beans from behind the smith shop. I planed Mrs. Abraham Penner's *Kohlholtz*[?]. I was there after *Vesper*. Yesterday Peter Friesens finished their harvest.

31 Sun. +12, day +16, *Vesper* +16 1/2, evening +12. Quite calm; rain in the morning until 9 a.m.; in the afternoon clear with a cold north wind. The church service was here in the old house, or school. Heinrich Reimer preached the main sermon. Brotherhood until 2:30; Klaas Friesen, Steinbach, was again accepted [into membership]. Also Klaas Friesen and Peter Töws, Steinbach, were discussed. Johan Reimers, Steinbach, were at Abraham Penners' for lunch.

September 1879

1 Mon. +8, day +18, *Vesper* +22 1/2, evening +15. Clear. Also Abraham Friesen, Steinbach, came home August 21 in the afternoon. He brought $200.00 worth of notes to Winnipeg. On Thursday 8 a.m. he again went to Winnipeg with an agent with 10 dollars and came home on Saturday evening. He brought a chiming clock along for 6 dollars, 2 [yellow chairs?] for 3 dollars and 60 and one *Klauer Zuk*[?].

2 Tues. +12 1/2, day +20, *Vesper* +22 1/2, evening +14. Was quite calm and cloudy. The day before yesterday Johan Reimers were here for *Vesper* and brought us a rooster and 2 cabbage heads and 1 ripe [sour?] melon. Lisbet and Ana, daughters of Abraham Reimers, were here for lunch and *Vesper* at Abraham Penners'. Yesterday I was at Abraham Penners' and at the young Mrs. Peter Töws'. In the morning today I was at Abraham Penners'. Sunday Klaas Reimers from Steinbach were here. Today Klaas Reimer from Steinbach was here for lunch.

3 Wed. +10, day +18, *Vesper* +20, evening +10. Calm, some clouds. Yesterday Klaas Reimer and Franz Kröker from Steinbach brought 2 men from the city to Peter Töwses' and they were there for lunch. One was Rutal [?] and the other Scheinrichden, a teacher. They were here to visit all the Mennonites and in the afternoon Peter Töws drove them to Bergthal. The young Peter Töwses slaughtered a hog, which was somewhat sick. It yielded 1 1/2 inches fat. Klaas Reimer bought it. The meat was good and yielded 7 cents a pound.

4 Thur. +8, day +18, *Vesper* +23, evening +13. South wind. Also on Tuesday, the day before yesterday, I went with the old Peter Barkman from Steinbach to Steinbach. He had come the day before yesterday to Peter Töwses', as she was very sick. He came Tuesday 7:30 to Abraham Friesens'; there I stayed overnight. Klaas Reimer and Peter Friesen came home on Sunday 6 a.m. from Winnipeg. Yesterday I was at Peter Töwses' for lunch and *Vesper*.

5 Fri. +12, day +12, *Vesper* +12 1/2, evening +11 1/2. During the night it rained from 11 p.m. until today 11 a.m., so that everything is wet. And it still rains off and on. Cloudy with a north wind. Yesterday I stayed at Penners' overnight and for lunch I was at Klaas Reimers'. In the afternoon at 2:30 I left Steinbach and home at 5 p.m. Today Abraham Reimers slaughtered a hog that yielded a half inch of fat.

6 Sat. +6, day +12, *Vesper* +12 1/2, evening +10. Wind north and a cold rain. Abraham Reimers' hog yielded 2 pails full of lard. Heinrich Reimer helped. They started at 1:30 yesterday. My wife went at 3 and I went for *Vesper* until supper. Yesterday the new maid came to Abraham Penners'; Katrina is to receive 25 dollars a year.

7 Sun. +10, day +12 1/2, *Vesper* +16, evening +10 ... Quite clear, north wind. The church service was in Grünfeld. Since the day before yesterday my wife was at Abraham Penners'. I was at Abraham Penners' in the morning. Today the young Peter Töwses came at 2 p.m. to our place and stayed for *Vesper* until 5. At 4:30 Abraham Friesen from Steinbach came; they had been at Juhnkes' for *Vesper*. Then they were at Johan Warkentins' and Abraham Friesen went home at [no time] o'clock.

8 Mon. +2 1/2, day +17. A little hoarfrost in the morning, but without any damage. Also Johan Jahnkes from Blumenhof were yesterday at Abraham Penners' for lunch and *Vesper*. Today I was at Abraham Penners'. She was 3 days sick in bed. Last week Wednesday I helped Johan Reimer eat a ripe watermelon. Then I was at Peter Reimers', who again has many ulcers on his side.

9 Tues. +6, day +18, *Vesper* +20, evening +14. South wind in the afternoon, quite clear. We had green beans. Last night Abraham Reimer was completely sick. He could hardly sleep during the night. He was outside frequently because of the ulcers on his side. Yesterday he could hardly walk or eat. Today at 7:30 he went to Steinbach and got home at 3 p.m. Peter Töws came in the afternoon to Abraham Penners' for *Vesper*.

10 Wed. +12, day +19, *Vesper* +16, evening +14. Very overcast, rain in the afternoon, south wind. For *Vesper* yesterday Abraham Friesen from Steinbach was at Abraham Penners'. We were there also after *Vesper*. Abraham Friesen left at 7 for home. Peter Töws was for the night at our place and in the afternoon he walked home. Wednesday morning of last week our old cat ran away and came home Friday morning; she had been away 2 days and 2 nights.

11 Thur. +11, day +16, *Vesper* +18, evening +10. Quite clear, south wind. Since Monday of this week we took everything out of the room here *als das Essen schaft nicht* [?] and then my wife whitewashed the entire room with lime, including the entrance. And it was all only a little [work?]. Today Abraham Penner planed their rolling chair at Peter Reimers'.

12 Fri. +6, day +16, *Vesper* +14, evening +8. North wind. Very cloudy and rain. Peter Reimer began in the afternoon to cut grain with the machine. I sawed firewood. Johan Ens from Grünfeld came here in the afternoon for a little while. Today I visited Abraham Penners and we began to burn grass. Yesterday I fastened more securely the [copper?] tin.

13 Sat. +2 1/2 and there was hoarfrost. During the day it was +8, *Vesper* +10, evening 6. North wind and some clouds. I cut firewood and in the afternoon I was at Peter Reimers'. My [wife] began to sew at dawn. And the day before yesterday Peter Reimer finished his grain and hay harvest. He received 45 loads of hay. Heinrich Reimer finished his grain and hay harvest yesterday. He received 50 loads.

14 Sun. +4, day +12, *Vesper* +14, evening +12. Quite calm; clouds after *Vesper*. Communion was held in Steinbach. I and my wife were there. I left after *Vesper* at 5:30 and got at 7:30 to Klaas Reimers'. Here I stayed overnight. I and my wife were at Klaas Reimers' on Monday and for *Vesper* at Peter Friesens'. I left at 5:30 and got home at 7 p.m. and in the morning my wife with Abraham Reimer and Peter Reimer also went with them. They got home at 6:30.

15 Mon. +7, day +13, *Vesper* +16 1/2, evening +11. Westerly wind, very cloudy and rain. In the morning yesterday Heinrich Reimers went with the spring buggy to Steinbach. They had not been in the church service for over a year due to sickness and weakness. The old Mrs. Peter Barkman from Steinbach, who had not been in the church service for 5 weeks because of sickness, was there too. But now she is able to do a little walking and a little talking. Since the day before yesterday Peter Reimer finished cutting his grain.

16 Tues. +6, day +10, *Vesper* +12, evening +6. There was north wind; very cloudy; and it rained off and on. Yesterday Heinrich Reimer threshed his grain. Last week Wednesday Abraham Reimer finished his hay and grain harvest. He had 65 loads of hay. Yesterday I was at Abraham Penners' in the afternoon.

17 Wed. +2 1/2 with a little hoarfrost. During the day it was +8, *Vesper* +10, evening 6. It was very cloudy with a cold northwest wind. Yesterday morning at about 8 o'clock Johan Ens from Eigenfeld was here again. [I] helped a little. At noon yesterday they began threshing at our place and I rolled up a piece of cotton thread. In the evening I also was at Abraham Penners'. Afternoon I picked the ripe, in other words white, beans behind the smith shop.

18 Thur. +8, it had been freezing. During the day +9, *Vesper* +12, evening +4. Wind northwest and very cloudy. At 3 p.m. Abraham Reimer had completed all his threshing. From 35 acres he received 216 bushels wheat and from 7 acres barely it gave 100 bushels and from 11 acres of oats, seeded actually only from 6 acres, he received 146 bushels. Peter Penner received from 16 acres 148 bushels of wheat and from 7 acres of barley 98 bushels and from 2 acres 48 bushels.

19 Fri. +2, day +12, *Vesper* +14, evening +1/2 a degree. Quite calm, clouds in the morning, clear thereafter. I picked all the ripe white beans – 2 containers full. I sawed some firewood. Today I was at Abraham Penners'. All day today they were threshing at Peter Wiebes' and at Abraham Reimers' they threshed for a good 2 days and at Heinrich Reimers' a day and a half. Today Jacob, son of Johan Kops, came home and the old Peter Töwses and Klaas Reimers from Steinbach also came home at 8 from Winnipeg.

20 Sat. +4, day +12, *Vesper* +16, evening 10. Quite calm; somewhat cloudy. Also Johan Reimers and P. Töwses, Steinbach, came here at about 12 o'clock on a spring wagon [pulled] by Johan Reimer's horses. Johan Reimers were at Abraham Penners' for lunch and at our place Peter Töwses were for lunch, but for *Vesper* we were however at Abraham Reimers'. Also at about 2 o'clock I walked to Blumenhof to old Cornelius Plett's; I was there for *Vesper* and Peter Reimers drove in the afternoon to Steinbach to Klaas Reimers and they came home at 7.

21 Sun. +4, day +12, *Vesper* +16, evening +10. Quite calm, a little cloudy. Johan Reimer came for lunch at about 12 noon and Peter Töws, all on Johan Reimers' [spring wagon?]. The Communion was at Grünfeld. And from [here] there were only Heinrich Reimers. And Peter Wiebes and Peter Töwses came here for lunch and Johan Reimers were at Abraham Reimers' for lunch. For *Vesper* we all were there. Johan Reimers gave us 2 roosters and at 7 the guests went home.

22 Mon. +3, day +8, *Vesper* +11, evening +5. It was quite calm, somewhat cloudy. Yesterday Mrs. Peter Töws was at Abraham Penners' in the afternoon to visit a little. Mrs. Johan Warkentin and Mrs. Aron Penner from Blumenhof were at Abraham Penners' for *Vesper*. In the evening yesterday my wife was at Abraham Penners' and I was also there in the evening. Also the old Johan Klassens were at Abraham Reimers' and after *Vesper* at our place ... The day before yesterday Cornelius Penner threshed and received 95 bushels of wheat. Today Martin Penner is threshing and received 60 bushels of wheat.

23 Tues. -4 cold, and there was frost covering the windows and at places it had frozen, -5. The ice had frozen 1/3 inch. Quite calm, somewhat a north wind, some clouds. Yesterday at about noon Peter Reimer walked with their children to Blumenhof. I sawed and split firewood. Yesterday afternoon Peter drove with about 14 bushels of wheat to Point des Chesne and this morning at about 7 o'clock Abraham Reimer took 18 bushels of wheat to Point des Chesne and came back at 5:30 and it had all milled.

24 Wed. +3 1/2, day +10, *Vesper* +16 1/2, evening +6. Quite clear, south wind. Peter Reimer came home this morning from Point des Chesne with his flour. He had stayed there overnight as they needed their flour. Abraham Reimers slaughtered a hog, their best. It had 3 1/2 inches of fat and yielded about 4 pails full of lard. Peter Reimers were there also and we were there for *Vesper*. I sawed firewood. Abraham Penners' *groszaltes Peter von sie da al uber Jahr gelegen hat* [?].

25 Thur. +3, day +18, *Vesper* +19 1/2. Wind south. Clear. At 4 a.m. Abraham Reimer went with Klaas to Winnipeg with 1 wagon and 2 horses and 2 hogs and 6 bushels of wheat and 15 dozen eggs, and Heinrich Reimer went with 2 cows – 1 sold for $30.00 and 1 for $25. The hog sold for $20, it weighed 252 pounds, at 8 cents a pound. Wheat sold for $.65 a bushel and barley for $.45, oats $.45, the butter for 16 cents, the eggs sold for 18 cents. Klaas Reimer from Steinbach went yesterday to Winnipeg.

26 Fri. +6, day +16, *Vesper* +20, evening +10. Calm. Cloudy. Abraham Penner threshed his grain yesterday and today. From 20 acres he has 200 bushels of wheat and from 3 acres of barley 23 bushels and from 4 acres of oats 41 bushels of oats and potatoes 16 bushels. I split firewood. At 2 a.m. the old Peter Penner came here for my wife. He sent Johan here with the buggy and got my wife and at 6 a.m. the son Jacob was born and at 6 a.m. my wife walked home.

27 Sat. +6, day +20, *Vesper* +20, evening +12. Quite calm, clear. Also, Abraham Reimer came home from Winnipeg in the morning at about 1 o'clock. He had bought 2 12-inch ploughshares for $15.00, a heating stove for $7.00, a barrel of salt of 20 pounds for about $6.00 for 1 1/2 cents a pound, a box of soap for 60 cents, coffee at $4.00 a pound and 7 cents. We bought also for 50 cents and 7 Par [?] cloth, 1 pair of shoes for 6 ... and 2 small articles ...

28 Sun. +10, day +16, *Vesper* +19, evening +16. Quite overcast, but with a south wind. There was here, in the old school, the church service. Peter Barg from Grünfeld preached. In the afternoon *Ältester* Peter Töws conducted the Communion at Abraham Penners' because of all the sick women, that is, Mrs. David Tiessen and Mrs. Peter Friesen. And at our place were Johan Reimers for lunch; and Klaas Reimers and Peter Töwses' daughters, Lisbet and Ana, as well as Johan Reimers were here for *Vesper*. The Abraham Friesens were at Abraham Reimers' for lunch and for *Vesper*.

29 Mon. +12, day +17, *Vesper* +19, evening +12. It was quite calm, a bit of south wind; overcast in the afternoon. Yesterday at Abraham Penners' there were 5 men and also 6 women for the Communion. Last week they did much ploughing and in Blumenhof they all did much ploughing and old Cornelius Plett has already finished his ploughing. Last week my wife took on the task of making a fur coat for the old Penner. And in Steinbach Klaas Reimer has already finished all the grain and today ...

30 Tues. +4, very *fruan*[?], day +16, *Vesper* +20, 8 evening. There was fog and it was quite smoky; quite calm; a southerly breeze. Then Peter Klassen and Peter Löwen began to thresh their wheat. Also Heinrich Reimer today really began separating his crop. Yesterday and yesterday evening the young Mrs. Peter Töws was very ill. And I was at Mrs. Abraham Penner almost every day this week as she was very weak and suffering.

8   Moses S. Bowman (1819 to 1898)

Mannheim, Ontario

Diary selection: 1 January to 29 April 1890

Age: 71

Moses S. Bowman, born in 1819, was the eldest child of pioneers Benjamin and Susannah (Bechtel) Bauman, who came from Pennsylvania in 1818 and settled in Waterloo Township, three kilometres southeast of the Berlin townsite (Kitchener). In 1844, he married Anna Cressman (born in 1828), another Pennsylvania Mennonite descendant, who lived in Freeport, about eight kilometres distant. A year after their marriage, Moses and Anna moved to a farm on Bleams Road North, in Wilmot Township, near Mannheim, about three kilometres from where he grew up. Eventually they had a family of 12 children: six girls and six boys. The eldest son, Menno, died at the age of 21 in 1870.

This diary selection covers January to April 1890, and Moses mentions all but one of his surviving 11 children: nine of these were married to Mennonites and resided on farms not far from the Bowmans' own farmstead. Louisa, born in 1845, was married to David Bergey and lived near New Dundee; Leah, born in 1847, was married to Henry Baer and lived near Mannheim; Annie, born in 1851, was married to Wendel E. Shantz and lived near Berlin; Moses, Jr., born in 1855, was married to Lydia Shantz and lived near Mannheim; Barbara, born in 1857, was married to David Shuh and lived near Berlin; Susannah, born in 1859, was married to Menno Shantz and lived near New Dundee; Aaron, born in 1861, was married to Sarah Bricker and resided on his parents' old farm near Mannheim; Noah, born in 1864, was married to Mary Bricker and lived near Mannheim. This made for a compact kinship network. On 9 April, for example, four of these siblings – Louisa, Leah, Moses, and Lydia – met at their parents' place for spring housecleaning. The elder Bowmans relied, either by gift or purchase, on foodstuffs from the households of their sons Moses, Aaron, and Noah. Moreover, there were frequent visits over "dinner" and sometimes overnight with the Bergeys, the Baers, the "Wendel Shanzes," and the "Moses Shanzes." In addition, there were many grandchildren – 36 by 1895.

Only one child moved away from Waterloo County: Samuel, born in 1852, who was married to Emma Shantz and resided near Brown City, Michigan, where many Waterloo County Mennonites had settled in the 1860s. The two youngest children, Lydia and Ezra, were single when this part of the diary was written. In September, Moses helped Lydia purchase household goods, possibly in preparation for her marriage to schoolteacher John Berry; Ezra, 17, was a student at the Berlin high school in 1890 and in the employ of his brother Aaron.

Moses's world was also linked to his and to Anna's extended families. There were visits throughout the year from Moses's younger brother Samuel, 56, and his wife Susannah, and from "Moses Sniders," the household of Moses's youngest sibling, Elisabeth, of Wilmot Township.

Moses was also closely identified and linked with the Latschar Mennonite Church, which was located two kilometres from the village of Mannheim. In 1853 he had been ordained deacon of this congregation, in 1857 he was chosen preacher in the wider Waterloo District Conference, and in 1873 he was appointed as the first church moderator of the Mennonite Conference of Canada. He was clearly a respected churchman; the family history notes, "He was a man of more than ordinary ability" whose "sermons convince[d] both friends and enemies." The diary indicates that in 1890 he was intricately involved in all church affairs, attending disciplinary meetings, paying visits to the households of parishioners, and holding services. He specifically conferred with Old Mennonite bishops Amos Cressman, in January, and Moses Erb, in April. A portion of the diary not reproduced here describes a four-week visit in May and June to Lancaster County, Pennsylvania, where Moses followed an exhausting schedule, participating in 30 worship services and visiting over 100 homes. A typical entry for the diary at that time was the one for Sunday, 18 May, when he noted the following: "From Isaac Landes to Franconia Me[e]ting. *Wo wir die Einigkeit Gielten* [where we held communion] with a Congregation of about 500 Members. From Me[e]ting to Michael Moyer for Dinner. From Moyer to Me[e]ting Cal[l]ed [at] Souderton [Pennsylvania], from Me[e]ting to John J Alderfer, from Alderfer to Josiah Clemmer (bishop) for supper. Over night to Abram P. Clemmer." Upon returning to Canada in mid-June, he spent another four days in church meetings and home visitations. Although he spent the next month "at home" doing little but milk one cow, he left again, on 15 August, for another extended church trip, this time to Godridge, Ontario, 100 kilometres to the west, on Lake Huron.

Moses Bowman was an elderly man in 1890. Most of the old farm had been taken over by son Aaron and his wife. Except for his trip to Pennsylvania, Moses's life was summarized by his frequent entry "at home." He still wrote some phrases in German; he seemed to have a repertoire of Pennsylvania Dutch folk sayings, and he often spelled surnames the way they sounded in Palatine German: Bare (Baer); Shans (Shantz); Gunggles (Kunkels); Pole (Poll); Jones (Jonas). It is not known what the coding for the entry of 9 January means. And, though he still travelled, Moses became less and less mobile within the county; in February, his horse, Polly, broke a leg and had to be shot, but there is no record of Moses obtaining another horse.

The diary, written in English, is located at the Mennonite Archives of Ontario, in Waterloo, Ontario. It was transcribed by Reg Good, of Kitchener; notes for the introduction were provided by Lorna Bergey, of Kitchener. For more information on Bowman, see Ezra Eby, *A Biographical History of Early Settlers and Their Descendants in Waterloo Township, 1895* (Waterloo, ON: 1971), 18ff.

January, Wednesday 1, 1890 We to Me[e]ting at Latschaws [later Mannheim Mennonite Church]. David Eshleman & [Old Mennonite Church Bishop] Amos Cressmans Paid us a visit. Rain all Day; Wind from south East.

January, Thursday 2, 1890 We at Home. I Mailed a Letter to My Son Samuel, Michigan. Warm Wind from South West. Henry Bares Paid us a visit.

January, Friday 3, 1890 We at Home. I Helpt [son] Noah to Make his Bridge Across the Creek in his Lane. Amos & Menno Cressman Stopt over night with us. The ground Bare.

January, Saturday 4, 1890 I went with Amos Cressman to Martin Bowmans for Dinner. In the Afternoon we went to Conestoga Me[e]ting House About Church Difficulties. Menno Cressman took Jacob Bergey along.

January , Sunday 5, 1890 We went from Martin Bowmans, to Me[e]ting at David Ebys [later Erb Street Mennonite Church], from Me[e]ting to Gunggels for Dinner, Home in the Afternoon.

January, Monday 6, 1890 I have been to Berlin. Settled with the Bank of Commerce took out All My Money. Send My Son Samuel a New York Draft of Eight Hundred Dollars.

January, Wednesday 9, 1890 We at Home. *Ich habe der Mann den Lebens Wetter aufgesetz* [One has to bend to the weather?].

January, Wednesday 8, 1890 I settled with Abram Buehler. He Paid his interes and $125.00 Dollars. I settled with [son] Moses he Paid Me his notes being $700.00 Dollars. Snow Storm to Day.

January, Thursday 9, 1890 BbbeBBb. BB bGbb. BB bbBBb.

January, Friday 10, 1890

January, Saturday 11, 1890 We at Home. Snow and Rain. very foggy. Wind from South East. [Son] Ezra to Dundee with 10 Dozen of Eggs. Bought 1 Dollar worth of Sugar and Lamp glass.

January, Sunday 12, 1890 I and Ezra went to the funeral of Martin Sniders Child Aged 3 Months and 2 Days. Buried at David Ebys. Some Rain.

January, Monday 13, 1890 We at Home. High wind from South West. Snow all gone. Highest Wind for this Winter.

January, Tuesday 14, 1890 We at Home nice weather to Day. Thawing.

January, Wednesday 15, 1890 ...

January, Thursday 16, 1890 ...

January, Friday 17, 1890 We at Home.

January, Saturday 18, 1890 We at Home.

January, Sunday 19, 1890 We to Me[e]ting at Latshaws. Brother Tobias and wife Paid us a visit and Abram Webers young people Paid us a visit. Heavy Rain.

January, Monday 20, 1890 We at Home. High wind. Freecing. No Sleighing.

January, Tuesday 21, 1890 We at Home. No Sleighing.

January, Wednesday 22, 1890 We at Home. No Slcighing.

January, Thursday 23, 1890 We at Home. Bought German silver teaspoons one Dozen for seventy five cts. No sleighing, but some snow to Day.

January, Friday 24, 1890 We at Home. I wrote to My son Samuel to Day.

January, Saturday 25, 1890 We at Home. No Sleighing.

January, Sunday 26, 1890 To Me[e]ting at Blenheim. Took Dinner with Isaac Brickers. Supper with David Bergeys and over night.

January, Monday 27, 1890 Dinner with [children] Menno Shanses. Vissited John Bucks. From Bucks to [New] Dundee for our spring goods then Home.

January, Tuesday 28, 1890 We went to Berlin. I bought A New York Draft of 2 Hundred and twelve Dollars, for My son Samuel. No Sleighing.

January, Wednesday 29, 1890 We visited Henry Baers.

January, Thursday 30, 1890 We visited David Cressmans. No Sleighing.

January, Friday 31, 1890 We at Home. Cold and frosty. No Snow.

February, Saturday 1, 1890 We at Home. Cold and frosty. No Snow.

February , Sunday 2, 1890 We at Home. Cold, no snow.

February, Monday 3, 1890 We at Home. Noah paid Me $230 Dollars and took up his note. Cloudy and foggy all Day. Not a Bit of Snow thawing.

February, Tuesday 4, 1890 We at Home. Cloudy & Foggy all Day, Some Rain, thawing, frost through the night.

February, Wednesday 5, 1890 I to Berlin. Depossited $230 Dollars in the Bank of Commerce than stopt at Wendel Shanses. We took Dinner there. Home in the Evening. No Sleighing.

February, Thursday 6, 1890 We at Home. *Der Mann den Lebens – Wetter aufgesetzt. Der Grund hart Gefroren. Die Wegen sehr Rauh* [One has to be conditioned to the weather. The ground is frozen solid, the roads are very rough.]

February, Friday 7, 1890 We at Home. Snow Storm to Day. The wind from East.

February, Saturday 8, 1890 We at Home. Snow Storm. The wind from North west. Snow about 5 inches.

February, Sunday 9, 1890 We at Home nice winter weather, wind Still to Day. A few cutters going. Aarons [son and his wife] went to Me[e]ting at Christ Eby's [later, First Mennonite Church] with Polly and Cutter, west Wind.

February, Monday 10, 1890 We at Home in the forenoon. In the Afternoon I went [to New] Dundee with 18 Dozen Eggs. Bought 3 gallons of Canadian Coal oil. Midlen [middling] good sleiging.

February, Tuesday 11, 1890 We at Home. Eshleman, David Smiths, Huber & his wife from Ca[y]uga [Halimand County, west of Niagara Falls and] and Sherk from Berti[e, Welland County, south of Niagara Falls], all Paid us a visit to Day.

February, Wednesday 12, 1890 We at Home. I wrote a letter to My son Samuel.

February, Thursday 13, 1890 We at Home. I Paid Pole 1 Dollar 15 cts for Mending Shoes 5cts for Post Stamps. I Drove up to Middle Street [later, Snyder's Road] throu[gh] [son] Aaron[']s Road. Came Back through [son] Noah['s] Road. Thawing, wind S. west.

February, Friday 14, 1890 We at Home. In the forenoon My Brother Samuel and Wife, Isaac Webers, Hubers from Ca[y]uga, Sherk from Berti[e], all took Dinner with us. So Did Gilbert Bearss from Berti[e]. In the afternoon we all went to Me[e]ting at Latshaws.

[Pages of the diary are missing here.]

February, Wednesday 19, 1890 We at Home. C[l]ear & Coldest Morning. Wind from North.

February, Thursday 20, 1890 We at Home. Snow Storm. Wind from North West.

February, Friday 21, 1890 We at Home. Snow Storm. Very cold wind from West. No good sleighing yet. The snow is blowing on heaps.

February, Saturday 22, 1890 We at Home. My Horse Had one of His hind Legs Broken this Morning by Kicking. We shot him.

February, Sunday 23, 1890 We at Home. We and Noahs took Dinner at Aarons'. Snowing.

February, Monday 24, 1890 We at Home.

February, Tuesday 25, 1890 We at Home. Foggy and Rain. In the forenoon Cleaning off. In the Afternoon thawing. Frost going out of the ground.

February, Wednesday 26, 1890 We at Home. It Rained some last night freecing this Morning. Snow all away. Wind from the West . . . &. Cloudy. [Purchased?] Chicken feet from Aaron: Oats, 16 bushels; Barley, 16 bushels; wheat, 4 bushels.

February, Thursday 27, 1890 We at Home.

February, Friday 28, 1890 We at Home. Rain this Morning. Very foggy.

March, Saturday 1, 1890 We at Home.

March, Sunday 2, 1890 We at Home. David Smith & Amos Shanses Paid us a visit. Cold March weather.

March, Monday 3, 1890 We at Home. Aaron fec[t]hed a girl to work from near Erbsville. In the Afternoon we went in the bush to look for the timber for the shed; we found some on mine and some on his [Aaron's] 8 Acres.

March, Tuesday 4, 1890 We at Home. Snow Storm to Day. The wind from South West.

March, Wednesday 5, 1890 I have been to the funeral of the Wife of Jonathan Krupp; she was Buried at Geigers [later, Wilmot Mennonite Church]. Aged 35 years, 5 Months & 8 Days. Poor Sleighing. Some with Bug[g]ies, Some with Cutters. Clear all Day.

March, Thursday 6, 1890 We at Home in the forenoon. In the Afternoon I went to Dundee with 24 Dozen of Eggs. Clear all Day. [Stamp of Moses Bowman's Name].

March, Friday 7, 1890 We at Home. [Stamp of Moses Bowman's Name]. Clear all Day.

March, Saturday 8, 1890 We at Home. Cold and Clear the wind from North East. No Sleighing but about 3 inches of snow. 166 2/3 Squers [?]. Cash amount 286.63. Bunches 480. Clear all Day.

March, Sunday 9, 1890 We Have been to Me[e]ting at Christ[ian] Ebys [later, First Mennonite Church] Berlin. Took Dinner with Daniel Wismers. Visited Peter Webers. Clear all Day.

March, Monday 10, 1890 We at Home. My son Noah's wife Paid us a visit. Foggy and Snow.

March, Tuesday 11, 1890 We at Home. Foggy and Rain.

March, Wednesday 12, 1890 We at Home. Foggy and Rain. Snow all gone. Wind from south west. Bees were fliing for the first time for this winter.

March, Thursday 13, 1890 We at Home. Clearing up. Wind from West. Sat one Hen.

March, Friday 14, 1890 We at Home. I Helpt Aaron. Tapping sugar Trees. Sap is running.

March, Saturday 15, 1890 We at Home. I and Aaron Made the wall for the sugar pans in the forenoon. In the afternoon I boiled sugar. Cold wind from West no sap to Day. We got 100 lbs flour from Aaron.

March, Sunday 16, 1890 We to Me[e]ting at Latshaws. Jones [Jonas] Goods, Menno Shanses, David Shus, took Dinner with us.

March, Monday 17, 1890 We at Home. I bound some Sap Buckets. Cold and Snowy. Wind from south west. No Sap to Day.

March, Tuesday 18, 1890 We at Home. I Bound Sap Buckets. no Sap to Day. Cold snow all gone. Wind from west.

March, Wednesday 19, 1890 We at Home. Wind from East. Freecing.

March, Thursday 20, 1890 We at Home. Wind from South west. Thawing, Cloudy and a little Rain in the Afternoon. March, Friday 21, 1890. We at Home. I am Boiling Sugar. Sap is Running. Wind from West.

March, Saturday 22, 1890 We at Home. I am Boiling sugar. Sap is Running. Wind from East.

March, Sunday 23, 1890 We at Home. Cold and Snowing. Wind from North.

March, Monday 24, 1890 We at Home. Sugaring off.

March, Tuesday 25, 1890 I have been to the funeral of Isaac Wambold; their only child was Buried at Latshaw aged 11 Months. Rain. Cherry a calf.

March, Wednesday 26, 1890 We at Home. I have been Boiling Sugar. Sap Running. Wind from west. David Bricker Moved to Day.

March, Thursday 27, 1890 We at Home. I have been Boiling Sugar. Sap Running. Wind from West.

March, Friday 28, 1890 We at Home. A Severe Snow Storm from East and Cold. I Sugard off. no sap to Day.

March, Saturday 29, 1890 We at Home. Cold wind from North West. No sap today.

March, Sunday 30, 1890 I Have been to Me[e]ting at Geigers. Visited Jonathan Hupp in the Afternoon. Wind from West.

March, Monday 31, 1890 We at Home.

April, Tuesday 1, 1890 We at Home. I am Boiling Sap to Syrup. Sap Running.

April, Wednesday 2, 1890 We at Home. I am Boiling Sap to Syrup. Sap Running. Send 2 Dollars to Salser, Wisconsin, for garden seeds.

April, Thursday 3, 1890 We at Home. I am Boiling sugar. Sap Running. Some Rain.

April, Friday 4, 1890 We to Me[e]ting at Latshaws. No frost this Morning warm and foggey. Heavy Rain at noon. *Eharfreitag* [Good Friday].

April, Saturday 5, 1890 We at Home. Sugaring off. Clear and frost. Wind from North west.

April, Sunday 6, 1890 We at Home. *Wir den Lebens Wetter aufgesetzt* [?]. Frost in the Morning. Looking for Rain. Wind from South West. Easter Sunday to Day.

April, Monday 7, 1890 We at Home. Easter Monday. Rain this Morning.

April, Tuesday 8, 1890 We at Home. Rain in the Morning. 150 + 30 + 14 = 194 + 15 = 209.

April, Wednesday 9, 1890 We at Home. Scrubt [scrubbed] the Me[e]ting House and our House. Louisa, [A]Melia [her oldest daughter], Leah and her 2nd Daughter Nancy, Moses, Lidia, Sarah [Aaron's wife], were all with us to Help.

April, Thursday 10, 1890 We at Home.

April, Friday 11, 1890 I went with My Son Moses to Conference.

April, Saturday 12, 1890 We to Meeting at Latshaw's in the Afternoon. I Paid one Dollar to [John F.] Funk [the Indiana publisher] by Samuel Herner for German *Herold* this Day.

April, Sunday 13, 1890 We to Me[e]ting at Latshaws. Joseph Hallman, Jes Cassels, Moses Sniders, Menno Shanses, and John Nargangs Paid us a visit.

April, Monday 14, 1890 We at Home.

April, Tuesday 15, 1890 Moses Erbs Came to us, and We went with them to Amos Cressmans for Bonnets for our wifes. Clear and Warm.

April, Wednesday 16, 1890 We at Home. Grafting Jerrys [cherries]. Clear and warm.

April, Thursday 17, 1890 We visited old Sweitzer. Clear and Warm.

April, Friday 18, 1890 We at Home. Jinni, A Colt. Started Yanky Pump. Clear and Cold. North Wind.

April, Saturday 19, 1890 We at Home. Clear & North wind, the ground was frozen about 1 inch this Morning.

April, Sunday 20, 1890 We to Me[e]ting at Blenheim [later, Nith Valley Mennonite Church]. Visited Abram Hallmans. Old Joseph Hallman and Menno Shanses then Home. Nice Clear Weather. Roads Dry.

April, Monday 21, 1890 We at Home.

April, Tuesday 22, 1890 We at Home.

April, Wednesday 23, 1890 We visited my Brother Samuel. Took Dinner there in the Afternoon. We stopt at Moses Erbs'. Then to Berlin and Bought

Ezra a watch for 11 Dollars. Bought our Valleace [valise?] for to go to Pen[n]sylvania and some other articles.

April, Thursday 24, 1890 We at Home.

April, Friday 25, 1890 We Have been to the Funeral of Benjamin Rudy at David Ebys, Aged 52 years. In the Afternoon we was to the funeral at Samuel Sniders, his wife was Buried at David Ebys [Meetinghouse], Aged 65 years.

April, Saturday 26, 1890 We at Home.

April, Sunday 27, 1890 We Have been to the funeral of Elias Snider. He was buried at Martins, Aged 75 years.

April, Monday 28, 1890 We at Home.

April, Tuesday 29, 1890 We at Home. I wrote 5 Letters: one to Henry Bower, Lansdale P.O., P.A.; one to Henry Cressman, Lansdale P.O.; one to Christian Allebach, Culpsville P.O., P.A.; one to Henry Gottshall, Landsdale P.O., P.A.; one to [brother-in-law] Christian Haist, Fonthill P.O., Ont.

The flour mill of Elias Eby and partners in Bridgeport, Ontario, about 1900. The mill was later purchased by Peter Shirk and Samuel Snider. The photograph was taken in about 1900. (Courtesy Lorna Bergey)

Merchant Fathers

IV

9 Elias Eby (1810 to 1878)
Bridgeport, Ontario
Diary selection: 8 January to 20 December 1874
Age: 63

Elias Eby was born in Berlin, Ontario, on 22 February 1810. He was the second son of the prominent bishop and founder of Berlin, Benjamin Eby, and his wife, Maria Brubacher. After Elias's marriage to Anna Weber in about 1835, the young couple started farming just to the northeast of Eby's Meetinghouse in Berlin. In 1851, Elias Eby and Barnabas Devitt purchased the Lancaster Mills of Bridgeport, four kilometres to the north, and Elias and Anna moved there. They eventually had 10 children, seven of whom reached adulthood. Of these seven, however, three died in their twenties, and hence only four children eventually married and had families. In 1869, the Ebys sold their share in the mill but continued to live in Bridgeport. By 1874, the health of Anna was waning, and three years later she died. Elias died in 1878.

Elias Eby's diary is an unusual notebook. The diary was composed in two columns, the first comprising a daily weather record (which is not reproduced here), and the other (transcribed here) a "visiting register," which listed the important social encounters and social events of the community. In May he noted the tragic death, a suicide, of his cousin Elias Brubacher. In July he recorded the details of a botched ordination, when John Snider declined the lot designating him minister and with that temporarily upsetting the ordination of three other designates – Noah Stauffer, Jacob Gingrich, and Elias Weber. But most important was the April schism in the Mennonite Church that followed the evangelistic work of Daniel Brenneman of Indiana, a man Elias Eby described in 1874 as a "self-styled peace messenger" who had gone "astray," wishing not to be a servant but a "ruler and regent." (For a different viewpoint of Brenneman in 1874, see diary 3.) The actual division occurred on 2 April, when Elias noted that Brenneman's "freethinkers," the "New Mennonites," had left the "Old Mennonites," violating their "bonds of baptism." Another important event in 1874 was the passing through of the "Russian Mennonites" from Europe en route to Manitoba; in July Elias was part of the Waterloo delegation that met the first group in Toronto; this group included the Kleine Gemeinde Mennonite minister Peter Baerg. Then, at the end of July, Eby noted the coming of a Bergthaler Mennonite group led by the minister, Heinrich Wiebe. Finally, Elias carefully noted each crossing of Ontario's Old Mennonite Church boundaries. In February he attended the services of Reverend Benjamin Shupe and Reverend Wendel Hallman, both "River Brethren" (later, Brethren in Christ) preachers, and in August he attended a funeral at a "New Mennonite" church where Reverend John McNally and Peter Geiger preached.

The Mennonite community, and not kinship, seems to have been Eby's primary concern and interest. Elias's own children are noted only on special occasions. "Ben and Anna," that is, Elias's daughter Ann and her husband, Benjamin Reesor, of Markham, Ontario, are mentioned in early March because they came to visit from a distance. Elias's own son Benjamin is mentioned only three times, one of the references relating a land-scouting trip he took to Kansas and another to the convalescence of his wife, Hannah, who was away from home for seven months nursing a broken leg. Daughter Magdalena, referred to as "Lena" or, when in the company of her husband, manufacturer Isaac Shantz of Berlin, as "Isaacs," is mentioned seven times, but Veronica, called "Frene," may have already been living in Winnipeg with her husband, Aaron Shantz, and is mentioned only once, on 2 March. The name of the youngest child, Elias Eby Jr., who was 26 in 1874, is not found in this selection of the diary; he is reported to have remained unmarried and in residence in South Valejo, California, until just before his death in 1883, when he moved to his brother Benjamin's home in Michigan.

For further information on events and people in this diary, see: Reginald Good, *Frontier Community to Urban Congregation: First Mennonite Church, Kitchener, 1813-1988* (Waterloo, ON), which provides background to the schism that Elias refers to on 26 February; Elisabeth Ziegler Kolb (b. 1811), letters to Jacob B. and Mary Mensch, Montgomery County, PA, 1874-1895, translated by Isaac Horst (Waterloo, ON: n.d.). A photocopy of the translated portions of Eby's diary was located at the Mennonite Archives of Ontario, Waterloo. The original German diary is in the collection of the Waterloo Historical Society, Kitchener Public Library.

January 1874

8. Noah Schantzes visited us today. Last week, their children were with Anna, and brought word that little Harvey lies quite sick with whooping cough. Towards evening, Joe W. Webers of Michigan came, then went to Isaacs', and later to Ben's.

11. This afternoon we were at the burial of old Jacob Schupp's wife, and mother of Mrs. Thomas Schmitt, Mrs. D. Reinhart, and Mrs. John Meyer. A young minister from Waterloo held suitable services for a large number of people. Age 72 years, 5 months, and 2 days. Tonight Solomon Sittlers came overnight, and went to Waterloo next morning.

17. David Sherks were here this afternoon, accompanied by his sisters, Susanna of Iowa, and Elizabeth of Blenheim.

24. Ludwig Krueger, a young Mecklinburger, died. He lived in Berlin and district for 6 years, working as hired help, and was married four months ago to a young English girl. They lived in one of my houses in Berlin. Age 26 years, and was buried in the Lutheran cemetery.

25. We stayed at home. Isaacs were in meeting at Schneider's, where Daniel Brenneman preached. B.B. Schneiders visited us for dinner.

February 1874

6. Solomon Kauffmanns visited us today, and went home to Blenheim in the evening.

8. We stayed at home this forenoon, then we went to Caspar Wagners' where B. Schupp and Wendel Hallmann preached.

9. I went to Peel and Maryborough on business, and stayed at Solomon Sitlers' overnight.

12. This afternoon we visited Noah Webers and Nancy. Daniel Brenneman of Indiana, Joseph Kressmans and Isaac Webers were also there.

14. This afternoon we visited Anna, Peter Erb's widow. Her son, Henry, married Daniel Burkholder's daughter, lives on the old [Bridgeport] farm. Nancy was with us.

18. Hannah came here today for the first time since she broke her leg, seven months, less 3 days; still goes on crutches.

21. John Krafts and family visited us for the last time tonight. They are going to Kansas. Caspar Otterbeins visited us too.

22. We were at Schneider's [meetinghouse, later, Bloomingdale Mennonite Church] where Moses Bauman's wife of near Bloomingdale was buried. She was old Abraham Clemens' daughter. By the nice weather and good sleighing, a large crowd gathered. Wismer and D. Brenneman preached, Revelations, chapter 14, verse 13; "Blessed are the dead," etc. Age 52 years, 3 months and 26 days. Lived in matrimony 30 years, 9 months, 12 days. Had eight children, 7 living. She died with the testimony of going to her eternal peace.

23. Today we buried old Joseph Schneider where many friends and acquaintances gathered. The weather and roads were good. He was a son of old Christian Schneider and came as a youth in 1805 from Pennsylvania in this Canadian wilderness, and helped to change it into a nice region. Was married to Maria, daughter of old Joseph Bauman. Raised one son and one daughter, lived with first wife 18 years, and with second, over 34 years. A. Martin and Sem Weber held suitable funeral sermons. Age 78 years, 1 month, and 8 days.

24. This afternoon, [Reverend] Sem Webers visited us, and went home late. Much was discussed about disunity in the church.

26. We visited [Bishop] Joseph Heges today. The wilful brethren cause this old bishop much sorrow and unrest. Too bad that peace has been lost. Since January 23, D. Brenneman of Indiana is in this district, where he and D. Wismer hold meetings by day and night, in schools, here and there in meeting houses, and in private dwellings, with would-be Mennonites, United Brethren, Methodists, in short, with anyone who accepts them, they carry on their work, in German or English, without turning to our church rules and regulations; but they wish to retain the Mennonite name, because they know that it stands fast and immovable. Too bad, that such men, who have united and avowed themselves to this firmly grounded rule by their baptismal vows, and later through a decent walk of life gained the respect of the church, according to the church rules and regulations were called and installed as ministers of the Word, as teachers, ministers, and shepherds of the flock, which they also diligently practiced for some time, by God's blessings; now have strayed so far that they commune with men who despise our nonresistant faith, with the church rules. Now, I ask, how can it be possible that these men wish to be our ministers, and commune with those with whom they cannot be in agreement? Is this not being unequally yoked together? What can be the reason of all this confusion? Is it not wilfulness and exaltation? Instead of servants, they wish to be rulers and regents! That is not the meek spirit of Christ! Brenneman handed out posters by which he advertised that he would be at a certain hall in Berlin on the evening of the 24th to proclaim Peace. Too bad that this self-styled peace messenger did not begin at home.

March 1874

1. We were at Ebys' in meeting where Hunsperger of the Twenty [Niagara Penninsula], and D. Brenneman preached. Ben and Anna went along too.

2. Bens, Lena and Frene went to Ben and John Webers', and Joseph Geges, and home in the evening.

4. Parting! This morning, our old neighbours, John Krafts, and family left to seek their future home in the state of Kansas. They lived here all their lives in prosperity and blessings; what awaits them there in a strange land, time will tell. They stayed in Michigan until the 9th. Isaac's Benjamin went along as hired man, and our Ben followed on the 6th to satisfy his curiosity.

7. [Son-in-law] Ben [Reesor] went home today [to Markham]. [Daughter] Anna is staying with us another week.

15. We were at Ebys' [meeting house] in meeting, where A.C. Weber and Niels Holm preached.

17. Today Anna went by cars [streetcar?] to Markham, then 4 1/2 miles to her home at Cedar Grove. She has been here since February 28.

21. We received a letter from her. She arrived safely at home at 8 o'clock, and found all healthy.

23. This morning Joseph M. Weber came here with a written petition, composed by Elias Schneider and others, to be presented to the semi-annual conference on April 2. The contents in short are this: that all those whose names appear below, are willing to hold firm and steadfast to the old rules, regulations, and confession of faith under which we pledged ourselves through the bonds of baptism; and that we cannot accept Solomon Eby, D. Brenneman and others, as brethren, and much less as our preachers, etc.

24. Widow Anna Erb and Jim Devitt's wife visited us tonight and stayed overnight.

29. We were at Ebys' in meeting where Abraham Weber and Hege preached. Then we visited [druggist] John W. Ebys in Berlin.

April 1874

2. The semi-annual conference was held at Ebys', where many ministers and deacons gathered to see whether peace and unity might be restored, but all seemed to be in vain. Reciprocal charity and confidence have so far declined, many harsh accusations are made, yet no one wishes to accept it. [Reverend] Moses Bauman and others expressed the wish to let the so-called freethinkers go their way, since they can no longer function together, but he (namely Bauman) believed that they would regret this serious step before 5 years had passed. Isaac Weber surmised that they would regret it in less than three years. Evening came, and the meeting dispersed without solving the matter, a division was pronounced.

4. Tonight Benjamin came safely home again from Kansas. The district suited him well. They took 3 to 4 days for the trip out there. Summer comes a month earlier there, but that land has its drawbacks too, so that it is hardly worth the expense to move there from this district with a family. Tonight, Sem Webers brought [Reverend] Sem Hubers from Markham. Hubers stayed overnight.

5. We went with them to Kressmans' [later, Breslau Mennonite Church] where Huber and Hege preached. Communion was held there.

16. Today we were at the burial of Abraham Kolb near Breslau, where Moses Bauman and Hege held suitable sermons. Text 2 Corinthians, ch. 5, v. 1: We know that our earthly house of this tabernacle were dissolved, etc. He was born June 13, 1806, married Licy Ziegler November 3, 1829. Lived in matrimony 44 years, 5 months and 11 days. Raised 4 sons and 3 daughters. Age 67 years, 10 months and one day. He had a form of consumption. One of the daughters, widow of Jacob C. Bauman, lives in Michigan. The rest of the family live in this district.

18. This morning, Agnes's sister came from Branchton by railroad, and went on the 20th by stage to Preston, and from there by cars.

May 1874

1. [Brother-in-law] John Webers visited us today, and brought John Kochs from Markham. They plan to go to the States from here, and don't expect to be at home before October.

9. Today, Jacob Erb of Clarence [Centre, New York] came here. He brought his elder brother, David, $30 as a gift for his support. Next morning he went along to Ebys' in meeting. Tonight, John Webers brought John Webers, now living in Indiana, and Henry Martins, earlier of Ohio, now also of Indiana, and both cousins to my wife, for the night. Weber's wife is Christian Zimmerman's daughter, and also in the relationship. Both men are ministers, and went along to Ebys' the next day, where they preached.

Dreadful deed!! Saturday morning May 9, at one o'clock, cousin Elias Brubacher [of near Breslau] left his home, in a disturbed state of mind, went to his son-in-law, Elias Shantz in Breslau, then to [cousin] Henry Brubacher, Jacob Y. Shantz, where he took breakfast with them, then to uncle [deacon John] Brubacher, complaining to each one that his creditors are after him, and want to jail him, and could not be convinced that his fears were groundless. In the afternoon he hurried home, taking the way by [cousin] David Webers, asked for a drink of water, went to the river in four feet of water, where he cut his throat with a razor, apparently sinking into the water in a moment, and died. No more was heard until the 12th at 5 p.m. [when] he was noticed in the water by a boy. He was pulled from the water, his throat cut, and still holding the razor in his hand. An inquest was held next morning, then he was buried at Kressmanns' just as he was found. May God protect us from such a death!

15. I wrote a letter to his relatives. Age about 60 years. Leaves a widow, 5 sons and 3 daughters to mourn his sad death.

17. We visited John Webers, and in the afternoon we went to Breslau where Jacob Bauman held an appropriate [United Brethren] funeral sermon for the unfortunate Elias Brubacher in the English language.

20. I went to brother Isaac in the afternoon, and planned to take him home with me. The family was busy packing in preparation for moving to their new home in Berlin the following day. Isaac was already quite weak, and rather than become too tired from moving, he was going to stay with us a day or two. He prepared himself, went to the other part of the house to bid goodbye to Moses Betzner, the new owner of the place, came out again hurriedly, sat on the doorstep, and began to bleed, spurt upon spurt, from mouth and nose, and in four minutes his spirit had fled, and his lifeless body lay in our arms. Then we carried him into the house. This was a sudden death, and an example anew of the uncertainty of our life. Oh, Man! Consider your end!

23. We laid the dear brother in his grave, where Hege and Niels Holm preached to a large number of funeral attendants. Age 65 years, 9 months and 20 days. Had 8 sons and 2 daughters; 3 grown sons passed before. Father and sons died of consumption. David Scherks came with us from Isaac Eby's funeral for the night. The next morning they went with us to Ebys' in meeting, where Wismer and Scherk preached. Aaron, son of Moses Schantz, married to Leah, daughter of B.B. Schneider, came home with us from the meeting.

31. This afternoon we visited Benjamins. Hannah is still quite lame, and is unwilling to go without crutches.

June 1874

1. David Martin and his cousin Henry Martin of Indiana visited us today. Martin and his travelling companion, John Weber, are going home to Indiana on the 5th.

3. This afternoon we visited the widow Liza Kolb. Her son, Jacob, now lives with his mother.

4. Jacob D. Schumachers visited us today, going from here to the carding machine [in Bridgeport], and then home.

13. Sus[an Brubacher] Weber was in Waterloo and brought Lena Kraft, now wife of ... Donald along. The poor woman is quite weak with consumption and must rely on the mercy of kind people for her support. She has 5 children. The man is a drunkard and has long since left her.

17. This morning at 9 o'clock, my wife had a stroke while she was in the woodshed, where Nancy found her, and it was soon apparent that her left side was lame, and quite useless, likewise her tongue; but her eyes, hearing, and mind suffered nothing. During the first week she complained of pain, but was soon better; but she still cannot move her left side.

20. Joseph E. Schneiders visited us. John Webers were also here a short while. Joseph Hege came a little in the evening.

21. Jacob Brubachers, Joseph Webers and Daniel Webers visited us today.

22. Many of our neighbours were here today. Anna Erb, Mary Ann Schumacher, L. Schetter and wife. She is a cousin to Nancy, and lives near Chambersburg, Pa. They went to Jacob Groffs for the night.

23. Joseph L. Webers visited us today.

24. Sem Webers visited us this afternoon. In the evening, Elias Brubacher's widow came and stayed overnight.

30. Betz Burkholder and Joseph Hege were here. John Weber's wife took the above-named Lena Kraft home with her, where the poor woman is to be cared for by friends as long as she lives, which by all appearances, may not be long. According to her desire, she was baptized early in July by Bishop Hege, and is willing and ready to follow the precious laws and commands of our dear Saviour.

July 1874

4. Nancy went with Isaacs to Ebys' in meeting today, where Woolner and Amos Kressman preached. Towards evening Elias Schneiders visited us. His letters from

Russia say that the [Mennonite immigrant] brethren will soon land at Toronto, and then travel to Manitoba on the Dawson Route.

Abraham C. Weber was born where Berlin now stands March 14, 1817. He became the owner of his father's farm, which he sold in 1853 to Sherriff Grange for $24,000, and bought the farms of B. Schantz, John Stafford, S. Bricker, Isaac Hege, and others. Enough land for seven farms, where his sons live. In 1850 he was chosen by lot as a minister of the Word, and remained a faithful minister until his death. Was married to Judith, youngest daughter of the old Peter Martin family, 1839. Raised 16 children, 15 still living. Died the 6th and was buried near Berlin on the 9th, where ministers Hege and Amos Kressman preached to a large number of people. With this departing, the sorrowing widow must miss a faithful husband, the children a loving father, and the church an earnest and sincere minister. He was still in meeting the day previous, but very weak. Age 57 years, 3 months, and 22 days. He was esteemed and loved.

11. [Reverend] George Schmitts visited us this afternoon. They went to Jacob Brubachers' in the evening, and to David Ebys' [meetinghouse, later Erb Street Mennonite Church] in meeting from there.

15. Dianna visited us today. In the evening Richard fetched her.

18. This afternoon I went to Toronto to meet the Russians who are on their way to Manitoba. G. Schmitt, D.Y. Schantz, E. Schneider, John Schuh, Hen Brubacher, Sem Schantz, I.E. Schantz, Andreas Weber, and D. Scherg also went along.

19. At 8:30 320 souls came to Toronto on the cars, where they unloaded at the immigration sheds and stayed until Tuesday afternoon at 2 o'clock, July 21. From here they went by cars to Collingwood. Then per Allen Line by steamers to Duluth, etc. This company is from southern Russia; consists of 69 families. Among them is one man of 76 years, down to children of 25 to 16 days old. They seem to be innocent, peaceful and modest people. In the large dining hall an afternoon worship service was held. For the opening they sang a hymn in soft and humble tones. Schmitt made a suitable introduction. Scherg then spoke further, and Heinrich Berg [probably Peter Baerg], a preacher of their party, concluded the service with well chosen remarks. Monday, some men chosen among us are gathering 60 hams and other provisions. From Collingwood on they have to support themselves. They are cheerful and seem healthy. Weigh from 180 to 220 and 250 lbs. They have close to $60,00[0] cash along altogether. Some have as little as $25, but they help each other. From 2 to 9 children per family. Another good point they have: *they use no tobacco!!*

19. Nancy went with Sem Rudy to Ebys' in meeting where Sem Weber and Moses Erb preached.

21. Today we took Mother from home for the first time since her stroke, and went to John Webers', where Lena Kraft now lies, weak with consumption. Everything went well.

26. Today we went to Joseph Webers'. Lately he had a hard attack of dysentery, but is better again. Mother endured it well.

28. This afternoon we took Mother to Benjamins'. She can bear the driving well.

29. This afternoon John Martins visited us. I received a dispatch that Henry Wiebe with 160 families are coming to Toronto tomorrow from southern Russia. From there they all want to go to Manitoba. Martin is going to see them.

August 1874

Misfortune! On Sunday, July 5, Tilman Schneider was driving near Dundee in Wilmot, along with two women, when his horse shied and started to kick. He jumped off and broke his leg, which was so bad that by the next Saturday he was a corpse, and was buried on the 13th, where ministers Schmitt and Moses Bauman held suitable sermons before a large gathering. Age 24 years, 1 month, and 24 days. He was single. His father was a son of Benjamin Schneider, Ox Bow [between Conestoga and Salem Swamp], and his mother was Susanna, daughter of old David Eby.

5. A.C. Weber's widow stopped by, but soon went home again.

8. Abraham Groffs visited us. Isaacs were at Schneiders in meeting. R. Quickfalls came home with them. Towards evening, Moses Springers also came and went home late in the evening.

10. Today we visited David Webers, possibly for the last time. We have now visited all my wife's brothers and sisters, to satisfy her. As she keeps growing weaker, we will likely not go away again.

16. Nancy went with Isaacs to Ebys' in meeting. Oberholtzer and Hege preached. Veronica Horst and Ben Brubacher's widow came along home. In the afternoon Hege held meeting here. The house was well filled.

18. We buried Henry B. Bauman [father of Waterloo MP Isaac E. Bauman] of Berlin, where he has lived for 40 years. He was buried in the old cemetery near [east of] Berlin where Daniel Wismer gave a suitable sermon. He leaves 3 sons and 2 daughters, all grown. Age 68 years, 10 months, and 9 days.

22. This afternoon Bill Hunspergers of Wilmot visited us, and went to Isaac Ebys' overnight, and tomorrow to P. Sauders' in Dunker meeting.

22. The long deceased Christian Reichert's widow was buried today. She was one of the first inhabitants of this county. She came as a young woman from Pennsylvania in 1800, to this Canadian wilderness, where she helped to share in the inconvenient bush life. The last 30 years she lived in Wilmot. She was 96 years, one month and 20 days old. [River Brethren minister] Niels Holm preached.

26. The 40 years deceased Jacob Sherk's widow was buried at Kressmann's cemetery [now Breslau Mennonite Church], where John McNally and Peter Geiger preached. She was a daughter of Jacob Bechtel. She had a large family, but few left in their fatherland. The rest are scattered through the western States. Age 74 years, 11 months and one day.

27. Doctor William Pipe, inhabitant of Berlin, was buried. He came as a lad with his destitute parents from England to this district, and worked as a farm hand, until he was strong enough to learn the turning-craft, although his inclination was to become a doctor. He gained the confidence of Samuel and Isaac Schantz, and Dr. Ephraim Willson, who helped him through his studies with money, and became a famous doctor. This summer he went to Europe to reclaim his ruined health, and came home to die. Age 39 years.

28. We visited Uncle Brubacher's this afternoon. They were busy gathering apples.

October 1874

4. [Nephew and wife] Andrew Webers visited us today. We were all at home.

10. Peter E. Weber's wife was buried in the old cemetery near Berlin. She was a daughter of Abraham D. Clemens, Breslau. She had been sick over two years with a form of consumption. Age a little over 30 years, but had no children. Ministers Hege and Woolner held suitable funeral sermons. [Servant] Nancy and [daughter Magda]Lena went to the funeral.

11. Nancy and Josiah went to Ebys' in meeting where communion was served.

15. Today I went with Nancy to her father, who now has his home with his son, Jacob. He is in his 83rd year, and as spry as one of fifty.

16. I and Pitt Sherk went to Webers' (Strasburg) meeting house [later Pioneer Park Christian Fellowship] where an ordination was to take place. Since John B. Schneider was unwilling to go through the lot, it was seen as not expedient to go ahead with it. Noah Stauffer, Jacob Ginrich, and Elias Weber were also in the lot.

18. Old David Erb's wife and daughter Susanna who lives near Widder Station visited us.

23. Today, Isaac Berge's widow from Michigan, formerly Nancy Huber, and her sister Kette, wife of Jacob Schlichter of Chicago, both cousins to Nancy, were here on a visit.

26. Seventeen Mennonite families from Russia came to Berlin today. Word of their arrival was sent from Quebec by telegraph, which gave us opportunity to make preparations for fetching them at Berlin, and quarter them for the winter in this area. By April they want to continue their journey to Manitoba. They seem to be honest and diligent people. The local inhabitants are doing their utmost to make their condition as comfortable as possible. Six families went from Toronto to Markham with Sem Risser to winter among the brethren there, and are going along to Manitoba in the spring.

29. Our governor appointed a Thanksgiving day for today, in his whole province; in consequence of this, meeting was held at our usual meeting places. I was at Ebys' where Steckle and Sherk preached.

November 1874

5. Ben Weber's [Widow Anna Schantz Weber] sale.

7. This afternoon we visited Benjamin B. Schneiders, and went home in the evening.

8. We were at Ebys' in meeting where Moses Erb and Woolner preached. Joseph S. Martins came home with us.

11. A family of Russian [Mennonites] came to Berlin today, named Klassen, consisting of ten persons, whom we quartered in Sem Brubacher's house in Lexington. They plan to go to Manitoba in the spring, to their acquaintances.

15. Today we visited Benjamin Schuhs. The 88-year-old David Schantz is there, and still quite spry.

22. We were at Ebys' in meeting where Elias Schneider and George Schmitt preached. There were a nice number gathered together, among them quite a few of the Russian brethren who now live in this district.

27. David Weber was here today. He came home from Markham a few days ago. He was with Anna at Cedar Grove, and found them all well.

December 1874

10. We buried old Benjamin Bauman in the old cemetery near Berlin. He came from Pennsylvania to Waterloo in 1809, then still a wilderness; was married to Susannah, daughter of old preacher Joseph Bechtel. He remained a faithful brother in the church. The ministers Hege and Schmitt preached to a large number of funeral attendants. Age 87 years, 9 months, and 22 days. I, my wife, and Nancy went to the burial. From there we visited Peter Brickers, who moved to Berlin from Blenheim in February.

20. We and Nancy went to Ebys' in meeting where many were gathered. Menno and Amos Kressman and Moses Erb preached. Menno Schantz, who was ordained deacon 2 months ago, was here the first time, and read the chapter. Afterwards we visited Bill Meyers. Moses Erbs were also there.

10 Klaas R. Reimer (1837 to 1906)

Steinbach, Manitoba

Diary selections: 31 October 1885 to 12 February 1896

Age: 47 in 1885

Klaas R. Reimer was the most powerful merchant in early Steinbach, Manitoba. Although his grandfather had been the relatively well-to-do farmer/bishop Klaas Reimer, founder of the Kleine Gemeinde Church, his own parents, Abraham Reimer (see diary 7) and Elisabeth Rempel of Petershagen, Molotschna Colony, New Russia, were poor. Soon after Klaas married Katherina Willms in 1857, however, he became relatively prosperous, and, after a move to Borosenko Colony, Klaas became a respected wheat farmer, sheep raiser and local plough manufacturer.

Although Klaas fathered 24 children, 19 of whom reached adulthood and several of whom became leading second-generation Steinbach, Manitoba, businessmen, he had a difficult family life. His first wife, Katherina, suffered from a debilitating mental illness and died in 1875, just six months after the great migration to Canada. His second wife, Helena Warkentin, died in 1885 in childbirth just nine years after their marriage, and three children from his third marriage to Margaretha Klassen died from various illnesses in a single year, 1894. A family history also notes that Klaas became disillusioned with living in Manitoba and in 1876 considered moving to Kansas or Nebraska. He changed his mind when his mother reminded him that "the dear Lord ... protected us on our journey here." Over the next 30 years, Klaas became one of the East Reserve's wealthiest men: in 1893 his store made $14,000 in sales, and 10 years later sales were double that. In 1906 when he died, he left not only a farm and business, but $2,300 to each of his surviving 17 children.

Still, Reimer is remembered as a devout man who was close to his community, relatives, and fellow Mennonites in other settlements. Klaas's notebook describes not only ties to an immediate community and extended family, but also his links to a wider world. They contain notes about letters that he sent to and received from relatives: his uncle, Bernard Rempel (1820-1891), his mother's youngest full brother in Russia; his cousin, Margaretha Reimer, a 28-year-old servant from Jefferson County, Nebraska; neighbour Jacob J. Friesen on 21 March 1886; his first wife's uncle, Gerhard Willms in Minnesota; Johan Willms, his first wife's brother in Kleefeld, Russia. Then, too, there are descriptions of letters to Peter Fast, Peter Friesen, Heinrich Ratzlaff, Heinrich Loewen, Peter Harms, and Jakob Enns from the sister settlement in Jefferson County, Nebraska. Other notes describe letters written to unrelated Mennonites in Manitoba's West Reserve, such as to well-to-do Gretna merchant Erdman Penner, as well as to customers in Minnesota, Kansas, and Ontario.

Most of the diary entries reproduced here are notes about letters written between 1885 and 1896. As a summary of the letters' contents, the notes often serve as a daily account of Klaas's life and offer frank viewpoints on community developments. The fact that the letters are not always in exact chronological order suggests that Klaas's notes were sometimes written days after the letters were posted. Then, too, the fact that the destination of the letters was usually written in German phonetics – rendering Scratching River as Krätschen Riefer, Plum Coulee as Plum Kulle, Gretna as Grätnau – illustrates the mindset of a person deeply rooted in his own community.

The notebook was preserved by John C. Reimer, Steinbach, Manitoba, and was translated by Peter U. Dueck, Steinbach, in 1987, with the sponsorship of Peter J. Reimer, Steinbach. For more information on Klaas Reimer see: Delbert Plett, *Storm and Triumph: The Mennonite Kleine Gemeinde, 1850-1875* (Steinbach, MB: 1986), which reproduced Reimer's autobiography (21-24); and Delbert Plett, *Pioneers and Pilgrims: The Mennonite Kleine Gemeinde in Manitoba, Nebraska and Kansas, 1874-1882* (Steinbach, MB: 1990), which contains the notes reproduced here (115-126). See also: Royden Loewen, "Klaas R. Reimer: From Rags to Riches but not from Village to World," *Historical Sketches of the East Reserve, 1874-1910*, edited by John Dyck (Steinbach, MB: 1994), 304-312.

Here are the letters that were written:

October 31, 1885: A letter to Bernhard Rempel

Dear Uncle and Aunt; May the peace of God, physical and as well as spiritual health, a never-ending hope, a very firm hope, be yours. This is my wish for you with all my heart and with a sincere Amen.

Dear Uncle; Quite some time has passed since I wrote you, and since you wrote us. What the actual reason for this is, I am almost unable to give a name to; it could be called laziness, for I still always feel it in me. That which I really want to do, I do not do; but that which I don't want, I do. That is how it is with my writing, when I have been encouraged by your letter; I make up my mind, having been quite excited about the letter, to answer it immediately; but if I wait for a while for a more suitable time. Ah, yes, this time has come after much hesitation; but it was through misfortune, not fortune, that the time and opportunity has come. However, one thing after another has befallen me.

First, you will have already heard that my dear wife died [11 months earlier, on 1 December 1884]. It was during childbirth, after the delivery, that she died a sudden death. At 8 o'clock in the evening she brought forth a son Martin and at 7 in the morning she was dead. Oh, what a hard test this was, to lose my dear wife who had been so dear to me! Concerning my first wife I had prayed the Lord to be merciful to me and take this heavy burden from me, and He did. But how much I prayed in this case, I cannot say, but God's will was otherwise. A person makes plans, but God leads. But when my wife said she was ready to die, that she had crossed all mountains and did not want to be here any longer, saying "Good-bye" with confidence. Oh, how they went right to heart. I thought about myself and examined myself, if I should have come to this point that I had complete confidence that I would be in eternal bliss, there could be no greater blessing either in this world or the next than to die.

Dear Friends, I must report to you that I have married again, [this time] to Margaretha, daughter of Johan Klassens, for which I am obliged to thank the Giver of all good things and pray that He, the Almighty God, would bless me and give me well being in the right love and trust in God. I am married since March 19 and have been well, praise God, till August 10, when I had the misfortune of falling into the basement, breaking my leg almost off. That scared me and I didn't know what to do. I thought, who would set the bone in my leg? There is no good bone-setter here, like Diedrich Wiebe, Lichtfelde. One does not know of anybody like him around here. However, I sent for a man, his name is Heinrich Dick, Rosengart. He set my bone but I still can't walk or stand. I sit and write and read, although I haven't had much pain, and I can walk with crutches. I do hope that I'll soon be able to walk again, God willing.

Dear Uncle, I must tell you that my dear parents are still living and dear Father, as is his habit, quite often walks from Blumenort to Steinbach. Our dear mother is very weak and sickly already, but work and sew she still does. They still have their cow, which she still always milks. They also kill their own pig every year, it gets extremely fat [as] it is looked after very punctually.

Oh, dear ones, how often we talk and think about you and wish that you could be here in our midst. From what we read in your first letter, one is amazed at all that is going on there, and at all that you have experienced because of the differences in the church. I suppose the whole world is in strife about church matters, and especially among us Mennonites. Everyone thinks he is alone, and no one else is right, forgetting that the Lord said He would gather his own from all the four corners of the world.

I must also inform you that Abraham Friesens were in Nebraska. Also, they were at Gerhard Willms' place in Minnesota and found them all to be in good health. However, the old uncle cannot forget his wife, whenever she is talked about, the eyes become teary. It seems as if he is also getting ready to enter eternal life. What he is so concerned about is his former life. Living such a life would prevent him from entering heaven. One also notices immediately that . . . he is committed. He used to be so attached to his tobacco pipe, which he could hardly be without. And this, as I have heard, he has not used for several years. One can imagine what an effort it takes to quit such a habit. Otherwise they are not doing too badly, and always have enough to eat and drink. Uncle Gerhard Rempel was also still up and around, but his strength is failing and he has aged very much. He has sent greetings to everyone.

Well, dear Uncle, I would like to ask you, if you are not thinking about coming here, even if only to visit for a year, or to move here for good? You would be well received here. And about travelling expenses, you can do it. I heard that Martin Barkmans of Nebraska are planning to travel to Russia in the next coming year. Their last trip had not cost them anything. He had so much income from trees and aprons that it had paid for his trip. I would think you could do the same, but I would first write and let you know what you should bring for our area, which should not pose any problems for you. In this I could be of much assistance to you.

Well beloved, I must close this time. Greetings from us and all your friends: Abraham Friesen, Widow Töws, Johan Reimers, Abraham Reimer, Peter Reimers, Abraham Penners and my dear parents. Also hearty greeting from us, including children and wife. Klaas and Margaretha Reimer. [This was] a letter written to Bernhard Rempel in Alexanderwohl, the 30th of October.

March 1, 1886 A letter written to Margaretha Reimer, [Jansen] Nebraska. It dealt with [my invitation] that she should come here with the wages that Anna had earned and that she need not work on the fields. Also that brother John would want to have company, for he will probably consent to staying in Manitoba. If that is the case, it is thought that she might also stay here. That is the content of the letter.

March 2, 1886 A letter to Uncle Gerhard Willms in Minnesota [from] Manitoba, Steinbach, on the 2nd of March [from] Klaas Reimer.

Dear Uncle Gerhard Willms: My wish for you is that you would have peace, well-being and blessing as well as health in body, but more so in soul. Amen. For a long time I have thought of writing and at last feel I have to write you a few lines and pay you a visit, although my writing is not perfect. To pay a personal visit is always difficult, especially for my nature. First, to leave my family that is so dear to me, and secondly, to leave the friends around here. This caused a lot of tears to fall, for by nature I am quite soft-hearted, so it is quite hard for me, especially parting from friends and family.

February 1, 1890 Wrote a letter to Uncle Bernhard Rempel, a friendly letter, about this being the third letter I have written him, [and wondering] whether he was dead already, that he should let us know whether he is still living. Also wrote about the ages of myself, my wife and my parents and each person's weight. Also greetings from all, also the parents.

February 20 A letter to Uncle Gerhard Willms, regarding our state of health, the parents' health, the number of children and their health. Also that his children, the Siemens, have come from Russia and what a joy this had been for him; also how much greater joy it will be in that eternal land along with all. Greetings from parents and siblings.

February 10 A letter to Penner, Gretna, Manitoba, regarding the 10 dozen shawls which he has not paid for yet, and he asks payment for the 52 lbs. of cherries. They could be considered to pay for the former items, so everything was settled. Erdman Penner, Gretna.

February 10 A letter to Mr. Neufeld, Plum Coulee [Manitoba], Post Office, regarding the printed aprons, of which I do not need any this year.

February 10, 1890 A letter to Abrams and Esau, Gretna, regarding the cheese money that they still owed, $34.20; and that this was already received.

February 20 A letter to Peter Isaaks, Nebraska, regarding the 17 aprons and shawls for $27.00. Then also, a friendly letter, regarding the large amount of snow, the many cases of sickness and influenza that occur here in almost every family; now and then also deaths occur.

A letter on February 10 to Peter Harms, Nebraska, for Harms the elder. How he finds such a marriage in his old age, in his 80th year with a wife of 38 years. That it is often not good when this happens; that such a thing should rather not happen, as the consequences are seldom good.

To Nebraska, 1890 A letter on February 20 to Heinrich Ratzlaff. I sent him 6 aprons at 60 cents each, [totalling] $3.60 and a letter whose subject matter was the 3 feet high snow trails and about going a roundabout way to church on such a snow road. Also that we all want to go to heaven and indeed there is only one way there, what he thought about his. Asked him to answer soon. Also about 10 weeks of rheumatism and influenza.

February 21 [To] Minnesota, Bingham Lake: Sent goods to Johan Görtzen: 3 aprons at 55 cents equals $1.65; and 9 shawls at 25 cents equals $2.25; and seeds for $3.90. In case they did not want these goods, they should give them to old Gerhard Willms, as a present for the cousins. Encouraged him to order good. I have a contract with the cheese factory, and how much butter sells for 13 . . . And 12,000 lbs.

February 1 Letter to Isaak Harms, Rosenort: Contents of which were $20.00, taken over from A. Friesen, Blumenort.

March 1, 1890 A letter to Johan Willms, Kleefeld, Russia. It concerned [my admission] that we had waited far too long till we wrote. About the passing away of Jakob Görtzen, his lovely letters and also our visit to Minnesota in 1884. And that I am asking brother-in-law, J. Willms, for some information about Kleefeld. Who of those in 1864 are still living there? And about Bernhard Rempel, whether he is still living? Also how are things going as far as temporal matters are concerned? With whom we own the mill: P[eter] Bark[man], A[bram] Reim[er], and K[laas] Reim[er], and P[eter] Reim[er]. That in six months in their cheese factory they can make 30,000 lbs of cheese and process 4,000 lbs. milk into cheese in 6 hours. The cheese sells for 9 to 10 cents a pound, they pay 65 cents a 100 lbs for the milk. The people realize that this is a third more than if they make butter, and only half the work. I asked for information about our friends. Greetings from the parents, that they are well, the siblings as well as the parents, we all send many greetings. Goodbye.

Helpful Hints for House and Farm:

Using cheap paint on rough wood. Take sweet milk and enough cement to make it thick enough to paint with a whitewash brush. This works very well.

If one of your cattle gets bloated, take hay-twine and turn it till it is as thick as an arm, put this in the mouth and tie it up on top of the head. Leave it standing till the bloating it gone, repeat until the sickness is completely gone.

For a wound caused by piercing or cutting or any other painful wound, take unwashed wool, put it on live coals, then fumigate the wound till the pain abates.

For deafness: If someone is deaf, take a hot freshly-baked bread, bore a hole through the crust so that the small end of a funnel fits into it; slowly pour a glass of whisky containing a high percentage of alcohol into this bread; hold over the hole so that it will become absorbed or bathed; repeat.

March 1, 1890 [To] Plum Coulee: A letter, often repeated, to Krause regarding the $20.00 that he promised to pay but has not yet; it seems the last one is worse than the first one was.

March 8, 1890 [To] Scratching River, Rosenort [Manitoba]. A letter.

Dear brother-in-law, Isaak Harms: Four weeks ago I sent a letter where I enclosed $21.00. You have not sent me any information or receipt, is this not worth the trouble? Someone knows where it is?

March 8, 1890 [To] Scratching River, Rosenhof, a letter to Gerhard Warkentin, about his moving away from here, having sold his property for $700.00 and that he still owed me $32.25. I would think he would have been too honest to move away like that, also that it is 6 years that I have left it without interest. At 6% up to 1890 it would already amount to $212.25, which I would grant him if he would pay me. Greetings.

March 8, 1890 To Feschbok, in Western Denmihren [?]. A letter for Eva Schareina, that I sent $10.00 for her to Feschbok.

March 14 [To] Kansas: A letter to Widow Dörksen. Sent her the wool and six shawls, dropped the price 10 cents for the defects in the aprons. I also wrote her what the prices were. Concluded with greetings from us and the parents.

March 15, 1890 [To] Kansas: A letter to the aunt, Mrs. Esau, to encourage her in bearing the cross that she has because of her husband. Out of sympathy I sent her material for a dress, for an apron and a shawl. Concluding greetings.

March 20, 1890 [To] Minnesota: A letter from Unrau, Katherina Willms, the contents of which were very spiritual, that in their conscience they have been truly converted, with the Saviour. Nothing about temporal matters.

March 30, 1890 [To] Kansas: [I sent the] widow Dörksen 1 dozen cashmere shawls at $3.00 a dozen. I also sent her a statement giving the total amount owing.

[April 1, 1890] A receipt from Heinrich Plett, Blumenort: I acknowledge with my own signature that I have duly received the capital with interest to April 1, 1890, of Elisabeth Reimer, wife of Heinrich Plett. Total amount is three hundred seventy-six dollars and eighteen cents ($376.18). [Signed] A.S. Friesen.

April 5 [To] Minnesota, Bingham Lake: Received a letter from Johan Görtzen with a cheque for $3.90. He ordered goods again, 1 dozen aprons and 1 dozen shawls. I also sent shawl samples.

April 10 [To] Minnesota, Bingham Lake: Wrote him a letter that we sent him goods for $16.00. Also about the weather, that we had sleigh roads till Easter and are planning to start seeding by April 14.

April 10 [To] Pembina, Reinland P.O.: A letter to V. Niesen's Johan in response to his letter of March 26, that he wants to purchase the place in Rosenort. He can have it for $500.00, a bank transaction for $400.00 to be made up with Joh. Klassen. He is to trade building lots with Kornelius Rempel, because of old Mrs. Rempel's illness, and make a down payment of $100.00.

April 10 [To] Minnesota, Heinrich Unrau: A letter to brother-in-law. It concerned my dissatisfaction with myself as far as my soul is concerned, as he expresses himself in his writing. No! Much rather that even if we would have done everything, we are still unprofitable servants. He says he is converted and does not have to live a life of temptation any longer, which one would wish.

April 19 A letter from Nebraska, from Heinrich Ratzlaff. A letter that was quite kind-hearted, about uniting. He asks for true brotherly love even though we do not belong to the same church.

April 25 A letter to Nebraska, to Heinrich Ratzlaff: Many thanks for the love shown in the letter, also for the cheque for $3.90. There shall be no party spirit about church matters. Also about the senior Mr. Harms's infirmities of old age.

April 25, 1890 [To] Russia: A letter from uncle Bernhard Rempel written March 15, stating that he is rapidly getting more and more feeble, and does not expect to write very many letters any more.

May 10, 1890 A letter to Russia to Uncle Bernhard Rempel. It concerned my response about church matters, how the separation [in] the Nebraska church came about. Also regarding our parents' health and their feebleness of old age, the number of children, about earthly matters and seeding time. Wrote about Ungers, that they are here, and how we enjoy being with them, etc. Also sent them 25 envelopes.

August 9, 1890 A letter to Nebraska, to Peter Isaak, that the cheque was received. About the hail we had on August 1, two thirds of the grain crop was destroyed.

August 9 A letter to Kansas, to Widow Dörksen, stating that I do not want to force the deal on her, but if she wants me to I will send her the goods.

July 10 Nebraska, Peter Fast, Nebraska: A letter written about my childhood and youth in Rosenort, Russia, where my cradle once stood and then [following my life story] to the present time. Sent 2 packages of shawls. Also about parents, siblings and acquaintances.

September 6, 1890 A letter from Nebraska, from Peter Fast, which he had written on August 25. He had enclosed a draft for $12.45. Also about his 4 siblings, where they ... and how they are faring, and how himself is doing.

September 6 Received a letter from Cousin P. Friesen of Nebraska, which he had written on August 28 [and in which] he told about their sickness and rheumatism, also about friends and acquaintances.

[No date] A letter from Nebraska, Peter Isaak, written by him on September 1, 1890. He ordered 4 dozen shawls. He also wrote about his health. A greeting to A.S. Friesen, that he should answer his letter.

September 1 A letter from David Klassen, Rosenhof, Morris, of August 26. It concerned his report that he has had a serious problem regarding work animals. He would very much like to borrow or buy an ox. He states that they are well, requests leniency concerning his debts.

September 1 Wrote a letter to David Klassen, Rosenhof, Morris. That he can have the ox until November 1, 1891, and then return same with the others again, which Klaas Brandts were to bring back.

September 6, 1890 Wrote a letter to Peter Friesen, Nebraska. Wished him better health. Described the kind of harvest we had. We canned 20 gallons of fruit, at a cost of 50 lbs. sugar. We made 50,000 lbs. of cheese, sold it for 9 cents a lb. A certain amount was figured for the work, leaving 2 cents. Parents were well, thank God, but very weak.

In 1890, on October 6 Sent Klaas Wiebe, Nebraska, a draft for $5.00 for the elder Harms, to help him in his need that he addressed to me.

October 8, 1890 To my address, a letter from David Hiebert, Nebraska, and a draft for $70.00 for the elder Isaac Harms.

October 11, 1890 [To] Nebraska: A letter from Cousin Peter Friesen, Nebraska. He writes that Mrs. Dietrich Isaac died on October 9, at 8 in the morning, after being very sick for 4 weeks following childbirth. She is my cousin, Peter Rempel's daughter.

The 25th of October 1890 I [wrote] a letter to Klaas Wiebe, Nebraska, as a receipt for the $5.00 cheque, also greetings from old Harms and from us.

The 25th of October 1890 A letter to Nebraska, to David Hiebert, with a receipt showing that I had received the $70.00 draft for old Isaak Harms; also that I had paid the $3.00 to Abraham Friesen; also about our health.

1891 A letter to Kansas, to Widow Dörksen, and a receipt for $20.00, also $5.00, also $10.23; and that we are well.

[No date] A letter to Nebraska, to Jakob Ennses, and also to the others [?]. Sent a package of goods for $3.66. Also a package of needles as a present.

January 2, 1891 A letter to Peter Isaaks asking them to make a silk net for Elisabeth, and to send it to us in a letter or somehow.

January 24, 1891 A letter from Russia, from Johan Willms. He scolds me for not writing enough, he thinks I have not answered him once. He also writes that Peter Engbrecht died in November, having been married for 29 years, that he died in 1890.

January 24 A letter from Maria Dörksen, Kansas, stating that they are well and that they have received their Christmas gift from us, without duty and say thank you.

January 24 A letter from Peter Isaak, Nebraska. Contained an order for a few shawls. All are well, except Abraham, he was very sick. Enclosed the silk net for Elisabeth, for 2 small pretty shawls.

January 24 [To] Nebraska, Heinrich Löwen, a letter that he wants 6 shawls with narrow borders.

January 31, 1891 I wrote a letter [to] Russia, Johan Willms, Kleefeld. I wrote that it was much better here than in Russia. Wrote about the milking machines and how many cows we have. Also that he should explain how Hein. Willms got 226 *Tschwert* wheat [1 *chetvert* = 5.7 bushels] from one farm. About Kornelius Willms, why he is so poor, whether he has had much misfortune? Asked where Jakob Berk, my [former] employer, lives? Also asked how Uncle B. Rempel is getting along? Requested that he inform me about everything, for which I enclosed a package of needles and a 25-cent bill.

January 30, 1891 [To] Minnesota: A letter to old Gerhard Willms, Minnesota, and to all cousins. Promised that whoever will write back first, will receive a present.

January 31 [To] Nebraska: I wrote a letter to Heinrich Löwen, also sent him 6 shawls with narrow borders.

[Recipes for ailments]: Eating an onion with salt or vinegar is good for a cold or a cough, the mucus will loosen up immediately. Also the centre of a red onion, fried till well done is exceptionally good for when children have ear aches. Push the same into the ear as hot as possible. Boiled onions are the best vegetables and ward off many sicknesses going around among children. For a compress on the legs, one boils onions, cuts them into small pieces and puts them into goose fat. Place these onions onto the child's feet, as hot as it can stand it. Also apply this on the chest. Onions are also good blood cleansers, for boils and skin disorders (rashes). If one suffers from a cough, apply a raw onion and the mucus will dissolve and the coughing will stop right away.

February 8 [To] Russia: [I] wrote a letter to Bernhard Rempel. Sent five small sheets of paper and a package of needles. Reported about the siblings and parents. Reminded him that he promised to answer. Invited him and his children to come here. Also many greetings. Also about Ungers, how they are making out.

February 21 A letter [to] Minnesota [to] Johan Siemens. Sent him a gift of $5.00 and a package of needles. Informed him that I was unable to lend him the $50.00 because money was scarce. The silver coins I was going to lend him now again have their full value also here. Received a letter from him on February 14.

February 14 Received a letter from Minnesota, Johan Kwierrink [Quiring?]. I responded on February 21, that we and also the parents were well, thank God. I sent along a package of the new style of needles.

February 7 and 12 Received a letter from Minnesota, Kornelius Willms [relating] that they are well. They each wrote one sheet full. They got 275 bushels of wheat from 25 acres, 630 bush. Oats, barley 179 bushels, potatoes enough. Everything seems to be well.

February 21 Received [two] letters from Kornelius, one from February 12 and the other from February 13. The first one I did not like as well as the last. I had written him a letter earlier on February 9 that it was saddening that he had gone to get his schooling in Winnipeg, which I had not given him permission to do. Higher education often results in pride. As well, the wisdom of this world is often foolishness before God. I wrote 3 sheets full, advising him as well as I was able, to come back. I also confessed my error that I had allowed him to go to Winnipeg too often on business where he had become too well acquainted with the big merchants.

May 9, 1891 A letter arrived from Russia, from Johan Reimer, Alexanderwohl, which he wrote on March 24. The content of which is that Uncle Bernhard Rempel has died. He had been sick for 4 months, one month he had eaten nothing. He writes that Uncle Bernhard starved to death; yet in the end he had hope of dying and entering into the state of greater bliss. He died on February 20, and I had written him [a letter] on February 8, which he had not read. I had also sent him a package of needles, with an open eye on the end, but this had disappeared on the way. Uncle Bernhard had reached an age of 71 years, being the youngest one of Mother's brothers and sisters. I corresponded with him a great deal, but now this has come to an end with him.

Two letters to Johan Willms, Russia, on January 6, 1892. The contents of one letter were 4 packages of flower seeds and two pictures for the girls. The other letter was about moving here, the property by Ranke is said to be valued at $2,400.00. About Kornelius, the flowers; translated into English. The second letter on the same date.

December 28 Received a letter from Johan Willms, Kleefeld, Russia. He would like very much to come to America. They caught the five rascals that killed an official in Orhloff, but let them go right away. He writes that it is quite evident that the Russians are filled with animosity. Also about getting 350 *tschetwert* wheat, over 10 *tschetwert* [1 *chetvert* = 5.7 bushels] from 1 *desjatien* [1 *desiatina* = 2.7 acres], valued at 850 rubles, and 2 *desjatien* potatoes at 2 rubles per *tschwert*.

January 28, 1893 [?] Received a letter from Jakob Berg, Russia, stating that he was planning to move here for the fall. He would leave his wife there and return later to get her and the money he had coming. Wrote to him immediately on July 1, 1892, that he should surely come; that it is very good here, but . . .

January 29, 1893 [?] A letter to Jakob Berg, Russia, asking why he did not answer my letter of last July, or what had happened to him? Offered to sell the store to him for 20% less than market price, for 10 or 11,000 dollars; half of it in cash.

January 30, 1893 [?] I wrote a letter to Johan Willms, Russia, [noting] that he should surely come here. I would sell him the store at 20% less than market value and that there were some 300 customers and [that we have] monthly sales of 1,200 dollars.

January 29, 1893 A letter to William Schneider, Waterloo, regarding the 2 moose horns, in size they are 3 feet and 9 inches, with 11 tips. The asking price for the two – $20.00.

January 30, 1893 A letter to Peter Harms, Nebraska, about the debts still owed here by old Mr. Harms. That they should bear in mind that we had taken good care of him and that they had mentioned paying everything in a previous letter.

January 16 Wrote 1 letter to Johan Willms, Kleefeld, Russia, about how we were doing, that the children had died and also Mother and Father.

December 10, 1894 Wrote a letter to Johan Warkentin. Sent him money with Peter Barkman's son: $2.00; Old Barkman $1.00; myself $7:00; and Blacksmith Peter Töws $2.00; for a total amount of $12.00. This was sent for a need to Colorado, Johan Warkentin. [Note in margin] Received a reply that he has received the money.

February 2 1895 A letter to Isaak Thiessen, Russia: That I have had 3 wives and that my family, as God has willed, numbers 20 children and that my hair now is white on account of my many troubles that I have encountered in my life. And that we have a [flour] mill and how much the mill produces. And that Abraham has a saw mill and [that he operates] 20 miles from here. Also that the two sons have three cheese factories within 10 miles and that they make $15,000 worth of cheese in 5 months and that we still work the farm and that we have 30 cows, 15 young cattle and 7 horses. And ordered from him 2 lbs *Borstlen* [?] and I sent him a 25-cent money order . . .

[Commencement of daily diary]

January 26 [1895] Heinrich Friesens were home and stayed for the night, they sold the Töws property to Peter for $1,000.00.

January 28 It was -30 and Friesens went home.

January 31, 1895 It froze 28 degrees and very windy. Mr. Sprague was here and bought 500 bushels of oats to be delivered to the camp for 35 cents a bushel. He also has 1,200 bushels lying at the slough for which he will pay 10 cents for delivering it.

February 1 -40 and very nice weather.

February 4 -44. Brother Johan Reimer drove Katherina and Elisabeth to *Jantseit*.

February 3 -45, nice weather.

February 4 -46, but no wind.

February 5 -40. Gerhard went to Sprague's camp with 7 loads of oats, 460 bushels that sold for 35 cents. Two Englishmen and two Frenchmen and two of Johan Friesen's boys [served as teamsters].

February 6 -22 and very windy. A letter from minister Johan Friesen, Rosenhof.

February 14 -20. 13 bushels went to Sprague's tree-felling camp. Gerhard brought 2,300 lbs. of meat at 6 cents to the camp, and 2,500 lbs. beef at 4 cents. Also 600 bushels of oats for 42 cents and 4 sleighs at 35 cents per hundred. The cartage for the oats was 12 cents.

February 16 A letter to the *Rundschau* concerning the letter to Isaak Thiessen, Rosenhof, Russia, that he should trace it. Also about *Paradise in the Years of Youth*. Greetings to Peter Janzen and the aged Mr. Harms in Kleefeld, also to Funk and Peters, and to Editor Harms.

February 18 14 loads of oats to Sprague, 1,200 bushels at 42 cents.

February 27 I was in Winnipeg. Rain and +12. I sold 4,000 lbs. of butter to Finkelstein for clothes and crockery.

[Notes on 1895 letters continued]

February 4 Received a letter from Johan Friesen, Minister, Rosenhof. He greatly saddened me, as he points out to me the matter of greediness that Peter Peters [Dutch Mennonite Pieter Pietersz wrote *Spiegel der Gierigheydt* (*Mirror of Greed*) in 1638] writes about doing business; [Son-in-law and business partner] Peter Barkman wrote an answer to the letter on February 10.

March 9 A letter to Heinrich Friesens, Rosenhof, about church matters; regarding business deals, what all this will come to if they are blaming me, while they keep forgetting how much unrighteousness occurs because of poverty when the sheriff is even taken to help; that does not seem right to me, and one wonders what all this is coming to. Greetings to the ministers. I have read my letter to [my] brother [Reverend] Peter Reimer.

[Daily diary for 1895 continued]

March 11 -25, but sleigh roads are good. On March 9 Gerhard came home from Sprague, he had gone on the 5th: 190 50-lb. bags flour, 2,100 meat at 4 cents [a pound].

March 12 -25. Ewert of Gretna was here for the night. He had come to visit the schools together with young Janzen, formerly of Tannenau.

March 13 -33. Ewert went to Blumenort.

March 14 -20. Jakob Barkman has gone to Winnipeg with 200 dozen eggs and butter and 1 calf.

March 15 -20, thawing at noon. Barkman came back, he had received 20 cents for the eggs and 11 cents for the butter.

March 16 -20. Sold the bull from Lichtenau for $10.00. The sorrel mare had a little foal.

March 17 -15. Peter Barkmans and Heinrich Reimers went to Grünfeld to church.

March 18 Thawing. Jakob Kröker and Johan Friesen were here for church in Steinbach. They conducted the examinations for baptism. There were two services, Johan Friesen preached in the afternoon.

March 19 Thawed a lot. The articles were read and [agreed that] Mrs. Günther [would be] received into the fellowship of the church [through baptism]; [Mr. Günther] has been excommunicated for two years [and wishes to be reinstated into membership].

March 20 Mrs. Günther was baptized and [Mr. Günther] was accepted into the church again. The ministers returned home [to Rosenort]. There was much thawing and a lot of water.

March 21 Thawing. Jakob Barkman went to Winnipeg with eggs and butter; the price of the eggs is 15 cents and for the butter 11 cents a lb. There is also much water in the creek.

March 22 Thawing. Sleigh roads are disappearing in Steinbach, very much water in our river. Bred 2 cows.

March 29 I and the children went to Peter Reimers in Grünfeld for the funeral of their little son Klaas, who died on March 27.

April 2 Jakob Barkman and Gerhard went to Winnipeg with 700 dozen eggs and 400 lbs. butter. We pay only 8 cents for butter and for eggs 8 cents. [Son] Abraham Reimer came home from the bush [camp] with all his workers.

April 4 Built a hot bed, planted cabbages in it.

April 11 Jakob Barkman went to Winnipeg with butter at 8 cents, eggs at 8 cents, chickens at 20 cents and onions at 3 cents. Very nice weather.

April 17 Barkman went to Winnipeg with butter and eggs and skins. Nice weather.

[Notes on 1895 letters continued]

April 1, 1895 Letter from Isaak Thiessen, Russia, dated February 27, Train Depot, L.S.D. Station, Sofiehke. Very warm, some frost at night.

April 15 Wrote a letter to Heinrich Friesen. Dearly beloved friends: Loving, heart-felt greetings. Wish that these lines would find you in good health as they also have left us. Also my wish for you, as well for us, that we would meet up yonder in that place of rest, where there will be no more parting for ever and ever. This is what the dear Saviour has wrought for us by his suffering and dying, and opened the way for us, of which we have again been reminded by our ministers yesterday and today, Easter. Also everything is green, the trees and the meadow, in this new season of the year, give us a cheerful outlook to the summer ahead. People have done a lot of seeding already; some are even finished; it looks very promising. We also had rain, after yesterday's dust [storm], which we seldom have here.

My dear friend, I want to reply to your letters. Several years ago I heard that your father in Blumenort read a letter, which said that you had changed your Sunday over to Saturday. Are you with the Seventh Day Adventists now, or where do you consider yourself to belong, to which church? I forget the places where you lived then, nor can I remember where you live now. It was also read to the brotherhood, two times this year already, concerning the need that you and your family are suffering. I feel sorry, for your family especially, that you are so far away from relatives and acquaintances, also from the church, and have left everything, so that you, as well as your wife and children, have become so poor that you have nothing to eat nor have a light or oil for a lamp. That reminds me of those 5 young virgins, who had no oil and couldn't find the door to eternal life. In a similar way you are experiencing this in the temporal. Perhaps your light has gone out, so that you cannot see where you would be able to make a better living with your family. That isn't so easy, to go haphazardly into a country where there is no way of earning a living. Here in Manitoba where you didn't like it at all, and where, according to your letter, you had lived nine years and nine years too long, such a thing has, as far as I know, not occurred yet, where one didn't have enough to eat or the necessary oil for a lamp.

It is true, many have left Manitoba, claiming that it is too cold and summer is too short. However, letters confirm that northern regions have more bread than many other southern regions. This winter it was especially remarkable how many letters came in from needy people, asking for help. And everything is scarce here too, particularly cash money.

Food is very inexpensive here and there is much of it on hand. If you would still be here on your old place, where Kornelius Fast lives, your children would find employment and have bread enough, although there are poor people here, temporally as well as spiritually.

Well, dear friend, since money was to be collected for you on the first Easter day, your father gave me the money that had come in; this was only $1.05. However, having pity for your family, as well as for you, I am adding so much that the total amount comes to $5.00, so that you will understand how it is with me. Although I don't feel rich, especially do I feel poor and sick spiritually, I want you to know that you can gladly come into my house with a letter, whenever you are in need. I love you. Everybody makes mistakes, in temporal matters as well as in the spiritual. In conclusion, many greetings from your parents as well as me, my wife and children, also from friends and acquaintances. Goodbye. Farewell. Also do let us know whether you have received this letter and the enclosed money. Amen.

Do read this letter to your children and ask their advice. Perhaps matters will improve for you, both temporally and spiritually, or you will come back. Goodbye.

[Daily diary for 1895 continued]

May 4 Planted the earliest potatoes. One pound cost 1 dollar, they are supposed to be ready for eating in 33 days. Had the brown mare bred by Kornelius Fast's stallion. Planted 1,000 cabbage plants. The plum trees are blooming. Finished planting all the potatoes.

May 9 Our son David was born, all well and chipper.

May 10 Frost ice as thick as a pane of glass.

May 11 Frost again one quarter inch thick. The seeding is finished.

[Notes on 1895 letters continued]

February 15 Wrote a letter to Johan Bärg, Morden, that he may have a job in the mill.

February 14 A letter to Jakob Enns, about the principal that I owed old Mr. Kornelsen.

February 14 To Heinrich Ratzlaff, Nebraska, about the 2 notes that he still has here. I am willing to extend them, but I want him to pay Jakob Ens the $25.00 that I owe him.

February 15 Wrote a letter to Johan Görtzen in which I enclosed $2 for the cards he sent here. My wife also sent a stamped apron for sister-in-law Görtzen.

February 18 A letter to Isaak Thiessen, Russia, concerning my negligence in letter writing.

February 15 A letter in response to one of February 8, received from Johan Willms, Kleefeld [Russia].

[Daily diary for 1896 continued]

February 12, 1896 My wife together with her parents went to Minnesota. She and our small two children, Martin and David, were gone for not quite 2 weeks. They came home safe and sound with the two children on November 25. Their parents stayed 3 weeks longer and also came home from their journey.

February 18 Has always been very cold, one day, on the 10th it was down to -42. The next day to -30 with much snow and wind. No one has gone to Sprague in the last two weeks. [On February] 14 two sows had piglets and over half of them died. Again 2 sows had piglets of which over half died. So from those 4 sows only 13 remained alive. We put a stove in the barn for the day time, this is good. [On February] 17 a sow had piglets in our heated barn and now 10 of 11 remained alive.

Married Men and their Work

V

11 Ephraim Cressman (1855 to 1911)

Breslau, Ontario
Diary selection: 1 January to 31 December 1890
Age: 35

Ephraim Cressman was born on 4 October 1855, near Doon, Canada West, to Isaac Cressman and Barbara Schneider, Mennonites whose parents had come from Pennsylvania earlier in the century. At age 21, in 1876, he purchased and began working a farm (German Company Tract lot #105) about three kilometres east of Breslau. He became especially known for his skill at fattening steers for export and added to the farm income by harvesting logs on his farm. Six years later, in 1882, he married Susannah Betzner, and together they moved to the Breslau farm, where they lived until Ephraim's death in 1911.

In 1890, Ephraim was a young family man, father to two children, Myra Ellen, six, and Laura May, three. He mentioned both with reference to illnesses. Although their nuclear family was small, both Ephraim and Susannah came from large families. Not only did most of Susannah's nine siblings and Ephraim's 10 siblings live in Waterloo County, but there were also a number of single siblings in both families. Ephraim thus encountered his married sisters Mary Biehn and Barbara Schweitzer, his married brothers Josiah Cressman and Allen Cressman, and unmarried siblings, Adam, Minerva, and Sarah. Then, too, Susannah's siblings dropped by for visits: Mary Stauffer was her eldest sister, and Ellen and Norman were Mary's children; Noah Stauffer was the husband of the second sister, Barbara, and Ida and Obal were their children; Isaac Betzner, Moses Betzner, and Samuel Betzner were Susannah's brothers; Aaron Cressman was married to sister Magdalena; Lydia Ann Betzner, the youngest sister, who married Ozias Snyder on 29 January 1890. Ephraim's youth also meant that he was intricately tied to the household of both sets of parents: "Dad Betzner" refers to Susannah's 72-year-old father, Jacob Betzner, of Breslau, and "Ma Betzner" refers to her 61-year-old mother, Maria. "Dad's" refers to Ephraim's 60-year-old father, Isaac Cressman, and his 56-year-old wife, Barbara. Most of these family members lived within a few kilometres of Ephraim and Susannah.

Ephraim was also actively involved in the wider community. He visited prominent community members like Moses and Rebecca (Hagey) Kraft, who owned and managed three large farms, and Levi Stauffer, a member of the United Brethren Church, who was manager of the North Waterloo Farmers' Mutual Fire Insurance Company from about 1880. He also carried on a variety of business dealings with neighbours, including Peter Reist, the eldest son of Daniel Reist, from whom Ephraim originally purchased his farm. And, like so many other Mennonites, there were ties to the United States, drawn by visiting ministers from Michigan and Virginia, and "Ma's" relatives from Indiana. Finally, Ephraim moved easily in the wider non-Mennonite world, visiting a debating club in February, attending a lecture on Canada-United States trade in June, and actively campaigning in the Ontario provincial election later that month.

An original copy of the diary, handwritten in English, is located at the Mennonite Archives of Ontario in Waterloo. It was transcribed by Reg Good.

1890 January

1 New Years Day. At Home. Rain.

2 Writing & opened water courses. Heavy rain last night & this forenoon [the weather] changed. Fine.

3 Haul[ed] wood to Breslau & Berlin. Fine.

4 To Berlin Market & [hauled] wood. In afternoon visitors, Barbara & Minerva Cressman. Fine.

5 **Sun.** To Cressmans' Meeting[house for church service];Visitors,William Krafts, Ellen Stauffer & Lydia Ann Betzner. Rain.

6 To Breslau & Moses Kinzie's. A terrible heavy rain last night, some more in forenoon. Very very wet & muddy.

7 Cutting wood & logs & [went to] Breslau with wood. Fair.

8 To Breslau with wood &c. Snowing & Storming.

9 Haul[ed] wood to Breslau & Berlin. More snow.

10 To Breslau with chopping & again with wood. Snow.

11 To Berlin Market &c. Rain & sleet. Sleighing now but poor.

12 **Sun.** At Home cloudy. Foggy. [A] little rain. Sleighing used up.

13 Helped to wash & churn Butter. Heavy rain last night, very windy & snow flurries. Visitors.

14 To Berlin with wood &c. Fine.

15 To Breslau & Berlin with wood. Visitor, Mrs. Eph Weber. A little rain & snow.

16 To Berlin with wood & Blustery cold.

17 To Berlin with wood &c. Fine.

18 To Berlin Market, 20 cts. for butter & [to] Breslau again. Roads good for wheels. Fine.

19 Sun. To Cressman's church. Visitors: Abr. S. Clemmers, Norman Stauffer, Ozias Snyder, Abr. Snyder, Melinda Clemens, Lizzie Snyder & Lydia Ann Betzner. Fine mild weather.

20 To Berlin with wood &c. Rain during night. Changed colder.

21 To Breslau 3 times. [Two-and-a-half-year-old baby daughter] Laura sick with Influenza. Cold blustery, snow flurries.

22 To Berlin with wood. Bot. a fur Overcoat for $22.00. Fair.

23 To Berlin with wood & more snow.

24 To Breslau &c. Freddie & [six year old daughter] Myra down with La Grippe. People sick with it all over the country, it originated in Russia. Fair.

25 To Berlin Market & Waterloo Co[unty] Farmers Mutual Fire Insurance Annual Meeting. Fair.

26 Sun. At Home. Foggy, some flurries.

27 To Breslau & Berlin with wood. Fair.

28 To Berlin with wood & [to] Natchez School House meeting for the purpose of organizing a Farmers Union.

29 To Wedding of Ozias Snyder & Miss Lydia Ann Betzner. Fine.

30 To Berlin with wood &c. Soft, foggy.

31 To Breslau with wood & chopping. Heavy snow in morning, changed. Fine roads. . . .

February

1 To Berlin Market. Fair hard frost.

2 Sun. To Cressmans' Meeting & Levi Stauffer's. Cold.

3 Took Ellen Stauffers to Abr. Biehns Mild road. . . .

4 Churning Butter. Splitting wood &c. Jerry Schantz & Annie Snyder married. Foggy, a little rain.

5 To Moses Betzner's & Debating School in evening at Breslau School House. Very windy, cold.

6 Splitting wood & [to] Breslau farmers Union meeting in evening; joined the Union. Fee for joining 25 cts. The object of the Union being to purchase supplies & dispose of our products to the best advantage. Fair.

7 Chopping wood & [to] Breslau. Cold east wind, some Snow.

8 To Berlin Market &c. Sleighing now, but not very good, both waggons & Sleighs going. Snow flurries. Visitors, Allan & Mary Ann Eby over night.

9 Sun. At Home. Visitors, Aaron Betzner & Ellen Stauffer. Fair.

10 Haul[ed] wood out of bush. Fair.

11 To Waterloo Fair & Farmers Union Meeting. Willie Kramp & Lizzie Schroeder married. Fine.

12 Haul[ed] wood & logs out of bush & [at] Breslau Literary Society in evening. Fair.

13 Haul[ed] wood out of bush & [took] 1 load of logs to Breslau. Robt. Bracey died. Very fine. Sleighing used up.

14 To Breslau, got [feedgrain] chopped & [to] Farmers Meeting in evening at Breslau.

15 To Breslau Market & Cressman's burying ground. Helped to Dig grave for Mr. Bracey. Fine.

16 Sun. To funeral of Bracey & [to] Abr. S. Clemmer's. Fine.

17 Haul[ed] wood out of bush &c. visitors, Uncle Amos Cressman's. Foggy.

18 Haul[ed] wood & stakes out of bush. Damp, foggy.

19 Haul[ed] wood out of bush. Cold east wind.

20 Haul[ed] wood to Breslau & [brought] ice home. Sleighing again. Blustery.

21 Haul[ed] wood to Breslau & ice home. Both waggons & Sleighs on roads. Blustery.

22 To Berlin Market & Haul[ed] wood to Breslau & ice home. Fine.

23 Sun. Out for a drive. More snow.

24 Haul[ed] wood to Breslau &c. Sleighing used up again. Soft Rain.

25 To Breslau with chopping & [to] Geo. McAllister's Sale.

26 To Breslau with wood, Berlin in afternoon & Breslau Literary Society in evening. Cloudy soft.

27 Haul[ed] Wood to Breslau. Dark, cloudy.

28 Writing. Rain Soft.

March

1 To Berlin Market with A.S. Clemmer. Cold.

2 Sun. To Cressman's Meeting & Uncle Jake Betzner's. Fair.

3 Helped to wash & haul[ed] wood to Breslau. Snow flurries.

4 Haul[ed wood] to Breslau. More Snow.

5 To H. Maertz's Butchering; 2 Hogs Sold, 1 for $5.75 per cwt [100 pounds] dressed weight. More Snow.

6 To Daniel Wenger's for a servant, unsuccessful, & [to] Breslau, Bot. corn @ 46 cts per bush[el] Cold clear. 14 Deg. below Zero.

7 Cleaned wheat & took 26 Bush[els] to Bridgeport. Sold @ 81 cts per Bush. Bot. bran @ 65 cts. Per cwt. Fine, but cold in morning. 16 Deg. below zero.

8 To Berlin Market & Kossuth. Fine.

9 Sun. To Dad Betzner's. Fine.

10 Haul[ed] wood out of bush &c. Some Snow.

11 To Waterloo fair & Bloomingdale Union Meeting. Foggy, rain.

12 To Breslau for chopping & Took a cow to Josiah Snyder's, sold for $35.00. Foggy. More rain.

13 To John Shaw's sale. Roads very heavy. Fair.

14 To Breslau &c. Fair.

15 To Berlin Market & haul[ed] wood out of bush. Cold.

16 Sun. At Home. Stormy.

17 Took cow to Berlin sold at $24.00 Bot. cow from Peter Reist for $28.00 & haul[ed] wood out of bush. Some Snow.

18 Haul[ed] wood out of bush & [to] Breslau. Fair.

19 Feeding & Sale at Jacob Kramp's. Visitors, Sam Sweitzers. Fine.

20 Feeding & haul[ed] wood out of bush. Cloudy a little rain.

21 Feeding & [to] Breslau. A little rain in morning. Fine.

22 To Berlin market & feeding. Visitors, Bro. Josiah, Jonah Berge, Mary Brubacher & Susannah Musselman over night. Fair.

23 Sun. At Home. Blustery.

24 To Breslau & feeding. Fair.

25 To Berlin & Breslau Farmers Union Meeting in evening. Cloudy, rain.

26 Abram S. Clemmer & Ellen Stauffer.

27 To Harriston & back to Jonah Bear's. Fine.

28 To Hanover to Cousin Menno Cressman's. An awful Stormy day, snowing & drifting all day, some roads blocked.

29 To Baden via Stratford to Isaac Betzner's & home. Fine.

30 Sun. To Josiah Nahrgangs. Fair.

31 Haul[ed] wood out of bush. Fine.

April

1 Haul[ed] wood out of bush & [to] Breslau. Bot. clover seed @ $4.00 per bush. Fine.

2 Haul[ed] wood out of bush. & Breslau for Sawdust. Fine.

3 Greesing Harness & sowing clover seed. Some rain.

4 Good Friday. At Home. Rain.

5 To Berlin Market &c. Roads bad. Fine.

6 Sun. Easter At Home. Cloudy, a little rain.

7 Easter Monday. To School Meeting, a special meeting held to elect a trustee in place of Elias Schantz, [who was] removed & I. W. Wamboldts Brot. Miss Isabel home as servant. Visitors, A. S. Clemmer's, Dad Betzner's & Mrs. Mary Stauffer. Rain in morning, changed fine.

8 To Berlin.

9 Greesing harness & Breslau. Showery.

10 Tinkering around. Showery.

11 To Moses Kinzies; exchanged seed oats & [to] Jos. Zuber's & Jos. Hummel's for seed peas. Fine.

12 To Berlin & Waterloo & Breslau. Got chopping done. Very fine, warm.

13 Sun. Cressmans' Meeting. Visitors, Moses Betzner's Abr. S. Clemmer's. Fine warm weather.

14 To Breslau got chopped [grain]. Cloudy, colder.

15 Started ploughing & Bot. seed peas from Jos. Hummel at 55 cts. per bush[el].

16 To Breslau & [then began] ploughing sod. Hired man started gangploughing.

17 Ploughing, harrowing, & Sowed two Bush[els] Spr[ing] wheat. Fine.

18 Sowing Oats, Harrowing & [to] Breslau farmer's meeting. Cold raw wind.

19 To Berlin Market. Got 20 cts. per lb. for butter, 10 cts. per doz for eggs. Cold, ground froze hard last night.

20 Sun. To William Krafts. Cold frosty nights. Clear weather.

21 Ploughing & haul[ed] manure.

22 Ploughing. Fine warm.

23 Ploughing & harrowing. Some rain.

24 Harrowing & sowing oats. Bot. Apple, pear &c. trees from J. Janzen, Berlin. Fine.

25 Sowing peas & oats & planted some trees. Fair.

26 Haul[ed] manure & sowing some oats & [to] Breslau. Rain.

27 Sun. To Cressman's Meeting. Pre[acher] Elias Snider buried. Fair.

28 Ploughing, harrowing, & sowed a few Oats. Sold lambs to Charles Reichart for $3.50 per head, to take away beginning of Sept. Fine.

29 To Breslau & spreading manure. Rain.

30 Harrowing. Fair.

May

1 Ploughing. Heavy rain last night. Fair.

2 Ploughing & harrowing. Fine.

3 Ploughing & spreading manure. Warm.

4 Sun. At Home, visitors Ozias Snyder's. Cloudy.

5 Ploughing. Cloudy some rain.

6 Ploughing & sowing peas cold. Cloudy, some rain, a little snow in evening.

7 Sowing Barley. Ploughing & Breslau cool. Cloudy.

8 Took 4 head cattle to Waterloo sold to Jos. Snider at 4 cts. per. lb. live weight for 3 head & 4 1/4 for 1 head average weight 950 lbs. & sowed some barley, a hard frost last night. Cold.

9 Sowing Barley & harrowing. Cloudy, rain.

10 To Berlin Market; got 18 cts for Butter, 10 cts for eggs, 70 cts per bag for potatoes. Heavy rain.

11 Sun. To Cressman's Meeting; visitors Abr. Bohn, Eli Schantz's. Ground froze hard last night. Fine.

12 Sowing barley on fall wheat ground which was winter killed. Finished sowing & B . . . Cloudy, rain in afternoon.

13 To Breslau, got chopped [grain] & planted a few potatoes. Cloudy cool wet weather not much growth yet.

14 Ploughing. Ridging for & sowed carrots & mangolds. Fine.

15 Ascension Day. To Breslau & Rolling. Fair.

16 Rolling & digging Garden. Cool windy.

17 To Berlin Market [and to] Jos. Hummel's & Digging Garden. Very windy cold.

18 Sun. To Dan Groh's with Abr. S. Clemmer's. Rain.

19 Working in berry patch & planted a few sugar beets. Cloudy.

20 To Breslau. Bot. Salt & planted potatoes. Rain during night, cloudy cool.

21 [Finished] planting potatoes &c. Cold cloudy weather. Hard frost last night.

22 To Breslau. Bot. corn at 53 cts. per bush. & Digging in Garden. Fine.

23 To Breslau &c. Heavy rain last night. Fine today.

24 To Berlin Market, 18 cts. for Butter, 2 cts. per doz. for eggs & [to] Breslau for clothing. Fine.

25 Whit. Sun. At Home. Heavy rain.

26 To Berlin & Waterloo heard Erastus [Neiman] speak on trade relations between U. States & Canada land very wet. Local Showers.

27 Repairing fence &c. Fine.

28 Making [fence] & Rolling. Fine.

29 Making fence & digging in garden. Warm.

30 Making fence &c. Rain.

31 To Berlin market & Dad Betzner's for supper & Reform Committee meeting at our School house. Moses B. Betzner's babtized. Fine warm growing weather.

June

1 Sun. To Dad Betzner's. Cressman's meeting in evening, Bro. [Samuel] Cofman from Virginia & Bro. J.F. Funk from Elkhardt Ind. [preached].

2 Washing Sheep [at?] Abs. S. Clemmer's &c. Very warm.

3 Picking out potatoes. Local thunder Showers, heavy rain.

4 To Guelph with Dad Betzner & [to] Breslau political meeting in evening. Heavy rain & thunder storms.

5 To Breslau School House, kept talley of voters coming in to vote [in] Local Election. John D. Moore, Reform, & Allan Bowman, Con[servative], Candidates for south riding & E.W.B. Snider, Ref[orm], & J.M. Scully, Con[servative], in north riding J.D. Moore elected by 400 Maj; E.W.B. Snider by 750 Maj. [Ontario provincial] House sustained by 24 majority, i.e. Reform [Oliver] Mowat, Government. Local Thunderstorms.

6 Cleaning & ploughing fence site. Local thunder storm.

7 To Berlin Market & funeral of Mrs. Ben. Shoemaker & Breslau. Visitors, Dads. Very wet cold cloudy.

8 Sun. To Cressman's Meeting & Simon Scheidel's in evening. Visitors, A.S. Clemmer's, Henry, Ben, Mary & Katy Brubacher, Lizzie Martin, Susannah Musselman & Josiah. Frost last night. Cool.

9 To Cressman's Meetin[g] house. Helped to build fence around grave yard & [to] Eby's Meeting in evening. John S. Co[f]fman from Virginia & [John F.] Funk from Elkhardt Ind. Preached. Warm.

10 To Breslau, Geo. H Clemen's, Peter Reists, &c., giving notice of the death & funeral of Mrs. Simon Scheidel & Spudding thistles. Cloudy, a little rain.

11 Spudding thistles & digging grave. Local thunder Showers.

12 To funeral of Mrs. Scheidel. Assisted as Pall bearer. Fine.

13 Spudding thistles & Breslau Farmers Union Meeting. Fine.

14 To Berlin market, .16 per lb. for butter, .12 per doz for eggs. [To] L. Spitzig's & spudding thistles. Fair.

15 Sun. At Home. Visitors, Albert Snyder's. Fair.

16 Ridging for & sowing turnips. Very warm.

17 To Breslau, got chopped [grain] & spudding thistles. Thunder Showers.

18 Scuffling mangolds & carrots & chicopee. Sold wool at .25 per lb.

19 Took cow to Waterloo, sold to Josiah Snyder for $46.00. Home via Berlin & spudding thistles. Fine.

20 Spudding thistles.

21 To Berlin market & spudding thistles. Rain in morning.

22 Sun. to Jacob's. Rain in morning.

23 Spudding thistles & cleaning mangolds. Very hot.

24 Scuffling potatoes & cleaning carrots. Fine.

25 To Conestoga for Shorts & Midd. & cleaning carrots. Fine.

26 To Henry Maertz's sold him 7 hogs at .06 1/4 per lb. dressed weight & Breslau. Fine.

27 Spudding thistles & Breslau farmers union meeting. Bot. Binder Twine Manilla at 13 1/4 cts. per lb. Fair.

28 To Berlin Market & went visiting with Abr. S. Clemmer to Titus Bingeman's for supper & Abr. Cressman's over night. Very hot.

29 Sun. To Jno. Betzner's, Plattsville, for dinner. Eph. Weber's Strasburg for supper & home. Local thunder Showers, very hot.

30 Spudding thistles. Awful hot.

July

1 Spudding thistles & [to] Abr. S. Clemmer's. Very hot, thunder Showers.

2 Spudding thistles. Local thunder Showers.

3 Spudding thistles & [to] Breslau. Cloudy cool.

4 Hoeing potatoes & spudding thistles. Cool.

5 Hoeing potatoes & funeral [for] one of Jos. Hagey's children. Fine.

6 Sun. At Home. Visitors, Aaron Cressmans. Cloudy, Showery.

7 To L. Spitzigs & Breslau with A. Cressman & spudding thistles. Fine.

8 To Berlin & Waterloo & scuffling potatoes. Brot. twine home. Local thunder showers. Hot.

9 Started morning & Paris greening potatoes. Very cool.

10 Mowing & haul[ed] in hay & poisoning potatoe [potato] bugs. Fine.

11 Mowing & haul[ed] in hay & Breslau. Fine.

12 Mowing & haul[ed] in hay. Very warm.

13 Sun. At Home. Very warm.

14 Mowing & haul[ed] in hay. Very hot.

15 Mowing & haul[ed] in hay. Very warm.

16 Mowing & haul[ed] in hay. Warm.

17 To Breslau & cleaning carrots & haul[ed] in 1 load hay. A little rain.

18 Scuffling potatoes & finished with hay got 29 loads. Fine.

19 To Berlin, Bridgeport & cleaning mangolds. Cool.

20 **Sun.** To Cressman's Meeting. Visitors, Jos. Nahrgang's. Fine.

21 Scuffling turnips & mowing thistles. Fine.

22 To Berlin & mowing thistles. Fine.

23 To Breslau Farmer's Union Meeting. Also cut a little wheat. Local thunder Shower's; no rain here.

24 Ploughing Sod &c. Thunder Showers.

25 To Breslau & cutting a little wheat. To[o] wet to cut much, broke a small spring on Binder. Thunder showers.

26 To Berlin & Waterloo, got spring for Binder, & cutting wheat. Fine.

27 **Sun.** To Abr. S. Clemmer's & Cressman's Meeting in evening Noah Stauffer's over night. Very warm.

28 Finished cutting wheat. Very warm.

29 Ploughing sod. Warm.

30 Ploughing sod &c. Rain.

31 Paris Greening potatoe bugs & haul[ed] in wheat. Fine.

August

1 To Breslau & finished haul[ing] in wheat. Got 807 Shocks, a very poor crop. Fine.

2 To Berlin & cutting barley. Fine.

3 **Sun.** At Home. Very hot 90 Deg[rees] in shade Local thunder showers.

4 Cutting Barley & [to] Breslau. Awful hot. Local thunder showers.

5 Finished cutting barley & cleaning turnips. Some rain.

6 Thrashing at J.S. Betzner's & started cutting peas. Fine.

7 Cutting peas & haul[ed] in 2 loads barley & scuffling turnips. Fine.

8 To Breslau got [grain] chopped. Haul[ed] in barley & cradled around a piece of Oats. Warm.

9 Cutting Oats & haul[ed] in peas. Fine.

10 Sun. To Abs. Snyder's & Dad Betzner's. Cool cloudy.

11 Haul[ed] in barley, finished, & cutting Spr[ing] wheat. Windy.

12 Cutting Oats. Sold two colts, 1 2-yrs-old, the other 3-yrs-old, for $225.00 to Obel Stauffer. Fine.

13 Cutting Oats & peas. Visitors Mrs. A.S. Clemmer & Mrs. Oswald. Fine.

14 Finished cutting Oats. Fine.

15 Thrashing at A.C. Schantz's & haul[ed] in Oats. Fine.

16 Haul[ed] in peas & oats. Fine.

17 Sun. To Breslau to Dad Betzner's. Some rain.

18 Thrashing at home & at P. Reists. Grain not turning out very well. Fine.

19 Haul[ed] in peas. [To] Breslau, got chopped. Rain.

20 Cleaning turnips & haul'd in Spring Wheat. Fine.

21 Harrowing &c. Heavy rain.

22 Harrowing & Gang plowing Bot. 2 furrow Gang plough for $12.00, [the plough is a] Teaswater make. Cool.

23 To Berlin & finished with peas & haul'd in 1 load Oats. Fine.

24 Sun. To Abr. S. Clemmer. Funeral of Mrs. Noah Schantz & Jerry Sander's. Fine.

25 Haul in Oats.

26 Haul in Oats. Finished harvest, got 829 Shocks Oats. Cloudy.

27 To Breslau & haul[ed] manure. Windy, cool.

28 Haul[ed] manure. Fine.

29 Spreading manure. Breslau got chopped & Started ploughing for Seed. Moses Weber buried at Eby's burial ground Berlin. Cloudy, some rain.

30 Spreading manure & ploughing. Visitors, Rev. Daniel Wismer's. Cold.

31 Sun. To Cressman's Meeting & Isaac C. Schantz's. Cool weather.

September

1 Home to Dad's for seed wheat. [To] Berlin & Waterloo. Hard frost last night.

2 To Breslau for tiles & [then began] ploughing. Fine.

3 Ploughing & Farmer's Union meeting. Warm.

4 Ploughing & Breslau for tiles, got ditcher's [machine]. Very warm.

5 Sowing wheat (Democrat, Manchester & Golden Cross); sowed about 9 [bushels?]. Warm.

6 To Berlin & Gang ploughing Some rain. Warm.

7 Sun. To Cressman's Meeting in evening. Visitors, Eph Weber's, Silas Eby's, Ed. Dabels, & Dad Betzner's. Hot.

8 Gangploughing. Cloudy.

9 To Berlin & Waterloo & Gangploughing. Fine.

10 Took a load of hogs to Waterloo for Ab. S. Clemmer & [then went] gangploughing. Mrs. Isaac A. Wamboldt buried. Fair.

11 Gangploughing & thrashing at Carl Wagners. Rainy.

12 Gangploughing. Fair.

13 To Berlin & home to Dad's. Cool, Local Showers.

14 Sun. to Webers Meeting. Abr. Bergy's Noah Stauffer's, Dad's for supper & home. Fine.

15 Burning brush & haul[ed] 1 load tiles from Breslau. Got Ditchers draining, 1,200 [feet?], field north side of railroad. Fine.

16 Drawing out furrows for drains & haul[ed] tiles from Breslau. Cloudy.

17 Haul[ed] tiles from Breslau. Fine.

18 Haul[ed] tiles from Breslau. Fine.

19 Haul[ed] tiles & ploughing. Very windy some rain.

20 To Berlin market: 14 cts. per lb. for butter; 15 cts. per doz. for eggs & ploughing. Very cool.

21 Sun. To Berlin & Cressman's church in evening. Visitors, Jos. Nahrgangs & Cousin Menno Cressman's. Fine.

22 Sowing Timothy Seed, pulling pears & ploughing. Fine.

23 Made Cider. Cool.

24 Boiling apple butter & [to] Breslau. Cool dry frost last night.

25 Working on road hard frost. Fine.

26 Finished working on road. Some rain.

27 Picking pears & ploughing. Visitors, Jacob Snider's. Cold.

28 Sun. To Abr. S. Clemmer's & Dad Betzner's. Fine but cold.

29 Ploughing & harrowing &c. Fine.

30 Digging potatoes & haul[ed] tiles. Fine.

October

1 Haul[ed] tiles & digging potatoes. Fine.

2 To Breslau & pulling apples. Fine.

3 Cleaning wheat & [to] Conestoga with 12 Bush. sold at 83 cts. per bush. Bot. Bran at 60 per cwt. Shorts at 70 per cwt. Heavy rain last night & this morning. Fine.

4 To Berlin market & digging potatoes. Fine.

5 **Sun.** At Home. Visitors, Maggie Snyder, Mary Ann Eby, Susannah & Obel Stauffer, Sammy Cressman, Allen & Melinda. Cloudy.

6 Digging potatoes. Pulling mangolds. [To] Breslau &c. Rain.

7 To Breslau for chopp & pulling apples. Cloudy showery.

8 Pulling apples. Digging potatoes & [helped] H. Maertz butchering a pig. Fine.

9 Finished taking up potatoes & pulling mangolds. Fair.

10 Thrashing beans & pulling mangolds. Thunder & Rain.

11 To Berlin Market & pulling mangolds & carrots. Fine.

12 **Sun.** At Home visitors Moses Cressman's. Rain.

13 To Breslau & finished with carrots, got 4 loads, a fair crop. Visitors, Abr. S. Clemmer's, Jacob Stauffer & Samuel Betzner. Cloudy, rain.

14 Pulling apples & [to] Breslau.

15 Picking apples. Fine.

16 Finished with apples &c. Rain.

17 To John Snyder's, Waterloo. Got Jelly boiled & [to] Berlin. Fair.

18 Ploughing & covering drains. Visitors, Lydia Ann & Lenah Stauffer over night. Fine.

19 **Sun.** At Home. Visitors, Norman Stauffer & Abram Snyder. Rain.

20 Ploughing & making fence. Visitors, Ma Betzner & John Sechrist & wife from Indiana. Fair.

21 Ploughing & [to] Breslau for tiles. Fine.

22 Ditching & started at turnips. Sold 3 hogs to H. Maertz at $6.00 per cwt. Dressed weight, $95. Fair.

23 Ditching &c. Rain.

24 Making fence on line between Maders. Cloudy.

25 To Berlin & Dad Betzner's, to family Gathering. Made them a present of 2 Chairs valued at $22.00. Fine.

26 **Sun.** To Cressmans Church & Abs. Snyder's. Cloudy cold.

27 To Breslau. Bot. Shorts at 70 per cwt & pulling turnips. Cold, cloudy, Snow flurries.

28 Picking stones. Measuring drains. Pulling turnips & [to] Breslau to Dad Betzner's in evening. Snow flurries.

29 Finished with turnips, a poor crop, got 14 loads & picking stones from drain. Fair.

30 To John Brohmann's, H. Maertzs, J.S. Betzner's & Dad Betzners in evening &c. Cloudy cold.

31 Ploughing in drains & ploughing snow flurries.

November

1 To Breslau & ploughing. Snow changed to rain.

2 Sun. At Home. Snowing heavy nearly all day but soft, about 3 in. snow on ground tonight.

3 Preparing for & thrashing. Fair.

4 Finished thrashing, not a very good crop, got: 1,600 Bush. Wheat, 123 Bush. peas, 337 Bush. Barley, 755 Bush. Oats, total 1355 Bush. Fair.

5 Ploughing. Snow nearly all gone again. Fine.

6 Ploughing. Thanksgiving day. Fair.

7 Thrashing at Peter Reists & [to] Breslau. Fine.

8 To Berlin & ploughing. Fair.

9 Sun. At Home. Visitor, Mrs Mary Stauffer. Heavy Rain.

10 Ploughing. Fair.

11 Ploughing. Fine.

12 Ploughing. Fine.

13 Ploughing. H. Maertz & Farmers Union Meeting in e[vening]. Fine.

14 Haul[ed] manure. Very fine.

15 To Berlin Market with potatoes, got 70 per bag & haul[ed] & spreading manure. Cloudy. Rain.

16 Sun. At Home. Fine.

17 Cleaning Wheat &c. Heavy Rain.

18 To Breslau with wheat, sold wheat at .90 per bush. Bot. shorts $14.00 per. ton & spreading manure. Fair.

19 To Breslau & ploughing. Finished. Blustry.

20 Making water course, &c. Fair, a little snow last night.

21 To Jos. Hummel's. Bot. 50 bush peas & haul[ed in wood. Fine.

22 To Berlin & Dad Betzner's. Cold Blustry.

23 Sun. To Cressman's church & A.S. Clemmer's. Visitors, Simeon Brubachers & John Nahrgangs overnight, voting for preacher & deacon. Cold.

24 Haul[ed] in wood & Jos. Hummel's for peas. Bot. at .60 per bush. Fine.

25 To Cressman's Church: candidates for preacher I.A. Wamboldt; candidates for Deacons, Ben. Shoemaker, David Shuh, Abr. Weber. & Abs. Snyder. Ben Shoemaker ordained. Snow flurries.

26 Thrashing at A.C. Schantz's. Fair.

27 Cleaning wheat & took to Breslau, sold at 90 per bush. Cold, ground froze hard.

28 To Breslau & David Bowdy's Sale. Bot Hay Raker for $11.25. Fine.

29 To Berlin &c. Visitors, cousins Moses Cressman's & Eliz Good's. Fair.

30 Sun. At Home. Visitors, Norman Stauffer & Moses Betzner's. Fair.

December

1 To Abr. S. Clemmer's & J.S. Betzner's &c. Cold snowing.

2 Feeding &c. Ground covered with snow, fair.

3 To Fischer's Blaksmithshop &c Snowing, but not enough for sleighing.

4 To Breslau &c. Some snow, sleighing not good yet.

5 Feeding cutting wood &c. Fine.

6 Cutting wood. Berlin & Aaron Cressman's now living in Strasburg. Fine.

7 Sun. To Eph. Weber's, Dad's & Noah Stauffer's. Fine, but cold.

8 Home via Berlin. Fine.

9 To Breslau, got chopped [grain]. Fine.

10 Cutting wood & Berlin with wood. Visitor, N. Stauffer.

11 To Guelph fat stock show. Fine. Little snow in evening.

12 To Berlin with wood & haul. [Brought] Bran home from Breslau Station. Bot. at $12.35 per ton delivered there from Goldie's Mill Guelph. Cold.

13 Haul[ed] Bran home & [to] John Schrader's; we [they?] being very sick. Fair.

14 Sun. At Home. Visitors, Ozias Snyder's. Very fine.

15 Cutting wood. Fine.

16 Cutting wood. Fine.

17 To Berlin with wood & Farmers U. Meeting in E[vening]. Fair.

18 To Berlin with wood &c. Fair.

19 To funeral of John Schrader & Breslau. Very fine.

20 To Berlin & cutting wood. Fine.

21 Sun. To Cressman's church & David Gimbels. Soft. Foggy.

22 Cutting wood & making logs. Fine.

23 To Berlin &c. John Shirich & Barbara Schantz married. Very windy, snow flurries.

24 Making saw logs. [To] Blk.smith shop & Breslau. Snow.

25 Christmas At Home. Visitors, Dad Betzner, Abram C. Schantz's, Abr. S. Clemmer's & Mrs. Mary Stauffer.

26 To Breslau got chopped. Cloudy a little snow.

27 Cutting wood & haul[ed] 1 load to Breslau. More snow.

28 Sun. To Dad Betzner's & Cressman's church in evening, John Nyce preached. Poor sleighing. Fair.

29 To Berlin & nomination at Township Hall of Reeves & Councillors. Fair.

30 To funeral of Mrs. Robert Bracey & cutting wood. Visitor Aaron Betzner. Fine.

31 To School meeting & New Germany [later, Maryhill] municipal election meeting in evening. Visitors, Adam & Irving Moyer from the Twenty [Niagara Peninsula]. Jerry Souder & Rev. John Nyce's from Michigan. Dark, foggy, all day.

12 Heinrich Friesen (1842 to 1921)

Hochfeld, Manitoba

Diary selection: January to March 1896
and April to December 1898

Age: 56 in 1898

Heinrich Friesen was born in the village of Schoenthal, Bergthal Colony, New Russia. He was the fifth of seven children born to Jakob and Helena (Dyck) Friesen. Heinrich's parents had moved there from Nieder Chortitza, Khorititsa Colony, in 1837; their own parents had, in 1778, been among the first Mennonites to leave West Prussia and settle within the Russian Empire. At the age of 20 in 1862, Heinrich Friesen married 19-year-old Agatha Hiebert. The young couple settled close to Agatha's parents' farm, in the village of Schoenthal, where they farmed and where Agatha gave birth to the first five of her 13 children. In the summer of 1874, Heinrich and Agatha migrated to Canada. In the spring of 1875, two of Heinrich's siblings – Jakob and Abraham – and their families, including their elderly, widowed father, Jakob Sr., also arrived in Canada. The two brothers, Jakob and Abraham, however, moved at once to a settlement near Butterfield, Minnesota. Heinrich and Agatha remained in Manitoba, settling in Hochfeld, literally "high field," in the East Reserve. In his last years, Heinrich's elderly father lived on their yard in a retirement house until his death in 1886. Here in Hochfeld the Friesens had another eight children. Only seven of the 13 children reached adulthood.

Heinrich was a farm householder and, as the diary shows, his wife and children comprised his immediate world. In 1898 the Friesens still had most of their children at home. They included: Jakob Jr., 28; David, 26; Heinrich, 20; Abraham, 17; Maria, 12; and Katherina, adopted, 14. Each of these children worked on the farm, although the older boys worked for short periods of time as servants for the Friesens' neighbours. In November, little Anna Penner, from an outlying area, came to live with the Friesens so that she couldattend school in Hochfeld village. By this time, Agatha, 23, was married to Peter Harder and Helena, 33 to Johan Schultz. The Schultzes and Harders lived on their own farmyards, some 18 kilometres to the west near Niverville. Daughter Maria eventually married Jacob Enns of Blumengart, and it was here that Heinrich Friesen spent his last years.

Heinrich was not only a householder, but also a churchman. His biography notes that he was a conservative and communitarian Mennonite: a "devout and peaceful man who had a strong faith rooted in ... history." In an 1895 statement, Heinrich criticized pietistic and progressive Mennonites as creating "ostentatious and brilliant displays in such impressive ways that even the Word of God and Christ is considered insufficient." In 1881, he was elected as a deacon in what came to be known as the Chortitzer Mennonite Church of the East Reserve, and just four years later as a minister. His obituary notes that he served in this capacity for almost 36 years, preaching 998 times and officiating at 71 funerals and 25 weddings. This activity required frequent interactions with fellow ministers – Heinrich Doerksen, Cornelius Friesen, Johann Neufeld, Johann Wiebe, Peter Toews; in the diary they are referred to as the *Ohms*, that is, the council of preachers and deacons of the East Reserve Chortitzer Churches. He also worked with the *Aeltesten*, the bishops Gerhard Wiebe and David Stoesz. He travelled often to the two main church buildings at Grunthal and Chortitz where all communion, baptism, and ordination services were held during this time. These were the only churches that had weekly Sunday services; smaller villages had rotating services that were held in the school buildings. Among Heinrich's duties, too, as minister, was the annual March school inspection of the Chortitz Church-run parochial schools: ministers evaluated the schools for order, the quality of books, and the effectiveness of the teacher. His duties also called him to prepare the congregation for communion, that is, to ensure that all members had previously sought forgiveness from fellow members whom they might have offended.

As a farmer and family man, Heinrich also encountered a larger community. He regularly drove to Steinbach to obtain binder parts, flour, bricks, and tools. In turn, East Reserve residents travelled to Hochfeld; during 1898, for example, Grunthal chiropractor "Dr." Johan Peters visited the village at least twice to "work on" a Hochfelder. There were also visits outside the East Reserve: to the Franco-Manitoban parishes of St. Pierre and Ste. Anne (known as *Pontischien*, a Germanization of the popular *Point des Chesne*); to the Métis lands (the *Französen Steppe*) just a few kilometres north of the village; and to the market in Winnipeg. Encounters with non-Mennonites in 1898 include: an occasion in March when Heinrich sought to purchase a horse from a Mr. Prefontaine of St. Pierre; the day in October when he accompanied "Penner" to Mr. Krause, a land conveyancer, at "Oak Bush" near Iles des Chesne; the times of negotiation with the village herdsmen, German Lutherans, Märks, Kohlschmidt, and Fuchs; the visits from Jewish peddlers, Löb, Joseph, Isaac and Herschke. Finally, Heinrich's world extended beyond southeastern Manitoba. There was a visit, for example, from Andreas Lilge, a Moravian Brethren pastor from Fort Saskatchewan, Alberta, who, in July, came to begin paying off a loan of cattle and money offered his group in 1894 by the Chortitzer Church. And then there was news from the outside: in May, Heinrich noted a newspaper report of war between the United States and Spain and offered an earnest prayer for peace.

The entire extant diary covering the years between 1893 and 1918 is massive, comprising 21 notebooks. With the exception of several notebooks that have not been located, including the notebook covering the period from 24 April 1896 to 30 April 1898, the diary has been translated in its entirety by Irene Enns Kroeker and Marie Enns, Steinbach, Manitoba, and published in John Dyck, ed., *Historical Sketches of the East Reserve, 1874-1910* (Steinbach, MB: 1894): 597-608. It includes poetry, personal thoughts, descriptions of dreams, food recipes, and copies of favourite written works. The poems that follow each month were written in German, with a rhyme scheme of a-b-a-b. These poems have been translated for content only and do not reflect the creativity of Heinrich Friesen. For more information on Heinrich Friesen, see Irene Enns Kroeker, "Prediger Heinrich Friesen," *Historical Sketches*: 329-337.

January 1896

Jan 1 In the morning there was a beautiful sunrise. In the forenoon it started snowing with an east wind. There was church in Hochfeld. It was not very cold. God bless us in this new year.

Jan 2 -26. Cold with a cold north wind and blowing snow.

Jan 3 Fri., -29. Cold with a cold N.W. wind.

Jan 4 Sat. -35. No wind. The breeze was from the south.

Jan 5 Sun. The frost was somewhat lighter, but the snow was from the S.E. In the afternoon we had blowing snow.

Jan 6 Epiphany. The weather was nicer but there was blowing snow from the S.W.

Jan 7 Tuesday. Little frost but still blowing snow from the S.W. Dr. Peters was in the village.

Jan 8 Wed. Clear and very mild, almost warm. The wind was from the west. I went to Steinbach to the store.

Jan 9 Thurs. Very mild. Today J. Dörksens from Bergthal were here. Abram was *geschnellt*[?]. In the evening there was some rain from the S.W.

Jan 10 Friday. Mild but cloudy and humid. David went to Burwalde. Abram Görtzen (my great grandfather from my mother's side) brought us our daughter Katharina (they adopted her: she was 3 years old).

Jan 11 Sat. The morning was clear with a temperature of -18 and a north wind. At noon it became cloudy. Mr. Görtzen went back in the afternoon and David came home from Burwalde.

Jan 12 -25, N.W. wind.

Jan 13 Less frost with a N.E. wind. We went to Krauses'.

Jan 14 -28. Light north wind.

Jan 15 -21. Blowing snow from the north. Soon after dinner it cleared. Dr. Peters was at Peter Hieberts'. Heinrich had his shoulder bone set.

Jan 16 Thurs. Clear and -29. Light north wind.

Jan 17 Fri. Snow with light blowing snow from the north.

Jan 18 Sunny and very cold. I went to Grunthal. The road was not good. For night I went to Bergfeld.

Jan 19 Sunday. Strong blowing snow from the south. I did not return home.

Jan 20 Monday. Clear and cold N.W. wind. I returned home. The way was difficult.

Jan 21 Light blowing snow from the south.

Jan 22 Wed. Cold with a N.W. wind. David went to Osterwick to get some hay for Johann Schultz. Peter and Agatha came here.

Jan 23 Thurs. -29. North wind. The Jewish peddlar, Löb, was here and we owe him 20 cents.

Jan 24 -16. During the day it was very mild with a light wind from the east.

Jan 25 Sat. Cold with a north wind. -29. We sold two young oxen for $47.50 for both. We have to bring them to Klaus Reimers', Steinbach, in two weeks.

Jan 26 Less frost with a S.W. wind.

Jan 27 Clear and not too cold. A light south wind.

Jan 28 Tuesday. Mild with a S.W. wind. I and Jacob went to the sawmill, the Löwen sawmill.

Jan 29 Wed. Somewhat cold with a S.W. wind. David went to Steinbach. Heinrich Wiebes were here.

Jan 30 Thurs. Not too cold, but cloudy and foggy with an east wind. We went visiting in Burwalde during the day.

Jan 31 This morning it snowed a lot and it was cloudy, but otherwise mild with a N.W. wind.

This is the end of the first month of the new year. We thank God for His care.

Feb 1 Sat. Mild with a south wind but cloudy with a little snow. I went to Neubergfeld. Franz Peters from Schönsee came with me.

Feb 2 Sun. Clear and very nice. South wind. Came home from NeuBergfeld.

Feb 3 Monday. Cloudy with a north wind but not cold. We went to Osterwick. Andreas Lilge was here during the day. It snowed in the afternoon.

Feb 4 Tues. Cloudy and mild with a N.W. wind. There was much hoarfrost and in the evening we had fog.

Feb 5 Wed. Very mild with no wind, but somewhat foggy. David came from Burwalde with firewood today.

Feb 6 Thurs. Cloudy but not very cold. It snowed periodically all day, so that there was much loose snow. Jacob and Heinrich went to the sawmill during the day. Towards evening it cooled down.

Feb 7 In the morning it was clear and cold with a temperature of -27 but no wind. A breeze came from the west. The boys came from the sawmill with boards. The best [boards, equalled] 450 ft. Before we had 338 ft. Altogether [we have] 788 ft. The second best [boards equalled] 275 ft. making 232 ft. Altogether [we have] 1,063. Altogether [we have] 1,020 [?].

Feb 8 Sat. Brought the oxen to Steinbach that I had promised old Klaus Reimers. One pair of two-year-olds and one pair of 3-year-olds; we got $47.50. It was clear and very cold with a west wind. Jacob Giesbrecht died suddenly, without having been sickly, quickly and without warning.

Feb 9 Not very cold with a south wind making blowing snow. Towards evening the wind picked up making blowing snow. During the night the wind changed to the N.W. and became very strong.

Feb 10 Cloudy with a north wind, -12. It cleared very quickly but we had quite some blowing snow and cold winds.

Feb 11 Cold with a north wind and blowing snow.

Feb 12 Wed. Cloudy and cold. We cooked syrup today. Blowing snow from the south.

Feb 13 Thurs. No wind but much snow. We cooked syrup again. Today we received a bull.

Feb 14 Blowing snow from the west and cold.

Feb 15 Sat. Very cold -35, no wind. We went to Burwalde. In the evening the wind turned to the south.

Feb 16 Cold and blowing snow from the south. I went to Rosengart to Church. The afternoon we returned and the wind was stronger. There was a storm at night.

Feb 17 Monday. Milder. The wind changed to the N.W. and a large snowstorm settled in. After a short time it cleared but we had snow falling all day.

Feb 18 Clear and cold with a north wind.

Feb 19 Wed. -29. N.W. wind. Today we were at Johann Dörksens'.

Feb 20 Thurs. South wind. -25 in the morning. During the day Peter came here.

Feb 21 Friday. Clear and not very cold. -15. Bought 6 sheep from Peter. The wind was from the south during the day. It was very mild.

Feb 22 Sat. Very mild – almost thawing. David went with a load to Rosengart for A. Janzen who moved to their land.

Feb 23 Sunday. Mild with a north wind.

Feb 24 Mild but cloudy with a S.W. wind.

Feb 25 Tuesday. Clear and mild so that there was some water standing in the yard. Jacob and Peter went to Pienehill [Pinehill]. David went to Steinbach to the mill. We got 4 lambs, making 7 altogether.

Feb 26 Wed. Thawing. Peter and Jacob came from Pinehill. They had left the wood on the way because the roads were too bad.

Feb 27 Strong blowing snow from the N.W. but very little frost. Towards evening it cleared and became cold. The bull was taken away today.

Feb 28 Friday. Clear with a N.W. wind and -21. Peter and Agatha returned home.

Feb 29 Saturday. Cloudy and cold N.E. wind. We went to Steinbach to get the flour. This is the end of this month.

March 1 Sunday. Cold north wind so that there was blowing snow. I was in Chortitz for church.

March 2 Monday -23 north wind. Jacob went to Pinehill again. We went to Heinrich Penners'.

March 3 Tuesday. Less frost but foggy. Some snow fell. North wind. Jacob came from Pinehill.

March 4 Wed. Cloudy but not very cold. David went to the woods for firewood. Jacob Hiebert came back from West Reserve. In the evening Johann Schultz came here. He wanted to go to Winnipeg with David Schultz the next day.

March 5 Thurs. Snow all day with a light east wind and little frost. David came back from the woods.

March 6 Friday. In the morning cloudy but not very cold. The wind turned to the north and it became colder. Blowing snow.

March 7 Clear and not very cold with a light north wind.

March 8 Sunday. clear.

March 9 Monday. In the morning Jacob went to Winnipeg. It was mild with a light east wind. Small Abraham Dyck came here in the evening. He needed help in the way of food. The village helped him out.

March 10 Tuesday. Somewhat colder with a north wind that turned into blowing snow. Late in the evening Jacob came from Winnipeg. He received 53 cents / bu. for the wheat.

March 11 -26. Light north wind in the morning. David went to the woods. He is to bring the wood to Steinbach and then pick up a load of wood for Johann Schulz. He wants to break down the house he bought from Johann Klassen and take the wood to his farm in Niverville.

March 12 Thurs. Clear and cold with a north wind. We were at a meeting at David Stösz regarding the building of a church [probably Chortitz]. Our Brotherhood Meeting is to be held on the 22nd. David came home from the woods.

March 13 Friday. Clear and cold with no wind. David went to get a load for Johann Schultz.

March 14 Sat. A little blowing snow from the north. I went to Grunthal, but went to Gnadenfeld for night.

March 15 Sun. Not very cold with a light south west wind. Came home from Grunthal. Visited a little at Bluemstein.

March 16 Mon. *Ohm* K. Friesen and I went to visit the schools – Hochfeld and Blumengart. Cold wind from the west.

March 17 [Visited] Bergthal and Chortitz [schools] today. Not very cold with a S.W. wind. Towards evening it started snowing.

March 18 Wed. Strong blowing snow with a N.W. wind. Colder and clear. We were in Osterwick and Strassburg. There was no school being held in Schönthal.

March 19 Thurs. Mild with a S.W. wind. My wife came to get me from Schönthal.

March 20 Strong blowing snow from the south but not very cold. The old Johann Funk, Bergthal, was buried. He died on the 17th, Tuesday in the morning. It had been a difficult cross to bear for a long time. In the evening it thawed. The schoolteacher came to board at our house.

March 21 Sat. Strong blowing snow from the north. Cold wind. -12. Toward evening it cleared and the wind died down. The wind changed to the N.W. and it is getting colder.

March 22 Sunday. It is getting somewhat milder. South wind. There was a Brotherhood Meeting in Chortitz after the church service regarding the building project and other things.

March 23 Mon. Not too much frost but a strong wind from the south. Jacob and I went to Steinbach.

March 24 Tues. Clear and nearly thawing weather. Peter and Agatha came here. In the evening it started to freeze. The wind shifted to the north.

March 25 In the morning there was blowing snow from the north. In the afternoon it cleared and there was frost.

March 26 Thurs. Clear and mild with a south wind. It started melting. The boys are supposed to get the seed grain ready. Heinrich and Maria were sick.

March 27 Friday. Thawing. South wind. I went to Johann Töwses' to get seed oats. Abraham was *geschnellt* [?]. It rained toward evening.

March 28 Sat. Foggy and snow with a N.E. wind. There was quite a bit of water in the low areas. Towards evening it stopped snowing but there was much fog. Otherwise it was mild. I did not go to Strassburg to church because the roads were too bad.

March 29 Sunday. Foggy but not cold. I was in Hochfeld in church. There was quite a blanket of newly fallen snow. In the evening it turned colder.

March 30 Monday. It had frozen hard. North wind and cloudy. We threshed rye. Jacob went to work in the cheese factory in Steinbach at noon. Toward evening it started clearing. There was no wind.

March 31 Overcast and cold. The ice did not thaw. I walked to Bergthal. The water flowed over the dam. The *Ohms* were to come to David Stöszes' for a meeting, however could not come because of the road conditions.

We have again ended a month through the grace of God.

Apr 1 Cloudy with a north wind. Towards evening it cleared up but it did not thaw.

Apr 2 Thurs. Clear and cold with a N.W. wind.

Apr 3 Good Friday. Mild weather with a south wind so that there was a little thawing during the day. I went to Chortitz to church. The schoolteacher took leave as he had closed the school [for the academic year].

Apr 4 Sat. Overcast with a light south wind. Schultz came over towards evening.

Apr 5 Easter Sunday. Clear with a cold north wind. During the day it thawed just a little. I went to Chortitz to church. In the morning the ice was almost strong enough to drive on.

Apr 6 Clear and cold with no wind. It was a difficult drive to Chortitz in the sleigh.

Apr 7 Easter Tuesday. During the night it had frozen. During the day there was a mild breeze from the S.E. It clouded over in the west. We had Johann Schultz's Peter here. His grandmother is not well and he will stay here to help her. During the night we had blowing snow from the south.

Apr 8 Wednesday. In the morning there was snow with a strong south wind, however it was mild. Peter Hiebert got the machine shed with the sleigh from Bergthal.

Apr 9 Thursday. South wind. I collected money for the church building here in Hochfeld. Peter came here towards evening. The wind turned to the west. I collected $75.57.

Apr 10 Friday. In the morning it had frozen. There was a cold wind from the north. I collected $41.50 from Blumengart. We branded our lambs – 50 ewes and 12 male. Total 27 lambs. We have 34 old sheep altogether, not counting the lambs.

Apr 11 Sat. Rain with a N.E. wind. Towards evening we had a heavy rain.

Apr 12 It had frozen in the morning and it was very foggy. It was difficult driving to Chortitz.

Apr 13 There was a heavy snowfall from the N.E. It was quite mild though, with little wind.

Apr 14 Mild with a light N.E. wind. During the day it was warm. We were at *Ohm* David Stösz's for a meeting regarding the building of the Church. We collected $372.00 and $163.00 pledged. Altogether $535.00. We could count on more.

Apr 15 Wed. Cloudy and cold with a north wind. During the day David went to work for Peter Hieberts'.

Apr 16 Cloudy and rainy with an east wind. Quite cold.

Apr 17 In the morning it had snowed a little with a cold north wind.

Apr 18 Sat. In the morning it had rained a little with a strong east wind and overcast. Today David got sick. In the afternoon the wind turned to the south and became stronger, but the clouds parted so that the sun peeked through the clouds once in a while.

Apr 19 Sunday. Cloudy with a cold S.W. wind. It had frozen so much in the morning, we had trouble getting to Chortitz because of the water.

Apr 20 Cloudy with a cold west wind. It had frozen in the morning again. Every once in a while we had a light blowing snow. Heinrich and I went to Steinbach to the store. Heinrich bought a dress [suit?]. There was so much water that we sank deep into the ground.

Apr 21 Tuesday. It had frozen again. In the morning it was cloudy but it cleared soon in the west. It cleared so that we had sun for a long time. We laid a floor into the pantry.

Apr 22 A mild spring day. South wind. Towards evening it clouded over in the S.W.. It dried a lot today.

Apr 23 Thurs. Much cloud and a little rain with a S.E. wind, otherwise it is not very cold. We had a lot to do on the yard.

March 1898

March 1 Tues. -15. Strong N.W. wind. Went to Blumstein [20 kilometres distant] to the home of *Ohm* K. Stösz. We had a meeting to get things ready for discussion [at Brotherhood Meeting]. As I returned home, the Jews, Löb and Joseph [Winnipeg-based peddlers], were here.

March 2 Not very cold. Overcast. Light wind from the south. [Son] Jacob went to Burwalde [13 kilometres distant] and the next day to the sawmill. In the evening there was light blowing snow.

March 3 Clear and -11. Light wind from the west. It soon became overcast. Jacob returned home from the sawmill in the evening.

March 4 Mild with a S.W. wind. Harders and Schultzes [daughters' households] were here. Dr. [Johan] Peters [of Grunthal came and] worked on Mrs. Schultz's back. They returned home during the day.

March 5 Sat. Mild with a light S.W. wind. I went to Grunthal. I took *Ohm* David Stösz along. There was Brotherhood Meeting during the day. We went to Blumstein at noon, then to Jacob Klassens'. His son tethered the horses and from there we went to [St. Pierre] Jolys to Mr. Prefontaine to buy a horse. I couldn't make a deal, so we went to Peter Giesbrechts' for night.

March 6 Sun. There was Brotherhood Meeting in the church in Grunthal because of: 1) repairs to Grunthal Church; 2) [someone wishes] to purchase a recipe from Dr. Russell; 3) may the people from [close quarters in] towns buy fire insurance [in the Mennonite agency]? The first item was accepted, the second rejected and the third was left for further discussion. We returned in the afternoon. It was very mild; almost thawing weather.

March 7 Mon. In the morning only a little frost. Clear and very mild. No wind. Jacob went to Niverville with the wheat. He received 83 cents per bushel. He was supposed to return with feed for the cattle but no one was there.

March 8 Tues. Not much frost but blowing snow all day from the north. A rough wind. To this point in this year six cows have freshened.

March 9 In the morning there was much snow and it is still snowing with a strong wind and blowing snow. Toward evening it stopped snowing.

March 10 Thurs. It was not very cold with a north wind. Jacob and I went to Steinbach [14 kilometres distant]. The sleigh tracks were so full of snow, the likes of which we have not yet experienced this winter. I bought five sacks of Strombecker flour: $2.15/100 lbs; 500 lbs. cornmeal at $18.50/tonne.

March 11 Overcast, but mild with a south wind. Yesterday, that is, the 10th, David Schultzes [from Hochfeld] moved to Osterwick [11 kilometres distant].

March 12 Sat. Not cold – almost warm. [Son-in-law] Peter Harder brought the horse we had bought for $50.00.

March 13 Sun. Very mild with N.E. wind. During the day we had Brotherhood Meeting in Chortitz.

March 14 Mon. Mild but overcast with a strong wind from the south. In the morning *Ohm*. K. Friesen came and we went to visit schools – today in Hochfeld and Blumengart [2.5 kilometres distant]. In the evening it started snowing. It had rain mixed in with it. During the night we had a strong storm from the N.E. with rain and snow.

March 15 We went to the schools in Bergthal [2.5 kilometres] and Chortitz [9 kilometres]. It stormed all day and rained. We went to Strassburg [22 kilometres] for night. There was quite a bit of water in the low areas.

March 16 Wed. In the morning it snowed, with blowing snow from the north. It started freezing. We were in Strassburg in the morning and Osterwick in the afternoon. For night we went to Schönthal. In the evening it cleared up.

March 17 Tues. Clear with a cold N.W. wind. In the morning we visited Schönthal and in the afternoon [son] Heinrich came to pick me up. Jacob went with Johan Schultz to Heinrich Penners' for wood. Franz Giesbrecht's Franz had been here for seed grain while I was not at home. In the evening Jacob and Johan returned.

March 18 Fri. Overcast with a cold north wind. *Ohm* K. Friesen went to Jankes' and dropped in here. In the afternoon I went to Steinbach. Travelling was good but there was some ice in the low spots.

March 19 Sat. Cloudy with a light wind from the north. In the afternoon a snowfall with a west wind. *Ohm* K. Friesen was here to trade seed oats.

March 20 Sun. In the morning it had frozen. It was cloudy with a south wind. We drove successfully to Chortitz as there was a light blanket of snow overall. During the day we had blowing snow from the south, but it was mild. For night Löb and Joseph were here. In the evening it cleared and became colder. The wind turned to the north.

March 21 Mon. It was overcast with a cold wind from the north. Peter Harder came for night.

March 22 Tues. There was a cold wind from the west again. Peter Harder and Johann Schultz went to the woods [20 kilometres east]; came here for night.

March 23 Wed. The wind was from the N.W. It was cold and there was much frost.

March 24 -10 in the morning with a very cold wind from the north that turned to blowing snow. Today we went to Osterwick to visit the children. I went straight to the Widow Kliewer and bought an old *Zinder* [worn-out ox] for $20.00. We took it along right away.

March 25 Fri. Little frost with the wind from the north. In the morning I met David Friesen, Sommerfeld [of the West Reserve], at [brother-in-law] Peter Hiebert's.

March 26 Sat. Cold wind from the north that turned to blowing snow. I went with [brother-in-law] Johan Hiebert to Steinbach.

March 27 Sun. Less frost. Strong blowing snow from the north. I went to church in Hochfeld. Heinrich Penner's son Abraham was also here. [The German Lutheran] Märks, the herdsman, was also here for lunch, from Blumengart.

March 28 Mon. Not very much frost; cold wind; and during the day we had strong blowing snow from the north.

March 29 Not too much frost but still blowing snow from the north. Somewhat less wind.

March 30 Wed. Clear and very mild. Our children, Harders were here. They had arrived yesterday. Jews, Löb and Joseph, were also here.

March 31 Thurs. Clear and mild. During the day we returned the material we bought from [the Jewish peddler] Isaac for $2.50. We still owed 32 cents and bought apples for 50 cents. After this we still owed the Jew 82 cents. *Ohm* K. Friesen came to get the last of his oats. Our children Johann Schultzes were here. Abraham went to the woods with David.

The month has ended through the grace of God.

> Lord we thank you;
>
> It is without hurt or pain
>
> that you have, with your mercy,
>
> guided us through the month of March.

April 1898

April 1 Clear and mild with a cool west wind. It was Friday. At noon [our youngest son] Abraham returned from the woods. Where there was sunshine it was thawing.

April 2 In the morning foggy. The trees were heavy with hoarfrost. During the day it was mild with a N.E. wind.

April 3 Sun. Sunny again with a cold north wind. I went to Chortitz. It was icy in the low-lying areas and from Bergthal to Chortitz it was good travelling, but it was difficult to travel in the villages and on the plowed fields.

April 4 Mon. Cloudy with a cold north wind. At noon it cleared but it was still cold. During the day Märks began threshing rye.

April 5 Tues. In the morning it was overcast with a north wind, but somewhat milder. During the day it was nice.

April 6 Wed. It started thawing. During the day, we worked on the platform for the kettle.

April 7 Thurs. I finished. It was "Green [Maundy] Thursday" and very mild with a strong south wind. I went to Rosengart [15 kilometres distant] in the afternoon. I took the wagon. There was much snow in many areas but it was thawing fast.

April 8 Good Friday. Very mild. In the afternoon I returned home. The snow was almost gone. The dam at Bergthal is overflowing somewhat.

April 9 Sat. Mild. Wind from the south. During the day the snow melted, except in the bushes, and the water ran off. We had our school program for the end of the school term today.

April 10 Easter Sun. In the morning it had frozen and the wind came from the north. We could travel easily to Bergthal but after Bergthal there was a fair bit of ice. During the day it was clear and very mild.

April 11 There was no frost in the morning and [it was] very mild. It is drying well. In the afternoon it clouded over in the S.W.

April 12 Sharp wind from the N.W. People are thinking of seeding.

April 13 Wed. Clear and warm. People are getting ready for seeding. Some are starting to seed. In the evening it clouded over in the west.

April 14 Thurs. Overcast but quite nice; strong wind from the south. Today we started seeding. The cows were sent to the pasture for the first time.

April 15 Fri. Mild with a light wind from the north. We seeded 11 bags of wheat in two days. We delivered the cattle we had sold.

April 16 Sat. In the morning it had frozen somewhat. Otherwise it was mild and clear. We did not seed, but harrowed.

April 17 Sun. It had frozen in the morning again. During the day it was mild with a cool N.E. wind. Travelling went well, the entire way to Chortitz. It was almost dry.

April 18 Mon. It had frozen a little in the morning; cloudy with a south wind. In the evening [the senior] *Ältester* Gerhard Wiebe [and his wife] came for night.

April 19 Tues. It rained a little in the morning but not so much that it interfered with the seeding. During the day there was much cloud with a sharp wind from the north. We had done a lot of field work by noon by the [section of the open field system bearing the] large numbers. We also seeded some rye.

April 20 Wed. The last of the wheat was seeded. In the morning it had frozen considerably, but during the day it was clear and warm. In the morning the wind was from the N.W. and at noon from the south.

April 21 Cloudy with a cool wind from the south. In the afternoon a light overall rain. We had to postpone the seeding. Towards evening it stopped raining.

April 22 Fri. Cloudy and cool with a north wind. We could seed again. We seeded oats. At noon it cleared, but it was not warm.

April 23 Sat. Mild with a N.E. wind. We harrowed [the part of the field] that we had seeded until noon. In the afternoon we did not seed. David Dück came to pick up the last of the seed grain.

April 24 It had frozen somewhat in the morning. It was cloudy with a cold south wind. The road was dry to Chortitz. During the church service it rained a little. At noon the wind changed to the north.

April 25 Mon. It had frozen hard in the morning – cloudy with a light north wind. Jacob plowed in order to seed oats. David and I went to Steinbach in the storm.

April 26 Tues. Strong windstorm from the south so that the wind was thick and dark with dust on the summerfallow. The wind scattered the seed of the summerfallow. Towards evening the storm died down somewhat, but it kept on blowing all night.

April 27 Wed. [There was] still wind from the south but not as strong. In the afternoon it started raining. The wind died down. It rained only a little. Our first thunderstorm of the season. We did not work the fields. We want to wait until the weeds come up, then we will seed barley and oats. Towards evening it rained a lot; so that there was much water standing.

April 28 Thurs. Clear and cool with a west wind. We went to *Ohm* David Stösz regarding Heinrich Fast. It was difficult travelling past Bergthal.

April 29 Fri. In the morning it had frozen hard. Cloudy with a cold N.W. wind. We wanted to get the manure ready, however it was so frozen that we wasted a lot of time.

April 30 Sat. Clear and cold wind from the N.E. Today we visited Janches'. On the way back we stopped to visit the shop of the clockmaker Reimer in Blumenort whose wife has been sick for a long time. The man showed us his wife's wound in her side, and I was shocked. The Lord stay with her and keep her at his side.

> Lord give us your blessing
>
> It is your hand that rules the world
>
> Bless us with the cleansing rain
>
> For our hearts and for the fields.

May 1898

May 1 Sun. Clear with a cold north wind. The road was quite dry to Chortitz.

May 2 Mon. Cold with a N.W. wind. We plowed our own garden in the morning and in the afternoon plowed [Lutheran neighbour] Kohlschmidt's garden. Heinrich Wiebes from Chortitz were here.

May 3 Tues. In the morning it had frozen hard. There was a cold wind from the north. In the afternoon we walked to Johann Neufelds'. The elderly Tante Töws was depressed because it was taking her so long to die.

May 4 Wed. Mild and almost warm. No wind. In the afternoon it cooled somewhat with a light wind from the north. We began building the machine shed. We ploughed a furrow over the field in order to make a garden in the afternoon.

May 5 Thurs. Morning was cloudy. The clouds left and it was mild with a cool north wind.

May 6 Fri. Arbor Day. In the morning it had frozen hard again. The wheat has sprung up and has received some frost. We planted potatoes in the field. It was warm during the day with a light wind from the west.

May 7 Mild with a warm S.W. wind. We harrowed the potatoes, seeded the feed beets and ploughed the *Vorgarten* [front herbal garden].

May 8 Sun. Warm with a west wind. Johann Schultzes were here and came with us to church. In the afternoon Johann Wiebes were here. Towards evening it cooled off. Schultzes returned home.

May 9 Mon. We started seeding again. We wanted to seed a few acres of oats and a bit of rye and 5 acres barley. It was mild with a west wind. In the afternoon it clouded over. In the evening a little rain. The wind changed to the S.W.

May 10 Tues. It had frozen in the morning. During the day we had a cool N.W. wind. Otherwise it was mild. We seeded the last of the oats in the forenoon and plowed the field for the rye in the afternoon.

May 11 Wed. I went with *Ohm* David Stösz to Bergfeld. A calf was born in the morning. It was cloudy with a cold north wind and night frost.

May 12 Thurs. We all went to Kronsgart [27 kilometres south] to help with some problems with God's help. We were largely successful through God's grace. It was clear and mild with a cold wind from the north. We returned home in the evening and arrived late.

May 13 Fri. Clear with a night frost. Cold north wind. We ploughed some more land for barley. We had already seeded the last of the oats and some barley.

May 14 Sat. warm with a S.W. wind. We seeded the last barley and this ends the seeding. May the Lord give us his blessing.

May 15 Sun. warm again with a west wind. The youth [in preparation for baptism] said their first Catechism recitations. It was a large group. Harders came here.

May 16 Mon. Hot with a south wind. Overcast. There is a lot of news regarding the Spanish-American War that has been going on since April. May God lead us to peace. I went with Peter to Steinbach. We made plans to go to Winnipeg.

May 17 Warm and overcast again. S.E. wind. Jacob and Abraham went to Winnipeg. In the afternoon we went visiting in Bergthal to Gerhard Kehlers'. We wanted to visit Bernhard Dyck from Minnesota but he had gone to Winnipeg. Towards evening it clouded over in the west.

May 18 Wed. Cloudy with an east wind. In the morning it rained, however it did not last long. Towards evening Jacob and Abraham arrived from Winnipeg. The price of the wheat was $1.15. This is the highest it has been since we have come to America.

May 19 Ascension day. Mild but overcast. East wind.

May 20 Fri. Mild but cloudy with an east wind. We went to Steinbach with the wool. We had 101 lbs of wool. Jacob is working at the village well.

May 21 Sat. It clouded over in the morning; east wind. We finished building the machine shed, and ploughed for Ungers. At noon it started raining, but only a little. It kept going until evening.

May 22 Sun. Cloudy with a light wind from the north. It cleared up fairly soon and was pleasant.

May 23 Very warm with a light east wind. We seeded some barley today, ploughed the beets, painted our house and so on.

May 24 Tues. Warm with a S.E. wind. We tightened the steel tires for the wagon. Heinrich and Abraham were sick.

May 25 Wed. Cloudy with a south wind. Abraham ploughed the field but Heinrich was sick. We went to David Stöszes' for *Faspa*. It started raining on our way home. For night Dr. Peters came to Peter Hieberts' [Mr. Hiebert had injured his back permanently]. In the evening we had a nice rain and later in the evening even more. As far as we can see, this rain has been good for all types of growth.

May 26 Tues. Foggy with a cold north wind. During the day we straightened the wheels on the wagon. Cloudy all day but no rain.

May 27 Fri. Cloudy all day with a cold wind from the north. We built a lean-to onto the shed for the bakeoven.

May 28 Sat. Mild and warm. Today we built a gate onto the street and more.

May 29 Pentecost. Mild with a S.W. wind. I was in church in Hochfeld.

May 30 Pentecost Monday. There was baptism in Chortitz. 26 people were baptised. There was a large gathering. It was mild with a S.W. wind. In the afternoon I went with the *Ältester* to Grunthal. We travelled to Gnadenfeld [28 kilometers]. In the evening it clouded over in the west. There was a light rain in the evening. I went to Jacob Funks' for night.

May 31 Baptism services are held in Grunthal where 7 are to be baptised. It was cloudy with a S.W. wind. In the afternoon we returned. We were greeted with rain in Blumstein. There was also some thunder. We stayed there until the rain ceased. From then on the road was very wet, however it had not rained that much in Hochfeld. Heinrich was also in Grunthal, but Jacob and Maria had gone to Osterwick. In the evening it was cloudy again in the west.

We have ended the month of May
O Lord through your faithfulness
your mercy and your goodness
Give that furthermore your help,
While we are on life's journey,
might not be taken from us.

June 1898

June 1 Wed. Frost in the morning. During the day it was cloudy and humid. Abraham ploughed the summerfallow. Cold N.W. wind.

June 2 Thurs. In the morning it had frozen hard; the frost had not done a lot of damage. It was still cloudy with a N.W. wind. Towards evening it cleared and became milder.

June 3 Fri. Mild with an east wind. Before lunch I went to Steinbach to get a *Pfluchbaum* [plough hitch]. After lunch Johann Töws' came and I had to repair a plough for them. In the afternoon the wind was from the N.E.

June 4 Sat. Mild with a north wind. We worked on our sod-breaking plough. In the evening we went to look at the windmill that had been raised a few days ago.

June 5 It started raining in the early morning. It rained all day with a strong rain from the south. In the evening it died down. There was much water.

June 6 Cloudy. In the afternoon it rained a little, but in the west we saw large thunderclouds. It passed us by. In the afternoon I went to Blumengart to repair my plow. The road was very difficult.

June 7 Mild with a cool north wind. Jacob was sick. I walked to Johann Neufelds' in the evening. I met Heinrich Friesens and Jacob Thiessen from the West Reserve and also others from here.

June 8 Wed. Wind from S.E. It was mild. In the afternoon we both went to Blumengart to get the plough. We went visiting to Johann Peters' and Abraham Enses' [father to future son-in-law Jacob, who later married daughter Maria]. Mrs. Ens was just out of the hospital in Winnipeg. She had been there for 6 weeks because of sore eyes.

June 9 Thurs. Warm and no wind. The work on the road in Hochfeld began. Jacob was still sick so Heinrich had to work. In the evening we went to Bergthal. For dinner the herbal doctor, Dermunn, came here. I bought some kidney poultice and other medicine from him. He left at *Faspa* time.

June 10 Frid. Cloudy and warm with a S.W. wind. At noon I pulled weeds in the grain field with the children. We had been in the field a short time when a storm cloud came from the west. There was rain with hail, but it did not rain much. Most of it passed by on the north.

June 11 Mild with a west wind. We weeded the grain field in the afternoon and it was cool. We herded the calves.

June 12 Mild with a S.W. wind. Today was Communion in Chortitz; 249 people attended. A nice gathering. In the evening it clouded over in the west.

June 13 Mon. Cloudy with a cold N.W. wind. The children and I pulled the weeds in the grain fields. Mother with the older children made bricks. In the evening the Jews, Löb and Joseph, came here.

June 14 Tues. Cool N.W. wind but otherwise mild. We were in Schönwiesse at Derk Penners' today. Towards evening it clouded over in the west.

June 15 Mild with a south wind. We took the bakeoven out of the workshop and placed it in the new place we had built for it.

June 16 Warm and very humid. We finished our bakeoven and organized the shed. It clouded over in the west. We saw lightening. At midnight a thunderstorm passed over with much thunder and strong rain.

June 17 Clear and mild with a west wind. I went to Blumenort in the forenoon to the store. I wanted to speak with the Bachelor Heinrich Friesen. I talked to him about buying his land, but we could not agree on a price. The boys are getting ready to break sod [on the] new land. In the afternoon cloudy but warm. The boys went to plough.

June 18 Very warm with a south wind. We went to our children today. We also visited in Schöntal at [Estates Administrator] Cornelius Friesens'.

June 19 Sun. We went to church in Osterwick. In the afternoon we visited at Cornelius and Peter Friesens'. After *Faspa* we returned home. It was warm again. Wind from the south.

June 20 Warm with a east wind. The boys ploughed the new land. I did not feel very well. Today Mrs. Jacob Kehler was very sick. I had to go to Steinbach to tell Mr. Kehler to return. I met him on the road close to Steinbach. For night Löb came here and he brought Hörschke with him.

June 21 Tues. Warm with a south wind. Löb said that I should write down that Joseph wanted to go to Oregon on the 26th. It was cloudy in the west. It started raining. A thundercloud from the west passed over and it kept on raining hard. The biggest rain we have had this year. We wanted to weed the potatoes but we couldn't because it rained. It rained in the evening with much thunder. This was a 10-hour thunderstorm.

June 22 Wed. Cloudy and very hot. No wind. We worked at home. It was clear in the evening. It only clouded over in the west a bit. The elderly Jew was here for night.

June 23 Thurs. Warm again, but somewhat milder. Before lunch, Dörksen and I went to look for hay. In the afternoon we had another rain overall. There was some thunder. The cloud came from the south and the wind from the N.E. Yesterday Abram Janches went to Peter Dörksens'.

June 24 Cloudy all day with a nice rain from the N.E. Cool.

June 25 Still cloudy and rainy. Very fruitful weather but some people are saying it is too wet. God knows what is best. It will turn out all right. Today it is very cool.

June 26 Sun. Church was in Hochfeld. There were few people because of the unfriendly weather. It rained until noon. It was drizzling from Tuesday noon to Sunday noon. At noon the rain stopped, but it was still cloudy. In the evening the sunset was beautiful. During the night it stopped entirely.

June 27 Mond. Clear and mild with a south wind. The warmth of the sun is refreshing after so many days of rain. In the afternoon I went to look at the grain. There was much water in low-lying areas and little water in the higher areas under the grain. In the creek there was much water.

June 28 Tues. Threatening rain; overcast, but it did not rain here. In the afternoon the children went to weed the potatoes on the hill. We had wanted to weed the grain field but it was too wet in the forenoon. Towards evening the wind changed to the west and became stronger.

June 29 Wed. Cloudy and small strips of rain. Strong cool wind from the west. In the forenoon the children worked in the potato field. In the afternoon they ploughed [on the] new field. We went to Johann Neufelds'. It was hard going. As we returned we stopped in at Peter Hieberts' Bergthal to pick up a songbook that we had ordered through Simmons [Publishing House]. He had left it there.

June 30 Thurs. Cloudy and mild N.E. wind. We weeded in the field again. It was wet in places. In the afternoon it cleared, but it was cloudy in the evening in the west. So we have ended the month without problems. We give God the glory for this.

> Everlasting sunshine in life
>
> will never bring a blessed crop
>
> If sunshine interchanges with rain
>
> flowers will bear the lovely fruit
>
> That is the way of nature.
>
> Therefore God has wisely sent
>
> His blessing in the month of June
>
> After sunny days He sends the mighty rain.

July 1898

July 1 Fri. It rained all day with an east wind. It was a pleasant rain and not a hard rain, more wet than dry.

July 2 More rain from the east. In the afternoon the wind changed to the north. In the evening it stopped raining and it started clearing. I did not feel well during the day and became ill at night.

July 3 Sun. I could not go to Chortitz to church (even though it was my turn [as minister] to be there) because I was too sick. Johann Schultz was here. He wanted to take my wife to Harders'. Agatha [Harder, daughter] was sick. She had given birth to a son the 29th of June but because I was sick, [daughter] Maria went [with mother]. It was mild, cool and very muddy.

July 4 Mon. Warm with a south wind. The boys broke 4 acres of new land altogether this year. We started weeding. In the afternoon the Stöszes and Johann Peters were here, also Mrs. Märk. In the evening it clouded over in the west and at night we heard thunder in the distance; however, it passed by us. It only rained slightly at our place. It was very hot and humid. During the night the wind turned to the west and was very strong. After a while it died down somewhat.

July 5 Tues. Clear and warm with a strong wind from the south. The children weeded. I felt a little better. In the evening it clouded over and in the west we could see some lightening. In the night we heard thunder.

July 6 Wed. The wind was from the west and the clouds were threatening rain. It did not rain here, but it cleared soon and was pleasant and bright. During the day the children cultivated the potato field for the first time. It was a little wet but we managed.

July 7 Thurs. Clear and mild wind from the west. We weeded the grain. The last cow calved.

July 8 Fri. Wind from the N.W. and otherwise clear and mild. I went to help weed the grain for the first time since I became sick. The mosquitoes were intolerable.

July 9 Sat. Very warm with very little wind. The breeze was from N.W. We went to Steinbach to get some bricks, etc.

July 10 Sun. Warm with N.W. wind. There were some wet spots driving to Chortitz. My wife went with David to Osterwick to our children.

July 11 Mon. Mild with a warm wind. We broke up our [brick] oven. Soon the wind turned to the south. In the afternoon a thundercloud passed by to the north. It rained, but not here.

July 12 Tues. Foggy. It did not last long. It was very warm during the day. The wind was from the south and it was threatening rain. We made a [new] oven. Löb came for night. The mosquitoes were bad. We planted potatoes. In the evening a thundercloud passed by us to the N.E. but it did not rain much. There was a little hail with the storm.

July 13 Wed. [During the] morning the wind was from the south. It was warm and clouding over in the north. It is not raining, but it is very hot and humid, day and night.

July 14 Thurs. In the morning the wind was from the west, cloudy and hot. Abraham started ploughing the summerfallow for the second time. Jacob went to work in the [Hochfeld village] cheese factory yesterday and today.

July 15 Fri. Warm with a south wind.

July 16 Sat. Cloudy and humid with a north wind. I went to Grunthal. The way was good but there were too many mosquitoes. I went to Peter Funks' for night.

July 17 In the morning the wind from the N.E. shifted to the south and became stronger. In the afternoon I returned home. The mosquitoes were not quite so bad. In the evening it clouded over in the N.W. It rained a little and we heard some thunder towards sunset.

July 18 Mon. It clouded over in the south with an east wind. It rained only a little. It is still very hot.

July 19 Tues. Clouded in the west, but it rained very little. The wind turned to the north. It cooled off quickly and during the night it was cool.

July 20 Pleasant and cool with a north wind and cloudy. We wanted to spray the potatoes yesterday, but didn't because of the threatening rain. We will try again today afternoon. It is now 12:00 and we have finished spraying the potatoes.

July 21 Thurs. Pleasant and cool and cloudy with a west wind. We drove through the potatoes with the machine to heap the potatoes.

July 22 Fri. Pleasant. Towards evening *Ältester* Andres Lilge [of Edmonton] came to visit.

July 23 Sat. Pleasant with a west wind. I went with Lilge to Janches'. In the afternoon Abram Dücks came from Burwalde. Lilge went to Töws's.

July 24 Sun. Pleasant with a N.W. wind. Lilge was at church, but did not preach. Abraham Dücks went home in the afternoon.

July 25 Mon. Warm with a S.W. wind. In the forenoon we, Friesen, Dörksen and Falk, went to look at hay grass. We decided to buy it. I went to Gröning to borrow money. I borrowed $100 to buy land.

July 26 Tues. In the morning it was cloudy with a south wind. It rained a little in the morning. We took the mower into the field. In the evening it became very cloudy in the N.W.

July 27 Wed. Warm with a S.W. wind. We weeded the school section, the ploughed land, and in the afternoon, as we were weeding wild oats out of the wheat field, I noticed that there was rust [in the wheat]. It clouded in the N.W. H.F. went to buy the land.

July 28 Thurs. Dark and humid with a cool wind from the north. We put new windowsills onto the windows.

July 29 Fri. Cloudy with a cool N.W. wind. During the day we went to look at the land that we bought, Dörksen, Falk and myself; namely [the] Quarter

Section, 9 N.E., and the 80 acres of Section 16 S.E., Township 8, Range 5, for $300 per lot.

July 30 Sat. Warm with a N.W. wind. We started making hay today. Both of us went to Strassburg for night to Jacob Hieberts'.

July 31 Sun. Warm with a west wind. Forenoon we went to Strassburg to church and went home in the afternoon.

> Now we have, through the Lord's grace
> from this our life's path
> ended the month of July
> In which we received many blessings.

August 1898

Aug. 1 Very warm with a S.W. wind.

Aug. 2 Tues. In the morning it was foggy. It cleared quickly and was very hot with a south wind.

Aug. 3 Wed. Always hot with a south wind. We brought 11 loads of hay home.

Aug. 4 Wind from the south. It looks like rain. In the night we had a strong thunderstorm from the west.

Aug. 5 Fri. Very wet. We couldn't do anything with the hay. It was wet all day with a south wind.

Aug. 6 Nice, clear and pleasant with a west wind, but we will not be able to do much with the hay. In the afternoon we replaced one axle on the hay rack.

Aug. 7 Sun. Pleasant with a N.W. wind. My wife and I went to Chortitz to church. It had rained less in Chortitz.

Aug. 8 Mon. Pleasant with a S.W. wind. We are busy with the hay harvest. In the afternoon it clouded over in the west. In the evening we had a little rainfall.

Aug. 9 Tues. Foggy, cloudy and humid all day with a west wind. Towards evening it cleared up. We mowed for the herdsman all day.

Aug. 10 Wed. Pleasant with a N.W. wind. We brought hay home from the Schultz quarter section. We had to drive via Bergthal because it was too wet here. Towards evening it cooled very quickly.

Aug. 11 Thurs. In the morning clear and mild with a cool north wind. Abram had to work at the Kohlschmidt's, the herdsman, bringing in the hay. By midday today, we have gathered 30 loads of hay. Tomorrow we will cut some barley, God willing.

Aug. 12 Fri. Cool. There was some frost during the night. Some say it has frozen, but nothing has been harmed by the frost. During the day [it was] pleasant with a light N.W. wind. We have begun our harvest. We have cut the oats.

Aug. 13 Sat. In the morning it was foggy and cool. The fog cleared quickly and it was clear and warm and a light N.W. wind. We mowed the rye.

Aug. 14 Sun. Pleasant and mild with a west wind. The wheat is not very ripe.

Aug. 15 Mon. Cloudy and cool and N.W. wind. We cut oats. We broke the binder towards evening. It clouded over in the west and there was some rain at night.

Aug. 16 Tues. Mild with a S.W. wind. We cut the first of the wheat. It was not very ripe.

Aug. 17 [During the] morning it was foggy again. It cleared quickly. Today we cut the barley. The wind was from the S.W.

Aug. 18 Thurs. Mild and warm with a south wind. During the day we began cutting "the field with the high numbers" [a designated field within the Hochfeld village district]. In the evening the binder broke.

Aug. 19 Fri. Warm with a south wind. In the forenoon we went to Steinbach in order to buy parts to repair the binder. In the afternoon we continued cutting.

Aug. 20 Sat. Mild with a S.W. wind. We have cut the wheat [on the] "field with the high numbers" but have not quite finished it today. The air was heavy with humidity.

Aug. 21 Sun. Warm with a south wind. I went to Blumengart to church. The air was humid again.

Aug. 22 Mon. It was cloudy and humid all day with an east wind. We finished our "field with the high numbers" by noon. The wheat was really quite green, but the time for harvest was here so we continued. We also have 3 acres of summerfallow wheat that was still green and we will wait with cutting this. We also have 2 acres of oats that were seeded late. The rest is all cut.

Aug. 23 Thurs. In the morning it had rained. It is very cloudy so that we cannot start anything until it clears. The wind was from the south.

Aug. 24 Wed. Cloudy and humid with a south wind. In the afternoon we cut the last of the wheat. In the evening the rain came from the N.W. but it was not a strong thunderstorm.

Aug. 25 Thurs. Morning, cool and very cloudy with a N.W. wind. In the afternoon it was mild. We cut the last of the oats and finished cutting the grain in the afternoon. We do not have enough hay cut yet.

Aug. 26 Fri. In the morning it was cloudy, otherwise mild with a N.W. wind. Jacob drove to the *Franzosen Steppe* [Métis lands in the Ste. Anne Municipality, just to the north] to cut hay. We loaded hay steadily and stopped towards evening. It cleared in the evening.

Aug. 27 Sat. Clear and a strong south wind so that the weather hindered gathering hay. Jacob went to the back field to cut the grass and Abram and Maria are loading hay. Heinrich has to rake the hay.

Aug. 28 Mild with a north wind. Very pleasant.

Aug. 29 Mon. Mild with a strong wind from the south. We went to the other farm to gather hay but, because of the storm, it was not pleasant.

Aug. 30 Tues. We gathered the last of the hay on the *Franzosen Steppe*; 10 loads. The wind was calm and it was humid.

Aug. 31 Wed. Cloudy and warm with a east wind. We started to bring in the grain. Towards the afternoon raindrops fell and towards evening it rained hard enough that we could not bring home the grain.

> The month of August has passed,
>
> In which the Lord has done much good.
>
> Our body and soul He has blessed
>
> For that we want to praise the Lord.

September 1898

Sept. 1 Thurs. During the night it had rained a little. In the morning there was fog. I can't haul grain. I went with my neighbour Dörksen to Steinbach. The fog cleared but it stayed cloudy. Towards evening it was mild. We started hauling grain but it clouded over right away. We heard thunder once in a while, but it passed by on the north.

Sept. 2 Fri. In the morning there was fog. The fog cleared and it became mild. In the afternoon we gathered oats and one load of barley.

Sept. 3 In the morning it looked like it would be nice but it soon clouded over with a south wind. I went to Bergthal because of a meeting held at David Stöszes'. In the forenoon it rained a little. I went to Burwalde in the afternoon. The wind turned to the west. It rained with a strong west wind towards evening.

Sept. 4 Sun. In the morning cool, but mild. In the afternoon I left Jacob Friesens'. We went to look at cherries. The bushes were very full and we picked some. It looked like rain. Before we got home it had rained. In the evening we went to visit the elderly Peter Ginter in Rosengart who has been sick for a very long time.

Sept. 5 Mon. It looks like it will be a nice day with a west wind. It is too wet to haul the grain. The boys went ploughing. The wind is cold and strong. In the afternoon we hauled wheat. It was not very dry.

Sept. 6 Tues. Cloudy and cool with a strong N.W. wind. We hauled wheat until noon and in the afternoon it rained again. We had several rain showers in the afternoon that hindered our work.

Sept. 7 Wed. In the morning it was still cloudy but no rain. We ploughed until noon. We brought a load of feed home, but before we could get to where we were going it rained again. We could not work with the grain because of the rain. Towards evening it cleared and became cold with a N.W. wind.

Sept. 8 Thurs. The first real frost covering the ground this year. During the day it was mild and cloudy. It is almost noon. We want to haul wheat if it stays nice.

Sept. 9 Fri. Mild and no wind. It had frozen heavily in the morning. This was the first day we could work all day. We brought some stacks home. The grain was dry today.

Sept. 10 Sat. Strong frost again. Mild with a strong west wind. I want to go to Grunthal. In the afternoon we both [my wife and I] went to Grunthal. We stayed at Peter Giesbrechts' for night.

Sept. 11 Sun. Mild with a S.W. wind. We visited at Franz Peters' in the afternoon in Schönsee.

Sept. 12 Mon. Mild and warm with a south wind. During the day we brought the last of the sheaves home with God's help, for which the Lord should be thanked.

Sept. 13 Tues. Cloudy and humid. In the daytime we worked with the hay. Jacob and Abraham went to the *Franzosen Steppe* to look at the hay. We ploughed a strip of land to prevent fire. Heinrich mowed the grass here.

Sept. 14 Wed. In the morning it had rained, N.E. wind. We are ploughing because we cannot begin working with anything else.

Sept. 15 Thurs. In the morning it was cloudy with a light N.W. wind. It started clearing quickly. In the afternoon we cut the last of the hay. The last of the hay is in. It was very mild. We put the [mowing] machine into the shed.

Sept. 16 Fri. Clear and mild with a light wind from the west. Today we hauled and stacked the hay.

Sept. 17 Sat. Cool with a N.W. wind. We have collected hay. Heinrich, Maria and I went to Osterwick in the afternoon. In the forenoon Bernard Wiebe and I had gone to Greenland [the Holdeman Mennonite community just to the north of the East Reserve] to a threshing machine meeting. The air is humid and in the evening we had a thunderstorm with hail.

Sept. 18 Sun. Cool with a strong N.W. wind. We went to church at Osterwick in the forenoon and returned home in the afternoon. It cooled quickly in the evening. The air is full of smoke.

Sept. 19 Mon. In the morning it had frozen. During the day mild, but humid air with a S.W. wind. Jacob went to Johann Neufelds' to help thresh, Heinrich ploughed, Abram and Maria collected hay.

Sept. 20 Tues. Much smoke in the air and a strong wind from the south. We ended the hay gathering at noon. In the afternoon we dug potatoes.

Sept. 21 Wed. At noon we had finished digging potatoes; 29 bags. It was cloudy with a west wind. Jacob came home from threshing.

Sept. 22 Thurs. Cloudy again with a N.E. wind. We harvested the feed beets in the field. In the afternoon Jacob and Heinrich went to Johann Schultz to help thresh.

Sept. 23 Still cloudy and cool with a S.W. wind. In the evening a strong rain passed over with thunder from the S.W.

Sept. 24 Sat. I went to Neubergfeld. The wind was N.W. [In the area] from Schönfeld to Kronsthal it had rained a lot. There was quite a lot of water on the road.

Sept. 25 Sun. I returned home. It was clear and pleasant but the wind was N.W.

Sept. 26 Mon. No wind. Clear and warm. Heinrich came home on Sunday. He had been threshing at Schultzes' and Harders', but Jacob had stayed to help Peter.

Sept. 27 Tues. Clear and mild with a strong wind from the south. Peter brought Jacob home at noon.

Sept. 28 Wed. Mild with a strong wind from the west. Today we finished ploughing at the "Wide Numbers" [section of the open field system]. We also took in some heating manure.

Sept. 29 Thurs. Cloudy and it started raining. A light and soft overall rain. It continued almost all day. Towards evening it cooled suddenly.

Sept. 30 Mild with a S.W. wind. Today Peter Hieberts threshed on Janches' farm. Towards evening it clouded over in the S.W. It has been raining on and off all month.

> Now the month of September has passed
>
> O that we might not in our mind
>
> forget the Lord our God
>
> He who richly measured our crops in this season
>
> Let us thank Him graciously.

October 1898

Oct. 1 Sat. Mild. During the night we heard a steady thunder and also in the morning there was thunder, but little rain. The thunder stopped in the morning but it was cloudy and wet with a cold wind from the east. The rain kept on all day. They closed the cheese factory. During the night we had strong thunder again with a strong wind from the N.E. and pouring rain.

Oct. 2 Sun. Still rainy, but the wind came from the S.E. There was lot of water while driving to Chortitz. In the afternoon the wind sprang to the N.W. The wind became strong and in the evening a storm passed over.

Oct. 3 Cloudy and mild with a cold west wind. Today they, Heinrich Falks, started to thresh. The carrots were dug.

Oct. 4 Tues. In the morning it had frozen. Cloudy with a N.E. wind. Towards evening it started snowing and snowed heavily.

Oct. 5 Wed. In the morning it was cloudy with a west wind. Soon it cleared in the west. At noon we brought the threshing machine to Johann Hieberts'.

Oct. 6 Thurs. Mild with a S.W. wind. Today Johann Hieberts finished threshing. After *Faspa* the threshing machine came here.

Oct. 7 Fri. Mild and cool with a west wind. We finished threshing. We have, with God's help, finished threshing without problems. We have 44 loads of wheat from 24 acres; 464 bushels of wheat; oats 13 loads from 8 acres, making 264 bushels; barley 10 loads from 5 ... acres, making 162 bushels; rye 4 loads from 1 ... acres, making 18 bushels; total, 908 bushels.

Oct. 8 Sat. Clear with a N.W. wind. We went to Osterwick to the children in the afternoon.

Oct. 9 Sun. There was frost in the morning, but the wind came from the south. Peter Harder came with me to Strassburg to the church service. I left for home in the afternoon. It clouded over in the west. I arrived at home in the evening. It started raining and rained all night.

Oct. 10 Mon. It is still raining in the morning; cold north wind. There is lots of water. We cannot thresh. In the afternoon the rain eased up, but it is still cloudy and rainy. It rained until evening. It has rained for 24 hours straight. There was a cool wind and rain from the north.

Oct. 11 Tues. Mild again with a N.E. wind. Jacob and Heinrich went to Steinbach to the mill. It was hard going – much water and much mud. They threshed in the afternoon.

Oct. 12 Wed. We threshed at Peter Wiebes'. It was mild with a south wind. It started clouding over in the north at noon. The wind turned to the N.W. Today my wife cooked syrup.

Oct. 13 Thurs. Very mild and no wind. Jacob Hieberts threshed. *Ohm* David Stösz had a meeting because of Abraham Görtzen. My wife made syrup again.

Oct. 14 Fri. During the night there had been frost, but during the day it was mild and clear.

Oct. 15 Sat. Cloudy, but otherwise mild with a strong wind from the south. We finished threshing at Peter Hieberts'.

Oct. 16 Sun. Cloudy with a cold wind from the west. Communion [service] was held in Chortitz. It was difficult driving.

Oct. 17 Mon. Very cloudy with a cold wind from the north. We started threshing at Bernhard Wiebes', but we didn't finish.

Oct. 18 Tues. In the morning there was a thick layer of snow on the ground. It is still snowing, but mild. The wind was from the north. We cannot thresh.

There are so many interruptions in our threshing that our patience is being tested. Winter is almost here and there is much to thresh as yet. In the afternoon we were able to thresh a little.

Oct. 19 Cloudy and rainy all day. We did thresh, however, we did not make much time. The wind was from N.E. We threshed at Jacob Kehlers'.

Oct. 20 Still very cloudy. Cool wind from the north and rainy. We finished threshing at Jacob Kehlers'. Today the sheep have been brought in from the pasture. It is extremely muddy.

Oct. 21 Fri. It is still cloudy, but not raining. In the forenoon we did not thresh as the threshing machine broke down in the morning. Threshed at Abram Gerbrands' in afternoon. The wind was from the north and in the evening it cleared so that it was freezing. Such a long, sad, rainy time.

Oct. 22 Humid with a south wind, but we could see the sun coming.

Oct. 23 Sun. Mild, but very wet while going to Chortitz. The wind was N.W.

Oct. 24 Mon. Mild, but cool with a west wind. Threshing is somewhat better, but it is cloudy again.

Oct. 25 Tues. Cloudy, but otherwise mild with a west wind. We threshed at Schultzes'.

Oct. 26 Wed. Cloudy and cold wind from the south. We finished threshing, with God's help. We went with Heinrich Penner to look at the land he wanted to buy. We went to Johann Schultzes' at noon. In the afternoon we went to the *Franzosen Steppe* to look at land. He [Heinrich Penner] bid on the [hay] lot that bordered John Schultzes' land. We stayed for night.

Oct. 27 Thurs. In the morning it had snowed and there was a thick blanket of snow. The wind came from the south and the snow soon melted because it was mild. We went to the Oak Bush [30 kilometres to the N.W., near Iles des Chesnes] in the morning. Penner wanted to speak with Johann Roon about buying land. He was not at home. Johan Schultz and David Dyck also went to discuss the calves. From there we went to [land conveyancer] Krause's and arrived at 2:00. Because Krause wanted to help Penner with the land purchase, they left for Winnipeg directly, and I walked home. I came home late at night. The apple trees we had ordered had come.

Oct. 28 Fri. Cloudy with a west wind otherwise mild. In the forenoon we planted the apple trees. In the afternoon we brought in the manure blocks [heating blocks], however, they were not very dry.

Oct. 29 Snow had fallen again. No frost. The wind came from the north. Cloudy.

Oct. 30 Sun. There was heavy frost, but the wind came from the south. I walked to Blumengart to church.

Oct. 31 Mon. Mild with a south wind. Jacob and I went to Steinbach to the mill. Travelling was difficult. Heinrich and Abram went with Bernard Wiebe to help thresh at Krauses'.

November 1898

Nov. 1 Tues. Cloudy with a north wind, but not very cold. There was a little snow falling today, but it melted right away. Towards evening it became colder.

Nov. 2 Wed. Cloudy with a cool wind from the south, otherwise it was mild. Today Heinrich Penners brought Anna to board at our house so that she is able to go to school. This is the first day of school.

Nov. 3 Thurs. Mild with a south wind. I went to Heinrich Penners' with Abraham Janzen. He wanted a house to live in and found one.

Nov. 4 Fri. Clear and mild with a strong wind from the west. We ploughed the garden. We want to plant plum trees. We planted some in the afternoon, the rest we planted later in the day. In the evening a little snow fell.

Nov. 5 Sat. Cloudy with a N.W. wind, but otherwise mild, except for a cold wind. I went to Grunthal. It had frozen a little. Where it was a little wet the ice was not strong enough to hold us, however it was not too bad driving today.

Nov. 6 Sun. Cloudy, but otherwise very mild with a west wind. At noon it began clearing. Towards evening it clouded over in the west and became colder.

Nov. 7 Mon. Blowing snow from the east. In the afternoon the wind turned to the north. All day there was light blowing snow.

Nov. 8 Tues. Humid with a cold wind from the north, -7. Jacob went to Niverville with a load of wheat. Cornelius Friesens had a wedding at their house. We did not attend because we were not feeling well.

Nov. 9 Wed. Clear, but -15 with a south wind. We helped Jacob Hieberts butcher pigs. There was not enough snow on the roads to use the sleigh.

Nov. 10 Clear and mild. The wind was from the S.W.

Nov. 11 Fri. Clear and mild with a S.W. wind. Jacob had to help butcher pigs at Kohlschmidts'. We went to Janches' and bought a bushel of apples for $1.90. Heinrich Penner came here with [son] David.

Nov. 12 Sat. Mild with no wind. Soon the wind picked up and came from the west. Penner went to Niverville to look at some land.

Nov. 13 Sun. Cloudy in the morning with a little snowfall and a cold wind from N.W. A Brotherhood Meeting was held in Chortitz. Mrs. Penner came to get Heinrich Penner.

Nov. 14 Mon. Cloudy with a S.W. wind. We got ready to butcher pigs.

Nov. 15 Tues. Cloudy, but mild with a S.W. wind. We butchered pigs.

Nov. 16 Wed. Mild with a N.W. wind.

Nov. 17 Thurs. Cloudy, but mild with a S.W. wind. Jacob went to the mill in Steinbach. I went with Peter Klassen from Niverville to Heinrich Penners' [to discuss the] land purchase.

Nov. 18 Fri. It was very icy. It was cloudy, but not cold with a N.E. wind.

Nov. 19 Sat. Cloudy, but not cold with a south wind. Jacob went to Niverville with wheat. He got 51 cents a bushel.

Nov. 21 The first frost, -14.

Nov. 20 Cloudy and snow with an east wind, but not cold. At noon the wind came from the north and became stronger so that there was blowing snow. Towards evening blowing snow and cold.

Nov. 21 Cloudy and cold wind from the north. The first very cold day this fall, -14.

Nov. 22 Clear and cold with a N.W. wind. We went to Heinrich Dörksens' in Schönthal. He was ill. We had to drive with the wagon as there was not enough snow to take the sleigh. We got ready to tan the leather. It was -18 in the morning.

Nov. 23 Cloudy with a cold wind from the N.W.

Nov. 24 Thurs. Humid and cold with north wind. We had a wedding [in Hochfeld] – Johann Hiebert with Susanna Kehler in Blumengart.

Nov. 25 Fri. Clear, but a cold west wind. We had a *Waisenamt* meeting at *Ohm* David Stöszes' regarding the problem of Wilhelm Schwartz.

Nov. 26 Sat. We had to meet at *Ohm* Cornelius Stösz's in Blumstein regarding Schwartz. It was a cold and strong south wind so that there was a storm in the evening. I stayed in Chortitz for night.

Nov. 27 Sun. Very mild with a light wind from the north.

Nov. 28 Mon. Not very cold, but a heavy snowfall from the south that continued all day.

Nov. 29 Tues. Strong and cold wind from the N.W. and blowing snow. We had a Brotherhood Meeting in both churches regarding Rempel's things. We decided to send two men to Winnipeg.

Nov. 30 Wed. In the morning clear and mild all day. The wind was from the north. Both men, Cornelius Dyck and *Ohm* Peter Töws from Bergfeld went to Winnipeg. Löb and Herschke were here for night.

December 1898

Dec. 1 Thurs. In the morning foggy, but mild during the day. We went to visit at Krauses'. The wind was from the west.

Dec. 2 Fri. There was hoarfrost on the trees. Clear and -19 in the morning; the wind from the N.W. Abraham went with Johann Hiebert to Winnipeg. Jacob and Heinrich went for hay. Fuchs was here to apply for the job of herdsman. Heinrich Penner was here with Janches' Bill.

Dec. 3 Cloudy, but not very cold. Jacob and Heinrich are supposed to go for hay. The wind is from the N.W.

Dec. 4 Foggy all day. The wind was from the S.W. We went to Blumengart to church. It was not cold.

Dec. 5 Mon. Cloudy and light snowfall all day. The wind was from the east, but not cold. We butchered a cow today. Towards evening the wind was from the N.W.

Dec. 6 Tues. Humid, but not very cold; the wind from the north. The wind is light, but the snow is drifting into the sleigh tracks. We got two loads of hay.

Dec. 7 Clear and light wind from the N.W. Again we got two loads of hay. It was moderately cold.

Dec. 8 Thurs. Moderately cold again with a light north wind. There was a little blowing snow. Jacob went to *Pontischien* with wheat, but returned with the load as no boxcars had been there. Heinrich got the last of the hay.

Dec. 9 Cold wind from the S.W. that made blowing snow. Jacob and Heinrich went to *Pontischien* with wheat, Heinrich for us, and Jacob for Jacob Kehlers. The wheat buyer did not have money. In the evening Peter came here.

Dec. 10 Sat. Moderately cold with a light wind from the S.W. I went to Rosengart for night.

Dec. 11 Sun. Not very cold with a N.W. wind. I came home in the afternoon. Towards evening it became colder.

Dec. 12 Mon. Cold north wind with -16 in the morning. We went to Steinbach to the store.

Dec. 13 Tues. Wind was S.W., -23. An auction sale was held at the Widow Peter Ens's in Blumengart. I bought a cow for $18. During the day it was milder.

Dec. 14 Wed. Moderately cold with a west wind. Jacob and Heinrich went to *Pontischien* with wheat. The price was only 47 cents. Towards evening I went to Schönthal. The travelling was good.

Dec. 15 Thurs. Not very cold with a south wind. Cornelius Friesen and I visited the school in Schönthal and Osterwick and then went to Franz Dycks', Niverville, for night.

Dec. 16 Fri. Wind from the south and mild. In the forenoon we visited Strassburg school. In the afternoon we went home. Towards evening the wind picked up. During the night there were strong winds from the south. We brought barley to Blumenort to the feed mill.

Dec. 17 Sat. Wind was west and it was unusually mild, almost warm. Jacob is supposed to get the chop.

Dec. 18 Sun. Mild with a west wind. Hochfeld hosted the church service; however, I went to Chortitz. *Ohm* Cornelius Friesen was here and stayed for night.

Dec. 19 Mon. Somewhat colder with a S.W. wind. Abraham and David went to the bush. We visited the school in Hochfeld in the forenoon, and Blumengart in the afternoon.

Dec. 20 Tues. The wind is from the S.W. We visited the school in Bergthal in the forenoon and Chortitz in the afternoon. This completed the visitations of the schools. The weather was mild.

Dec. 21 Wed. Wind from N.W. and not very cold. Heinrich went with Krauses [to Winnipeg].

Dec. 22 Thurs. Some hoarfrost. Cloudy during the day, but not very cold. The wind was from the west.

Dec. 23 Fri. A little colder with a west wind that caused blowing snow.

Dec. 24 Sat. Christmas Eve. In the morning cold, but the wind was from the south. It was cloudy and snowed a little in the morning.

Dec. 25 Sun. Christmas Day. Strong wind from the south with blowing snow. I went to Chortitz to church in the morning and in the afternoon I travelled with *Ohm* Peter Töws to Bergfeld for the night.

Dec. 26 Mon. The Second Holiday. There was blowing snow from the west as I travelled to Grunthal. At noon it cleared and became colder. Strong N.W. wind with blowing snow. I went to Blumstein for night.

Dec. 27 Tues. In the morning it was cold with a north wind. *Ohm* Cornelius Stösz and I went to the municipal [head office at Chortitz] to register new births and deaths. During the day it was mild. I returned towards evening.

Dec. 28 Wed. Mild with a south wind. Heinrich Wiebes were here.

Dec. 29 Thurs. Cold wind from the north and blowing snow. It is getting colder.

Dec. 30 Fri. -30. Clear with a light wind from the N.W.

Dec. 31 Sat. Very cold -32, wind from S.W. I went to Rosenbach to visit the children. At noon I went to Peter Harders'. In the evening I went to Strassburg and then to Jacob Krahns' for night. The cold abated somewhat.

> The time flies and passes quickly
> like a wave being pushed by the wind
> the clock has already turned
> telling us to write eighteen hundred and ninety eight
> eternity is drawing nearer
> urging us to better our lives

An "Old Mennonite" church building: the Christian Eby Meetinghouse, built in 1833. (Courtesy Mennonite Archives of Ontario)

J.R. and Maria (Reimer) Friesen's wedding in 1903. J.R. Friesen opened western Canada's first Ford car dealership in about 1914, causing *Aeltester* Peter R. Dueck great anguish. (From *Preservings,* December 1996, 73.)

Bishops and Evangelists

VI

13 Levi Jung (1841 to 1905)
Center Valley, Pennsylvania
Diary selection: 7 November to 31 December 1863
Age: 22

Levi Jung (Young) was born on 12 October 1841 in Northampton County, Pennsylvania. He was the first child of David and Barbara Jung. By the 1850s, the Jung household comprised Levi, his four siblings – Susanna, Elizabeth, Samuel, and Jonathan – grandfather Peter Jung, great-aunt Susanna Hiestand, great-uncle John Hiestand, and labourers Mary Rohm and Charles Edelman. In April 1857, the Jung family sold their farm to Stephen Trumbauer and moved to a another community, Center Valley. Within a short time, however, Levi returned to the old farm to work for the Trumbauers. Here he experienced a conversion to evangelical Christianity through an Evangelical Mennonite itinerant preacher, Eusebius Hershey. Jung was subsequently drawn by Hershey to leave the Old Mennonite Church and associate with the Evangelical Mennonite Association (later the Mennonite Brethren in Christ). In March 1863, Jung looked back to a time six years earlier when he was still at home: "Then I was serving Satan and I was respected by my father, but now as I am serving God I have lost his esteem, but thanks to God that I have learned to love the Lord and [that] I became willing to resign my heart to Christ."

In the midst of the Civil War, in June 1863, Levi Jung attended a conference of Evangelical Mennonite Association ministers held in Zionsville, Pennsylvania, and heard about the work of revivalism. As he noted later, the chairman, Eusebius Hershey, "laid upon the hearts of every servant the urgent need at the present time for more travelling preachers, and that God would expect more from our small society since we have a reason to believe that souls are being lost, which otherwise could be saved with the help of God and more willing itinerant preachers." When Jung attended another conference in October of the same year, he was recruited by Hershey to accompany him to Canada that winter. Jung agreed. Although he was found "able for soldier" on 10 October, he avoided military service by paying a $300 commutation fee. Thus, on 10 November he departed by train for Philadelphia, Buffalo, and Canada.

Once in Canada, he quickly linked up with "Brother Hershey" and prepared for two months of revivalism in the Niagara Peninsula and Waterloo communities. In the Niagara Peninsula Mennonite community of "The Twenty," Jung and Hershey encountered other evangelistic Mennonite leaders: Jacob Albright, a one-time deacon in the Old Mennonite Church; Daniel High, the founder of Ontario's New Mennonite Church, now "silenced," or excommunicated, by the Old Mennonites; Jacob Gross, a one-time Old Mennonite bishop at "The Twenty" but now a member of a church group known as the Evangelical Association. While at "The Twenty," Hershey and Jung also looked up Dilman Moyer, the local Old Mennonite bishop.

On 18 November, Jung and Hershey moved on to Waterloo County, where they linked up with a third Evangelical Mennonite Association revivalist from Pennsylvania, Jonas Schultz. The three evangelists commenced a six-week period of preaching, visiting ministers, and making house calls. They visited New Mennonite preachers John McNally and Samuel Schlichter, but they also encountered the old guard, and at one juncture listened to a sermon by Old Mennonite Reverend Moses Erb. Most of the visiting revivalists' preaching took place in Mennonite homes and schoolhouses, but the revivalists also visited some Catholic and Lutheran families, noted by Jung as being more open to personal prayer than some "cold" Mennonite homes. Clearly, each visit was important, since Jung (or an editor) enumerated these visits, beginning with the number three on 15 November and continuing to number 129 on 30 December.

After returning to Pennsylvania, Jung received public acknowledgement for his work from Hershey. Two years later, Jung made public his call to be an itinerant preacher and subsequently was licensed by the Evangelical Mennonite Church for this ministry. Seven months later, however, he withdrew from the Evangelical Mennonites and associated with the Godshall Group, a radical Mennonite church that rejected the ordination, Sunday schools, and other "man-made rules." Jung eventually married a woman named Susannah; 1880 census records indicate that they had four children – Emma, Floyd, Palmer, and Mark – and lived in Petersville, Pennsylvania. Levi Jung died in 1905.

Jung's diary is contained in the collection of the Schwenkfelder Library, Pennsburg, PA. The diary was transcribed by Richard Taylor, Wallingford, PA. For more information on Levi Jung see: Richard Taylor, ed. "Revival in a Young Man's Life, Levi Young, 1863," unpublished paper, 1996; Richard E. Taylor, ed., and Frank Litty, trans., *Verhandlungen, 1859-1895* (Coopersburg, PA: 1989).

November 1863

Sat. 7 Today I made preparations to get ready to start next week for Canada. I wrote a letter for Sarah Frick of Quakertown or near there and one to my grandfather to Uncle Auro and to Uncle Live. Towards evening I fetched my clothes from Mrs. Kiefer and paid her yet 63 cents for washing and mending. After supper I went to Schafer's and read a sermon of Hofacker on Luke 18: 31-43 in presence of Mrs. Beaver and her daughter. Mrs. Klepping, R. Beaver and W. Klepping came also when I was done ready but I prayed yet in their presence. Merle Bauer soled my boots this evening which I took home. Trumbauer paid me $5.30 for work and gave me 50 cents in silver this evening. I enjoyed God's presence today very much and felt so far confident that it is God's will that I should go to Canada.

Sun. 8 This afternoon I was at home and spent the time in reading, praying and singing, etc. In the afternoon I was in Oxford Sunday School. We closed it for the present season. I went home with Jos. Schmick where I took supper. We went to A. Bleam's where I exhorted on John 1. I felt God's presence and His assistance. To Him be all praise and honour. Many tears were shed, some I trust were tears of penitence. Jos. Schmick was inclined to God to give me $1. I stayed during night with Bleams.

Mon. 9 This morning I returned to Trumbauer's and made ready to leave. Mr. T. gave me $2 without my asking. He left home this morning. After dinner I departed, though we sang and I prayed before I left and had a most serious time. Farewell tears were shed. I took my baggage to S. Funk's and went with him to Bethlehem. Mrs. Funk handed me a handkerchief which Mrs. Sam'l Smith bought for me. Indeed how good is God to give me all I need thus far. I was with Daniel Young a short time and went on the evening train to Centre Valley to the house of bro. Chas. Gehman.

Tues. 10 This morning I left Gehmans' and went with first train to Sellersville and walked to my uncle Reuben to see sister Susanna but who had gone home. I went at about 11 o'clock in the cars at Sellersville and came to Philia. about 1 o'clock. I then went to the Tract House and bought for $1 tracts, and was also at the office of the "Sunday School Times" and also bought a black book for a diary next year for 62 cents. I went to the house of Len Landis today over night. I agree with Cooper, "God made the country, men made the city."

Wed. 11 This morning Len Landis gave me $1 unasked. God is indeed giver and holds His promises but I am unworthy. At about 9 o'clock I left Landis's and went with my baggage to 13th and Callow Hill Sts. where the Pa and RR depot is. I was in the Phila. Noon day Prayer meeting and felt God's presence there. I then went to corner 6th and Chestnut Sts. and bought a ticket to Niagara Falls for $7.75 and from there I went a[nd] bought a Port Folio and Pocket Testament for $2.50 and then went to the American Sunday School Union House and bought *Mine Explored* for 90 cts and from there went to the depot at 13th and Callow Hill Sts. The prayer meeting was at 1011 Chestnut St. and just when I came out on the pavement a brass band passed and I felt serious. I was thinking while the band was playing of the music in heaven, of which I by God's grace expect to be a partaker. I also saw a funeral procession pass through Chestnut St. this afternoon. I left Phila. at 3:30 o'clock arrived in Reading at 6 and in Port Clinton at about 7, in Tamaqua at 9 and in Williamsport at 2 o'clock or a little before that time and slept in Parker Hotel in Pine St. Thanks be to God that He thus far brought me safe. I paid 40 cts. for my bed. I left Williamsport at about 8 o'clock and arrived at Elmira at noon.

Thur. 12 I left Elmira N.Y. at half past 2 o'clock p.m. and came to Hornelsville at half past 6 o'clock, a distance of 60 miles and nearly the whole way from Elmira to Hornelsville I was in the baggage car on account of the uncleanness in the Emigrant cars. I left Hornelsville at 7 o'clock in the evening and arrived at 10 in Buffalo the distance of the latter place being about 90 miles. I lodged in the "Reitz House" kept by a German.

Frid. 13 This morning I paid 37 cents for lodging in the "Reitz House" and then when I came to the Depot to go to the Niagara Falls, I saw the cars going but was to[o] late. Now I have to go with the next train. The sinner who is unprepared when death comes must go with it over Jordan to Hell and no train for ever will come to take him to heaven, a sad truth indeed. My resolution by God's grace to serve Him faithfully that death will bring me safe in the heavenly mansions. At half past 2 o'clock I left Buffalo for Niagara Falls and came to the Falls at about 4 o'clock and there I was taken to the Suspension Bridge by a man who [rowed] me and charged me $2. Thus I paid something to learn which I will not soon forget. In Buffalo at the Depot I met with a man by the name of Thos. D. Rutter who confessed that his condition was not safe and asked I should write to him which I promised if I could possibly. I took a view of the Falls and crossed the Suspension Bridge and then went [with] the cars on "Great Western Road" and went to Jordan and from there went to the house of Bro. Jacob Albright where I came till dark. Thanks be to God that he has brought me safe into Canada.

Sat. 14 This morning while eating or just when done breakfast Bro. Hershey came here. When I came to Canada I had $1.12 left and faith in God that He will provide. I had 60 cents more . . . than above stated when I treaded on Canada's soil but had to pay that for fare from Suspension Bridge [Canada-United States border] to Jordan Station. Soon after dinner we sang and Bro. Hershey prayed and then we left and went to the house of Bro. Daniel High. Bro. Albright gave $2 to Bro. Hershey for paying our fare to Waterloo Co. At present we are in Lincoln Co., Lowth [Louth] Township.

Sun. 15 This forenoon we had meeting in "Union Meeting House" where Bro. Hershey preached on Math. 6:9[.] I was when I entered the M. House a little downcast but after sermon I made a few remarks and was assisted from on high and refreshed and closed by prayer. After meet[ing] we went to the house of Bro. Jacob Hoch (3) and took dinner and then went to the house of Bro. Daniel Hoch [or Hersh] and Bro. Hershey preached on Rom 8:31 and I exhorted a little and closed by prayer. I was during night at the house of Bro. J. Hoch and B. Hershey at Bro. Albright's.

Mon. 16 This morning I wrote a letter for Mr. Trumbauer and at 1 o'clock had meeting at the house of Bro. ... Hoch (4). Bro. Hershey preached on Psalm 73:72-76. I closed by making a few remarks and prayer.

Tues. 17 This morning I have the letter I wrote yesterday to Bro. Hoch who [took] it to put in P. O. and offered to pay for it. We left his house this morning and were a short time in the house of Bro. Fry (5). At 10 o'clock we had meeting at the home of Bro. Jacob Hoch and here for the first time undertook to preach in my great weakness. Text Psalm 25:15. I did not speak very long and was succeeded by Bro. Hershey by appropriate remarks and prayer. This morning I commenced reading in the beginning of my Ger[man] and E[nglish] Testaments and intend to read in them in both languages at the same time. In the afternoon I wrote a letter to Thos. D. Rutter and visited Bro. Jacob Oberholzer (5) and took supper there. We visited also a short time Bro. Daniel Hoch and prayed in their family and Bro. H. and I spoke a few words to their children. We returned to the house of Bro. Jacob Hoch.

Wed. 18 This morning Bro. J. Hoch gave me $1. We were a short time at the house of Dilman Moyer (6). We had meeting at the house of Bro. J. Oberholtzer (7) and Bro. H[ershey] preached on Rom 12. I closed by exhorting and prayer. We took dinner at his son's house. In the afternoon we were a short time at the house of Bro. Jacob Albright and from there visited a family by the name of Saml. Moyer (8) and then went and visited an aged sister in the Lord named Keipple [?] who will be 92 years till next 26th of Dec. We came a little before night to the house of Bro. Jacob Gross (11) a preacher of the Evan[gelical] Ass[ociation]. Here we spent a happy evening.

Thur. 19 This morning we left the house of Bro. Gross and visited a short time Bro. A. Moyer (12) and then Bro. Saml. Moyer (13) and from there to the house of Bro. A. Hunsberger (14) where Bro. Hershey preached on Heb. 4:9 and we had indeed a very serious time. I exhorted a short time and had the assistance of God to whom be the glory. I closed by prayer. I was very much refreshed this forenoon and felt alive which I not often do for immortal souls. In the afternoon we visited Jos Nesh [Nash] (15), Jacob Nesh [Nash] (16), Bro. Grenzenbach (17) and took supper at the house of Bro. Houser (18). In the evening there was meeting in the Evan[gelical] church. Bro. H. preached on Rom. 5-1 and I exhorted a short time. After meeting we went to the house of Br. Sm M. Moyer who gave me [a] book, one containing sermons of R. Weaver and the other on "Christian Perfection" by Wesley.

Frid. 20 This morning Bro. Moyer took us to Beamsville Sta. and from there we started for Preston, Waterloo Co. This morning I wrote a letter to my sister Susanna. We came to Preston at noon where Bro. Saml. Bauman (19) met us and took us to his house where we me[t] Bro. Jonas Schultz. After dinner Bro. Schultz, H[ershey] and I went to see Bro. John McNelly [McNally] (20) where we took supper and after that were taken to a meeting in a school house where Bro. H. preached on Dan 6:16 and I exhorted a little and Bro. Schultz closed by prayer. After meeting we went to the house of Bro. John Detweiler (21).

Sat. 21 This forenoon we visited 6 families and came before noon to the house of Bro. A Detweiler (28). In the afternoon we went to the house of Bro. S. Bauman (29) and after supper went to Bro. Benj. Bauman and were in meeting in Carlisle [Blair] School House where Bro. H. preached on Acts 22:10 and I exhorted and Bro. Schultz closed by prayer. We were during night at the house of Bro. B. Bauman.

Sun. 22 This morning we were a few minutes in the house of Bro. J. Schlichter (30). This forenoon Bro. J. McNelly's son took us about 13 miles to the house of Bernhard Devitt (31) where we got dinner and after dinner Mr. Devitt took us 3 miles further out to St. Jacobs in Woolwich T[ownship], Waterloo Co., where Bro H[ershey] preached on Rom 8:31 and I exhorted. We were over supper with John Weitman (32) and in the evening I had a s[h]ort discourse in my weakness also in the school house where the meeting was this p.m. Bro. H[ershey] closed by exhortation and prayer. During night we were with Bro. Daniel Reutlinger (33).

Mon. 23 This forenoon I wrote a letter to Chas. Gehman and one to Mrs. Schafer and in afternoon to Bro. Shelly and enclosed the letter with Bro. Hershey's letter and we also visited 2 families and took supper with Bro. John Bauman (36). This evening when we went to meeting we hear[d] that a man who was last evening in meeting had suddenly changed time for eternity. Bro. Hershey preached on Proverbs 6:9. I exhorted and prayed. Bro. H[ershey] asked the males in meeting the hope that is in them and I gave all who desired tracts. May the Lord bless them to the conversion of souls for Christ's sake. After meeting we went home with Bro. Jacob Weber (37).

Tues. 24 As it rained we did not leave Weber's till this afternoon when we went to see . . . Hoch (38) a Mennonite preacher and from there to the house of Bro. Adam Seybert (39) and took supper with Bro. Reutlinger. In the evening Bro. H[ershey] preached on Acts 10:34-35. I exhorted a short time. After meeting we went Jno. Weitman's.

Wed. 25 This forenoon we attended the funeral of Christian Martin who died so sudden last Monday evening. Rev. Moses Erb [of the Old Mennonite Church] preached on 2 Cor. 5:5. Mr. Martin was in meeting last Sunday evening and had then drunk some liquor as I got from his smell. He died almost in a moment. This occasion should cause hope [and it] will always make me when speaking in public or private to sinners urge them to decision. May the Lord give me grace for Christ's sake. This noon we got dinner with J. Weidman. In the afternoon we visited 5 families (44) and one which was Catholic and indeed a very miserable one. May the Lord enlighten them. We got supper with Bro. Daniel Reutlinger. In the evening Bro. H. preached on Dan. 6:16 in English and I closed by exhorting in German. We went home with Bro. Otwein [?](45).

Thurs. 26 This forenoon we visited 5 families (49) and were over dinner with B. Devitt. In the afternoon Bro. H. preached at the house of Devitt on Psalms 37:37 and I closed by exhortation and prayer. After meeting we went to the house of Rev. Staufer (50) and took supper and then paid a short visit to Daniel Martin (51) and then to St. Jacobs where I had a very short discourse on Isa. 3:10-11, and Bro. Schultz and Hershey also exhorted. After meeting we went to the house of Bro. Christian Weber (52).

Frid. 27 Today after dinner Bro. H[ershey] and Schultz left Bro. Weber and visited 5 families (57) though Schultz went to St. Jacobs and therefore was not in all families which I and Hershey visited. I and Bro. Schultz took supper with Bro. Reutlinger. Bro. Schultz preached on Jer. 17:14 and Bro. Hershey exhorted and prayed. Many of the brothers and sisters made confessions and I also was much refreshed. To God be all the honor. After meeting we went home with Bro. J. Bauman.

Sat. 28 This forenoon we visited 3 families (60). We got dinner with Bro. J. Bowman. In the afternoon we had prayer meeting at the house of Bro. Ottwein and visited 3 families (63) and got supper with Bro. Reutlinger. In meeting Bro. H. preached on Rom. 8:18 and I closed by exhortation and prayer. We got dinner with Bro. Singkern (64). In . . . we went home with Bro. A Seybert.

Sun. 29 This forenoon Bro. H. preached on Acts 24:14-16 and I closed by exhortation and prayer. We got dinner with Bro. Singkern (64). In the afternoon Bro. H[ershey] preached on 2 Tim. 4:5, an interesting sermon and I closed by exhortation and prayer. I felt very serious and had God's assistance while speaking and to Him be all the glory. We got supper at D. Eby's Hotel (65). There Bro. H[ershey] and I had the opportunity to offer prayer alone . . . at the table. It is indeed singular that a hotel keeper gave me more liberty in this respect than my father who is a professor of religion. In the evening I was in meeting in the Evangelical Church where Bro. Stabler preached on Zech. 14:9. Bro. P. Winkler closed by exhortation and prayer. After meeting we went to the house of Bro. Isaac Bowman.

Mon. 30 Today after dinner we went to visit and were in 7 families (72) and took supper with Bro. Reutlinger. In the evening Bro. H. preached on Isa. 55:6 and I exhorted a short time. 2 souls were this evening deeply concerned about their souls' salvation and we prayed on their behalf. They were both young females. After meeting I went to the house of Bro. Jac. Weber whose daughter is one of the penitent. Bro. H. went to another place as he intends to attend a conference [of the New Mennonites] in Carlisle tomorrow.

December 1863

Tues. 1 Soon after dinner I left the house of Bro. J. Weber though I prayed with them before I left and left three of his children in tears and they appeared to be in distress about their salvation. I went to the house of Bro. Reutlinger and wrote a letter to Jos. A. Weaver. This evening I had a sermon on Matth. 5:4. I did not speak very long and Bro. Reutlinger exhorted. We prayed for 4 souls this evening who were deeply distressed about their soul's salvation. One professed to have found peace by believing in Jesus. After meeting I went home with . . .

Wed. 2 This forenoon I conversed with Weitman and also read to him John Yoder answers and read etc. In the afternoon I wrote a letter at Bro. Reutlinger's for Jos. Schmick. I was over supper with Bro. J. Bowman. In the evening, Bro. H[ershey] preached on James 4:10 and I exhorted a little. 3 souls were distressed about their souls' salvation. After meeting we went to the house of Bro. Reutlinger.

Thurs. 3 This morning I wrote a letter to Bro. Saml. M. Moyer and Bro H[ershey] wrote] one to Bro. J. Albright and I also wrote a few lines in the latter. We visited then 14 families (86) today. We [had] dinner with a family with the name of Cress. I took supper with J. Weidman. This evening Bro. Schultz preached on Psalm 118:5 and Bro. H[ershey] exhorted. After meeting Bro. H. and I went home with Bro. J. Weber.

Frid. 4 This forenoon I wrote a letter to Daniel Young and one to Uncle Daniel Geissinger. In the afternoon we had a prayer meeting here. Bro. Schultz opened the meeting and read the 42nd Psalm. 3 of Bro. Weber's and other young girls were deeply distressed about their salvation and the 2 daughters of Bro. J. Weber found peace by believing in Jesus. It was indeed a serious time which I shall not soon forget. After meeting we went to the house of Bro. G. Wells. Bro. H. preached on Rom. 10:1 and Bro. Schultz exhorted a short [time]. 2 persons were in distress seeking the Saviour and 4 profess to have found peace in believing in Christ.

Sat. 5 This forenoon we visited one family and then (87) I wr[o]te a letter for Harrison Seiple in the forenoon yet. In the afternoon we had prayer meeting in the school house and had a happy time. After meeting to the house of Bro. Jac. Weber where I got supper. Bro. Schultz preached on 1 John 2:2 and I exhorted and also Bro. H[ershey]. One soul was penitent and cried for mercy. After meeting we went to the house of John Weidman.

Sun. 6 This forenoon Bro. Schultz preached in English on John 3:7 and I exhorted in German and offered closing prayer. At noon I was at the house of Bro. J. Bowman. After dinner we were 12 in number all young in years who had a prayer meeting before the meeting in the school house and had a very happy time and which I shall not soon forget. Two of the number were penitent and wept on account of their sins. This afternoon Bro. H[ershey] preached and had for his text the 1st Psalm. I exhorted a short time and Bro. Schultz offered the closing prayer. I took supper with Bro. Reutlinger. In the evening Bro. preached on Psalms 40:1-4 and Bro. Schultz exhorted. After meeting I went to the house of Bro. Jacob Weber.

Mon. 7 This morning I went to the house of Bro. J. Bowman where I met Bro. H[ershey]. Then we went to visiting and took dinner with Bro. John Detweiler and supper with Bro. Spiess. We visited 6 families (93) to day. In the evening I in my great weakness had a short discourse on Matth. 11:28-30. Bro. H[ershey] exhorted. 5 souls were penitent and cried for mercy. I felt much seriousness. Today a son of Bro. Spiess gave me Five cents which was an encouragement for me that the Lord hears my prayers and provides for my bodily wants. To Him be all the glory and honor and thanks for what He has done to my soul. After meeting we went to the house of Bro. Reutlinger. When I went towards this village I was in spiritual darkness and also at times since I am here but the Lord was also pleased at times to let my soul be refreshed. I now plainly see that our work has thus far been blessed by the Lord. My prayer is for a humble and sincere heart and grace to serve my Maker fully the remainder of my pilgrimage through this vale of tears that I may be ultimately saved in the celestial city above. Amen.

Tues. 8 This forenoon we had prayer meeting at the house of Bro. Reutlinger and had a happy time. Five souls were penitent and in distress about their souls' salvation though none obtained pardon. In the afternoon we were a short time at B. Devitt's and visited a short time Bro. Houck (94). I took supper at Weidman's. In the evening Bro. H[ershey] preached on 1 Cor. 7:29 and I exhorted. 7 young souls were in distress about their salvation though none obtained peace and pardon of their sins. After meeting we went home with Bro. Christian Weber's where we had a happy time yet before we went to bed.

Wed. 9 This forenoon I spent in reading and conversation and soon after dinner we left Bro. Weber's for St. Jacobs and visited 3 familes (97). We took supper with Bro. Reutlinger. In the evening Bro. H[ershey] preached in English on John 9:4 and Bro. Schlichter followed and spoke in German on Jer. 37:9. There were five penitents this evening and Daniel Weber seemed more or less to have some hope in Christ. After meeting I went to the house of Bro. J. Bowman where also Bro. Schultz. This evening I did not feel quite as happy as I did this afternoon at Bro. Weber's as there I enjoyed the presence of my God while I sat there singing as I seldom do.

Thur. 10 This forenoon I went to the house of Bro. Jac. Weber. In the afternoon I was in prayer meeting at the house of Bro. J. Bowman and had a very happy time. Four souls were penitent and cried for mercy. After meeting I went home with Bro. Reutlinger. This forenoon Bros. Schlichter, Hershey and Jac. Weber spoke to each other and Bro. Weber could not altogether agree with Bro. Hershey. I went upstairs and opened a Bible for consolation and opened Nahum 1:3 and then I prayed to the Lord and after that opened the Bible again and my finger pointed to a picture of Martha, Mary and Jesus, but my finger was on Jesus. This was a great consolation to me. Christ is "all in all." This evening Bro. Schultz preached on Heb. 11:1 and Bro. Schlichter exhorted and also Bro. H[ershey] a little. 7 souls were penitent and two for certain obtained peace by believing in Jesus and found Him precious to their souls. After meeting Bro. H[ershey] and I went to J. Weidman's.

Frid. 11 This forenoon we went to the house of Bro. Reichard (98) and took dinner there. I read here awhile in Bishop [John] Seybert's Memoir. In the afternoon we visited 3 families where we have not been before (101) and also at the house of Schafer whose maid is penitent. We spoke a few words of encouragement to her. Bro. H[ershey] preached on Micah 2:13 and I exhorted. There was only one penitent soul present. After meeting we went home with Bro. J. Bowman.

Sat. 12 This morning we went to the house of Bro. Reutlinger and read there etc. and after dinner went in the church of the Evangelist's where Bro. S. Weaver preached on Psalm 26:8. We got supper at the house of Bro. Isaac Bowman. This evening I preached on John 12:35. and Bro. H[ershey] exhorted. There were a few penitents. After meeting we went to Bro. Reutlinger's.

Sun. 13 This forenoon we were in the Evangelist's Church where Bro. Sol. Weaver preached on Acts 26:22-23 and after sermon they had the communion of the Lord's supper. This noon I went home with Bro. Anthony Reitzel where we [helped] a few young pilgrims towards Zion. After dinner [we] s[a]ng and prayed with each other. In the afternoon I was in meeting in the School house where Bro. H[ershey] preached on Ps. 119:165. On the 19th of March 1862 I heard for the first time Bro. H[ershey] preach and saw him for the first time. It was at the house of Bro. Charles S. Gehman in Saucon, Pa. We took supper at the house of Bro. Reutlinger. In the evening Bro. H[ershey] preached on Rev. 22:17 and I exhorted and then we prayed for penitents and one obtained peace by believing in Jesus. After meeting we went home with Bro. Reutlinger. 8 souls have now found Jesus precious to their souls and 4 are yet in distress.

Mon. 14 This morning Sister Reutlinger informed me that she and Sister Weidman intend to make a shirt for me. This was quite unexpected, though it strengthened my weak faith that God will provide for me if I do faithfully the work He wishes me to do. We visited this forenoon Bro. Henry Seibert, who gave each of us 50 cents. Sister Reutlinger also gave me 50 cents this morning. We then went in the forenoon yet to the house of Bro. Jac. Weber and visited a family on our way (102) before noon. In the afternoon we visited a family (103) and took supper with Bro. Speiss. This evening I in my great weakness preached on 1 John 2:17. Bro. H. exhorted. This evening it appeared that Jacob Weber found Jesus precious to his soul. After meeting we went to the house of Jno. Weidman.

Tues. 15 This morning Weidman gave me a $1. We then went to Bro. Reutlinger's. We took dinner with Bro. Gilpin (104) and in the afternoon we visited some of our brothers and sisters and one family (105) we had not visited before. Bro. J. Bowman gave me $1 and Bro. Felsinger 10 cents. Thus it appears the Lord will provide. Thanks be to Him. We were also this afternoon in the Evangelical Church where an infant of Mr. Schroter and wife was buried aged 10 months 22 days. Bro. Stabler preached on John 14:4. I felt serious during sermon. Ah! how soon my frail life may end. Soon I shall breathe my last. May the Lord give grace that I may always be prepared for death and eternity. This evening Bro. H. preached his farewell sermon to our fellow travellers to eternity on Psalm 37:37. The school house was pretty full. I exhorted also and gave my parting exhortation and felt serious. We gave our parting hand to each person in the school house and while doing so many tears were shed. We have good evidence that the effort I put forth in St. Jacobs for the good of precious souls was not in vain as 12 young souls expressed a desire to come on the Lord's side and 7 we [k]now that profess to have found Jesus precious to their souls and 2 are not quite satisfied that God is their friend and 3 others expressed to seek the Saviour till found. I received $3.12 ... unasked for this evening and Bro. H[ershey]. $2.85. We went home after meeting with Barnabas Devitt.

Wed. 16 Today we visited 12 families, 3 of which we had visited before (114). We took dinner with Bro. David Stauffer and supper with Bro. Houck. This evening we had meeting at the house of Barnabas Devitt where Bro. H[ershey]. preached on Mark 10:28-30 and I closed by exhortation and prayer. We had a very serious time.

Thurs. 17 Today I wrote at Devitts' a letter to L.J. Pflueger and one to Saml. M. Landis and a letter before night. We went to the house of Wm. Bomberger where we had meeting this evening. Bro. H[ershey] preached on Matth. 6:33 and I closed by exhortation and prayer. We stayed with Bomberger over night.

Frid. 18 This forenoon Bro. Houck took us to the house of Peter Erb (115). We took dinner with Bro. Wismer (116). We visited 2 families (118). We wrote [rode] today in the sleigh as it snowed last night. This was the first sleigh ride I had in Canada. This evening we took supper with B. Devitt. In the evening we had meeting [in] the school house near Devitts' where Bro. H[ershey] preached on Micah 6:8 and I closed by exhortation and prayer. We went after meeting to the house of B. Devitt.

Sat. 19 This morning early Bro. Hershey left to go with Wm. Bomberger to Carlisle. I went today to the house of Bro. Christian Weaver and returned in the afternoon again to the house of B. Devitt where Bro. H. soon also came and had 4 letter[s] which are the first I received since I am in Canada. They were from John Trumbauer, Chas. S. Gehman, Jos. A. Weaver and my sister Susanna. This evening Bro. H[ershey] preached on 2 Cor. 5:1 and he was very serious while preaching. I exhorted and closed by prayer. Bro. D. Stauffer gave me this evening quite unexpected unasked for 50 cents. Bro. H[ershey] received a letter today of Bro. Wm. N. Shelly.

Sun. 20 Last evening our meeting was in School house again but after meeting a letter was handed Bro. H[ershey] certainly a notice that we are not allowed to preach any longer therein this day. This forenoon Bro. H[ershey] preached on Matth. 23:35 a very solemn sermon and Bros. Schultz and Schlichter exhorted and I also and Bro. Schlichter closed by prayer. At noon Bros. Schultz, Schlichter and I went with B. Devitt to St. Jacobs to meeting and Bro. H[ershey] stayed at Devitts'. This afternoon in St. Jacobs Bro. Schlichter preached on Matth. 22:42 and Bro. Schultz exhorted and I closed by prayer. The bros. returned to Carlisle and I took supper with John Weidman and was in the evening in prayer meeting at the house of Bro. H. Seybert. I opened the meeting and read the 2nd chap. 1 Peter and made a few remarks. We had a happy meeting and felt the presence of our Saviour. After prayer meeting I went home with Bro. Daniel Reutlinger.

Mon. 21 This morning I left Reutlingers' and walked to Devitts' where I learned that 4 souls were penitent last evening and cried for mercy in meeting in the school house. Bro. H[ershey] is gone to Cyrus Bauers' today and he was the only minister last evening in the school house. This afternoon I went to the school house and brought a letter to the teacher to give to Bro. Reutlinger and I gave a short address to the scholars. Then I went to Bombergers' and soon bro. H[ershey] came. Then we went to Devitts' again. This evening I made the attempt to speak on Proverbs 8:17 and Bro. H[ershey] exhorted. The meeting was at Devitts'. 2 souls were penitent though did not obtain peace.

Tues. 22 This morning we rode with Wm. Bomberger and went to the house of Bro. Christian Weber. After dinner we left Webers' and visited several (120) and took supper with Wm. Bomberger. In the evening Bro. H[ershey] preached on Gen. 7:1 a very serious sermon. I exhorted a short time. 2 souls were penitent. We went home with Bro. Daniel Stauffer.

Wed. 23 This forenoon we visited a few families. Met one where prayer was denied us (121). At noon we were at Devitts'. In the afternoon I read a short time in Lorenzo Dow's work and was refreshed while reading some experiences of this man of God. O may the Lord guide me by His spirit and give me grace that I may work with more zeal for the good of immortal souls. This afternoon we visited a little and returned before night to Devitts'. In the evening Bro. H[ershey] preached on Ecc. 9:10 very solemnly and I exhorted a short time. I felt very serious this evening.

Thur. 24 This forenoon I also wrote a letter to father and a few words to mother. This forenoon we walked to the town of Waterloo and took dinner at the house of Jacob Bricker (121). In the afternoon we went back again and took supper with Bro. Jos. Weber. This evening Bro. H[ershey] preached in Luke 12:32 and I exhorted.

Christmas

Frid. 25 This forenoon we were in the Old Mennonite Meeting where Bro. Wismer preached on 2nd Matth. In the afternoon Bro. H[ershey] preached at Devitts' on Isaiah 9:6 and I closed by exhortation and prayer. After meeting we rode with the sleigh to the house of Bro. C. Weber and returned to Devitts' again where Bro. H[ershey] preached in the evening again on Eph. 3:14-15. I exhorted a short time and closed by prayer. We had a serious time. We closed the meeting now at Devitts' and went home with Bro. C. Weber. 2 young girls profess to have found the Saviour during our meeting at Devitts'.

Sat. 26 This forenoon I was in a Lutheran Church in Heidelberg where Rev. Stahlschmidt preached on Isa. 9:6. In the afternoon I was at Webers'. In the evening we had meeting in a school house near Webers' where Bro. H[ershey] preached on 1 Tim 1:15 and I exhorted and closed by prayer. After meeting we returned to the house of Bro. Weber.

Sun. 27 This forenoon we had prayer meeting in Bro. Weber's house. Bro. H[ershey] read part of the 95th Psalm. We had the presence of our Saviour. Elizabeth Weber at the close of the meeting found the Saviour precious to her soul. In the afternoon I in weakness had a discourse in the school house on Ps. 37:4. Bro. H[ershey] closed by exhortation and prayer. We took supper at the house of John Moyer. In the evening Bro. H[ershey] preached a very interesting [sermon] on Luke 15:18 and I exhorted and a few of the Brethren closed by prayer. After meeting we went to the house of John Moyer.

Mon. 28 This forenoon we went to St. Jacobs with Moyer's sleigh and horse to visit B[rother] Jno Bowman and several other families. Sister Bowman was sick though happy in her Redeemer. In the afternoon we returned to Moyers' and then left for Bro. C. Weber's. While on our way thither visited a Catholic family (122) where Bro. H[ershey] had the opportunity to pray. It is indeed remarkable that Catholics give more liberty in this respect than Mennonites. We visited Mennonites who refused to us prayer in their house before leaving. O that God by His Spirit may awaken souls dead and cold professors of religion before it is eternally too late. This evening Bro. H[ershey] preached on 2 Cor. 6:10 and I exhorted and prayed. There were only about 2 hearers though we felt the presence of God. After meeting we went to the house of Bro. C. Weber.

Tues. 29 This forenoon I wrote a letter to Jno Trumbauer and enclosed a tract published by the London Religious Tract Society. This afternoon we visited several families (126) and [a] Mennonite family where prayer was refused to us. May God have mercy on such dead professors of religion. We also spoke with a school teacher who believes that man doth not receive reward or punishment till after judgment day and I had some temptations about this man's doctrine. May the Lord guide me into all truth by His spirit. This evening Bro. H[ershey] preached on Proverbs 3:5-6 and I exhorted a short time but was in spiritual darkness while speaking as also during Bro.'s sermon. After meeting we went home to the house of John Moyer.

Wed. 30 This morning we walked to Bro. C. Weber's and then to the school house where Bro. H[ershey] preached on Psalm 126:3 to 5 hearers but I was refreshed again in Spirit and felt the presence of God and also exhorted a short time. John Moyer's two daughters were of the 5 hearers and they shed tears so I trust tears of repentance. May God bless them for Christ's sake – Amen. We took dinner at Bro. C. Weber's. This afternoon we visited several families and in Lutheran families we had the liberty to pray and received thanks for doing so while in some Mennonite families prayer was refused to us. Singular indeed!(129) We took supper with Jno. Moyer. In the evening Bro. H[ershey] preached in the S. House on Acts 16:34 and I exhorted and offered prayer and Bro. C. Weber also offered prayer. After meeting we went home with Weber's.

Thurs. 31 This day I spent in reading and wrote yet a little and enclosed it with the letter I wrote for Jno Trumbauer a few days ago. In the evening we had meeting at the house of John Moyer where Bro. H[ershey] preached on 1 Cor[inthians] 7:29 and Rom. 12:11 and I exhorted and offered prayer. I felt very serious this evening. We stayed at Moyers' house over night. During the past year the Lord has blessed me both in soul and body. It pleased the Lord to give me through the past year $231.92 through friends for my bodily support without my asking as answers to prayer. I also received articles of clothing to the amount of about $3.50. I have cash on hand $6.70. We had preaching 59 times since we are in Canada and 6 times prayer meeting. 9 times I made the attempt in my great weakness to preach. 129 families we visited in C[anada]. I am not able to thank the Lord as I ought to do for the goodness He has shown against me during the past year as well as from my infancy up to the present moment. And I, perhaps amen ...

> Thus far the Lord hath led me on,–
> This far his power prolongs my days;
> And every evening shall make known
> Some fresh memorial of his grace.
> Much of my time has run to waste,
> And I, perhaps, am near my home;
> But he forgives my follies past,
> And give me strength for days to come.

My resolution is by the grace of God to serve the Lord to the end of my pilgrimage through this vale of tears that the crown of glory may be mine in the mansions of the skies. Lord, help me to this end for Jesus's sake, Amen.

14 Peter R. Dueck (1862 to 1919)

Steinbach, Manitoba
Diary selection: 1 January 1910 to 5 December 1913
Age: 47 in 1910

Peter R. Dueck was born in 1862 to Reverend Jakob L. and Maria (Rempel) Dueck of Gnadenthal, Molotschna Colony, New Russia. In 1875, he joined his parents in their move to Manitoba, where they settled in Gruenfeld on the East Reserve. In 1888, Peter married Sara P. Kroeker of Steinbach and moved there. At first, the young couple farmed across the road from Sara's parents, the well-to-do farmers Franz M. and Margaretha (Plett) Kroeker (see diary 15). In 1911, however, as Steinbach was rapidly changing from a farm village to a commercial centre, the Duecks purchased a farm one kilometre south of town. Here they raised a family of 10 children. In the meantime, Peter Dueck was elected a minister in the Mennonite Kleine Gemeinde and in 1901 the *Aeltester* [bishop] of the East Reserve churches – Steinbach, Blumenort, and Gruenfeld (later, Kleefeld). In January 1919, at 56, after having served as *Aeltester* for 18 years, Peter Dueck died suddenly of a heart attack. He left a widow and six children under 15. He also left a church struggling to contest an encroaching outside world.

The diary reproduced here is a church diary kept by Peter Dueck. It lists the location of the revolving church services and notes which of the four East Reserve Kleine Gemeinde preachers – Peter W. Loewen (Neuanlage), Cornelius L. Plett (Blumenhof), Peter R. Reimer (Blumenort), or Peter R. Dueck himself – presented the Sunday sermons. More important, the diary portrays the work of the *Bruderschaft*, which we have translated as Brotherhood, comprising all baptised male members (usually 21 and over), who gathered when summoned, usually monthly, to discuss and enforce the Anabaptist principles of the simple life. The word *Bruderschaft* refers to such meetings. Members who fell into adultery, premarital sex, incest, drunkenness, or theft were excommunicated. Members who supported the establishment of a public school or the purchase of cars proved especially troublesome and seem to have been pressured to resign, a severance that usually did not result in shunning. During these years, several members left the Kleine Gemeinde on account of these issues and joined the more progressive Bruderthaler or Holdeman churches in Steinbach.

The diary records historic changes in the Steinbach-Hanover Mennonite community. The first car was purchased in May 1910 and the first indication of the establishment of a public school in Steinbach came in April 1911, five years before provincial law made such schools mandatory for all Mennonite communities. A further sign of change came in October 1911, when the Kleine Gemeinde Church was refused entry into the schoolhouse that it, itself, had constructed for religious services and parochial education; the school by public petition had been turned into a state-run school, and church services could not be held in Steinbach until a new building had been completed. There were other events that indicate that Steinbach was a quickly ascending trading centre. They include the proliferation of telephones, business enterprises at Giroux, the rail depot 10 kilometres to the northeast, the opening of a guesthouse and even a store selling tobacco and musical instruments. A sign of this encroaching world was J.R. Friesen's resignation from membership on 7 April 1912. Friesen, later reputed as being the owner of western Canada's first Ford dealership, seems to have renounced and resigned his membership in the Kleine Gemeinde over the issue of either "worldly weddings" or car ownership. Contrary to local folklore, it appears that Friesen was not excommunicated and banned for his actions.

The diary also reveals the nature of proceedings at a Mennonite Brotherhood meeting: the *Aeltester* and ministers warned and admonished but did little ruling; not until a consensus was reached could the Brotherhood act. It was because the Brotherhood was divided on the public-school and automobile question that the ministers could not act as decisively as they seem to have wished. The debate on these issues continued to the year of Dueck's death in 1919. Another issue that shows the nature of Brotherhood deliberations was the request in December 1912 by young widower Johann G. Barkman to marry the sister of his deceased wife, a practice once prohibited in the wider Christian church. The Brotherhood debated the issue for six months. The ministers were loath to make the change, but scripture evidently did not support the prohibition, and in June 1913 the change was made. The decision came too late for Johann, for his love seems to have waned during the long deliberations, and he married his deceased wife's cousin instead.

Finally, the diary defines social boundaries for the conservative Kleine Gemeinde. The East Reserve church communities – Steinbach, Blumenort, and Gruenfeld – were bridged by networks that extended to two sister communities: *Jenseit*, that is, the Kleine Gemeinde community on the "other side" of the Red River, at Rosenort and Rosenhoff near Morris; and Meade County, Kansas, the location of the American chapter of the Kleine Gemeinde Church. Both church communities offered and received assistance from the East Reserve churches during these years. The East Reserve church, however, was linked to a wider world within Manitoba; Ninette's Sanatorium, Brandon's Insane Asylum, and St. Boniface's hospital were institutions that the church supported financially. Reports of famine in India and Russia solicited similar benevolence from it.

For more information on Bishop Peter R. Dueck and his work in the Kleine Gemeinde, see: Royden Loewen, "Aeltesten, Revivalists and the Urbanizing World," in *Family, Church and Market: A Mennonite Community in the Old and New Worlds* (Toronto: 1993): 237-261; John Dueck et al., eds., *Descendants of Jacob and Maria L. Dueck, 1839-1986* (Steinbach, MB: 1986), 71-118.

This is a personal diary; it is an informal set of notes, hastily written at Dueck's home according to Dueck's recollection after, and sometimes several days after, the church meetings. This means that the entries are not always in chronological order. The diary was preserved by Peter's wife, Sara, and the Dueck children. In 1948, when she was an elderly widow, Sara Dueck, along with her grown children, moved to Chihuahua State, Mexico, and they took the diary with them. It was retrieved to Canada by Dueck's son, Reverend Cornelius P. Dueck (Blumenort), where he and Henry Loewen (Steinbach) also transcribed it from the Gothic handwriting. It was translated by Peter Dueck's grandson, Peter U. Dueck (Steinbach), and by Royden Loewen. A photocopy of the original diary is located at the Evangelical Mennonite Conference Archives, Steinbach, Manitoba.

1910

Jan. 1 Worship service was held in Blumenort; ... preached.

Jan. 2 Worship service was held here in Steinbach; I preached the New Year's sermon. There was also Brotherhood and so Johan Goossen was [re]accepted into our church. And also about a brother who ... turned against his father and wanted to physically take him into a rear room. But as the father had many reasons for his behaviour and as the son had been to both the father and the church [for forgiveness] so he was forgiven. Preparation was also made to vote for a *Waisenman* [estates administrator], as David Löwen [of the Holdeman Mennonites] no longer wanted to undertake this [inter-church] task.

Jan. 6 *Heilige Drei Könige* [Epiphany] was celebrated in the Blumenort service; C. Plett presented the sermon and in Grünfeld, P. Reimer.

Jan. 9 Worship service was held in Steinbach; P. Löwen presented.

Jan. 12 Mrs. G. Kornelsen was buried here in Steinbach; she had been lying ill for 5 days and died on January 9 in the evening; A. Eidse of Morris preached.

Jan. 23 Worship service in Steinbach; P. Reimer preached and two letters, namely from *Ältester* [Bishop] A.L. Friesen and C. Löwen were read.

Jan. 30 I preached in Grünfeld on the text, I Peter 5:8-9, and in Blumenhof, C. Plett preached.

Feb. 6 C. Plett preached in Steinbach on the text, I Timothy 6:12. He also married the bridal couple, namely Martin W. Friesen with Johan ...'s [daughter].

Feb. 13 I preached in Blumenort, on the text, I Peter 5:8-9. There was also Brotherhood about the *Waisenverordnung* [Mennonite Estates Administration] which has become ineffective [no longer recognized by Manitoba's Surrogate Court] and as we have elected a new man who does not want to take on this task in the present state of confusion, that is, if it is not established on a firmer foundation. And so we were all in agreement to restructure the [*Waisenverordnung*]. Also we spoke about the weddings, on which we had as much as possible counselled earlier, but as many now hold *Nach Hochzeiten* [wedding parties] ... much [unrighteousness is occurring].

Feb. 20 I preached the sermon in Steinbach on the text, I Peter 5:8-9; a bridal couple was also married, Jakob I. Dück with Anna K. Klassen.

Feb. 17 A wedding was held at A.S. Friesens', as their Elisabeth married Johan D. Goossen and they were married by me. Their bans were read in Blumenort on the 13th.

March 6 P. Löwen preached in Steinbach.

March 13 P. Reimer preached in Blumenort, text, John 10.

March 20 Worship service was held in Steinbach, P. Reimer preached; there was also Brotherhood about the *Waisenverordnung*, whether we should [legally] incorporate this organization or how we wish to structure it in the future. Also about the collection of money for the Brandon Insane Asylum, as $54 have been collected; so we agreed to take in another $75 and send it. Also we decided to begin work again with the youth. About the incorporation [of the *Waisenverordnung*, following the example of the Bergthaler Mennonites], however, we first want to confer with the Holdemans and the brothers at *Jenseid* [literally the "other side" of the river, that is, the Rosenort community, asking] whether this would be good for us, because it . . .

March 26 We presented the Good Friday sermon in Blumenhof and P. Löwen preached in Grünfeld.

March 27 Easter Sunday; C. Plett preached here in Steinbach.

March 28 Easter Monday, P. Löwen preached in Blumenort.

April 3 I presented the articles [of faith for the benefit of the youth] here in Steinbach. To date, 20 youth have indicated [their intention] for baptism, eight male and 12 female. There was also Brotherhood [and] the youth were presented for the first time.

April 10 C. Plett preached in Grünfeld and P. Löwen preached in Blumenhof.

April 17 P. Reimer preached in Steinbach.

April 24 I presented the articles [of faith] in Blumenort and in the afternoon we had a Brotherhood [about] a brother who has renounced the church and the youth were . . . presented and another two souls have come forward [for baptism].

May 6 Martin Barkman died and was buried on the 9th. I preached.

May 1 P. Löwen preached in Steinbach. There was Brotherhood about A. Töws; he wishes to be accepted again [by the church], and it was seen as advisable if we first discuss his situation with the family that he has offended, and so it was decided to reaccept him on Thursday in Blumenhof.

The 5th Ascension Day [was celebrated] in the Blumenort worship service; C. Plett preached and after the service the brethren remained behind and so the brother was removed from excommunication, and in Grünfeld P. Reimer preached.

May 15 Pentecost Sunday; C. Plett preached in Blumenort.

May 16 Pentecost Monday; I preached in Steinbach and at the same time married the bridal couple, Jakob Schellenberg and Aganetha Kornelsen. In the afternoon there was a Brotherhood meeting and the youth were presented for the last time; one [of the youth] has withdrawn completely and more is wished [by us] of another two. And so we should speak more with the two, which we [at the time of this writing] have already done and have found an understanding. We also talked about the automobile, which a brother has purchased for himself for $480 [?]. While most of the congregation does not see this as a good thing, that is either to use it or for brothers to purchase it [and] while it does not fit our [objective] not to assimilate too much with the world [we opposed it]. . . .

May 22 I preached in Grünfeld, the text II Corinthians 6:1-2 and in Blumenhof . . . preached.

May 29 P. Reimer presented the Spring Sermon here in Steinbach and so, too, the youth were instructed [about baptism] during the service. In the afternoon there was Brotherhood concerning the use of automobiles and so the same brother promised to sell it as the church deemed it as detrimental for securing *Seelenheil* [salvation], as it is so much of an assimilation with the world and by and large too innovative and costly, and [leading to] arrogance and pride. Also C.K. Friesen was presented as he wishes to [re]join the church. Also we encouraged [members] to prepare [their hearts] for *Einigkeit* [communion service].

June 5 I presented the articles [of faith] in Blumenort and asked the questions and in the afternoon J.K. Friesen of Morris preached on the text, I John 4:1-3.

The 8th The elderly Mrs. Johan Janzen was buried, and [it was] on the 5th, in the evening that she died. Joh[an] Friesen of Morris preached.

June 12 The youth were baptised by me in Steinbach. The baptised youth included: C. Krökers' Cornelius; Johan Reimers' Johan; G. Kornelsens' Wilhelm and Abram; Widow M. Barkman, her Cornelius; I.J. Löwens' Isaak; H. Pletts' Cornelius; P. Reimers' Klaas; Joh. F. Reimers' Johan. And the girls include: our Margaretha; Mrs Johan Dück, her Margaretha and Maria; Klaas I Friesens' Katherina; and H. Reimers' Katherina; Widow H. Brandt, her Justina; P. Klassens' Gertrude; Widow Martin Barkman, her Helena; Widow A. Reimer, her Anna; A. Pletts, their Anna; and Jakob Pletts, their Margaretha; and Jakob Barkmans' Margaretha; in total 21 souls were baptised.

June 19 Peter Löwen preached the Spring Sermon in Grünfeld and in Blumenhof C. Plett presented the Preparatory Sermon. We drove to Grünfeld.

June 26 P. Löwen preached in Steinbach and in the afternoon there was Brotherhood, as G.G. Kornelsen has resigned from the church and has had himself baptised by the Mennonite Brethren and also about a brother who had overly ... June 26, there was also Brotherhood about preparing for communion and great concern [expressed] about pride. And also we discussed the telephone, but without success as there is too much support for it.

July 3 Worship service in Blumenort; P. Reimer preached the Preparatory Sermon. In the afternoon there was Brotherhood about A. Töws's unchaste way of life, but [action] was postponed as he had not come [to Brotherhood]. Also C.K. Friesen was reaccepted into membership.

July 10 Worship Service was held here in Steinbach; C. Plett presented the Preparatory Sermon. The bridal couples were also presented. In the afternoon Brotherhood concerning A. Töws and so it was hoped that with patience there will be an improvement. Also a discussion about the automobile and withholding permission [to purchase it]; also a warning about the [federal] government election, [a warning] not to vote; also about pride, several points.

July 3 [Mrs.] David Kröker has died in the maternity bed and was buried on the 5th.

July 17 I preached in Morris, the text, II Corinthians 6:1-2 and in Blumenort Peter Löwen preached and in Grünfeld Peter Reimer preached. Tuesday, the 19th, I preached in Rosenort.

July 24 Peter Reimer presented the Preparatory Sermon in Steinbach and there was also Brotherhood meeting about the automobile and about the one brother who was asked to come to Brotherhood meeting but for the second time has not come. So it was decided to request him [to come] for another time and if does not come he will be excommunicated. Also about rebuking and rejecting pride.

July 31 P. Löwen preached in Blumenort and in the afternoon there was Brotherhood and so the brother [owning the car] did come and acknowledged [his wrongdoing] and promised to improve. Also about the government [election] in which several brothers participated, but some of the same [brothers] now see it as wrong and so several confessed at Brotherhood and those [brothers who voted but were] not present we approached [after the Brotherhood], and so we agreed [that we could now] hold communion.

Aug. 7 Communion service was held in Steinbach.

Aug. 14 Communion service was held in Grünfeld.

Aug. 21 Communion service was held in Blumenort. Today, the 21st, the youth are to be baptised at *Jenseit*, that is if no obstacle has arisen. It has been long postponed because of the measles, which the youth contracted after our last trip [to Rosenort]. There are eight souls there, but one has withdrawn, leaving H. Friesens' Heinrich, Johan Friesens' Heinrich, Jakob Krökers' David, and I. Harmses' Peter, Jakob Klassens' David and D. Friesens' David, and the girls are Johan Löwens' Elisabeth, A. Löwens' Margaretha and Anna, and Kornelius Rempels'. . . .

Aug. 28 There was Worship Service in Blumenort; P. Reimer preached the Thanksgiving Sermon, on Colossians 2:6-7.

Sept 4 There was Worship Service here in Steinbach, C. Plett had the Thanksgiving Sermon, on Romans 12:1. There was Brotherhood in Steinbach concerning A. Töws who, wishing to be married to an unbelieving girl, and thus resigned from the church the previous Sunday. He has been the subject of counselling during the entire summer and at one point was excommunicated, and after that, in intense counselling, and yet before communion promised the best, attended communion and then after communion resigned and drove to Winnipeg to get married. Also [we discussed] those members that did not attend communion, . . . also about Widow Giesbrecht's hay harvest and so several committed themselves to take a day and [help her?]. . . .

Sept. 11 I preached the Harvest Sermon in Blumenhof and in Grünfeld C. Plett presented the sermon.

Sept. 18 P. Löwen preached in Steinbach.

Sept. 25 C. Plett presented the Harvest Sermon in Blumenort.

Oct. 2 I presented the Harvest Sermon in Steinbach.

Oct. 9 I presented the Harvest Sermon in Grünfeld and at the same time married the bridal couple, Dietrich Bartel with Helena Klassen, and in Blumenhof C. Plett preached.

Oct. 21 We drove to Morris as we received the news that *Ältester* Jakob Kröker and H.L. Friesen were seriously ill and so on the 23rd I preached there in Rosenort about the apathy of the 10 virgins. There was also Brotherhood about Anna Harms who stands excommunicated and so she was reinstated. On the 24th we returned home. In Blumenort C. Plett preached and at the same time the bridal couple, namely John Reimers' Abraham with David Pletts' Helena, were married.

Oct. 30 There was Worship Service in Steinbach. In the forenoon P. Kröker, Morris, preached on the text, Matthew 11:2-12. In the afternoon Johan R. Friesen preached on the text . . .

Nov. 6 P. Reimer preached in Blumenhof and in Grünfeld P. Löwen preached. At the same time the bridal couple was accepted, J. Reimers' Johan with Maria Dück.

Nov. 13 I preached in Steinbach, the text, II Corinthians 6:1-2; and also married the bridal couple, Johan R. with Maria Dück in the service. Also at the time we had Brotherhood. A brother had carried about with a rifle and fired it, which we see as an offense. Also about weddings, that alcoholic drinks should not be [served] and the youth shall not be allowed to participate and they shall not be served. . . .

Nov. 20 Worship service in Blumenhof; P. Reimer preached.

Nov. 27 Worship service in Steinbach; C. Plett preached.

Dec. 4 Worship service in Grünfeld; P. Reimer preached and in Blumenhof P. Löwen preached. On December 1 the elderly H. Friesen at Morris died and was buried on the 4th.

Dec. 11 P. Reimer preached the Advent Sermon in Steinbach. At the time we held Brotherhood concerning the rifle which a brother has in his possession and about the one who wished to borrow it; it was dealt with and in the future it is not to happen again. Also about the *Poltern* after the wedding, or [the time in which] the youth extort money [with threats to embarrass the bridal couple] – what to do? So it was decided that when members' children take part in these events the fathers are to be told so that they are not ignorant [about this]. But if they are strangers [non-Mennonite labourers] and there is no other way, their [demands] are to be satisfied, but they are not to be employed or given lodging until they make good and promise better. Moreover, members should not attend these parties (unless they are obligated to) so that they do not represent a bad light to the youth and thus undermine the salvation of the youth and make them unable to resist the evil way.

Dec. 18 I presented the Advent Sermon in Blumenort.

Dec. 25 In Steinbach P. Löwen presented the Christmas Sermon.

Dec. 26 I presented the Christmas Sermon in Blumenhof.

Dec. 31 A ministerial meeting at P. Reimers' in Blumenort and so we planned another ministerial meeting at C. Pletts' on February 4.

1911

Jan. 1 I presented the New Year's Sermon in Steinbach.

Jan. 6 C. Plett presented the Epiphany Sermon in Blumenort.

Jan. 8 C. Plett preached here in Steinbach and married a bridal couple.

Jan. 15 I preached in Grünfeld, the text, I Peter 5:8-9; in Blumenhof P. Löwen preached, and married the bridal couple, namely Johan N. Koop with Aganetha Siemens.

Jan. 22 P. Reimer preached in Steinbach, the text, Romans 8:12-14; also held Brotherhood concerning Klaas Töws's guesthouse and about the banquet which he put on in the beginning of January in his house and which was attended by high officials according to worldly ways and which several of our brethren attended, having paid a $1 entry fee. But as they all said, they had not known the nature of the gathering when they went. Also about the brother who wrote for a patent for an improvement he invented on the sleigh. [Patents mean that people] are to take note of [the invention] and protect it against copying. But the [patent application] had gone to the wrong [government] department and had been returned and with this [the application] was cancelled. [Moreover], he was repentant and acknowledged [his error]. Also much that dealt with warnings about [the danger of] Sunday Schools and lengthy oral prayers. And two brothers exhorted the church to be more accepting [of these innovations] but because of a number of issues [which our church opposes] they wish to join the other [more progressive] church. Also some [discussion] about the many debts and the indifference about them.

Jan. 29 P. Reimer preached in Blumenort, the text, Romans 8:12-14. After the service brother C. Siemens was presented, as he has come from Herbert [Saskatchewan] and would like to join our church.

Feb. 4 We ministers were at C. Pletts' where we discussed many issues.

Feb. 5 P. Löwen preached in Steinbach; there was at that time Brotherhood concerning C. Siemens, as he wishes to join our church and so it was decided that he should be accepted on February 19. Also we decided to collect money for the [Brandon] Insane Asylum for four Sundays. Also we discussed the church building construction and so it was decided that there shall be two Sundays to note on a roster how much each [member] is willing to contribute. This will happen on February 11 for which Brotherhood will be planned to decide how and where the church building shall be built [but already before that date] it was decided to build it here in Steinbach, 72' x 36'.

Feb. 12 P. Löwen preached in Grünfeld and in Blumenhof C. Plett preached.

Feb. 19 I preached in Steinbach and after the service an acceptance, namely, C. Siemens and afternoon Brotherhood to see if [there was enough interest] to begin with the church construction and so it became apparent that over $2,200 had been pledged and so commencement is to be undertaken.

Feb. 26 P. Löwen preached in Blumenort.

On the 1st of March we held a ministerial meeting at P. Löwens' in Neuanlage.

On March 5 C. Plett preached in Steinbach, the text ...

March 12 I preached in Blumenhof, the texts, II Corinthians 6:1-2, and at the same time I married the bridal couple, namely Cornelius Siemens with Jakob Pletts' Katherina. In Grünfeld P. Reimer presented the sermon.

March 19 Johan Friesen, Morris, presented the sermon in Steinbach, and married the bridal couple, I.C.B. with M. Dück. There was also Brotherhood meeting about the brother who drank too much during harvest and seeing it was not premeditated, has not happened to him before and that he was repentant, we forgave him. And also concerning the site for the church [building] ...

March 21 Worship service was held in Blumenort, Johan Friesen presented the sermon.

The 26th Worship service was held in Blumenort; P. Löwen presented the sermon.

April 2 Worship Service was held in Steinbach; P. Reimer preached and then, too, Brotherhood meeting about the school question, as here in Steinbach there is much support for a [public] District School and so several [residents] from outside our church, also several from within our church, have without discussion raised the flag, and by this act commenced the District School. But the majority in the congregation see this as very wrong for us and for our descendants and [thus] work against it. Also there was more discussion about the church building site and as there has been some dissension on this matter, so a reconciliation will be procured.

April 8 I drove to Morris as [my] brother B. Dück had written that their little daughter Anna was very sick and also that *Ältester* Jakob Kröker was very weak and as I dearly wish to speak with him and visit him there, so I went over there, and on the 19th in the forenoon I presented the sermon in Rosenort on the text Luke 15:11-24 and in the afternoon in Rosenhof [and also attended] the funeral of B. Dücks' Anna. And here in Grünfeld C. Plett presented the sermon and in Blumenhof, P. Reimer presented the sermon.

April 14 P. Löwen presented the Good Friday sermon here in Steinbach.

On April 16 On Easter Sunday, I preached in Blumenort.

On April 17, Easter Sunday C. Plett preached in Steinbach on the text from Matthew[?]:1-8.

April 20 Brotherhood was held here in Steinbach concerning the District School which has been established by some without discussion. This, however, does not seem right to us and so requires much diligent work [opposition, even though] it is not something illegal. But it is a dubious prospect to have a school just for ourselves; it would cost a lot and be such an unpleasant thing [for the community]. Yet there are those amongst us who want to support the District School as there is not enough knowledge or learning [in the Parochial School]. ...

April 23 C. Plett preached in Blumenhof.

April 28 I preached in Grünfeld on the text of Luke 15:11-24.

On May 1, I preached in Steinbach on the text of Luke 15:11-24.

May 7 C. Plett preached in Blumenort and in the afternoon Brotherhood concerning the District School, but which has become so rooted [infected] here in Steinbach, no way has been found for us to get rid of it. Also concerning Esaus' Marie who was brought to a Winnipeg hospital to see if she can be helped from her feeblemindedness, but subsequently it appears that she cannot be helped, as it stems from an inherent birth defect.

May 14 C. Plett preached in Steinbach.

May 21 I presented the articles [of faith] in Blumenhof and married the bridal couple, namely W[idower] P. Barkman with K. Koop [?]. In Grünfeld P. Löwen preached.

May 25 Ascension Day, Peter Reimer preached in Steinbach and in the afternoon Brotherhood and so seven youthful souls who wished to be baptised were presented to the brethren. Also about purchasing cars and driving them too fast, which two brothers have. We, however, have worked against this, first, because as Christians we are not to assimilate to the ways of the world and shall not desire [such a] mighty and elegant thing which bears a majestic image and which here in this region is something new and ostentatious. And, second, because [the car] travels so quickly and frightens so many horses, so that many accidents have occurred resulting in collisions and annoyances. However, [the car] is supported by many brothers and [our concerns are] looked upon as self-made rules and so we were unable to come as far as we wished. Also decided to have a two-Sunday offering for the Sanatorium in Ninette [Manitoba] which the [Hanover] municipality has requested; also one Sunday for . . .

On the 28th of May I presented the articles [of faith] in Blumenort.

On the 31st of May there was a funeral at Jakob Dücks' in Grünfeld so I preached there on the text of Revelation 2:10-11.

On June 3rd there was a gathering [of ministers] at P. Reimers' in Blumenort to discuss several points. First, we discussed and [came to a decision] on the matter of the District School and automobile, that we want to discuss how we want to approach this with the ministers from *Jenseid*. And secondly concerning P.F. who has treated his family so severely, so we want to speak with him. And also something about the church building construction. And about the brethren who live such a great distance from others.

June 4 Worship service in Steinbach, C. Plett preached.

June 5 P. Löwen preached in Blumenhof and in Grünfeld P. Reimer preached. A collection for the hospital in Ninette was held in Blumenort, $3.50, and in Steinbach, $11.75 1/2.

June 11 P. Reimer presented the Spring Sermon.

June 18 P. Reimer presented the Spring Sermon in Blumenort and in the afternoon Brotherhood. First, we presented the youth and after that [we] discussed the District School and automobile driving and so we decided that we ministers, all four, should travel to *Jenseid* on the 21st to seek the advice of the ministers there, and also have discussions there with the brethren, [asking] if we want to have this amongst us, and also whether we could, freely in our faith, [forcibly] pull the flag out of the school. So we went over there by train on Wednesday and on the 22nd we had a ministerial meeting at A. Eidses' and considered both points and agreed to work against both with great resolve in order to break away from both.

June 22 After *Vesper* there was a Worship Service in Rosenhof and P. Reimer from Blumenort presented the Spring Sermon.

June 23 I preached in Rosenhof and in the afternoon there was Brotherhood, to an extent concerning the District School, together with the flag, which from their unanimous [perspective] was declared a danger to our faith. Secondly concerning brothers owning and driving automobiles, also unanimously declared unsuitable for the *Nachfolger Christi* [followers of Christ] and it too shall not be tolerated.

On the 24th C. Plett preached in Rosenort and in the afternoon we returned by train.

On July 1 I returned to *Jenseid* to help with the youth as the one *Ältester* cannot do this on account of his weakness and on July 2 the youth in Rosenort were instructed. I preached and then, too, there was Brotherhood and so a brother was excommunicated from the church whose secret life has brought suspicion and great slander on the church. After *Vesper* another worship there and the [Catechism] questions were put to the youth [who wished to be baptised].

On July 3 the youth were baptised there in the morning and then, too, Brotherhood concerning preparation for communion and about the parents who defend their children and others who do not believe anything bad about their children. And after *Vesper* the Preparatory Sermon was presented by Johan K. Friesen.

July 4 In the morning we held communion in Rosenhof.

July 5 Communion was held in Rosenort.

July 6 I left there for home.

July 9 I presented the articles [of faith] in Steinbach and presented the questions [to the youth]. And in the afternoon there was Brotherhood concerning District Schools and attendance at the circus to which many admitted.

July 10 Worship service in Blumenort where Peter Kröker of Morris preached and in the afternoon A. Eidse preached.

July 11 Johan K. Friesen preached in the forenoon and in the afternoon Brotherhood was held concerning the District Schools and we agreed to diligently work against, although as it seems our efforts so far have not been successful as the newly hired schoolteacher of the District School is not for private schools. We also worked with those who own automobiles and so several promised to abstain, however not sincerely enough.

July 12 We [as ministers] met separately in the evening with the Steinbach brethren concerning the school question, but nothing came of it because we wanted first to get the other church leaders' opinions, to see if they were going to talk their people into abstaining from the District School or if the new schoolteacher also wants to teach in the private schoolhouse. Thus we talked with the teacher, but he declined, and so we will no longer work with this case.

July 16 The Youth were baptised in Blumenort, nine souls: first, W. Giesbrechts' Johan; Klaas Reimers' Klaas (Blumenort); Johan F. Reimers' Jakob; Gerhard Schellenbergs' Johan and Johan Reimers' Maria; C. Krökers' Katherina; Widow H. Brandt, her Margaretha, and Widow M. Barkman, her Katherina; Gerhard Dörksens' Sara.

July 23 Worship Service in Steinbach, P. Reimer preached and in the afternoon Brotherhood concerning the schools.

July 30 I preached in Grünfeld and C. Plett preached in Blumenhof.

August 6 C. Plett preached in Steinbach.

August 13 P. Löwen preached in Blumenort.

August 20 P. Löwen preached in Steinbach.

August 27 P. Löwen preached in Steinbach.

Sept. 3 I preached in Steinbach.

Sept. 10 C. Plett preached in Blumenhof and in the afternoon there was Brotherhood where we discussed whether we could hold communion service. Also [we] spoke about the school and about the business in [the railroad town of] Giroux in which a number of brethren have invested but which we do not see as good. Also, it was announced that Johan Goossen has resigned from the church as he wishes to join the Schmitten [Bruderthaler] Gemeinde; C. Löwen has declared that he too wishes to join that church. Because our Steinbach brethren were not at the Brotherhood meeting we decided to have another Brotherhood meeting next Sunday in Steinbach.

Sept. 11 The elderly Mrs. P. Barkman died at six o'clock in the evening and was buried on the 14th. I preached.

Sept. 17 P. Reimer preached in Steinbach and in the afternoon there was Brotherhood meeting where communion was discussed; two other families have left the church – namely Jakob D. Barkmans and Benjamin Janzes who are joining the Bruderthaler.

Sept. 24 I preached in Blumenhof, text, Luke 15:19-25, and in Grünfeld P. Reimer preached.

Oct. 1 Worship service was held in Blumenort because new desks are being installed in the Steinbach school and because the new schoolteacher no longer wants church services to be held in the school as it has been turned into a district school and so the worship services will be held in Blumenort until the new church building [in Steinbach] is completed.

Oct. 15 Worship service in Blumenhof, P. Löwen preached.

Oct. 22 C. Plett preached in Grünfeld.

Oct. 29 P. Löwen preached in Blumenort.

Nov. 5 C. Plett preached in Blumenort on the text, I Corinthians 13.

Nov. 12 Worship service was held for the first time in the new Steinbach church; C. Plett presented the Harvest Sermon, along with a short addition about the Mennonite Brethren Church.

Nov. 26 Worship Service in Steinbach, Johan K. Friesen preached on the texts of Matthew 13:24-30: "A man planted good seed." Then, too, there was Brotherhood. First, about Brotherhood meetings, should they always be held in conjunction [with worship services] in winter time. Then [a discussion] about church debts. And so we should take note that what is not coming in should be borrowed. Also Old C. Fast was engaged to heat the church and look after it. Then, concerning H.R. who has rented part of his lot to A.B. who wants to set up a barber shop where he will also sell tobacco and musical instruments. He was strictly admonished and told to see if he could buy his way out. Also concerning his daughter who had her picture taken with an English boy and because she was repentant it was forgiven her. Also much discussion about the car, which we do not want in the church but as several brothers had not come to Brotherhood meeting [any action] patiently had to be postponed. Also concerning the District Schools, but there is not much to say about it. And [we] also spoke more about matters dealing with assimilation with the world.

Dec. 1 We ministers gathered in Blumenort at P. Reimers' and discussed many things, how we can advance the spiritual work.

The 3rd Worship Service was held in Blumenort, P. Reimer preached.

The 10th Worship Service was held in Steinbach, P. Löwen preached.

The 17th I preached in Grünfeld and in Blumenhoff.... preached.

The 24th Dec. I presented the Advent Sermon in Steinbach.

The 25th Dec. I presented the Christmas Sermon in Blumenort.

The 26th P. Reimer preached in Steinbach, on the text, Luke 2:1-14.

On Dec. 31 I presented the New Year's sermon and P. Reimer preached in Grünfeld.

During this year we held 16 Brotherhood meetings and two I [held] in Morris. There were nine souls baptised this summer, on July 16. And four couples were married. I married C. Siemens with Katherina Plett, and P. Löwen has married Johan N. Koop with Aganetha Siemens, and married P. Barkman with Katherina Koop, J. Friesen (Morris) [married] C. Barkman with Margaretha Dück. And having died are, the elderly sister P. Barkman on September 11 (I preached there). And resigned from the church are the following people: Johan Goossens, Klaas W. Reimers and Jakob Barkmans, Benjamin Janzes. Also eight souls and C. Siemens were accepted by our church.

1912

Jan. 1 There was worship service in Steinbach. C. Plett gave the sermon.

Jan. 2 We ministers had gathered at C. Pletts' to deliberate on the spiritual work; it was decided that those brethren who had an automobile should come to Brotherhood to renounce it. Included were those who used a rifle. It was determined to have Brotherhood on January 15. We discussed the heating in the church. Warning was expressed that our members and their children should not attend [meetings that present] strange teachings or attend Sunday School [at the Bruderthaler or Holdeman Mennonite churches] as well as all seemingly harmless meetings, thereby losing appreciation for the simple preaching of the Word, or support the new [ways].

Jan. 6 P. Löwen brought the Epiphany Sermon in Blumenort.

Jan. 7 P. Löwen brought the Epiphany Sermon in Steinbach.

Jan. 14 C. Plett brought the sermon in Grünfeld and ... in Blumenhof.

Jan. 21 I delivered the sermon in Steinbach, the text, Luke 15:11-24.

Jan. 21 A.P. Reimer is said to have married the widow, Mrs. Jakob Friesen of Meade, Kansas. They were married in Meade.

Jan. 28 C. Plett delivered the sermon in Blumenort.

Feb. 3 Brotherhood was held in Steinbach (about five hours). First on the agenda was the matter of Esaus' Maria, who is mentally handicapped. She is to go from place to place in the church community, one month at a time. Secondly, there was discussion again regarding those who have used rifles; they were openly chastened; these promised to do better. Thirdly, it was decided to collect money for the needy in Russia on the next four Sundays. Fourthly, the financial report for the church was read and we decided that the required $1,200 be supplied by means of personal loans amongst us. Fifthly, we talked about owning cars.

Feb. 4 P. Reimer brought the sermon in Steinbach.

Feb. 11 P. Löwen presented the sermon in Grünfeld. I was there, also ... preached in Blumenhoff.

Feb. 18 C. Plett preached in Steinbach.

Feb. 24 I and C. Plett went to *Jenseid* on the sleigh.

Feb. 25 I brought the sermon in Rosenort; text was 1 Peter 2:5; in the afternoon C. Plett preached at the same location. He also did so in Rosenhof on the 27th.

Feb. 25 There was a worship service in Blumenort.

March 3 P. Löwen presented the sermon in Steinbach.

March 10 I preached in Grünfeld; the text was 1 Peter 2:5.

March 11 Brotherhood was held in Steinbach about a matter that took place about three years ago between a man and a widow, both being very remorseful. . . . When the matter was presented to the brethren, it did not meet with their approval. We [thus] confessed it [publicly] before marrying the people in question. Secondly, other matters were presented: that $100 had been collected for the needy in Russia, the matter about school districts and about cars. However, nothing was accomplished.

March 17 I delivered the sermon in Steinbach, with text being 1 Pet. 2: 5.

March 19 A funeral was held in the Steinbach church. Abraham, a son of G. Kornelsens, had died on March 16, having reached the age of 22 years, 8 months and 10 days. Johan K. Friesen, Morris, presented the sermon. There was a cold north wind.

March 24 I presented the sermon in Blumenort, based on I Peter 2:5.

March 31 P. Reimer preached the Palm Sunday sermon in Steinbach.

April 1 We ministers were together to discuss several things regarding our service at weddings of non-Christians . . . and taking part in them; also about the Friesens [and the] Winnipeg school [?].

April 5 I delivered the Good Friday Sermon in Blumenhof and P. Reimer preached in Grünfeld.

April 7 C. Plett brought the Easter Sermon in Steinbach. Immediately after the service there was Brotherhood which concerned those brethren that attend the weddings of unbelievers and help them prepare meals and thus encourage them in their evil intentions. And so Jakob R. Friesen [J.R. Friesen] renounced the church. And then we also discussed Abram B. Friesen who boarded at P. Löwens' during the winter; he has been committed in Winnipeg by a brother as he was becoming insane. He was so dangerous, having several times spoken very angrily and threatened to shoot with a revolver, and so they have ordered him to be brought to Winnipeg. Since he was not a church member, since the government did not allow us to keep such people here and since he was dangerous, we knew of no better advice. If such a case should come up again, we will first consult with the church ministerial [to consider] the best response. It was also decided that three collections be made for the insane asylum [in Brandon], since only $63 had been collected so far. There was also discussion regarding some brethren, and young people also, who failed to observe the practice of turning around [and kneeling] for prayer during the worship service. They should be more orderly in this respect and should if possible all turn around and fold their hands, resting them on the seat of the pew and hold their heads on folded hands. Also, more attention should be given when the blessing [that commences the worship service] is pronounced.

April 8, Easter Monday P. Löwen preached in Blumenort. I stayed at home because of bad roads.

April 14 I presented the sermon in Steinbach; text based on 1 Peter 5: 8-9. There were no other ministers present, except C. Plett. It was rainy and the roads were very poor.

April 21 C. Plett preached in Grünfeld; P. Reimer preached in Blumenhof.

April 28 P. Löwen presented in Steinbach.

May 5 C. Plett preached the Word in Blumenort, and I held a service in Steinbach in the afternoon. At the same time I also married the engaged couple; namely, G.E. Kornelsen with the widow Mrs. M. Barkman.

May 16 C. Plett delivered the Ascension Day sermon in Blumenhof and P. Löwen delivered the Ascension Day sermon in Grünfeld.

May 19 I presented the articles [of faith]. In the afternoon there was Brotherhood dealing with the "eggs and butter" matter in the store. However, the matter had been somewhat exaggerated; it was retracted; so one brother acknowledged his fault. Several had already settled the matter in the store, having been somewhat indifferent about the matter, as it seemed. The whole matter was to be taken as a general encouragement and the matter closed. Three young persons were presented who wanted to be baptized.

May 26, Pentecost P. Reimer presented the Pentecost sermon in Blumenort.

May 27, Pentecost Monday C. Plett preached in Steinbach.

June 2 C.L. Friesen, Nebraska, delivered the sermon in Grünfeld and P. Löwen in Blumenhof.

June 3 The funeral of Aganetha Wiebe (living at Jakob Reimers') was held in the Steinbach church. I presented the sermon, based on 1 Peter 1: 24. . . . She died on June 1st, at five o'clock in the morning, having reached the age of 27 years and 3 months. On the 7th of June the old Mrs. Giesbrecht died at four o'clock in the morning at the age of 86 years, 11 months. She was buried on the 9th; Johan K. Friesen, Morris, brought the sermon.

June 9 *Ältester* Jakob Kröker had the sermon, based on Rev[elation] 22:12-13. The funeral for old Mrs. Giesbrecht was held in the afternoon, with Johan K. Friesen presenting the Word.

June 10 There was a worship service in Blumenort; A. Eidse brought the sermon. In the afternoon we ministers met in the school to deliberate on how we could come to one mind again with respect to district schools, automobiles and assimilation with the world. We decided to have Brotherhood meeting and see if those concerned [i.e., supporters of public schools] would be willing to resign themselves to private schools and to put away other things and if this did not work out, an ultimatum would be given, that if they would resign themselves to our presentation and accept our counsel by the time Communion Service [*Einigkeit*] was to be held, we would be willing to work further with them and hold communion. Those that could not agree to this would no longer be members of our church.

June 12 Brotherhood was held in Steinbach where we strove hard to come to one mind regarding schools, automobiles and assimilation with the world – but those concerned did not say much although we presented it with all earnestness and declared that they should make a decision by communion time and recommended that they follow our counsel. However, the church is at this time not ready to deal with them according to II Thess[alonians]3:14 [that is, to shun with the purpose of shaming], but rather according to the sixth verse in the same chapter.

June 13 P. Kröker presented the sermon in Steinbach.

June 16 There were two worship services in Blumenort. In the forenoon *Ältester* Jakob Kröker had the introduction and Johan K. Friesen had the text. In the afternoon Johan Friesen had the introduction and Jakob Kröker the text.

June 17 There was Brotherhood in Steinbach again where the same matters were discussed as last time. Several brethren declared their willingness to go along with the Brotherhood and accept their advice.

June 23 Worship service was held in Steinbach.

June 30 I preached in Grünfeld, while C. Plett preached in Blumenhof.

July 5 We ministers met at our place to discuss several matters.

July 7 There was a service in Steinbach. C. Friesen from Kansas presented the text. I married the bridal couple, Johan Giesbrecht and K. Reimer. In the afternoon there was Brotherhood where the baptismal candidates were presented for the second time. It was decided that the candidates be instructed in Blumenort in the presence of the congregation. Also other matters were dealt with. Saturday, July 6th, there were two *Verlobungen* [engagement parties] at P. Reimers' and Jakob Reimers'.

July 14 There was a worship service in Blumenort where I preached and instructed the youth. In the afternoon there was a service where the bridal couple, P. Reimers' son Klaas and A.P. Reimers' daughter Anna, were married by P. Reimer. On July 16th there was a wedding at Jakob Reimers': C. Krökers' son Cornelius with Judith Wiebe. I married them.

July 21 I presented the articles [of faith] in Steinbach and asked the questions [of the baptismal candidates]. In the afternoon there was Brotherhood; firstly, concerning Abram Töws, who wants to come back into fellowship [with the church] which he had renounced two years ago [when] he married an unbaptized girl. As she wanted to be baptized we were able to examine him and found him to be honest and repentant. It was decided to receive him [back] into fellowship right after the baptism. There was also discussion regarding pride and schools, also about the musical instrument shop: the brother who had [the dealer] on his yard [as tenant] should [break the rental agreement]. . . .

July 28 Four persons were baptised in Steinbach and one man was accepted into fellowship. Baptised: Jakob Dücks' daughter Anna; Mrs. Abram Töws; John Reimers' daughter Susanna; Jakob Pletts' daughter Helena.

August 4th The worship service was in Steinbach; C. Plett preached.

August 11 Worship service was held in Blumenort and Peter Löwen preached. Brotherhood was held in the afternoon. Firstly, it was about the matter between John R. and C.R. This point of controversy could not, even after lengthy persuasion, be settled completely.

August 18 Worship service was held in Steinbach; P. Löwen preached. Brotherhood took place in the afternoon, for C. Reimer had renounced the church in writing, because of the quarrel he had with J.R. So the matter was discussed again and upon J.R.'s promise to mend his ways, he was forgiven. There was also a repetition about the musical instrument shop and H.R. [the landowner] had to promise to continue to try hard to get rid of him [the shopkeeper] even though [H.R.] had rented the parcel of land to him for five years. The taking of photographs by brethren was forbidden. Since these obstacles had been cleared away it was decided to have communion, first in Blumenort on September 8th if nothing else intervenes.

August 25 P. Löwen brought the sermon in Blumenhof; the text was Psalm 22:27. P. Reimer brought the sermon in Grünfeld.

Aug. 24 Old Mrs. A.L. Friesen died of a kidney illness that lasted only four days. She was 62 years old; her funeral was on the 26th. Johan K. Friesen had the sermon, based on Matt. 25: 1-13.

Sept. 1 P. Reimer preached the Preparatory Sermon in Steinbach. After the service Brotherhood was held to see if there was anything that would keep communion from being held, and so it was decided to hold communion on Sept. 8th in Blumenort, next in Steinbach and then in Grünfeld.

Sept. 8 Communion was first held in Blumenort, five members having died from last communion till now: one brother & four sisters; namely, Abram, son of G. Kornelsens; old Mrs. P. Barkman; Aganetha Wiebe (single); the widow Mrs. G. Giesbrecht; and old Mrs. A.L. Friesen.

Sept. 15 Communion was held in Steinbach.

Sept. 22 Communion was held in Grünfeld. Roads were very bad.

Sept. 29 Worship service was in Steinbach, where C. Plett had the Thanksgiving sermon, based on Romans 12:1.

Oct. 6 The worship service was held in Blumenort; P. Reimer preached.

Oct. 20 Worship service in Grünfeld with C. Plett presenting the sermon. We had also gone there. Presenting the sermon in Blumenhof was . . .

Oct. 13 P. Löwen presented the sermon in Steinbach. On the 27th, P. Reimer delivered the Harvest Sermon in Steinbach. In the afternoon there was Brotherhood regarding those that had not attended communion. Twenty-one members [of about

400 members] had not attended because of matters like district schools, automobiles, and other matters such as assimilation with the world [with which they were] not willing to accept our advice. Eight members could not find it in themselves to attend, although they still desired to be one with the church. Five were absent because of sickness. There was discussion about one absent brother who had used a rifle to shoot his neighbour's ox. We decided to be patient with him and continue to deal with him. There was also a discussion regarding the [financial] shortfall for the church construction and we were encouraged to give more, $1,000 was still needed. It was decided to collect this in the month of November.

Nov. 3 C. Plett preached in Blumenort; the Harvest Sermon.

Nov. 10 I presented the sermon in Steinbach, based on Philippians 4:8. In the afternoon there was Brotherhood, where this brother's ox-shooting was discussed. Since he recognized his error, we forgave him. After that we took up the matter of [premarital sex of] two members who [we then] excommunicated. The sister belonged to the church already, but at the time of the act the brother was not baptised yet. But since he had not confessed it before he was baptised, not even [when] he married another woman, and [because he] was not [open] about this matter and very indifferent about it, so [he] was declared to be guilty and was excommunicated.

Nov. 17 Jakob J. Friesen, Meade, Kansas, preached in Blumenhof. He was [one of] four men from Kansas who had come here on November 7, including M.T. Dörksen, Jakob J. Friesen, and Jakob and Heinrich Reimer, to seek counsel about variations in the church polity and views of faith. So they preached with the intention of uniting with us [on these matters]. P. Löwen went to hold a worship service in Grünfeld with M. Dörksen.

Nov. 21 Thursday, M. Dörksen held a service in Steinbach and so there was also Brotherhood regarding the excommunicated sister who was repentant and desired to be reaccepted, which we did. A.P. Reimers left for Meade, Kansas on the 22nd of November.

Nov. 24 There were two services in Steinbach; Jakob J. Friesen preached in the forenoon and M.T. Dörksen Meade, Kansas in the afternoon. On the 25th they went to Morris.

Nov. 30 C. Plett, and I also, went to Morris.

Dec. 1 I presented the sermon in Rosenort in the forenoon and C. Plett in the afternoon; the ministers from Kansas were not allowed to preach; they were to settle their matter at home first.

Dec. 4 We left there in the afternoon, but because a bridge had broken, the train could not go [and so we] had to stay in Winnipeg overnight. So we came home on the 5th, at three o'clock in the afternoon. In Blumenort P. Löwen had preached on the 1st of December.

Dec. 8 C. Plett brought the sermon in Steinbach; none of the other ministers were there in the service. It was quite cold.

Dec. 15 I presented the Advent Sermon in Blumenhof and P. Reimer preached in Grünfeld.

Dec. 17 We met at P. Reimer's in order to deliberate on several matters.

Dec. 22 P. Reimer preached in Steinbach, and so there was Brotherhood where we accepted C.T.K. again. Also there was a discussion about marrying the second sister; but, since there were differing views about this we decided to discuss the matter with the Morris and Meade churches. The matter of English readers: to select those that were more in accordance with what we basically believe and have them printed.

Dec. 26 C. Plett presented the Christmas Sermon in Steinbach.

Dec. 29 I delivered the New Year's Sermon in Grünfeld; and in Blumenhof C. Plett preached.

1913

Jan. 1 I delivered the New Year's Sermon in Steinbach.

Jan. 5 P. Reimer presented the sermon in Blumenort. Immediately after there was Brotherhood, for a young brother was burdened about his youthful sins, not having confessed them before he was baptised. He was remorseful about it, but he had not fully committed the act so he was forgiven. The female person was at that time already a member, and after more questioning it was learned that she had later lived in more serious sins. So she was excommunicated.

Jan. 6 C. Plett delivered the Epiphany sermon in Steinbach.

Jan. 12 P. Reimer delivered the sermon in Blumenhof; C. Plett in Grünfeld.

Jan. 19 P. Löwen preached in Steinbach; the text was Rev. 14: 13.

The 26th P. Reimer preached in Blumenort; the text was Luke 15:1-10. Also, there was Brotherhood where M.E. was accepted into membership and J.B. was excommunicated because of adultery, although the act had not been completely carried out.

Feb. 1, Saturday There was Brotherhood in Steinbach where J.B. was received into membership again. Also about J.P.'s daughter, Helena, who had been coming together with unconverted boys; however, since she seemed to be repentant and promised to mend her ways, she was forgiven. The way young people are getting together was sharply portrayed and reproved. There was also discussion about the deception in a wheat deal; but improvement was promised, that is, that he would settle up with that dealer. It was also decided that money would be collected on four Sundays for the insane asylum in Brandon.

Feb. 2 P. Reimer preached in Steinbach; the text being Luke 15: 1-10.

Feb. 9 I brought the sermon in Blumenhof, with text I Peter 2: 5; Peter Löwen brought it in Grünfeld.

Feb. 14 We ministers met at P. Löwens in order to discuss several matters. First, the matter of marrying the second sister [i.e., the traditional prohibition of marrying the sister of one's deceased wife].We agreed to hold it off [i.e., changing this practice] as long as possible. Second: about the dissension in the church at Meade [Kansas] and the fact that they wanted us to come and help them.

Feb. 15 The engagement of the widow took place, Mrs. M.D. Barkman with the bachelor, C.L. Friesen of Morris.

Feb. 16 Worship service was held in Steinbach. Minister Johan K. Friesen presented the sermon and published the banns of the bridal couple. Right after that there was Brotherhood where the matter of marrying the second sister was discussed, and it was evident that there was a wide variation of opinion. Evidently, too little scriptural evidence could be given to convince the opposing party [the man wishing to marry his wife's sister] that it was wrong, for that party was represented by some very strong brethren. So we decided to discuss the matter with the ministers in Morris, before we would allow it. Concerning the matter in Meade, it was resolved that we would first write them and see if both sides would resign themselves to whatever was....

Feb. 17 Johan K. Friesen held the worship service in Blumenort.

Feb. 18 Johan K. Friesen held the worship service in Grünfeld.

Feb. 23 P. Löwen held the worship service in Blumenort; then also married the bridal couple. There was also Brotherhood concerning J.K.'s unchastity with his daughter, and so he was excommunicated.

March 2 I preached in Steinbach, with text based on I Corinth[ians] 13:1-13: Though ... There was also Brotherhood meeting, so he (J.K.) was received back into the church. Not many brethren were present.

March 9 C. Plett preached in Grünfeld. I did not feel very good; had severe toothache last week and one side of the head was swollen. In Blumenort the sermon was brought by P. Löwen.

March 16 C. Plett brought the sermon in Steinbach; there was also Brotherhood meeting regarding the District Schools. The [supporters of public schools] intended to hold an election for borrowing money from the municipality. The Reeve had asked C.K. to be in charge of this but we decided that C.K. should see if they would release him from the responsibility. We did not want to have anything to do with the matter. (They did release him.) The matter of marrying the second sister was dealt with and so Brotherhood was planned for Friday in Blumenort. Furthermore it was decided to have a collection, one time around, for a poor sick man, said to be incurable. Also, a letter from M.T. Dörksen, Meade, was read....

March 21 Good Friday. C. Plett brought the sermon in Blumenort. In the afternoon Brotherhood was held which concerned the matter of marrying the sister. After a lengthy discussion the concerned persons were reminded to consider how difficult it was for many of us to allow this and that they should sincerely call upon the Lord to help them do His will in this matter. But, since they [the couple in love] cannot let go of each other, the membership thought it best to permit it, as peace could not be maintained any longer. However, the Lord has led otherwise; also, He has changed the minds of the persons concerned [and they will not marry after all]. Also, a letter by J.J. Friesen, Kansas, was read in which he asked for forgiveness of whatever he had done or said that was wrong; but since we as a membership could not think of anything amiss, it was decided to forget everything. There was also some discussion about the excommunicated Mrs. Bröski [Maria Radinzel, the first female schoolteacher on the East Reserve] who is feebleminded.

March 23 Easter Sunday – P. Löwen preached in Steinbach.

March 24 Easter Monday – I delivered the sermon in Blumenhoff, that is, the Easter Sermon; P. Reimer preached in Grünfeld.

March 27 Rev. P. Reimer, C. Plett and I went to Mrs. Bröski in order to talk with her about the shunning, for she doesn't show up very often in our midst. Besides that she is feebleminded and it is many years ago that she was excommunicated; so it wouldn't hurt her nor the church if the ban was lifted. We sensed also that she had some desire to be relieved of the ban before we left, and so we shook hands and left.

March 30 P. Reimer preached in Steinbach. Right after there was Brotherhood concerning the letters by M.T. Dörksen & A.L. Friesen [Kansas], for they have reached some reconciliation, excepting [?] the ministerial, where they held a vote of non-confidence against M.T.D., J.J. Friesen and Deacon Jakob Reimer, on Palm Sunday. This seemed like very harsh treatment to those concerned so they asked us for advice. We deliberated on this for a while, but decided to accept whatever had transpired, although we had a different view about the matter. Also the matter of Mrs. Bröski was presented. About participation at District School meetings, we declined [the invitation].

April 6 I brought the sermon in Blumenort, based on I Corinthians 13:1-3. After that a Brotherhood was held regarding the letters from Meade, and it was ...

April 13 I brought the sermon in Steinbach with II Corinthians 6:1-2 as text. After the service the young people were asked to apply for baptism.

April 20 I preached in Grünfeld, with text based on I Corinthians 13:1-3 in Blumenhof. ... preached.

April 27 The articles [of faith] were presented for the first time by me in Steinbach. Also there was a discussion about collecting money for supporting Mrs. I. Plett in building her own house.

On the 26th Our children had their *Verlobung* [engagement party] at our place with Klaas D. Reimer, and so their wedding banns were read on Sunday in Steinbach.

May 1st, Ascension Day P. Reimer preached in Blumenort.

May 4 C. Plett brought the sermon in Steinbach; after which I married our children, Klaas [D. Reimer] and Margaretha [Dück]. Brotherhood was held in the afternoon where some more baptismal candidates were presented (some had already presented on the 27th) - a total of 19. Also the Meade letters were read and discussed, since they urged us to come over and help them in their matter; also to carry out a baptismal service. But we wanted to wait and do some work here, also baptize the candidates.

May 11 I Preached in Grünfeld and married the bridal couple, namely, Johan R. Schellenberg with Ana Dück, Grünfeld.

May 12 P. Löwen brought the sermon in Steinbach.

May 18 I presented the articles for the second time in Blumenort. Brotherhood was also held, where two more young people were presented as baptismal candidates. Also the Meade case was discussed.

May 25 C. Plett preached in Steinbach.

May 30 We ministers went to *Jenseid* in order to talk about several matters.

June 1 I preached in Rosenhoff and P. Reimer preached there in the afternoon. On the 3rd C. Plett preached in Rosenort and on the 4th we had a meeting there to talk about going to Meade. However, we decided to delay for a while till there would be more hope for an agreement. Also, in the matter of marrying the second sister, it was decided that this should no longer be a point of controversy. As long as their conscience is not harmed, or [the conscience of] the one solemnizing the act, or the ones who want to get married. [It is] similar to what we are told in Romans 14 and I Corinthians 8, about [consuming meat once] offered to idols, [it is permitted] if it can be done without causing too much offense. We have very little scriptural support to disallow [marriage to the second sister] and yet [we want to maintain the] love.

June 8 Worship service was held in Steinbach; . . . was preaching. After this there was Brotherhood concerning two members who had committed the offense of adultery. Both of the [parties], J.U. & S.R., were excommunicated.

June 15 I presented the articles in Blumenort and asked the questions of the baptismal candidates. After lunch there was Brotherhood where the disciplined persons were received into membership again. Other matters were dealt with that had to do with preparing for communion.

June 22 The candidates were baptised in Steinbach – 20 persons. One candidate was so severely tempted that he withdrew. Also, afterwards he fell into great temptation (P.P. Friesens' son Jakob); his father came back from the insane asylum on the 23rd of June, where he had been for about two months.

June 22 At 1:00 p.m. the beloved *Ältester* Jakob Kröker died at the age of 76 years, 1 mo., 20 days. He had faithfully served his congregation for 40 years: five years as a deacon, five as a minister and 30 years as *Ältester*. He was buried on June 24th. C. Plett and I, along with several members, had gone to the funeral where I brought the sermon. We came back on the 26th. On the 25th there was a service and a short Brotherhood meeting.

June 29 I preached in Blumenhof, and Peter Löwen . . .

July 1 We ministers were together at our place to discuss several matters on how to prepare for communion, about automobiles, marriages and other work.

July 6 The worship service was in Steinbach, where P. Reimer preached. In the afternoon there was Brotherhood regarding J[ohan G.] B[arkman]'s marriage: he wants to let go of the second sister and marry someone else. He had already been given the freedom to do it, but he had settled it up with her and her relatives, as he didn't quite have peace of mind about Mrs. A. Reimer ['s daughter], even though it hadn't been completely disallowed (marrying the sister); so it was left up to him to decide. Furthermore, we discussed matters relating to preparation for communion. The case of A.S. Friesen was also presented; he went over to the Peters' Church [Bruderthaler Mennonite Church] in order to marry a widow, Mrs. Solomon Ediger.

July 8 I went to Morris by train in order to hold communion there. So there was a service on the 9th in the forenoon and Brotherhood after that regarding Jakob K. Kröker, who had drunk too much; he was excommunicated. He had already written to ask for cancellation of membership, but since he had already been dealt with on the matter, [the resignation] was not accepted. There were discussions that had to do with getting ready for communion; and so it was decided that the Preparatory Sermon be presented on the morning of the 10th, then on Friday in the forenoon to hold communion in Rosenort, and in Rosenhoff after *Vesper*. On the 12th I came home from Morris.

July 13 Worship service was held in Blumenort. Rev. P. Kröker presented the Preparatory Sermon. In the afternoon there was Brotherhood in preparation for communion, where several declared themselves and confessed their sins.

July 20 Worship service was held in Steinbach where Rev. P. Kröker delivered the Preparatory Sermon. Then in the afternoon there was a Brotherhood meeting where we got so far with communion that we decided to have it in Grünfeld the following Sunday, then in Steinbach, and in Blumenort on the 3rd Sunday. I should mention that P.W. Reimers were received into membership during the worship service in the forenoon. At first they were members in our congregation for a while; then they canceled their membership in writing and later joined the Brudertaler [Church]. However, they soon left that church, and so they are back now....

July 27 Communion was held in Grünfeld.

August 8 Communion was held in Steinbach.

August 10 Communion was held in Blumenort.

August 17 Worship service was held in Steinbach, where Johan K. Friesen, Morris, brought the Thanksgiving Sermon.

August 24 The worship service was held in Grünfeld; P. Reimer preached and I married the bridal couple: Widower Johan Barkman with Sarah Reimer. Also, at that time, the banns were read for another bridal couple, who, however, later began to doubt and separated [nullified their engagment]. In Blumenhof C. Plett brought the sermon.

August 31 P. Löwen preached in Steinbach.

Sept. 7 P. Löwen preached in Blumenort.

Sept. 14 C. Plett brought the sermon in Steinbach.

Sept. 21 P. Löwen preached in Blumenhof and C. Plett in Grünfeld.

Sept. 28 P. Reimer preached in Steinbach.

Oct. 1 We ministers met at P. Löwens and talked about the lawsuit that arose concerning the [criminal act against the] Dörksens' girl; but, since the [Dörksens] had not originated it, we would not be able to forbid them to go and testify as this might cause problems for them. Also we talked about those who had not attended communion, about school matters and the letters from Meade, whether we should go there in order to help them reconcile. We couldn't decide, [although we] wanted to let one brother be responsible [?].

Oct. 5 Worship service was held in Blumenort and Brotherhood meeting right after that, where those that had not been at communion were somewhat summarily admonished. Also, concerning the letters from Meade that were read, two from *Ältester* A.L. Friesen and one from M.T. Dörksen, requesting that we come there, as they are so divided. But we didn't decide about going there, as several members were of the opinion that it would not do any good. So we decided that the matter should first be discussed with the ministers at Morris. Also discussed whether or not we wanted to be included [?] with the school commission at Pembina. We agreed to decline....

Oct. 12 I brought the sermon in Steinbach; the text was based on Matt. 15.

Oct. 19 P. Löwen preached in Grünfeld and in Blumenhof... preached.

Oct. 26 P. Löwen brought the sermon in Steinbach.

Nov. 1 We ministers met at Plett's to discuss several matters: first, about reporting a break-and-entry to the authorities, whether it wouldn't be against our principles of faith, although we could not accuse any person specifically; second, whether our schoolteachers who are brethren should meet with the District [school] teachers for conferences (both cases were to be presented to Brotherhood for the deliberation); third, it was decided that we talk with the brethren about the excessive use of the automobile; also with the brother who had traded in [sold] a car. It was also decided to make an appeal for the debt on the church construction, as this has not been entirely paid for.

Nov. 2 Worship service took place in Blumenort; P. Reimer preached.

Nov. 9 Worship service was held in Steinbach; C. Plett brought the sermon.

Nov. 16 I delivered the sermon in Grünfeld; it was about the prodigal son. In Blumenhof P. Reimer preached.

Nov. 17 Monday – there was Brotherhood in Steinbach concerning the debt on the church; so we are going to collect till New Year; about $900 are needed. Also about the automobile. One brother had traded... in for an old one, but he wants to sell it if he can. We were also warned against hiring those with an automobile, [that is, those] who forsook the church [on this matter]. It was also considered to be dangerous to hold [teacher] conferences together with the District School teachers. Finally, we discussed our going to Meade; we agreed to go.

Nov. 12 Mrs. Peter Löwen died; she was buried on the 14th. JKF preached.

Nov. 23 Mrs. C. Plett died at 6:30 a.m.; she is to be buried on the 25th of November. Death probably due to heart attack (or stroke).

Nov. 23 P. Reimer preached in Steinbach.

Nov. 25 Mrs. Cornelius Plett was buried. I presented the sermon at the funeral in the Steinbach church.

Nov. 27 Johan K. Friesen, Morris, and I left for Kansas in order to bring reconciliation to the church there. And so we went – also A. Eidse, Jakob Bartel, and Abraham and Jakob Kornelsen, and Jakob Friesens of Morris – and got there Sunday, November 30, at noon. On Wednesday, December 2, we held two services. I presented the Word in the morning and in the afternoon Johan K. Friesen presented it, and Thursday, December 4, we had another service and A. Eidse presented.

Dec. 5 We ministers were in a meeting with both parties at Jakob Isaaks' and sought to understand their differences. Then Rev. C. Plett with A. Plett came there too, as they had only left home on December 1. Then, on December 6, there was Brotherhood there in the village [settlement] and so after a five-hour Brotherhood we came to a peaceful conclusion. And so the three ministers who had done the excommunicating were removed from their offices [with the condition] that when they had the grace to acquire the trust of the membership they could once again acquire their positions. And so new elections for minister were postponed. A service was decided for December 7 in the North Church and so C. Plett preached there. And Tuesday, December 9, there was another worship service where I preached. Thursday, December 11, there was yet another service with A. Eidse preaching and after the service we had Brotherhood about Communion Service, where we mentioned the District Schools. And so we decided to hold services on the 13th and 14th in the village. And so Johan K. Friesen preached in the morning, that is on December 13, and on Sunday, December 14, we had Communion Service twice in the village. In the morning C. Plett preached and in the afternoon A. Eidse preached.

Farm Women

VII

15 Margaretha Plett Kroeker (1842 to 1920)

Steinbach, Manitoba
Diary selection: 1892
Age: 49

Margaretha Plett Kroeker was born in Kleefeld, Molotschna Colony, New Russia, in 1842. Her parents were Cornelius S. Plett, the village mayor, and Sara Loewen, the sister of Cornelius Loewen (see diary 1). In 1861, she married widower Franz M. Kroeker of the same village, and some time in the mid-1860s the young couple moved to Steinbach, 100 kilometres to the west, in Borosenko Colony. A decade later, in 1874, they joined the migration to Manitoba, becoming one of the first 18 families to settle in Steinbach, which was the namesake of their village in Europe. In Steinbach, Manitoba, the Kroekers quickly established themselves as leading farmers, taking out a "double farm" and erecting a spacious house/barn that was large enough to host all Steinbach church services until 1882. By 1883, the Kroekers farmed the village's largest farm, which was 480 acres, of which 125 acres were cultivated. The family history notes that the Kroekers "were generous people having been known to give of their property to help poorer families," and that Margaretha was "a capable independent person" who continued farming after Franz died in 1905. In 1915, she left the farm and moved into a small retirement house on the yard of her daughter, Sara, and her husband, *Aeltester* Peter Dueck (see diary 14). She died at the Dueck residence in December 1920.

Only three of the Kroekers' children reached adulthood, and by 1892 all three had married and established their own households, although all three lived within close range of the Kroekers at the southern end of Steinbach's main street. Cornelius, 30, was married to Katherina Toews, and they had three small children, ages six years to six months. He, too, established a reputation as a successful farmer and was especially noted as a horseman. Margaretha, 29, was married to Johann R. Dueck, who came from Gruenfeld to settle in his wife's village: they had two children, one of whom was born in 1892 on 10 March. Sara, 21, had married Peter R. Dueck (Johann's brother) in 1888 and by 1892 they, too, had two small children; Sara and Peter lived just across the street from the Kroekers until 1911 when the agrarian village system ended in Steinbach and they established their farm on their own quarter section just to the south of town. These three young couples, referred to as "Kroekers," "Johann Duecks," and "our Peter Duecks," comprised a tightly knit work and social unit.

The immediate household of Margaretha and Franz, however, also included other individuals: according to census records, the Kroeker household in 1891 included 13-year-old Katrina Penner, a presence confirmed by this diary and by a family history that notes that the Kroekers had a foster child named Penner. According to the diary, in 1892 the Kroeker household also included an older handicapped woman named Margaretha Harder, a German Lutheran servant named Paul brought from Winnipeg, and a female servant, Katerina, from the village of Burwalde, 10 kilometres south of Steinbach.

In 1892, Margaretha also interacted regularly with her elderly parents and her siblings, most of whom lived in the village district of Blumenhof, some seven kilometres to the north. The siblings included the families of her brothers, Reverend Cornelius L. Plett, Johann L. Plett, Peter L. Plett, Abram L. Plett, and Jacob L. Plett. Another brother, David L. Plett, lived in nearby Neuanlage, his wife's village. Then there were the families of Margaretha's younger sisters: Anna, who was married to Gerhard Siemens of Rosenort, west of the Red River; Maria, who was married to Reverend Peter Reimer of Blumenort; and Katerina, who was married to Heinrich Wohlgemuth of Blumenhof. Many of these families visited the Kroekers' home on the Sunday each month in which the service of the Kleine Gemeinde Church was held in Steinbach. One sister, Sarah, had remained in Russia with her husband, Jakob Thielmann. Franz did not have close relatives in Steinbach but had two prominent brothers, Reverend Peter M. Kroeker and *Aeltester* Jacob M. Kroeker, who lived at Scratching River Reserve, west, "on the other side," of the Red River, and who visited in December.

The original diary, in German Gothic handwriting and covering the years 1892 to 1911, was preserved by the Cornelius P. Kroeker family and inherited by Margaretha's great-grandson Ben K. Plett, of Landmark. It was translated by Ben Hoeppner of Winnipeg. For more information on Margaretha Kroeker, see Delbert F. Plett, *The Plett Picture Book* (Steinbach, MB: 1981), 33-40.

January 1892

The 1st of January, the service was in Blumenort. It was very cold. The 10th, the service was here. Cornelius Pletts were here. The 14th, slaughtered an ox and [our children] Johan Dücks [slaughtered] 2 cows. The 12th, Cornelius Krökers slaughtered an ox. The 14th, Johann Dück went with the meat to

Winnipeg. The 18th, the senior Mrs. Berg, Blumenort, had an auction sale. The 25th, we were at the parents' [in Blumenhof] and [at brother] Peter Pletts'.

The 24th, the service was here. The parents, Cornelius Pletts, H. and Peter Reimers were visiting us.

The 26th, Abraham Kornelsens came here for the night. The 27th, Cornelius Pletts were visiting us. Elisabeth Kröker got very sick. At 5 a.m. we went over for 5 hours. A stroke. The 31st, the old Peter Ennses visited us.

February 1892

The 1st of February, an auction took place at Johann Friesens' in Blumenort. Johann Klassens were here. On the 31st of January we received letters from Nebraska, from [*Ältester*] A[braham] F[riesen] and A. Sawatskys. On the 1st of February Johann Klassens were here. The 2nd, the Wohlgemuths. The 3rd, the old and young Schellenbergs visited. The 3rd, Mall [the cow] calved. The 4th old Löwen was here. The night of the 4th to the 5th Elisabeth Kröker died and was buried on the 6th. The parents and Cornelius Pletts stayed here for the night.

The 7th, the service was here [in Steinbach]. Abraham Dücks were here for lunch. The 8th, the old cow calved. The 4th, Abraham Friesen went to Nebraska [and] Kansas. On the 24th we were in Blumenort for the service and were also at Peter Reimers'.

The 16th, old Cornelius Friesen died and was buried on the 20th. The [cow] Dälli [Dolly] calved. The 18th, [our children] Joh. Dücks borrowed the cow.

The 21st, the service was here [in Steinbach]. Cornelius Plett and Helena [his eldest daughter, age 18] and the old Jakob Dücks came for the night with all the children, Mrs. Plett was here too. The 23rd, Peter Pletts [the family of a brother-in-law] were here for the night. [Our children] Cornelius Krökers got the cow. The 26th, Heinrich Reimers of Grünfeld were here. The 28th, we were at Heinrich Brandts'.

The 26th, Mrs. Heinrich Friesen died. Peter Reimer and Cornelius Plett went to the West Reserve. She was buried March 1. We were in Neuanlage at David Pletts' and old Koops'. Reimer and Plett came back home Mar. 1.

The 29th, old Töws and Vogt here for lunch. In the afternoon I went to Mrs. Töws's and Abraham Friesens'.

March 1892

The 4th of March, another cow calved. It is thawing much. It is mild and there is much water. The 6th, the service was here. Peter Pletts, Jakob Pletts and Cornelius Pletts and Helena were here. The snow road is very bad. The 8th, it began to rain and to snow. Much wind in the evening and it was freezing a good deal. On the 2nd it was -19 and [there was] much wind. It was blowing much. Cornelius Kröker went and spent a night in the forest [some 20 kilometres to the east, for purposes of logging or obtaining firewood] for the first time.

The 13th, we were in Blumenort for the service and at [my sister's] Peter Reimers'. The old Abraham Reimers were both sick in bed. On the 14-16 Abraham Schellenberg [born 1878 or 1839] worked here for 75 cents a day.

The 20th, the service was here. The parents and Cornelius Pletts and Mrs. Jakob Plett and Cornelius Krökers were here as guests.

The 23rd, Father and Dalke went for poplar wood.

The 24th, we went to Blumenhof to the parents' and Cornelius Pletts'.

The 25th, we went to Grünfeld to Jakob Dücks' to get the old Magaretha Harder. The 28th, Monday, [our children] Peter Dücks slaughtered a hog. The 29th, they [Peter and Sara] began to build, also the posts for the well. The 31st, they put on the rafters.

April 1892

The 1st of April, it began to rain. The 2nd, [it began] to snow and to freeze. The 3rd, it began to thaw very much. The service was here. Cornelius Plett and Helena were here. The 2nd, [Cheesemaker] Klaas Reimers' [son] Heinrich died [on the very day of his birth]. The 7th, it was snowing. The 8th, the windows were white [with frost].

The 9th, Abraham Schellenberg worked here.

The 12th, it was snowing very much. The 11th, Johann Klassens visited us.

The 10th, Abraham Friesen was here as guest.

The 12th, Father came walking to our place and had *Vesper* here.

The 12th, at 12 o'clock, 12 midnight, Abraham Reimer, Blumenort, died in the morning. He was 87 (see diary 7). The funeral was on the 14th. We were there also.

On Good Friday, April 15, the worship service was here. Jakob Dücks, Abraham Dücks, our P. Dücks, Peter Pletts, C. Plett, Hel. C., the old Mrs. Berg, and Mrs. J. Plett, Cornelius Krökers were our guests.

The 16th, H. Wohlgemüts were visiting us. Peter Dück smashed his foot while drilling the well. On Easter, the 17th, the first holiday, we were at the old Barkmans'.

On the second holiday, the 18th, the service was here. The visitors here were the old Mrs. Berg, Cornelius Pletts, David Pletts, Peter Reimers, Isaak Löwens.

On the 20th, they were cutting wood at Johann Dücks', and after *Vesper* they started at our place and the rest on the 21st and then at Krökers'. On the 22nd of April we began to seed.

On the 24th, we were in Blumenort to attend the service at Peter Reimers'.

The 27th, it was raining much, so that the seeding was halted. Father sheared all 10 sheep. After *Vesper* it began to snow very much and to freeze. On the 28th in the morning it was -10.

May 1892

On May 1st, there was worship service here. Cornelius Plett with Helena was here. The road is very muddy. On May 2 it was snowing again a little. Around 5 it began to rain again and to snow and continued all night to the 6th forenoon. On the 4th I began to rake the garden. On the 5th I began to dig and [plant] the first potatoes. On Saturday, the 8th, we were at Johann Klassens'. [During the night] from the 9th to 10th he died. He was buried on the 11th. We also were there. In the forenoon Father went to Burwohl and got Katharina for a month for $4.00. On the 13th we began to dig the flower plot.

On May 14, the sheep were brought to the pasture in Rosengart. On the 9th the parents were here as guests.

On the 15th, the service was here. Jakob Wiebes, the young Mrs. Wiebe, Abraham Pletts, Cornelius Pletts, Helena, Cornelius and Peter Dücks were our guests. On the 17th it began to rain all night through. On the 18th it rained again. On the 19th water froze.

The 20th, Mrs. J. Dörksen got stuck with Maria.

On the 21st, the yearlings were brought to Lichtenau.

The 24th, we were in Blumenhof at the parents'.

The 26th, the service was here on Ascension Day. Cornelius Pletts, Helena, and we went to Peter Dücks' for *Vesper* and then to Johann D[ücks'].

The 28th, it began to rain and during the night it rained very much.

The 31st, Tuesday, we began to whitewash and to clean all week long.

June 1892

Friday, the 3rd, after *Vesper*, we planted potatoes. The 4th of June, Katharina went home.

The 5th, the first holiday of Pentecost, the service was here. Cornelius Pletts were here. On the 4th, Cornelius Fasts, of Pembina, were here as guests. Klaas Brandts, Heinrich Brandts, Heinrich Friesens were here also. Abraham Eidses were here on "this side" [the East Reserve] during the holidays. For the 2nd holiday we went to Blumenort to attend church, and [sister Maria] Mrs. Peter Reimer and I were at Johann Reimers' for a little while. The 8th, Heinrich and Klaas Brandts and the two Pletts were here visiting. The 9th, Mrs. Töws and Heinrich Friesen were engaged. The 10th, the bridal couple were here for *Vesper* and for the night. The 12th, the service was here. Isaak Plett was accepted [back into church membership]. The parents, Cornelius Pletts and Helena were here as guests.

The 13th of June, Father, Cornelius and Johann went to Winnipeg with potatoes, during the night of 15 [they returned]. He got 35 cents for the potatoes.

July 1892

July 13, 1892, [Father] brought a servant along from Winnipeg for a month, for $6.00 plus laundry. His name is Paul.

The 16th, Krökers' David [Franz's nephew] came around here. The 18th, we went to Blumenhof.

The 20th, Father and Peter Dück went to Winnipeg. David went along with potatoes. 75 cents for old ones, 60 cents for a pair of chickens, and 30 cents for a pair of rabbits. The 24th, the service was here. The parents and Cornelius Pletts and [their son-in-law] Gerhard Dörksen were here, and after *Vesper* the old Barkmans also.

On the 25 and 26, there was street work. The 27th, to Winnipeg with wheat. Bought 1 bag of flour and 75 lbs. of potatoes, 18 dozens of eggs for 13 cents. The 30th, finished the fence. Johann Friesen helped. Cost $3.00 wages.

The 31st, went to the service in Blumenort. For lunch at Peter Reimers', for *Vesper* at Mrs. Berg. The *Ohms* are all gone to *Jenn Seit*, except the old Berg and Peter Plett.

August 1892

August 1, began cutting hay and on the 3rd began hauling it. The 5th and 6th, it rained very much until the night of the 7th and forenoon of the 8th. [On the 7th] the service was here. The parents, Cornelius Pletts, A. Plett, Jakob Plett and Peter Plett, Peter Reimers, Jakob Dörksen, Cornelius Fasts, Peter Reimers' boys and our Peter Dücks.

The 12th, it rained heavily. On the 13th we began to cut barley. The 14th, we visited the schoolteacher Kornelsens'. [From] the 15th [to the] 16th forenoon, the mill burnt down, and in the afternoon a very hard thunder and lightening storm ensued.

The 16th, afternoon [we] began to cut wheat.

The 17th, it rained after *Vesper* and then through the night, at times heavily.

The 18th, mild and strong wind. Barkowski helps to level the manure on the yard and ploughed it in the evening. The 19th and 20th made a fence. During the night much rain. Cut wheat in the afternoon. The 21st there was much wind. Cornelius Pletts and A. Pletts were here. From the 25th to the 26th, rain again. In the forenoon began to cut oats. Finished it on the 7th at noon. In the afternoon hauled the last of the hay. During the night had much rain. We went to the service in Blumenort. Because of the heavy rain, few people were present. Today, the 29th, it is stormy in the morning, but mild by lunch. The 30th, after *Vesper* we began to cut barley.

September 1892

The 31st and the 1st of September, began hauling wheat to the yard. Then during the night much rain again. On September 1 Aron Penner [of Blumenhof] was struck by lightning and killed. The funeral on the 4th. Rain on the 3rd and

4th. The service was here on the 4th. Peter Pletts visited us. During this week it rained several times. On the 1st we were in Neuanlage at David Pletts' and the old Koops'. He is sick in bed. The 13th, at *Vesper* time we finished gathering the grain. After *Vesper* Kröker again left [us].

The 14th, Peter Dücks drove [grain?] all day long. The 14th and 15th, we had a little frost. The 15th, I began digging out potatoes. Father helped Gerhard Giesbrechts with threshing. The 15th the cattle began grazing on the ploughed land. The 9th, we attended the funeral of [9-month old] Gertrude, daughter of Jakob Pletts, of Blumenhof. Then Paul left and went to Johan Wiebes'.

The 17th, after *Vesper*, he helped Johann Barkmans.

The 18th, the service was here. The parents, Cornelius Pletts, Peter Pletts, Heinrich Pletts, Johann Janzens, Abraham Kornelsen, Jakob Dück, were here. From the 19th until *Vesper* they threshed at Burkowskis' and then to Krökers' until the 20th in the afternoon and then at our place: 182 bushels of wheat. The 21st, the barley, 22 bushels, and oats, only 3 loads [or] 80 bushels; [we threshed at our place] until the afternoon. Then at Johann Dücks' until the afternoon of the 22 until *Vesper*. Then to Peter Dücks' until the 23 until *Vesper*. ... The 24th repaired the fence. In the afternoon we hauled 3 loads of hay. The 25th, we drove to Blumenort to attend the service. In the afternoon we were at Jakob Wiebes'.

The 26th, we had 2 loads of hay. The 27th, we also had 2 [loads]. Peter Dück hauled 3 loads. The 28th, we had 2 and he also had 2 [loads]. The 29th, a strong wind. Then we had only 1 load.

The 30th, 2 [more loads]. Oct. 1 – also 2. 30 loads all told. The 30th of September, Cornelius Krökers went to *Jenn Seit*.

October 1892

On the 2nd of October, the service was here. Cornelius Pletts, Peter Reimers and Johann Friesens, of beyond Heuboden, were here visiting. In the evening we went to Peter Dücks'. The 3rd, we began to dig out potatoes and carrots. Father began to plough. The 4th, Krökers came back. The 5th, Johann Dück and Peter Dück went to Winnipeg.

The 8th, we were in Lichtenau visiting the old Mrs. Kornelsens'. He is very sick in bed. The 9th, we visited the parents in Blumenhof and Jakob Pletts'.

The 11th, the old Mrs. Kornelsen died.

The 11th, finished harvesting all vegetables and storing them.

The 13th, the funeral was held. We also went.

The 14th, it rained. The 16th, the service was here. The parents, Cornelius Pletts, Jakob Pletts, Peter Löwens and Peter Pletts and the old Cornelius Löwens were here as visitors. The night of the 16th to the 17th we had a severe thunder storm. The 17th, we had a big storm. On the 21st of October, we and the old Peter Barkmans went to *Jenn Seit*. The 27th we came back. At 5 o'clock we got to Johan Esaus' in Rosenort [?].

On the 27th, I turned 50. The 28th, Peter Dücks went as far as Grünfeld. The 29th, to *Jenn Seit*. We had our Katharina [Penner] to take care [of their children?]. On the 15th of October Klaas Friesen and Katharina Janzen had their *Verlobung* [engagement get-together]. The 23rd, they were married in Blumenort.

22 October, Dörksens' Bernhard and Helena Plett, of Blumenhof, had their *Verlobung*. The 30th they got married here in the service. For lunch they came here as visitors, as did their parents, Cornelius Pletts, and Peter Pletts and David Pletts and Ab. Pletts and the old Gerhard Schellenbergs and the old Johann Esaus and Johann Janzens, C. Pletts, Cornelius and Peter Reimers' Maria. In the evening we visited Cornelius Löwens.

November 1892

The 31st of October and the 1st of November, we hauled away the manure. Borkowski helped. The 2nd of November we slaughtered hogs at Johann Klaasens'. The 1st of November Elisabeth Braun died. She was 46 years old. The 4th we... The 5th, I mailed a letter to Nebraska. The 6th, Sunday and the night, [we] had snow and storm and frost. We did not have all of the cattle at home. The 7th, we got all of them at home. We had already gotten the weak [cattle] home on November 3 from Rosengart. The 9th, we slaughtered hogs at Cornelius Krökers'. The 10th, Cornelius Kröker and Joh. Dück went to Winnipeg. It was raining and snowing and blowing.... The 13th, it was snowing heavily. Only a few people in the service. The 15th, we slaughtered 2 hogs and 2 oxen. The 17th, Johan Dück, Peter Dück and Kröker went to Winnipeg. They took the oxen and hogs along. The 18th, we were in Blumenhof at Jakob Pletts', who slaughtered hogs. The oxen and the smallest hide netted $44.50, the hog $5.45. The 20th, heavily snowing in Winnipeg. The 21st, we slaughtered 10 roosters. The 22nd, Johann Dücks slaughtered 2 hogs and we 3 oxen. The 22, Johann..., Peter Dück and Kröker, Heinrich went to [?] Winnipeg. Heinrich had our 3 oxen..., and Johann Dück sold it with the hide for $55.40.

The 24th, we were at Cornelius Töwses'. The 25th, we slaughtered hogs at Cornelius Goossens'. It snowed all day. The 26th, snowing. The 27, the service was here. Cornelius Pletts and Jakob Dück were here for lunch. After lunch the old Peter Barkman and Johann Dück for *Vesper*. The 28th, Krökers again slaughtered a cow. Peter Dücks took a quarter of the meat for 3 cents. $11.50. The 29th, the children drove to Winnipeg. Kröker loaded the hind quarter of the cow and sold it for $11.35 and 2 hides for $3.00.

December 1892

The 1st of December the old Magaretha [Harder] visited us. The 3rd of December we slaughtered 4 ducks, one we sold for 54 cents to... The 4th, went to Peter and Abraham Pletts'. Took the parents along. The 8th [my brothers, Rev.] Peter [M.] Kröker and [*Ältester*] Jakob [M.] Kröker came [from *Jenn Seit*] as far as Grünfeld. On the 10th [they returned] home. The 11th, the service was here. The parents, Cornelius Pletts, Peter Reimers, Johann Klassens,

Abraham Plett and all children, and Jakob Dücks were our visitors. There was a funeral at Dahlkis'. His daughter had stumbled down and died 3 hours later. The 12th, the service and Brotherhood [meeting] was in Blumenort. The 13th, again [a] service. The 15th, they [Peter and Jacob Kröker?] went as far as Grünfeld. The 16th, [they went] home. It was very cold. The 17th, snowing heavily and blowing. The 16th, visited Wohlgemüts and Gerhard Dücks. The 18th, we visited the old Ennses'. The 20th, we slaughtered 2 hogs at Johann Dücks'. The 21st, he went to Winnipeg. From the 20th to the 21st [daughter-in-law Katherina was in labour and] at 3 o'clock Krökers received an infant son, Franz. The 24th, Jakob Rempels, of *Jenn Seit* came here. They stayed here 2 nights. Jakob Siemens came on the first holiday and stayed 2 nights. Peter Krökers' Peter and Jakob Krökers' David were here for the holidays. The 29th, we and Peter Dücks went to Blumenhof to Cornelius Pletts'. The parents came also.

The 30th, Krökers' Heinrich helped haul in 2 loads of hay. The 25th, the first holiday of Christmas, Cornelius Janzen and Agatha Friesens were married. The 31st, Koops' Peter and Schellenbergs' Magaretha had their *Verlobung*. The 31st, I mailed a letter to Nebraska.

16 Laura Shantz (1883 to 1969)

New Hamburg, Ontario

Diary selection: January to December 1918

Age: 34

Laura Shantz was born in 1883, the oldest child of Noah and Susannah (Cassel) Shantz. After completing elementary school, Laura remained in her parents' home, keeping the house and working on the farm. In 1899, at 16, she was baptised and joined the Blenheim Church. When she was 23, she was engaged to be married to Ezra Bergey, a local schoolteacher, but shortly after the engagement Ezra died of consumption. Five years later, Laura had another suitor, but he lost his life in a tragic sawmill accident. At the age of 36, on 5 November 1919, she was married to Tobias Shantz, a 45-year-old bachelor. Laura and Tobias moved to the town of Waterloo, where they renovated a large house. Although they had no children of their own, they became known as "Uncle" and "Aunt" to the children of their neighbours; moreover, their nieces and nephews stayed with them while attending Winter Bible School in town. Laura Shantz died in 1969 at 86.

Laura's diary is a rich record of the interaction of the kin and neighbours. Most frequently noted are members of her immediate family. She lived not only with "Ma" and "Pa," but with her brother Walter, who married Selina

Shirk of Bridgeport in 1920, and she lived with her sister Mary Ann Shantz, who travelled to Saskatchewan in November and who married Reuben Steiner the following year.

Other couples, invariably addressed by the male's first name, comprised a kinship network that was closely linked to the Shantz household. "Con's" is the household of Conrad Hable, a German Lutheran immigrant who had once worked for the Shantzes and after marrying Noah's niece came to be considered one of the family. "Eph," or "Uncle Eph," was Laura's uncle, Ephraim Cassel, who was married to Hannah Bricker. "Uncle Ezra's" refers to the household of Ezra M. Cressman (New Hamburg); he was the husband of Laura's aunt Louisa, Noah Shantz's sister. "Uncle Dave's" was the household of Dave Shantz, Noah's brother. Warren Bean was Noah's nephew. Curtis Cressman, who returned from college in Kansas in May, was the child of Noah's sister, Louisa. The Rosenbergers were neighbours and kin; Titus was married to Pa's niece and Menno to Pa's cousin. The Tohman family was related more distantly; 85-year-old Sam Tohman was only a second cousin to Laura's mother, but as an elderly neighbour he was referred to affectionately as "Doddy Tohman."

Laura also lived within a wider Mennonite community. There were church services. And there were tragedies. The person referred to as "Jane Doe" in this diary was an unwed Mennonite woman, who, after having indirectly caused her baby's death, was baptized in the Blenheim Mennonite Church in 1918, after having made a public confession and being assured of the community's and of God's forgiveness.

Laura's diary, however, is also a document of a growing interaction with a wider non-Mennonite world. Fred Miller, who married Ida Bergey, daughter of David Bergey, was not a Mennonite and went to France as a member of the Canadian armed forces (although it is said that he returned an avowed conscientious objector and joined the Blenheim Mennonite church); Sam Humphrey, who was one of the English "home boys" who had been given a home by a Waterloo Mennonite family, joined the Canadian army and left for overseas in July; Minnie Humphrey, who came to work for the Shantz household in January as a 16-year-old servant, was Sam's sister, who was baptised in the Blenheim Mennonite Church in July, shortly after seeing Sam off to Europe and before she endured spine surgery in Toronto and married a Mennonite, Clarence Weber; "Nurse," who took care of "Grandma," was Alice Smith, a medically trained person from Stratford, Ontario; Martha Frank was a non-Mennonite servant from the greater Waterloo community. A similar connection took Laura on her longest trip during this year: a June road trip to Painesville, Ohio, a town east of Cleveland, where her neighbour Nora Rosenberger's sister lived, having married a non-Mennonite American.

The original diary, handwritten in English, is in the possession of Lorna Bergey, Kitchener. Background information was provided by Mrs. Bergey. The diary was transcribed by Reg Good.

January 1918

Tuesday 1 Agnes Cressman was buried at Biehns [later, Nith Valley Mennonite Church].

Thursday 3 Ed. Hess started meetings at Geiger church [later, Wilmot Mennonite Church].

Saturday 5 Jake Schneider cut Straw here. Menno Shantz's baby died at Roseville, 11 mos old. Miss Alice Smith, Walter & I had last car ride to Stratford.

Sunday 6 Mr & Mrs Albert Smith, Peace River [Alberta], & Mr & Mrs J.C. Hallman called on us a few min. yesterday.

Monday 7 Gordon Hallman's a son.

Tuesday 8 Bible Conf. at Geigers.

Wednesday 9 Bible Conference at Geigers. Elmon Shantz married to Lizzie Roth.

Saturday 12 Severe blizzard. Joe Shantz was to Kitchener Market and couldn't get home till Sun. P.M. He walked from Manheim.

Sunday 13 Snow storm all day.

Monday 14 [Jane Doe's] baby girl almost frozen, [as it] was pitched out the window. Henry Roth came to help Walter cut wood here. First train thru Baden this eve after blizzard Sat. & Sunday.

Tuesday 15 Walter killed old Tom [a horse or a dog].

Wednesday 16 Marria Gofton married to Myrle Pogs. Benj Bowman came to thrash.

Sunday 20 Mrs. B. Bowman & Mr & Mrs T. Rosenberger here to dinner.

Monday 21 Harry Rothaernel to cut wood.

Tuesday 22 Linc went to Moffat to fetch Minnie Humphrey on 2 wk's trial.

Wednesday 23 Annie Good married Angus Eby. Mr & Mrs Geo Hoffman's here to dinner, Lizzie Hartman & U. Eph called this P.M.

Thursday 24 Henry & I were to Hamburg after dinner.

Friday 25 Grandma had hemorage this morn. Ben Bowman's thrashed from Wed. noon till Fri 5 o'cl. Gottfried Franke died 89 yrs 9 mo & 20 days.

Saturday 26 Grandma had hemorage this eve.

Sunday 27 Dr Gillespie was here. Walter & Miss Smith & I were to Tob's for dinner.

Wednesday 30 Eph's butchered 5 pigs, 1 for Mother Shantz. Mrs Elam Axt had operation at Kitchener Hosp. appendicittis.

Thursday 31 Pete Gingerich & Barbara Gasho married. Melvin Shuhs a son, the 3rd boy. Lincs butchered 3 pigs. Grandma had hemorage Last night. Our water pipes froze from tank to house today. Also rain water all.

February

Friday 1 Grandma had hemorage this morn & this P.M. again. Dr G. was here. 11 below zero. [Jane Doe's] baby died.

Sunday 3 Mary Tohman had operation for appendicitis was burst. Wesley Battler's scarlet fever.

Monday 4 Pa & Walter opened water pipes from Tank to house.

Tuesday 5 25 below zero this morn. Grandma had hemorage last night. Pa & I were to Baden to S.S. Cressmans.

Wednesday 6 "Buzzard cow," calf.

Thursday 7 Gordon Hamacher started this noon cut wood. Elmer Hess at Geigers this P.M. & Baden Mission this eve.

Saturday 9 Dr Gillespie & Dr Anderson consulted Grandma's case. Rained last night.

Sunday 10 U. Sam's & U. Dan Shantz's, Roy, Barbara & Ada Rosenberger here dinner. Mrs Adam Cassel died this morn. Dom. Aliance speaker at Blen[heim].

Monday 11 Mooly heifer calved.

Tuesday 12 Goldwin died this morn of convulsions. Israel Brubacher married Urias Martin. Leafy started work at Eph's yesterday.

Wednesday 13 Orph Hofstettlers sale yesterday. Christ Gasho's sale today.

Thursday 14 Very mild. Goldwin's funeral. Annie Hastings buried at Hamburg. Thunderstorm & heavy rain this eve. Alvin Snider married at Kossuth.

Sunday 17 Lincs & Minnie here to dinner & Eph's yet for tea, Christ Schrag preached at Blen. A.M. Elvin Shantz has mumps & Mose B. congestion of the lungs at Kitchener.

Monday 18 Elmer Shantz & Arthur Snider came to cut wood this morn. Fine day. Geo Milne's a daug., "Alice Lousie".

Tuesday 19 Rained all day, high water.

Wednesday 20 (First lamb. 2 more). Cold & windy. Pa fetched 1/4 beef at Mervyn Becthel. Roads very icy.

Thursday 21 Mr & Mrs Alvin Cressman's, Ceylon, Sask. visited here to dinner. Arthur & Elmer went home this eve. 4 below zero this morn.

Friday 22 Took out 7 heifers to Baden. Dr Gillespie put me to Bed for 1 wk.

Saturday 23 Minnie came over for 1 wk.

Sunday 24 Mr. & Mrs Geo Hallman & Mr & Mrs Israel Cressman here [for] dinner. Lincs & Eph's called.

Monday 25 John Seiberts sale at Lexington. Cloudy, & severe high wind by eve & all night, took corner of Christ[ian] Rosenbergers barn roof.

Tuesday 26 Dave Shuh's sale.

Wednesday 27 Mary Tohman had 2nd operation. Young Howling stole cigars & money from Till at Kavelmans store & caught this eve.

Thursday 28 Uncle Eph Cassel sold his farm for $7,500.

March

Friday 1

Saturday 2 Herman Shantz had operation for appendicitis. Walter had sore ear.

Sunday 3 Dr. Gillespie ordered me out of bed. Stauffer & Minnie were to Norman's to dinner.

Monday 4 Ida Bergey married Fred Miller, Toronto. Uncle Sam Cassel was here to dinner. Johny Stauffer's boy was killed in bush cutting down tree.

Tuesday 5 Eli Weber's sale.

Wednesday 6 Ada Rosenberger & David, & Mr & Mrs Titus Rosenberger's & Annie Bowman & Mary Ann Shantz left for Guernsey Sask.

Friday 8 Minnie came to clean & help wash on monday.

Monday 11 Minnie was here to help wash. Walter had 2nd bunch of little pigs in oven this morn.

Tuesday 12 Nurse & I were to Edna's quilting.

Wednesday 13 Mrs Jacob Hunspergers sale of stock & implements.

Thursday 14 Tellphone wires broke. Severe ice storm broke off 3 big limbs poplar tree in yard. Landreth Bingemans moved to Christ Cressman's [and] Elias Bingeman's [moved] on Landreth's [farm?].

Friday 15 Ice still on the trees & cold. Boys putting harness together in washhouse after greasing. Pa was to Aaron Bender's sale.

Saturday 16 Ice still on trees, milder. Pa was to Aaron Bender's sale. Grandma came downstairs this P.M. first time, Dr Gillespie called before dinner.

Sunday 17 Walter & Nurse & I were to Morris Gofton's to tea. U. Eph's here dinner, Ma had sick headache.

Monday 18 Pa & Linc were to Urias Nahrgangs sale. Grandma weighed 118, Ma 154, Nurse 161, Laura 144. Elvin Shantz left for West to Manitoba.

Tuesday 19 Men tapped. Leafy was here to help wash. Arthur Lautenschlager's cow sale. Elmon Shantz's a daughter.

Wednesday 20 Dave Hillgartners sale at Wilmot Centre. Fred Miller, Ida's [husband], went to Halifax & on to England.

Thursday 21 Mose Groff's sale.

Friday 22 Mose H. Shantz's sale fine day. Mr & Mrs John Seibert came for the night. Pa took 10 head of cattle out to Baden.

Sunday 24 Eph's here to dinner, had taffy [candy made from maple syrup]. Lincs & Minnie & Joshua Shantz's here to tea. Mary Tohman's nurse, Miss Moranda Master's left.

Monday 25 Washed; fine day. Nurse & I went out to see Linc boil syrup in bush.

Tuesday 26 Cold. Harry Copler's sale. Moses H. Shantz's moved to Baden.

Wednesday 27 Fine but cold. Mr. Veitch to Gertie Freed. [Reverend] Oscar Burkholder [of Breslau Church] married Mary Reesor. U. Eph's sale today. Miss Alice Smith left for Stratford this noon. Amos Good's moved on M. Groff's farm.

Thursday 28 Sam Tohman's 85th birthday with best of health. Stella Schweitzer has mumps. Geo Schmidt's [of] Upper Str. a son.

Friday 29 Uncle Isaac Bricker was here to dinner. Good Friday, fine day.

Saturday 30 Mose H. Shantz's here to tea. Mrs Levi Shantz died at Baden.

Sunday 31 Mary Stauffer & Vera & Lorne R. here to dinner. Mr & Mrs Dave Bergey & Herb & Ida here to tea. Mrs Peter Nafziger died, Noah Snider's at Waterloo a son.

April

Monday 1 Mrs Levi Shantz's funeral at Baden, rained.

Tuesday 2 Hamburg horse show. Uncle Eph's moved to Hamburg in Grandma's house. Apr 3rd, fine day.

Wednesday 3 Aunt Annies sale at Dundee.

Thursday 4

Friday 5 Martha Frank came out this eve, untill Monday morn. Angus Martin's baby buried.

Saturday 6 Grandma weighed 128 lbs.

Sunday 7 Martha, Frank, [and] Edith Rosenberger, Lila Pfohl, & Mrs Adolph Hofstetter here dinner & tea.

Monday 8 Men took sap buckets in, worked on land first day. Sam Humphrey sick. Pearl went home to make coat. I had 1st treatment at Dr Gillespies.

Tuesday 9 Minnie was here help wash. Stauffer was sick in bed. 2nd treatment.

Wednesday 10 Baden horse show. East wind. Walter took load of pigs out to Baden. Cleaned atic [attic] today

Thursday 11 3rd treatment. Addis Cressman's a daughter. Wilfred Lashinger died at home 21 yrs old.

Friday 12 I was to call on Mary Tohman & is still in bed.

Saturday 13 Lincs cattle & our 4 steers & roan heifer left. 4th treatment. Pa & Ma were to Kitchener, [to] U. Sam's [for] dinner & to Eliab Betzner's to tea. Creamery team knocked U. Dan Shantz out of his buggy at Baden.

Sunday 14 Aunt Mary & Rebecca here dinner. Percy Weicker here to tea. Abram Good's a son.

Tuesday 16 5th treatment.

Wednesday 17 Rained all day & damp. Mary Klinkman drowned herself in woods.

Thursday 18 Pa & I were to Hamburg. Cleaned Shanty & scrubbed big porch. Snowing.

Friday 19 6th treatment. Ground white with snow. Mrs (Barbara Cressman) Magus, died at Guernsey, Sask. G. Hanley returned from war. I set 3 hens in corn crib this eve.

Saturday 20 Pa fetched new Ford.

Sunday 21 Walter & Stauffer & I were to Abram's to dinner after S.S. (Ma had severe neuralgia). Rained. Mary Gimbel died 9 o'cl this eve.

Monday 22 Mrs. Irvine Gimbel died 2 o'cl this morn at David Gimbel's. Eph's bot rocking chair from Grandma for $1.00.

Tuesday 23 Snowed & cold this eve.

Wednesday 24 7th treatment. Sybilla & I went to Breslau to Gimbel's funeral. At Andrew Bender's to dinner & Sam Schweitzers tea. Still cold.

Thursday 25 Scrubbed church at Blen. Boiled soap this morn. Old Ruben stopped here 1st time. I got a flower slip at Sim's.

Friday 26 Set 1 hen in corn crib.

Saturday 27 8th treatment. Dr Gillespie was down to see Mary Tohman, again.

Sunday 28 Communion Sunday at Blen. We called at U. Eph's for dinner. Will Oberer's 2 yrs old son buried at Waterloo, from Allan Hallman.

Monday 29 Allan Cassel left for Toronto this morning. Pa & Con & Andrew Calannan [?] were to Brantford in new car. Rained this eve.

Tuesday 30 Mrs. Jake Schweitzer died at Hosp. Mrs. Hamacher helped wash & churn, rained. Men finished seeding, replanted Chesnut trees to lane.

May

Wednesday 1 Pa & Walter, Linc & Eph motored to shorthorn cattle sale at Seaforth. Gotlieb dug garden this P.M. Set brooding hen [on eggs in] corn crib. Henry Schlichters twins girl & boy Apr. 30.

Thursday 2 9th treatment. Dr. G. was here from Heimpels to examine Ma, & found pleurisy. Minnie ironed & helped clean storeroom. Con's bot Maxwell car.

Friday 3 Pa fetched Lightheart repair water wheel this morn. Pa & Linc went to Kitchener for seed corn at Eidts & fertilizer for Linc's beets.

Saturday 4 Kate a colt.

Sunday 5 10th treatment. Grandma weighed 136 lbs., Ma 157, I 144. Quite warm. Cherry calf. Mr & Mrs Allan Becthel & his mother called on Grandma.

Monday 6 Will Egerdee started new roof on Linc's silo.

Tuesday 7 Rained.

Wednesday 8 11th treatment. Mrs G. Hamacher & Lizzie Hartman & Leah Hunsperger cleaned upstairs.

Thursday 9 Ascension day. Mrs. Toby Bowman died. Pa took Ben's to Kitchener this morn. Ma had severe headache in bed & also next day.

Friday 10 Oiled Kitchen floor.

Saturday 11 12th treatment. Gib Wallace died. 45 yrs old. Took out 30 chicks from corn crib. Planted onion seeds & beans by cherry tree. Leafy's 20th birthday.

Sunday 12 Rainy. Isaac Bingeman died this eve. Eph's here to tea.

Monday 13 Fine day. Pa & Geo went to Gib Wallaces funeral & I called at Mary Tohman's. Set 6 hens. Still in bed.

Tuesday 14 Fine. Leah helped wash woollens. Grandma went to U. Eph's.

Wednesday 15 Leah helped wash. Isaac Bingeman's funeral.

Thursday 16 Ma & I washed slips & mats. Pa's 59th birthday.

Friday 17 Pa fetched I[saac] Lightheart for Linc's pump & ours also till noon.

Saturday 18 Rubens arrived this morn from Bluffton & Montana. Mrs. Menno S. went West. Jacob Schweitzer burried clipped sheep. 13th treatment.

Sunday 19 Mr & Mrs Clayton Scheifley here to dinner & Linc's & Minnie.

Tuesday 21 Rubens & Eph's & we all but Pa were to Guelph sale. Bot Stauffer's suit. Rubens's stayed at E. Betzner's.

Wednesday 22 Sam Humphrey had to report at London.

Thursday 23 Pa & Ma fetched Rubens at Kitchener & called at Uncle Noah Stauffers. Auntie had sick spell day before.

Friday 24 Pa & Ma & Rubens visited at U. Moses to dinner & U. Ezra's to tea.

Saturday 25 14th treatment & last for a while. Curtis [Cressman] arrived home, Hesston [College, Kansas]. John Seiberts came for the night. Lady a colt this eve.

Sunday 26 Rained. Rubens called at U. Dan's & to Linc for tea.

Monday 27 Rubens called at U. Dan Cressman's & fitted Rubens suit at Lederman's.

Wednesday 29 Ruben left for Ohio.

June

Saturday 1 Weston Bowman's a son Mich.

Sunday 2 David Garber's meetings at Blenheim church. We were to Rev. Stevens meetings. Jack Frances a daughter "Violet".

Tuesday 4 Pearl [Linc's wife] took pneumonia & Dr. called every morn for 1 wk.

Thursday 6 Blen. conference 1 day. Mrs Landreth Bingeman died.

Saturday 8 Joshua Heintz burried.

Sunday 9 Wanda Hostettlers funeral. Noah Webers & Abr. Sniders here to dinner. Emanuel & Eph Schmidts here to tea.

Thursday 13 Nora R. Scheifle & I left Ayr this morn for Painesville, Ohio.

Saturday 15 Cloise's motered us to Cleveland, Elma & Nora [Rosenberger to visit Nora's sister] & I on Sunday morn.

Sunday 16 David Garber closed meetings at Blenheim. Urias Nahrgangs here all day.

Wednesday 19 Nora & I went to Cleveland by Trolley.

Friday 21 Nora & I left Painesville for home, & I stayed at Ab's in Kitchener all night.

Saturday 22 Registration day. Card No. 73-6-81. We were to Kitchener to Rev. C.F. Derstines meetings.

Sunday 23 Old Madter burried at Blenheim. We took Marian to Betzners for tea. Called at Goods & Martha.

Monday 24 Virgil was sick from toothache in bed 2 days. Minnie Humphrey's [foster child from England] 17th birthday.

Tuesday 25 (Virgil was to Dr. Winn, Wed. Morn.) Oscar Martins a son, Roy Franklin Martin.

Thursday 27 Marian & Virgil & Mar . . . left for Big Timber this P.M. from Bright, Ont.

Sunday 30 Pa & Ma visited at Warren Bean's & Menno Nahrgang's (thunderstorm). Mr & Mrs Amos Shantz & son Leslie & Mrs Malinda Shantz & daughter Viola of Kitchener came in for the night.

July

Monday 1 Shantz Family dinner at U. Mose Cressman's. U. David Shantz's arrived from West [Didsbury, Alberta]. Sam Weber's & Sol. Sniders came for the night.

Thursday 4 I planted beans in little orchard.

Friday 5 Walter caught swarm of bees in the field.

Saturday 6 Uncle Dave's came this eve.

Sunday 7 Tob's & Walter & I visited Sherk's at Bridgeport, & Sam Schweitzer. Dave Bingeman & Judith & 2 sons were here to dinner. [Baptism] Instruction meetings at Blen.

Tuesday 9 Walter took U. Daves to W. Erb's this eve.

Wednesday 10 Herb Kropf's a daughter Ruth Eileen Kropf.

Friday 12 Hubert Sherks' took Minnie along to London Camp, as Sam left for England this eve.

Sunday 14 Walter & Stauffer & Minnie & I were to instruction meeting at Mannheim & Mannassah Hallman's dinner.

Thursday 18 Minnie Humphrey had xray Examination by Dr Gillespie on her spine. I varnished oil cloth in 2 rooms.

Saturday 20 Pa & Ma fetched U. Dave's at Aunt Mary A's & had dinner at Abram Good's & to Bethel C[hurch] in the afternoon.

Sunday 21 Pa shot skunk at chickens last night. Stauffer & Minnie were baptized at Blen C. today. All were to Bethel church. U. Dave preached. Very warm & dry.

Monday 22 Pa & Ma took U. Daves to Joh Seiberts.

Tuesday 23 Pa took Lincs & Minnie to Kitchener this P.M. & had been to Hamburg & Baden this A.M.

Wednesday 24 Wes Wolf's barn struck & burnt. Minnie left at Baden for Peterboro[ugh] Hosp. this P.M. Severe thunder storm. Mr & Mrs Eliab [?] & Mrs Joe Steiner & Mr. & Mrs Calvin Geigers here to tea.

Thursday 25 Cut first wheat yesterday afternoon. Rudy Gingerich's team ran away with hay wagon yesterday P.M. & hurt him.

Saturday 27 George Hoffman died this eve 62 yrs old.

Tuesday 30 Geo Hoffman's funeral. Sara Seibert came with us until Friday.

Wednesday 31 U. Daves came here this noon also Mr & Mrs Dan Stauffer & Ruby for tea.

August

Thursday 1 Mr & Mrs John Hoffman & Mrs Christ Shantz here to dinner & then called at Simeon's & up to Ben Bowman's tea. Old Rudy Gingerich died.

Friday 2 U. Daves called here this P.M. with U. Daves rig. Then Pa took them to Aunt Mary A's after tea.

Saturday 3 144 lbs. Mr & Mrs Jacob Shantz & his sisters Mrs Weber & Mrs Snider here to tea.

Sunday 4 Mrs. Henry Rohr died this noon. David Christner took Uncle Dave Shantz's to Hanover today to visit Mr Perchbacker's.

Monday 5 Eph's & Walter & Mabel Weber, Genevieve & Ruth Betzner, Maggie Shantz & Ada Sherk & we went to the River to dine. Civic holiday. "Very warm."

Tuesday 6 Ford Wilson married Jennie Good.

Wednesday 7 Pa & Ma & Maggie Hoffman & I went to Mrs H. Rohr's funeral, Clarence Hallman married to a Miss Russel. Roy Hewitts barn burnt by thrashing machine this P.M.

Thursday 8 Very warm & dry, but had rain this P.M.

Friday 9 Pa & Ma & U. Dan's were to Uncle Moses to spend the eve with U. Dave Shantz's.

Saturday 10 Uncle Sam & Eph took Grandma Cassel to Baden to Adolph Hofstetters. Uncle Moses took U. Dave's to Dilman Erb's.

Sunday 11 Lincs & Walter & I visited Oscar Martins to dinner.

Tuesday 13 Wesley Wolfe's raised new barn today.

Wednesday 14 Ben's thrashed 1/2 day & broke seperator at noon. Anson Hallman married to Esther Shantz.

Thursday 15 Thrashed here this forenoon at Linc's afternoon & engine leaked, had to start again next day. Sow has 8 pigs in sheep pen.

Friday 16 Pa & Ma were up to Dilman Erb's this P.M. to see U. Dave's again.

Saturday 17 U. Dave's leave for their home by boat to Calgary, Alta.

Sunday 18 Old Mrs Sam Hallman died this morn. Pa & Ma were at D. Sniders & Joshua's. Walter & I at Vera Rosenbergers's to dinner.

Monday 19 Mose[s] H. Shantz was operated for appendicitis at Hosp. last eve., had preached at Blen church in the morn. Norman Kropf's a son.

Tuesday 20 Pa & I brot U. Eph's to haul oats. Went to Mrs Sam Hallman's funeral at Blen.

Wednesday 21 U. Eph helped haul in Oats all day & Aunt H. helped peel onions for pickling. Junia Shantz married Clara Bectel.

Thursday 22 Put Grandma's room down. Pa took U. Eph's home this morn had rain yest eve.

Friday 23 Minnie came back from Toronto & Peterborrow [Peterborough]. We thrashed this P.M. U. Sam brot Grandma this P.M. from Susan Adolph's.

Saturday 24 Alice Smith came this eve. Mrs. Noah Snider, "Leak" Bowman, burried at Hagey's Ch[urch, later Preston Mennonite Church] this P.M.

Sunday 25 Walter & Stauffer & Nurse & I motored to see Roy Hewitts & I[saac] Battlers remains of barn's. Grandma weighed 124.

Tuesday 27 Sam came on 6 wks harvest leave, from Brockville Camp. Sewing circle at Dave Bergey's. Nurse went to Eph's.

Thursday 29 Walter Hostettler's a son.

Friday 30 Dr Bock [veterinarian] was up to see Billy [the horse] & said was paralized.

September

Sunday 1 Clint Habel was here to tea. Ada Burkholder came from Y.P.M. at Blen[heim Church?].

Monday 2 Baden S.S. Conf. in Tabernacle. Amos Shantz's came for the night from Waterloo. Melvin Bear's a son Elmer Russell.

Tuesday 3 Aaron S. Bowman's a son.

Wednesday 4 Mrs. Peter Bricker died 60 yrs. Barbara Cressman & Linda Becker & I went to Toronto Ex[hibition?] this morn for 2 days & were at Irvine Witmers, ...McKenzie Cresent.

Thursday 5 Vera Hallman [Roseville] left for [Hesston College,] Hesston, Kansas.

Friday 6 We filled dry house apples. Pearl & Minnie helped.

Saturday 7 Ma was sick all day.

Sunday 8 Jake Schmidts, Eph Sniders, Herman Shantz's, & Dady Reist here to tea.

Monday 9 Eph's filled our dry house. Minnie was to see Dr. Gillespie.

Tuesday 10 Pa & I & Pearl & Minnie were to see Dr. Wardlaw at Galt. Mrs Will Sherk died at Galt Hosp. this morn. A.D. Schmidt came & 3 men for the night and put new rods on barn till noon or 4 o'cl.

Wednesday 11 Eph's were here fetch snitz [dried apples]. "Jew dress goods peddler here."

Thursday 12 Minerva & I were to Mrs. Will Sherk's funeral, rained all day. Dr. Bock was here again yester.

Friday 13 Boys 4 First prizes for calves at Hamburg show.

Saturday 14 Pa bot honey, 30 lbs at Facey's. Boys sawed wood at Linc's. Mose[s] Hostettler bot 4 lambs at $15 & also "Dave" [the] Bull for $150.00.

Sunday 15 Pa & Ma visited at Joe's for tea.

Monday 16 Boys sawed wood here 1/2 day. U. Sam brot plums for elderberries. Ab Gingerichs at Elmira a daugh. Mrs. Fred Frank died this eve 146 Water St. Kitchener.

Tuesday 17 Filled dry house 2nd time.

Wednesday 18 Bell Co. put new Batteries in Linc's & Moses were to Vineland for peaches at $1.10. basket.

Thursday 19 Pa bot coal oil heater. Boys finished saw wood also Mrs. Geo H. is thrashing. First Singing school this eve. Pa took Minnie to Kitchener Hosp. for operation on spine.

Friday 20 Minnie had operation today.

Saturday 21 Mrs Oliver Bergey burried at Dundee.

Sunday 22 Lincs were here dinner Pa & Ma went to Norman's [for] tea.

Tuesday 24 Sara Seibert came out to help us this wk. Eph's filled our dry house.

Wednesday 25 Lincs thrashed all day, finished.

Thursday 26 Lincs filled silo.

Friday 27 We filled silo. 2nd eve Singing Class [at] Blen[heim Church].

Saturday 28 Percy Weicker & Olive Kalbfleich married & went to Sask for trip. Eph's filled silo after dinner. John & Wesley came out for Sara. Jesse Clemons died this eve New Dundee.

Sunday 29 Communion at Blen. Noah Cressman & Mary Gingerich here dinner & Noah Snider & Annie Snider here tea.

Monday 30 Walter Kraatz died of influenza near Petersburg. 19 years old. John B. Biehn died at Port Huron Mich. 59 yrs. old.

October

Tuesday 1 First heavy frost this morn. Took up potatoes in truck patch.

Wednesday 2 Sewing Circle at Ed Witmers. School Fair at Haysville.

Friday 4 Minnie came to Moses from Hosp. 3 singing class. Linc's fill silo & Bing's also.

Saturday 5 Mrs Allan Heist burried at Kitchener 49 yrs old.

Sunday 6 Pa & Ma were to Sim's dinner & U. Dans for supper.

Monday 7 Mrs Webourne Doeer died of Spanish Influenza. 26 yrs old & her husband also the next day. (Mrs) Daniel Martin burried at Conestoga, (Mary Hoffman).

Tuesday 8 We filled dry house. St. L. [?].

Wednesday 9 We washed. I had treatment at Dr Gillespie. Minnie came home from Moses this eve.

Thursday 10 Old Ben Shoemaker died at Kitchener. Fred Helfer died at K. & W. Hos. 26 yrs. old, & wife very sick. We filled dry house, St. L. [?].

Friday 11 C. Beckman's son-in-law buried. Christ Rosenberger's filled silo. 4th singing class. Irvine K. Weber sick with Spanish flue & Irene.

Saturday 12 Mose B. Shantz & his mother came home from West. Dr Gillespie sick in bed. Clinton Shantz very sick with Spanish flu. Also Vina Mose [married to Moses B. Shantz] Plattsville, baker, quite [sick].

Sunday 13 Pa & Ma & Grandma had dinner at Betz, & called at Doddy Tohman's. Walter & I had dinner at Abram Cressman's with Christ Habel.

Monday 14 Thanksgiving Day. Clinton Shantz died 21 yrs old at Waterloo of Influenza. Alvin J Forler of Baden died of "flu" at West Minster.

Wednesday 16 Abram C. Hallman died 60 yrs. Fell down thru silo day before. Alfred H. Ratz to Florence A. Zoeller. Wesley Spaetzel married to Nellie Edna Wildfong, Doon.

Thursday 17 Edna took sick. Boiled apple butter at noon & I went to Eph's, Sara Seibert came out.

Friday 18 Another batch this morn. 5th singing class. Eph took sick also. Albert Cousins of Avonbank died of "flu," 26 yrs old.

Sunday 20 I came home from Eph's sick this noon.

Monday 21 Elmer Hallman married Miss Forester of Sask this wk.

Tuesday 22 Word was recieved of the death of Pte Elgin Eby in Action overseas 71 Battalion machine gun section.

Wednesday 23 Mrs Dr Brodrecht died of flue at Spokane, Wash. Uncle Mose Cressman fell from wagon & apple barrel on his head.

Thursday 24 Ralph Shantz died at Calgary 29 yrs old leaving wife & 3 children. Mrs Harold Perkins Rush died. Mrs Wm Loehr died of "flu" 33 yrs 20 days.

Friday 25 No singing class cause of flu. Had 14 crocks of applebutter boiled at Baden & for Lincs. Sam Alderfer died. Pa.

Saturday 26 Pa & Linc fetched cattle at Dave Hunspergers.

Sunday 27 Was in bed all wk got up today. Henry Pfohls all in bed & Allan Hallman's also. Pa & Ma were to see Mose. Norman Kropf was out to see for potatoes apples – butter & etc.

Monday 28 Dr R.W. Faulds died at Elmira 36 yrs of influenza. Mrs. Kate Oliver died at Leander Cressman's 66 yrs old.

Tuesday 29 Lawrence Bingeman took sick.

Wednesday 30 Mrs Dan Wismer died 81 yrs old. Miss Alice Smith came from Dr Hagemeyers, to sleep this P.M.

Thursday 31 Nurse called at Eph's this P.M. & to Dr Gillespies tea. Dr. Gillespie was down to see Minerva again this eve.

November

Friday 1 Linc has sore throat. No Sing Class yet. Charles Stuart's barn burnt early this morn west of Plattsville. Had apple molasses boiled.

Saturday 2 Linc's sugar beet car at Baden yesterday. Pa, Walter & Stauffer hauling beets, Linc is sick.

Sunday 3 Walter & Stauffer were to S.S. again this morn. Lawrence Bingeman was in bed all wk got up today. I, 142 [pounds], M[a] 150, Grandma 134 lbs., St [?] 121 lbs.

Monday 4 Dr Morrison calls at Pfohls ever day till Sat. Marian & Margaret have flu this wk.

Tuesday 5 We washed.

Wednesday 6 Mary Roth died of flu at Haysville, 20 yrs old. We filled dry house last time.

Thursday 7 Mrs Herb Hallman died in Sask. of flu. Pa was to Kitchener apples & potatoes for Norman K. & Marth.

Friday 8 Peace declared on trial for 48 hrs yesterday noon. No Singing class.

Saturday 9 Clayton Shantz Carstairs Alta. died this eve. Mr & Mrs Jno Seiberts came this noon. (Hunters in bush.)

Sunday 10 Pa & Ma & John's were at Abram Cressman's dinner & Joshua's for tea.

Monday 11 Peace declared. Kaiser went to Holland. Sara cleaned Kitchen upstairs.

Wednesday 13 Sara & Lizzie cleaned Kitchen.

Thursday 14 Mrs. Jesse Clemens sale. Mr. & Mrs D.K. Erb & son John & Grandma Erb & Mrs Lizzie Hilborn dinner here. . . .

Friday 15 Bessie Rosenberger died of flu at Guernsey Sask 25 yrs less 2 days. Mr & Mrs Edwin Daniels & Mrs R. Puddicombe & Robert called this P.M. No singing class.

Saturday 16 Walter took Sara & Wesley to their home & Minnie to H. Sherk's. Elvin & John came home from West.

Sunday 17 Rained most all day. Pa & Ma were to see U. Moses. Pa & Ma were to Con[rad Hable's, a German Lutheran and former employee of the Shantz] to tea.

Monday 18 Isaac Becthel died of weak heart. Ma bot shirting at Dundee 46.4 yd. Linc clipped Jim [the horse].

Tuesday 19 Blen Sewing Circle here.

Wednesday 20 Lucinda Becthel.

Friday 22 Judith Shantz died of flu at Carstairs Alberta. 7th singing class.

Saturday 23 Celina Shantz had operation at Hosp. for appendicitis, Kitchener. Walter took "Billy" to Burschatzkis.

Sunday 24 We called at U. Eph's this P.M. Aunt Hannah is at Toronto yet.

Monday 25 Started thrashing here this noon.

Tuesday 26 Fine day.

Wednesday 27 Finished thrashing by 2.30 o'clock. Sandy Fraser & U. Eph called here. 8th singing class.

Friday 29 9th singing class.

Saturday 30 Pa & St. took 2 loads lambs to Bright. Eph's thrashed all day.

December

Sunday 1 Pa & Ma & I were at Eph's roast.

Monday 2 Aaron Bender repaired engine all day at Eph's.

Tuesday 3 Sewing Circle at S. Sniders. Eph's finished thrashing this P.M.

Wednesday 4 10th sing class.

Thursday 5 Pa & I & Linc's were to see Sugar factory Kitchener

Friday 6 Sam Rohr died, 86 yrs old. Orkney (Cressman) Shuh died of flu. 11th Sing class.

Saturday 7 Pa took 2 baby beefs to Bright. Lily a calf this eve.

Sunday 8 Pa & Ma were at Con's 21st anniversary dinner. Breslau Conf starts, S.F. Derstine instructor.

Monday 9 Very fine day. Mrs Elroy Hawes died at Ayr.

Tuesday 10 Cold east wind & rain & icy by eve. Mose Hostettler died. Linc took 20 old hens to Plattsville, 113 lbs. Pa & Ma went to Waterloo Conference. R.L. Hartzler & Geo J. Lapp instructors.

Wednesday 11 Rain & fog. Stauffer went to Guelph show. Mrs Oscar Sweitzer died of flu. Jessie Mcdonald died of flu. No sing class.

Thursday 12 Con's butchered 4 pigs.

Friday 13 Rained. No sing[ing] school. Emery, Mary Ann & Annie came home from Sask. Mose Hostettlers funeral, 31 yrs 9 mo.

Saturday 14 Ada Brunk died of flu.

Sunday 15 Roy Cressman died in Alta & barried at Breslau today. Mose Bears here to dinner.

Monday 16 Fine day, we butchered. Manassah Shantz's a son.

Tuesday 17 Fine day. Washed. Postponed Bean Conf., "flu". (Minerva Cressman had accident. Coach burned near Fort William.) Herb Brunk died of flu.

Wednesday 18 Willie Bergey, Eldon Snider sick flu. No sing[ing] school.

Thursday 19 Baden Conf. postponed, flu. Minnie has flu this morn.

Friday 20 Brindlle a calf.

Saturday 21 Stauffer did chores for Linc yest & today, sick. Rained.

Sunday 22 Cloudy. Hannah & Isaac Snider have flu. Pa & Ma & I called at Ben B's. Tob sick in bed also Christ Leidty. Layton very sick, pneumonia.

Wednesday 25 Roy & Milford have flu.

Thursday 26 Linc's here, goose roast.

Friday 27 Ben's thrashed this P.M. Nurse & I called at Edna's.

Saturday 28 Called Dr Anderson for Grandma, but not serious. Clarence Shantz burried at Kitchener, died of flue 22 yrs old.

Sunday 29 Ben Bowman's & Menno Rosenberger's here to dinner. Mrs Jake Karcher died at Mose Tohman's.

Monday 30 Nurse & I called at Mrs. Dr. Gillespie.

Tuesday 31 Old Mrs. Goettling died. Old Mrs. Poth's funeral.

17 Maria Reimer Unger (1875 to 1955)
Blumenhof, Manitoba
Diary selection: 1 January to 31 December 1919
Age: 43

Maria Reimer was born in Blumenort, Manitoba, to Peter and Maria (Plett) Reimer just a year after the 1874 migration to Manitoba. Maria was the eldest of seven surviving children from Peter's second marriage. Peter and Maria Reimer were successful farmers, and Peter was a minister in the Kleine Gemeinde Church. In 1895, at the age of 19, Maria married 28-year-old Johann F. Unger, who came from a poorer family in the neighbouring district of Blumenhof. Just 10 and half months after their marriage, their first child, Maria Jr., was born. By the time Maria was 43, she had given birth to 13 children.

After their marriage, Maria and Johann established a small farm in the Blumenhof district. In 1904, however, they purchased a much larger farm from Johann's uncle and aunt, Gottlieb and Helena (Friesen) Jahnke, who moved to Herbert, Saskatchewan. By 1906, the Ungers had a sizeable farm, with 95 cultivated acres and six milk cows. In 1915, they purchased another quarter-section when a neighbour, Aron W. Reimer and his family, joined a Mennonite migration to Texas. Their farm now included 205 cultivated acres and 12 cows. They lived on this farm until Johann's death in 1938. After assisting her third-eldest daughter, Elisabeth, and her husband, Isaak F. Loewen, to take over the family farm, Maria married widower Heinrich Brandt of Morris. When he died in 1942, Maria returned to the Blumenort district and lived on a few acres of bushland where Blumenort, the trade centre, was later established. She lived there until her death in 1955.

By 1919, the year of this diary, Maria and Johann had come to represent a prominent Blumenhof-district farm family. As the diary notes, both Maria and Johann were active in the community; Johann was the local Mennonite *Brandschulz* [fire-insurance agency commissioner] and Maria was a respected midwife. Their eldest daughter, Maria, was a single schoolteacher who lived at home occasionally (she married local farmer Peter F. Wiebe in March 1920). Justina was married to Peter K. Dueck, the son of *Aeltester* Peter R. Dueck of Steinbach (see diary 14), and lived close to her in-laws, south of Steinbach, but continued to visit her parents regularly, an event usually designated in Maria's diary as a visit from "Peter Duecks." Sons Johann Jr. and Peter, 17 and 13 respectively, handled many of the heavy chores on the farm. Daughters Elisabeth, 19, Anna, 16, and Tina, 14, assisted their mother at every turn, both with housekeeping and with the work of the farm. Finally, there were the five younger children, ages 10 years to one year – Sahra, Lena, Cornelius, Abraham, and Greta – who were mentioned less frequently in Maria's diary.

Maria Unger lived in a tightly knit community, ordered by the congregational boundaries of the Kleine Gemeinde Church. It was an identity that she cherished, even employing the term "uncle" to identify church leaders. And on Sundays, when the rotating church services were held in Blumenort, the regional church district to which Blumenhof belonged, the Ungers hosted many couples from within the wider congregation, most of whom were not close kin. Such congregational networks alerted her to the news of death, illness, marriage, and birth in Blumenort, Steinbach, Gruenfeld, and Rosenort. Only occasionally were other Mennonite churches mentioned. One exception in 1919 was the allusion on 9 March to *Aeltester* Wahl, an Old Colonist Mennonite, who was preaching in Steinbach. Another exception was the close relationship the Ungers had with the family of Gottlieb and Helena Jahnke, who had joined the Chortitzer Mennonite Church after Gottlieb married his deceased wife's sister in 1877, an act forbidden by the Kleine Gemeinde until 1913. Maria recorded Helena's ("the dear aunt Mrs. Jahnke") death on September 8.

As in most of the diaries reproduced in this volume, kinship lines were even more important than were church lines. Hog-butchering bees, such as the one held on 23 January, brought together only relatives: Peter P. Reimer, Abraham P. Reimer, Cornelius P. Reimer, and Johann P. Reimer were Maria's brothers; Heinrich Plett was her brother-in-law, the husband to her half-sister Elisabeth; Peter Unger was the brother of Johann, Maria's husband; Peter U. Dueck was the husband of her daughter Justina. Kinship ties also linked Maria via Johann's mother, Justina Friesen Unger, to Adolf Jahnkes, Uncle Radinzel, "Aunt Mrs. Peter Plett," "Mrs. Klaas F. Penner, and "Aunt Broesche" (Broesky). Maria was linked by Johann's paternal side to his brothers, Cornelius F. and Peter F. Unger, both local farmers with families of 12 and 15 children respectively. She was linked by her mother, Maria Plett Reimer, to the large Plett clan that had founded the Blumenhof district: Maria's uncles included Reverend Cornelius L. Plett and other patriarchs of large families, including Peter, Abraham, David, and Jakob, each a farmer within Blumenhof and each the father of 15 children. Maria was further tied through her father to an even larger Reimer clan that dominated Blumenort and Steinbach. Thus, even families that do not bear the Reimer, Plett, Unger, or Friesen names, such names as Cornelius Siemens, Johann J. Loewen, Johann Klassen, and *Aeltester* Peter R. Dueck, refer to households in which the women were first cousins of Maria. Moreover, the name Wohlgemuth referred to Maria's aunt and Cornelius Kroeker to a cousin. Finally, in 1919, Maria had 57 nieces and nephews, most of whom lived within six kilometres of the Unger household. A final anchor of the Unger household was "Grandmother," or *Grossmutterchen,* as Maria wrote it; this was her widowed mother, Maria Plett Reimer, 69, at this time in residence at her son

David P. Reimer's farm, two kilometres away. In other years, *Grossmutterchen* lived with the Ungers.

Maria was in touch with a wider world, too, noting frequent market-related trips to the train depot, Giroux, seven kilometres to the east, and to the larger market, further afield, in Winnipeg. A few non-Mennonites were encountered from her home; a Mr. Halles, and Tom Mooney, a neighbour, dropped by for visits. Although Maria's world was a German one, there are hints of an encroaching English world. They are found in the names of the cows – Bonni, Gerti, Flora – and in English designations such as zement (cement), mikzer (mixer), stohr (store), lamm (lamb), miting or mieting (meeting), zeiding (siding), traktor (tractor), telephon (telephone), and lods (loads).

An original copy of the diary, written in Gothic handwriting, was obtained from Peter U. Dueck, Steinbach, Manitoba. It was translated by Margaret Toews, Winnipeg, and by Royden Loewen.

January

Wed., the 1st, New Year We were in the Blumenort church and Peter Dück preached. For lunch Johann F. Reimers, with their Elisabeth and Klaas Friesens' Johann were here, and for *Vesper* Peter Brandt with his sister Margareta came here, and in the evening we drove to A.D. Reimers'.

Thurs., the 2nd The school began again, also Brindal became fresh [bore a calf].

Fri., the 3rd We helped butcher one pig and two cows [heifers] at C. Reimers'. The weather was cold, with the wind from the south.

Sat., the 4th There was Brotherhood Meeting in Steinbach; also Maria moved several things over to the school, and also drove to Steinbach.

Sun., the 5th [?] Worship services were held here [in our church]; we were instructed by Heinrich R. Reimer and Klaas R. Friesen. Also we had guests: Jakob E. Schellenbergs and Peter K. Dücks and A.P. Reimers, also Susanna and Jakob Reimer were here a little, and in the evening Heinrich and Johann Plett were here a little. Also we heard that the aunt, Mrs. Peter Kröker, and Mrs. Gerhard Brand, also the young The Peter Kröker, also Tina W. Brandt, are said to have died from the 'flu in Morris.

Mon., the 6th [?] We were in Neuanlage at Johann Klassens, also at Mrs. Peter Löwen; in the evening Johann H. Dörksen was here.

Tues., the 7th We heard that our *Ältester* [Bishop] Peter Dück is to have died during the night, around one o'clock. Also, the girls began to do the laundry, and Johann went [to the Giroux railroad station] with the milk, also they hauled in the straw. And in the evening Maria [came home] and brought a letter from Lena Jahnke. It was windy with only a little frost.

Wed., the 8th The girls did the laundry, while Papa did the accounting, and in the evening A.R. Penner with his daughters were here. The weather was pleasant and clear.

Thurs., the 9th We drove to P.R. Dücks'; also we were at Radinzels and at the store. The weather was quite pleasant. Papa ordered lumber for the barn.

Fri., the 10th The girls finished the laundry, and Papa did the figuring [accounting]. In the evening C. Ungers were here and helped adjust the telephone. The weather was pleasant and windy.

Sat., the 11th Papa and the children drove to Steinbach for the funeral and in the evening they brought the medicine from the mail.

Sun., the 12th There was worship service in Steinbach. Then we drove to *Grossmutterchen's* and also to Mrs. Klaas R. Penner. We heard that Heinrich Töwses', their Elisabeth, died at one o'clock in the afternoon. The weather was pleasant and calm.

Mon., the 13th P.P. Reimer was here with the fire insurance book; also Uncle Jak. Barkman from Heuboden was here to settle up; also P.K. Dücks were here, and picked up the geese and one pig. The weather was very pleasant.

Tues., the 14th Uncle Jakob A. Wiebe was here, also Cornelius Siemens, and in the evening there was a telephone "miting"; also the wives were along, namely Mrs. Klaas P. Reimer and the Peter and Mrs. Cornelius Unger, also Heinrich Pletts' Peter and Heinrich were here and helped mangle [the damp laundry].

Wed., the 15th Mrs. David Friesen was here, she picked up a horse; also Adolf Jahnke came here, and Papa was in Steinbach and picked up [some] flour. The weather is very pleasant and calm, only five degrees.

Thurs., the 16th Johann J. Löwens were here; in the evening the children drove with Adolf to Peter K. Dücks'; also we heard that Abraham Löwens' Franz of Morris died. The weather was pleasant, a little snow. Johann R. Töws has been in Winnipeg since Monday; he has had surgery. Also we received a letter from G. Jahnkes.

Fri., the 17th Papa drove with the milk; also he got shingles from Johann, and in the evening it began to storm, overall it was [a] pleasant [day]. Also, Uncle Radinzel died.

Sat., the 18th Papa drove to Osterreich with Adolf Jahnke; he obtained some wood. And in the evening the children drove to Steinbach with Adolf. Also we obtained a calf, the Bonni. The weather was pleasant and windy, with a little snow.

Sun., the 19th Worship services were held here [in our district] – P[eter] Kröker preached – and in the afternoon there was the funeral. The children attended. And in the evening Cornelius P. Reimers, as well as Johann and Elisabeth Brandt and Peter and Katherina Klassen from Neuanlage [were here]. The weather was very pleasant.

Mon., the 20th We were in Steinbach. We heard that Mrs. Klaas I. Friesen was very ill. Also, Johann was in Winnipeg with Adolf Jahnke; and, also, Papa brought the bull to C. Ungers'. The weather is very pleasant.

Tues., the 21st We were in Steinbach at *Ältester* P[eter] Dück's funeral. Bernard Dück preached. The weather was pleasant; it was windy in the evening.

Wed., the 22nd Papa brought in straw; drove to H. Pletts'; he also drove to A.P. Reimers'. B. Dück was there. Also D.P. Reimer was here; Johann P. Reimer was here and mangled. The weather was pleasant and it was calm.

Thurs., the 23rd We butchered five pigs. Peter, Abraham, and Cornelius Reimers and Heinrich Pletts, Peter Ungers, Cornelius Siemens, and Peter U. Dücks helped us. The weather was pleasant and windy. Also the school inspector was here.

Fri., the 24th Papa went to fetch the siding. And we brought the scraper to our side. The weather was pleasant.

Sat., the 25th We attended to the laundry, pickled the meat, smoked the sausage, and hauled the straw [home]. In the evening C. Ungers were here a little. The weather was pleasant.

Sun., the 26th Worship services were held in Steinbach. Maria and Elisabeth drove there; also, Lisbet was at Mrs. Peter Dück for lunch and we drove to A.R. Penners after lunch. In the evening a little to Johann Töwses'. The weather was pleasant. The children – Johann, Anna, Tina – had driven to H. Pletts'.

Mon., the 27th We did the laundry; Papa began to haul dirt [as a footing for the new barn?]. We got four "lods." The weather was quite stormy, but eventually Johann Töws also came home.

Tues., the 28th The boys hauled two loads of gravel and in the afternoon the boys drove to Steinbach to have the horses shoed. In the evening there was "miting" in the school; also, Peter was a little unfortunate. The weather was pleasant and still.

Wed., the 29th The boys drove three times and got six "lods." And in the evening we drove to H. Pletts'. The weather was pleasant, but windy. Johann drove Elisabeth to Justina's.

Thurs., the 30th The boys went again three times for gravel. Also we were invited to the funeral at H.W. Töwses'. Also, Jakob A. Wiebe was here with Sahra. The weather was pleasant, but windy.

Fri., the 31 The boys went another three times for gravel and we visited the widow Mrs. P. Dück. C. Krökers were also there and for *Vesper* P.U. Klassen was here. Also Papa brought visitors from Giroux, namely *Ohm* Johann K. Friesen and Rev. Abraham Eidse. The weather is somewhat cool and windy.

February

Sat., the 1st So, Papa drove the guests to Heinrich R. Reimers and for *Vesper* Jakob Bartels came to our place and stayed for the night. In the morning we received a fresh cow, Gerti. The weather was pleasant and it was calm.

Sun., the 2nd Worship services were here, in our church; also [there was a] wedding, namely P.R. Reimer and the widow Mrs. Gerhard K. Schellenberg. And for lunch, Klaas R. Friesens and Mrs. Franz Plett were here. Also, Justina and Peter were here a little and Elisabeth came home. In the evening the children drove to Aunt Wohlgemuth's. It was cold and calm.

Mon., the 3rd There was a brotherhood meeting in Steinbach. Papa went along with Peter Unger. Also we heard that the elderly Aunt Mrs. Abrah. Friesen had died Sunday morning. It was calm; in the morning it was 20 below and cold.

Tues., the 4th The boys went twice for gravel; the girls did the laundry and I wove. In the evening we took the lard to A.P. Reimers'. It was cold and clear.

Wed., the 5th Worship service was held twice in Steinbach and Papa and Elisabeth attended. The boys went another three times for gravel; so, in total, there were 40 "lods" here and the boys walked home. It was cold and calm. Klaas I. Friesen got two "lods" of straw. The children – Johann and Peter and Anna – drove in the evening to P. Ungers'.

Thurs., the 6th I wove a little, the girls did the laundry, and Papa spent the morning accounting and in the afternoon he hauled in straw. And in the evening Jakob Pletts' girls – Gertrude and Anna – were here; also, H. Pletts' Cornelius and Klaas were here to mangle. It was cold and calm. Yesterday we received a "lamm."

Fri., the 7th We were in Steinbach; also at Justina and Peter. The girls did a little sewing. The weather was pleasant.

Sat., the 8th I began to weave [wool] for Papa's socks; Elisabeth sewed a number of things; Anna was busy; Katerina had a sore finger; and Maria spent the entire day in Steinbach at the [teachers'] conference; Papa and Johann drove the wheat to Giroux. The weather was quite pleasant. In the evening, Johann R. Töws was at our place; also Mister Hales was at our place. Yesterday we had a bad . . .

Sun., the 9th In the morning we were at the worship service in Steinbach and Uncle Abraham Eidse of Morris instructed us and in the afternoon *Grossmutterchen* came with us. In the evening we drove here to Johann F. Reimers'. The girls – Maria and Elisabeth – were at Isaak Löwens' for lunch. Maria had come along with us in the evening. And P., Kati and Sahra were at Wohlgemuths' in the evening. The weather was very pleasant. In the evening it was quite windy.

Mon., the 10th Papa and Johann hauled wheat; I wove; Elisabeth sewed; Anna sorted [?] laundry. In the evening Papa was very busy with the accounting. The weather was very pleasant, but there was much wind and there was much dust blowing.

Tues., the 11th We received two *Lämuer* [lambs?]; also, the girls did the laundry and Papa and Johann hauled wheat; I wove and baked. And in the evening we were at the young David Pletts'. Maria drove to Neuanlage for the night. Also Mrs. Peter Sawatzky was here a little. The weather was very pleasant and calm.

Wed., the 12th Papa drove to Steinbach in the morning. The girls brought . . . the laundry in. Bernard Dörksen milled [feed grain at our place]. Two lambs died. In the evening, we drove to P.P. Reimers'. Also, we heard that A. Esaus' Sahra had died. The weather was pleasant; in the evening it turned windy.

Thurs., the 13th A.T. Löwen [of Steinbach] was here for lunch. The girls did the laundry; I wove and prepared food; Johann fixed up [made tight] the henhouse. Also they got the telephone ... here. Also, the girls received letters from Satanta. In the evening we drove to Uncle Jakob Plett. The weather was pleasant and windy.

Fri., the 14th Papa brought in straw in the morning. For lunch, Jakob A. Wiebe came here and got several papers [fire insurance claims?]. The elderly aunt accompanied [him] and [he] was feeling somewhat better than in earlier times. Also, Papa drove to Altona [West Reserve]. The weather was pleasant and windy.

Sat., the 15th Papa drove to Giroux in the morning and on to Morris; the trip is to be extended to Altona. The girls cleaned [the house]; I baked and wove; and Maria sewed and moved to the school with her things; the boys did the chores and harnessed and drove the yearling.... In the evening Johann was at H. Pletts'. The weather was pleasant and calm; in the evening there was wind. Yesterday, C. Kröker had the misfortune of having 20 sheep die during the night. However, I still do not know how it happened. He had had the sheep outside.

Sun., the 16th Worship service was here and we were instructed by Klaas R. Friesen. But, I drove to Johann Reimers where ... after a while, a son was born. For lunch, P.K. Dücks and Heinrich and Margaretha Fast were our guests and in the evening Jakob U. Kornelsen and P.R. Plett were here and Elisabet, Johann and Anna were the evening in Neuanlage. The weather was very pleasant and it thawed much.

Mon., the 17th The girls took care of the laundry. In the evening they mangled, Jakob F. Löwen helped a little; and I wove. The weather was pleasant and still.

Tues., the 18th The girls patched and I wove. Also, I was at C. Siemens and Johann was the evening at Johann Töwses'; also, Jakob R. Plett was here. The weather was ...

Wed., the 19th It snowed during the night. Johann hauled in barley chaff. The girls sewed and I wove. And in the evening Papa came home. Peter P.D. Reimer was the evening at our place. The weather was pleasant and calm.

Thurs., the 20th We were the morning at H. Pletts' and in the afternoon we, with P.P. Reimers, drove to Heuboden. Also, Jakob R. Plett helped haul in straw at our place. The weather was very pleasant.

Fri., the 21st We were the night at Jakob Kornelsens' and for lunch we were at A. Kornelsens' and for *Vesper* at Franz Goossens' and in the evening we returned safely home with Peter P. Reimers. In the evening, Maria and Johann had driven to Steinbach for "Mieting." The weather was very pleasant. Yesterday we were at C. Siemens' for *Vesper* and in the evening at Jakob Kornelsens' with P. Reimers and Jakob Dücks together.

Sat., the 22nd In the morning we were at C. Siemens' and in the afternoon we were a little at J.P. Reimers'. I did a little laundry there; in the evening Papa did some writing and I wove; Maria sewed and the others did a little baking and held Saturday [cleaned the house]. The weather was a little cold and windy.

Sun., the 23rd The children drove to C. Jahnzens' and Johann Löwens' after lunch and we were at Peter Ungers'. Johann had visitors in the evening. It was cold and [there was] a slight north wind.

Mon., the 24th I wove and the girls sewed and Papa was in Steinbach at [the meeting of the] Brotherhood. Also, P. Unger, C. Unger and J.R. Töws were here for *Vesper*. The weather was cold and stormy and in the evening, our cow, Fwor [?], gave birth.

Tues., the 25th I wove and the girls did the laundry and baked and Papa began to ... the wood together with Bern. Dörksen. I spent the afternoon at C. Siemens'. It was very cold.

Wed., the 26th I wove; the girls did the laundry; and Papa was a little ill and Johann repaired the sled and in the evening C.P. Reimers were at our place. It was very cold.

Thurs., the 27th I wove and the girls sewed and Bern. D[örksen] hauled in straw and in the afternoon we drove to C. Ungers' as they had the "flu" there. In the evening P.U. Klassens were here a little and got a ... for C. Ungers. It was very cold.

Fri., the 28th Johann drove with the milk and Bernard ... axed [?] wood; I did a little weaving, also Anna wove and Elisabeth sewed and in the afternoon we drove to Steinbach and were also at the Widow Mrs. Peter Dück's and in the evening Jakob R. Plett and Johann H. Dörksen were here. Also Johann went to get a load of wood from the bush and Maria drove to C.P. Reimers' for the night. It was quite cold.

March

Sat., the 1st The boys got two loads of wood; Papa was at Jakob Pletts' in the morning and in the afternoon [he] hauled in straw and in the evening he did the accounting and Maria sewed at C.P. Reimers'; and the other girls, they cleaned [the house]; and I sewed and did a little weaving. In the evening the boys were a little at H. Pletts'. The weather was quite pleasant; in the afternoon it was cloudy.

Sun., the 2nd Worship services were here and H. Dück preached and Peter K. Dücks were our guests and in the evening we were at H. Pletts'. It was cold and calm.

Mon., the 3rd We were in Steinbach at the "stohr"; also at the Aunt Radinzel's; also at the Aunt Brösche's; and in the morning I wrote a letter to the Jahnkes'. The girls did the laundry; and in the evening David L. Pletts were at our place, also Uncle Jakob Barkman; he also stayed the night. It was very cold and in the morning it had snowed very much.

Tues., the 4th Papa drove to the auction sale with Jakob Barkman and in the evening Johann Barkmans came here.

Wed., the 5th Papa and I wrote a letter in the morning; I wrote to the Jahnkes and Papa to Uncle Luppki [?]. In the afternoon we drove to *Grossmutterchen*'s. Papa also was a little while at Johann P. Reimers'. The weather was quite pleasant. Johann hauled in straw; also, we had a calf that died.

Thurs., the 6th I and Papa drove to *Grossmutterchen*'s for lunch as Abraham D. Löwens were there and in the afternoon we drove to Steinbach with Mrs. David Reimer; also J.R. Plett was here to exchange some mash. Also, I wove and the girls did the laundry. The weather was pleasant.

Fri., the 7th Papa hauled in straw; Johann hauled wood; I wove; Elisabeth sewed. In the evening Mrs. Heinrich Plett was at our place; Maria was with C.P. Reimers' children; also, A.P. Reimers' girls were at our place. The weather was quite pleasant.

Sat., the 8th Papa got two "lods" of wood and Johann got one "lods" of wood in the morning; he went with the milk; the girls baked and so on; in the evening H.R. Reimers were at our place with A.D. Löwens; also, C. Siemens were at our place. The weather was pleasant

Sun. the 9th We were in Steinbach; Uncle A. Eidse instructed us and after lunch from *Ältester* Wahl, who had met [Reverend] Jakob R. Dück. The weather was very pleasant.

Mon., the 10th I and Papa drove to the [special] worship service in Steinbach in the forenoon and in the afternoon I worked in the kitchen and in the evening I wove and Papa picked up a pig in the afternoon; Johann went to pick up one load of wood; in the evening Peter Ungers' children were at our place; also, the girls began to wash the laundry. The weather was quite pleasant; in the evening it was somewhat windy.

Tues., the 11 Papa and Johann drove to the ... mill for wood and the girls did the laundry; I wove; in the evening I was a little at C. Siemens'; also, Johann R. Dück came here for the night. The weather was very pleasant.

Wed., the 12th I wove, the girls did the laundry and Papa drove with Johann R. Dück visiting; in the evening Jakob A. Wiebe came here and Bernard D. ...

Thurs., the 13th I and Papa drove to P.K. Dücks'; also, we had Mrs. Peter Dück with us. Bernard split wood and Johann went to fetch one load of wood. The girls dried the laundry, and also mangled it, Johann R. Plett helped. The weather was pleasant, somewhat windy.

Fri., the 14th Johann and Papa got two loads of wood and Bernard D. split wood. The girls cleaned [the house] and baked. In the evening Maria R. Barkman was at our place and Papa was at Cornelius P. Reimers'. The weather was very pleasant. In the evening there was a very strong wind, and late evening there was a lot of thunder and lightning. I wove.

Sat., the 15th It was rainy, so the Bernard Dörksen walked home and Papa did the accounting, the girls cleaned the house and I rewove numerous items. Also we received a letter from Aunt Mrs. Peter Plett.

Sun., the 16th Worship service was here [in Blumenort] and we had a guest for lunch, namely Johann F. Plett and later, Maria K. Penner came here; and in the evening Klaas F. Penners were at our place; also, Maria, with C.P. Reimers' girls and Peter were at our place. The weather was pleasant and calm. C.T. Kröker was also here.

Mon., the 17th Papa and Johann drove to Giroux for wood and I wove. The girls patched and dyed wool; also, they were a little at Maria's at the school. B. Dörksen finished hacking the wood and in the evening Papa and I were at Uncle Jakob Plett's. The weather was pleasant, with [only] a little freezing.

Tues., the 18th Papa drove for a load of wood in the morning; and for lunch Peter K. Dücks came here; and in the afternoon they drove to Gre[e]nland for an auction sale; and Johann R. Töws and Maria also came here for supper. The weather was pleasant.

Wed., the 19th Papa and Johann drove for wood twice; and in the evening we drove to the Widow Mrs. K.R. Penner's. Elisabeth sewed; also, Anna sewed; and I baked and did some patching, also wove. It was very windy, but mild and somewhat cloudy.

Thurs., the 20th Papa and Johann got the last of the wood from the bush; I walked to C. Siemens' in the afternoon. The girls sewed and in the evening they drove to C.P. Reimers'. Also we heard that the Aunt Mrs. Jakob J. Friesen is supposed to have died in Meade, Kansas. It was pleasant and calm. It is rather, Mrs. Jakob R. Friesen.

Fri., the 21st I sewed a little and so too did the girls. In the afternoon we drove to Peter P. Reimers, as Bernhard Dörksen[s] were there, and we also brought *Grossmutterchen* back home with us. Also, we heard that Uncle David Klassen in Herbert is to have died. The weather was pleasant, with somewhat of a south wind.

Sat., the 22nd I first worked with the beds and then did some patching. In the afternoon we drove to Steinbach; I was also a little at Mrs. Jakob Reimers'. Elisabeth sewed; the other girls cleaned [house], also baked. It was pleasant and calm, also we had a heavy snowfall.

Sun., the 23rd We were in Steinbach in the church and were instructed by Bernard Dück [Morris]; and for lunch we were at Jakob W. Reimers'; and in the evening Maria was at home with C.P. Reimers' children. The weather was very pleasant. It was very pleasant. Maria and Elisabeth were at Margaretha Fast.

Mon., the 24th I and the girls sewed; Papa was a little ill. Johann was at H. Pletts' with the harrow.... It was very rainy.

Tues., the 25th I and the girls sewed; Papa and Johann hauled wood to the granary building site. It was somewhat cool and rainy.

Wed., the 26th I and Elisabeth sewed and Tina made ... and made food; and Papa and Anna drove to Peter K. Dücks' for oat seed. It was somewhat cool and rainy.

Thurs., the 27th Papa and Johann drove twice to Giroux for "Zement" and also we sawed wood; and Peter and Cornelius R. Plett cleaned barley here. Also, Johann P. Reimer was here a little and I patched and Elisabeth sewed something new. The weather was pleasant. The chickens fully began to lay eggs.

Fri., the 28th Johann drove for "Zement"; also we ended the sawing of the wood; and I and Elisabeth sewed. It was pleasant; a little snow. Also, we received a wonderful letter from Aunt Mrs. Jahnke.

Sat., the 29th Johann R. Plett milled [feed grain] here. Papa and Johann hauled in hay; I patched and also made a straw bed. The girls held Saturday and Sahra was at Maria's. It was pleasant in the morning; in the evening it was colder and clear.

Sun., the 30th We had worship service here in our church and were served from Jakob R. Dück. For lunch, Katherina T. Kröker was at our place and in the afternoon Elisabeth drove with her to C.P. Reimers' and also to Neuanlage. And we drove to H. Pletts'; he had just returned from Kansas. The weather was pleasant.

Mon., the 31st There was the *Prüfung* [annual public examination] here at the Blumenhof school. For lunch, Peter K Dücks and Katerina and Justina U. Klaassen were at our place. The weather was very pleasant and thawing....

April

Tues., the 1st Papa helped C. Ungers saw wood in the morning and in the afternoon he got a load of straw and then we drove to *Grossmutterchen's*. Elisabeth sewed and I patched and for night G.G. Kornelsens came [to our place]. It was thawing very much [making it appear] that the sled driving will be over.

Wed., the 2nd Papa and Maria had driven to Winnipeg and I and Elisabeth sewed and Johann had driven to H. Pletts' to have the harrow teeth sharpened and Anna baked and Tina washed. It thawed very much.

Thurs., the 3rd Papa hauled in straw in the morning; I and Anna and Elisabeth sewed; Tina patched; and in the afternoon I and Papa helped butcher pigs at C. Siemens'. It thawed.

Fri., the 4th Papa smoked meat; I [reworked] his clothes; Tina and Anna made blankets; Elisabeth sewed a dress for herself; and in the evening I and Papa drove to C.P. Reimers'. It was very pleasant and . . .

Sat., the 5th I cooked up soap; Maria sewed; the boys split wood; Papa was ill. It was very rainy. I.P. Löwen [the neighbour] was here a little while.

Sun., the 6th Worship services were in Steinbach, however no one from our place went. In the afternoon Peter R. Plett came here, also A.P. Reimers. They related to us that in Steinbach a bridal couple had been married, [banns?] namely Agata Janzen and Heinrich Fast. Also, it was very . . . but pleasant and still.

Mon., the 7th The girls began to wash and Papa and C. Siemens and the boys split wood and one turkey began to lay. It was quite windy; in the evening it began to snow.

Tues., the 8th The boys drove the milk in the morning and in the afternoon they cleaned out the chicken barn. Papa made goose . . . The girls, Lies and Anna, washed; I patched, also baked. It was pleasant and windy.

Wed., the 9th I sewed a little in the morning; Papa smoked hams; the girls dried the laundry; and we drove to Steinbach in the afternoon. It was sunny.

Thurs., the 10th We were at the *Prüfung* [public school examination]; for *Vesper* Peter Ungers were at our place. It was cloudy and windy.

Fri., the 11th Papa did the accounting; the girls looked after the laundry and mangled; the boys, with C. Siemens, completed the wood-splitting; also I did a little weaving and Papa sharpened a saw. It was pleasant and warm.

Sat., the 12th The girls cleaned house; I baked and prepared the pots for soap cooking, also wove and Papa smoked hams. It was pleasant. In the evening Johann and Maria drove to Heinrich Pletts'.

Sun., the 13th Worship service was held here in our church; there was a wedding, namely H. Fast and Agata Janzen, and for lunch Peter . . . Dücks were here and in the evening Johann . . . Plett was here and Johann was at A.P. Reimers' in the evening. It was very pleasant, also very *kotig* [?]. Sahra drove along with Dücks; also a bridal couple was married, namely Peter F. Löwen from Neuanlage and Tina Fast of Steinbach.

Mon., the 14th We all sewed and Papa cleaned [seed] grain with the boys and C. Siemens separated [?] wood and in the evening Jakob A. Wiebe was here. It was very pleasant.

Tues., the 15th I sewed in the morning and in the afternoon I cooked soap with Mrs. C. Siemens. The girls all sewed and Papa and the boys cleaned grain and C. Siemens completed separating [?] the wood and Johann and Anna drove to Steinbach after *Vesper*. It was clear.

Wed., the 16th I completed the cooking of soap; the girls sewed steadily; Papa did repairs on the drill and the boys repaired and oiled the harnesses. It was nice.

Thurs., the 17th The girls whitewashed the kitchen; Johann drove the milk and brought the cleaning mill till the school; I wrote letters in the morning and in the afternoon I washed. It was very pleasant and calm.

Fri., the 18th The children – Johann, Peter, Maria and Elisabeth – drove to Steinbach for worship service and for lunch they were at Peter K. Dücks'. I and Papa drove to Johann R. Töwses'. It was very pleasant.

Sat., the 19th I sewed in the morning and in the afternoon I and Papa drove to Uncle Klaas Friesen's; the girls did the Saturday cleaning. The boys did some straw hauling. It was very pleasant.

Sun., the 20th We had worship service here [in Blumenort] and were instructed by Heinrich R. Dück. Also Peter F. Löwen and Tina L. Fast were married [banns?] and for lunch Anna R. Dück and Peter and Maria P.D. Reimer were at our place. And I and Papa drove to C. Ungers' this afternoon. The girls had driven a little to Neuanlage. It was pleasant and clear.

Mon., the 21st I and Papa and Tina and Maria, also Johann Barkmans, drove to Steinbach for worship service. There we were instructed by H.R. Reimer. For lunch we were at the aunt Mrs. Johann Reimer's. Also there was Brotherhood Meeting. It was stormy.

Tues., the 22nd The first thing after breakfast Papa drove to I.P. Löwen; also P.P. Reimer was soon here and Peter went harrowing and Papa and Johann left for Giroux at about 10 to unload wood; Anna began to wash and Elisabeth, Tina and Maria began to pile up wood (also they smoked hams) and Maria began to sew; also Maria K. Plett was here a little. Also it was cold and windy; and we received a letter from G. Jahnke.

Wed., the 23rd Papa and Johann made two trips for wood to Giroux and in the evening the girls – Maria and Elisabeth – drove to *Grossmutterchen*; also Jo. R. Töws was here to trade eggs; also Johann R. Plett was here a little. It was quite cold and windy. During the day, the girls had sewed a variety of things.

Thurs., the 24th In the morning Papa loaded wood and did accounting and in the afternoon the boys drove for the wood; also Peter K Dück picked up potatoes and after *Vesper* we drove to Steinbach. The girls hung up the wash to dry. It was cold.

Fri., the 25th The boys drove for the wood and I and Papa drove to Heuboden; the girls sewed and laid together the wash, also piled the wood. . . . It was a little windy and cold.

Sat., the 26th Papa hauled the milk and picked up wood. The boys were on the field. Also Uncle D. Plett was here a little, and Peter P. Reimer. The girls did the Saturday cleaning; I did a little sewing and weaving. I finished the little Peter Dück's . . . socks. . . . It was cloudy and calm; it rained a little. The first wheat was sown.

Sun., the 27th Worship service was held here; we were instructed by Jakob R. Dück and for lunch Peter K. Dücks and Sahra K Dück, also Franz Duck, were here; also the aunt Mrs. Peter R. Dück was here a little and in the evening Kornelius R. Plett was here and Maria drove with Peter K. Dück and Lara [?] came home. It was nice.

Mon., the 28th We did a variety of things. The girls cleaned two rooms upstairs; I sewed a little on the bed and sorted the potatoes; the boys worked on the field; the weather was nice and calm; also Elisabeth drove to Steinbach.

Tues., the 29th The boys worked on the fields and the girls cleaned three rooms upstairs; also I set one hen on turkey eggs; I wrote a letter to G. Jahnkes in the morning; and afternoon Papa and I sorted potatoes; the weather was very windy and rainy; also Papa picked up a load of wood and Fritz Schulz picked up a load of shingles. C. Siemens picked up the soap.

Wed., the 30th The girls moved upstairs and began to cleanup up there and I and Papa worked in the basement; also Papa was a short time at C. Ungers' and Johann P. Reimer and Jakob F. Penner were here for *Vesper* and Jakob Penner sheared the sheep and stayed for night. The boys worked on the field; today they completed the seeding of 30 acres of wheat; it was nice; in the evening a cold wind [began].

May

Thurs., the 1st The girls began to clean *Grossmutterchen*'s house; and Papa and Abraham drove to Giroux with potatoes in the morning; I fried a . . . in the morning and in the afternoon I baked. The boys worked on the fields and in the evening we bought five pigs for 37 dollars apiece from a couple of hog dealers. It was pleasant. Also I set a hen on goose eggs.

Fri., the 2nd We were in Steinbach in the morning and in the afternoon Papa did the accounting and I washed and in the evening I and Papa *ein 1/4 Ring* . . . *entzwar gemacht* [?]; also we unloaded the pigs; the girls completed cleaning *Grossmutterchen*'s house. The boys cultivated; the weather was very . . .

Sat., the 3rd Papa hauled away the pigs; and the girls painted the floor inside here and in *Grossmutterchen*'s house; and I canned; also I and Papa sorted some potatoes; and after *Vesper* Papa sowed grass by hand; the boys worked on the field; the weather was windy and cloudy; also we took several [vats of?] *Seife* upstairs and yesterday we set two hens on chicken eggs; also we baked and did the Saturday cleaning.

Sun., the 4th [Worship services] were in Steinbach; I and Papa and Elisabeth and Anna drove to church and for lunch we came home; Peter Löwen and Elisabeth and Neta came here; also Dave P. Reimer and *Grossmutterchen*, also Mrs. Johann Barkman and H. Pletts were all here for *Vesper* and in the evening Elisabeth and Anna went over to Heinrich Pletts' a little. The weather was cloudy. . . . [May 5 to June 3 missing]

June

Wed., the 4th Immediately after breakfast Uncle G. Kornelsen came here, and then Heinrich Plett; and for lunch the widow Mrs. Peter Dück with her daughters, and Peter K. Dücks and Maria; also, Mrs. C. Siemens came here. Papa and Johann helped the workers work in the old barn. It was pleasant and calm.

Thurs., the 5th The workers completed setting up the forms and the boys, J. and P., cultivated. I, with Lies, prepared food and baked; in the morning Elis. and Johann drove to Steinbach. Anna washed. It was pleasant.

Fri., the 6th The workers finished putting up the walls of the barn completely. J. and P. worked in the fields; I did the laundry. The girls prepared food; also the cow, the Flora, had a bull calf. It was cold and calm; very useful for cement work.

Sat., the 7th The boys – J. and Peter – completed the field work. Justina picked up Peter and brought Abraham home. It was very pleasant.

Sun., the 8th I and Papa and Elisabeth drove to Steinbach for worship service; Elisabeth drove to Neuanlage for lunch and we, after *Vesper*, drove to *Grossmutterchen*'s. The weather was somewhat rainy.

Mon., the 9th Worship services were held here [in Blumenort] and also we had C. Friesen with his daughters as guests; also, P.R. Plett was here a little, also D. Reimer and P. Brandt; also Maria came home for a while and Elisabeth went to *Grossmutterchen's*. The weather is pleasant.

Tues., the 10th The workers worked on the barn, also they began to scrape [around the barn]; I, with Anna, did the laundry; Peter cultivated; Elisabeth made food. The weather was very pleasant and warm.

Wed., the 11th More work on the barn and so on. Papa drove to Giroux with wood; Tina worked on the field; I did the laundry and so on. It rained. Also, we had a sheep die.

Thurs., the 12th The first thing [in morning] Papa killed the dog that bit our sheep; and I and Anna brought all the wash outside. In the morning it was rainy. The workers worked diligently on the barn.

Fri., the 13th Papa was in Steinbach for the wood. H. Enns came to pick up the [cement] "mikzer." I cooked a little soap and made food. Papa was at the *Brandordnung* [Fire Agency meeting]. The weather was rainy, but pleasant.

Sat., the 14th I [spent] the morning helping to prepare food and in the afternoon, we and Elisabeth were in Neuanlage at the *Verlobung* [engagement get-together]. In the evening we had a severe storm, and also a pleasant rain. Johann drove [along] with Peter Dück for night and Maria came home; Papa did the accounting until late.

Sun., the 15th I and Papa, with Lies and P., also Johann, were in the Steinbach church; we were instructed by P. Kröker. For lunch we were at C. Krökers'; then we drove to Jakob A. Wiebe. The weather was very warm.

Mon., the 16th Johann drove to Steinbach with the milk. For lunch, we had guests, C. Kornelsens and the widow Mrs. Jakob Kornelsen. After *Vesper* Papa drove to Steinbach for communion service. The bridal couple was at our place. The workers spent the entire day working on the barn. The weather was quite hot.

Tues., the 17th Papa did the accounting. I tended to the laundry. Elisabeth and Anna did a little hoeing; Johann ploughed the summerfallow; overall, our work was similar to yesterday's. The weather was rainy.

Wed., the 18th The workers nailed the barn roof over with boards; I and Papa drove to Steinbach in the afternoon; Johann ploughed. The weather was pleasant. Also, I wrote a letter to G. Jahnkes'.

Thurs., the 19th The workers nailed the shingles and Papa drove to Gre[e]nland and afternoon he drove to Giroux with barley and brought back [some] flour. Tina and Anna hoed; Johann was ill; Peter and Abraham herded the cattle. The weather was very pleasant.

Fri., 20th Shingles were nailed. Papa hauled barley to Giroux; I baked; Anna and Tina hoed and tended a little while to the laundry; H. Pletts were here to mangle; also we sold eight pigs. The weather was quite warm.

Sat., the 21st The barn roof was completely finished. Maria and Justina were both home; and Johann cultivated; we baked and so on. The weather was cloudy, but then in the evening it began to rain.

Sun., the 22nd We had worship service here in our church, also a wedding, P.P. Reimer's Peter with Katherina Klaaszen; also, there was the [baptismal] instruction of the youth. In the afternoon the girls and Johann were in Neuanlage. We spent the entire day home alone. The weather was very pleasant.

Mon., the 23rd Papa spent the morning helping with the work on the barn; and then he worked a little with the haying, also he hauled rocks. I did a variety of things; Elisabeth sewed; the other girls helped prepare food. For the evening, Peter Ungers were at our place. The weather was very pleasant. The goose's eggs hatched.

Tues., the 24th Papa, with the boys, worked on the barn; Johann ploughed; I baked; Elisabeth sewed; Anna, Tina hoed. In the evening, Jakob Barkmans were here to mangle. The weather was very pleasant.

Wed., the 25th Papa worked with the workers; Johann and Elisabeth were in Steinbach over lunch; overall, the children worked in the garden; also, *Grossmutterchen* was here and stayed for the night. The weather was very pleasant. The milk is [again] being directed to Giroux.

Thurs., the 26th Papa drove to Giroux with the milk, also with the barley. Overall, the work was similar to yesterday's. In the evening P.P. Reimers were at our place. The weather was pleasant, somewhat cold.

Fri., the 27th I and the girls [spent time] making food, baking and hoeing. Johann completed ploughing the summerfallow, and Papa was in Giroux twice with barley. The weather was pleasant.

Sat., the 28th Papa and Anna [went through] the potatoes; Johann and Peter cultivated; I and the other girls made food and did the laundry. Also we had guests for *Vesper*, Franz Goossens and the Old Cornelius Fasts, also the Aunt Radinzel. It was quite windy.

Sun., the 29th The children drove to Steinbach for worship service; also they were at Peter Dücks'; I and Papa had guests, Johann P. Reimers and Johann R. Töwses; also Peter Ungers were here a little while, and Martin Friesens from Morris were here in the evening. The weather was warm and there was a strong wind.

Mon., the 30th Papa [drove through] the potatoes in the morning with Anna; Elisabeth and Maria made the food; Peter cultivated. In the afternoon, Papa drove to Steinbach; I and Anna did the laundry. Workers, there were only six today; Johann also worked on the barn. The weather was quite warm and windy in the morning; in the evening it began to rain, and it rained heavily till 10 o'clock; also there was a lot of lightning. Also, sold four pigs for $36 apiece. Also, my brother, Cornelius P. Reimer had a misfortune and inhaled too many kerosene fumes and became quite ill as a result.

July

Tues., the 1st I washed the clothes together with Anna. Maria and Elisabeth made the meals. Papa and John helped the men build the barn. Tina planted some cabbage, etc. The weather was so rainy before, but now the moon shines.

Wed., the 2nd It was raining very hard and Johann went to Steinbach. Maria and I were sewing. Papa was working on his accounts, and made a report on papers to be mailed to several places. The builders worked inside the barn. We also heard that Mr. P.D. Ginter drowned.

Thurs., the 3rd Papa delivered four pigs to St[e]. Anne and also stopped off at the Heinrich Pletts'. Anna and I dried the whole wash and mangled most of it. The others all worked at the same things as yesterday. The weather was quite nice and dry.

Fri., the 4th I ironed wash in the forenoon and Papa went to Steinbach to get some supplies for the barn. In the afternoon we sprayed the potatoes first thing, and I sewed a while. Also Papa and I and Lena, Abraham and Margaretha were a little while at the P.K. Dücks'. The girls cleaned, baked and weeded. The weather was beautiful. Also we got a letter from the K.P.L. Reimers in Kansas, and we were for a little while at the C.P. Reimers'.

Sat., the 5th I worked again with the wash. P. Dücks were here awhile. Some of the workers have already been paid and left and also some of the construction equipment has been removed. Elisabeth and Maria went to the Peter K. Dücks for night so they could look after the animals while the Dücks are away.
...

Sun., the 6th We were here in Blumenort to church and Rev. Heinrich R. Reimer preached. Maria and Anna Koop came over for lunch and for the afternoon lunch A.R. Pletts came. Also P.K. Dücks came for a little while.

Mon., the 7th It has rained a bit and there was a strong wind. So Elisabeth and I sewed. Johann went to get some cement from Giroux. Papa has been lying down all day because he was sick. We also have heard that it rained very hard south of us and that the Seine River is too small. It is overflowing badly so that much grain is standing in the water. The G. Dörksens had to move out of their house because the water was coming in. It's the same situation at the neighbours'. In fact the water has already reached P.G. Töws' land. Such a flood is not supposed to have happened for the last 19 years. Today only three men worked on our new barn.

Tues., the 8th Today we moved all *Grossmutterchen*'s things out of her house and D.P. Reimer and Johann U. Brandt raised it off its foundation. We got seven new piglets from one sow today. We also got five new piglets from another sow yesterday.

Wed., the 9th We did various things. In the forenoon Papa and I went to Steinbach. We also visited a little bit at C.P. Reimers'. The boys have already brought the horses into the new barn. We also got more new little pigs. The weather was very nice.

Thurs., the 10th The workers have all left today and the barn is more or less finished. Papa has worked on different things in the barn together with the boys Johann and Peter. I worked a little with the wash, made butter, and made soap, and also put most of it in the barrel for summer. It was ready for that. Anna and Tina and Sahra worked. The weather was very nice and there was no wind.

Fri., the 11th Mrs. C.T. Goossen was here, also Aron Reimers and *Ohm* A. Enns. I was at the Johann R. Töws' place. The girls worked in the garden and the boys worked on the barn. Papa brought hay into the barn and we got seven more new piglets. The weather was a little rainy in the morning. In the evening it was nice.

Sat., the 12th We worked with the weeds in the garden and on the field. Elisabeth worked inside. I went to Johann R. Töwses' for a while. In the evening Johann U. Kornelsen, Tom Mooney and Cornelius R. Plett were over. We also got seven more new piglets. The weather was nice.

Sun., the 13th We were in Steinbach at a baptism service. Also the children, Johann, Tina, Anna, and Elisabeth came along. The children went home at noon and we went to Peter K. Dücks'. After evening lunch there was another service. Then Rev. Johann Friesen from Morris led the communion service. We got another seven new piglets today. Altogether we now have 39 piglets.

Mon., the 14th In the morning Papa worked on the road and in the afternoon he had a visitor. I was at Johann R. Töwses' place. The children went away to pick fruit. The weather was nice. Also Papa wrote a letter to the Jahnkes in Saskatchewan in answer to one received.

Tues., the 15th Johann took the milk to Giroux and Papa worked on the road. I made soap and later we were for a while at the Heinrich Wielers and in Steinbach. Also Johann R. Töws was at our place a little bit. The weather was nice.

Wed., the 16th Sewed in the morning. Elisabeth cleaned the blueberries. In the afternoon the girls hoed. I was at Heinrich Pletts' and picked fruit there, and Papa worked with the earth in the hay mow. Johann tidied up the new barn. In the evening Papa came to Pletts' also. He settled an account there. The weather was beautiful. We got a letter from Jahnkes.

Thurs., the 17th Peter W. Reimer came over because we had a sick horse, but it died. I put the soap out to dry. In the afternoon Papa and the boys buried the horse and after that Papa and I went to Jakob U. Wiebes'. The weather was nice.

Fri., the 18th Justina and Maria came home to visit. The Peter P. Reimers came over for lunch and A.P. Reimers came for *Faspa* [afternoon lunch]. Also Maria and I sewed. The weather was rainy. In the evening it was nice. Very many mosquitoes.

Sat., the 19th I sewed. The girls did the Saturday cleaning. Papa got gravel from the pit and improved the road. The boys cut forage and cultivated.

Sun., the 20th There was church service here in Blumenort and we were instructed by Rev. Jakob R. Dück. For lunch Johann W. Reimers and Peter K. Dücks were here. Also Tina and Maria F. Dück came. For afternoon lunch we went to Johann R. Töws' with Johann Reimers. In the evening Heinrich P. Töwses and C.K. Siemens came over. The weather was fairly good.

Mon., the 21st Elisabeth and I picked raspberries in the morning. Then she canned them. I made butter. The other girls hoed the potatoes. Papa and Anna cultivated the potatoes in the forenoon. The boys cultivated in the morning and then Johann cut the hay and raked it. After the evening lunch Papa and I and Margaret went for a short visit to *Grossmutterchen*. Also I wrote a letter to Klaas P.L. Reimers in Kansas. The weather was very nice.

Tues., the 22nd Jakob P. Penner took me to the Edward Mankes' because Mrs. Manke had burnt herself very badly. I also visited at the Johann F. Reimers' a little while. Papa and the girls hoed and gathered the hay into piles. The boys cultivated. The weather was nice.

Wed., the 23rd We went with *Grossmutterchen* and Mrs. Peter Löwen to visit Cornelius Barkmans'. The children worked in the garden, cultivated and gathered the hay. The weather was very nice.

Thurs., the 24th Papa first completed the water run-off trench for the well and then he and the boys dragged earth with the scoop and horse. In the forenoon Elisabeth and I went to the Edward Mankes'. In the afternoon Elisabeth, Anna and Abraham went to Peter K. Dücks'. In the evening H.L. Fast came and got medicine for Mrs. Manke. The weather was nice.

Fri., the 25th In the forenoon Papa dragged some more earth. Elisabeth and I picked berries and in the afternoon the girls worked in the garden. Papa and I went to Steinbach. For afternoon lunch we were at Johann W. Reimers' and later a little while at the Aunt Radinzel's. The weather was rainy.

Sat., the 26th We had very stormy weather, wind and rain. So we couldn't do much outside. Elisabeth canned berries. Johann put a new floor in the pantry. Also he worked in the pig barn. Papa has been lying down all day because he didn't feel well. The weather became quite nice in the evening. We also heard that Mrs. Edward Manke died.

Sun., the 27th The children Johann, Elisabeth and Anna, went to church in Steinbach. We were alone at home all day. In the evening the Johann R. Pletts were here. The weather was very nice.

Mon., the 28th Papa worked on the pig barn. Johann has started to cut the grain with the binder. Elisabeth and Anna washed. Tina and Sahra worked in the garden. I worked inside. The weather was nice.

Tues., the 29th We all continued our various jobs the same as yesterday. I baked and made meals. Papa went to Gre[e]nland in the forenoon to estimate the storm damage at C.W. Töws' where the wind had toppled over the windmill. We also received the medicine we had waited for. The weather was nice.

Wed., the 30th I went to Steinbach with *Grossmutterchen*. We went to see Mrs. Franz Kröker and Mrs. P.R. Dück. The girls have dried much wash. Johann was cutting grain. Peter cultivated. Papa fixed the hayrack and got some hay. We also heard that Isaak P. Löwen's "babi" died. The weather was nice.

Thurs., the 31st In the morning Johann took the milk to Giroux. Papa stooked sheaves. He also had a visitor – Uncle Jakob Barkman. I picked raspberries in the garden. The girls dried wash and ironed it. They also picked cranberries, etc. The weather was nice.

August

Fri., the 1st Johann cut grain and Peter cultivated on the land. The girls were working with the wash. Papa and I stooked sheaves till seven o'clock in the evening. Then we went to the Heinrich Wielers' to get butter and also stopped at P.P. Reimers' to consult about threshing matters. We got a letter from G. Jahnkes. The weather was nice.

Sat., the 2nd Johann has completed cutting 30 acres of wheat and Papa and Peter stooked sheaves. Peter also raked. We worked busily indoors. The weather was nice but quite windy. We have . . .

Sun., the 3rd We were here in church and Peter Kröker preached. For lunch Peter K. Dücks' and also Maria and Lena were here and for afternoon lunch we went to Peter Ungers' with the Dücks. Maria had guests – Margaretha Brandt and P.U. Klassen. The weather was fine.

Mon., the 4th Papa went for a little while to the H. Pletts'. The girls and I worked some more with the wash. Johann was cutting oats with the binder and then I and Elisabeth, Anna, Peter and Papa stooked sheaves. Also A.P. Reimer came and got some oats. The weather was fine.

Tues., the 5th Johann W. Reimer came and got two little pigs in the morning. Peter cut the grass and Johann or Elisabeth cut the grain. The rest of us stooked sheaves. I also picked a pailful of cucumbers. Tina pickled them and cooked the meals. The weather was hot and quiet. In the evening there was some wind and rain.

Wed., the 6th Last night there was a good rain. Justina was home and took three little pigs back with her. I wrote a letter to Jahnkes. Papa repaired the coffee grinder. Johann repaired the binder and then cut grain, and the others set up sheaves in stooks. In the evening Papa and I went to *Grossmutterchen's* for a little while. The weather was nice but there was a cool wind.

Thurs., the 7th Papa took the milk to Giroux and the rest of us were harvesting grain. In the afternoon Papa was cutting the grain because Johann was at Johann T. Reimers'. The weather was nice.

Fri., the 8th We harvested grain all day and stooked sheaves. Peter cultivated. Mrs. C. Siemens was here. They finished cutting the oats. The weather was quiet and nice. Some north wind.

Sat., the 9th Papa went to Steinbach and got some flour. Johann was cutting grain. The girls stooked sheaves in the forenoon and then they worked inside. Peter was cultivating. In the evening Papa raked the hay. I picked five pails of cucumbers and pickled them and did other things like that. The weather was fine.

Sun., the 10th The girls, Elisabeth and Anna, went to Steinbach to church and because it was raining so much, the rest of us stayed home in the forenoon. Then Papa, I, Peter, Tina, Sahra, Abraham and Greta went to Steinbach and visited Peter K. Dücks. In the evening Jakob U. Kornelsen and P.R. Plett were here. The weather was rainy in the morning but nice in the evening.

Mon., the 11th We all did various things because it rained last night. J.R. Plett came here to grind some grain. In the afternoon the girls stooked sheaves. Papa finished cutting the wheat. Johann cut the hay. I was at David P. Reimers'. There I have *Kapfst gesetzt* [?] for Mrs. D. Reimer and also got some plums. The weather was quite nice.

Tues., the 12th Johann finished setting up the hay sling and track in the hayloft and then brought in two loads of hay. The girls were stooking sheaves. I picked cucumbers and prepared a barrel full to ship to Herbert, Saskatchewan. I also wrote a letter to Jahnkes in Saskatchewan.

Wed., the 13th First Johann took a cow to Giroux and sold it for 67 ... dollars. The binder has been busy all day. In the afternoon Papa raked hay, and Peter cultivated today. The girls canned plums in the forenoon and then stooked sheaves. I worked in the garden in the afternoon. The weather was very warm.

Thurs., the 14th I worked in the garden and baked. The others worked in the barley field and cultivated. C. Barkmans were here for afternoon lunch. They had come to get a piglet. The weather was rainy after lunch.

Fri., the 15th I picked cucumbers in the morning. The girls and boys were stooking sheaves. Papa worked in the barn loft. In the afternoon it was rainy and we went to Steinbach to the store. We also visited at J.W. Reimers', H. Wielers' and Johann Klassens'. Also J.R. Plett and Johann R. Töws were here.

Sat., the 16th Johann took the milk to Giroux. Papa repaired a barrel for me and did some accounting. He also wrote some letters. One was to A.A. Löppky. In evening he went to a school meeting. I made mustard pickles and picked cucumbers. The girls did various things. The weather was quite rainy and humid, making us feel sluggish. Papa was suffering because of a boil. Also both of my brothers, David and Johann, were here.

Sun., the 17th We were here in our church and K.R. Friesen preached. For lunch P.K. Dücks and Maria were here. For the afternoon lunch C. Ungers, C.P. Reimers and C. Kornelsens came over. Later the Jakob Plett girls were here a little while. Also there was a small meeting here about church matters. The weather was nice.

Mon., the 18th First Johann went to Steinbach and then he went away to thresh. Papa was cutting grain all day with the binder. The girls stooked sheaves.

Peter cultivated in the forenoon. I worked with the cucumbers in the afternoon. The weather was beautiful. We also received a letter from G. Jahnkes.

Tues., the 19th Papa cut the grain all day. The girls stooked sheaves. I was in Neuanlage in the afternoon. I also wrote a letter to Jahnkes. The weather was nice. In the evening it got windy.

Wed., the 20th Papa finished all the grain cutting by afternoon lunch time, and then Elisabeth went to Steinbach. I brought some plums to Giroux in the afternoon. In the evening I picked some cucumbers. Also Uncle J.U. Wiebe with Sahra were over in the evening. The weather was nice and a little windy.

Thurs., the 21st We threshed today. Also Justina and Maria were home. The weather was very warm.

Fri., the 22nd We threshed till two o'clock in the afternoon and Mrs. P. Löwen was here for lunch. And for afternoon lunch we walked together to Johann R. Töwses' place. Papa raked the hay and brought one load home. Peter cultivated the land. The girls moved everything out of the kitchen. The weather was nice.

Sat., the 23rd Papa brought hay into the hayloft. Peter worked the land with the cultivator. The girls made ketchup and pickles and canned cherries and blueberries. We also put cucumbers in brine and dill for winter. The weather was quite windy.

Sun., the 24th Papa and I were in church in Steinbach and Jakob R. Dück instructed. We were all home for lunch. Johann had guests. In the afternoon we went to Johann Klassens'. Elisabeth is at A. R. Pletts'. The weather was nice.

Mon., the 25th In the morning Papa brought hay into the hayloft. Peter cultivated. Johann went away to help thresh where the community machine was threshing now. I sewed and in the afternoon we went to Steinbach. The girls canned plums. Peter was cutting hay. A.T. Löwen was here a little while and we were at C. Siemens' for a short time. The weather was quite windy around noon, otherwise nice. Tina walked to Johann P. Reimers'.

Tues., the 26th I worked with the cucumbers. Elisabeth canned some more plums. Anna started to do the washing. Papa and Peter worked with the hay. Towards evening I was at A. Reimers' and C. Reimers' for a little while. The weather was a little rainy in the morning, otherwise nice.

Wed., the 27th Papa and Peter worked with the hay. The girls laundered the wash. I made the meals and canned some pickles. The weather was very nice. We had some frost already.

Thurs., the 28th Papa and Peter finished mowing the hay. The girls were washing. I did various things inside. The weather was rainy after tea, so Johann and C. Kornelsens' Gerhard came home, because the threshing had to stop. Johann R. Töws was here.

Fri., the 29th First Papa went to Neuanlage and to Klaas C. Penners' and then he worked all day with his accounts. The others couldn't do much today because it was so rainy. The ... barley dried. In the evening P. and C. Plett came to mangle their wash. I sewed a little.

Sat., the 30th In the morning Johann and G.S. Kornelsen went to Steinbach. Papa worked on his accounts in the forenoon and then he worked with the hay. Peter ploughed. Johann went threshing again in the afternoon. The girls worked with the wash and did the Saturday cleaning. I baked and sewed. The weather was very good.

Sun., 31st Papa and I were here in church and the rest of the day we were alone. Elisabeth was in Grünfeld. In the evening J.R. Plett was here a while. The weather was very nice.

September

Mon., the 1st Papa took away the milk and brought back some berries, so Elisabeth canned them. I and the other girls picked beans. Peter raked hay all day. Papa also raked in the afternoon. I had a visitor – Mrs. Johann R. Töws. The weather was good but quite windy.

Tues., the 2nd Papa with Anna, Elisabeth and Peter together stacked the hay. I and Sahra, Abraham and Greta were at Justina and Peter's place, also Maria. They were threshing. The weather was fine.

Wed., the 3rd Papa finished stacking the hay and also took some to the barn. The children helped him. I was at Klaas P. Reimers' and also got some hops plants there. Also the P. Reimer women were here to mangle their wash. The weather was good.

Thurs., the 4th Papa and Elisabeth worked with the hay and Peter ploughed the land. Anna worked with the wash. I was at A.P. Reimers'. The weather was nice and quiet. Also we got a letter from G. Jahnkes.

Fri., the 5th Papa worked with the hay and Peter ploughed. I and the girls did various things in the garden and inside. The weather was good. And I wrote a letter to G Jahnkes.

Sat., the 6th Papa nearly finished transporting the hay. I brought a barrel of cucumbers to Giroux. I also baked and was a little while at H. Pletts'. Peter plowed. The girls did various things in preparation for threshing. The weather was quite hot.

Sun., the 7th It rained in the night so we did not go to church. Johann and Elisabeth went to P.K. Dücks' but did not find them at home. The weather was cloudy and windy.

Mon., the 8th Johann took away the milk. Papa went to Johann Löwens' and brought the plough back with him. And in the afternoon we went to Gre[e]nland to the Martin Penners'. The weather was quite warm. We also heard that the dear Mrs. G. Jahnke died today.

Tues., the 9th I was at D.P. Reimers in the night. Then Papa and I went to Steinbach in the morning. In the afternoon Papa went to Herbert [Saskatchewan], also C.F. Unger. The boys started ploughing with the tractor plough. The girls mangled the wash, etc. The weather was good. Also Johann Klassens were here awhile.

Wed., the 10th It rained very hard in the night. Justina and Maria came home to visit. Also Mrs. Jakob Kornelsen was here and brought Johann home. Johann ploughed for a while. The weather was nice but windy.

Thurs., the 11th We threshed today and Papa was not at home. The weather was very warm.

Fri., the 12th We threshed till nine o'clock in the morning. Then I went to Steinbach and also worked a little in the garden. Johann plowed the land. The girls were busy inside. And for supper Uncle Isaak Löwen and Mrs. C.D. Barkman were here. The weather was very nice. We sold three crocks of lard.

Sat., the 13th It rained a lot again in the night, so we couldn't do much outside. Johann was milling some grain for feed.

Sun., the 14th It rained again in the night, and we and Elisabeth went to church. For lunch Peter K. Dücks were here. Also Johann R. Plett was here for a while. The weather was cloudy and humid.

Mon., the 15th Johann fixed fences in the morning. The girls started to wash. They also worked in the henhouse and canned tomatoes and brought in the watermelons. In the afternoon Johann went threshing and we went to Heuboden to see the J. and C. Kornelsens. The weather was very warm.

Tues., the 16th Papa and I went to Steinbach in the morning and were at Johann Klassens' for lunch. Then Papa helped at the threshing machine and Johann came home and ploughed till evening. I and Maria brought in beans, tomatoes, etc. The other girls washed. The weather was very warm.

Wed., the 17th Johann ploughed on the land. The girls finished washing in the forenoon and then they took Maria to P. Dücks'. I was at *Grossmutterchen's* place, also at Johann P. Reimers'. Papa came home from threshing at noon. The sheaves were all threshed. Then he went to Giroux for oil. The weather – very warm.

Thurs., the 18th Papa took the milk to Giroux. Johann ploughed with horses. I did various things in the kitchen. The girls ironed and mangled the wash with Gertrude Plett. Also Mrs. C. Siemens was visiting here. The weather was quite cloudy and rainy.

Fri., the 19th Papa built a fence around the haystacks. Johann was in Steinbach, and later he and Peter ploughed. The girls finished doing the wash and in the evening Elisabeth and Anna went to Heinrich Ennses'. I baked. Peter Ungers were here for a little while. The weather was nice.

Sat., the 20th Papa built two milking stools. Johann ploughed. The girls did the Saturday cleaning. I worked on various things in the bedroom. The weather was nice.

Sun., the 21st Papa, I, Elisabeth, Katharina and Peter went to church in Steinbach and Rev. H.R. Reimer preached. We all came home for lunch. For afternoon lunch Papa and I went to the Peter B. Krökers'. The girls had visitors. Sahra, Lena, and Peter walked to the widow Mrs. Klaas R. Penner's. The weather was nice.

Mon., the 22nd Papa harvested *Alsranken* [?]. Uncle Jakob Penner has started to paint the barn. The girls dug some potatoes. I worked inside, and pressed the juice out of the ripe tomatoes. Johann ploughed ten acres today. The weather was a little cool and windy.

Tues., the 23rd Papa got two hayrack loads of *Alsranken* from the field and then he also helped paint the barn. The others all continued with yesterday's work. I and Elisabeth went to Jakob U. Wiebes'. The weather was good.

Wed., the 24th Papa was painting the barn in the forenoon. So was Johann. The girls whitewashed the walls upstairs. I was busy in the kitchen, and also cooked ketchup and *Heffe* [?]. Mr. Johann R. Töws visited here a while. In the evening we brought in beans. The weather was cool and windy.

Thurs., the 25th Papa and Jakob Penner painted the barn all day. Johann got some kerosene in the morning and then he ploughed till 9:30 in the evening. Peter was cultivating again. I made meals, baked, washed, and cleaned some hens for cooking. The girls finished cleaning the upstairs. The weather was very nice and quiet.

Fri., the 26th Papa and Jakob Penner painted the barn. Johann ploughed. Peter cultivated. The girls dug up the potatoes. I made meals and baked. In the evening Papa and Jakob Penner went to Blumenort. The weather was nice.

Sat., the 27th Papa took the milk away in the morning and Jakob Penner painted. P. Dücks came for lunch and brought Maria home, and then Maria went with C. Ungers to Morris. They were at the funeral of Mrs. Jakob Kröker. Also "Zentral" Töws [Peter; he was called "Zentral" because he ran the local telephone central station] was here and Papa went with him to fix a telephone line. Johann ploughed and Peter cultivated. The girls cleaned floors in the forenoon. The weather was very nice.

Sun., the 28th We and the children here in church and Heinrich R. Reimer preached. For lunch only Johann had visitors. Franz K. Dück and Jakob P.D. Reimer were over. Then Papa and I went to C. Brandts'. For afternoon lunch J.R. Plett and *Ältester* Reimer were here. Also Maria came home from Morris.

Mon., the 29th Papa and Jakob Penner painted the barn. David Dörksen was here for lunch and in the afternoon Papa went along with P.P. Reimer to Osterwick. The girls dug potatoes. I was busy inside. Johann ploughed and Peter cultivated. In the evening we cleaned one kind of beans. The weather was nice.

Tues., the 30th Papa and Jakob Penner finished painting the barn. I worked in the kitchen and also prepared the ... The boys both worked on the land. The girls finished digging the potatoes and also brought many in from the garden. The weather was cloudy and cool.

October

Wed., the 1st The girls cleaned the henhouse and whitewashed it. Johann ploughed and Peter cultivated. In the afternoon Papa and I went to Steinbach. Johann went to Giroux for kerosene. The girls hoed in the garden. The weather was nice but a little rainy in the evening.

Thurs., the 2nd Papa worked in the granary with the grain. Johann ploughed and went to plough at C. Ungers' after late afternoon lunch. Peter finished cultivating the fields. The girls washed. Elisabeth mended and sewed for the topbuggy. I made the meals. The weather was nice but windy.

Fri., the 3rd Papa and Peter cleaned a load of wheat and brought it to Giroux. I and Elisabeth and Anna worked on the buggy top, and also baked. Work was also done with the wash. The weather was good.

Sat., the 4th Papa went twice to Giroux with wheat. Johann finished ploughing at C. Ungers'. The girls painted the henhouse. I worked with a large bed. Maria was sewing at the Siemens'. In the evening Papa was sick. There was good weather.

Sun., the 5th The children, Anna, Elisabeth, Peter, and Tina went to church in Steinbach, and for lunch to the widow Mrs. Peter Dück's. In the afternoon we had visitors. Mrs. C.F. Friesen and Mrs. C. Barkman were here. Also P.K. Dücks came later. In the evening Maria and Elisabeth walked to H. Pletts'. The weather was good.

Mon., the 6th Papa went twice to Giroux with wheat. Johann ploughed. Peter cleaned wheat. Also he and Anna, Tina, and Maria brought in wood for winter. I and Elisabeth did some canning. In the evening Papa and I went to C. Ungers' to trade geese. The weather was nice.

Tues., the 7th Papa made another two trips to Giroux with wheat. Johann ploughed. The girls brought in wood. Elisabeth and I canned fruit. In the evening C. Siemens came over. Maria and Elisabeth were at Heinrich Ennses' place. The weather was good but quite windy in the evening.

Wed., the 8th Papa was in Steinbach and Johann ploughed. Peter and Tina went along with Papa to P.K. Dücks'. The girls sealed the windows with putty. In the afternoon Elisabeth went to Jakob U. Wiebes'. We had visitors for lunch at noon. Jakob R. Dücks and Mrs. D. Isaak were here. For afternoon lunch we were all at C. Siemens'. The weather was quite windy.

Thurs., the 9th Papa took the milk away. Johann ploughed. In the afternoon Papa took the wheat to Giroux and Johann took the ploughshare to Steinbach. The weather was quite windy but nice.

Fri., the 10th Papa and Johann moved the buggy shelter to its right place. The girls cleaned house. The weather was a little cool.

Sat., the 11th Papa went to get the cattle from Heuboden, the summer grazing ground. Johann ploughed after the late afternoon lunch. In the evening Elisabeth and Anna went to the P.K. Dücks'. The weather was nice.

Sun., the 12th Church was here in Blumenort and we had no visitors. In the afternoon we went to J.P. Reimers'. The weather was very nice.

Mon., the 13th I was at Johann T. Reimers'. Papa brought chopped feed into the barn. The girls washed. Johann ploughed. The weather was nice.

Tues., the 14th Papa took away another load of wheat. Johann ploughed. I and Maria went to Steinbach. The girls did various things, like ironing the wash, canning tomatoes, cleaning and sealing the windows, etc. We also heard that Joseph, son of J.B. Reimers, died. The weather was nice.

Wed., the 15th Papa worked on his accounts in the morning and then went to Steinbach and I went along to C.P. Reimers'. In the evening we went to visit *Grossmutterchen*. Johann ploughed the garden. The girls sewed. The weather was sunny but a little cool.

Thurs., the 16th Johann ploughed. The girls sewed again and Papa and I went for night to Jakob E. [The days 17 to 20 inclusive are missing.]

Tues., the 21st We came home in the evening and we had good weather during the whole trip. We also heard that the widow Mrs. C.D. Barkman has married Edward Manke.

Wed., the 22nd Papa, Johann, and P.K. Dück went to an auction sale in Hochfeld. Justina was here. Papa bought two sheep at the sale. The weather was quite windy with some snow and rain.

Thurs., the 23rd Papa worked on the henhouse. The girls cleaned the kitchen and did various things. I sewed and also wrote a letter to B. Dücks. In the evening we were at the H. Pletts'. The weather was cool and cloudy.

Fri., the 24th Papa worked on the pig barn. Johann was repairing various things. I and Elisabeth and Maria sewed. Anna cooked ketchup. Tina cooked, etc. Johann T. Reimer and C. Siemens were here for a while. In the evening Johann and Peter went to H. Pletts'. The weather was quite cool and snowy.

Sat., the 25th Johann went twice to Giroux with a load of wheat. Papa, I, Elisabeth and Maria went to the funeral. C.R. Penners' son Johann was being buried. We also did the Saturday cleaning and baked. In the evening H. Pletts' sons, Cornelius and Peter, were here and picked up their last pay for building the barn. The weather was quite cool and clear.

Sun., the 26th Church was here and we were instructed by Klaas R. Friesen. For lunch we had visitors: P.K. Dücks, P.P.D. Reimers, and Jakob B. and Susanna Reimer were here. For the afternoon lunch Mrs. Peter Löwen and Margareta came over. Also H. Pletts and uncle Jakob Plett were here. In the evening Jakob U. Kornelsen came over. The weather was quite cool but clear and quiet.

Mon., the 27th Johann took the milk to Giroux. We also shipped a load of cabbages to Herbert [Saskatchewan] and Papa went along to the Jakob Pletts'. He also cleaned up various things on the farmyard. They also brought some chopped forage into the barn. The girls sewed and I darned socks. The weather was a little snowy.

Tues., the 28th The Peter Löwen boys moved *Grossmutterchen*'s house from here, but didn't get very far. Papa and Johann had to help them. I darned stockings and washed and baked. The girls sewed. In the evening K.F. Penners and Peter Ungers were here. Papa was at a school meeting. The weather was windy.

Wed., the 29th Papa and Johann helped move *Grossmutterchen*'s house to David Reimers'. I and Anna and Tina sewed and darned stockings. Elisabeth painted the kitchen floor. Maria has started to teach school. Also the Siemens boys were here for a visit. The weather was very nice.

Thurs., the 30th Papa and Johann and Peter were milling grain for feed. Also Jakob U. Wiebe came to visit. I was knitting. Anna and Elisabeth were in Steinbach. Tina baked, etc. The weather was fine in the daytime. In the evening it snowed. It was one degree warm.

Fri., the 31st Papa and Johann went to Peter Ungers' to mill grain. Also Papa went to I[saak] Pletts'. In the afternoon we went to P.K. Dücks'. The children, Maria, Elisabeth, Anna and Peter, went to J.G. Barkmans' in the evening. The weather was quite stormy.

November

Sat., the 1st Johann was milling grain for feed at Johann R. Töwses' place. The girls cleaned house and baked. Papa helped to lay a brick chimney at Dücks'. The weather was nice.

Sun., the 2nd We went to church in Steinbach with Maria and Elisabeth. We were instructed by P Kröker. For lunch we were at C. Fasts'. Later we went to see the Aunt Radinzel. In the evening Anna, Johann and Elisabeth went to David Reimers'. The weather was quite nice but rather windy in the evening.

Mon., the 3rd Papa worked on his accounts in the forenoon, and in the afternoon uncle Jakob Barkman from Heuboden visited. In the evening the Aron W. Reimers were here. The girls were sewing during the day and I knitted. Johann was milling grain again with our feedmill at J.R. Töwses' place. I sent a letter to G. Jahnkes. The weather was cool and windy.

Tues., the 4th We helped butcher three pigs at Peter Ungers'. The girls washed. The weather was quite nice.

Wed., the 5th Johann was milling grain at Johann R. Töwses' place, and at H. Ennses' and J.W. Reimers' in Blumenhof. Papa worked on his accounts. Also Papa and I went to Steinbach. In the evening I knitted. Papa worked on his accounts. The girls were butchering geese at Peter K. Dücks'. The weather was cloudy and mild.

Thurs., the 6th Papa and Johann were milling feed grain for others. Then Papa brought the feedmill home and Johann went to Steinbach. Elisabeth sewed. The other girls washed and I knitted and baked. I also went to A.P. Reimers'. The weather was nice.

Fri., the 7th Papa and Johann installed water pipes in the barn for watering the cattle. Then Papa worked on his accounts and wrote fee collection letters to the members of the fire insurance guild. Johann and Elisabeth went to Steinbach and I knitted. Elisabeth also sewed some and Anna and Tina ironed the wash and folded it. In the evening Maria cut out dresses from material for sewing and also was at Johann R. Töwses' for a while. Peter Ungers' children visited here. The weather was mild.

Sat., the 8th Papa wrote letters and did accounts in the morning and then did various things in the barn. Maria and Elisabeth sewed. I knitted and spun wool. Anna and Tina did the housecleaning. In the evening H. Pletts and Johann and Klaas came over. The girls mangled some wash. The weather was snowy.

Sun., the 9th Church service was here today but we all had no visitors during the day. Rev. B. Dück preached this morning. For afternoon lunch we went to A.P. Reimers' as Rev. Dück was visiting there. In church marriage banns were announced for two couples. The girls were out visiting. Anna and Tina were at Mrs. P. Löwen's place. Elisabeth was at the P.R. Penners' and Maria went to visit the widow Mrs. Klaas R. Penner. Also Elisabeth and Cornelius, children of Johann F. Reimers, visited us in the evening. The weather was mild.

Mon., the 10th Johann took the milk to Giroux and we butchered pigs today. C. Ungers and P.K. Dücks helped us. The weather was very stormy, so the Dücks had to stay for night.

Tues., the 11th Johann took Justina home. I knitted and spun. Elisabeth and Anna sewed. The weather was clear and cold with 11 degrees frost. Papa worked on the accounts and wrote letters.

Wed., the 12th We didn't do any out-of-the-ordinary work. The weather was a little stormy. Papa and I went to visit at the David Reimers' and Johann Reimers'.

Thurs., the 13th Papa made the pig barn more airtight for warmth. He also brought in a load of hay and smoked the sausages. In the evening Maria, Elisabeth and Johann went to visit the widow, the Aunt Wohlgemuth. I did some spinning and Elisabeth sewed. The weather was quite cold, 15 degrees frost.

Fri., the 14th We helped butcher pigs at C. Ungers'. The weather was quite cold but quiet. In the evening the wind blew from the south. In the morning there was a 21-degree frost.

Sat., the 15th Papa went to Steinbach and the boys brought wood to the house. They also brought the window shutters upstairs and fastened the storm windows. Elisabeth did various things in her room, and pickled some cabbage. Maria sewed and I spun. Anna and Tina cleaned house and baked. The weather was quiet and mild. We also heard that Martin, son of Klaas P. Reimers, died in the night at one o'clock.

Sun., the 16th There was church in Steinbach and in Grünfeld. But we stayed at home. The David P. Reimers came to visit. Maria and Elisabeth went to a double wedding in Grünfeld. Dietrich, son of Jakob Dück, married Elisabeth R. Schellenberg, and Johann, son of the widow Mrs. David Friesen, married Maria F. Dück. They were married by the father, Jakob R. Dück, in the Holdeman church. The weather was unusually mild, about one degree below and very quiet. In the evening it got windy.

Mon., the 17th Papa, Elisabeth and Johann went to Winnipeg. I did some spinning. Anna and Tina brought chicken feed and straw into the henhouse. The weather is very mild, nearly four degrees warm.

Tues., the 18th We helped butcher two pigs at David Reimers'. The girls did various things. Elisabeth sewed. Anna and Tina worked for a while in the henhouse. The weather was quite mild, two degrees cold.

Wed., the 19th Papa wrote letters. I was spinning. The girls sewed and made sauerkraut. The weather was mild and quite windy, four degrees cold. Also Klaas P. Reimers came home from the States today.

Thurs., the 20th We helped butcher two pigs at C. Siemens'. In the evening J.R. Töws was here for a while. Papa also worked on his accounts and I was spinning. The girls did various things. Elisabeth had a bad headache. The weather was quite mild.

Fri., the 21st Peter K. Dücks and his mother came here and then we all went to the funeral of Martin Reimer. In the evening I worked with the wool. The weather was mild.

Sat., the 22nd Papa and the boys cleaned some grain. Johann took the milk away in the morning. I washed, and also washed wool, and baked. Maria sewed a lot. The other girls cleaned house. In the forenoon Uncle Johann B. Koop was over and in the evening Martin F. Barkmans were here a little while. And later we went to visit Klaas P. Reimers. The weather was quite mild. In the morning it was one . . . degree warm.

Sun., the 23rd We were in church here [in Blumenort] and Rev. Heinrich R. Reimer preached. For lunch, Johann D.F. Friesen was here. In the afternoon, Maria and Elisabeth went to visit A. Pletts and we went to Johann Barkmans'. In the evening Johann D. F. Friesen and P. and H. R. Plett were over. The weather was mild.

Mon., the 24th Johann took the milk to Giroux and Papa brought in a hayrack full of hay. The girls sewed and I mended clothes. In the afternoon we were at I.W. Reimers' because the Aunt Reimer was sick. The weather was quite windy with snow from the north.

Tues., the 25th Papa and I helped butcher two pigs at Klaas D.F. Friesens'. Elisabeth sewed. Maria has stopped teaching school. Johann took a load of wheat away to sell. The weather was quiet and cold, about 23 degrees below.

Wed., the 26th We helped butcher three pigs at H. Pletts'. Maria and the other girls sewed. Johann brought in some straw. The weather was quite cold, 23 degrees below.

Thurs., the 27th Papa and Johann brought in feed for the animals. Anna washed. Maria and Elisabeth sewed. I knitted and also wrote a letter to B. Dücks. Tina made meals, etc. The weather was quite cold and windy. In the morning there were 15 degrees frost; in the evening, 10 degrees.

Fri., the 28th First thing in the morning Papa went to see Jakob J.G. Barkmans. Then he cleaned wheat with Johann. In the afternoon Johann went to Giroux. Papa and I and Maria went to Steinbach and in the evening we went to visit *Grossmutterchen* who came home from Kansas this morning. The weather was quite mild, a little windy with 10 degrees frost.

Sat., the 29th Johann took another load of wheat away. Papa and Peter brought in feed, etc. The girls, Elisabeth and Maria, sewed. Anna ironed the wash and I knitted and baked. The weather was not very cold but stormy.

Sun., the 30th Papa and I went to Neuanlage to visit Peter P. Reimers, also I.P. Löwens in Blumenort. The children, Johann, Maria and Elisabeth, went to H. Pletts' in the evening. The weather was quite cold and windy. There was a strong north wind and 23 degrees frost.

December

Mon., the 1st Papa shoed two horses. Johann worked in the henhouse, etc. The girls were all sewing. Maria sewed for Mrs. Johann R. Töws. I knitted various things and dyed the prepared wool. In the evening Uncle Jakob Barkman from Heuboden visited here. The weather was quiet and cold, 24 degrees frost in the morning.

Tues., the 2nd Johann went to Giroux with a load of wheat. Papa worked with the stovepipes. The girls were all sewing. I was knitting. The weather was cold with 22 degrees frost.

Wed., the 3rd Papa and I helped P.P. Reimers from Neuanlage butcher three pigs and one ox. Maria and Elisabeth sewed. Johann went to Steinbach. The weather was mild.

Thurs., the 4th In the forenoon I was at the Isaak P. Löwens'. Papa and Johann cleaned some grain and then Johann went to Giroux with a load of wheat. I and Papa went with *Grossmutterchen* and Mrs. P. Löwen to Johann F. Reimers'. Maria was at C.P. Reimers' and Elisabeth did some sewing. In the evening the H. Plett children were over and mangled their wash. The weather was quite mild.

Fri., the 5th We helped butcher pigs at Johann P. Reimers'. In the evening Klaas F. Penners were here. Maria was in Winnipeg today. The girls did some baking and housecleaning. The boys were at H. Pletts'. The weather was quite mild.

Sat., the 6th We went with *Grossmutterchen* to visit the widows Mrs. Peter Dück and Mrs. Franz Kröker. We also were at the C. Krökers'. The boys were milling grain for feed. Maria sewed and the other girls did the Saturday chores. The weather was quite mild. We also got a letter from Uncle G. Jahnke.

Sun., the 7th Church was here [in Blumenort]. Papa, Johann, Maria, and Elisabeth attended. Johann U. Kornelsen was over for lunch and Klaas R. Plett came later for afternoon lunch. In the evening Johann, Maria, and Elisabeth went to visit the Jakob Pletts. The weather was very stormy but in the evening it became cold and quiet with 22 degrees frost.

Mon., the 8th Papa worked on his accounts and wrote letters. Johann went to Giroux with the milk. The girls sewed and I knitted. In the evening we went to the Aron W. Reimers'. The weather was very cold. In the morning there were 27 degrees frost, and in the evening, 25 degrees.

Tues., the 9th Papa worked on his accounts. Johann R. Plett was here to mill some grain. Peter F. Wiebe was here and pulled a tooth from one of the horses. Also Kornelius and Abraham, sons of Jakob Koops, visited here a little while. I knitted and the girls sewed. The weather was very cold with 27 degrees frost.

Wed., the 10th Papa had visitors. Uncle G. Kornelsen, also Uncle I. Plett and P.P. Reimer were here. Also Uncle Kornelius Töws from Gre[e]nland came. Jakob E. Schellenberg came and got Maria to help in their home. I knitted and the girls sewed. The boys were milling grain for feed. The weather was 27 degrees cold and somewhat windy.

Thurs., the 11th Papa worked in the account books. Johann R. Plett was grinding feed grain here till late afternoon lunch time. The girls sewed and I knitted. In the evening I did some spinning. C.R. Plett came to visit. The weather was a little milder, 18 degrees frost.

Fri., the 12th In the morning Uncle Johann P. Janzen was here. I was spinning and the girls sewed. In the afternoon Anna and Elisabeth went to P. K. Dücks'. I and Papa were in Steinbach. For afternoon lunch we were at Mrs. Jakob W. Reimer's place. Johann repaired the manure sled. The weather was 18 degrees cold.

Sat., the 13th In the forenoon Papa brought one load of straw into the barn, and then he made preparations for butchering pigs. The girls baked and I knitted. The weather was 23 degrees cold.

Sun., the 14th We went to church in Steinbach and H.R. Dück brought the sermon. For lunch we were at C. Krökers' and for afternoon lunch C.P. Reimers came to our place. In the evening Johann R. Töws and the boys were here a while. The weather was cold – 27 degrees in the morning and 23 degrees in the evening. H.R. Dücks came home on Thursday from the States.

Mon., the 15th We butchered two pigs and one ox: H. Pletts, P. P. Reimers, A.P. Reimers and Peter Ungers came to help. In the evening Peter R. Plett came to visit. The weather was very cold – 27 degrees and 26 degrees in the evening.

Tues., the 16th Papa stored away the fresh meat and smoked the sausages. Elisabeth also helped to take care of the meat. I knitted mittens. Also Johann R. Penner and Mr. Halles were here. Papa went to see Johann R. Töws a little while. The weather was cold and quiet with 24 degrees frost.

Wed., the 17th We helped butcher two pigs at Johann R. Penners' place. The girls washed and Elisabeth sewed. Johann got some more loads of straw for the barn. In the evening he was at the H. Pletts'. The weather was 20 degrees cold.

Thurs., the 18th Papa went to Morris. The girls washed and Elisabeth sewed. I looked after Margaret who was sick, and did some knitting. Johann looked after the cattle. The weather was fairly mild with 13 degrees frost. There was a little snow and some wind.

Fri., the 19th I was knitting and the girls took care of the wash. In the evening Johann and Elisabeth went to get Maria from Johann B. Reimers'. Papa came home from Morris and brought along Uncle Johann K. Friesen. The weather was mild with six degrees and four degrees frost.

Sat., the 20th Papa went to Steinbach with Uncle Johann K. Friesen [a minister]. The boys brought fodder into the barn. The girls did the Saturday work. I darned stockings. Johann and Peter went to Steinbach in the evening. The weather was very mild with zero degrees frost.

Sun., the 21st Church was here in our district and Uncle Johann K. Friesen preached. For lunch the K.R. Töwses and the P.K. Dücks were here. In the afternoon Peter Dücks' Sahra and Elisabeth, Frank and Gertrude Penner, and Margaret Fast were also here. In the evening the Johann R. Töwses and J. Plett visited.

Mon., the 22nd Johann brought the milk to Giroux. In the morning Father brought the big water kettle to the church and Anna and Elisabeth helped clean the church. Maria washed the curtains for it. Papa and I went to Steinbach in the forenoon. In the evening the children brought the curtains to the church and hung them. The weather was mild.

Tues., the 23rd Papa went to Giroux in the forenoon, and in the afternoon we went to the funeral of Katharina Reimer, daughter of Johann F. Reimers. In the evening we went with the school children, and Johann and Tina, to the Christmas Fest in the Blumenhof school. I also did some baking today. The girls did a lot of sewing. It was nine degrees cold.

Wed., the 24th The girls baked and made various preparations for Christmas. Papa and I went to our children, Peter K. Dücks, and brought them a supply of apples. The weather was very mild but stormy with seven degrees frost. Also C.S. came to visit.

Thurs., the 25th Christmas day, and the church service was in Steinbach, but no one attended. Everyone was home till the afternoon, and then we all went to *Grossmutterchen*'s place. The weather was very mild. In the evening there was sleet.

Fri., the 26th We had church service here [in Blumenort] and were instructed by H.R. Reimer. P.K. Dücks were here for lunch. In the evening Anna and Elisabeth were at the Klaas P. Reimers'. The weather was very mild with six degrees frost. Yesterday Maria was at Tom Mooneys' for a little while. We also heard today that Mrs. Dietrich Isaak had died.

Sat., the 27th Papa and Johann worked with the pigs and brought in feed. In the evening we were at Peter Unger's. Maria was at P.K. Dücks' and for night Cornelius Kornelsens came to us. The weather – very mild with 11 degrees frost.

Sun., the 28th The children, Johann, Anna, Elisabeth, Tina and Peter, and Johann R. Plett, went to P.K. Dücks'. Maria came back home with them. Papa and I went to see Mrs. A. Penner a little while. In the evening C. Siemens were here. Also the children had visitors. Elisabeth, Johann, and Aganetha Brandt were here. C. Kornelsens left before noon. The weather was quite mild with eight degrees frost.

Mon., the 29th We went to the funeral of Mrs. Dietrich Isaak in Grünfeld. We also visited a little while at Johann W. Reimers' in Steinbach. The weather was very mild and windy with one degree warm.

Tues., the 30th Papa went to H. Bartels' in the morning. The girls were sewing and I knitted. In the afternoon Papa and I were in Steinbach. I was a little while at P.R. Friesens'. The boys got in loads of straw. The weather was quite quiet with a few degrees cold.

Wed., the 31st The weather was quite cold with 21 and 20 degrees frost. Yesterday C. Unger brought back our ram. The end of 1919.

18 Judith Klassen Neufeld (1869 to 1952)

Ebenfeld, Manitoba

Diary selection: 1 May to 31 October 1922

Age: 53

Judith Klassen was born in 1869 in Schoenthal, Bergthal Colony, New Russia, to Johann Klassen (1820-1907) and Maria Stoesz (1823-1897) (see diary 4). She was the youngest in a family of 15 children. In 1874, at age five, she came to Manitoba with her parents, who settled in Ebenfeld on the East Reserve. In about 1890 she married Peter B. Neufeld (1866-1939) and established a household on a farm that they rented from his elderly parents in Ebenfeld. Between 1891 and 1910, Judith gave birth to 10 children.

Even though they still did not own their farm in 1922, during this year Judith and Peter continued to oversee the establishment of sub-households for their married children. This was the year that Peter's 101-year-old father died (on 21 October), and now their attention turned to helping raise their grandchildren. Judith's life was especially intertwined with that of her daughter Maria, 28, and her husband, Jacob Wiebe; her daughter Anna, 26, and her husband, Aron Schultz; her daughter Susanna (or San, pronounced Zaun), 24, and her husband, Kornelius Stoesz. Contrary to custom in both Manitoba and Ontario, Judith often referred to her married children by the names of both wife and husband, that is, as "Aron and Anna" and "Kornelius and San." The daughters were obviously very close to their mother. On several occasions Judith noted that "the girls" came home to help, and when they gave birth, as Susanna did on 5 August, Judith rushed over to help.

The sons, unlike the daughters, still lived at home in 1922. Johann, 21, worked on the farm and the farms of neighbours and enjoyed leisure in the form of skating, hunting, horse riding, and even visits with the English neighbour, Drury.

Jacob, 19, was also at home, and he, too, had his times of leisure, Judith even noting the day he slept until noon to recover from a party that lasted until 6 a.m. Heinrich at 15 appears to have been the darling brother, helping with sister Anna's baby and with sister Maria's hog butchering; in addition, he attended school, helped out at his grandfather's, and worked successive days in the community threshing bee. Abram, 12, seemed very closely linked to Papa, spending many days in joint tasks with him when not in school.

Beyond Judith's immediate household lay a world ordered by kin and congregation. In 1922, she had eight sisters and one brother, but she was especially close to Helena, 75, who was married to Peter Falk; Maria, 66, who was married to Abraham Kehler; and Sara, 58, who was married to Heinrich Neufeld. It was a kin-based world that in 1922 was experiencing great upheaval. Abram Kehler had an auction sale in October, probably indicating an intention of moving to Mexico. Judith's sister Margaretha, who was married to Peter Penner, appears to have lived in the West Reserve and in 1922 moved to Mexico. Another sister had already moved to Didsbury, Alberta. Her sister Sara, the wife of Heinrich Neufeld, was obviously close to Judith, but they lived in Steinbach, where in 1915 Heinrich was listed as owning 60 acres of land, two kilometres west of town. Her sister Elisabeth and her husband, Peter Funk, also lived in Steinbach, where Peter likely worked as a wage labourer. Still another sister, Aganetha, and her husband, Peter Wiebe, lived in Langham, Saskatchewan.

Judith's own household was no more stationary than those of most of her siblings. The year 1922 was one of particular instability. For example, Peter attended "Mexico meetings" in May, September, and October, hearing reports of plans to migrate following Manitoba's assimilative School Attendance Act of 1916. In addition, the Neufelds were forced to move off the farm they had rented from his elderly parents because they could not afford the selling price. Although their feelings are not recorded, the difficult task of entertaining "Winnipeg" prospective buyers, seeing the farm sold to the English Drury family, seeking rental property in Steinbach and Niverville, and, finally, moving from the farm on 22 June are noted. With the move from the farm ended the household work for sons Jacob, Johann, and even Peter, the father. The men now worked on community threshing crews, and in November Jacob seems to have obtained a job in the town of Niverville. Judith, meanwhile, bolstered the household's income by providing lodging, on 25 different occasions during 1922, to a Jewish peddler named "Farmer." Family lore has it that later in the 1920s, when the Drury family defaulted on their farm loan, Judith and Peter purchased the family farm and returned to the land. Judith and Peter never did move to Mexico.

A photocopy of the diary written in German Gothic script is in the possession of Irene Enns Kroeker, Steinbach, Manitoba, and was initially translated by Ben Hoeppner, Winnipeg. For more information on Judith Klassen Neufeld see: Irene Enns Kroeker, "Blumengart," *Historical Sketches of the East Reserve* (Steinbach, MB), 100.

May 1922

1. Mon. Clear, but in the evening rain with lightning for a short time.

2. Tue. Mild. The Jew came for lunch. In the afternoon Aron came. It is very warm. In the evening Kornelius and San came here.

3. Wed. Cloudy. Our Stripe [cow or horse] died. It is 1:30. Rain sets in. The Jew was here overnight. He left today. The rain has stopped. Mild.

4. Thur. We drove to Steinbach. It was very pleasant [weather]. At 6 a.m. we drove home.

5. Fri. We drove home. Cloudy, but no rain. We had supper at San's. Arrived home at dusk.

6. Sat. It was mild. Johan ploughs the garden. Papa drove to Niverville. The Jew is here for lunch. He wants to go home. In the afternoon Aron and the children came here. Jacob rode to Heinrich Derksens' in the evening.

7. Sun. Warm. Jacob rode again to Schröders'. Johan drove for a visit and Heinrich went visiting by *Beizekel* [bicycle]. Abram walked to Heinrich Penners'. We had visitors: the junior Stöszes.

8. Mon. Cloudy and windy. Johan drove to Blumengart for seed and brought Abram Kehlers a load of wood.... At 10 rain set in for the day. In the evening Jacob went hunting wolves.

9. Tue. At a.m. lightning and raining: a big storm. Gerhard Neufeld got his piglets from our place, 4 dollars apiece.

10. Wed. Rain again. Much water on the fields. Heinrich Derksen came here to get 7 piglets. The Jew again came for the night.

11. Thur. Raining heavily. The Jew stayed also for lunch. I cleaned the boys' room. Peter Funk brought his wife to Winnipeg; she is in the hospital. She has had surgery on her head.

12. Fri. Cool and cloudy. Papa and Johan and Wm. Hübert and Jacob went to Winnipeg by train. Jacob took them to the train. It is cooling off.

13. Sat. Mild. Cloudy. A good rain at places. A lot of water. In Winnipeg the water was flowing over the streets at places.

14. Sun. Mild. Rain during the night. In the afternoon we drove to Jacob Funks'. Cloudy in the evening

15. Mon. Mild. Johan went cultivating. Abram again went to school.

16. Tue. I [worked] in the garden. Rain at times. Brought potatoes out of the cellar. Have water in the basement.

17. Wed. When we got up, it was raining. At 10 a.m. it is still raining. Heinrich got the plough from Labke [Loeppky?]. Papa drove to Kronsthal. There is a man who has come from Mexico; he has called a *Mitting* [meeting] there. It gets cold and windy from the north.

18. Thur. Cold and cloudy. It still freezes at times. It is not mild. Johan and Heinrich are ploughing the barley field.... In the afternoon we drove to the senior Schultzes'; there was a *Mitting* about moving to Mexico. In the evening our children, Jacob Wiebes, came here.

19. Fri. The weather is still changeable, cloudy and raining. Johan and Heinrich are ploughing. Set a brooding hen. One hen hatched some chicks today.

20. Sat. Everything seems so different, it all seems to strange. Papa drove to Niverville. Johan seeds barley. Heinrich still ploughs. After lunch he harrows. Jacob is planting.

21. Sun. Windy and warm. We are at home. Johan went visiting. Jacob was riding and Heinrich and Abram walked. In the evening it got cloudy. Lightning.

22. Mon. When we got up, it was very cloudy. At 7 a.m. rain. Most of it passes by. Rain all day.

23. Tue. Mild. Windy. We did the laundry. Johan and Heinrich are ploughing the barley fields. Jacob completes the fence. Papa and Abram drove to Vollwerk to get flour.

24. Wed. Warm. Papa and Jacob drove to Niverville. Johan and Heinrich are ploughing.

25. Thur. Very warm. Johan and Jacob drove to Chortitz to church. We stayed home. After lunch Aron and Anna came here.

26. Fri. The senior Abram Kehler came here.... During the evening Papa and Kehler drove to Niverville.

27. Sat. He drove home. Abram Hübert [?] came here also. He had 3 brooding hens. It is warm and windy.

28. Sun. We had visitors: Abram Kehlers. Jacob Wiebes came from *Jennseit* [West Reserve] at 12 midnight.

29. Mon. We cleaned the [summer] kitchen. In the afternoon we moved into the [summer] kitchen. It is cool and windy.

30. Tue. We cleaned the cooking room [in the main house].

31. Wed. Did the laundry. Had visitors in the afternoon from Winnipeg. They wanted to buy our farm. Johan is sick with a headache. Seeded the last barley.

June 1922

1. Thur. Our children, Jacob Wiebes, and Aron drove to Winnipeg. They had hired Johan Wiebe. I want to clean the windows on the outside and to whitewash the hallway. Lightning during the evening and raining a little.

2. Fri. Mild. Jacob and Heinrich are harrowing. In the afternoon our buyer from Winnipeg again came to buy our farm and also Aron's farm. For the night they drove to Winnipeg. It looks like rain. There was lightning all night.

3. Sat. Warm. Windy. Peter drove with Peter Ungers for greenfeed [unripened oat plants]. Johan and Heinrich drove to Vollwerk. Papa and Aron drove to Niverville.

4. Sun. Pentecost. The children were all here for lunch. Johan went visiting and Heinrich drove to Bergthal [?].

5. Mon. The second holiday of Pentecost. Our children, Jacob Wiebes, drove with Jacob Stöszes to *Jennseit*. Windy. Afternoon we drove to Wm. Hüberts. During the evening the wind shifted to the north and it got cool and cloudy.

6. Tue. Cool and windy and cloudy. In the afternoon Heinrich drove to Penners'.

7. Wed. Rain. Jacob returned from *Jennseit*. We sold our calf for $10.00.

8. Thur. Rain in the morning [and it continued] until the afternoon. Heinrich Neufelds came here, as did Mrs. Peter Neufeld from *Ditzburi* [Didsbury, Alberta] and 3 children. Our land buyers drove home for the night. Rain. The Jew came here for the night. It gets cool and windy.

9. Fri. Mild. Papa and Aron drove to Steinbach. They are looking for living quarters. They bought a watermelon for 2 cents a lb., but it was not worth anything for it is completely decayed. They found nothing in Steinbach. The houses are all occupied.

10. Sat. Papa and Abram went again. Johan Kehler is sick, as is also Abram, the son of Gerhard Neufelds, and their Katharina. I made butter for the first time.

11. Sun. It is very hot. We drove to church in Reinland. In the afternoon we had visitors: Jacob Wiebes from Chortitz, and the Unger boys from Steinbach. Johan Kehlers' and Neufelds' boys are still very sick. It looks precarious.

12. Mon. Neufelds' Katharina died during the night. Jacob is again seriously sick. Drove to our children's, Jacob Wiebes. He has sprained his ... Had visitors, the senior Aron Schultzes and our children.

13. Tue. I did the laundry. Had visitors all day: Senior Jacob Stöszes and the senior Mrs. Stösz. Finished doing the laundry.

14. Wed. We drove with Peters to the funeral; Gerhard Neufelds' Katharina has died. She was 25 yrs. and 9 months and 23 days. She was sick 3 days. After *Faspa* Peters and we drove to Steinbach.

15. Thur. Cloudy. Heinrich took Jacob to Wiebes'. It began to rain. Papa and Aron drove with Peters along to Winnipeg. Anna is here with her children all afternoon.

16. Fri. We drove to Niverville hunting houses. In the afternoon the people [the buyers] from Winnipeg came here again. They took Papa along and drove to Steinbach. That man has bought an *Inschen* [an engine or tractor]. In the evening San came.

17. Sat. Kornelius Friesen came with the *Inschen* and the people [the buyers] also came here. Papa and Aron drove to St. Adolphe in the morning and after lunch Papa and Abram drove to Niverville. Heinrich wants to get Jacob from Jacob Wiebes.

18. Sun. It rained in the afternoon and there was also a little hail. Afternoon to Jantzes to have a look at the seniors' house. It is to be had for $5.00 a month. Cool in the evening.

19. Mon. Jacob again drove to Wiebes'. Papa drove to Niverville. Johan ploughs. . . .

20. Tue. I did the laundry and the baking and cleaned the house into which we want to move. Papa also drove there.

21. Wed. They took all chairs down there. The [married] girls all came to help. It is very hot.

22. Thur. We moved from our farm. Johan and the Englishman drove to Winnipeg to get loads [of his furniture?]. It is very hot.

23. Fri. In the morning there was a severe storm and some rain. . . . Papa and Heinrich drove down there to hoe potatoes.

24. Sat. Warm. Papa drove to Niverville.

25. Sun. Mild. All children came in the afternoon. In the evening it got very cloudy. There was lightning and thundering, but we received only a little rain.

26. Mon. Heinrich Neufelds came here and Johan.

27. Tue. The senior Stöszes and Kornelius Derksens came all at once. They wanted us to get ready and go with them to the West Reserve. We were ready in 15 minutes. We had a fine day at Peter Penners'. At 10 in the evening we were home again. Heinrich . . .

28. Wed. Papa drove to St. Adophe. Brought some sugar. "Farmer" [the Jew] came again for the night.

29. Thur. Cloudy. The rain bypasses us again. It is very dry. In the evening it rained a good deal.

30. Fri. Clear. Papa and Abram drove to Grünfeld in the afternoon to have the buggy repaired. I did the laundry. Jacob has been sick a week. Peter K. Friesen was killed in Steinbach while cutting down a tree. A piece of iron struck his head. He lived until the next day. He died at 7 a.m. He slept all the time.

July 1922

1. Sat. Windy. Papa and Abram did some haying. Papa cut wheat. I made butter. The senior Schultzes were here a little at Gerhard Stöszes'. There they are sick again. The senior Neufeld is completely down in bed. Ben also, but Suse is able to walk about. Jacob went in the evening to the children, Aron Schultzes'. After afternoon Papa and Abram drove to Niverville. He bought cheese.

2. Sun. Mild. In the morning Papa drove to Gerhard Neufelds'. He is very sick. . . . After lunch we drove to our children, Korn. Stöszes'.

3. Mon. Papa took a chair to Neufelds'. His condition has not changed. They are raking hay. Franz Schröder was here overnight. Schröders had gone to Blumengart. [His] mother is very sick. In the afternoon Jacob drove to Schröders'. He is doing some haying there. Anna came here after lunch. Maria and San also came. It is hot.

4. Tue. Cloudy. Papa and Heinrich are sharpening the scythe. Papa wants to do some more cutting. The beloved elderly aunt, Mrs. Jacob Stösz, died last evening. Afternoon cloudy and rain until the evening. Jacob came home for the night. Jacob Wiebe has . . .

5. Wed. Mild and windy. Kornelius's young son came here. He wants to have Jacob to help him. . . . Heinrich is to help at Kehlers' in the afternoon.

6. Thur. Had visitors for lunch: Johan Friesens and Johan Hildebrands from the West Reserve. In the afternoon we attended the funeral of the elderly aunt, Mrs. Jacob Stösz. She was 86 yrs., 3 months and 28 days. She was sick 7 days. After we had arrived home, the senior Schulzes came here and informed us that Gerhard Neufeld had died at 6 and Ben, their son, is still completely sick. It is cold and windy.

7. Fri. Papa went by train to Winnipeg. Jacob is raking and Heinrich helps again Grandfather. He . . . for the Small Jantzes. Fairly cool.

8. Sat. Papa harvested [hay] on the road allowance. In the evening rain set in and continued through the night. Good deal of thundering.

9. Sun. Rain at times. In the afternoon we attended the funeral of Gerhard Neufeld. The rain continued until the evening

10. Mon. We attended the after-funeral service. It is clear and mild. In the afternoon we drove to our children, Aron Schulzes'. On the way home we took the young boys along. In the evening Kornelius and Maria came. It is quite cool.

11. Tue. The son of the senior Mrs. Töws, Jacob, came here. Jacob took Peter Friesen to work, and Heinrich is again well. In the afternoon the children, Aron Schulzes, came here to pick up the little boys.

12. Wed. Papa and Abraham got two loads [of hay] with Kornelius's wagon: . . .

13. Thur. Very cloudy and raining. Papa drove to Winnipeg. Druri took him along on a car. They all went, including Aron. In the evening he brought them home again. Johan came also. I did the laundry and ironing.

14. Fri. Warm. Papa and Abram hauled hay. Very hot in the afternoon.

15. Sat. Not as hot. Papa and Abram hauled the last fodder in the a.m. Afternoon very windy. After lunch Papa drove to Niverville. Jacob came in the afternoon

16. Sun. Cool and showers with rain. We drove to church in Reinland, but no minister came. We had visitors in the afternoon: the senior Peters and Heinrich Friesens from the West Reserve. After lunch the senior Schultzes came, as did our children, Kornelius Stöszes.

17. Mon. Windy, cool and cloudy and windy. At times rain. Papa drove to Osterwick. Jacob rode to Stöszes' in Blumengart. Henry is again at Janzes'. In the afternoon we drove to our children's, Aron Schulzes'. There also were the Hüberts. Hübert has returned from Mexico.

18. Tue. Warm. In a.m. Papa drove along with Görtz to Niverville. Upon arriving home, he noticed he had forgotten the hitch for the rake. Hence he had to go again. . . .

19. Wed. We drove to Steinbach. Warm. We had lunch at Heinrich Neufelds'. In the afternoon we drove to the Unger Parents'. Their Abram is very sick. For night we drove home.

20. Thur. Cloudy and windy. Heinrich has finished helping Görtzes. Papa drove to our former farm. In mid-morning he drove to the senior Schultzes'. Jacob Kehler from Ebenfeld was there also, he took our Jacob to Hüberts' to do some work there.

21. Fri. Cloudy. I washed in the forenoon and afternoon.....

22. Sat. Still cloudy. Jacob rode to ... In the afternoon Abram went there also. Papa drove to Franz Schröders', but he returned at once. They had gone to Niverville.

23. Sun. Warm. No visitors. In the evening our children, Jacob Wiebes, and Franz Schröders came here. Lightning and thundering....

24. Mon. Cloudy and at times rain. In the afternoon Heinrich Neufeld came here and brought us cucumbers. In the evening we drove to our children and got a pail of potatoes.

25. Tue. Warm. Jacob cultivates at Görtzes'. Papa drove to Schultzes'. I pickled cucumbers and washed the towels. In the afternoon we drove to Blumengart.

26. Wed. Cloudy. Jacob drove to Chortitz to get firewood. Heinrich is again at Görtzes' to cultivate. We drove to our children's, Aron Schultzes'. Farmer, the Jew, came here for the night. We bought something.

27. Thur. Heinrich cultivated at Görtzes'. Papa and Jacob drove to our former farm to haul the barley to Heinrich Penners' to have it crushed. It is warm. I hoed....

28. Fri. Heinrich walked again to Maria's and Jacob ... at Görtzes'. Papa got the crushed barley from Penners'. After lunch San came here. Kornelius drove to Niverville....

29. Sat. Hot. After lunch Papa drove to Niverville. He bought several items with our children together; 100 lbs. sugar and cheese and other items.

30. Sun. We drove to church. Upon returning, we received the news that Ben Neufeld had died at 10:30 a.m. In the afternoon Gerhard Kehlers and our children, the Aron Schultzes, were visiting us. In the evening a shower with hail by-passed us for the greater part.

31. Mon. Warm. Papa drove to Niverville to get flour. Heinrich is again at Jacob [Wiebe]'s. [Our son] Jacob is at Görtzes'. In the evening the children, Jacob Wiebes, came here, as did Aron Schultzes....

August 1922

1. Tue. Warm. In the afternoon we attended Gerhard Neufeld's funeral. He was sick 6 weeks. He was 22 years, 3 month and some days. It was a big funeral. We heard that the senior Mrs. Peters has died due to dropsy.

2. Wed. Jacob is shocking sheaves at Görtzes'. It is warm. In the evening a Jew came here and bought 3 dozen eggs for 22 cents per doz. In the evening Papa drove to Wm. Hüberts'.

3. Thur. We drove to Steinbach for lunch. Lunch and *Faspa* we were at Funks'. After lunch we drove to Heinrich Neufelds'. At 8 in the evening it was cooler. I got some cucumbers and plums. When we got home we had visitors: Jacob Funks, and Farmer, the Jew, stayed here overnight.

4. Fri. Warm. I did the laundry. Cloudy. Rain in the afternoon until after lunch. After lunch Johan's [house] burned down. Cause is unknown. In the evening we drove to our children's, Kornelius Stöszes'. Getting cooler.

5. Sat. Very foggy. In the afternoon Jacob Wiebe got me to Korn. Stöszes'. They have an infant son, Jacob. During the night Anna came here.

6. Sun. In the morning we drove again to Neufelds'. In the afternoon we drove home. We received visitors: Peter Ungers and Peter Funks. It's raining, at times heavily....

7. Mon. Mild. I stayed here overnight. Maria and Jacob had gone to Chortitz yesterday to buy 4 pails of cherries for 25 cents a pail. In the evening Papa came to get me home.

8. Tue. Papa and Jacob drove to Cor. Schulzes' to shock sheaves. It is warm. I pickled cucumbers and de-stemmed the cherries.

9. Wed. Shocking again at Görtzes'. In the evening we again drove to the children's. It is cooling off. We took Heinrich back home.

10. Thur. Heinrich is again at Görtzes'. . . . Papa and Jacob drove to Cor. Schulzes'. Abram has gone to San's. I am home alone. I did the laundry. Hot and windy.

11. Fri. It is very hot. Heinrich is harrowing.

12. Sat. The last grain is being cut. Jacob and Heinrich shock sheaves.

13. Sun. Hot. In the afternoon we drove to Stöszes'. In the evening the children came here. It looks like rain. It is still warm. There is lightning and thundering.

14. Mon. Jacob shocks the last grain at Görtzes'. Heinrich cultivates at Görtzes'. After lunch we drove to San's and Kornelius'. Kornelius came in the morning to saw wood. I pick cucumbers at San's. In the afternoon Heinrich helped with shocking.

15. Tue. The children, Aron Schultzes, moved home. In the evening Johan also came home. Görtz helped to thresh at Schulzes'.

16. Wed. Rain in a.m. Johan is home again for the night. The people [who bought the farm] are in Winnipeg so Papa drove there to our [former] farm to feed the chickens. In the afternoon Papa and Jacob drove to Franz Schröders' to help with the threshing. It's warm.

17. Thur. They went threshing again. It is windy. In the evening Maria and Jacob came here. They have gathered all the grain. Johan again came for the night.

18. Fri. A little rain. Farmer, the Jew, came here. Heinrich has worked since Tuesday at Kornelius's. Our people again threshed at Schröders'. Johan came for the night again.

19. Sat. They threshed until lunch at Franz Schröders'. Then they drove to Gerhard Schröders'. They threshed here 100 bushels. Johan came again for the night.

20. Sun. Raining. Kornelius and San are here. Kornelius and Heinrich drove to Grünfeld to church. The old Peter Harder got away Saturday with horses and hayrack. They are searching diligently for him. He drove home from the threshing scene.

21. Mon. It is too wet. Papa drove to our [former] farm to get grain. Heinrich cultivates at Görtzes'. Here they found Peter Harder. He was completely confused. He found his way home.

22. Tue. Cloudy, but they went threshing. Jacob drove to Derksens' to repair his machine. Heinrich had to go to Gerhard Schröders'.

23. Wed. The [threshing] machine came to Görtzes'.

24. Thurs. They are again threshing at Görtzes'.

27. Sun. Church. Heinrich Derksen . . . drove in the afternoon to Abram Friesens'.

28. Mon. Threshing at Görtzes'. Jacob is again at Gerhard Derksens'.

29. Tue. Threshing at Görtzes'. They finished by evening.

30. Wed. They are threshing at Schröders'. We do the laundry. I scalded my foot with boiling lye. Heinrich Neufeld and Heinrich came in the afternoon and brought us plums and watermelons and melons. I had much pain until evening and then the burning sensation abated. I applied a sweet . . . and the white of an egg.

31. Thur. I ironed all day.

September 1922

1. Fri. They went with the machine to our childrens', Jacob Wiebes'. I and Anna also drove there. In the afternoon the rain set in. Hence we drove home.

2. Sat. They went threshing in the afternoon; Kornelius and San also were threshing. They did so with Peter Friesens' machine. It is hot.

3. Sun. We had visitors: Peter Wiebes and Gerhard Friesens. After lunch Maria and Jacob came also. Hot.

4. Mon. Papa and Heinrich drove to Jacob's to thresh. They finished it by lunch. Then they drove to Johan Harders'. The senior Schultzes were here. . . .

5. Tue. Raining. Papa went threshing. In the afternoon Heinrich got him home. Mrs. Franz Schröder drove to Mrs. Gerhard Neufeld and Abram's in the afternoon. It is cloudy. [We were] at our children's, Kornelius Stöszes'.

6. Wed. Mild, but too wet for threshing. In the evening Jacob Stöszes came here. It's cool and clear. The heaviest rain of the season came down. It was lightning and thundering.

7. Thur. Weather is fine. The senior Schultzes came here.

8. Fri. Rain again during the night. Since Tuesday the senior Schultzes have the [threshing] machine, but have not done any threshing. Too wet. Jacob and Anna drove . . . Since Wed. they have hauled chaff into the shed.

9. Sat. Today Mrs. Peter Harder, Halbstadt, was buried.

10. Sun. Cool and mild. We had visitors: Aron Schultzes, the junior Jacob Peters, Wm. Hüberts, Heinrich Derksens, Jacob Funks, Abram Kehlers, the small Stöszes, the senior Mrs. Johan Derksen, her Sana and Johan, Abram Derksens, Peter Friesens, Jacob Hüberts, and from the West Reserve Heinrich Schultzes and also another senior bachelor, Peter Falk and yet another carfull of several [people], Diedrich Derksen and Tulgus [?] Harder and a Sawatzky.

11. Mon. Jacob took Papa to Johan Harders. . . . Derksens' Gerhard picked up Jacob again to . . . I and Anna drove to Jacob and Maria's to help with the threshing. Heinrich cultivates at Görtzes'. . . .

12. Tue. A Jew was here. He [sold?] apples and beets. Jacob got Papa for threshing in the afternoon.

13. Wed. We drove to Steinbach, and then first to Mother, who is very sick. I stayed overnight and left in the morning.

14. Thur. Were at Peter Funks' for a little while. Then we drove to Heinrich Stöszes' and had lunch there. After lunch we drove home. There was a funeral in Grünthal. Rev. Kornelius Friesen had died from cancer.

15. Fri. Cool and windy. Jacob rode to Druri's to thresh and Heinrich as well. In the evening the children, Jacob Wiebes and Kornelius Stöszes, came home.

16. Sat. Papa and Abram drove to Steinbach to get watermelons from Heinrich Neufelds. Heinrich again rode to Druri's in the afternoon.

17. Sun. Rain in the afternoon. It ceased in the evening. Papa drove to Schultzes'. Jacob went visiting.

18. Mon. Papa and the senior Schultz drove to Kronsthal. There is a *Mitting* again as a man from Mexico is there. Jacob and Heinrich and Anna and their children also went to dig their potatoes.

19. Tue. Warm. Papa makes visits. In the evening he drove to Niverville to get Görtzes. . . .

20. Wed. Very windy. Peters began threshing yesterday. Jacob and Heinrich help threshing at Druri's. Papa and Abram drove in search of hay, but found none. In the evening he again drove to Niverville.

21. Thur. Windy. We did the laundry in the afternoon. Papa and Abram drove in search of grass. Later we drove to our children's, Jacob Wiebes'. Heinrich drove again to Jacob Neufelds' to plough. In the evening we had visitors: Heinrich Friesens.

22. Fri. In the afternoon the Gerhard Neufelds began to thresh. Papa helped.

23. Sat. We drove to church. In the afternoon we drove to Jacob Peters. It's getting colder.

24. Sun. Jacob drove to Gerhard Neufelds' to thresh. Papa with a horse to Schultzes', helped Schultzes' Franz with his work.

26. Tue. We drove to Chortitz to attend the Brotherhood. I went along as far as Jacob Wiebes'. In the afternoon Wiebe took us to Steinbach to the parents'. Mother is still very sick.

27. Wed. The old Mrs. La... was buried. Maria came here.... In the evening Jacob came home. He has again finished threshing. Stormy.

28. Thur. We did the laundry. Farmer, the Jew, came for lunch. He has cloth for 39 cotton shirts for 27 cents a yard....

29. Fri. Papa took the boys to Niverville. They went by train to Winnipeg. They bought themselves overcoats: Johan for $15.00 and Jacob for $20.00. They also bought caps.

30. Sat. Papa drove to Wm. Hüberts'. Johan and Jacob are home.

October 1922

1. Sun. We drove to Heinrich Penners'. It is very hot. Jacob and Maria drove to Steinbach.

2. Mon. We preserved apples. In the afternoon Anna sewed her dress. Papa drove along with Wilhelm Hübert to Kronsthal, where there is again a Mexico *Mitting*. Hot.

3. Tues. Johan brought 2 ... to Reinfeld. Abram helped him. Johann hauled firewood which was attained at the Big Kornelius Neufelds' and William ...

4. Wed. Jacob went along with Aron to Niverville and wants to work there. I and Anna are sewing.

5. Thur. We do the laundry. Cloudy. The Jew was here for the night. He bought 5 heads of cattle. In the evening Schultzes' girls came here.

6. Fri. Cloudy. Looks like rain. Jacob went along with the Jew to town. He took our hornless cow and white heifer along. After afternoon Maria and San came here. In the evening we drove to Gerhard Neufelds'. David Neufeld died due to typhus fever. The funeral is on Thursday.

7. Sat. Cold and cloudy. In the morning Papa drove to Schultzes'. There was again a funeral in the Chortitz Church. Johan Wiebe had died. Papa drove to Niverville. Jacob drove to get him, but he did not come along, as he had gone along with Johan Schultz.

8. Sun. We went along with the small Stöszes to Schönau. It is mild. Anna and Aron drove with Peter Ungers to Neufelds'.

9. Mon. Papa and Jacob drove to Winnipeg. Anna drove with her children to Schultzes'. It is mild.

10. Tue. Mild. We drove with Wilhelm Hüberts to the West Reserve; to Penners' for night, in the morning . . .

11. Wed. . . .

12. Thur. We did the laundry and sought to make the . . . , clean[ed].

13. Fri. We attended the funeral of the senior Mrs. Thiessen. She was 80 yrs., 9 months and some days.

14. Sat. Cloudy. Snow and rain. Jacob drove for wood. Papa and Abram drove to . . .

15. Sun. Snowing until noon. All the children are visiting. . . .

16. Mon. Everything was white when we got up. Snowing during the night. Jacob drove with Aron to Niverville. He wants to work for Brandstein. Aron has finished his work contract for the parents, but he still works there. Anna moved with her children again into her house. Papa and Heinrich moved them. It is cold. There was a funeral again on Sunday. The old Mrs. Peter Funk from Schönwiese had died.

17. Tue. Jacob and Heinrich drove for wood. It is cold.

18. Wed. We drove to Blumengart to Abraham Kehlers'. He has his auction sale. It was good.

19. Thur. Clear and cold. A good frost visible on the windows. Papa drove in the a.m. to Franz Schröders'. In the afternoon we drove to Niverville.

20. Fri. Farmer, the Jew, came for lunch. In the evening . . .

21. Sat. Mild. In the evening Jacob and Maria came with news that Father had died at 1 in the afternoon. Jacob and Heinrich went visiting.

22. Sun. When we got up, everything was white. At 10 a.m. it still is snowing and melting. The boys have gone visiting. We are at home.

23. Mon. Papa drove to the children's, Aron Schultzes'. He helped bring home their chickens. Mild, but cloudy and windy.

24. Tue. We drove to Steinbach. It is raining all day. We had lunch at Funks'. After afternoon we drove to Ungers' to help them. For the night we drove to Funks'.

25. Wed. We attended Father's funeral. Mild. It was a big funeral. For the night we drove to Neufelds'. Father was 101 years, 8 months and 23 days. He was sick 2 days. He died Sunday at 1 in the afternoon.

26. Thur. We attended the after-funeral. It was a sunny day. After lunch we drove home. We got here by 8 in the evening. Everything worked out well.

27. Fri. Not as mild. We did the laundry. In the afternoon we cleaned the kitchen. Mrs Janz and her children came here. Heinrich went along with Görtz to get wood.

28. Sat. Papa drove to Niverville and brought sugar and ... dozen ... The boys went in the evening to Schultzes'. Cloudy.

29. Sun. Mild. In the afternoon we had visitors: our children Aron Schulzes and Kornelius Stöszes. In the evening Görtzes were here.

30. Mon. Cloudy and rain at times. Heinrich drove to Blumengart for wood. Jacob slept until noon, as he attended the wedding last evening. He came home at 6 a.m. Jacob Wiebe began to teach in the school. We slaughtered a hen and a cow. We have a goose for lunch. Kornelius Neufelds, Peter Falks, Jacob Dücks came here. In the evening Kornelius Neufelds and our Jacob drove to Jacob Wiebes'. The others drove home after noon. It is clearing.

31. Tue. Maria came here. Neufelds stayed here for lunch. In the afternoon Heinrich Neufelds came here, as did Peter and Sara. After lunch Peter Neufeld and Kornelius Neufeld drove to Ungers'. In the evening Görtzes came here, as did Maria and Jacob and our Jacob.

Judith Klassen Neufeld and family. (Courtesy Maria Enns)

Helena Penner of Gretna in the West Reserve was among the first group of women to graduate from the University of Manitoba. She may well have served as a model to diarist Marie Schroeder, whose aspiration was to become a professional writer. (From F.G. Enns, *Gretna: Window on the Northwest* [Gretna, MB: 1987], 18.)

Cornelius T. and Gertruda (Dyck-Wiebe) Friesen and family. This was a blended family composed of Cornelius's four youngest children from his first marriage, to Katherina Friesen, and Gertruda's children from her marriage to Heinrich D. Wiebe. Cornelius's four sons (in the right half of the photograph), from oldest to the youngest, are: Martin C., Heinrich C., Jacob C., and David C. Friesen. Gertruda's children, lower left-hand corner, clockwise, are: Helena, Johann, Gertruda Jr., Elisabeth, Peter, Jakob, and Abram D. Wiebe. (Courtesy Irene Enns Kroeker)

Diverging Paths

VIII

19 Marie Schroeder (1907 to 1929)
Morden, Manitoba
Diary selection: October to November 1926
Age: 19

Marie Schroeder was the daughter of an East Reserve migrant to the West Reserve. She was born on 23 October 1907 in Kronsweide, West Reserve, the eldest child of Peter Schroeder and Susannah Banmann. Peter and Susannah, who had married in 1906, farmed near Lowe Farm on rented land during the summer of 1907, but a back injury forced Peter to give up farming. The young couple then lived with Peter's parents at Kronsweide, and it was here that Marie was born. Susannah wrote in her memoir that during a time when Peter's back became increasingly worse, ultimately forcing him into a wheelchair, "a lovely baby girl was born,... named Maria, after mother-in-law Schroeder." In 1918, after 11 years of life on Peter's parents' yard, the Schroeders spurned his parents and had their little house moved to the town of Lowe Farm, where the Sommerfelder Church offered them a lot. Here they could live more independently, and Susannah eked out a life with her handicapped husband and two small daughters. During the fall when young Marie was 11, she helped her mother build a 14-by-18-foot extension to the house. A short time later, during the 1918 influenza epidemic, Peter died. In 1921, Susannah married Abraham Hildebrand, a well-to-do Morden widower with 10 children, from the ages of 19 to a few months. Susannah wrote that her two daughters, Marie, 14, and Susannah Jr., 12, "did not want [her] to do this, but God did," having revealed His will in a dream in which a man resembling Abraham "stood at the foot of [her] bed and looked at [her]." That very year, Marie signalled her interest in academics by completing grade eight in school at a time when it was customary to leave school after grade seven. After Susannah's marriage to Abraham Hildebrand, she and her daughters moved to the large 320-acre Hildebrand farm, some 10 kilometres north of Morden, and here they lived in a "huge [house] made of fields stones and mortar with a wood burning furnace in the basement," and Susannah could at last "work for [her]self and not for other people." Over the next seven years Susannah gave birth to six more children, giving Marie and Susannah 10 step-siblings and six half-siblings. In 1929, at 28, Marie died in the Morden hospital after a short illness.

Despite her interest in academics and expressed yearning to be a writer, Marie's life was rooted on the farm north of Morden. Her sister, Susannah (or Susie), was her closest companion. But she also associated closely with her step-sisters Maggie (Margaretha), 19, and Tina (or Cathy, Katherina), 16, and her step-brother Willie (Wilhelm) Hildebrand, 23, and his new wife, Lizzie Zacharias. She also related to cousins, including some that had recently relocated to Mexico, and to friends from other districts, such as Plum Coulee, some 20 kilometres to the west.

Marie's personality is vividly portrayed in her diary. Her younger sister Susie provided the following description of Marie:

> Marie was named after Grandma Schroeder and consequently she was her favourite, but I always felt Grandpa loved me just as much as Marie. He did not play favouritism with anyone. . . . Marie was not such a tomboy as I. She was a dreamer, especially after mother married again. She was always up first and to bed last. If she was reprimanded for "burning the midnight oil" her reply used to be, "I am also always up first." She was slimmer and much prettier than I was. She had blue eyes and lovely curly brown hair. . . . Marie's ambition was to get an education and be a writer – she was always "scribbling" as she called it. She always stood first in her class and passed into Grade 9 [on] August 19th, 1921. When Mama re-married, she was very protective of me and she even stood up to our step-father. She was often blamed for things she never did. She was not as impulsive as I, so did not have to be reprimanded as often. I still have quite a bit of her writing, some diaries and some fiction.

Marie Schroeder's diary is unusual in several ways. It seems to have been written with the intention of mailing it to a friend, cousin Annie. Then, too, it is the only Manitoba diary in this collection that was originally written in English. It was discovered by Irene Enns Kroeker at the residence of Susannah Schroeder Janzen, Steinbach, Manitoba, and transcribed by Irene Enns Kroeker. For more information on the Schroeder family, see: Royden Loewen, "'As I Experienced Them Myself': The Worlds of German-Speaking Prairie Women," *A Chorus of Voices: German Canadian Identities*, ed., Angelika Saurer, et al. (New York: 1998).

1926

Oct. 22
    Annie dear what is the matter—
    That I have not received a letter?
    I've waited for one every day,
    But, "None for you," the mailmen say.
    So now of you I must inquire:
    Did it get stuck in mud and mire?
    Or didn't you write one at all—
    Not *one* letter this muddy sticky fall?

I composed this little rhyme while milking my daily three cows. It is for my cousin Annie, who hasn't written to me for ever so long. I've wanted to write to her ever so often but always put it off in the hope of hearing from her soon. To-day is Friday. Always considered unlucky but I mean to start my diary anew again, even if it is. I started one last Christmas but kept up only about 3 months because I decided I did not experience anything worth writing. I have changed my mind since then, eho!

Yes, and Willie, or Bill, as he is usually called, will be married on Sunday. We have been busy making preparations all this week. But I hope we'll have better weather than we've had so far. So good-night. Marie.

Oct. 25 In spite of the fact that I resolved to make an entry every day I have neglected to do so. We were so very busy on Saturday. Dad wanted to go to Morden and, as I did not have wedding present yet, I wanted him to bring one. This he did not want to do, so I went along and got one. I bought a calendar. I wanted something to use in the kitchen and something somebody else would not be likely to bring. Before we left for Morden, Mrs. Herman Hildebrand from Mexico arrived. She only stayed till the afternoon. Miss Tena Dyck arrived in M[orden] by train. In fact we went to meet her. Sunday morning found us up bright and early. Preparations that could be done the day before, had all been finished. Dad, Mom, Susie, Tina and I left for church in our car. The married-to-be's and Maggie left in Will's flivver [?] coupe. Several Plum Coulee folks arrived in church for the wedding ceremony. That done, we proceeded home for lunch consisting of *Plumenmos* [a plum compote] and boiled veal and bread. Then we all gave them our presents. There were quite a few, considering the number of guests there were. Then we sang two songs and then served a lunch of chocolate drops, home-made ginger snaps, and cookies, and buns, with sugar and coffee. Then somebody played the organ and we sang. Then we did our chores [milking nine cows]. They have to be done whether we celebrate weddings or not. Then supper by the lunch menu. That cleared away, we sat around for an hour till we sang hymns, accompanied by the organ. Then K & I played some lively pieces on the organ. This was followed by fun dances and that was the end. To-day we threshed some flax and the floors had to be scrubbed. There was so much dust. I must go to bed as it is pretty late already. Must add that we had fairly good weather Sunday. It was somewhat cloudy but the sun broke through now and again. Marie.

Oct. 27 To-day is my birth-day and a real sunshiny day it was. If the following year will contain as much sunshine, I need not dread it. I hope it does. Tina Dyck went back to Plum Coulee to-day. She was tired of us – mostly because she had no one to romp around with I suppose; because Willie is married now and things have changed somewhat. She gave me a very pretty buffet set (three-piece). Susie gave me a lovely hanky; one she had embroidered herself. I have a strand of imitation pearls from Betty Fehr. And a hanky from Cathy. They brought the presents Sunday night. Susie had injured a shoulder and her arm in a sling now. Not very comfortable. I know for I have experienced it myself. One year when we made cordwood I had to help and strained my right shoulder so much that I had to have it set and it would not stay in place unless I bedded it in a sling.

I love to write and have a secret hope that I may write things that have a real worth someday; things that are worth printing, and things that other folks would love to read and pay for. Yes – that is only a hope, but I do so wish it may be realized. Sometimes when I work about the house or outside perhaps, I long to take pen or pencil, then and there, and jot down my thoughts. But I can't then, and afterwards – my pencil is not as eloquent as my thoughts were. If anybody knew that I was writing this, they'd think me silly and near to losing my senses. Perhaps I am, but then I certainly can't help it. Oh! but losing one's senses seems terrible to me. More terrible than being blind, or a cripple, or deaf, or dumb, or even both the latter. I certainly hope I'll never go crazy. That is something I'm much afraid of.

Yes I've rambled on and on regardless of time, but it's quarter past ten and so, to bed I go. Good-night my diary. You are a friend indeed. Marie.

Oct. 28 Yes what shall I write to-day? Oh, now I know. I received another birthday present. A salt shaker from Will's Lizzie. I had a letter from Mrs. Ed. J. Funk too. She's my cousin, you know. Poor Susie. I promised her I'd come up and rub some medicine on her sore shoulder but when I wanted to go up she wasn't quite ready and now I stayed down too long. She is asleep already. I wonder if she did it herself or if the shoulder had to go without. I presume it is the latter, but bygones is bygones, as the saying goes and a person can't do anything once the opportunity has passed. So good-night. Marie Schroeder.

Oct. 29 Winter made its entrance with all the farmers . . . to-day. Or so we thought at least. For, the ground was almost covered with snow when we got up this morning. And a real north west wind was blowing, making pretty uncomfortable weather, but we should miss such weather, were we not to have any of it all winter. In an hour the storm abated, the snow stopped falling and melted. Fall had triumphed once again and we are not sorry it did. But we can't expect Fall to keep up his fight much longer, as its almost Nov. but not quite half of Fall's allotted term gone yet, though it seldom can manage to keep all of it.

I was in Morden to-day. Had to go and see a doctor about those sores on my foot I've had for about two months now. He can't do much about them. There was a One cent sale on at Veu Allens, the corner drug store. You can buy any article included in the sale for its usual price and another just like it for 1 cent. I bought 2 packages of envelopes. Can't think of anything more just now. So good-night my diary. Marie

Nov. 4 I haven't made an entry for several days now. Mostly because I did not think of anything worth writing. Will and his wife moved into the school house to-day. They seemed very happy. We had a letter from Martha Epp too to-day; she changed her place of work; is a nurse to four children ranging in ages from 1 to 7 years, now. She must also take care of upstairs rooms. She is quite pleased with it. Had a letter from Annie Wiens Oct. 30. Also a hanky for a birthday present. She thought maybe it had been I who was married to Bill several days already. Now another item that would only happen on a farm. Now here's the big news. Listen so you won't miss it! We had a new little calf. He was quite frisky in spite of the fact that he was born outside in six inches of newly fallen snow. Goodnight my dear diary. Marie

> My Weekly Evening Program Hours 7.30 to 9.30
> *Sun.* Anything except work
> *Mon.* Fancy Work
> *Tue.* Reading
> *Wed.* What's most Important to me.
> *Thur.* Reading
> *Fri.* Fancy Work
> *Sat.* Cleaning Up

No I'm not married yet and I don't expect to be either.

Nov. 17 I find that I have neglected my diary for nearly two weeks now. How lazy I've been. Certainly a lot of things have happened since my last entry was made. For instance Dad took sick with appendicitis about a week ago. We called the doctor. He made Dad go to bed without food for 2 days. Doc. also examined Sue who had pleurisy, he said. Poor Sue! sick for more than three weeks now.

We killed pigs yesterday. 4 big ones and 2 small ones. Had invited John Hieberts (P.C., Plum Coulee) Isaac Fehrs, Frank Zacharias, Willie Hildebrands, Jacob Heppners, Henry Janzens Sr. and Jr. both also Lizzie Janzen and Hans J. We got there quite early. Mother and Dad were in Winkler and Morden to-day. Mother had her tooth pulled in Morden. It had tortured her for ... [page missing].

Morden, Man   April 29, [19]28

Dear Anna

Have you a few minutes time for me? Yes? Oh that's splendid then we can have a nice little talk. I've mislaid your letter and that means your questions (if there were any) will go unanswered unless I find it soon.

Well what'll I say first. To-day being Sunday, Dad and four of the girls were at church. We always take turns, as we can't all go at once, and next Sunday is my turn again. Anne is joining the church this year and so has to go every Sunday. I suppose people think it kind of funny that I'm not, as I'm older, but I won't just because somebody else will. If its done in that spirit, I don't think it'll do anyone any good. And what about you?

Oh Annie, is Jacob Falk back in dear old Manitoba, already? I expect he is, as April is pretty nearly gone. I was so surprised when I read that, but I'm very very anxious to see him, should he really be back. Didn't we and those cousins of ours always have loads of fun though! I'll never forget it. I hope he comes to see us too, even if only for a day. Annie, you will see him sooner than I, so just "invite" him over to our house. As I would love to see some of that Mexican sunburn on him and ask loads and loads of questions too. About Nettie and Aunt Nettie and the younger boys and girls too. We have not had a letter from any of them since last summer.

We celebrated Katie's birthday last Sunday. We would have enjoyed ourselves more tho' if the P.C. girls and our crowd had not insisted on mixing something like oil and water. And we had two rather unexpected visitors besides. They were Martin and John Friesen, my cousins from Lowe Farm. I wish you would give us a pleasant surprise like that in the near future. You'd be welcome any day. When may we expect you then? Or won't your old Ford go anymore; if not, just get one like ours and it'll go. Do you know that we have a Ford coach model now? It is much nicer than the old one.

Dear Alee (Elfrieda):

Just a few lines to let you know that we received your letter and was delighted to hear from you. I don't blame you for not writing often as I can well imagine that you are busy most of the time. So have we for that matter. At least for the last two months. As we have done all the haying, harvesting, and threshing during that time. The busiest part of the farm year is over once again, I am glad to say. Not so much besides the plowing to do now, and I don't do that. Annie plows with horses. Sue or Dad with the tractor. I am planning to do some work after we have finished everything. Though I'm not quite sure yet. If I do I expect it will have to be domestic work as I am not qualified for anything else.

Had Lowe Farm visitors last Sunday, and the week before that. Once it was Wiens' and Annie too, of course. Do you know that she had applied for assistant nurse at Ninette Sanitorium? She was expecting to go any day and may be gone already for all I know. Last Sunday John Schroeders were over. Sure enjoyed myself those two Sundays. Tien Schroeder sure is a fatty, but lively too, oh boy!

Bought myself from August 1, 1926 to September 1, 1927

1 toque at	.35			
1 pair gloves @	.69	Aug. 1, 1926		
helped pay sweater	.95	Clothing my parents bought for me		
1 gingham dress @	1.20	1 Print Dress 4 yds at 25	1.00	
1 pair shoes @	2.75	1 pair bloomers @	.35	
Total for 1926-27	$6.34	1 pair work boots @	2.95	
		1 pair dress boots @	3.75	
After Sept 1 1927		1 pair silk and wool hose @	.79	
1 winter hat @	2.95	2 Flannelette shirts 5 yds @	1.50	
1 pair stockings @	.40	1 sleary [?] Eiderdown		
1 Summer Hat @	2.95	Petticoat 2 yds @ .80	1.60	
1 slicker @	3.25	1 pair moccasins @	1.50	
1 pair shoes @ 3.50 I paid	2.45	Wool for feet on stockings @	.25	
1 pair stockings @	.35	1 pair drawers @	1.00	
1 pair rubbers @	.75	1 sweater 95 cents I paid myself	3.00	
1 pair bloomers @	.37	1 apron 2 yds @ 20	.40	
1 dress buckle @	.15	1 gingham dress 4 yds @ 2	1.00	
after Sept. 1 1928	13.62	1 pair stockings @	.40	
1 silk scarf	.89	1 shirt 2 yds @ 20	.40	
1 dress buckle	.25	1 garden hat @	.40	
2 aprons 4 yds at 30 cents	1.20	1 Sunday dress 4 yds		
1 pair of stockings (fine)	.50	@ .59 + .45 trim	2.80	
1 pair stockings @	.30	1 apron 1.5 yd @	.40	
1 broadcloth dress @	1.60	1 pair stockings @	.35	
1 dress (Christmas present)	1.50	Total cost for 1 year + 1 month	23.84	
Dad paid on shoes	1.85	Sept. 1927,		
1 pair bloomer	.87	1 pair wool stockings @	.65	
Sept 1928		1 pair drawers @	.95	
total cost of 1927 - 1928	11.52	1 pair work boots	3.18	
		1 shirt 2 yds at 20	.40	
1 pair bedroom slippers	.69			
1 shirt 2.25 yds flannel				
at 25 a yd	.57			

Catherine	Betty	Tena D.	Annie W.	Susie S.	Lizzie H.
received					
B. Hanky	B. Pearls.	b. Buffet Set	B. Hanky	B. Hanky	B. Salt sh.
					P. Hanky

20 Cornelius T. Friesen (1860 to 1929)

Osterwick, Manitoba

Diary selection: 1927

Age: 66

Cornelius T. Friesen was born on 20 August 1860, in the village of Bergthal, Bergthal Colony, New Russia. At 16 he came to Canada with his parents, Cornelius B. Friesen (1833-1909) and Anna Toews (1834-1899), who settled near Osterwick, East Reserve. Cornelius worked on the farm until he married Katherina Friesen, from the nearby village of Schoenthal. They established a large farm in his village, Osterwick, and here they raised a family of 12 children. In 1909, a year after Katherina died, Cornelius married Gertruda Dyck Wiebe. They lived in Osterwick until he died in 1929.

His contemporaries remember Cornelius as a quiet and strong man who was the president of the Chortitz Mennonite Church's *Waisenamt,* its estates, and its credit institution, between about 1906 and 1925. Serving as *Waisenvorsteher* was a tradition that had been in his family for two generations. As business officer, banker, and paralegal he was in charge of administering the Mennonites' traditional inheritance system, and specifically of managing the inheritance monies that "orphans" (meaning children who had lost either a mother or a father) were entitled to upon reaching the age of majority. Beginning in about 1924, the *Waisenamt* carried the added responsibility of transferring the estates funds to Paraguay, the new home of many East Reserve Chortitzer Mennonites. As Cornelius Friesen's workload increased dramatically, he is said to have doubted his own capabilities, expressing these in letters written to the congregation. He served as *Waisenvorsteher* for 19 years, after which his grandson filled the office.

In 1927, Cornelius was no longer at the height of his role as community leader. However, it is clear from the many visits he received from neighbours and friends planning to move to South America that he was still a venerated man. During 1927, he met a parade of community officials – *Aeltesten*, ministers, and *Waisenmänner* – from not only the East Reserve, but also the West Reserve and the Mennonite colonies in Saskatchewan. A frequent associate was Martin C. Friesen, a minister who had been chosen *Aeltester* of the East Reserve Chortitzer church in December 1925 and who, during 1927, became a leader in the emigration to Paraguay, leaving with a contingent of Chortitzer Mennonites amidst a tearful farewell on August 23. (Martin C. Friesen later became the *Aeltester* of the Mennonite church in the Chaco in Paraguay.) In Martin C. Friesen's absence, it was *Aeltester* H.J. Friesen of the Sommerfeld Mennonite Church in the West Reserve who came to conduct the October Communion Services on the East Reserve. Heinrich G. Klippenstein, another frequent visitor, was one of the men who had been elected as *Waisenmann* in 1925 to take over from a retiring Cornelius T. Friesen. Diedrich Wiebe, Peter K. Toews, and Peter F. Wiebe were ministers in the Chortitzer Church. David F. Doerksen was a minister from Main Centre, Saskatchewan; Anna Schulz was the wife of Heinrich Schulz, another Main Centre minister, and she was also Cornelius's daughter.

Clearly, Cornelius's long term in office was still remembered. Over the course of the year there were several visits from and to widows; Cornelius knew at least one of these widows – Maria Pries – by her first name. He also recorded events, not only of death but also of times of illness, within the congregation community; in April he noted that the wife of Peter Wiebe had collapsed with only a cow near her, and in June he noted that someone (not named) was rushed to the Franco-Manitoban village of Ste. Agathe for medical treatment.

The most remarkable aspect of the diary of this Chortitzer Mennonite is his chronicle of the emigration of the Chortitzer and Sommerfelder Mennonites to Paraguay's Chaco region in 1926 and 1927. It was he who kept the careful roster of the migration of Chortitzer Mennonites; he recorded the departure of 191 families, or almost 1,200 people, about 15 percent of the total emigration of Manitoba Mennonites to Latin America in the 1920s. The significance of the migration is measured by the constant flow of people – neighours, dignitaries, and friends and relatives from the West Reserve – who passed through the Friesen home in 1927 to bid their farewells. It is also measured by the emotional farewell services; during one in August, Cornelius Friesen speculated on the slim possibility of ever again seeing his friends and neighbours. Finally, it is measured by the stark juxtaposition of names; the Mennonite villages of Reichenbach, Reinland, Vollwerk, Bergthal, Grunthal, Chortitz, and Osterwick are the origins of people who find themselves in a succession of places that include Chicago, New York, Bermuda, Buenes Aires, Asuncion, and even Puerto Casado, Paraguay.

The diary was kept within a large writing book that also served as a primary site for Friesen's deep sense of history. Included in the book are many hymns that Friesen copied. There is also a handwritten version of the deceased *Aeltester* Gerhard Wiebe's 1900 book entitled *Ursachen und Geschichte der Auswanderung der Mennoniten aus Russland nach Amerika*, an account of the 1874 migration from Russia that really serves as an apologia for it. And there is a copy of the venerated *Privilegium*, the German translation of the June 1873 letter that the Mennonite immigration delegates received from the Canadian government; as the Mennonites saw it, the letter promised not only military exemption and block settlement, but the freedom to operate parochial schools, a promise that they believed had been broken by Manitoba's School Attendance Act of 1916. For the Mennonites, the migration to South America was an act by which they contested the culture of the wider society and an act, too, of religious commitment. It seems natural, then, that in December 1927 the Chortitzer Brotherhood committed itself to reform; the members agreed to stop brewing spirits, to stop the bawdy street singing of the youth (known as *Poltern*), and to guard against fashionable haircuts. Significantly, there is no prohibition of smoking, a practice that Cornelius Friesen engaged in during his years as *Waisenmann*; he notes in a 1924 entry that he had stopped smoking, something he had attempted to do three or four times before that.

For a family history of Cornelius T. Friesen, see Katherine Friesen Wiebe, "Waisenmann Cornelius T. Friesen," *Preservings: Newsletter of the Hanover Steinbach Historical Society* (June 1996): 36-40. The original Gothic handwritten diary is in the possession of Irene Enns Kroeker, of Steinbach, Manitoba. It was translated by Ben Hoeppner and Royden Loewen.

Jan. 1 Johan B. Harders, both of them, were here to visit with his father [and mother, the] Jacob Harders. In the evening Jacob Fehrs were also here to visit.

Jan. 2 Heinrich G. Klippensteins were here to visit. At 4:30 Klippenstein drove to Niverville and picked up his sister, Mrs. Abram D. Doerksen. She has come to visit her siblings and they all stayed here for supper.

Jan. 3 Peter D. Wiebe of Sommerfeld [West Reserve], and Widow Maria Pries arrived here. They wished to stay the night at H.P. Doerksen. On January 4 he returned to the West Side [West Reserve] to Winkler to visit his parents to take their farewell, as they are emigrating to South America.

Jan. 5 Abram Kehler was here as a guest, also Jacob D. Wiebe. Peter F. Hieberts were not home, so Abram Kehler stayed at our place.

Jan. 7 Peter D. Wiebe of Sommerfeld and Maria Pries of the West Side. . . . [visited] Martin C. Friesens', and from there they returned home.

Jan. 9 Martin C. Friesen drove to the West Reserve, to Letellier, and in the evening on the 13th of January he returned, via Winnipeg.

Jan. 15 Andres Blatzes were at Abram K. Friesens' of Reinland for *Vesper*. They were here for about 3 1/2 hours in the afternoon and at 8:45 p.m., that is 1/4 before 9, they returned home.

Jan. 16 We were at Jacob G. Goertzens'. F.H. Giesbrecht, M.C. Friesen, and H.F. Toewses [were also there].

Jan. 19 In the afternoon at 5, Andres R. Sobering took our Cendo [a vehicle?] to Niverville and returned home at 8 p.m.

Jan. 24 Jacob P. Funk was here in the evening with his father, Jacob Funk of Bergthal . . . and at 9 p.m. they returned home to Schoenthal. [During the day] I was again at Klippensteins'.

Feb. 6 David D. Falks were at our place to visit us.

Feb. 9 We were visiting at Abram F. Hieberts'; there was a gathering.

Feb. 12 Heinrich G. Doerksens, Gretna, came in the evening and Andres Sobrings got them from [the train station in] Niverville with our wagon. They arrived at 9 p.m. and stayed overnight.

Feb 13 They also came for the night at 6 p.m.

Feb 14 At 9:30 a.m we took them to Ab[raham] and Gerhard Neufelds' place in Kronsthal. From here they went to see Peter Giesbrechts, then to Jacob D. Goertzens'; from there to Hein[rich] P. Doerksens', Reinland; from there Hein[rich] D. Penners' [went to] Niverville, and then by train to Winnipeg. [Note added later] On February 17 in the morning to Gretna....

Feb. 15 In the afternoon we were visiting at Hein. F. Toewses'.

Feb. 16 Completely by myself, I was visiting at Jacob Hildebrands'; sold 42 bushels of wheat to Jacob Hildebrand.

Feb. 20 Peter F. Wiebe was installed to his office as preacher and ordained as preacher, and Abram P. Schroeder was installed and ordained on the same day as deacon.

Feb. 20 [Note added later] Peter F. Funk died this morning and was buried on February 24.

Feb. 26 Andres R. Sobering with C.C. Friesen's sleigh drove to Steinbach; they returned on Feb. 27.

Mar. 8 Peter A. Braun and Glenn Bodger came here in the evening and got the moveable articles of Martin C. Friesens. At 9 p.m. they went to Pet. T. Hieberts and did the same thing. They stayed overnight at Abram F. Hieberts' place.

Mar. 10 Johan H. Löppky was at Martin ... Friesens' and Peter T. Hieberts' for the afternoon and for *Vesper*.

Mar. 12 Mrs. Andres R. Sobering's two brothers from the West Reserve came here. Peter Giesbrecht [got] them. Heinrich W. Dueck, Mexico, Ben and Solomon W. Doerksen, Rosenfeld, were here Sunday afternoon.

Mar. 13 David D. Falks arrived at Peter T. Hieberts' at 5:30 p.m. and left for home at 8:45 p.m.... Also Peter T. Wiebes were both here. David D. Falks were here for supper.

Mar. 14 Solomon went home in the morning. Peter Giesbrecht took him to Niverville. Hein W. Doerksen went along with Martin C. Friesen to Johan Schroeders' place. He wanted to go to Steinbach to visit his two aunts. Since March 12 H.W. Doerksen is here from Mexico visit his parents in Gretna.

Mar. 16 Martin C. Friesen went to Winnipeg, as did Jacob D. Wiebe and stayed 2 days and returned.

Mar. 18 Preacher Peter Harder of Kronsthal died at 5:50 p.m.. He was 61 years, 4 months, and 2 days old. Funreral was held on March 22. He had been ill for 16 days, 3 days seriously ill.

Mar. 22 Abram A. Brauns, both of them, were driven here from the funeral by Jacob Hildebrand. They spent the night at Martin C. Friesens'. First thing in the morning they drove to Kronsthal to the post-funeral [gathering]. [For] night [they went to] Peter Harder....

Mar. 26 I copied the "Ordination Sermon" for Martin C. Friesen. He had borrowed it from H.J. Friesen for copying.

Mar. 29 Martin C. Friesen again went to Winnipeg.

Mar. 30 Martin C. Friesen had a meeting with the emigrants ... so that all can go. Thus, they were ...

April 6 David and Abram went to drive Widow Maria E. Pries, she with the children, to our place, and they arrived here on the 7th at 12 noon. They used two buggies; very bad roads.

April 7 We were at Abram F. Hieberts' place to say farewell. A farewell took place on April 10 here in the school in Osterwick. Martin C. Friesen conducted a service.

April 7 At 10 a.m. Abram A. Braun, David A. Fehr and Heinrich G. Klippenstein arrived here to [discuss] the emigration. They stayed till noon. In the afternoon they drove to Arm F. Hiebert's. For night they were at Martin C. Friesens'.

April 8 All three, Martin C. Friesen, Abram A. Braun, and David A. Falk, drove to Winnipeg with our Democrat. They arrived [back here] at 8:45 p.m. They again stayed the night and on the 9th at 9 a.m. they returned home via St. Pierre, where they did banking business.

April 10 Here in the Osterwick school there was a farewell service for those who are moving to South America. *Ältester* Martin C. Friesen conducted the farewell sermon. In spite of the bad roads, 125 to 140 [persons] were present.

April 12 At 7:30 a.m. we brought Widow Gerh. E. Pries to Niverville with some suitcases and 3 children: Gerhard, Jacob and Maria. Abram did the driving. Jacob D. Wiebe also went along. Martin C. Friesen, Heinrich A. Hiebert, Abram C. Hiebert and Jacob D. Wiebe went along up to Emerson [the American border]. At 7:30 a.m. they were back in Niverville and arrived home at 11.

April 12 At 1 p.m. to Niverville, also Martin C. Friesen took Elisabeth along. And we and Jacob C. Friesens took Gertruda with satchels to Niverville. We travelled over 2 hours. We had to clean the wheels several times. So muddy were the roads. We had 2 pairs of horses for one big wagon with little freight. The wheels clogged that they would not turn.

April 13 At [precisely] 3:33 a.m. they left Niverville. Martin C. Friesens escorted them up to Emerson, as did Jacob Wiebe and several others. They arrived there at 5:30 a.m. They returned with the "Flier" [the express train].

[Entry made at a later date] April 13, 1927, the 4th group left Niverville at 3:33 a.m. from Niverville and reached Emerson at 5:30 a.m. Some who had gone along to Emerson came back to Niverville. They reached Asuncion May 13 and Puerto Casado May 15.

April 16 Andres R. Soberings drove to the West Side, to Gretna, as their parents are there. [Entry made at a later date]. On April 22 they returned home and Peter Giesbrecht went to pick them up in Niverville.

April 18 Mrs. Peter H. Toews died in the evening. Both had gone to look at the water [the spring runoff] in the creek and then the cattle came and all at once, P. Toews looked around, and there was his wife, sitting, with a cow near her and.... Then she still had [been able to] walk in [to the house] and P.T. Toews helped her into bed. Half an hour later she died.

April 22 The funeral took place. She was 66 years and 4 months.

May 3 A Brotherhood meeting took place in Chortitz dealing with emigration. On May 4 a Brotherhood meeting about emigration took place in Grunthal.

May 4 Preacher Peter D. Funk died in Steinbach, and was buried on the 7th of May. He reached the age of 52 years, 4 months. [Added at a later date] on May 14 Peter F. Hiebert's mother-in-law also [died?].

May 10 We received a telephone message from Bones Eires [Buenos Aires] from the last group and also letters from Peter T. Hiebert, Barbados.

May 13 The emigrating group is said to have arrived in Asuncion and May 15 they are to have disembarked in Puerto Casado.

June 7 Jacob Neufelds and Heinrich Hieberts arrived here and in the evening for supper they were at Martin C. Friesens'. At 10 p.m. they drove home. Heinrich Hiebert purchased three bottles of *Aplenkräuter* for $3.65.

June 9 David C. Friesen drove to the West Reserve to Jacob Wiebe, of Plum Coulee; *im Dienst gegangen* [went on behalf of the church?].

June 12 Johan ... Doerksens, the both of them, were here at ... Friesens', and also at our place to visit.... [They] left for home at 6:45 p.m.

June 14 Heinrich J. Friesens, the *Ältester*, of Altona and Jacob W. Peters of Vollwerk and also Widow Jacob P. Doerksen of Schoenwiese came for lunch. They left at 12:45 for home, but first drove to Steinbach.

June 18 Peter C. Friesens came here at 2 p.m. and stayed overnight at Hein C. Friesens' place.

June 19 They had communion service and for lunch they came to our place. Immediately after lunch they went to C.C. Friesens' place. From Peter C. Friesens', C.C. Friesen and Hein C. Friesen at once went to the doctor, Erdmann P. Penner. Mrs. Penner at once said that she would not accept the case. Then they went to St. Agathe. E.P. Penner went along. He drove and the doctor gave an injection and applied hot water. In coming back they went to Hein F. Toewses' place.

June 20 They came here and to Johan Neufelds' place, Schoenthal. For the night they were at our place. During the night we had a heavy rain which lasted into the morning.

June 23 David A. Falks, both of them, of Bergfeld, Post Office St. Pierre, came to Martin C. Friesens' for night, for a visit and they left for home in the afternoon. And in the south, towards Grunthal, it rained heavily, with thunder and lightning.

June 26 Peter F. Friesens, also their father, Heinrich A. Friesen, were here in the afternoon, they left for home at ...

July 2 Abram H. Duecks came here in the evening and stayed for the night and on the 3rd of July they were at Cornelius C Toewses' of Strasberg [Strassburg] for the night. They wanted to leave for home on the 4th. His address is Post Office Box 73, Morris, Manitoba.

July 4 We visited at Jacob P. Funks', also at his father's, the senior Jacob Funk, who is staying with them. Also [drove] to Johan B. Neufelds'; Jacob P. Funk came with us; the senior Jacob Funk came for him an hour later.

July 11 Heinrich L. Friesens, both of them, came here at 12 noon and an hour later they left for Schoenthal for their parents', Heinrich Doerksens. Heinrich A. Friesen brought Cornelius Friesen here for night at 6 p.m.. On the 12th at 8 a.m. I drove him to Schoenthal, with a stop at Jacob Fehrs'; he also wanted to drive to Gnadenfeld; from there he wanted to depart for home, with H.L. Friesens.

July 12 Peter Dycks and Gerhard W. Dycks of Kronsgart [near] Plum Coulee, came to our place at 10:30 a.m. [and stayed] for lunch. In the afternoon they all drove to Widow Jacob Wall, and we too. Heinrich H. Gerbrandts were here for supper.

July 13 Peter Dycks and Gerhard W. Dycks drove to Widow Johan Loeppky's. From there they wished to go home. They [Heinrich Gerbrandts] came here from Bergthal where they had spent the night at Widow [?] Johan Toews'. They were at Jaocb G. Goertzens' for lunch and they departed from our place at 2 p.m. for Jacob Duecks'.

July 17 Jacob D. Funks of Schoenwiese were here at our place to visit. Also David D. Falks were at our place to visit. Also Cornelius Harder of Lowe Farm was here for a short while, about one hour.

July 21 We, C.T. Friesens, were at Cornelius H. Peters, Reichenbach, for the wedding. We were at Jacob W. Peters' for lunch.

July 22 We met Johan Funks of Herbert at the funeral at Jacob P. Funks'. They came to visit here by car.

July 23 I met them again at the Widow Abram Funk's, of Bergthal. From there they wanted to go . . .

July 24 Cornelius Stoeszes and Abarm Thiessens came to our place for *Vesper* at 2:30 p.m. and left for home at 7:30 p.m. They each have two children. Abram Thiessens had two children with them, also Mrs. C. Stoesz.

Aug. 1 Both us drove to Steinbach. We had lunch at H.W. Reimers' and were at Jacob B. Peters' for *Vesper*. We arrived there at 3:30 p.m. and left at 6 p.m. Purchased from Heinrich Harder a pair of *Karken* for my wife.

Aug. 6 Johan S. Rempel and Jacob D. Wiebes of Chortitz visited us in the afternoon.

Aug. 7 Johan F. Wiebes, Johan P. Hieberts, Jacob H. Hildebrands, Peter Toewses, David K. Hieberts, Peter F. Funks, Abram Funks, Widow Abram Funk, Jacob P. Funk, Jacob Funk, Abram P. Funks, Jacob G. Goertzens, Wilhelm Giesbrechts of the West Reserve, C.C. Friesens, David Falks' three girls, that is, Maria, Agatha, and Gertruda [were at our place]; also Jacob Vehr was here in the evening.

Aug. 10 Rev. Peter Dycks from the West Reserve visited us to say their farewell from Martin C. Friesens, as they are going to South America.

Aug. 11 Johan F. Reimers of Steinbach, Abram A. Brauns, Peter F. Wiebes, and Widow Johan L. Kehler of Reinland were here in the afternoon; Johan F. Reimers, however, were here for lunch.

Aug. 12 Martin R. Friesens of Lowe Farm, the West Reserve, were here after after *Vesper*. And on Aug. 13 Heinrich G. Klippensteins, David F. Wiebes, Jacob R. Funks, Peter Harders, Peter Giesbrecht of Osterwick, ... Abram P. Schroeders, ... Diedrich Wiebe, and Jacob Wiebe [were here?].

Aug. 17 Cornelius P. Ennses of Altona were here; Peter Dueck with David Doerksen, Peter D. Falks, Jacob K. Kehlers, Bernhard H. Giesbrechts, Heinrich F. Falks, Jaocb G. Goertzen, Peter F. Hieberts [and] Peter W. Friesen [were here].

Aug. 18 David F. Doerksens and Anna Schulz, Herbert, Sask. came here. At 2 p.m. Abram D. Doerksen had gotten them from [the train station in] Winnipeg. *Ältester* David F. Doerksen went in the evening of Aug. 21 to Niverville. Jacob H. Harder brought Peter C. Friesen down there.

Aug. 25 They want to go to Winnipeg. David C. Friesen took C.C. Friesen, Jacob G. Görtzens and Mrs. H. Schulz to the train [station], which left at 10:30 p.m.

Aug. 19 For the farewell of Senior Peter F. Wiebe, Hein F. Toewses, Isaac Hildebrand, Cornelius W. Friesens, and Franz Giesbrechts were here.

Aug. 20 At our place were Rev. Peter Giesbrecht, Died. Wiebe and Jacob Wiebe, Chortitz, C.F. Friesen, Peter K. Hiebert, Jacob T. Hiebert, Peter D. Duecks, Hein C. Friesen, Hein A. Hieberts and Jacob Hildebrand.

Aug. 21 At our place were Peter C. Friesen, Corn. Stoesz, Hein F. Friesen, Corn. F. Friesen from the West Reserve and G. Goertzen.

Aug. 22 Visiting us were: Jacob Fehr, Rev. Peter F. Wiebe, Jacob P. Funks, Jacob Funk, Peter F. Hiebert, Peter K. Toews, Hein Enns, Abram Peters, *Ältester* Unrau, C.C. Friesens, Hein C. Friesens, Susana Harder, Hein F. Toewses, Johan W. Harder, Aron Schulz and David Peters, Martin T. Friesens, Abram A. Hieberts, Peter F. Hieberts, Jacob L. Rempel, and Peter Dyck, who went to H.F. Toewses' place for the night. Johan Giesbrechts were here for supper. Johan Giesbrechts went to Jacob G. Goertzens' place for the night. [For the night] Hein H. Doerksen and Peter D. Toewses were here.

[A note written at a later date] And there was a great farewell. Many people were present. Many took their farewell of Martin C. Friesen and said, *Aufwiedersehn*. And if not here then up there in eternity. Many tears of separation flowed and many well-wishes were extended until the train started moving and left. It arrived on the 24th in St. Paul, August 26, 11 a.m., in Chicago, Aug. 27 in New York at 7 a.m. Then they embarked on the ship, which was to leave at 12 o'clock from New York. Sept. 9 they arrived in Rio and Sept. 23 in Puerto Casado, Paraguay.

Aug. 23 [A note written at a later date] August 23, 1927, the 5th group left from Carey station at 6:30. We escorted Martin C. Friesens and Abram D. Wiebes. There were 8 cars in a row. In the 9th car were C.A. Hieberts. When we and all the children escorted them to the Carey station; . . . there were only 3 cars.

Sept. 4 The senior Jacob Hildebrands were here to visit.

Sept. 6 Abram A. Braun, Peter A. Falk, and Jacob N. Doerksen, stopped by here as they came from the Niverville train station.

Sept. 12 C.C. Friesens, Heinrich F. Toewses, Heinrich Friesen and Jacob G. Goertzen, were all here in the evening to decide about the threshing.

Sept. 25 We visited at Heinrich F. Toewses'. And David K. Wiebe of Bergthal were at our place in the evening and also at Jacob C. Friesens'.

Oct. 4 We had lunch at Hein G. Klippensteins' place. At 1:30 we visited Diedrich Toewses to say farewell, as they are going to South America.

Oct. 10 We installed a stove.

Oct. 13 Jacob Hildebrand died at 5 p.m. due to the choleric. In the morning after getting up he received pain in the chest which continued until he died. He was 56 years, 7 months and 6 days. He died Oct. 17, 5 a.m.

Oct. 18 I went along with Gerhard Hildebrand to Altona to attend the funeral of Peter Friesen, my cousin. He was [buried on?] Oct. 19. He got to be 62 years minus a day. Twice he was stricken with a stroke.

Oct. 21 I went home by train via Winnipeg. I got there at 7 o'clock. I paid G. Hildebrand $1.00 and $3.95 for the trip from Altona to Niverville.

Oct. 22 Johan Siemens came here at 9 a.m. and at 11:45 a.m. they left for Peter F. Hieberts'; from there they drove to Kopps' in Niverville, and from there they left for home. . . .

Oct. 24 Peter Duecks and *Ältester* Heinrich J. Friesen of Altona came here and Peter Dueck stayed the night and on October 25 *Ältester* H.J. Friesen served us with communion at Chortitz and on October 26 served communion in Grunthal and in the evening he returned home.

Nov. 6 We, C.T. Friesens, visited at Martin T. Friesens'.

Nov. 7 I, C.T. Friesen, was at H.G. Klippenstein with a letter.

Nov. 9 We were at Widow Jacob Hildebrand's for a visit; were there for *Vesper*. On October 22 we had also been at Widow Hildebrand's.

Nov. 13 Jaocb G. Goertzen, Jacob F. Wiebe of Niverville, Heinrich G. Klippenstein, and Johan K. Doerksen of Bergthal, were here in the evening (Jacob G. Goertzens were here during the day), all to visit. And we read a letter from Martin C. Friesen and Peter T. Hiebert of South America.

Nov. 14 Widow Johan Toews of Bergthal was here to hear the letter from South America.

Nov. 17 We were guests at ... Peter F. Wiebes'.

Nov. 21 David C. Friesen drove to the West Reserve to Gretna for the winter to chore [take care of a farm], but first to Winnipeg and from there on the 22nd of November to Gretna, and from there to Rosenort.

Nov. 23 The Brotherhood discussed: 1) the annual account up to the 28th and Jan. 2 the account of $220.43; 2) the levy of 50 cents from every eligible church member; 3) the fire insurance, that is, the Russian, ... which has not been settled; 4) Mrs. Martens's $10.00 to be sent to the West Reserve; 5) the medical expenses of the son of Jacob W. Wiebes, $40.00 for the hospital and $25.00 for the doctor to a total of $65.00; 6) concerning haircuts [fashionable hair cuts for either men or women?]; 7) each one is to have a transfer letter when moving from one church to another; 8) the request of Jacob Unger, Giroux, who wants financial assistance; 9) wedding banns [are] to be announced 2 times in church; 10) the interest in the *Waisenamt* is to be set at 3%; 11) concerning the brewing of spirits; it is not to be practiced any longer; 12) the ministers are to visit the schools twice a year, just as [they did] with the private schools; 13) no more ...; 14) buying of ... Bibles; 15) there is to be no more *Polltern* [a form of charivari] nor the playing [of musical instruments associated with this public spectacle?].

Dec. 11 Something which we had not done for two years, Katherina Wiebe, daughter of Jacob H. Wiebe, was at our place for *Vesper*.

Dec. 30 I, C.T. Friesen, was at Peter F. Hieberts' for a visit; all alone.

21 Ishmael Martin (1893 to 1980)

St. Jacobs, Ontario

Diary selection: January to June 1929

Age: 35

Ishmael Martin was born on 7 May 1893, to Noah and Rebecca (Martin) Martin. He married Fanny Snyder, who was born in 1898. Both Ishmael and Fanny were baptised in the Old Order Mennonite Church in 1918. By 1929, however, they had begun attending the more progressive Conestoga Old Mennonite Church. This is apparent in Ishmael's diary entries that mention his attendance at church every Sunday, which he would not have done as a member of the Old Order Church, which alternated services among different localities every four weeks. He also mentions attending Sunday school and Sunday evening services, meetings that were forbidden by the traditionalist Old Order Mennonites.

Despite leaving the Old Order Mennonites, Ishmael lived in a world quite separate from Canada's roaring, technologized, and industrialized 1920s. Only once, in 1929, did Ishmael record a trip to Toronto, and only four times did he ever go to Kitchener. His world was tightly cast by his immediate and extended family: The "kids" in the diary include Vernon Martin, the eldest son, 10; and Edna and Naomi, the younger daughters, probably eight and six. Nelson Snyder, 15, was Fanny's nephew, a son of "E.S." [Edwin Snyder], who also lived south of Conestoga; he worked as a hired hand for the Martins during 1929 and was an integral part of the household. Isaiah Weber, who worked occasionally as a day labourer, of course, had a different status.

Beyond the immediate household was an extensive kinship network of Snyders and Martins. The Martins included "Ma and Pa," or "Grandpa and Grandma Martin," Ishmael's parents; Jesse Martin, Ishmael's younger brother, who was married and lived with his family and his retired parents on the home farm across the river from Ishmael's; Joseph, Ishmael's younger brother, 22 and single in 1929; Preacher Urias Martin, Ishmael's half-brother; George Horst, who lived just south of Conestoga, east of Ishmael's farm, and who was married to Leah Martin, adopted daughter of Christian R. and Susannah Martin; Christian Horst, a carpenter, who lived with George and Leah; Uncle Jesse, Ishmael's uncle from Bridgeport; Christian R. Martin, Ishmael's neighbour; both Elam and Amos Martin, who were sons of Paul Martin of Erbsville. The Snyders included "Pa Snyders," or "Grandpa Snyders," which, despite its male designation, referred to Fanny's parents; Noah Horst, Sr., who was married to Fanny's sister and who farmed southwest of Elmira; Ephraim Snyder and Joseph Snyder, both Fanny's brothers; Isaiah Martin, who was married to Fanny's sister; Simon Martin, another carpenter, who was married to Fanny's cousin; Henry Horst, who was the father-in-law of Fanny's sister; both David Snider (a variation of Schneider or Snyder) and his wife, who lived near the Martins' meetinghouse and were Fanny's cousins; Menno Eby, who lived north north of St. Jacobs and was also Fanny's cousin.

Identified as neighbours and possibly related in some manner were the following: Sol Koch,, who lived two kilometres away; "Albert" (that is, Albert Habermachel or Habermehl) and his daughters, Ada and Edna, who lived just to the north of Ishmael and Fanny's; Amos Esch, who lived just to the north of Conestoga; Charles Koch, who lived north of Conestoga; Norman G. Martins, who lived north of Conestoga, near Winterbourne; Henry Martin, who was from Conestoga; Aaron Weber and his children, Levi, 13, Nelson, 11, Lena, eight, Edgar, six, and Aden, four, who were neighbours, living just to the east of Ishmael's; Manasseh Gingrich, who lived near Conestoga; Eli Marten, who lived in New Jerusalem; Deacon Menno Brubacher and his brother Bishop Moses Brubacher, who lived on the Heidelberg Road. A variety of farm tasks brought together other neighbours. In April Ishmael helped "grader the road," and in May he helped rebuild a 100-year-old bridge over the river near his place; in June, Louis Brox, an elderly widower, who may have lived in Conestoga with one of his daughters, came to help Ishmael hoe corn; in June, too, Ishmael helped fill the silo at either John Frey's or Tilman Frey's, both of whom were his neighbours; in August, Ishmael helped with the threshing at his non-Mennonite neighbour's, Fred Weppler. Then there was the larger Mennonite community, noted especially in times of tragedy: Alvin Martin, whose 10-month-old baby died in February, for example, was from Erbsville, 10 kilometres away.

Significantly absent in the diary is any mention of steam or gasoline power. Instead, the attention is on the cycle of manual and horse-powered labour. In January, Ishmael hauled "chop" to St. Jacobs mill; in February, he had the sleigh fixed; in March, he had Sally, one of the horses, bred at his brother Jesse's, place; in April, Ishmael hauled manure; and in May, when he "twitched" weeds from a Buckwheat field and harrowed and seeded, there is no indication of tractor power. Technology was employed on more progressive Waterloo Mennonite farmers, but not on Ishmael's: he had Johnny Hahn, the livestock jobber of St. Jacobs, ship out stock from the county by rail, and he sent livestock along with Erwin Dahmer who owned a trucking business. A sign, too, of the traditional life the Martins chose, was the overlapping work roles of husband and wife: while it is true that Fanny did attend "women-only" quilting bees and "rag bees," it is also noteworthy that on numerous occasions Ishmael "help[ed] with the wash" or "work[ed] in the garden." A final sign of old ways is Ishmael's reference to German place names; true, Berlin is known as Kitchener by Ishmael, but the German Catholic hamlet of Maryhill, named during the heady days of World War I, is still referred to as "New Germany" by Ishmael.

A photocopy of the original diary, which was handwritten in English, was obtained at the Mennonite Archives of Ontario. It was transcribed by Reg Good.

January

Jan. 1 Wet day. We was at home. [My wife] Fanny [Snyder Martin] had the flu. Ma. & Pa. was here.

Jan. 2 Cold & Stormy forenoon helped ... Ma was here washing. P.M. was to Conestoga.

Jan. 3 Nice A.M. Stormy P.M. A.M. Took hogs to St. Jacob's [Johnny Hahn for shipment by rail]. P.M. took Ma Home.

Jan. 4 Nice Day. A.M. chored around at home. P.M. took some [grain for] chopping to St. Jacobs mill [&] back.

Jan. 5 Damp day. A.M. fetched [the] chop in St. Jacobs. P.M. chored at home. Funeral Jacob Schweitzer.

Jan. 6, Sun. Cold & Stormy day. A.M. was in church. P.M. Was all at home.

Jan. 7 Very cold & stormy. A.M. chored. P.M. fetched children from school an[d] voted for township election.

Jan. 8 Very cold & stormy A.M. chored. P.M. was to sale of Tilman Martin.

Jan. 9 Mild day A.M. chored. P.M. team in blacksmith shop.

Jan. 10 A.M. Mild chored P.M. Stormy. [Day labourer] Is[a]iah Weber helped clean wheat and took the team to St. Jacobs.

Jan. 11 A.M. cold, P.M. stormy, A.M. took pig to A. Esch. P.M. took wheat to Conestoga.

Jan. 12 Very cold & stormy. A.M. was in St. Jacobs P.M. fetched hog at Amos Esch [north of Conestogo].

Jan. 13, Sun. Cold & Stormy A.M. I an[d] [eldest son] Vernon was in church then we went to Til[man] Freys.

Jan. 14 Very cold A.M. Chored & help washing. P.M. got chopping done at Conestoga.

Jan. 15 Cold Day. A.M. chored P.M. Is[a]iah was here working in the bush.

Jan. 16 Cold day. Is[a]iah was here all day working in the bush.

Jan. 17 Rainy day. A.M. took the children to school. PM was in Conestoga and Arron [Aaron] Weber.

Jan. 18 Nice A.M., rainy P.M. A.M. Is[a]iah was here in the bush. P.M. fetched Kids from school.

Jan. 19 Cold day. A.M. took cow (Bo[i]se) to St. Jacobs. P.M. chored at home.

Jan. 20 Sun. Cold & Stormy. A.M. all in church. P.M. was at home. [Neighbourhood girls] Ada & Edna [Habermehl] was here.

Jan. 21 Nice day. A.M. chored. P.M. got chopping done at Conestoga.

Jan. 22 Nice A.M. Cold P.M. A.M. chored P.M. took Fanny to Cha[rlie] Koch [just north of Conestoga]. Quilting and fetched her in the evening.

Jan. 23 A very stormy day. A.M. took kids to school and fetched them in P.M.

Jan. 24 A nice day. A.M. chored. PM got chopping done St. Jacobs.

Jan. 25 A stormy day A.M. chored was at Ed Snyders [Fanny's brother, two kilometres south of Conestoga]. P.M. fetched kids.

Jan. 26 A cold day. A.M. was in St. Jacobs also funeral of [Nancy] Mrs Til[man] Brubacher [wife of St. Jacobs' jeweller]. PM hauled wood.

Jan. 27, Sun. A cold & stormy day. A.M. was all in church. P.M. at home.

Jan. 28 A nice day A.M. helped washing. PM hauled wood.

Jan. 29 A cold day. Was all at Jesse Martins butchering.

Jan. 30 A nice day. Hauled wood all day.

Jan. 31 A nice day AM was at W. Martin. P.M. fetched sow at Wendall Martin for butchering.

February

Feb. 1 A nice cold day. A.M. hauled wood. P.M. fetched binder at N[orman G.] Martins.

Feb. 2 A cold stormy day A.M. was in St. Jacobs. P.M. fetched butcher tools at [brother] Jesse['s].

Sun. [Feb.] 3 A nice day. A.M. was all in church. P.M. was at home. Menno Ebys here.

Feb. 4 A nice day. A.M. chored at home. P.M. took chopping to Conestoga.

Feb. 5 A nice day. A.M. chored. P.M. took pig to [Bishop] Norman Martins [of Montrose] for butchering and fetched chopping and took pig to Amos Esch.

Feb. 6 A nice day Pa [and] Ma was here all day, butchering.

Feb. 7 A snowy day. A.M. was at Conestoga. P.M. worked at home. Henry Martin [of Conestoga] was here for milk.

Feb. 8 A snowy day. A.M. chored and took red heifer to Arron Webers. P.M. hauled manure and was at Conestoga.

Feb. 9 A nice day. A.M. was at St. Jacobs. P.M. got chopping done at Conestoga.

Sun. [Feb.] 10 A nice day. A.M. was all in church. P.M. was at home. Arron Webers children were here & Marr & Tina Schmid's. Vernon [age 10] was at Charles Koch.

Feb. 11 A cold day. A.M. help washing. PM hauled manure.

Feb. 12 A cold day. A.M. hauled manure. P.M. hauled gravel 5 hrs.

Feb. 13 A nice day hauled gravel all day.

Feb. 14 [A nice day hauled gravel all day.]

Feb. 15 A cold [day, hauled gravel all day.]

Feb. 16 A nice [day]. A.M. was in St. Jacobs. P.M. was to Conestoga got sleigh fixed.

Sun. [Feb.] 17 A nice day. A.M. was to church then to Manasseh Gingrich for dinner.

Feb. 18 A cold day hauled gravel all day.

Feb. 19 A cold day. A.M. chored. P.M. helped Albert skin a horse.

Feb. 20 A very cold day, 20 below. A.M. chored. P.M. was at Jesse. Hauled manure.

Feb. 21 A cold A.M., a stormy P.M. Hauled manure all day. Jess & George Horst helped.

Feb. 22 A cold day. A.M. was in St. Jacobs. P.M. hauled manure, Jess & Pa helped. Selina was here P.M.

Feb. 23 A cold day. A.M. chored. P.M. was at Jesse hauling shit.

Sun. [Feb.] 24 A nice day. A.M. was in church. P.M. was to funeral of Alvin Martin [of near Erbsville] child age 10 months. Abe & Sus Brubacher was here for supper.

Feb. 25 A nice day. A.M. helped washing. P.M. took red sow to Arron's.

Feb. 26 A wet day. A.M. chored. P.M. was to Jesse & Conestoga.

Feb. 27 A cold windy day. Was to sale of Nellson Snyder [near West Montrose, Woolwich Township] all day.

Feb. 28 A very nice day. A.M. was to St. Jacobs. P.M. we was in Kitchener at St. Marys hospital [to] visit Mrs. Manasseh Gingrich.

March

March 1 A very nice day. A.M. chored and helped Albert. P.M. was to Conestoga with chopping.

March 2 A nice day. A.M. was in St. Jacobs. P.M. helped Albert and fetched beef at Norman's [Norman Martin, a butcher] for sausage. Henry Martin was here for cream.

Sun. [Mar.] 3 A nice day. Was all in church and at Norman Martins for dinner.

March 4 A rainy day. Was butchering. Ma. & Pa. and Simeon Martin helped. P.M. was to Conestoga for Caustic [needed for making soup from the offal from butchering]. Sleighing about all gone.

March 5 A mild day. A.M. fetched pigs at Alberts and cleaned out his stabel. P.M. put out ashes and put out meat.

March 6 A nice day. A.M. chored and was to Albert's. P.M. took ma home.

March 7 A very stormy day, worst of season. A.M. chored. P.M. was to Albert's.

March 8 A cold day. A.M. chored and at Alberts. P.M. took chopping to St. Jacobs.

March 9 A very cold day. A.M. was at St. Jacobs.

Sun. [March] 10 A cold day, all at home.

March 11 A nice day. A.M. chored helped wash. P.M. was to Conestoga.

March 12 A nice warm day. A.M. chored. P.M. took red sow to Arron Weber's. Grandpa Sniders here all day.

March 13 A nice day. Rainy in evening. A.M. Fanny was to funeral of Mrs. Addison Freeman [Selina Bauman]. P.M. I and A[aron] was to Roy. Snider and Conestoga.

March 14 A Rainy A.M., a nice P.M. A.M. chored. P.M. was down to river, the bridge went away.

March 15 A nice day. A.M. chored. P.M. was to D[an] E. Martins and St. Jacobs.

March 16 A stormy A.M., a nice P.M. A.M. chored. P.M. to St. Jacobs and fetched mare at Dan Martins and took Sally to Jesse Martin.

March 17, Sun. A nice day. We was at home all day, no visitors.

March 18 A nice warm day. A.M. chored. P.M. got Neddy shod at Conestoga.

March 19 A snowy A.M. A rainy P.M. A.M. chored. P.M. got chopping done.

March 20 A cold day. A.M. chored. P.M. went to sale of Roy Snider. Fanny was to Albert's rag bee.

March 21 Snowy A.M. Nice P.M. A.M. chored. Took kids to Conestoga. P.M. Is[a]iah was here cutting wood.

March 22 A nice day. Is[a]iah was here all day cutting wood. P.M. took cow, Roany, to Jack Burnett.

March 23 A nice warm day. A.M. was to St. Jacobs. P.M. was to Eli Sauders & D. Kramer [of Three Bridges, northwest of St. Jacobs] looking for cows.

Sun. [March] 24 A nice day. A.M. was all in church. P.M. all at home.

March 25 A nice day. Rain at noon. A.M. was to Angus Martin. Bought a heifer. P.M. split wood. Is[a]iah helped.

March 26 A nice day. A.M. chored. P.M. got Pete shod and was to sale of H[enry]. Halle New Germany.

March 27 A nice A.M., a rainy P.M. A.M. got chopping done Conestoga. P.M. worked at home. Ervin D[ahmer, trucking business] brought cow & took black heifer.

March 28 A cold windy day. A.M. chored. P.M. St. Jacobs & Elmira with Jesse.

Good Fri., 29 A nice day (good Fri.). Was all at home. Aaron Weber's kids was here.

March 30 A cool cloudy day. A.M chored. P.M. fetched salt at St. Jacobs.

March 31, Sun. A cold day. A.M. I and Vernon was to church. P.M. all at home. Joseph [brother] was here.

April

April 1 A very stormy day. A.M. chored P.M. was to sale of Eli Sauder.

April 2 A cold day. A.M. was to Ed Snyders, fetched [hired hand] Nelson. P.M. cleaned grain.

April 3 A nice day. A.M. cleaned grain. P.M. graded on the road.

April 4 A rainy A.M. A nice P.M. A.M. chored and opened ditch. P.M. spread shit.

April 5 A nice a.m. A rainy P.M. A.M. spread Sh[it]. P.M. was to St. Jacobs.

April 6 A nice day. A.M. took corn to A.W. and fetched a load of Aaron's grain in St. Jacobs. P.M. fetched barley at Sol[omon] Kock's [located between St. Jacobs and Conestoga] and was to Conestoga.

April 7, Sun. A nice day. Was all in church, then home.

April 8 A nice day. A.M. helped washing. P.M. was to Conestoga. Nelson took chopping to St. Jacobs.

April 9 A nice warm day. Hauled gravel all day.

April 10 A windy day. Spread manure all day.

April 11 A cold day chored all day. Picked out potatoes. P.M. was to Conestoga.

April 12 A nice day. A.M. cleaned root cellar. P.M. took cows to West Montrose.

April 13 A rainy day. A.M. St. Jacob's. P.M. got chopping done Conestoga fetched cow at Albert's.

April 14, Sun. A nice day. A.M. was all in church. P.M. home. Uncle Jesse Martins here.

April 15 A cold day. Was at [Jesse's] cementing all day.

April 16 A cold day. Worked at the bridge all day.

April 17 A cold day. A.M. sawed wood. P.M. worked at bridge.

April 18 A cold day. A.M. Nelson got chopping done at St. Jacobs. P.M. both plowed.

April 19 A cold day. A.M. got chopping done at Conestoga. P.M. Nelson plowed. I to St. Jacobs.

April 20 A rainy day. Chored and took binder apart.

Sun. [April] 21: A cold day. Nelson & Vernon to church. We and Aaron's was to Bloomingdale at Elo Sniders [between Maryhill and Bloomingdale] for dinner.

April 22 A nice day. A.M. took calves to St. Jacobs. P.M. cultivated.

April 23 A nice day. A.M. fetched disc at Aaron's. P.M. we cultivated and started seeding.

April 24 A nice day. Sowed & cultivated.

April 25 A rainy [day]. A.M. was in Conestoga. P.M. worked home.

April 26 A cool day. A.M. helped ma and piled wood. P.M. was to St. Jacobs and harrowed.

April 27 A nice day. A.M. [helped ma]. P.M. cultivated and harrowed.

Sun. [April] 28 A rainy day. A.M. all in church. P.M. all at home.

April 29 A cold day. A.M. took cow to St. Jacobs. P.M. picked stones.

April 30 A.M. chored and hauled in wood and helped white washing. P.M. repaired fence.

May

May 1 A warm day. A.M. dug post holes. P.M. harrowed. Sol Koch & Jesse [and] grand ma martin [his mother] was here.

May 2 A cold rainy day. A.M. fetched cow at Sol Koch's. P.M. was to Conestoga.

May 3 A wet day. A.M. to Conestoga. P.M. got chopping done took cow to A.W.

May 4 A nice day. A.M. to St Jacobs. P.M. to S. Koch. Nelson got chopping done. Mare in Blacksmith.

Sun., May 5 A nice day A.M. Sun[day] Sch[ool]. N. Horst for dinner. Eli Martin's for supper.

May 6 A nice day rain in evening. A.M. got chopping done Conestoga. P.M. cultivate[d] an[d] Sowed.

May 7 A nice day. A.M. plowed. P.M. cleaned out garden.

May 8 A nice day. A.M. cultivated & plowed. P.M. sowed & harrowed.

May 9 Ascension [Day]. A nice day. A.M. was in church. P.M. disced & Harrowed.

May 10 A nice day. Sowed & harrowed all day.

May 11 A rainy A.M. A nice P.M. Shower at night. A.M. was to St. Jacobs & E. Spatez. P.M. C[hristian] M[artin] was here [to] patch roof.

May 12, Sun. A nice day. A.M. was all in church. P.M. was at home & went down to the river.

May 13 A nice day. A.M. hauled manure. P.M. worked in garden.

May 14 A rainy day. A.M. was to Albert's sowing and cultivating. P.M. Fetched Kids and to Conestoga.

May 15 A nice day. Worked at the bridge all day. Nelson got chop.

May 16 A cold day. A.M. at bridge. P.M. digging post holes.

May 17 A nice day. A.M. plant[ed] garden. P.M. sowed & cultivated at Albert Habermahel.

May 18 A nice day rainy eve. A.M. was to St. Jacobs. P.M. picked stones an[d] to Conestoga.

May 19, Sun. A nice day. A.M. was to church. Nelson was [at] E.S. [for] dinner. P.M. was to funeral of J. Heer.

May 20 A nice day. Hauled manure all day.

May 21 A nice day. Sowed at Alberts.

May 22 A nice [day.] A.M. hauled manure. P.M. worked in garden & disked.

May 23 A nice day. A.M. was to Conestoga. P.M. both [Nelson and I] plowed. Red sow to A[mos Esch].

May 24 A nice cool day. Planted potatoes.

May 25 A nice day. A.M. took cattle to J. Burrnet & was to St. Jacobs. P.M. Plowed & disked.

May 26, Sun. A nice day. A.M. was to church. P.M. was at home. W.B. [and] H.W. was here all day.

May 27 A warm day. A.M. plowed & disked. P.M. fetched roller and disck.

May 28 A rainy day. [In] Toronto all day.

May 29 A very warm day. A.M. took sow to Amos Esch. P.M. . . .

May 30 A nice day. A.M. was to Conestoga. P.M. made fence. . . .

May 31 A nice day. Made fence all day.

June

June 1 A nice day A.M. in St. Jacobs. P.M. fixed fence. . . .

June 2, Sun. A cool day. Was to Eden Martins dinner.

June 3 A [cool day.] Fixed fence all day.

June 4 [A cool day. Fixed fence all day.]

June 5 [A cool day. Fixed fence all day.]

June 6 A nice day. A.M. was to Conestoga. P.M. fixed fence.

June 7 A nice day. A.M. was to St. Jacobs. Nelson got chopping done. P.M. Plowed.

June 8 A nice day. Was to Jesse all day hauling stones. Nelson plowed.

June 9, Sun. A warm day. Was [in] church. Jesse for dinner.

June 10 A [warm day.] Plowed all day. Church even.

June 11 [A warm day. Plowed all day.]

June 12 [A warm day.] A.M. disked. P.M. sowed turnips.

June 13 [A warm day.] A.M. [disked] P.M. plowed.

June 14 [A warm day.] A.M. sowed buckwheat. P.M. raked of[f] twitch roots.

June 15 A nice day. A.M. Was to St. Jacobs. P.M. was to Conestoga.

June 16, Sun. A warm day. A.M. was to church. P.M. was at home. Nelson was to church all day.

June 17 A very warm day. A.M. plowed & cultivated corn. P.M. hoed thistles.

June 18 A nice day. A.M. plowed & disked. P.M. hoed thistles.

June 19 A very warm day. Hoed thistls.

June 20 A very hot day. A.M. sowed buckwh[eat]. P.M. took team to pasture. Grand pa's was here for supper.

June 21 A very hot day. A.M. was to St. Jacobs and got chopping done at Conestoga. P.M. hoed thistles.

June 22 A hot day. A.M. worked in the corn. P.M. hoed thistles.

June, Sun., 23 A nice day. A.M. was to church. P.M. was to Ed. Sniders.

June 24 A nice day. A.M. hoed corn. P.M. hoed thistles.

June 25 A hot day. Hoed corn all day, L. Brox helped. P.M. to St. Jacobs.

June 26 A.nice day. Hoed corn all day. Shower at night.

June 27 A cool day. A.M. hoed corn. P.M. cultivated. Nelson to Prima [?].

June 28 A cool day. A.M. hoed corn. P.M. to St. Jacobs an[d] hoed corn.

June 29 A cool day. Hoed corn all day. P.M. was to Elmira.

June, Sun. 30 A cool day. Nelson was to church. We was at home was down to river.

Notes

Preface

1 Robert Fothergill, *Private Chronicles: A Study of English Diaries* (London: 1974), 2.

Introduction

1 Fothergill, *Private Chronicles*, 2.
2 Ibid., 2 & 10.
3 Tamara Hareven, "The History of the Family and the Process of Social Change," *American Historical Review* 96 (1991): 116.
4 Brian W. Beltman, *Dutch Farmer in the Missouri Valley: The Life and Letters of Ulbe Eringa, 1866-1950* (Urbana: 1997); William Boelhower, "Dutch-American Fictions: Learning to Read the Signs," *European Contributions to American Studies* 17 (1990): 131- 153; Charlotte Erickson, *Invisible Immigrants: The Adaptation of English and Scottish Immigrants in 19th Century America* (Ithaca, NY: 1972); Walter D. Kamphoefner, Wolfgang Helbich, and Ulrike Sommer, eds., *News from the Land of Freedom: German Immigrants Write Home*, trans. Susan Carter Vogel (Ithaca, NY: 1991); Wolf D. Kindermann, "Asian-American Literary Perception of the United States, 1930-1940s," *European Contributions to American Studies* 17 (1990): 243-272; Robert Orsi, "The Fault of Memory: 'Southern Italy' in the Imagination of Immigrants and the Lives of Their Children in Italian Harlem, 1920-1945," *Journal of Family History* 15 (1990): 133-147; Tamara Palmer, "Elements of Jewish Culture in Adele Wiseman's *Crackpot*: A Subversive Ethnic Fiction Female Style," *Prairie Forum* 16 (1991): 265-285; Ira Robinson, Pierre Anctil, and Mervin Butovsky, *An Everyday Miracle: Yiddish Culture in Montreal* (Montreal: 1990); Regine Rosenthal, "The Cultural Work of American Jewish Immigrant Autobiographies," *European Contributions to American Studies* 17 (1990): 152-175; Roshan Roshan, "In Quest of a Habitation and a Name: Immigrant Voices from India," *International Journal of Canadian Studies* 6 (1992): 87-98.
5 James M. Nyce, ed., *The Gordon C. Eby Diaries: Chronicle of a Mennonite Farmer, 1911-1913* (Toronto, ON: 1982); Harvey L. Dyck, ed. & trans., *A Mennonite in Russia: The Diaries of Jacob D. Epp, 1851-1880* (Toronto: 1991).
6 The various archives in Ontario and Manitoba include: the Mennonite Archives of Ontario, Waterloo, ON; Doon Heritage Crossroads, Kitchener, ON; Manitoba Genealogy Inc., Winnipeg, MB; Evangelical Mennonite Archives, Steinbach, MB; Mennonite Heritage Village, Steinbach, MB; Mennonite Heritage Centre, Winnipeg, MB.
7 For a history of Hanover, see: Lydia Penner, *Hanover: One Hundred Years* (Steinbach, MB: 1982); Abe Warkentin, *Reflections on Our Heritage: A History of Steinbach and the R.M. of Hanover from 1874* (Steinbach, MB: 1971); John Dyck, ed., *East Reserve Village Histories, 1874-1910* (Steinbach, MB: 1990). See also relevant sections in E.K. Francis,

In Search of Utopia (Altona, MB: 1955); John Warkentin, "Mennonite Settlements in Southern Manitoba: A Study in Historical Geography" (Ph.D. dissertation, University of Toronto, 1960); Royden Loewen, *Family, Church and Market: A Mennonite Community in the Old and the New Worlds, 1850-1930* (Urbana and Chicago: 1993); Dennis Stoesz, "A History of the Chortitzer Mennonite Church of Manitoba, 1874-1914" (M.A. thesis, University of Manitoba, 1987).

8 *Census of Canada, 1901*, Table X.

9 For histories of Waterloo County see: Elizabeth Bloomfield, *Waterloo Township through Two Centuries* (Kitchener, ON: 1995); John English and Kenneth McLaughlin, *Kitchener: An Illustrated History* (Waterloo, ON: 1983); J. Winfield Fretz, *The Waterloo Mennonites: A Community in Paradox* (Waterloo, ON: 1989). A.G. McLellan, ed., *The Waterloo County Area: Selected Geographical Essays* (Waterloo, ON: 1971); Kenneth Cressman, "A Descriptive Summary and Analysis of the Changing Settlement and Occupational Patterns of the Mennonites and Amish Mennonites of Wilmot Township" (M.A. thesis, Waterloo, 1988); Ezra Eby, *A Biographical History of Early Settlers and their Descendants in Waterloo Township, 1895* (Waterloo, ON: 1984).

10 *Census of Canada, 1901*, Table X.

11 Ibid.; Hanover Municipality Tax Rolls, Rural Municipality of Hanover (hereinafter RMH), Steinbach, MB. Winnipeg, possessing some 42,000 inhabitants by 1901, lay a full day's travel by horse from the centre of the municipality.

12 English and McLaughlin, *Kitchener*, 53ff.

13 Royden Loewen, "Ethnic Farmers and the Outside World: Mennonites in Manitoba and Nebraska," *Journal of the Canadian Historical Association* 1 (1990): 195-214.

14 Adrian Wilson, "Foundations of an Integrated Historiography," *Rethinking Social History: English Society 1570-1920 and Its Interpretation* (Manchester: 1993): 293-335.

15 Ibid., 314.

16 Jack Goody, *The Interface between the Written and the Oral* (Cambridge, England: 1987), 300.

17 Walter Ong, *Orality and Language: The Technologizing of the Word* (New York: 1982), 42.

18 Ibid., 104; 81.

19 Matthew Innes, "Memory, Orality and Literacy in an Early Medieval Society," *Past and Present* 77 (1998): 3-36.

20 Werner Sollors, Introduction to *The Invention of Ethnicity* (New York: 1989), xiv; see David Gerber, "You See i Speak Wery Well English," *Journal of American Ethnic History* 12 (1993):56-65, in which he reviews Walter D. Kamphoefner et al.; Betty Bergland, "Postmodernism and the Autobiographical Subject: Reconstructing the 'Other'," in *Autobiography and Postmodernism*, edited by Kathleen Ashley, et al. (Amherst: 1994).

21 Harvey J. Graff, Introduction to *Literacy and Social Development in the West: A Reader* (Cambridge, England: 1981), 4.

22 Mark Zborowski and Elizabeth Herzog, *Life is with People: The Culture of the Shtetl* (New York: 1952), 32; Ira Robinson et al., *An Everyday Miracle: Yiddish Culture in Montreal*, 11; C.A. Dawson, *Group Settlement: Ethnic Communities in Western Canada* (Toronto: 1936).

23 Arnold Snyder, *Anabaptist History and Theology: An Introduction* (Kitchener, ON: 1995), 108; see also Arnold Snyder, "Orality, Literacy and the Study of Anabaptism," *Mennonite Quarterly Review* 65 (1991): 371-392.

24 Robert Friedmann, *Mennonite Piety through the Centuries: Its Genius and Its Literature* (Goshen, IN: 1949).

25 James Urry, *None but Saints: The Transformation of Mennonite Life in Russia, 1789-1889* (Winnipeg: 1989), 154.

26 Leo Driedger, *Mennonite Identity in Conflict* (Lewiston, NY: 1988); Urry, *None but Saints*; Peter J. Klassen, *A Homeland for Strangers: An Introduction to Mennonites in Poland and Prussia* (Fresno, CA: 1989); James T. Lemon, *The Best Poor Man's Country: A Geographical Study of Early Southeastern Pennsylvania* (Baltimore and London: 1972); Richard MacMaster, *Land, Piety, Peoplehood: The Establishment of Mennonite Communities in America, 1683-1790* (Scottdale, PA: 1985); Aaron Spencer Fogleman, *Hopeful Journeys: German Immigration, Settlement and Political Culture in Colonial America, 1717-1775* (Philadelphia: 1996).

27 François Furet and Jacques Ozouf, *Reading and Writing: Literacy in France from Calvin to Jules Ferry* (Cambridge, England: 1982), 190. See also Keith Thomas, "Numeracy in Early Modern England," *Transactions of the Royal Historical Society* 37 (1987): 103-132. I thank James Urry for bringing this article to my attention.

28 Urry, *None but Saints*, 138; Ingrid I. Epp and Harvey L. Dyck, *The Peter J. Braun Russian Mennonite Archive, 1803-1920: A Research Guide* (Toronto: 1996).

29 See Fogleman, *Hopeful Journeys*. Partible inheritance practice among Mennonites required equal division of property among all children, both male and female. Impartible inheritance prohibited division of property.

30 Fothergill, *Private Chronicles*, 14.

31 For standard accounts of the history of Canadian Mennonites see: Frank H. Epp, *Mennonites in Canada, 1786-1920: The History of a Separate People* (Toronto: 1974). For sociological analyses of the Waterloo County and East Reserve communities, see: Fretz, *The Waterloo Mennonites*; Francis, *In Search of Utopia*.

32 Fothergill, *Private Chronicles*, 35.

33 Cornelius Loewen, "Tagebuch, 1863-1892," Mennonite Heritage Village, Steinbach, MB. For other travelogues by East Reserve Mennonites describing the transoceanic voyage, see: Gerhard Doerksen, "Tagebuch, 1876," Bernard P. Doerksen, Blumenort, MB; David L. Plett, "Tagebuch, 1875," Betty Plett, Blumenort, MB; Peter Loewen, "Tagebuch, 1874," Evangelical Mennonite Conference Archives, Steinbach, MB.

34 Ezra Burkholder, diary, 1876, Mennonite Archives of Ontario (hereinafter MAO), Waterloo, ON.

35 Margaretha Jansen, diary, 1873-1874, trans. Anna Linscheid, Mennonite Historical Library, Newton, KS. For a history of the Jansen family, see: Gustav Reimer and G.R. Gaeddert, *Exiled by the Czar: Cornelius Jansen and the Great Mennonite Migration, 1874* (Newton, KS: 1956).

36 Maria Stoesz Klassen, "Tagebuch, 1887," trans. Irene Enns Kroeker, Steinbach, MB; Margaretha Plett Kroeker, "Tagebuch, 1892-1911," trans. Ben Hoeppner, courtesy Ben K. Plett, Landmark, MB.

37 Levi Jung, "Excerpts from the Diary of Levi Jung, 1863," edited by Richard E. Taylor, Schwenkfelder Library, Pennsburg, PA.

38 David Blackburn, "Between Recognition and Volatility: The German Petite Bourgeoisie in the Nineteenth Century," in *Shopkeepers and Master Artisans in Nineteenth*

Century Europe, edited by Geoffrey Crossik and Heinz-Gerhard Haupt (London: 1984); Clifford Geertz, *Peddlers and Princes: Social Change and Economic Modernization in Two Indonesian Towns* (Chicago: 1963), 142. See also James Urry, "Prolegomena to the Study of Mennonite Society in Russia, 1880-1914," *Journal of Mennonite Studies* 8 (1990), who notes that in turn-of-the-century Mennonite colonies in Russia "new ways of relating to various sectors of the community developed, with a degree of solidarity emerging among those who shared the same education standard, wealth, occupation and status" (64).

39 Elias Eby, diary 1876, trans., n.n., MAO.

40 Klaas R. Reimer, account of letters written, 1885-1896, trans. Peter Dueck, EMCA.

41 Ephraim Cressman, diary, 1892, MAO; Heinrich Friesen, "Journal 1896-1898," trans. Irene Enns Kroeker, *Historical Sketches of the East Reserve, 1874-1910,* edited by John Dyck, 477-501 (Steinbach, MB: 1994).

42 Moses Weber, diary, 1865, MAO; Heinrich Kornelsen, "Tagebuch, 1875," trans. Dave Schellenberg, EMCA.

43 Weber, diary.

44 H. Kornelson, "Tagebuch." Mennonite churches in both Manitoba and Ontario rotated their worship services during the course of the year from one village to another within the district.

45 Abraham F. Reimer, "Tagebuch, 1879," trans. Ben Hoeppner and Royden Loewen, EMCA.

46 Moses Bowman, diary, 1890, MAO.

47 Ibid.

48 Judy Simons, *Diaries and Journals of Literary Women: From Fanny Burney to Virginia Woolf* (Iowa City: 1990), 196.

49 Margaret Conrad, "Recording Angels: The Private Chronicles of Women from the Maritime Provinces of Canada, 1750-1950," *The Neglected Majority: Essays in Canadian Women's History*, edited by Alison Prentice and Susan Mann Trofimenkoff (Toronto: 1985), 52 and 58.

50 Margaretha Plett Kroeker, "Tagebuch, 1892" ; Laura Shantz, diary, 1918, in the possession of Lorna Bergey, Kitchener, ON; Maria Reimer Unger, "Tagebuch, 1919," trans. Margaret Toews and Royden Loewen, in the possession of Peter U. Dueck, Steinbach, MB; Judith Klassen Neufeld, "Tagebuch, 1922," trans. Mary Enns, in the possession of Mary Enns, Steinbach, MB.

51 Marie Schroeder, diary, 1925, in the possession of Susannah Schroeder Janzen, Steinbach, MB.

52 Cornelius T. Friesen, "Tagebuch, 1925," trans. Ben Hoeppner and Royden Loewen, in the possession of Irene Enns Kroeker, Steinbach, MB; Ishmael Martin, diary, 1929-1935, trans. Paul Hunsberger, Kitchener, ON.

53 Ishmael Martin, diary, 1929-1935, Paul Hunsberger, Kitchener, ON.

54 See: Clifford Geertz, *After the Fact: Two Countries, Four Decades, One Anthropologist* (Cambridge, MA: 1995; Hans Medick, "'Missionaries in a Rowboat'? Ethnological Ways of Knowing as a Challenge to Social History," *Comparative Studies in Society and History* 29 (1987): 76-98; Fredrick Barth, Introduction *to Balinese Worlds* (Chicago: 1993).

Bibliography

Barth, Fredrik. Introduction to *Balinese Worlds*. Chicago: 1993.

Beltman, Brian W. *Dutch Farmer in the Missouri Valley: The Life and Letters of Ulbe Eringa, 1866-1950*. Urbana: 1997.

Bergey, Lorna, et al., eds. *A Family History of Jacob and Elisabeth Eby Bergey*. Kitchener, ON: 1987.

Bergland, Betty. "Postmodernism and the Autobiographical Subject: Reconstructing the 'Other.'" In *Autobiography and Postmodernism*. Edited by Kathleen Ashley, et al. Amherst, MA: 1994.

Blackburn, David. "Between Recognition and Volatility: The German Petite Bourgeoisie in the Nineteenth Century." In *Shopkeepers and Master Artisans in Nineteenth Century Europe*. Edited by Geoffrey Crossik and Heinz-Gerhard Haupt. London: 1984.

Bloomfield, Elizabeth. *Waterloo Township through Two Centuries*. Kitchener, ON: 1995.

Boelhower, William. "Dutch-American Fictions: Learning to Read the Signs." *European Contributions to American Studies* 17 (1990): 131-153.

Buhler, Linda. "Ebenfeld." In *Historical Sketches of the East Reserve, 1874-1910*. Edited by John Dyck, 104-124. Steinbach, MB: 1994.

Burkholder, L.J. *A Brief History of the Mennonites in Ontario, 1935*. Waterloo, ON: 1986.

Cisar, Mary. "Mennonite Women's Autobiography: An Interdisciplinary Feminist Perspective." *Journal of Mennonite Studies* 14 (1996): 142-152.

Conrad, Margaret. "Recording Angels: The Private Chronicles of Women from the Maritime Provinces of Canada, 1750-1950." In *The Neglected Majority: Essays in Canadian Women's History*. Edited by Alison Prentice and Susan Mann Trofimenkoff, 41-60. Toronto: 1985.

Cressman, Kenneth. "A Descriptive Summary and Analysis of the Changing Settlement and Occupational Patterns of the Mennonites and Amish Mennonites of Wilmot Township." M.A. thesis, Waterloo, 1988.

Dawson, C.A. *Group Settlement: Ethnic Communities in Western Canada*. New York: 1936.

Dilley, Robert S. "Migrations and the Mennonites: Nineteenth-Century Waterloo County, Ontario." *Canadian Papers in Rural History* 4 (1984).

Driedger, Leo. *Mennonite Identity in Conflict.* Lewiston, NY: 1988.

Dueck, Abe J., ed. *Canadian Mennonites and the Challenge of Nationalism.* Winnipeg: 1994.

Dueck, John, et al., eds. *Descendants of Jacob and Maria L. Dueck, 1839-1986.* Steinbach, MB: 1986.

Dyck, Harvey L., ed. & trans. *A Mennonite in Russia: The Diaries of Jacob D. Epp, 1851-1880.* Toronto: 1991.

Dyck, John, ed. *Working Papers of the East Reserve Village Histories, 1874-1910.* Steinbach, MB: 1990.

_____, ed. *Historical Sketches of the East Reserve, 1874-1910.* Steinbach, MB: 1994.

Eby, Ezra. *A Biographical History of Early Settlers and their Descendants in Waterloo Township, 1895.* Waterloo, ON: 1984.

English, John, and Kenneth McLaughlin. *Kitchener: An Illustrated History.* Waterloo, ON: 1983.

Ens, Adolf. *Subjects or Citizens: The Mennonite Experience in Canada, 1870-1925.* Ottawa: 1994.

Ens, Anna Epp. *In Search of Unity: Story of the Conference of Mennonites in Manitoba.* Winnipeg: 1996.

Epp, Frank H. *Mennonites in Canada, 1786-1920: The History of a Separate People.* Toronto: 1974.

Epp, George K. *Geschichte der Mennoniten in Russland: Deutsche Taeufer in Russland Band I.* Lage, Germany: 1997.

Epp, Ingrid I., and Harvey L. Dyck. *The Peter J. Braun Russian Mennonite Archive, 1803-1920: A Research Guide.* Toronto: 1996.

_____. *Mennonites in Canada, 1920-1940: A People's Struggle for Survival.* Toronto: 1982.

Epp, Marlene. *Women without Men: Mennonite Refugees of the Second World War.* Toronto: 1999.

Erickson, Charlotte. *Invisible Immigrants: The Adaptation of English and Scottish Immigrants in 19th Century America.* Ithaca, NY: 1972.

Fogleman, Aaron Spencer. *Hopeful Journeys: German Immigration, Settlement and Political Culture in Colonial America, 1717-1775.* Philadelphia: 1996.

Francis, E.K. *In Search of Utopia: A Social History of the Mennonites in Manitoba.* Altona, MB: 1955.

Fretz, J. Winfield. *The Waterloo Mennonites: A Community in Paradox.* Waterloo, ON: 1989.

Friedmann, Robert. *Mennonite Piety through the Centuries: Its Genius and Its Literature.* Goshen, IN: 1949.

Friesen, Gerald, and Royden Loewen. "Romantics, Pluralists and Postmodernists: The Ethnic Historiography of Prairie Canada." In *River Road: Essays in*

Manitoba and Prairie History. Edited by Gerald Friesen, 183-196. Winnipeg: 1996.

Furet, François, and Jacques Ozouf. *Reading and Writing: Literacy in France from Calvin to Jules Ferry.* Cambridge, England: 1982.

Geertz, Clifford. *Peddlers and Princes: Social Change and Economic Modernization in Two Indonesian Towns.* Chicago: 1963.

———. *After the Fact: Two Countries, Four Decades, One Anthropologist.* Cambridge, MA: 1995.

Gerber, David. "You See i Speak Wery Well English." *Journal of American Ethnic History* 12 (1993): 56-65.

Good, E. Reginald. *Frontier Community to Urban Congregation: First Mennonite Church, Kitchener, 1813-1988.* Waterloo, ON: 1988.

Goody, Jack. *The Interface between the Written and the Oral.* Cambridge, England: 1987.

Graff, Harvey J. Introduction to *Literacy and Social Development in the West: A Reader.* Cambridge, England: 1981.

Hallman, A.G. *100 Years of Progress in Waterloo County, Canada.* Waterloo, ON: 1906.

Hareven, Tamara. "The History of the Family and the Process of Social Change." *American Historical Review* 96 (1991): 95-124.

Innes, Matthew. "Memory, Orality and Literacy in an Early Medieval Society." *Past and Present* 77 (1998): 3-36.

Janzen, William. *Limits on Liberty: The Experience of Mennonite, Hutterite and Doukhobor Communities in Canada.* Toronto: 1990.

Kamphoefner, Walter D., Wolfgang Helbich, and Ulrike Sommer, eds. *News from the Land of Freedom: German Immigrants Write Home.* Translated by Susan Carter Vogel. Ithaca, NY: 1991.

Kindermann, Wolf D. "Asian-American Literary Perception of the United States, 1930-1940s." *European Contributions to American Studies* 17 (1990): 243-272.

Klassen, Peter J. *A Homeland for Strangers: An Introduction to Mennonites in Poland and Prussia.* Fresno, CA: 1989.

Kolb, Elisabeth Ziegler. *Letters to Jacob B. and Mary Mensch, Montgomery County, PA: 1874-1895.* Translated by Isaac Horst. Waterloo, ON: n.d.

Kroeker, Irene Enns. "Blumengart." In *Historical Sketches of the East Reserve, 1874-1910.* Edited by John Dyck, 63-103. Steinbach, MB: 1994.

———. "Prediger Heinrich Friesen." In *Historical Sketches of the East Reserve, 1874-1910.* Edited by John Dyck, 329-337. Steinbach, MB: 1994.

Lemon, James T. *The Best Poor Man's Country: A Geographical Study of Early Southeastern Pennsylvania.* Baltimore and London: 1972.

Loewen, Harry, and Steven Nolt. *Through Fire and Water.* Scottdale, PA: 1996.

Loewen, Melvin J. *The Descendants of Cornelius W. Loewen and Helena Bartel.* Goshen, IN: 1994.

Loewen, Royden. *Blumenort: A Mennonite Community in Transition, 1874-1983.* Blumenort, MB: 1983.

———. "Diaries as a Source for Studying Mennonite History." *Mennogespräch: Mennonite Historical Society of Ontario* 9 (1991): 1-6.

———. "'The Children, the Cows, My Dear Man and My Sister': The Transplanted Lives of Mennonite Farm Women in Manitoba and Nebraska, 1874-1900." *Canadian Historical Review* 73 (1992): 344-373.

———. "Bright Lights, Hard Truth, Soft Facts: The Evolving Literature of Ethnic Farm Life in Canada." *Canadian Ethnic Studies* 28 (1997): 25-39.

———. "'As I Experienced Them Myself': The Autobiographical German-Language Prairie Women." In *A Chorus of Voices: German Canadian Identities.* Edited by Angelika E. Sauer and Matthias Zimmer, 119-142. New York: 1998.

———. *Family, Church and Market: A Mennonite Community in the Old and the New Worlds, 1850-1930.* Urbana and Chicago: 1993.

———. "Klaas R. Reimer: From Rags to Riches but not From Village to World." In *Historical Sketches of the East Reserve, 1874-1910.* Edited by John Dyck, 304-312.

———. "The Mennonites of Waterloo, Ontario, and Hanover, Manitoba, 1890s: A Study in Household and Community." *Canadian Papers in Rural History* 9 (1993): 187-209.

———. "Si son herederas de la gracia, más aún de los bienes temporales: El sistema de herencia igualitario entre los Menonitas de Canadá." Translated by Maria Bjerg. *Reproducción Social y Sistemas de Herencia en una Perspectiva Comparada Europa y los Países Nuevos.* Edited by Maria Bjerg, et al., 145-170. Paris: 1998.

MacMaster, Richard. *Land, Piety, Peoplehood: The Establishment of Mennonite Communities in America, 1683-1790.* Scottdale, PA: 1985.

Macnaughton, Elizabeth. *The New Agriculture in Waterloo County.* Waterloo, ON: 1990.

Martens, Katherine, and Heidi Harms. *In Her Own Voice: Childbirth Stories from Mennonite Women.* Winnipeg: 1997.

McLellan, A.G., ed. *The Waterloo County Area: Selected Geographical Essays.* Waterloo, ON: 1971.

Medick, Hans. "'Missionaries in a Rowboat'? Ethnological Ways of Knowing as a Challenge to Social History." *Comparative Studies in Society and History* 29 (1987): 76-98.

Nyce, James M., ed. *The Gordon C. Eby Diaries: Chronicle of a Mennonite Farmer, 1911-1913.* Toronto, ON: 1982.

Ong, Walter. *Orality and Language: The Technologizing of the Word.* New York: 1982.

Orsi, Robert. "The Fault of Memory: 'Southern Italy' in the Imagination of Immigrants and the Lives of Their Children in Italian Harlem, 1920-1945." *Journal of Family History* 15 (1990): 133-147.

Palmer, Tamara. "Elements of Jewish Culture in Adele Wiseman's *Crackpot:* A Subversive Ethnic Fiction Female Style." *Prairie Forum* 16 (1991): 265-285.

Penner, Lydia. *Hanover: One Hundred Years.* Steinbach, MB: 1982.

Peters, Jake. *The Waisenamt: A History of Mennonite Inheritance Custom.* Steinbach, MB: 1985.

Plett, Delbert F. *Plett Picture Book: A Pictorial History of the Children and Grandchildren of Cornelius Plett and Sara Loewen.* Steinbach, MB: 1981.

_____. *Storm and Triumph: The Mennonite Kleine Gemeinde, 1850-1875.* Steinbach, MB: 1986

_____. *Pioneers and Pilgrims: The Mennonite Kleine Gemeinde in Manitoba, Nebraska, and Kansas, 1874-1882.* Steinbach, MB: 1990.

_____. *Leaders of the Mennonite Kleine Gemeinde in Russia, 1812-1874.* Steinbach, MB: 1993.

_____. "Print Culture of the East Reserve." *Mennonite Quarterly Review* 68 (1994): 524-550.

_____. "The Chortitzer Church: Feature Story." *Preservings: Newsletter of the Hanover Steinbach Historical Society* 11 (1997): 1-7.

_____. *East Reserve 125: Hanover Steinbach, 1874-1999: Celebrating Our Heritage.* Steinbach, MB: 1999.

Plett, Harvey. *Seeking to be Faithful: The Story of the Evangelical Mennonite Conference* Steinbach, MB: 1996.

Redekop, Calvin H. *Leaving Anabaptism: From Evangelical Mennonite Brethren to Fellowship of Evangelical Bible Churches.* Telford, PA: 1998.

Regehr, T.D. *Mennonites in Canada: A People Transformed, 1939-1970.* Toronto: 1997.

Reimer, John C., et al. *Familienregister der Nachkommen von Klaas und Helena Reimer mit Biographien der ersten drei Generationen.* Winnipeg, MB: 1958.

Reimer, Gustav E., and G.R. Gaeddert. *Exiled by the Czar: Cornelius Jansen and the Great Mennonite Migration, 1874.* Newton, KS: 1956.

Robinson, Ira, Pierre Anctil, and Mervin Butovsky. *An Everyday Miracle: Yiddish Culture in Montreal.* Montreal: 1990.

Rosenthal, Regine. "The Cultural Work of American Jewish Immigrant Autobiographies." *European Contributions to American Studies* 17 (1990): 152-175.

Roshan, Roshan. "In Quest of a Habitation and a Name: Immigrant Voices from India." *International Journal of Canadian Studies* 6 (1992): 87-98.

Roth, Lorraine. *Willing Service: Stories of Ontario Mennonite Women.* Waterloo, ON: 1992.

Schroeder, William, and Helmut T. Huebert. *Mennonite Historical Atlas.* Winnipeg: 1996.

Scott, Stephen: *Introduction to Old Order and Conservative Mennonite Groups.* Intercourse, PA: 1996.

Simons, Judy. *Diaries and Journals of Literary Women: From Fanny Burney to Virginia Woolf.* Iowa City: 1990.

Snyder, Arnold. "Orality, Literacy and the Study of Anabaptism." *Mennonite Quarterly Review* 65 (1991): 371-392.

Sollors, Werner. Introduction. *The Invention of Ethnicity.* New York: 1989.

Steiner, Samuel J. *Vicarious Pioneer: The Life of Jacob Y. Shantz.* Winnipeg: 1988.

Stoesz, Dennis. "A History of the Chortitzer Mennonite Church of Manitoba, 1874-1914." M.A. thesis, University of Manitoba, 1987.

Taylor, Richard E., ed. *Verhandlungen, 1859-1895.* Translated by Frank Litty. Coopersburg, PA: 1989.

Thomas, Keith. "Numeracy in Early Modern England." *Transactions of the Royal Historical Society* 37 (1987): 103-132.

Urry, James. *None but Saints: The Transformation of Mennonite Life in Russia, 1789-1889.* Winnipeg, MB: 1989.

_____. "Prolegomena to the Study of Mennonite Society in Russia, 1880-1914," *Journal of Mennonite Studies* 8 (1990): 52-75.

Warkentin, Abe. *Reflections on Our Heritage: A History of Steinbach and the R.M. of Hanover from 1874.* Steinbach, MB: 1971.

Warkentin, John. "Mennonite Settlements in Southern Manitoba: A Study in Historical Geography," Ph.D. dissertation, University of Toronto, 1960.

Wiebe, Gerhard. *Causes and History of the Emigration of the Mennonites from Russia to America, 1900.* Translated by Helen Janzen. Winnipeg, MB: 1981.

Wilson, Adrian. *Rethinking Social History: English Society 1570-1920 and Its Interpretation.* Manchester: 1993.

Zborowski, Mark, and Elizabeth Herzog. *Life is with People: The Culture of the Shtetl.* New York: 1952.

Selected Index

accidents 27, 45, 72, 105, 106, 136, 240, 250, 254, 257, 260, 276, 279, 303, 309, 312
adoption 167, 238
Alberta 253, 255, 258, 295, 298
alcohol 23, 24, 26, 129, 202, 211, 217, 219, 234, 318, 325
Altona, Manitoba 267, 323-4
Amish 69
anger and arguing 42, 55, 62, 228
assimilation 78, 214, 220, 226-9, 295

Baerg, Peter (Rev.) 23, 124, 130
baking 63, 67, 267ff, 299
baptism 67, 146, 179, 214-6, 223, 228, 233, 245, 253, 276, 314
Baptist Church 67
Barkman, Helena Rempel (widow) 21, 29
Barkman Jacob M. (Rev.) 21, 28
barley 32, 75, 95, 99, 113, 155, 190, 242, 267, 271, 296, 301
barn construction 178, 255, 264, 274-8
beauty 310
Bergey, David (diarist) xv, 115, 117
Bergthal
–church 2, 213
–colony (New Russia) 70, 71, 164, 294, 316
–village (Manitoba) 70, 72
Berlin, Ontario xii, 41ff, 82, 85, 114-5, 117, 123, 132-3, 150-64
Bible 57, 65, 165, 125, 199ff, 205, 212ff, 247, 325
bicycle 296
birthdays 49, 64, 250, 312
blanket-making 270-1
Blumenhof, Manitoba 261ff
Blumenort, Manitoba 87, 89ff, 194, 211, 222, 261ff
Borosenko Colony, New Russia 21-26, 89, 134, 237
Bowman, Anna Cressman (spouse) 114ff
Bowman, Moses (diarist) 15, 114ff, 127

Brenneman, Daniel (evangelist) 8, 42, 44-53, 57, 67, 123, 125-7
Breslau, Ontario 149ff
Bridgeport, Ontario 123ff
bridges 43, 50, 101, 105, 116, 200, 229, 326, 330, 332
Brotherhood Meetings (*Bruderschaft*) 10, 93, 173, 193, 211ff, 304, 318, 320
Bruderthaler Church (Evangelical Mennonite Brethren) 211, 222, 224, 234
Burkholder, Ezra (diarist) 8, 29ff, 40
butchering 44, 73-74, 79, 96, 110, 113, 136, 153, 192, 238-9, 244-5, 247, 260, 262-3, 265, 288-90, 292, 295, 307, 313
butter 73, 75, 97, 100, 145-6, 151, 154, 278, 280, 299

California 124
calving 173, 239, 248, 260, 263-5, 274, 313
Canada, people of 69, 210
carpentry 101, 102, 103, 184, 240, 279
cars 196, 211, 214-6, 220-2, 224-9, 234-6, 251, 300, 314, 322
Cassel, Mary Ann Bricker (grandmother) 246ff
Catholic 202, 209
cattle 149, 250
–breeding 38, 98, 146
–marketing 84, 93, 106, 153, 155, 244, 259, 281, 305, 328, 322
–pasturing 82, 92, 95, 286;
charivaree (Poltern) 217, 307, 318, 325
cheese production 138, 140, 144, 171, 184, 189
Chicago 132, 317
chickens 74, 99, 109, 242, 259, 288
childbirth 21, 24, 95, 134, 135, 141, 148, 183, 195, 215, 245, 248, 251, 267, 294, 302
Chortitz
–church 165, 262, 316
–colony (New Russia) 70, 164
–village (Manitoba) 194, 195, 297, 321-2

Index

Christmas 44, 142, 195, 293
church building 171, 172, 218-220, 223, 229, 235
church elections (ordinations) 24, 63, 75, 115, 132, 162-3, 211, 213, 235, 319
church attendance 46, 49, 94, 112, 242, 293, 300, 325
class (social and economic) 3, 36, 69, 134, 142, 145
clothing (also cloth and textiles) 23, 43, 44, 49, 58, 60, 63, 67, 69, 72, 75, 87, 92ff, 121, 137-8, 144, 151, 172, 199, 206, 210, 250, 252, 255, 266, 270, 288, 290, 305, 315
clover 81, 154
code 86, 88, 117
Colorado 65, 144
communion 60, 61-2, 107, 109, 115, 181, 215, 222, 226-8, 233-4, 255, 275, 278, 317, 321, 324
corn 31ff, 251
courts 213, 235
courtship 50, 67
credit and debt 22ff, 116, 118, 128, 139, 144, 218, 266, 269, 273, 277-8, 282, 287-8, 292, 316, 325
Cressman, Amos (Bishop) 116
Cressman, Ephraim (diarist) xiv, 11, 149ff
Cressman, Susannah Betzner (spouse) 149
Crimea 23
crying 42, 49, 136, 137, 199, 203-210, 316, 323

dancing 311
death 50, 73, 74, 128, 135-6, 195, 233
Derstine, C.F. (Rev.) 17, 253, 259
diary-keeping 1, 21, 22, 30, 42, 54, 58, 67, 69, 70-1, 78, 86-7, 89, 90, 91, 93, 115-6, 135, 166, 199, 212, 246, 311-3, 317
dirtiness 66, 200
doctors (licensed and unlicensed) 38, 132, 136, 165, 173, 179, 180, 248-51, 253-4, 257-8, 313, 321
Doon, Ontario 149
drainage 159-60
dreams 43, 309, 310
Dueck, Peter R. (diarist) 10, 196, 210ff, 235, 261, 263
Dueck, Sara P. Kroeker (spouse) 210, 212, 237, 280
dust storms 177, 266

East Reserve xiii, 2, 12, 21, 22, 89, 210, 309, 316
Easter 59, 146
Ebenfeld, Manitoba 70, 294ff

Eby, Anna Weber (spouse) 123
Eby, Benjamin (bishop) 123
Eby, Elias (diarist) 10, 122, 123ff
education
–higher 13, 79, 114, 115, 143, 225, 255, 308, 310
–parochial 165, 170, 171, 174, 176, 194, 265, 271, 281, 317
–public 211, 219, 220-3, 225-9, 231-2, 235-6, 325
eggs 72, 99, 107, 113, 117, 119, 145-6, 251-2, 270, 273, 276, 297, 302
engagement parties (*Verlobung*) 227, 232, 244, 275
English 36, 46, 48, 63, 78, 128, 201-2, 205, 263, 310
English people 90-1, 100, 124, 132, 145, 246, 249, 251, 263, 293, 294-5, 299, 300, 302, 304
environment 13, 18, 31ff, 48, 63-4, 67, 146, 166, 182, 191, 199, 312
eternity 136, 143, 200, 202, 206, 323
Evangelical Mennonite Association 197, 201, 203
Evangelical Church 29
excommunication, 105, 108, 146, 198, 211, 214, 216, 221, 227, 229-30, 232-3, 235
exhibitions (circuses, fairs, shows) 152-3, 163, 221, 250, 255-7, 260

family
–blended 86, 308, 310
–conflict 53, 55, 143, 197, 310
–nuclear 30, 41, 70, 76, 78, 114, 134, 144, 149, 165, 197, 198, 211, 245, 261
feed milling 288, 292, 327-9, 334
fencing 83, 156, 242, 297, 333
fire 28, 242, 254, 302
flags 219, 221
flooding 99, 171, 174, 176, 189, 277
flour milling 35, 123, 144, 242
flowers 33, 37, 67, 94, 241
food (consumption of) 43, 270, 274, 276, 279, 282
–apple butter 257-8
–apples 32, 175
–beans 108-9
–buns 26
–cabbages 110, 146, 148
–carrots 190
–cheese 23, 299
–coffee 26, 92, 113
–corn 37
–cucumbers 94, 280, 282, 301-2
–dill pickles 282

–dried apples 27, 255
–flour 74, 173, 301
–honey 256
–ketchup 285, 287
–lard 27, 96, 284
–meat 27, 44, 92, 145, 260, 271-3, 289, 292, 330
–mince pies 45
–mustard pickles 281
–parsnip 91
–pies 33, 46, 50, 60, 53, 60
–plum compote 311
–sauerkraut 73, 290
–strawberries 100
–sugar 23, 26, 117, 301, 307
–syrup 168, 190, 249
–tomatoes 284-7
–watermelons 38, 111, 130
French Canadian (people and towns) 90, 94, 101, 106, 145, 165, 173, 186-8, 194, 299, 317, 320-1
Friesen, Agatha Hiebert (spouse) 164
Friesen, Cornelius T. (diarist) 19, 308, 316ff
Friesen, Gertruda Dyck Wiebe (spouse) 308, 316
Friesen, Heinrich (diarist) xvii, 11, 164ff
Friesen, Heinrich J. (bishop) 321, 324
Friesen, J.R. (car dealer) 196, 211
Friesen, Martin C. (bishop) 316, 319, 320-2, 324
fruit culture 36, 82, 103, 137, 148, 154-5, 161, 187, 191, 192, 255, 278-81, 283-4, 298, 303, 305
funerals 50, 51, 56, 73, 75, 78, 83, 119, 120, 122, 124, 125, 127, 128, 131-2, 152, 156, 202, 206, 213, 226, 241, 243, 264, 298, 300, 301, 304, 306, 319, 320, 329
Funk, John F. (publisher) 30, 156
furniture 22, 43, 99, 100, 110, 161, 251

gardening 91, 94, 95, 102, 109, 120, 146, 148, 155, 177, 241, 251-2, 275-7, 279, 283
gender (roles and relations) 3, 13, 15-18, 22, 47, 48, 55, 68, 70, 89, 129, 280, 314, 327
German 46, 78, 115, 135, 201-2, 204, 263, 327
Germans 125, 166, 175, 177, 183, 185, 192, 200, 238, 242, 246, 259, 279, 319
gifts 44, 45, 49, 64, 142, 161, 312, 315
Giroux, Manitoba 222, 263, 265, 270-1, 276-8, 280, 284
God (see also Lord or Jesus) 23, 61-2, 73-5, 128, 135-6, 143-4, 166, 168, 171, 178, 182, 185, 188-91, 197, 199-201, 205-10, 246, 309
Godshall Group 198
Gothic script 2, 22, 42, 87, 90, 212, 238, 263, 295, 318
government 25, 41, 59, 132, 231
Gretna, Manitoba 137, 138, 145, 235, 308, 325
Gruenfeld, Manitoba 21, 27ff
guns 38, 217, 224, 225, 229

haircut 108, 325
Hanover, Rural Municipality 2
haying 104, 107, 158, 185, 242, 276, 279-82, 300, 304, 314
health 29, 38-9, 138, 140, 151, 192, 216, 217, 229
–children's 27, 65, 66, 80, 95, 124, 134, 149, 151, 219, 280, 298, 300
–hospitals 180, 212, 220, 247, 251, 254-7, 296, 325
–medicine 264, 279, 303, 312, 320
–men's 69, 74, 102-8, 111, 128, 130, 132, 136, 143, 170, 180, 183, 211, 219, 231, 243, 245, 248-9, 259, 277, 279, 281, 313, 324
–mental 134, 213, 218, 220, 224, 225, 230, 232, 233, 303, 312
–prescriptions 139, 142
–Spanish influenza 257-60, 263, 309
–women's 17, 42, 45, 53, 60, 62, 91, 92, 96, 100-2, 105-8, 114, 129, 130, 132, 134, 141, 177, 228, 235, 239, 247ff, 290, 292, 303-4, 313, 320, 327;
Heatwole, Reuben J. (Kansas settler) 30, 37
Hershey, Eusebius (Rev.) 197, 198
High, Daniel [Hoch] (evangelist) 198, 200
Hildebrand, Abraham (farmer) 309
Hochfeld, Manitoba 164ff
hogs 93, 97, 98, 100, 148, 153, 156, 250, 255, 275-7, 277-8, 327-9, 330
Holdeman Church (Church of God in Christ, Mennonite) 211, 213, 224, 289
holidays 73, 132, 175, 298
horses 24, 43, 48, 81, 95, 99, 102, 106, 112, 119, 144, 146, 148, 169-70, 173, 220, 250, 252, 255, 264, 265, 277-8, 291, 303, 331, 333
hotelkeepers 203, 218
housecleaning 18, 63, 98, 111, 115, 121, 241, 249, 252-3, 258, 267ff, 297, 312, 331
hunting (shooting animals) 30, 34, 36, 144, 254, 294, 296
Hutterites 25
Illinois 32
Indiana 2, 46, 128, 150

Indians 59
inheritance 14, 22, 28, 88, 139, 181, 193, 316
insecticides 157-8, 184, 277
insurance 150, 151, 173, 261, 264, 267, 275, 279, 288, 325
Iowa 66, 67, 125
ironing (mangle) 52, 60, 102, 276-7, 282, 284, 286, 291, 303

Jansen, Cornelius (immigration leader) 8, 39, 41
Jansen, Helena Friesen (householder) 39, 41
Jansen, Margaretha (diarist) 8, 39, 41ff, 76
Jansen, Peter (immigration leader) 41ff, 53, 55, 68
Jesus (also Saviour, Christ; see also Lord) 47-9, 52, 146, 165, 197, 204-10, 221
Jews 22, 24, 145, 166, 167, 173-5, 181, 183, 255, 295-6, 299, 302-3, 305
Jung, Levi (diarist) 9, 197ff

Kansas 2, 29, 33-39, 94, 124, 127, 134, 135, 212, 229, 231-3, 235-6, 246, 256, 267, 270
kerosene 118, 285
kinship 22, 53, 55, 70, 77, 89-90, 114-5, 134, 137, 149, 161, 165, 210, 237, 246, 262, 326
Kitchener 247, 251-3, 259, 326
Klassen, Johan (spouse) 294ff
Klassen, Maria Stoesz (diarist) 9, 70ff, 294
Kleine Gemeinde xv, 2, 11, 21, 23, 89, 210ff, 261ff
Klippenstein, Heinrich G., (Waisenmann) 317, 319, 323-4
knitting 52, 288, 291
Kornelsen, Gerhard (schoolteacher) 86
Kornelsen, Heinrich (diarist) 13, 76, 86ff
Krimmer Mennonite Brethren Church 24
Kroeker, Franz M. (spouse) 25, 210
Kroeker, Jacob (Bishop) 217, 219, 226-7, 233
Kroeker, Magaretha Plett (diarist) 16, 210, 237ff
labour (wage) 151, 217
–female 23, 25, 31, 35, 93, 98, 102, 137, 154, 206, 238, 241, 247, 310, 314
–male 25, 31, 65, 148, 153, 171, 175, 184, 197, 238, 242, 305-6, 248, 326, 328, 331
laundry 43, 66, 67, 150, 249, 264ff, 297-9, 302, 306-7, 328, 331
laughter 42, 49
laziness 89
letters 43ff, 71, 122, 136ff, 201, 204, 207, 208, 232, 235, 239, 244-5, 263-4, 267-8, 273, 278, 287, 289-90, 311, 313-4
Lexington, Ontario 77ff

Lichtenau, Manitoba 86ff
Lincoln, Abraham (president) 82
literacy (see also reading) 4-6
Loewen, Cornelius (diarist) xviii, 7, 21ff, 237
Loewen, Helena Bartel (spouse) 21, 22, 27
Loewen, Isaak (deacon) 21, 25
Lowe Farm, Manitoba 309, 314, 322
Lord (see also God or Jesus) 44-5, 47, 50, 52, 54-7, 59, 62, 134, 136, 177, 180, 188, 197, 231
Lutherans 61-62,

Mannheim, Ontario 114
manure 82, 84, 154, 155, 159, 162, 177, 191, 242, 272, 292, 327, 329, 331, 333
maple sugar 60, 81, 120, 250
Markham, Ontario 124, 126-7, 132
marriage 138, 139, 151, 212, 223, 245
–to the second sister 213, 230, 231, 233-4, 262
Martin, Abraham (bishop) 77
Martin, Fanny Snyder (spouse) 325ff
Martin, Ishmael (diarist) 19, 325ff
mending (or darning) 48, 267ff, 287, 293
Mennonite Brethren Church 215
Mennonite Brethren in Christ 197
Mennonite Conference of Canada 115
merchandising 10, 134, 143, 222, 226
Methodist Church 29, 46, 55, 61, 65, 66
Métis 27, 186-8, 191
Mexico 2, 212, 295-7, 300, 304-5, 310, 314, 319
Michigan 115, 116, 124, 150
midwifery 109, 113, 261
migration 21, 26-27, 41, 70, 89, 114, 125, 130-2, 134, 143, 149, 164, 210, 237, 261, 317
military service 24, 198, 246, 252-3, 255
milking 44, 48, 50, 51, 63, 96, 97, 106, 136, 284, 311
Minnesota 134ff, 164
Missouri 33
Molotschna Colony 21, 23, 24, 89, 134, 210, 235
money 22, 23, 25, 28, 30, 39, 110, 116-8, 130, 138, 139, 142, 147, 210, 217
Montana 252
Moravian Brethren 166, 184
Morden, Manitoba 19, 309, 311, 313
mosquitoes, 183-4, 278
Moyer, Dilman (bishop) 198
mud 91, 92, 99, 150, 191, 241
murder 82, 143, 246, 247
music 46, 200, 211, 223, 227-8, 311, 325

Nebraska 41, 86, 90, 97, 108, 109, 134ff, 244-5
Neufeld, Judith Klassen (diarist) 16, 17, 70, 294ff
Neufeld, Peter B. (spouse) 294ff
Newfoundland 26
New Hamburg, Ontario 245ff
New Mennonites 30, 124, 198
New York 128, 317, 324
newspaper 30, 54, 59, 87, 121, 166, 178
Niagara, Ontario 53, 198, 199
Niverville, Manitoba 193, 297-9, 300, 305, 307, 318, 324
North Dumfries Township, Ontario xii, 58, 77

oats 23, 32ff, 75, 79, 83, 95, 99, 107, 113, 144-5, 154-5, 159, 190, 242, 255, 280
Ohio 14, 85, 246
old age 14, 89ff, 114ff, 136, 138, 140, 150, 165, 246ff, 262ff, 294
Old Colonist Mennonites 262, 266
Old Mennonites 115, 124, 196, 198, 208, 325.
Old Order Mennonites xiv, 325
open-field system 96, 176, 186, 189, 238
Oregon 180
Osterwick, Manitoba 316ff
oxen 24, 93, 99, 105, 141, 168, 174, 229

painting 138, 274, 285-6,
Palatine German 116
Paraguay 2, 19, 316-7, 320, 324
patents 37, 218
peas (production of) 83, 84, 154, 158
Penner, Erdmann (merchant) 99, 137
Penner, Helena (university graduate) 308
Pennsylvania 2, 6, 14, 29, 30, 77, 79, 114, 115, 122, 125, 131, 133, 149, 197-200
pets 51, 53, 55, 68, 93, 111, 247, 275
Philadelphia 63, 199
photography 223, 228
play 36, 42, 46, 52, 56, 66
Plett, Cornelius S. (parent) 23, 101, 237
ploughing 36, 82ff, 92ff, 154, 159, 162, 182, 187-8, 275-6, 284, 296-7, 305, 314, 332, 334
Plum Coulee, Manitoba 311, 314, 322
poetry 166, 175, 177, 180, 182, 185, 187, 189, 195, 210, 311
politics 29, 42, 131, 150, 156, 164, 215, 216, 231, 327
potatoes (production of) 83, 95, 99, 103, 107, 113, 143, 148, 155-8, 160, 162, 178, 182, 184, 188, 241-3, 257, 273-7, 279, 285, 296, 299, 301, 304, 331, 333
poverty 147, 224-5, 231, 237, 325
pranks 44, 56, 59, 64
prayer 136, 199ff, 218, 225
Pries, Maria (widow) 318
property purchase and sales 21, 23, 39, 139, 143, 181, 184, 191, 249, 261, 295, 297

Quakers 59
Quebec 27, 132
quilting 48, 52, 249, 327

reading 30, 36, 44, 49, 51, 54, 92, 108, 145, 152, 204, 205, 208, 313
Reimer, Abraham F. (diarist) 14, 89ff, 134, 240
Reimer, Elisabeth Rempel (spouse) 89ff, 134
Reimer, Klaas (bishop) 89, 134
Reimer, Klaas R. (diarist) xvi, 10, 15, 90, 167-8
Reimer, Margaretha Klassen (spouse) 134ff
Reimer, Maria Plett (grandmother) 261
revivalism 9, 48, 52, 54, 126, 197ff, 247
River Brethren 124, 131
rock picking 82, 162, 276, 333-4
root crops 85, 154-5, 157, 178, 189, 243, 251, 258, 304, 324
Rosenort (Scratching River, Jenseid, Rosenhof, Morris) 28, 88, 90, 91, 135, 212ff, 238, 245, 276, 278, 293, 322
Russia 6, 42, 48, 134, 137, 141, 148, 210, 225, 235, 238, 294, 316
rye production 171, 175, 186, 190
salvation 197, 203-4, 215, 218
Saskatchewan 218, 246, 248, 251, 258-9, 261, 278, 283, 287, 295, 316-7, 323
Satan 197
schism 23-4, 79, 123, 126, 127, 136, 235
schoolteaching 51-52, 62, 263, 288, 307
Schroeder, Marie (diarist) 19, 308, 309ff
secular organizations 31, 51, 68, 150-3, 157-9, 163, 188
seeding 36, 82ff, 91ff, 154ff, 160, 176ff, 251, 273, 297, 332
sermons 37, 47, 48, 115, 125, 127, 165, 199-210, 212ff, 319
Seventh Day Adventists 147
sewing 48, 89, 104, 111, 266-7, 282, 287
Sewing Circle 255, 257, 259, 273
sex 211, 221, 225, 229-31, 233
Shantz, Henry (Bishop) 77
Shantz, Jacob Y. (immigration leader) 40, 41ff
Shantz, Laura (diarist) xvi, 16, 17, 245ff
Shantz, Noah S. (father) xvi, 245ff

350 Index

Shantz, Susannah Cassel (mother) xvi, 245ff
sheep (wool, lambs) 24ff, 67, 83, 84, 134, 169, 172, 179, 240-1, 259, 267, 273
shocking sheaves 107, 280, 302
Schroeder, Marie (diarist) 309
Schroeder, Susannah Banman (mother) 309
silage 255, 278, 327
singing 45ff, 54, 68, 182, 200ff, 255, 311
smoke 188
snow 63, 92, 138, 190
soap-making 251, 270, 272, 275, 278
Sommerfelder Mennonite Church 309, 317
spinning 289-90
spiritual life 139, 147, 209
St. Jacobs, Ontario 325
Steinbach xiii, 10, 16, 27, 71, 73, 75, 86ff, 90ff, 134ff, 165, 167, 169, 173, 177, 180, 183, 186, 187, 190, 191, 192, 210ff, 237ff, 265ff, 295, 301, 322
Stoesz, David (Bishop) 70, 165
storms, 51, 74, 100, 106, 117, 120, 150, 153, 169, 174, 177, 243-4, 247-8, 275, 279, 296
students of Mennonites 110
suicide 123, 128, 251
summerfallow 84, 180, 184, 275
summer kitchen 179, 181, 183, 276, 297
Sunday school 44, 57, 65, 66, 199, 218, 224, 255, 325

technology (farm) 37, 94, 103, 105, 121, 134, 158, 180, 184, 185, 186, 188, 190, 191, 259, 270,   279-81, 283, 298, 314, 284; 300, 303-4, 322, 327-8, 332
telegraph 132
telephones 211, 215, 249, 263, 267, 285, 321
Texas 261
theft 211, 235, 250
threshing (or harvest)
–fall 37, 72, 107, 112-4, 158ff; 189, 216, 243, 255-6, 303, 312, 314, 327
–winter 79, 80, 247, 259;
tobacco 37, 130, 136, 211, 223, 318
Toews, Peter (bishop) 24, 93, 96, 98, 114
Toronto 22, 27, 32, 45, 130, 132, 246, 255, 326, 333
tracts 54, 69, 199, 202, 209
tragedies 21, 27, 28, 29, 101, 105, 123, 131, 242, 245, 246, 249, 257, 299
travel 56, 137, 148
travelogue 7, 22, 26ff, 30ff
Tunkers 68

Ukrainians 22, 43, 242

unbelievers 216, 311, 313
Unger, Maria Reimer (diarist) 16, 18, 261ff
Unger, Johann F. (spouse) 261ff
United States, images of 65, 292
United Brethren Church 47, 150

vaccination 60
vegetable marketing 73, 107, 148, 283
Virginia 150
war 178, 258
Washington 56
water pipes 247-8, 288
Waterloo
–county xii, 2, 3, 11, 12, 29, 143, 198ff
–town 31, 43, 80-1, 83, 85, 125, 129, 152-61, 208, 245
–township xii, 77, 114

weaving 266ff
Weber, Ann Martin (mother) 77ff
Weber, Rev. Samuel (father) 77ff
Weber, Moses (diarist) 13, 77ff
weddings 211, 213, 218, 225, 289, 307, 325
weeds 34, 39, 156-7, 177, 180-3, 277-8, 334
West Prussia 21, 41, 164
West Reserve 19, 72, 169, 174, 295, 298, 306, 309-315, 318ff
wet nursing 28
wheat
–marketing 24, 37, 72-3, 75, 83, 85, 113, 134, 151, 170, 173, 179, 194, 230, 242, 286-7, 290-1, 328
–yields, 32, 75, 112, 142-3, 190, 299
whitewashing 60, 98, 111, 285
widowhood 141, 216, 232, 264, 317
Wiebe, Gerhard (Bishop) 165, 176, 317
Wiebe, Heinrich (Rev.) 124, 131
Wiebe, Jakob (Rev.) 23, 24, 30, 37
wildlife 51, 86-88, 242
Wilmot Township, Ontario xii, 79, 114, 115, 131
Winnipeg xviii, 27, 72, 74, 93, 94, 98, 105, 107, 110, 113, 124, 143, 145, 169, 170, 178, 180, 225, 229, 241-2, 244-5, 264, 270, 289, 291, 296-8, 300, 302, 306, 318, 320, 325
Wisconsin 120
wood 21, 29, 34, 78ff, 97, 108, 112, 144-5, 149ff, 167-9, 173, 239, 247-8, 268-73, 305, 328, 331-2
Woolwich Township, Ontario xii, 77, 80, 202

youth 13, 77, 78, 96, 97, 104, 143, 178, 214, 222, 230, 232, 255, 294